THE DEATH OF THE CHILD VALERIO MARCELLO

D1482726

THE DEATH OF
THE CHILD
VALERIO MARCELLO

Margaret L. King

THE UNIVERSITY OF CHICAGO PRESS
CHICAGO AND LONDON

Margaret L. King, professor of history at Brooklyn College and the Graduate Center, CUNY, is the author of Women of the Renaissance *and* Venetian Humanism in an Age of Patrician Dominance.

THE UNIVERSITY OF CHICAGO PRESS, CHICAGO 60637
The University of Chicago Press, Ltd., London
© 1994 by The University of Chicago
All rights reserved. Published 1994
Printed in the United States of America
03 02 01 00 99 98 97 96 95 94   1 2 3 4 5
ISBN: 0-226-43619-5 (cloth)
0-226-43620-9 (paper)

Library of Congress Cataloging-in-Publication Data

King, Margaret L., 1947–
    The death of the child Valerio Marcello / Margaret L. King.
        p.   cm.
    English, Latin, and Italian.
    The illuminated ms., De obitu Valerii . . . , which is discussed in
this work is located in the University of Glasgow Library.
    Includes bibliographical references and index.
    1. Marcello, Jacopo Antonio, ca. 1400–ca. 1464.   2. Marcello,
Valerio, 1452–1461—Death and burial.   3. Nobility—Italy—Venice—
Biography.   4. Fathers and sons—Italy—Biography.   5. Venice
(Italy)—History—15th century.   6. De obitu Valerii filii
consolatio.   7. Consolation.   8. Mourning customs—Italy.
I. Glasgow University.   Library.   II. Title.
DG677.99.M37K56   1994
945′.3105′0922—dc20
    [B]   93-44666
                                                                      CIP

For Robert

Contents

ॐ

Illustrations

✣

Abbreviations

፟

Abbreviations for names of specific manuscripts and printed editions of consolatory works on the death of Valerio Marcello are listed in Texts II.A.

Abel   Eugenius Abel, ed. 1886. *Isotae Nogarolae Veronensis opera quae supersunt omnia*. 2 vols.; Vienna-Budapest: apud Gerold et socios.

Anon. Stu.   Anonymous Student. See Texts II.C.14.

Anon. Tut.   Anonymous Tutor. See Texts II.C.11.

Anon. Ven.   Anonymous Venetian. See Texts II.C.12.

ASI   *Archivio storico italiano*

ASL   *Archivio storico lombardo*

ASV   Archivio di Stato, Venice:
                AC-BO (Avogaria di Comun, Balla d'Oro); CLN (Collegio, Notatorio); CXM (Consiglio di Dieci, Miste); MC (Maggior Consiglio); SGV (Segreteria alle Voci, Miste); SM (Senato: Mar); SMI (Senato: Miste); SP (Senato: Privilegi); SS (Senato: Segrete); ST (Senato: Terra)

AV   *Archivio veneto*

BAV   Biblioteca Apostolica Vaticana

Ben.   Giovanni Benadduci. 1894. *A Jacopo Antonio Marcello patrizio veneto parte di orazione consolatoria ed elegia di Francesco Filelfo e lettera di Giovanni Mario Filelfo*. Nozze Marcello-Giustiniani (31 January 1891). Tolentino: Stabilimento tipografico Francesco Filelfo.

BHR   *Bibliothèque de l'Humanisme et de la Renaissance*

BMV   Biblioteca Nazionale Marciana, Venice

Chron.   Appendix Two: Chronology

CTC   *Catalogus translationum et commentariorum: Medieval and Renaissance Latin Translations and Commentaries.* Ed. Paul Oskar Kristeller and F. Edward Cranz. Washington, D.C.: Catholic University of America Press. 1960–.

DBI   *Dizionario biografico degli italiani.* Rome: Istituto della Enciclopedia Italiana, 1960–. 37 vols. and continuing.

Fam.   Appendix One: Marcello Family and Monuments

GSLI   *Giornale storico della letteratura italiana*

H   Ludwig Hain. *Repertorium bibliographicum, in quo libri omnes ab arte typographica inventa usque ad annum MD. typis expressi,* . . . Stuttgart: J. G. Cotta, 1826–38.

HC   Walter Arthur Copinger. *Supplement to Hain's* Repertorium bibliographicum, *or, Collections towards a New Edition of That Work.* London: H. Sotheran and Co., 1895–1902.

Iter   Paul Oskar Kristeller. 1963–91. *Iter Italicum: A Finding List of Uncatalogued or Incompletely Catalogued Humanistic Manuscripts of the Renaissance in Italian and Other Libraries. Accedunt alia itinera.* 6 vols. London: Warburg Institute; Leiden: E. J. Brill.

JHI   *Journal of the History of Ideas*

JMH   *Journal of Modern History*

JMRS   *Journal of Medieval and Renaissance Studies*

JWCI   *Journal of the Warburg and Courtauld Institutes*

Mon.   Monfasani, John ed. 1984. *Collectanea Trapezuntiana: Texts, Documents and Bibliographies of George of Trebizond.* Binghamton, New York: Medieval and Renaissance Texts and Studies.

NAV   *Nuovo archivio veneto*

NS   New Series

NYRB   *New York Review of Books*

PG   J. P. Migne, ed. *Patrologia graeca.* Paris: 1857–66.

PL   J. P. Migne, ed. *Patrologia latina.* Paris: 1844–55.

RIS   *Rerum italicarum scriptores.* RIS/1 = ed. of Ludovico Antonio Muratori (Milan: Societas Palatinae). RIS/2 = Bologna: N. Zanichelli and Città di Castello: S. Lapi.

RQ   *Renaissance Quarterly*

RSCI   *Rivista per la storia della chiesa in Italia*

SCV	*Storia della cultura veneta [SCV].* 1980. *III: Dal primo Quattrocento al Concilio di Trento.* 3 vols. Vicenza: Neri Pozza.
SLA	Scienze, Lettere ed Arti
SV	*Studi veneziani*
Texts	Appendix Three: Texts

Prologue

More than five hundred years ago, a child died: what is that to us? Approaching fast the end of the twentieth century, we see children die by the hundreds and the thousands. Around the world, they are dying by starvation and mortar shells. In my own country, they are dying of neglect and abuse and indifference. Each one of these deaths warrants scarcely a line in the daily newspaper. Here is a whole book. Yet I summon my readers to consider the case of Valerio Marcello, a child of power and privilege born to a leading family of Venice when, at the height of her power, she claimed to rule "a quarter and a half a quarter" of the old Roman Empire. Valerio fell ill and died at age eight and plunged his father into desperate, implacable grief.

The despair of Jacopo Antonio Marcello, Valerio's father, shocked his contemporaries. The father held firm against their rebukes, determined to persist in his desolation. The battle between the obdurate father and incomrehending consolers has left (this being the age of the Renaissance) a considerable textual footprint: a core volume of more than four hundred closely written manuscript pages, and as many again scattered in manuscript in libraries and archives. This ample testimony to the father's vision of his son and perceptions of his anomalous love has led this investigation in several directions.

First, this is a study of *childhood.* "Children are newcomers as a subject of literature, newcomers in the study of human physiology and anatomy, newcomers in the social sciences," wrote Margaret Mead nearly forty years ago.[1] They are newcomers no longer. Studies of the last two generations have taught us about their lives in families, their education, their significance for adults; their neglect, their abuse, their preciousness. The present work adds a little to that story. The Marcello literature provides a firsthand narrative (richly colored by humanist conventions and expectations) of the life of a fifteenth-century child. Other documents permit a reconstruction of the Marcello family and yield the picture of a household bursting with children and spanning three generations. Above all, the sources at hand give insight into patterns of sentiment: the love of the child for his father and siblings; the passionate involvement of the father in the life of his son; the striking absence of the mother. While the one case of Valerio Marcello is in no way representative of Renaissance childhood, it presents some features that must be considered in any comprehensive vision of that phenomenon.

Second, this is the study of one man's *career:* the career of Jacopo Antonio Marcello, Venetian nobleman and soldier, humanist and patron. Any detailed biography of a fifteenth-century figure can add to our understanding of the epoch of the Renaissance in Italy; there are not all that many at hand. But a consideration of Marcello's biography has further utility, because it has remarkable features. At a time when Venetian noblemen (though they might participate directly in naval positions in the maritime empire) hired mercenaries to wage their wars on their newly won land empire, Marcello was profoundly engaged in day-to-day military operations over a period of nearly twenty years before the Peace of Lodi (1454) put a brief halt to a state of chronic warfare. Not only did Marcello perform the duties Venetian representatives to the field normally performed (paying soldiers, hiring *condottieri,* writing endless letters back to the Senate), but he participated in battle, led troops, and began to think of himself as a *condottiere* himself: a mercenary captain like his companions. Given his adventurous past and sterling record of achievement, it is all the more surprising to observe the nobleman, in the years after Lodi, turning to a quite different agenda: the joys of study (showing a special penchant for Greek theological and geographical texts), of poetry, of painting, of the company of the learned and talented, of friendship, of fatherhood, of private pursuits over public responsibilities.

Third, this is a study of *patronage.* Trained in the new humanist curriculum (probably at the episcopal court of the university town of Padua), Marcello had both the talents and the wealth to participate in the cultural trends that made his century famous. Not only did he perform great deeds in the course of the Lombard wars, but he encouraged humanist writers to celebrate them. Not only did he love, create, and exchange books, but he hired artists of first rank to adorn them. Not only did he mourn for the death of his child, but he invited his literary friends to write to console him for his grief—which stack of consolations he resolutely rejected. Of all these events, Marcello was the center, the instigator, and the subject. His cultural activity, comparable to that of other key patrons of the age but better documented than some, is a key to understanding the mechanism of literary and artistic patronage in fifteenth-century Venice.

Fourth, this is a study about *death.* The men and women of the last medieval centuries (corresponding in Italy to the age of Renaissance) were profoundly concerned with death: a concern mounting to obsession. This is the age of shocking depictions of death and the dead in art and poetry, of elaborate tombs, of meticulous guides to those in fear of hell to making a "good" and pious death, of humanist consolations outlining a mix of Christian and Stoic "remedies" for sorrow. Our Marcello shares the fascination with death that characterized his age, but not its focus, fearful or hopeful, on the afterlife. Scarcely acknowledging the Christian framework of belief which shaped his generation, unimpressed with the image of Valerio as an angel in heaven and oblivious to images of the tomb or of hell, Marcello duels with death—almost challenging its power to remove from him the son in whom he had placed so much of his love and all of his hope.

Like Farinata in the sixth circle of Dante's *Inferno*, condemned for heresy, Marcello seems to mock the sovereignty of God. The unrepentant Ghibelline hero, rising towerlike from his open tomb, still airs in hell his aristocratic prejudice: "Who were thy ancestors?" he haughtily asks the pilgrim Dante (10.42). Yet on the day of judgment, the lid of his sepulchre will close shut, forever, and for having resisted the authority of the divine power, he will be triply entombed: locked in his grave, locked in hell, locked in the past. For Marcello, that moment had already come. The death of Valerio meant his own perpetual death. Even more than one's own, the death of a child closes the door to the future. Faith, hope, and love: the greatest of these is hope.

☙   ☙   ☙

I acknowledge with thanks the grants and fellowships that have enabled me to complete the research for this volume: from the National Endowment for the Humanities, a Summer Stipend (1984) and Senior Fellowship (1986–87); travel grants from the Gladys Krieble Delmas Foundation (1990) and American Philosophical Society (1991); and from the City University of New York, a PSC/BHE grant-in-aid (1990–91), a Brooklyn College Scholar Incentive Award (1986–87), and a Brooklyn College one-semester full-salary sabbatical award (1991). Many thanks are also due the editors at the University of Chicago Press, especially Douglas Mitchell and Kathryn Krug, for unfailing confidence and inspired criticism.

Many friends have helped me in my quest for the lost Valerio. Paul Oskar Kristeller first alerted me to the manuscript volume now in the University of Glasgow which lies at the heart of the Marcello story. His *Iter Italicum*, that indispensable catalogue of uncatalogued manuscripts, guided me to nearly all the others. Nancy Siraisi advised me on *Quattrocento* pediatrics, and Diana Robin valiantly critiqued the whole manuscript. John

Monfasani helped me avoid many errors, and sent me probing for references in the deepest cavities of the New York Public Library. Bridget Gellert Lyons, gifted with rare insight into things shadowy and obscure, raised for me the question of Valerio's missing mother.

O. B. Hardison and Elizabeth Hill pointed me to Paulinus of Nola's consolatory *carmen* for the infant Celsus (the "Urtext," said O. B.). From James Hankins and G. W. Pigman III came useful references, and from Pigman and George McClure, much guidance to the consolatory tradition. G. W. Knauer supplied information on Perleone's Greek scholarship, Margaret Bent introduced me to Fiordelise Miani and the music of the Paduan episcopal court, while my own student, Christina von Koehler (who reads Hungarian!), unlocked for me the literature on Janus Pannonius. Two Venetian gentlemen assisted me at the last moment by procuring needed photographs: the antiquarian Osvaldo Böhm, and the director of the Biblioteca Nazionale Marciana, Dott. Marino Zorzi. Richard Harrier, Debra Pincus, and Paul Rosenfeld put me on the track of some lost or missing monuments, and Patricia H. Labalme joined me in mental wargames on the Lombard plains.

In Venice in the summer of 1990, Dottore Girolamo Marcello welcomed me to his library and watched as I entered data about his ancient family, once honored by the *dogado,* into the portable computer I perched on the edge of an antique table. In the summer of 1992, Dottoressa Caterina Griffante, librarian of the Istituto Veneto di Scienze, Lettere ed Arti, offered me refuge and support when the Biblioteca Marciana closed its doors for *ristauri.* Later that summer, sitting with Professor Aldo Stella in the bar where he first met Fernand Braudel, overlooking the *bacino* and the island of San Giorgio (where the child Valerio was buried), I was privileged to hear the story of his young daughter's death, and to receive from his hands the book he composed in her memory. The readers of this book will understand the resonance of that moment.

As in the past, and I hope in the future if I do not strain my credit too far, my greatest debt is to my family. My parents provided space, warmth, counsel, and lunch; also proofreading and printing services, long-distance communications, and damage control. My children provided white noise and freed me from the burden of too much leisure in which I might have reflected on the deficiencies of this work. My husband shopped and chauffeured, led expeditions through every toy store in Venice, administered playdates, and put the children to bed on the nights when I fell asleep before they did. To that postmodern father this book is dedicated.

CHAPTER ONE

The Death of a Child

ᕛ

In a palace on the Grand Canal in Venice, surrounded by family, friends, and doctors, eight-year-old Valerio Marcello died on the first day of January, 1461.[1] His father, "like a stone," made the sign of the cross over the inanimate body, then fled from the light into darkness to grieve. The house was draped in mourning, Marcello robed himself in black, and the small corpse was clothed in white.[2] So common an occurrence, the death of a child, in the centuries prior to the twentieth! But this uncommon father continued to grieve long beyond the normal term. "And the rest of life has become for me a time of wretchedness; and when death won for him the eternal felicity and beatitude of heaven, it brought me enduring evil, and as long as life continues for me, I disintegrate in sorrow."[3] His sorrow may have extended to the last day of his life.

Marcello was sent to Friuli in the fall of 1462 and never returned.[4] The mission assigned him by the Venetian Senate was initially to govern the capital at Udine; later, to contain the Austrians who hammered at Istria. In military ventures of such strategic importance he was a veteran. But he had set off still encumbered by grief for the child buried nearly two years before. The father's distress caused eyebrows to raise in provincial Udine, as it had in cosmopolitan Venice. Months after the death, his friends chided him for his weakness, cautioned him not to become a public spectacle, begged him to free them all and the other members of Marcello household from the toil of unalleviated sadness. A year later, he had not been argued out of his depression. Two and nearly three years after the death of the child Valerio, undistracted still by administrative and military tasks, he was not prepared to let the matter go.

In a gesture that was for him characteristic, he gathered up a number of works, great and small, addressed to him in his bereavement: fifteen works by fourteen authors—letters, a poem, consolatory treatises, history, eulogy, and apology—perhaps the largest and most richly textured of the funerary collections of the Renaissance.[5] These he arranged in sequence and had them copied and bound as a book, dated from the field of battle. He gave the book to an artist to illustrate in gilt and brilliant color: a lush frontis-piece, and at the head of each component work a large and brilliant initial.

The exquisite book was never completed. The first several works open with illuminated initials, and are equipped with marginal glosses. Soon the marginal glosses disappear. Three initial letters are lacking (and initial frag-ments of the three works they were to open) leaving blank pages and unan-swered questions. On the patron's death (of old age? of wounds? of heart-break?), the project of illumination was suspended—to be resumed but not completed by Marcello's heirs. We are left with an unfinished book, telling of a child's unfinished life and his father's unfinished sorrow.

The book returned to Venice, perhaps with Marcello's other possessions to the palace where Valerio had died near Campo Sant'Angelo, a few steps from the vast piazza of San Marco. His branch of the Marcello clan still flourished there in the sixteenth century, and still held title to the building when it was sold, then razed, early in the seventeenth century. On its site was erected the theater where Goldoni's plays were staged and which Casa-nova graced. Now even the theater is gone: in Napoleon's wake, a ware-house took its place.

Before the palace of Jacopo Antonio Marcello suffered this fate, the book that had been the undertaking of his last years passed into the library of another member of the patrician Marcello clan, owners of several other and possibly more splendid Venetian palazzi.[6] In 1753 (three centuries after the death of Valerio) the bibliophile Apostolo Zeno saw and admired it in the palace of Federico Marcello. By 1767, the family that preserved a splendid library into the late twentieth century had nevertheless discarded the ele-gant volume memorializing Valerio Marcello. It awaited sale in a bookshop. There in 1767 the manuscript "di grande pregio" was viewed by Jacopo Morelli, the erudite head of the Marciana library that is housed today in the building designed in a Roman vocabulary to serve as the city mint by the master architect Jacopo Sansovino.

Within a few years, the codex of Marcello consolations reappeared in the personal library of a German bibliophile and New Testament scholar, Caesar de Missy, then posted in England as chaplain to King George III. It was listed among his books sold at auction on 18 March 1776 by the auc-tioneers Baker and Leigh, forerunners of the company known today as So-theby's. The manuscript was purchased by Dr. William Hunter, a fourth in this series of men who loved beautiful books. Hunter was a physician, better known for the work he had authored on *The Anatomy of the Human Gravid Uterus* than for his remarkable collection of rare coins, medals, shells, minerals, and books. When he died in 1783, his library was inherited by his nephew, destined to pass upon the latter's death to Glasgow University. In 1807, Hunter's volumes came to form the nucleus of the Special Collections of that university's library, one of Britain's largest manuscript repositories. Having left Friuli for Venice and Venice for London, the Marcello volume had accomplished a final journey to Scotland.

There it rests at this moment: an illuminated manuscript of 426 elegant pages from the full Renaissance, a monument to the thought and style of that age, and to a young child and his bereaved father. Refitted with a fresh leather cover in 1967, the book's fifteenth-century binding is represented by small sample patches glued to the inside back cover, alongside a note from the binder describing its condition. The lower right corner of each folio is trimmed in an arc to regularize the effects of a rodent's gnawing teeth, and small holes and irregularities in the parchment (carefully avoided by the scribe) are found throughout. Damp has damaged only two pages: the first two, the stain partly obscuring the frontispiece of the volume. Yet inside the verticals of a splendid Renaissance border of flowers and sworls there are still discernible two vignettes drawn in penwork on gold background: on the left, a boy, chin on hand; on the right, a bearded man with an open book, a lion peering over his shoulder. Surely this is the clever child Valerio listening raptly to the words of the patron of Venice, Saint Mark.

What follows is the story the book has to tell.

℘   ℘   ℘

The city of Crema, conquered in 1449, stood at the furthest point of Venice's westward expansion on the *terraferma*. There Jacopo Antonio Marcello was stationed as governor and military overseer of the western frontier from 1450 until the spring of 1452.[7] During that time Valerio was both conceived and born. That conception occurred under most favorable circumstances. Both parents, of continent and temperate habits, were in excellent health. Marcello particularly at that time, "in age, in mode of life, in health, color, habit, in dignity and majesty of body," was fit to beget an outstanding child.[8] The mother's mental condition also promised well. "I am convinced," the father later reflected according to a first-person narrative, "that when his mother conceived this son from me her husband, she was not imagining any human form or shape, which [the child] would resemble, but in her mind dwelled a certain excellent and unique pattern of beauty."[9] While the child still lay in that platonizing mother's womb, the father had visions of him: "a male child of most elegant form, replete with every kind

Damaged by moisture, the splendid opening page with blue background trimmed in costly gilt. In the margins, vignettes in pen on gold: left, a boy, possibly listening; right, a man with companion lion and book; bottom, the Marcello coat of arms. Glasgow University, Hunterian Museum Library, MS 201 (U.1.5), with permission of Dr. Timothy D. Hobbs, Keeper of Special Collections.

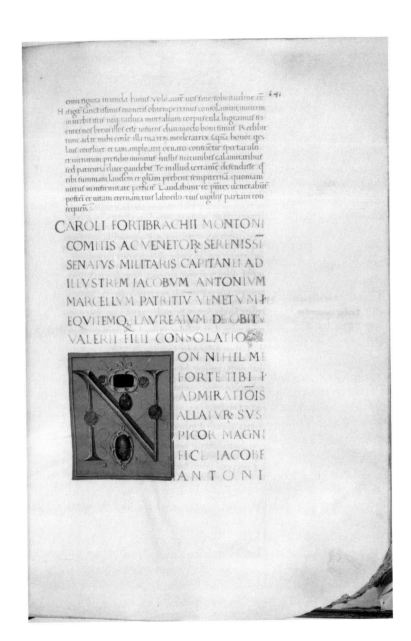

One of fifteen decorated initials in the Glasgow manuscript of Marcello consolations, all capitals in severe classical style on a variety of colored backgrounds adorned with flora, fauna, and gems. With permission of Dr. Timothy D. Hobbs, Keeper of Special collections.

of virtue."[10] The baby was destined to be not only beautiful and virtuous, but great; the father's military role at the time was an omen of the child's future glory.[11]

This privileged creature was born in Venice, perhaps on 24 April in the year 1452.[12] He came into the world suffering little from labor, and, far from crying, beaming at his mother. The happy news was raced to the absent father. "When you heard the news of the birth, you were so overwhelmed with pleasure, that the joy you expressed aroused wonder in all those present," wrote the humanist Francesco Filelfo. "So much hope did you conceive of his future worthiness, that you thought that a great quantity had been added to the sum of your happiness."[13] Since Marcello's public duties prevented him from attending to the matter himself, his wife diligently saw to the baptism and naming: "For he who was greatly to triumph (*valiturus*) beyond his years in mind and virtue was rightly named Valerio."[14]

Marcello returned to Venice when the infant was three months old. He found that Valerio exactly resembled the child of his vision: him whom "quiet nights had shown me, whom in my sleep I had closely embraced," in the words said to be his own. "I wonder at the boy's features—forehead, eyes, nose, mouth, his whole face—struck with admiration."[15] The first meeting of father and son had other notable features. Marcello had entered the house quietly, without the prior announcement that might have created a fuss in the household. As soon as Valerio saw the stranger enter, he pushed from his mouth his nurse's breast, the prize he had hungrily seized when aroused from sleep a few minutes before. He lifted his head and eyes and seemingly cocked his ears, as though some inner message had reached him that here was something especially worthwhile noting. Struggling from his nurse's arms he threw himself into his father's embrace, eyes wide, smiling sweetly, babbling "father," though he could not yet say the word. In all of antiquity, no father had received such a greeting from a son![16]

Marcello was surprised but delighted—Hector had returned from the fray and found a most amiable Astyanax—and bent to kiss the child.[17] The child returned his father's greeting with repeated kisses, and would not stop, and peered deep into his parent's eyes. The nurse reached for the infant but he rejected her. Finally coaxed away by his mother, Valerio turned his head sharply to see his father again, babbling vigorously sounds no one could understand. Marcello gazed on the boy with wonder, saying nothing, but rejoicing within himself that his son would surely be a great man and a great citizen. A special relationship between father and son began at this moment.

Valerio thrived. From the first he fed nicely, and suffered none of the digestive disorders common in children.[18] The image of his father,[19] he possessed great beauty. "This infant grew in the early years so handsome, his honest and open face so attractive, so splendid with charming beauty, that anyone who saw him was moved to admiration of his lovely form."[20] Beauty was not a merely incidental consideration, but a sign of greatness, and an attribute admired by the ancients. Helen, above all others, had been beautiful; Jesus Christ had been a beautiful child.[21] Valerio's exquisite eyes, nose, ears, hands, fingers, neck, mouth, tongue, were matched by the acuteness of the senses related to those organs: sight, hearing, touch, the beauty of his voice.[22]

That sweet voice was slow to form words, and Marcello longed ardently to speak with the child.[23] But then speech blossomed suddenly. Like Athis, the son of King Croesus of Lydia who spoke not at all until the sight of his imperilled father stirred him to instantly mature speech, Valerio did not begin (as do most children) with babbling. From the first, his speech was correct and eloquent: "For in him there was always the highest comeliness of words, and a certain flawless integrity of speech, a sweetness and smoothness of voice."[24]

Valerio was unusually precocious: like Hercules and Alexander, Theseus and Midas, Themistocles and Plato, and Augustus's beloved nephew Marcellus, who had all shown in early childhood the signs of their future greatness.[25] Several witnesses intone the theme. "In body he was . . . formed by a wondrous kind of disposition with a breadth of limb, a vigor, firmness and agility, above his age; the face of this adultlike child shone mature, grave, and noble . . ."[26] Such wisdom did he display, so rightly did he leaven serious thoughts with gay, that in every way "he exceeded his years in virtue."[27] He delighted those around him with words evincing prudence "beyond his age"; his studies were more profound than suited his "childish years."[28] His intelligence and industry were so great that they would be admirable even in an older child.[29] Where other children could be moved to do the right thing from fear of their parents or their teachers, Valerio was from the first his own guide.[30] He was gifted "beyond the standard of his age" with the greatest reason, grandeur of soul, moderation, prudence, and eloquence; those who knew him felt there was "some divine power, not merely human," at work in him.[31] He possessed gifts of body, of intelligence, of virtue, more befitting old age than childhood, and accomplished some feat each day "beyond his years, beyond nature."[32] He was indeed a "manlike boy," sheltering in his child's body "a manlike soul, a manlike strength, a manlike judgment."[33]

Precocious, Valerio showed his particular qualities in interaction with the other children of the Marcello household. Their example stirred him, while he was still an infant, to attempt walking, and later to greater athletic accomplishments.

> Already from infancy, Valerio was beyond beauty of form, and he so far exceeded others of his age in magnitude of body and limbs, that all admiringly judged that he would soon be able to walk. The strength and quality of this child's spirit was so great that when Valerio saw other household children playing, by his gestures and struggling to join them, he seemed to melt with love, and a wondrous desire to play, even when he was not yet strong enough. Therefore when he had not yet completed a year, the great nature of this generous soul first moved his body into play. . . . And beyond anyone's expectations, the boy entered the hall by himself, with no assistance, and contended with the others in competition, so that scarcely from morning to evening could he be called back by the nurse, and what is greater, to the incredible admiration of all, he began quickly and rightly [to do these things], even better than those who were three or four years older than he. Thus he showed from his tender years that he would not give himself over to be corrupted by laziness and leisure, but to the fullest extent that strength had been given him by nature, so much would he devote himself to study and exercise.[34]

With his kind and generous nature, he was able to kindle the love not only of his peers but even of the older children of the household.[35] He determinedly joined in their activities and sought to emulate them: "So did he insinuate himself in the activities of cousins, siblings, and other relatives, that he easily demonstrated how harmoniously he could join with those of that age, and what kind of life he was going to lead; and he imitated those older than he with a wondrous devotion and reverence."[36] In fact, he shone among them.

> Your scion, as you know, Jacopo Antonio, was among the other noble boys in the classroom, flowing curls encircling his milky neck, as the golden sun is among the lesser stars. Grave and modest eyes, kingly brow, rosy cheek and lip, his whole body resembled radiant Jove or Cupid, son of Venus. So much alacrity was in his members, so much strength, such swiftness, that in races he was always the winner. And in literary studies? He labored all the time with ambition to learn, while he daily stimulated his fellow students to exer-

tion. He sat near one bigger brother Lorenzo, younger by birth, whom he encouraged to learn not only by blandishments and occasional threats, but also with cookies and treats. . . . Wherefore he so fired the minds of the children with such benevolence that all venerated him as master, paid attention to him as to a father, and loved him as dearly as themselves. Often conflicts would arise among them over their games. Quickly, like a dictator, he would resolve them.[37]

Endowed with such native abilities, and fortunate to have a father who was himself an amateur of the new humanist learning and a thoughtful patron of arts and letters, Valerio would also be well taught. The most discerning care was taken to ensure that he was properly trained even before formal education could be begun. Of first moment was the character of the infant's nurse, considered critical for intellectual and moral development. Accordingly, Valerio was committed "to that kind of nurse who, upright and sober and imbued with the [Marcello] ancestral values, could cherish and nourish the tiny child, and could rightly guide his growth towards worthy manhood."[38] Soundly formed in the early years, he soon displayed the qualities of modesty and self-restraint that evidence the formation of moral character and the foundation for learning. "Valerio was thus trained in these disciplines and arts from infancy; these great and broad foundations of good living were so laid in him, and his childish soul was so informed by these counsels of virtue, that either he would listen quietly while others spoke, or, when he spoke, he would use few and truthful words; which skills are indeed the greatest and firmest ornaments, and testimony to the greatest virtues, not only of boyhood, but also of all the stages of life."[39]

Now it was time to introduce the rudiments of language, the cornerstone of liberal studies. These were to be mastered early in life, when knowledge could be fixed by strong roots, and when the concepts that were learned were indelibly imprinted on the soul.[40] Already at that tender age, only the child by nature predisposed to virtue would undertake the task of mastering the liberal arts with alacrity.[41] The worth of that enterprise was self-evident:

> For though many and various are the institutions and arts by which the human race is enriched and adorned, yet there is nothing of all human things except virtue which is either more favorable to utility, more excellent in dignity, more longlasting in durability, than the most excellent studies of letters, of which those are most splendid,

and should be judged the greatest, which have to do with eloquence joined to wisdom. For these are a guide when affairs are uncertain, an ornament when fortune is favorable, an aid when it is adverse, and in either kind of fortune bestow the use and understanding of the greatest things. These adorn the soul, sharpen the wit, strengthen the mind, and present to the good man the road to honor and glory (the greatest rewards, after virtue, that come to the wise man), and so present it, that not only does he act honestly and properly in civil duties, but he also ascends, as though by certain solid steps, to that point where is sought virtue and integrity of life, and duty and true wisdom.[42]

Above all, a good teacher had to be chosen—the father's responsibility. Marcello cheerfully took on that burden, as it appears from our first-person account: "When I considered how much men are aided in gaining honor and cultivating virtue through letters to the study of which they lend themselves, and how my son lacked nothing that might make him conspicuous in all virtues and in every regard perfect, it seemed best to hire the finest teachers, from whom he might be trained in the good arts from infancy."[43] One interested pedagogue praised Marcello's diligence in seeking a skilled teacher, without whom the benefits of natural intelligence and industry might wither: "I must make it clear at this point that I can't help but admire the diligence and prudence of Jacopo Antonio Marcello as much as I despise the negligence . . . of those parents who, when it comes to growing crops, training horses, building houses, sailing ships, and other lowly pursuits, select and handsomely pay those who are considered most skilled in that art; but in this highest duty of educating a child, we find they are incautious and negligent and faulty, so that without reflection they commit the minds of their children to be shaped and formed by some ignorant fool or other."[44] Nothing is more corrupting than an ignorant teacher, "who teaches not true knowledge, but his own foolishness."[45]

It was to one of his consolers that Marcello committed the education of Valerio at an early age: "For he was handed to me to be imbued with the first elements of letters when he had barely begun his sixth year, nor did he leave my side before he left this life. And indeed let me here dwell a little while on the reverence, and likewise on that incredible ardor of love with which the boy embraced me, and so embraced me, that he was never happy when he saw me sad, nor sad when I was happy."[46] Another observer concurred: it can hardly be expressed "with what reverence, what veneration, [the child] obeyed his teacher."[47] When Valerio died perhaps three years later, the esteemed tutor shared the father's grief: "You desire your sweet child, I my pupil; you remember his embraces and kisses, I his gentleness and reverence. While he lived he adorned you with the greatest glory of his accomplishments; while to me he gave immortality in all ages by his eloquence. Both of us, therefore, now equally bear just blame, if we suffer, if we let hair and beard go unkempt, if we stay at home and weep in our beds in the shadows."[48]

Under the tutelage of this committed pedagogue, Valerio flourished in the pursuit of liberal studies. Once introduced to them, he became discontented with the narrowly athletic training traditional for a nobleman, and "nothing delighted him more than the studies of the good arts."[49] "He so flamed with the desire to learn, he so bent himself to studies, he so grasped the rudiments of the good arts that there was no kind of knowledge that he did not yearn to master."[50] He burned with an insatiable desire to learn,[51] and labored, at that early age when vice had not yet beckoned, without relief.[52]

Idle hours abandoned by others to leisure, Valerio "devoted to some worthwhile business."[53] He left no time empty, but was either reading, or writing "with his tender fingers," or doing something. "Valerio, when will you relax?" his father would ask him. "When night comes, or death," the boy responded.[54] On his deathbed, he would promise his parent that, if he recovered, he would not exhaust himself so with studies.[55] His mother sometimes worried (as mothers indulgent towards their sons often do) whether he was studying so hard as to endanger his health: "he would stop for a while when his mother was present, but as soon as she left, for the sake of understanding more he would return to action."[56] Only a baby, Valerio had learned to balance the categories of action and contemplation so often discussed by the humanists!

Facilitating these studies was a powerful memory, an essential gift in the seeker of knowledge, for it "preserves all things tenaciously"; nor do we really know, unless we know through memory.[57] This gift Valerio possessed, so that "whatever was told him by you, when he was young, or by teachers, or whatever he saw or learned from others, he preserved tenaciously fixed in his mind."[58] This talent expressed itself in impressive feats of memory. At an early age he could recite a long poem, or, at age eight, recall in full the events of his infancy.[59] Among other examples, especially conspicuous was Valerio's deathbed recognition of the doctor Gerardo Bolderio. Valerio had met him only once, years earlier, when the physician came to Monselice to treat an older nephew, Girolamo. Barely clinging to life, Valerio recalled in detail the circumstances of that event of his early childhood. To that moment, and Valerio's recollection, we shall return.

Eager to learn and intellectually gifted, Valerio soon developed all the qualities of the consummate orator: "a pleasant and clear voice, sweetness of speech, charm of pronunciation combined with gravity, easy expression of any passage in either language [Greek or Latin] as though he had been born to it."[60] Latin *and* Greek: a stiff curriculum (so it seems to us) for a child who never reached his ninth birthday, but undoubtedly the one he followed. Mindful of his lofty goals, and since even the finest minds are corrupted by poor teaching, the diligent Marcello appointed for Valerio a tutor who was "most skilled in both languages."[61] With a fervor "most remarkable in a child of that age, thinking nothing of sleeplessness, toil, or hunger," Valerio labored in the study of Greek and Latin letters.[62] "He persevered in studying Latin and Greek at every opportunity given him by his father or his tutor, to such an extent that he never stopped reading."[63]

Valerio pursued his studies, his father as constant guide, beyond the confines of classroom and the discipline of memory and recitation. He was avidly curious, interested in everything, and "sought to know what his years denied him."[64] His active mind turned to great and small matters alike, and he would seek explanations for the causes of things from his father or other elders: "And having often seen triremes and biremes and various other kinds of ships, he would eagerly seek to know what their names were, and the names of all their armaments and equipment, and what was the disposition of the sailors and the art of navigation, so much that frequently those knowledgeable in these things, admiring his intelligence, could not answer his questions."[65]

The business of *terraferma* life also aroused Valerio's interest: hounds and horses. How were they to be fed and cared for? How could one tell which would be fleetest? Which suited for the battlefield? When mainland guests (his father's friends) came to visit, Valerio received them properly, inquiring politely, when the opportunity presented itself, as to "the size of their cities, the nature of their sites, the population and customs, and what made each region worthy and great."[66]

Valerio profited from other encounters with paternal visitors as well. When important men of the city came to the palace to salute Marcello or transact business, Valerio would greet them, if his father were out, ask their business, promise to convey their messages, and dismiss them courteously. These matters he would communicate precisely to Marcello on the latter's return, and to his stupefaction: "for they were all the words of a mature man, not a boy."[67] When some dark-robed senators, Marcello's colleagues in the government of Venice, complained during their visit to that notable of the fraud condoned by one of the governors their body had appointed, Valerio charged, when they had gone, that they, more than these events, were to be blamed; the responsibility was theirs.[68] This was one of many examples of Valerio's behavior "seen by me," reports one observer close to the family, who then reports also the next. Valerio's interests, like his father's, ranged beyond the political. Of some learned visitors to their palace, Valerio inquired politely about the structure of the heavens: "what the sky might be, and the sun and the moon and the stars, and by whose labor or command they were moved."[69]

Still it was his father's deeds and concerns that most aroused Valerio's interest. Often he asked about Marcello's military exploits and could retell the tales: "So smoothly and beautifully did he describe cities besieged, mountains overcome by ships, or assaults and victories in their proper order, that he seemed not to narrate the events but to perform them, not just to have heard of them but to have participated."[70] And Valerio yearned to know about the government and history of Venice: "He asked me" (Marcello's words are reported here) "to tell him by what means and by what persons the foundations of our city were built amid these waters and lagoons, and how, boldly, these piles of enormous houses and kingly temples came to be made and raised on these bars of sand; whether the governance of our republic had been from the beginning managed as it is now, and whether its regime had ever been interrupted."[71] The father responded by telling the tale of the history of Venice, as only in those years it was taking form in the hands of humanist scholars and propagandists.

Tutored by his father to assume civic responsibility in the patrician tradition of his ancestors, and by his teachers to admire the heroes of Greece and Rome, the young Valerio yearned to achieve glory himself. To that goal he turned "his whole mind and his eyes."[72] Winning the notice of posterity was the one consolation for the brevity of life, he believed, "by which it happens that when we are absent, still we are present, and though dead we are alive"; it was the one reward for the virtue that cost toil and danger.[73]

With the desire for glory Valerio was always so aflame, "so that even if there were other lesser ones, yet by this zeal of his, it appeared clearly enough that this was going to be his main and outstanding virtue, because there is nothing which more repels luxury, discord, avarice, pride, and other evil ways, but instead it urges continence, toil, liberality, affability, and other goods by which the body and soul are rightly guided to the good life, than the desire for praise and glory."[74] Viewing the military exercises of his elders and his father's soldier friends on one occasion (reported by a sole eyewitness), the remarkable child expressed his desire to excel with a quotation from Vergil.[75]

Among the many indications of the young boy's quest for glory is this memorable anecdote of an event that took place in 1458.[76] Fearful of plague in the city, the Marcello household took refuge in the monastery of San Antonio da Vienna at the furthest point of the city facing the island of Sant'Elena; on its site today, as a result of Napoleon's ordinances, stand the public gardens.[77] The learned prior, Michele Orsini, was one of the *letterati* of Marcello's circle, and a fond friend of the then six-year-old child.

> Valerio used to go daily into the church there for worship at his father's side. Once, when the service was over, he spied on the high altar an armed statue upon a tomb, and pointing, he asked, "Oh, father, who is that armed man, holding in his right hand a sword and the Venetian banner?" To whom his father replied, "He is Vettore Pisani, one of our nobles, famous for his glory in arms and deeds, who by his arms and his virtue restored Venice's fortune in the Genoese war, and by his industry and wit pressed with a wondrous siege the besieging enemy." To whom the boy said softly, "O fortunate man; and when will that day come, on which I, having deserved well of my country, may have such an honor decreed me?"[78]

Hero of the epochal Chioggian war (1378–80) fought successfully against the Genoese, Pisani was one of the few Venetians (outside of the *dogado*) honored by a monument in the early Renaissance.[79] The statue was erected by order of the Senate, ordinarily reluctant to cast glory upon merely human greatness: a rare prize understandably valued by the little boy who began to yearn for his own monument. By 1450, there was completed in Padua Donatello's peerless equestrian monument to the soldier Gattamelata—a valorous servant of Venice, and a man the elder Marcello had known well.[80] When Valerio saw it, he asked the same question he had posed of the Pisani monument: who was this man? Informed of that austere soldier's identity, Valerio once again expressed his yearning for greatness.[81] Two monuments of Renaissance sculpture, admired by us for their beauty, when they were still new moved the spirit of a sensitive child.

Of Valerio's own acts of daring one anecdote is told.[82] The architecture of Venice required that rich and poor inhabit the same neighborhoods; indeed the same buildings. So a young child of the nobility in Venice, unlike his counterpart in much of Europe, rubbed elbows daily with others of quite different social standing. One day Valerio encountered a group of rough youngsters who taunted and threatened him. He held them off, picking up stones as he walked backwards, and hurling them at his opponents in measured pace to cover his retreat. The sounds of this mêlée, as it proceeded from the Campo Sant'Angelo toward the Marcello palace, eventually reached through open windows into the large hall where that patriarch held conversation with his friends. The jurist Matteo Pandolfino, one of the company, leaned out the window to learn the cause of the commotion. Seeing it was the son of his host, he ran out, plucked the boy up, and brought him home.

His father commanded him to describe what had happened. Crying, he reported: "When I had vanquished the boys who were my equals in the piazza, father, moved by envy and also anger they hurled and slung right at my face base and degrading insults, and when in fact I had hit one of them hard in the eye with my fist, the others rounded up aid for their complaining fellow, and aroused a whole mob against me, when I was unaided, as you saw. The great man asked prudently: "Seeing them surrounding you, why didn't you . . . fly for home?" "Because," the boy replied, "it would have been shameful, and I decided it would be unworthy of you, my father, who have taught me never to flee, and of our whole family. For I have heard you often inveighing harshly against such cowards and urging that they should rather by fighting show themselves ready to die honorably than by fleeing to live basely. I wanted . . . to imitate your deeds and obey your words."[83]

"But why," asked his father, the veteran of many battles, "did you hurl stones against those who were unarmed?" "I didn't intend to harm anyone," Valerio replied, "but I threw rocks in order to hold them off with fear of injury, so that I could get to safety." Smiling, his father admonished him: "With such pure virtue, my son, this is the way by which one goes to heaven, where, mortal, made immortal, we live that which is truly life. But be careful henceforth about what you are undertaking. It is the act of a rash man, not a prudent one, to expose oneself to such evident peril with no purpose, with no clearly set public goal or mission—but for liberty, for country, for the common welfare, for loyalty, for justice, for religion, one must boldly and unflinchingly fight and not only not resist death itself, but, more, even desire it. This certainly is the duty of a brave and excellent man and citizen."[84]

Thus the child who seemed to be the image of his father strove to conform himself to his father's image, to gain identity with him in mind and spirit. For the two seemed as one: and just as Marcello recognized in his son his own face, the child seemed to know himself in his father, and like Narcissus, could not wrest himself away from the beloved face.[85] "What shall we say about our Valerio, or what shall we not say of him who . . . beyond the standard of his age, and beyond the character and nature of other infants, having before him the image of his father—and of a most excellent and constant father indeed—so bent his eyes and mind and soul on that image and with such constancy fixed on it, that, other concerns neglected and cast aside, all the time he wished, needed, and sought his father alone?"[86]

This relationship was surely intense beyond the norm, crowding out siblings, friends, and, conspicuously, the child's mother: she was barred from their duet much as the baby's nurse had been on the day that he first met his father. Her exclusion in part reflected contemporary assumptions about the father's greater role in creating life. "The father loves his child as an artist does his creation; and as much as nature exceeds art in its nobility and excellence, so much more intense is the father's love for his offspring— all the more so in that the principle of paternal virtue is principally responsible for the formation of the child; but the mother is involved only passively," as Aristotle, Galen, and Avicenna believed, and in their train the leaders of European thought.[87] Valerio's mother was sidelined because all mothers were seen as lesser than all fathers; and more, because this father infringed upon even that lesser role she played.

While the stern and hardened soldier gently nurtured his child, Valerio in turn revered him, fixed his eyes on his face, and clung to his side.[88] He would not be separated from his parent, as that parent's words report.

He grew in years with such force of love towards me, his father, that this was the infant's most amazing quality. Never did he babble, never could he attempt words, unless he saw me. He insisted, when I was at home, on hanging from my neck; and if I were somewhere else, he was struck as though by a blow, and was overcome with sorrow, he wailed, nor was he ever calm unless he saw that I was about to pick him up. Then if, annoyed with these demands, I put him back down, he clung to my knees, to my feet, so that pressed by these bold entreaties I would pick him up again in my embrace. If ever I was agitated with anxiety or perturbation, on account of which I pushed him away from me, he acted as if he thought of nothing other than me, he inspected me, I might almost say, to see when I might be free from these troublesome thoughts, from care, from pain, so that he could return to me, in whom alone he seemed to delight. Even at night, in bed, he never wished to be taken away from me.[89]

Later, infancy behind him, Valerio was still his father's shadow:

When you [Marcello] were at home, he was never very far from your side . . . ; he either stood next to you while you sat or followed you when you walked, observing whatever you did or said. He acutely inspected your face and every motion of your body in order to imitate them. . . . And if perhaps he noticed you from time to time wrapped in thought, as sometimes happened, silent he would attentively examine the motions of your eyes and of your whole body; then would ask his mother or the servants, "Is there anything bothering father? What is he thinking about in that way?"[90]

Marcello thought about Venice and glory, and Valerio probed his thoughts. He accompanied Marcello through the city, curious, questioning. The history of that state in which his father dwelt, the military lore in which his father was learned, Valerio wished ardently to share. "Above all he wanted to know," for this had been Marcello's climactic achievement, "by what art, by what genius those ships had been dragged from hill to hill, across dangerous chasms and paths, and lowered into the Lago di Garda. And when he learned that that accomplishment had been planned and completed by me, then he wished me to explain each detail, as if what his glorious father had attained for himself and posterity, from that standard . . . of life and virtue he [Valerio] would think it shameful to degenerate."[91]

Marcello was surely blessed: God had graced the Marcello family with an extraordinary child, worthy of his great father and his noble clan, destined to meet and exceed the standard set by a parade of heroic ancestors.[92] Valerio's father gloried in his son's radiant promise which showed so early in life, and nourished for him lofty hopes. "I could foresee that he would accumulate in himself by his acute mind the virtue of my ancestors, so that our whole posterity would be enriched by the glory of deeds well done."[93]

While Marcello looked forward to Valerio's achievements, Valerio dwelled in and through his father—preferring, as he once said, to die if that would spare his father's life. If his father were to die, Valerio lamented, "what would be left to me of life, what solace, what refuge, unless I die? so that within that embrace where, living, I joyously rested, dying, also, when the fates determined, I might reside? Oh, what a tragedy for the *patria* would his death cause, what grief to friends, neighbors, and family? so that without doubt I would rather give up my life, than with such grief lose my most excellent parent."[94]

৵   ৵   ৵

But it was Valerio and not his father who was fated to die first; and the father's life was spared, it seems, only so that he might view his son's demise. Soon after Easter of 1460, Valerio journeyed with his father and his tutor and their entourage by boat to Monselice, whose formidable *castello,* one of the most famous fortifications in northern Italy, had been purchased and refurbished by the Marcello family.[95] They, with Valerio's mother, were greeted by a crowd of local dignitaries (*cives primarii*) in the garden court-yard. "Here all turn their eyes upon Valerio, all salute him, all embrace and admire him." They entered the gate in full ceremony, delighting in air heavy with the sweetness of flowers and fruit and the songs of birds. Valerio pulled his tutor off for a tour of the castle, showing him all of the secret nooks and crannies he must have explored during lazy vacations over the years: "so that I rejoiced to see the boy exult with joy."

But there were thorns in that deceptive garden; in August, Valerio fell ill. A local doctor rushed in, and Matteolo, "prince of physicians," was summoned from nearby Padua, a center of medical learning.[96] They brought scalpels to bleed the child, a full equipage of bottles, iron, and fire. "At this the gentle and delicate boy paled, and feared to suffer the insolent wound." His father besought him, so that they might both be healed, to undergo the treatment. Persuaded, the child offered himself to the knife and the flame. His health apparently regained, Valerio returned soon after with the family to Venice, and there gladly resumed the studies that his illness had interrupted.[97] The fever in the end demanded its victim.[98] Defeated once, it seized the child again at Christmastime; its menace serious this time, it seemed, for like Hector who was defeated in the end not by Achilles so much as by Apollo, in Valerio's illness could be detected the hand of God. Returning to the house, Marcello felt the burning body and, terrified, summoned doctors immediately. First among them was Gerardo Bolderio, reputed as the Aesculapius of the day. He felt Valerio's pulse, comforted the frightened parents, provided herbal drinks and unguents, and employed all the resources known to the medical art; no greater care had been exercised in treating the wound of Menelaus! Valerio now noticed him. His father said, "Here is that Gerardo, my son, who recalls even the dead to life." The boy recognized him, for he had seen him before.

"When yesterday evening my father asked you to be called here," Valerio said, "I did not know you, nor nor did it enter my mind who you were, and the name I heard you called by I did not hear. But now, seeing you, I recognize you. Because you are he whom once at Monselice my father called in from Padua for the sake of our Girolamo (Valerio's nephew by an elder brother) who suffered from a grave illness. You came at night, however, at which time my father ordered that the gates of the castle be opened, and you wore a . . . cloak and a hat, and a . . . tunic, and on your feet red boots; your belt was black with a buckle and golden keys; a sword hung down from the belt, its hilt adorned with inlaid ivory and brass. In your right hand you carried a whip. Transferring the whip to your left hand, you remained silent for a moment. Then, after taking Girolamo's pulse and examining his urine, and you commanded my father and all present to be of good heart."[99]

Valerio's feat of memory impressed the doctor:

Gerardo was stupefied to hear this; and with his lips compressed and brow wrinkled, quietly he reviewed all in his own mind, then turning to those present confessed himself to be amazed that a child so sick could recall in exact detail with such accuracy and order things done so many years ago. . . . His father whispered, having quietly reckoned the time to himself, that Valerio had not yet completed his third year when these things were seen and heard and done at Monselice.[100]

As Gerardo continued to treat Valerio, the boy gave further evidence of his intelligence and powers of recall. The doctor inquired about the nature of his illness—what kinds of pains? intermittent or constant? in what part of the body? greater by day or by night, fasting or after meals? Valerio reported so precisely that Gerardo commented, amazed as before, that his description of the illness exactly matched Avicenna's.[101]

The illness so lucidly described by the patient was grave, and worsening. Gerardo and his assistant entered the room, and Valerio smiled at them, hoping perhaps that they now offered the help they had tried in vain to provide before, or perhaps that they might torment him a little less; and his concern was just, since the day before a surgeon commissioned to bleed his veins had cruelly tortured him. "The doctors came near, felt the vein, consulted, examined his urine. They said he was a little worse. In the midst of this, a Jewish doctor was called . . . , of whom the boy was terrified;" and the Jew, since Valerio would not allow himself to be touched by the man, examined a stool specimen in the chamber pot, then "discussed something secretly (I don't know what) with the other doctors; and then having tried to console you [Marcello], they departed."[102] Marcello grew desperate:

> When I saw him, I scarcely thought that it would result in death, that my son would desert me, his father; unthinking me, it never entered my mind. At that time I believed that the beginning of his illness was nothing, a trifle, and I thought that his good health would soon return. But when I saw that the situation slipped into serious illness, oh me! what effort did I expend to save him! How I exhorted the doctors to cure him! how assiduously I urged them! what vows did I offer for his safety not only with tears but with rivers of tears! I believe I canvassed all the judges in heaven in order to make all the saints friendly to me. I called for the help of mortals and immortals; vainly I tried everything. . . . I approached all the monasteries of our city, and all the most religious men of the religious orders I wearied with my importunity.[103]

The Marcello household ceased to hope. Valerio commended to his father's special attention a beloved sister, his favorite from birth. Marcello heard and, the muscles of his face rigid, "like a rock," stared at his son, stupefied.[104] "Miserable, I was stabbed by sorrow on sorrow; I could not speak, nor respond to his sweetest words; I could bring forth only tears, and sobs."[105] Weak though he was, Valerio collected his strength and raised his voice to heaven in prayer: in the name of Christ and the virgin Mary, he asked "that you remove this illness, if it please you, and restore me to my dear father and my beloved mother." And as a sign of his veneration, he pledged all his clothing and other personal ornaments to the poor.[106]

His father, touched, responded with his own vow. "If you recover," he told his son, "we shall both put on a mourning habit; and you shall wear one of silk for a year, but I of wool, and for my whole life." The remarkable child (who enjoyed luxurious garments) responded: "Stop, stop, my father. Indeed I shall wear mourning dress, and of wool, for that is fitting; but you shall wear elegant dress, as always, befitting a senator. For in you is expressed the honor not only of your family and your loved ones alone, but also of the republic."[107] When the child spoke these honorable words, he was one day away from death.[108]

Once-rosy cheeks now white, coral lips turned ashen, nose and chin trembling, the whole of his tiny body possessed by fever, Valerio fixed his eyes on heaven. Marcello stood by, helpless, wretched, weeping. "And do you cry, my father?" said the remarkable boy; "that is not worthy of a man."[109] "Don't dare to think any longer, dear father, that you can alter my fate with your tears. . . . You who are great with the glory of great deeds, do not allow yourself to look unlike yourself, base and common, and in this condition display yourself to the low and thoughtless foulmouthed mob."[110] Rebuked, the father fled from the room and in private collected himself; then returned to ask of his child a last embrace.[111] The boy kissed him, hugged him, called him "father," and with his own hands wiped the tears from his parent's eyes.[112] But now nearly lifeless, Valerio let out cries of pain so fierce that the walls themselves seemed to shake. "My son," you say, "these cries torture me." The boy heard, and suffered all the more, in silence. Evening came, and Valerio could speak no more; his pulse could no longer be heard.[113]

A priest hurried in. Valerio made his confession, kissing the offered cross held in trembling hands, bathing it with his tears.[114] He died, his eyes fixed on heaven, and a sweet odor (a sign of sanctity) filled the room. The cries of grief resounded through the household and neighborhood of the Marcellos.[115] "Oh, how my heart was wounded! Oh, how my body then without spirit, without any sensation, collapsed! Oh, how the whole gathering of relatives and household then believed that I had died with my son! . . . They are inhuman, they are impious, they are cruel, who view the deaths of their children with dry eyes!"[116] "For these are the sorts of things which cannot leave the souls of men unmoved."[117]

> Then you, his father, viewing the lifeless body of your son, stand in the black night like a stone; and having made the sign of the cross over the body, flee into the shadows alone, and grieve mightily. The whole palace is arrayed in black mourning, while heaven is adorned with festive banners. The mourning father dresses himself in black, and your son is robed in white, and borne to the funeral of the blessed angel Valerio. An angel, Valerio triumphantly enters the heavens; and we who are still on earth suffer. Unhappy, sorrowful, entombed by this calamity, we unwillingly live our lives.[118]

Though we suffer, we should rather rejoice: Valerio looks upon the face of Christ, and, released from this mortal prison, dwells in "palaces of immortality," in an untroubled holy city, "sacrosanct, immune, safe, impregnable, alive with concord, peace and tranquility."[119] He is not dead, but changed: alive and glorified. He has achieved blessedness, and in his present bliss awaits his aged father, destined soon to join him. Free of care, he exults amid the angel chorus, and prepares for his beloved father a home in heaven beside him:[120] "He has not deserted you, nor has he left his dear mother, his sweet brothers," but has gone to prepare your way.[121]

Yet Marcello wept. From heaven, Valerio looks down and is surprised: why, when he is so happy, was his former home still draped in mourning, beset with strife? He can be heard calling from heaven: "O father, is this your love for me? am I celebrated by your unkempt hair? by this uncut beard? I see mourning clothes; stop and congratulate me, who rejoice so, on my felicity, O father." "But I would prefer, my son, that you be here with me," replies the father, "that you kiss me and be the staff of my old age and at the last my heir." It is an impious father who begrudges his son such happiness, however; and for heirs, he may accept in his embrace the dead child's brothers and cousins. "And if you are Christian, if a worshipper of God, father, you should be gladdened no less to have given birth to an angel in heaven, than to have bestowed upon the republic those five preeminent citizens."[122] Though Valerio has not joined the ranks of the Venetian nobility, he has joined that "more glorious" order which reigns in heaven.[123] Such arguments do not solace Marcello. Not only to his glorified child, but to his friends and family, as well, were the hair, the beard, the pallor, the unremitting depression, an affront and a mystery.

The father would relinquish neither his grief nor his hold on life. An unlikely mourner, this veteran of twenty years of battle, this seasoned diplomat and statesman, this wealthy and proud aristocrat, grieved for his child publicly and defiantly. Eventually he expressed that grief and that defiance in the book that is his legacy and our window on the mind of a man who, like his son, is long since buried. The first fourteen works praise the dead and console the living. The fifteenth (apparently by Marcello himself) contains the father's response. The capstone of the collection, it defiantly confronts its companion compositions.

Marcello spurns the consolation offered him. He will face the charge of cowardice. The death of a child is a wound that cannot heal. He addresses his desperate apology, or *excusatio,* for his unceasing grief to the royal personage, the Frenchman René of Anjou, a longtime friend by correspondence and a comrade from the Lombard wars: "You decide, illustrious king, you judge my case. So many of the finest orators have written to me about the death of my son, and by their most eloquent letters, and not only by their letters and by their orations, but also by their books, they have tried to dry my tears, tried vainly to console me. But they have not yet been able to move me or change me: I could not be even in the slightest recalled from my grief."[124] "These consolatory books, therefore, for thus I now name them, gathered up and arranged in this volume, as they were written and sent to me, I send to you."[125]

Such is the book, and this account could stop here. But like all fine books, this one does not settle questions so much as raise them. Who is this Marcello, who liked to live in a fortress? who willingly rode into the midst of battle instead of watching, like most of his peers, from the safer sidelines? who liked paintings and books, theology and geography? who knew Latin and maybe Greek? who gathered about him a small academy of literati wherever he went? who had a wife and many children, and loved profoundly and mourned uncontrollably for, of all of these, this one son? Who are these writers who rushed to console Marcello? were they friends? were they bought? did they see the events they described? how did they propose to argue away the fact of death? Who was this child? why was he so beloved? can we find him amid the conventions and hyperbole of funerary rhetoric? And what of the book itself? is it simply a compilation of works, as it seems, or an artful and premeditated product?

The pages that follow address these questions about the man and his deeds, the father and his child, the author and his book.

CHAPTER TWO

The Birth of a Book

ॐ

To create the book that was the child Valerio's one enduring sepulchral monument, Jacopo Antonio Marcello recruited the pens of professionals hungry for profit and eager to dwell in proximity to power. The idea for the project grew slowly, originating in the spontaneous participation of the learned but falling gradually under the shaping hand of the patron and his agents.

Valerio Marcello had been dead less than a month when Niccolò Sagundino addressed to the bereaved father a letter of consolation.[1] That letter launched the project (never envisioned by the author) which would overshadow the nobleman's remaining years. In the manuscript book that now resides in the Hunter collection at Glasgow University, Sagundino's letter is the initial work of the series written on the death of Valerio Marcello. The volume bears a title, the creation of modern cataloguers, which reflects the preeminence of Sagundino's contribution: *De obitu Valerii Marcelli* [*consolationes*] *Nicolae Secundini et aliorum* (Consolations on the death of Valerio Marcello by Niccolò Sagundino and others).

The erudite and worldly-wise Sagundino was a likely person to spark this literary event.[2] Born in 1402 in the ancient city of Chalcis in Greek Euboea (called Negroponte by its Venetian overlords), he had entered the colonial bureaucracy at Thessalonica (Salonika) by 1430. To fill that position, he must have already acquired Latin literacy as well as an advanced Byzantine culture before he came to Italy to serve as translator during the Council of Ferrara-Florence in 1438–39. In the years that followed, he performed missions as papal secretary in both Italy and Greece. Knowledgeable in the events of the Turkish advance towards the kernel of old Byzantium, he served after the fall of Constantinople in 1453 with the title of ducal secretary as an important agent and trusted diplomat for the Venetians. It was their mission to alert self-absorbed Italian powers to the greater matter of an imminent Turkish threat in the east.

A deft politician, Sagundino was also a multilingual intellectual of considerable capacity, demonstrating in extensive works his power to translate

Greek philosophical concepts into the language of contemporary humanist Latinity: one of only a few men in the first half of the fifteenth century fully competent in both traditions. Sagundino appealed for and won the support of many Venetian patricians, patrons, and learned men, for his literary efforts, but had never been able to win sufficient assistance to free himself from the need to labor in that city's hardworking secretariat. Even though he may not have been an intimate of Marcello's at the end of 1460, to approach that nobleman directly with the offer of a small literary work was a step consistent with his past. He may also have been spurred to undertake a work in the genre of consolation because he had himself very recently undergone a momentous loss: that of his wife, his three children, and his books as the consequence of shipwreck. He was consoled for his loss by the humanist Pietro Perleone, a Marcello familiar, who reminded him of his benefits and urged him to think of the munificence of his patrons among the Venetian nobility. When Sagundino, that bereaved father, wrote to his counterpart Marcello, he may have hoped for and received the expected reward: it was the former's custom to hope, and the latter's to give.

Typical of Sagundino's works, his consolatory letter to Marcello is elegant, succinct, and intelligent. Sagundino will attempt to console Marcello, the letter opens, adding his humble gift to those already presented by other scholars and friends.[3] "Believe me, I was myself overcome with incredible pain and sorrow when I received the news of your son's death, nor, wretched, could I contain my groans and tears; I could not put out of my mind the fate befallen this excellent child, in form, spirit, mind, and birth illustrious and noble, especially when I recalled the loss of so many children which I myself suffered not long before."[4] There follows a eulogy of Valerio, including a brief story of his infancy and early growth, of the visits of doctors to his sickbed, and of his death. "You are justified in grieving his terrible loss," Sagundino says, and alluding to the community of learned friends in Marcello's entourage, he adds "we also who love you, serve you, revere you, grieve with you as well."[5]

Grief, nevertheless, must be moderated, cautions the humanist, and the noble and wise man must confront death with courage. While on earth, you must perform your duty to family, friends, and city, and understand that your son has moved on to a better life. In closing, Sagundino recommends himself to the nobleman while conventionally deprecating his own work: "I beg you, and pray that by your humanity and wisdom you may graciously and kindly accept this work however modest, even if not suited to one of your great reputation, nor in every way meeting your expectations, but measured rather by my good will and intentions. For in writing it, I assure you that I applied all diligence, concern, effort and good faith."[6]

Sagundino's consolatory work to Marcello was probably the first to be composed of the series of works eventually collected in the Glasgow codex by the bereaved father. But another and briefer letter not destined to appear in that collection may have been written even earlier than Sagundino's, or at least not long after. Perhaps it is one of those Sagundino had in mind when, so early in the history of the consolations of Marcello, he alluded to the works of "many" admirers who had already written in the attempt to lighten the father's sorrow.[7]

Its author Perleone has already been encountered.[8] Scion of a noble Riminese family born around 1400, he studied with Francesco Filelfo in the 1430s. Although not Greek-born like Sagundino, Perleone was nevertheless inducted into Italian Hellenism as the student of Filelfo who had mastered his Greek in Constantinople. A resident of Venice from 1436 to 1441 (where he gained limited citizenship *"de intus"* in 1438), Perleone journeyed himself to Constantinople to perfect his Greek under John Argyropoulos. An adept now of Greek as well as Latin literature, Perleone returned to Rimini as historiographer for the despot Sigismondo Malatesta. Later, he returned to Venice. In 1460,[9] he competed with George of Trebizond and Giovanni Mario Filelfo to win the position of public historiographer, which the Senate was then planning to institute. Much discussed, that position was not in fact created at this time. The main effect of the contest was to create enmity among its aspirants, all of whom would soon compete as well in consoling Jacopo Antonio Marcello.

When Perleone reached for the plum role of public historian, he already occupied a prestigious position in the Venetian social and cultural arena. From 1457 until his death (in 1462 or 1463) he taught at the publicly funded San Marco school.[10] One of the most famous of northern Italy's public schools, it had been created to train in humanist skills the future secretaries of the Venetian republic. In fact, it was attended in the early years by many young patricians through whom Perleone could have made valuable contacts with members of the city's ruling elite. Among his noble pupils there were the lifelong friends Pietro Barozzi and Pietro Dolfin, destined to become first-ranking prelates of the church, and the future doge Leonardo Loredan. Contacts with senior members of the families of these young men were not to be despised.

During these years, Perleone was a member of Jacopo Antonio Marcello's circle. Soon after Valerio's death he would write in haste a touching and revealing letter. Months later, he would write again of the tragic death. The later work exceeded the first one in length and depth and displaced it in Perleone's mind and Marcello's. The eloquent earlier letter was not included in the funerary collection, but it was copied and recopied nevertheless as a model of the genre.

It exists today in a scattering of miscellaneous collections of humanist works and letters: miscellaneous, though not featureless.[11] Of these, one is the Ferrara codex which also contains copies of other elements of the Marcello corpus. One is a Munich manuscript compiled by the indefatigable humanist Hartmann Schedel; here the Perleone letter is dated 1467, six years after its composition. One is a Venetian collection in several hands, among them that of the bibliophile and historian Marino Sanuto. Detached from the Glasgow texts, this little letter enjoyed considerable literary fame.

Perleone's letter opens with an apology. He writes in haste in order to fulfill promptly his duty to Marcello, overcome by the recent death. It is better, he explains, to write late than not to write at all; he cannot be blamed if the delay was due to his ignorance of the situation, and not to his negligence.[12] The author will address squarely what must have been the father's complaint of the unfairness of Valerio's death: "I do not think that you grieve that you have lost a son, who had been born to die, and to resist necessity would be alien to your wisdom; but rather that you lost him to a premature and sudden death." But all live a life as long as God has willed, Perleone counseled, and no longer. When Valerio died in his eighth year, he had reached, in God's eyes, "extreme old age," for that was the span of time assigned to him.[13] Rather than complain, Marcello should rejoice in all his blessings, and be content that after so many years, he had been asked to surrender only one son to God: "Indeed he is a dishonest debtor who refuses to pay, an ungrateful one who pays unwillingly."[14] Nor must Marcello think of Valerio's death as "violent" [*violens*], for Valerio died willingly [*volens*]. He died in the company of his father, his teacher, his peers, unaware of pleasures not yet tasted, confident of his place in heaven.[15] Marcello must therefore stem his grief, and give way to the wishes of those about him: "Yield therefore to your dignity and reputation; to your Valerio, who doesn't wish you to mourn; to all your other friends and children, finally, in whom sorrow is born of your sorrow, both because you have lost a son and because they see you in tears."[16]

Marcello was indeed unlucky. Valerio had died on the first of January, 1461. A mere three months later, a second child died: Marcello's daughter Taddea.[17] A consolatory letter written only six days later on 7 April by George of Trebizond, notes the second tragedy while it is concerned with the first.[18] Like Sagundino, George was born in Greek-speaking Byzantium (in the Trebizond or Trapezuntium of his name, a port on the Black Sea). Like Perleone, he had come to Venice to teach. His Venetian career and contacts reached back to the early years of the century. In 1460, George was back in Venice, where he became embroiled in one of the notable literary confrontations of the generation (as mentioned above), and engaged in a battle with the young and ambitious Giovanni Mario Filelfo.[19] Known to contemporaries as Francesco's son as well as for his own considerable talents, the younger Filelfo (not yet forty at this juncture) had impressed many with his brilliance, and came to impress most with his testiness.

In the spring of 1460, Filelfo was appointed as the first head of the last to be formed of Venice's public schools: the school of rhetoric. He had joined the competition for the planned position of public historiographer. His opponents included his two elders, the mild-mannered Perleone and George of Trebizond. The contestants fought tooth and nail, and Filelfo finished off the battle with a nasty invective against his competitors.[20] The senior participant, Perleone, wrote his old teacher Francesco Filelfo to complain of the vile behavior of the latter's son.[21] In the aftermath, both George and Filelfo left Venice for good.

When George wrote to console Marcello in the spring of 1461, these events had not run their course. George was still in Venice and, hopeful of advancement, was plainly seeking to secure Marcello's patronage. The nobleman's circle of literati already included Perleone, and would soon include the younger Filelfo, with whose father the nobleman had recently exchanged letters. George himself had previous literary contacts with Marcello. Before the first of March in 1457, he had translated Ptolemy's *Cosmography*, probably at that nobleman's bequest.[22] He sent his text with a dedicatory letter to Marcello, who rerouted the work on that date, rewritten and decorated, newly accompanied by a fine *mappamondo* and prefaced with his own introductory letter, to the royal Frenchman René d'Anjou.

Having found the Ptolemy translation acceptable, Marcello might be pleased as well by an elegant variation on the common theme of consolation. At the end of his work, George would accordingly place his bid for Marcello's attention: "I have written these brief remarks on account of your rare virtue, your unheard-of humanity, your kindness to me, and my duty to you as a faithful debtor. I beg that you gladly receive them as I gladly offer them."[23]

George's offering, like those that preceded his, is a simple letter: longer than Perleone's, briefer than Sagundino's. His central concern is Valerio's youth. Marcello complained that his son had been taken from him so young; but many have died young, George replies, and especially the gifted:

"However bright is the tremendous promise of the spirit of adolescents or even young boys who have not yet attained the age of adolescence, their life is often exchanged for death."[24] Hercules and Alexander died young, as did Marcello's own Roman namesake Marcellus, the son of the emperor Augustus's sister Octavia, at a mere eighteen.[25] And now Valerio has been seized by death from his father's embrace. In his infancy and on his deathbed, he had been extraordinarily close to his father, whom he resembled in intelligence and great accomplishments. Precocious in virtue and in learning, he could be compared with the finest ancient exemplars. Like other natural creatures who reached their maturity early, Valerio passed naturally to an early death: "For all animals that quickly achieve their purpose have a briefer life. . . . And . . . the trees and plants that earlier yield flowers and fruits the sooner meet their deaths."[26]

Just as it was Valerio's nature to flower quickly and die young, it is Marcello's to vanquish his grief as he has vanquished his enemies. For a man of his glorious reputation (won by his warlike deeds, which George here reviews), such excessive sorrow is shameful. "For all our perfection lies in this, that we do not depend on other or external things, but only on ourselves in whom we find all the principles of living well." These are found in the depths of the soul, but only in adversity.[27]

With this literary gift, and hopeful of some reward, George approached the beneficent nobleman. Perleone had already addressed his first consolatory letter (but not his longer work) to the bereaved father. Sagundino had submitted his lengthier one. George could well have known of these or other literary bids for the bereaved Marcello's attention: the Venetian humanist circle was small, and the events of Valerio's death and his father's grief were fully displayed in public. But he makes no mention of them in his own contribution to the consolatory series. And like his predecessors, George is unaware of the stacks of manuscript that would in the end come to be composed in memory of the child, or of the scope of the literary event that would emerge from the consolation of Marcello. Soon, writing in consolation of Jacopo Antonio Marcello would become the fashionable thing to do.

ℰↄ   ℰↄ   ℰↄ

The letters of Sagundino, Perlone, and George must have been circulated by the authors or by Marcello himself. The former were all professional humanists who promoted their literary progeny. The subsequent diffusion of texts (beyond the Glasgow manuscript) suggests that no little attention was paid them. But what of Marcello? He, too, may have shown the letters around, as part of a larger project conceived in these months. His later behavior suggests that he became about this time (although still in deep and desperate mourning) interested in acquiring a greater cumulus of literary attempts at consolation.

Regarding his interest there are two principal clues: the monumental manuscript that was eventually to result; and his message to Francesco Filelfo, transmitted orally by an intermediary (Marchesius Varisinus, Sforza's ambassador to Venice), before June 1461. Filelfo responded on 27 June. Varisinus had spoken to him of Marcello's wish, and although he would rather express his reverence for that nobleman on a happier occasion, nevertheless he would do what was requested: "I shall promptly bring into being that which you desire."[28] Only the date is uncertain, since Filelfo redated his letters misleadingly when he constructed his letter-book, less in accord with reality than the need to promote his career.[29] But the letter's contents point to a date, if not exactly the one it bore as it left Filelfo's hand, one very nearly the same.

The itinerant humanist Francesco Filelfo had already lived many years by his pen when Marcello approached him in 1461.[30] Italy's leading native Hellenist, Filelfo had been at home in Venice many years earlier, receiving citizenship there in 1420.[31] It was with the assistance of Venetian patricians that he soon afterwards journeyed to Greece to master its language and literature. To Venice he returned, laden with family and books in 1427. Receiving a chill welcome in Venice,[32] he proceeded the next year to Bologna, then Florence, Siena, and eventually Milan, for his middle years; ultimately his travels would take him to Rome, Naples, and back to Florence. Filelfo had established himself in Milan from June of 1439, summoned by the Visconti duke then fast engaged in war with Venice. With the accession of Sforza a decade later, he quickly changed coats to become tutor to the Sforza progeny[33] and court poet of a new dynasty.

For the new duke he wrote the epic *Sforziad,* and was rewarded by the largesse and the neglect that rulers customarily bestowed upon their learned clients.[34] Taking advantage of contacts made in these years, he arranged a promising position for his own son, Giovanni Mario. That young man joined the court of René d'Anjou in Marseilles, where from 1448 to 1450 he held the title of "juge du palais," organized the library and taught Greek (perhaps to the sovereign himself). From Milan, Filelfo issued moral exhortations and career advice to his son, and expressions of gratitude to the royal patron who had granted such opportunities to his brilliant but vagrant off-spring.[35]

In this milieu, Filelfo must also have encountered Marcello, who had for several years been Sforza's colleague. That encounter took place even before the death of Valerio, and is documented by a letter of 14 May 1460. Here, after some discussion of moral philosophical matters, Filelfo expressed his pleasure that he had heard "from the talk of many that I am most dear to you, and that you speak of me highly, and feel most cordially towards me."[36] For his part, he had the highest opinion of the Venetian: for "you are a great man, and exceptionally generous, and especially friendly towards those who, dedicated to the good arts [those *studia humanitatis* central to Renaissance culture], zealously seek immortality for themselves and assist others to gain it."[37] The links between Filelfo and Sforza and Filelfo and Marcello also involve those between Sforza and René, Sforza and Marcello, and Marcello and René, as later chapters will show. Of concern at the moment is that Filelfo was resident at the court of Milan, and disposed to accommodate his wishes when Marcello asked for a favor in the spring of 1461.

Before the end of that year, Filelfo had written a work vast in scale and importance, dedicated to Marcello: the *De obitu Valerii filii consolatio* (Consolation on the death of your son Valerio).[38] This fruit of Filelfo's pen may be considered for its humanist grace and philosophical range as one of the most important consolatory works of the age. Marcello thought so, too. Not only did he add the work to the pile he must by now have been assembling for inclusion in a single celebratory volume; but he also rewarded the author a few months later with a gift of immense value: a silver basin splendidly worked in gold weighing more than seven pounds and worth more than one hundred *zecchini*.[39] The gift is known from the story of its receipt by the wily Filelfo. The humanist ran to Sforza with the valuable cup and offered it to his master as a token of obedience: for himself, he desired not wealth but virtue. Filelfo deserved his gift, for the *Consolatio* is the jewel of the corpus of Marcello consolations: the only one to circulate broadly in many manuscript and printed editions beyond the Venetian circle to which it was aimed.

Much longer than the earlier letters (more than three times as long as Sagundino's, six times as long as George's), Filelfo's *Consolatio* is many things. It is a personal exhortation to the grief-stricken father, compassionate and intimate. It is a consolatory tract of undoubted originality and depth. It is a well-wrought biography of the child. It is a full-scale eulogy of Marcello and his city. With Filelfo's work, the genre of *Consolatio in obitu Valerii filii* takes on a new and irreversible dimension, although the model that author supplies will not again be equaled.

Filelfo was a veteran of child death.[40] Not long before such a tragedy

struck Marcello, Filelfo had lost his own eight-year-old son, Olimpio Gellio. Like Valerio, the gifted Olimpio spoke with an eloquence far beyond
his age, and possessed both unique virtue and beauty. Like Marcello, who
was his exact contemporary just as their sons were agemates (according to
the scholar's not quite exact reckoning),[41] Filelfo was overcome with grief.
"A companion stricken with the same disease, it should be recognized that
I myself must be consoled as much as I console you. For what counsel can
he give who cannot advise himself? What hope can he bring another when
he himself is in despair?"[42] In consoling Marcello in the work that follows,
Filelfo proposes also to console himself, wounded by the same blow.[43]

Yet Filelfo's profession should not be accepted uncritically. That poet's
literary past abounds with cases where he had manipulated his self-
presentation with the aim of self-promotion. His aim here may be the simpler one of performing the commission made him by Marcello rather than
(or at least alongside) the grander one of reaching out sympathetically to
another human being in need. Filelfo's loss is no doubt genuine (as no
doubt he genuinely mourned the many other deaths he experienced of his
children, his wife, his friends). Yet the record implies he would not have
written a full-scale consolation in the last months of 1461 if Marcello had
not asked him to do so.[44]

What then is the purpose of Filelfo's opening claims of the identity of
his condition with his patron's? It is to establish an equivalency between
humanist-for-hire and high-ranking nobleman, it can be argued, that will
permit a special intimacy. That intimacy builds upon the comradeship that
is also implied by humanist style and convention, whereby the lowly hack
and lofty patron companionably exchange the "tu" of the familiar form
and speak of friendship where they mean obligation. Thus Sagundino and
George of Trebizond had addressed Marcello as friends, where they were
clearly suppliants.

But Filelfo's approach to the nobleman is even more confident: he does
not so much address a treatise to Marcello as engage him in a conversation,
coaxing and cajoling where other consolers lectured and accused. Filelfo's
claim of relatedness to Marcello—not only as a friend and admirer, but as
a fellow-sufferer from the pain of grief—establishes the framework for the
Consolatio. In the interstices are mustered familiar consolatory arguments,
and the narratives of the lives of Valerio, his father, and of Venice.

Drawing Marcello into a dialogue, Filelfo presents arguments *in seriatim*
for the suspension of grief, and exhorts his interlocutor to assent. With this
tactic, Filelfo is able to run through the gamut of consolatory arguments,
at the same time maintaining a personal link to the bereaved parent whose

favor he seeks to win. Having concluded the argument, for instance, that Valerio died fortunately before encountering the perils and evils of this life, Filelfo turns to Marcello, still wrapped in sorrow in spite of the humanist's lengthy peroration: "I have resolved not to stop talking until I have restored you to yourself, as I in my grief have been restored to myself."[45]

Later, having demonstrated that Valerio now enjoys a place in heaven, Filelfo hectors the obdurate father: "Wherefore if you have decided to hear and obey Francesco Filelfo, who is himself in the same situation you are and who loves you greatly, you will not grieve for the death of your son Valerio but rather rejoice."[46] Free your friends from the pain of your grief, he exhorts, when he had run the course of his consolatory arguments: "All of us to whom you are dear lament your case. . . . So free us from the pain of sorrow, which you will be able to do by one single act, if we see that you have put an end to the bitterness of such great grief."[47]

In the Glasgow collection, as in other manuscripts and printed versions, Filelfo's substantial prose *Consolatio* is followed by a Greek elegy of a mere three pages also written by Filelfo for Marcello on the same date and on the same consolatory theme.[48] Marcello had amply displayed in the past his appreciation of the Greek tradition, having arranged for the compilation of manuscript books centered on a Greek text and its Latin translation.[49] Now it seems he esteemed Filelfo's verse as an adornment of the volume he intended to compile: the work of a fine contemporary poet in the still-living language of an ancient civilization.

Like its prose companion, the elegy stirred considerable interest, and was translated at least twice. The translation of Ludovico Carbone, following the original Greek in the Glasgow collection and in other versions, was composed at the behest of Borso d'Este, ruler of Ferrara.[50] A former student of Guarino Guarini Veronese's and court humanist at Ferrara, Carbone would later write his own consolation for Marcello, to be discussed below. An unrelated translation was also prepared by the Milanese Leonardo Grifo, a student of Francesco Filelfo's, panegyrist of Sforza, and subsequently prelate of the church.[51] The work appears in a Venetian miscellany alongside Carbone's, but did not attain equal note. It cannot be told whether Carbone's translation was preferred to Grifo's from the first, or whether Grifo's appeared after Marcello had already committed himself to the Ferrarese product. Both works appeared between December 25, 1461, and November, 1463: probably closer to the earlier date.

Even before Filelfo penned his precious elegy or his full-scale *Consolatio*, he had written to console Marcello on behalf of his employer Francesco Sforza, the duke of Milan.[52] That newcomer to the halls of power had known Marcello for more than twenty years when Valerio died. Though "more a warrior and politician than *letterato*,"[53] Sforza had received a courtier's education at Ferrara and Naples. His understanding of the importance of books is demonstrated by his active patronage of literary figures and support of the library inherited from his Visconti predecessors. That he wished to convey his condolences to his former companion in the language that nobleman best appreciated—a humanist text—is plausible in these circumstances, however odd on the face of it: as a ruler of one of Europe's foremost powers, Sforza would not normally have distributed communications of this sort to men, however elevated, who were not his peers.

But Sforza himself did not write Latin. He turned at this juncture to one of several humanists at his court who were competent to compose the very piece he desired. His stable of intellectuals included scribes and historians, diplomats and biographers: but none of the others possessed the linguistic gifts and intellectual depth of Filelfo. The first work Filelfo addressed to Marcello on the death of Valerio was accordingly written for Sforza, and partly in his voice. Filelfo has the former *condottiere* recall long-ago days: "For I remember the time when you waged war, as Venice's legate to her allies; no terror could touch your heart, no fear of arrows, no deadly dangers defeat you."[54] This undated verse consolation was never included in the Glasgow volume. Its place was taken by the later Filelfian works. These, the evidence suggests, were prompted by Marcello after he had read the earlier sample of the humanist's hand in the spring of the first year of his grief.

۵   ۵   ۵

Filelfo's consolation to Marcello has been considered here, a little out of turn, because of the (possible) June 1461 date of the commissioning letter. But between the agreement signaled by that letter and the Christmas Day completion of the *Consolatio* (if the hypotheses presented below are correct), there were attempted at least three other consolations of Jacopo Antonio Marcello. The first was offered by the Italian-born Hellenist Gregorio Tifernate, the inaugurator of Greek studies at the University of Paris: an *Oratio de obitu Valerii filii* (Oration on the death of your son Valerio), with accompanying epigram.[55] Like Perleone's first letter, his oration remains outside the corpus of works gathered into the Glasgow codex: a reflection not on the value of the work, but on the date and circumstances of its composition.

Teacher and translator of Greek, Tifernate resided at Sforza's court in 1456, where he was engaged in a monumental project: the translation of

Strabo's *Geography.*[56] In this effort he was Guarino's rival, for the Veronese giant was at that very time engaged in the same task, commissioned by the same patron, Pope Nicholas V. When the latter died in 1455, Tifernate had completed two of three parts (the *Asia* and *Africa*), while Guarino had nearly completed the *Europa*. Guarino's labors were completed under Marcello's patronage; Tifernate's were completed under Sforza's. Soon after, Tifernate left Sforza's court to go to Paris, to Mantua, and eventually to Venice. By the end of 1461, he had joined literary circles in that city (including that of Niccolò Sagundino, as the latter's *De finibus,* dedicated to Tifernate, attests),[57] and enjoyed the patronage of the wealthy Corner family. There he remained through September 1462, probably meeting Marcello as well before the latter's own departure at about the same date for Udine.

Tifernate was probably still in Mantua, working for the Marquis Ludovico Gonzaga, Sforza's former ally, when the news arrived of Valerio's death. Not far from Mantua, or Milan, or even Venice, he may have taken part in conversations about the Venetian's loss. His *Oration* (a literary piece, not meant for delivery) on Valerio's death probably dates from early 1461, although it could have been written at any time from 1461 to 1463. The author had received the news of the tragedy "late," Tifernate says at the opening of his consolatory oration. What does "late" mean in this context? so late that some time had elapsed since the death; not so late, as Tifernate's confident call for a stoic response to adversity indicates, that Marcello's fresh grief had settled into an unrelieved despair and become (as it did the following year) a *cause célèbre.*

Fearing condemnation for writing tardily or ineptly, Tifernate will proceed, as he explains, to write nonetheless: it is the duty of a friend, he believes, not to desert his comrade at a moment of adversity.[58] The author explains to Marcello the fragility of fortune: consider what has become of the great civilizations of the Greeks and the Romans, who could by themselves contend with the rest of the globe.[59] Why then do we grieve over the death of a single child, who by dying has avoided the miseries of this world? You had hopes, Tifernate addresses the grieving nobleman, that Valerio would grow to maturity and be an ornament to his country, his family, and his father. But you had no right to expect that happy outcome, given the unpredictability of all things: "because this life that we live is so perilous and fallible, full of such and so many hardships that we should rather expect an infinity of ills."[60] Marcello must now overcome his grief and content himself with his ample store of honors and wealth, the goods of family and country. While there are many more things that could be said in consolation, Tifernate concludes, he has written to Marcello in a mode "familiar and brief," not because he thought Marcello was distressed (Tifernate knew he was a wise man) but so that he could show his love and admiration for the nobleman whose splendid virtues he so esteemed.[61]

In the summer of 1461, a consolatory letter by Isotta Nogarola joined the swelling body of works that Marcello would collect to honor his lost son.[62] Its author was one of the foremost women humanists of the Italian Renaissance. She had known Marcello as the liberator of her native Verona a generation earlier, when alongside the *condottieri* Francesco Sforza and Gattamelata da Narni the Venetian had entered the city at the head of a victorious army.[63] From her earliest youth, she writes, she had "loved him as father, cherished him as master" for the "great kindness" that he showed her and the Nogarola family, one of the leading noble clans of that city.[64]

At that time she had been a young woman, trained in the *studia humanitatis* by Martino Rizzoni, pupil of her compatriot Guarino Veronese. Through him she was linked to Guarino's circle now centered in Ferrara. That circle included, among others, Jacopo Foscari, the son of the doge of Venice; Leonello d'Este, young ruler of Ferrara; Ermolao Barbaro the Elder, after 1454 bishop of Verona; and the humanists Battista Guarini (the master's son and eventual successor), Ludovico Carbone (who would deliver his funeral oration), Giorgio Bevilacqua, Giovanni Michele Alberti Carrara, Janus Pannonius, Tito Vespasiano Strozzi, Raffaele Zovenzoni, of all of whom more will be heard below.[65] Nogarola's entry into literary society (a female contender in a male club) had aroused a furor, occasioning both nasty gossip and serious correspondence. Since that time, she had matured. Rejecting marriage and the conviviality of Veronese life, she chose the solitary existence of a religious recluse and scholar. In 1451, she discoursed on points of theology and canon law with the Venetian noble humanist Ludovico Foscarini, who was undoubtedly in love with her. When she wrote Marcello ten years later, she was old: old for a woman (about forty-three), old in spirit. She had just buried her own mother and was only five years from her own death.

Unlike the authors who offered to console Marcello in the early months of 1461, Nogarola is aware she is entering a competition. "Many" others had already written to console Marcello; she does not wish to appear too bold: "I am concerned lest the multitude think I appear too audacious if amid the crowds of so many orators and so many philosophers . . . I also dare to try my hand."[66] But given her duty to the Venetian, because of his prior kindness to her family, and her daughterly love, she would rather appear bold than negligent. She will write, therefore, to alleviate Marcello's persistent grief of which she has heard "from many others" and from his own "pious writings."[67] Marcello himself had written Nogarola (so her words reveal; the letter is not extant), as he had written Filelfo the preceding June: had he solicited from her a *consolatoria,* as he did from the Milanese professional? And if so, from how many other humanists, of those who wrote in consolation and those who never did, did he request a literary memorial?

Like Filelfo, too, Nogarola had suffered a recent loss: that of her own mother, with whom she had shared a dwelling for the whole of her life, from whom she had never until then parted, who had provided her with the humanist education normally bestowed only on sons. "But how am I to console you, when I myself need the same consolation?"[68] She has forgotten the counsels of philosophy and religion, absorbed in grief for her mother's death, more painful than she had ever thought possible. She proceeds, nevertheless, presenting exemplars of stoical mourning, eulogies of Valerio and his father, exhortations to submit to the will of God and the natural limits of human existence: in all, a series of arguments as familiar and as persuasive as those of her male fellows in the profession of humanist consolation.

Nogarola's consolatory letter forms with the three composed earlier by Sagundino, Perleone, and George of Trebizond a small corpus united by type and tone: brief, elegant, learned, wise. While all four make their appearance in the Glasgow codex, they also achieved (like Filelfo's full-scale work) a readership independent of the Marcello circle—as is witnessed by their circulation in manuscript versions unrelated to that anthology. They really have no successors in this history. Later entries to the "competition" of consolation that Nogarola found herself hesitant to enter are mongrel works. Brief in some cases, not especially learned or elegant in others, they combine the features of a range of genres (the consolatory epistola, the dialogue, the oration, the treatise) and disciplines (philosophy, history, biography).

This mixture of forms typifies Filelfo's work. A pattern for the grand design of Filelfo's *Consolatio* is presented by the work of his former student Perleone: the *Laudatio in Valerium eius filium eximium* (In praise of his remarkable son Valerio), to which discussion now turns.[69] For Perleone's work is in some manner a match for his teacher's exquisite *Consolatio,* and anticipates it in some ways. The *Laudatio* was composed around the first of September of 1461. The author himself places the writing after the death of Marcello's daughter Taddea: "who five months ago now, unless I am mistaken, was snatched away by bitter death."[70] That loss occurred (as George of Trebizond testifies) on the first of April of that year, soon after

Valerio's on the first of January: as though destiny ordered the father's soul to be tested by sorrow, as silver and gold are by fire.[71] In the time since Perleone's antecedent letter (written immediately after Valerio's death), Marcello's grief had swollen beyond the ordinary tragedy, to be dispelled with kind words, to a depression and even obsession inviting a lengthy and more thoughtful response.

Long as it is (fifty-two pages in the Glasgow compilation, the third in rank of length), it is unfinished. The author's death prevented its completion, according to a notation on one manuscript and the statement of another of Marcello's consolers, the Anonymous Tutor, to be considered below. Perleone was still alive, though ill, on 13 June of 1462; six months after the labor of composing the *Laudatio* had begun, he could well have still been immersed in it. He had died before 22 April 1463; at that time the compilation of consolations for Valerio was already under way.[72] He had reached that part in the *Laudatio* where he described the impact of the father's example upon the young Valerio before he lowered his pen, "morte . . . preventus," stilled by death.[73]

Perleone's *Laudatio* is well-described by its title: more than an attempt at consolation, it is a eulogy of a child. He praises Valerio for thirty manuscript pages entire: some three-fifths of the text.[74] What distinguishes his eulogy from others in this age of formulae is its realism: this man knew this child. The realism is evident in the lack of anecdote as much as in its presence: no ornate pictures are found here of a virtuous or rosy-cheeked child. But in this work (matched only by that of the Anonymous Tutor, and with few parallels in all of humanist literature), there are glimpses of a real child and the elders who loved him. Perleone tells us of the child's intelligence and spirit, curiosity and character. He describes Valerio's journeys around Venice with a doting father who gives impromptu lessons in history and civics. He recalls the boy's life at home as a schoolchild, as a participant in the conversation of learned and important adult visitors, as a combatant of local toughs in the Venetian *calli*. Perleone's narrative is a complete portrait of the dead child.

Surrounding the portrait of Valerio are other narratives. These include valuable histories of the Marcello and da Leone clans (the ancestry respectively of the child's father and mother); of Jacopo Antonio's military career; of Venice. They include more conventional, but still moving, reflections on the nature of loss and grief. As a remedy for the latter, Perleone proposes his loving reminiscence of Valerio. Many others had attempted to console the bereaved father without success, reflects the author. Like a man overcome with stomach pain, the patient could not digest their delicate concoctions. So Perleone will cook up a different treat, in the hope that it will be tolerated and alleviate Marcello's condition. This special treat is the portrait of the child who was so loved: "And just as the lover's soul often delights in and is nourished by great sorrow, so your ailing soul may even take delight in this new bitterness and find peace in the recitation of the praise of the one whom you particularly loved."[75]

Perleone's close involvement with the Marcello family is witnessed by the warmth and fullness of his narrative. He died before it was completed, and another writer took up his pen to complete Perleone's story: "which heavy responsibility," he announces, "I have not refused to undertake."[76] This *Perleone Supplement* follows the *Laudatio* in the Glasgow codex, and lacking indication there of title or author, is easily misread as Perleone's own work.[77] Its author was Valerio's tutor from 1458 through 1460 (as the text amply demonstrates), and thereby earns the name granted him here: the Anonymous Tutor. Could he have been the poet and teacher Raffaele Zovenzoni, a Guarino alumnus, and resident in Venice in the late 1450s?[78] In 1463, while teaching in the northeast Italian outpost of Capodistria, Zovenzoni would have close ties with Marcello then engaged outside Trieste. Perhaps their relationship had begun when Marcello was the young man's employer, father of his charge, rather than patron. Since this is a possibility that, while plausible, cannot at present be confirmed, the author must remain anonymous.

Barely six years old, reports the Tutor, Valerio was committed to him "to be imbued with the first rudiments of letters," and from that time "never departed from my side before he departed from life." For nearly three years, the teacher recalls to the father, he had rich experience of the rare qualities of "our child," whose extraordinary qualities "no one knew better than I, nor more often admired them." Thus the tutor claims, alongside the father, a remnant of the child's attention. "You long for your child; I for my pupil."[79]

A resident in the Marcello household, the Anonymous Tutor knew Valerio better than any other of our authors. He provides vivid if fleeting images of the child in the classroom, outstripping the other children in skill and ardor, coaxing his brother Lorenzo to learn.[80] He describes the household's journey to Monselice in the spring of 1460, where the winsome Valerio was warmly greeted by the locals and showed the Tutor about the hidey-holes and secret passages of the castle.[81] He details, finally, Valerio's illness, treatment, and death: the procession of doctors, the Jew "who terrified the child," Valerio's fear of the knife, the shouts that rang through the whole neighborhood when the inevitable death ensued, the father's flight into the shadows.[82] There is little conventional in this brief biography (save the final summons to put aside despair) composed by the Tutor who wished he could "cut off the thread of his story" with the summer scene at Monselice, and not lead the grieving father from that garden into the thorny paths that lay ahead.[83]

The *Supplement* by the Anonymous Tutor is a fitting complement to Perleone's *Laudatio,* matching it in vigor and feeling to such an extent that its separate authorship is obscured. Appended to Perleone's work in the Glasgow codex after a break on the page but without new title, its placement misleads the reader about the circumstances of the *Laudatio's* composition. The *Supplement* (dated in the Glasgow codex Udine, 1 November 1463) could have been begun no earlier than June 1462. The *Laudatio* was begun (as has been seen) in September 1461, before Filelfo's *Consolatio,* but after the briefer letters of Sagundino, George of Trebizond, and Isotta Nogarola.

In its unfinished state, and unattached to the later *Supplement,* the *Laudatio* must have been circulated to other potential authors, probably at Marcello's behest. It could have been the source of the biographical material in later accounts and a stimulus to additional retellings of the tale by the nobleman's humanist friends. The texts themselves are testimony to the work's publication among likely humanist coteries: for the *Laudatio* provides details of the life of Valerio Marcello that would not otherwise be known to the professional humanists of Milan and Ferrara, Verona and Udine, who participated in the child's memorialization. Perleone's work, in effect, may have served as the "press release" that must be presupposed to explain the nature and existence of the later consolations of the father who invited but did not accept consolation.

It is, for instance, Perleone's dense account of Valerio's life that must have provided to Filelfo the data which he incorporated in yet another and more artistic confection. Perleone, his old friend and student, could have sent it to him (perhaps with marginal asides that have not reached us). Alternatively Marcello, also aware of the relationship between the two learned men, and now definitely (though still weeping) in the midst of a new literary venture, could have sent it to his Milanese client. Either of these modes of communication are possible. The only implausible reconstruction of events is that Filelfo, who had had no contacts whatsoever with the child, could have written his *Consolatio,* and designed his own moving portrait of Valerio, without such a document as Perleone's *Laudatio* at hand.

Filelfo's Christmas consolation of 1461 drew not only on Perleone (probably) for details of the life of Valerio, but also on ancient witnesses for the history of Venice, Marcello's *patria*. The resulting narrative occasioned a work in response. Entitled *Francisci Philelphi opinio de summa venetorum origine . . . improbata* (Critique of the view of Francesco Filelfo on the great origin of the Venetians), that work was composed in May 1462 by Michele Orsini, Marcello's longtime intimate.[84] Not essentially a consolatory work, Orsini's *Opinio* is a refutation of the theory of Venetian origins found in Filelfo's *Consolatio* which Orsini had read and, he professes, in all other regards admired. "I have read the book great in meaning, not in size, recently sent by you to the famous knight Jacopo Antonio Marcello, ornament both of the Roman aristocracy and the Venetian nobility," Orsini launches his *Opinio*.[85] Here at last is an explicit reference to a process that must have taken place, it can be inferred, in every instance when a consolatory work was sent to Marcello: the nobleman arranged for its circulation among his literary friends both for comment and as a stimulus to further efforts.

Orsini, with Perleone, was probably among the innermost circle of those friends and clients who formed the immediate audience for the consolatory works. Orsini points to the existence of such a circle when he describes Marcello as the "father" of an "academy" of literati.[86] Such a network is implied by the amicable exchanges between Orsini and Filelfo which postdate the former's critique of the latter's work. Filelfo wrote seven letters to Orsini between October 1462 and August 1464.[87] Among other pleasantries, Filelfo requests Orsini to inform him of events in the Peloponnesus, and shows him his *Sforziad;* and he recalls that epic portrait of his master "so that nothing be done against the will of the splendidly glorious knight Jacopo Antonio Marcello," who must have made objections to it.[88] Orsini was a bridge between Filelfo and the Venetian nobleman, who would have been in the Friuli and outside Trieste during the months that the two humanists discussed Filelfo's celebration of Francesco Sforza.

Certainly Orsini was regularly in contact with Marcello. From 1449 and for most of his long life, Orsini was prior of the monastery of San Antonio da Vienna in the Castello *sestiere* of Venice that the Marcello family often visited, according to Orsini's own witness, during Valerio's childhood in the 1450s.[89] Orsini in turn frequented the Marcello household of which he gives eyewitness reports. Although those reports are sparse and cannot match Perleone's for richness or power, they remain precious documents of the actual story of the Marcello family.

Marcello's relations with Orsini may have been more extensive even than these. Stationed as *provveditore* in the Veneto, the nobleman could have encountered the young cleric during the latter's university years in Padua. Orsini received his license and doctorate in law there in 1444, when he was recognized by Bishop Pietro Donato as the scion of the high-ranking Orsini family whose members had long been honored and promoted by the republic.[90] Orsini was already linked by his sister's marriage in 1426 to a nephew of Pasquale Malipiero: Marcello's provveditorial companion in the late 1440s to the early 1450s and, from 1457 through 1462, doge of Venice.[91] The link was still vital in 1497, when Orsini ceded (quite improperly) to his nephew Giovanni Malipiero the bishopric of Pola.[92]

The crux of Orsini's quarrel with Filelfo is this. The latter, following the Greek geographer Strabo (translations of whose work had been supported by Marcello himself, as has been seen, and his comrade Sforza), traced Venetian origins to the Gauls—ancestors of the contemporary French. Orsini, following the Latin historian Livy (seconded by the contemporary Leonardo Bruni) among others, traced them to the Trojans: themselves descended from the Paphlagonians of antiquity, a people who had never strayed from their native soil nor lived in servitude.[93]

Orsini's work takes its place in a long Venetian tradition where history served the political purposes of the community.[94] Beginning in the thirteenth century, Venetian chroniclers constructed the "myth of Venice," a particular reading of Venetian history which showed that city to be particularly favored, uniquely harmonious, splendidly ruled by a genuine nobility, divinely blessed, and certain to endure.[95] In the fifteenth century, these chroniclers were joined and succeeded in the forging of that myth by humanist historians. Of the many issues involved in this myth so central to Venice's historiographical mission, that which Orsini targets—the origins of the city—is surely pivotal. As early as the chronicler of the *Altinate,* as early as the chronicler called "Marco," the Trojans were chosen as the forebears of the Venetians—predating the Gallic invaders of antiquity or (their cousins), the barbarians of the post-Roman era. Whether the ancestors of the Venetians were of Gallic or Trojan or some other bloodline is unimportant to today's admirers of the city. But for these chroniclers, the issue was crucial. If the Venetians could trace their origins to the original settlers of northeastern Italy, their present claim to a mainland *imperium* became more credible. "Venice . . . [was] more ancient than Padua, more ancient above all than Rome, and built on land belonging to no one."[96] The land Venice seized in its march across the *terraferma,* the historian could argue, had once been theirs, and did not rightly belong to others.[97]

In addition, if the Venetians could trace their origins to a people who had always enjoyed personal and political liberty, who had never known subjection to another power or race, their own claim to original and essential liberty would be enhanced. Settled in the Euganean hills in earliest antiquity (from where they later took refuge from barbarian latecomers on the Adriatic littoral), the Venetians could be seen as the equals of Aeneas, offspring of the noble Trojans, heirs to indomitable freedom. From this origin there took immovable root "this Venetian liberty preserved immaculate and inviolate for more than one thousand years from the founding of the city."[98] So striking a claim, continuous with the Venetian chronicle tradition in the vernacular, is here announced for the first time by a Venetian humanist. Orsini himself would subsequently elaborate the claim in an autonomous full-scale history of Venetian origins: *De antiqua venetorum origine* (On the ancient origin of the Venetians). That work deserves to stand alongside the polemical treatises of Paolo Morosini and as a forerunner to Bernardo Giustiniani's famed *De origine urbis Venetiarum* (History of the origin of Venice).[99]

The body of Orsini's work (occupying twenty-two of twenty-seven manuscript pages) is concerned with these matters of history, geography, and ideology extraneous to the death of Valerio and the consolation of his father. Yet those matters are addressed in a brief and valuable middle section.[100] Like Perleone, Orsini had known the dead child personally. In daily visits to the household, he had watched Valerio grow from early infancy.[101] He reported the child's encounter with neighborhood toughs, his schoolroom triumphs, his intelligent exchanges with his father's important and learned visitors, and, uniquely, his passionate and telling comment on the memorial statue to Vettore Pisani, which stood in Orsini's own church.

Orsini's attachment to Marcello is further revealed in his expanded and mythicized account of the clan. He peopled with Marcello ancestors the last years of Rome and the dawn of Venice: Marcello martyrs for the faith, Pope Marcellus, Marcus Marcellus the patriarch of Aquileia, Doge Marcello.[102] The resplendent Marcello family, he claims, has flourished in Venice as it had once in Rome, just as Venice is now the legitimate heir to Roman power. The child Valerio gave special promise of being the brilliant ornament and worthy heir of this family made illustrious "by so many heroes on land and sea."[103]

With its focus on Venetian history, Orsini's work stands out as a maverick among the consolations of Marcello. Yet it was included in the Glasgow compilation. It did, after all, relate to the discussion that emerged from the child's death. And it was authored by one of the central figures in Marcello's literary circle. In that compilation, however, it did not appear with the date of May 1462, which an autograph notation insists was the date of composition. Orsini had written it then, but put it aside: "Now finally I send it late, though not for that reason less loving." He invites his friend to modify and improve it as he will. This second notation is dated by the author's hand 26 August 1462.[104]

Between author's draft in May and presentation in August, three months elapse: a span of time which hints of the gaps between creation and final transcription of the many other works in the collection. Orsini's *Opinio* was copied from its author's draft (or an intermediate version) to the pages subsequently gathered into the Glasgow codex. In that volume, it bears the date of its transmission from Orsini to Marcello (26 August 1462) which must have predated by some months at least its final transcription. Indeed, in the eventual volume Orsini's work occupies a place out of sequence. The dated works preceding and following Orsini's are in roughly chronological sequence, and the undated works plausibly fall into place. Could the compiler have decided late in the process, or been advised, to include the eccentric historical work amid the consolations?

Orsini's work alerts us to the intense elaboration of the literary project of the consolation of Marcello. Not only does this author engage another of Marcello's consolers in a dialogue (a dialogue meant for the public eye) but in full view he corrects his own work, which is again reworked (or at least transcribed) for insertion in to the final volume. What is known about Orsini's effort can be inferred about others. Spontaneous works of consolation are expanded (as by Perleone, Filelfo), translated (as by Carbone and Grifo), completed (as by the Anonymous Tutor), circulated (several?) and solicited (as was Filelfo's). These processes will be observed as clearly in the next group of Marcello consolations to be discussed.

ఴ   ఴ   ఴ

About the time that Orsini first composed his *Opinio* for Jacopo Antonio Marcello, there died the "peaceful doge" Pasquale Malipiero, known to them both.[105] A few days later, Marcello participated in the elaborate electoral process resulting in the choice of Cristoforo Moro as doge of Venice. That event marks his first reemergence into public life after the advent of Valerio's illness two years earlier. Soon he would serve as ducal counsellor, or *consigliere* (one of the highest magistracies in Venice), and by October of the same year, in a new office: *luogotenente,* or governor of Friuli. The history of the making of the Glasgow manuscript now shifts to that locale. The six consolations included in that volume and not as yet discussed were probably composed, or at least received by Marcello, after the summer of 1462. Two were addressed from Venice, one from Ferrara, one from Padua, and two from Trieste, within Marcello's jurisdiction at Friuli. Of the dated works, none is earlier than 1463.

When Marcello left Venice for Friuli, he took with him books and scribes and memories. In that outpost of Venetian empire from the last months of 1462 until the last weeks of 1463, the shape of the consolation project took form. That work of imagination was stimulated no doubt by the presence of a new group of literary friends and a heightened pace of conversation at the governor's court in Udine. Marcello's former colleague in the pacification of the *terraferma,* the learned Ludovico Foscarini, had just stepped down from the position of *luogotenente.*[106] During his occupancy of the governor's palace (which Marcello undertook to repair soon after his arrival), Foscarini had reveled in communion with learned men: among others, Guarnerio d'Artegna, the bibliophile whose library fueled so much discussion, and which still survives today.[107]

This coterie awaited Marcello upon his arrival late in 1462 with a military mission and sorrowing heart. Writing from Padua on 1 October 1463, a year after Marcello's arrival, an anonymous author (his own contribution to be discussed below) names three of the literati gathered in Udine, all bred in the Friuli: Leonardo, the reigning prince of the Thomists; the physician Geremia; Guarnerio d'Artegna, "the ornament of Latin eloquence." In addition to these, there was Georgio Bevilacqua da Lazise, whose Latin learning the writer's teacher Gian Pietro da Lucca had praised.[108]

The Veronese Giorgio Bevilacqua was a newcomer to the Friulian circle.[109] Born in 1406 to a noble Veronese family, he studied with Guarino Veronese in the 1420s, before undertaking university studies in law at Padua and Bologna. During these years, he befriended the Nogarola sisters, his compatriots, who circulated in the world of Guarinian humanism.[110] He found them, on his first encounter, with Cicero in their hands. Among the first to recognize the serious intellectual ambitions of the Nogarola women, Bevilacqua sent to them in 1436 a manuscript of Lactantius and in 1437 (probably) a life of the scholar-saint Jerome. For at least three decades more, Bevilacqua continued to pursue literary interests, corresponding with humanists especially in the Veronese and Venetian orbits.

Bevilacqua's larger works all targeted patrons in the Venetian elite. He composed a *Historia de bello gallico* (History of the Lombard War), dedicated to the learned Venetian nobleman Marco Donato.[111] That work chronicles the struggle between Filippo Maria Visconti and Venice from 1438 to 1441 which so convulsed his homeland. In 1466 or 1467, Bevilacqua addressed to Ludovico Foscarini a commentary on Cicero, and late in life, a collection of the "flowers," or finest sayings, of Saint Jerome, to Zaccaria Barbaro—both dedicatees being humanist amateurs of the same rank as Donato.[112] In 1456, Lorenzo Zane (another Venetian patrician humanist) dedicated to the Veronese a philosophical work *De difficilimae doctrinae palma capescenda* (On winning the prize of the most serious learning).[113] To the Veronese nobleman Antonio Nogarola, brother of the learned Isotta, Bevilacqua addressed a work on marriage, bound in a fifteenth-century manuscript today found in Toledo with Francesco Barbaro's famous *De re uxoria*.[114] To Jacopo Antonio Marcello, in addition to the consolatory work which is of principal concern here, Bevilacqua also wrote a laudatory Latin letter describing the soldier's leadership of Venetian forces at the siege of Trieste in 1463.[115]

These literary pursuits were accompaniments to a political career. Like the Nogarolas, Bevilacqua belonged to one of those leading patrician families on the *terraferma* who benefited from Venetian rule. He held public office under its aegis in his native city from 1437 until 1463, serving as counsellor, as state attorney, as administrator of the merchant corporation of his city, as *podestà* of the nearby city of Legnago.[116] While holding these honorific magistracies, he encountered various Venetian rectors of the city, including Ludovico Foscarini in 1450–51.[117] During those years he must also have been introduced to Marcello. The Venetian was a prominent figure in Verona in 1439 as liberator of the city (alongside Gattamelata and Sforza), in 1448 as its captain, and in 1454 as *provveditore*.[118] In 1463, Bevilaqua was in Udine, undoubtedly at Marcello's request. By November 1463, he boasts the title of Marcello's *vicarius*, or secretary.[119]

These literary stars of Marcello's Friulian circle must have gathered gladly for chats about the accumulating body of works written to comfort the wealthy and learned *luogotenente* who still mourned his son's death. Here it must have occurred to Marcello that the process of consolation should result in a product: a beautifully written and decorated volume, destined for the unseated king who grandly in Provence collected books, works of art, and courtiers. Possibly the idea was Marcello's own, since he had supervised similar projects (but none so grandiose) before.[120] Or possibly it was Bevilacqua's, whose cleverness of this sort reveals itself in a letter to Marcello to be discussed in due course.

In Udine, then, the man sent to guard the Venetian frontier managed at the same time a literary campaign: he reshaped the works written to console him for the death of his son into a monument worthy of his child and of the intensity of his grief. A scribe or scribes—Bevilacqua, one suspects— set to work recopying the earlier works in one continuous roll (each work

follows upon the end of the other, often without page breaks), and to adding, as they arrived and were judged worthy, the new ones. Word was sent
out to likely authors (along with sample manuscripts) that further entries
in this literary contest would be welcome. The process culminated (for it
was never completed) in November 1463, after Marcello had been ordered
from Udine to the battlefront at Trieste.[121]

It is in this environment that the inclusion of minor works in Marcello's
collection can be best explained: the shadowy Mascarello's, for instance, or
Fortebraccio's, a work which presumably under other circumstances would
not have been written, since its author wrote nothing else whatsoever. Why,
indeed, would Battista Guarini have taken up his pen in Ferrara, if a form
of "call for papers" had not been issued from Udine, inviting new submis-
sions to this literary project? Most of the authors whose works appear in
the Glasgow codex after Filelfo's consolations (excluding Perleone, Orsini,
and the Anonymous Tutor) had no personal knowledge of Valerio Marcello, and for some the time had long since past for a spontaneous response
to the news of his death. These writers who had never met Valerio, who
scarcely knew Marcello, who had no special knowledge of Venice or its
history, included in their works exact details of the child's death and of the
father's life. Incidents that had been included in the accounts of earlier writers reappear in these later works, and they betray a purely literary ancestry.
More than a "call for papers," a fact sheet must have been issued as well:
probably in the form of the earlier consolations (especially Perleone's) circulated to likely authors.[122]

Fortebraccio's consolation is the first in the sequence of those works appearing after the Filelfian works (*Consolatio,* Greek elegy, and translation)
in the Glasgow codex.[123] It was probably written after August 1463, when
both author and addressee were engaged in the siege of Trieste: Fortebraccio
twice refers to the camaraderie forged on the battlefield between the two
old soldiers.[124] Next come the works of Mascarello and Guarini, composed
before Fortebraccio's, but possibly not long before.[125] There follow (after
Perleone's *Laudatio* and the *Supplement* of the Anonymous Tutor) the work
of a second unknown author (here known as the Anonymous Venetian)
dated from Venice in July 1463; then Orsini's, dated 26 August 1462,
which like Perleone's must have been recopied from a file among Marcello's
papers. A consolatory letter dated 1 October 1463, attributed here to our
third anonymous author, the Student, may have just recently arrived from
Padua.[126] It was followed by the capstone work of the collection, completed
by Bevilacqua in Udine on 3 November, when it was sent to Marcello, and

copied into the Glasgow volume only ten days later on 13 November.[127] By Bevilacqua without question; but it pretended to be Marcello's own response, written from the field of battle, to all the previous works of consolation.

The father of Carlo Fortebraccio, Count of Montone, consoler of Marcello, was the formidable *condottiere* Braccio da Montone, arch-heretic and papal foe who secured for himself the lordship of Perugia and died excommunicate.[128] An unsavory character of heroic dimensions, Braccio was the recipient or subject of much Latin verse which testifies to his contacts in literary circles.[129] He was also the particular adversary of the pontiff's agent Muzio Attendolo, father of Francesco Sforza, who would one day share the field with Fortebraccio. Both sons of these mortal enemies would thus be eventually united (and with our Marcello as well) in serving the interests of Venice. Nearly forty years later, the aging Fortebraccio recalled the death of his notorious father.[130] In the third generation, Carlo's son Bernardo was to imitate his own father's respectability. He eventually inherited the latter's commission and troops as a standing captain in the Venetian land army.[131] The three generations of Fortebraccio warriors thus trace the pattern of the evolution of Italian warfare from the days of swashbuckling soldier of fortune to those of the regular army officer.

Carlo Fortebraccio himself served Venice as a fresh recruit in the years after 1440 until his death in 1479.[132] At many moments during the Lombard wars, Fortebraccio was named as one of the captains who led the campaign against Milan that Marcello steadily accompanied as *provveditore.* Fortebraccio's fame and status grew steadily. The respect in which he was held by the Venetian republic is indicated by an event in 1456. On 11 June of that year, he married Margherita, a daughter of Sigismondo Pandolfo Malatesta, the *condottiere*-prince of Rimini. Venice honored him by sending as their legate the high-ranking nobleman Girolamo Donato.[133] Marcello must have encountered Fortebraccio during the years of the Lombard struggle, when the latter served with the forces that the former supervised as *provveditore.* The warm relations between the Perugian-born captain and the would-be soldier Marcello are noted by Fortebraccio: "we have long been linked" by mutual affection at peace and in military service, he writes at one point; "you have known me since first I entered Venetian service," at another, referring to their "enduring friendship."[134]

Those relations were to continue through 1463 when, nine years after the peace at Lodi put an end to the struggle in Lombardy, Fortebraccio was sent to the field where Marcello commanded. On 30 August 1463, the

Senate ordered its agents in Vicenza to dispatch Fortebraccio to Trieste immediately. On 24 September, Marcello was ordered to Trieste to manage the siege as best he could until reinforced by Fortebraccio's troops, who had not yet arrived.[135] Soon after, the seasoned captain wrote his *De obitu Valerii filii consolatio* (Consolation on the death of your son Valerio), which refers to the presence of both soldiers before the walls of Trieste. Once again Marcello's comrade-in-arms, this soldier whose career gives no other indication of erudition wrote one of the works that attempted to console Marcello for the loss of his child.

Could Fortebraccio, who more familiarly held a lance than a pen, have written this effective and pious, sometimes moving consolation? The author speaks of the roughness of the culture of a man raised for war rather than study. "I approach this task, then, instructed with a rough military rather than polished eloquence, for our curriculum (as you know) is much more suited to prepare a man for drawing up battle-lines and planning encampments and exhorting men to fight and other such jobs than for soothing a friend's sorrows." Yet he will attempt the task, a friend's duty, "so that you might gain some tidbit of solace from this wholehearted exertion of my soul, even after receiving from others so many brilliant and monumental consolations." Again, he deprecates his own literary preparation: "I do not come laden with knowledge of literature, nor imbued with those humanistic studies (*studia humanitatis*). For from my very earliest youth committed to a military life, I barely absorbed the first rudiments of letters. But whatever understanding I have achieved from nature, from experience, from life, from reason itself, I shall share with you."[136]

Was this soldier son of a *condottiere* unlettered and incapable of writing the work that bears his name in the Marcello corpus? Sforza had others write for him—Giovanni Simonetta, with a coterie of secretaries, and Filelfo, who penned for his patron an elegy for the old friend of the new duke of Milan.[137] René d'Anjou and Marcello himself, as will be seen, were authors in their own right: yet they hired others to write for them, and may have on occasion put their own names to others' work.[138] Like them, Fortebraccio may have hired a surrogate to write in consolation of Marcello. On the other hand, Fortebraccio might have possessed a higher culture than he claims. Occasionally the dedicatee of humanist works, he may have mastered the rudiments of humanist style, and perhaps more than these.[139] Other *condottieri* are known to have been cultivated men. The great dynasts of Mantua, Urbino, and Rimini—the Gonzaga, da Montefeltro, and Malatesta—mixed the business of war with that of the arts. What was true of rulers could be true even of ordinary soldiers: such as the bibliophile Marsciano, Fortebraccio's lesser colleague in the Venetian army and participant in the assault on Trieste.[140] It is known that this Fortebraccio commissioned from Giovanni Antonio Campano a biography of his father that is a model of fine style and sound history.[141] The court of Perugia where Fortebraccio was raised, moreover, became in the generation after Braccio a center of culture.

Fortebraccio's own words further reveal that some literary activity was in evidence at that court, and that as a child he was consoled in writing for the death of his parent. It mustn't surprise you, he cautions Marcello, if I use some scriptural arguments to assuage your grief. "For I remember that on the death of my magnificent and glorious father some men learned in ecclesiastical discipline produced for my consolation their profound arguments, and others also did the same thing in their letters. All these things splendidly said or written by them I committed to memory, which are now put forward for your consideration."[142] In his way, Fortebraccio would compete with that fearful phalanx of the consolers of Marcello who had already written, trying diligently to root out the sorrow that had taken hold of the Venetian's heart, and leaving scarcely anything more on the subject to say.[143]

Fortebraccio's *Consolatio* contains in briefer scope the already familiar elements of Filelfo's work and others: a biography of the child, a biography of the father, and a series of consolatory arguments. The Valerio material focuses on the infancy and deathbed narratives. The discussion of Marcello's career repeats earlier accounts as well, though Fortebraccio was in a position to add a unique perspective. As promised in his allusion to the influence of those learned in the "ecclesiastical discipline," Fortebraccio's contribution offers distinctively Christian arguments for the cessation of grief. He exhorts Marcello to acknowledge the justice of God, and calls up the image of an angry Jesus who berates the nobleman for begrudging his Savior the sacrifice of his son.[144]

If the soldier Fortebraccio presents Marcello with mainly Christian admonitions, the obscure Vicentine Montorio Mascarello prods him with memories of military feats.[145] The *Dialogus consolatorius* (Consolatory dialogue) he composed for the Venetian is staged as a conversation between "Montorio" and "Marcello" in which the former encourages the latter to overcome his grief with the recollection of great deeds: those of the nobleman's ancestors and of his own military career. The author refers to the whole dialogue, indeed, as a "triumph," a parade in celebration of deeds done such as the Romans granted their heroes, in the tradition of the *Trionfi* (Triumphs) of Petrarch. He will display to Marcello his "triumphs," the author exclaims, in order to lessen his sorrows: "I believe this would be a most efficacious medicine for you, excellent knight and great-hearted man, if I place before your eyes the spectacle of your remarkable achievements so that you might observe, as it were, your own Triumph."[146]

Again, approaching the end of his work, Mascarello announces that he will "bring to a close this Triumph of ours"; and at various points in the text he proposes to describe "another triumph" accomplished by Marcello or his forebears.[147] These "triumphs" constitute the substance of the work, and include the deeds of Marcello's supposed ancestors (especially Marcus Claudius Marcellus, the opponent of Hannibal) and of the Venetian himself. The material is drawn, as the author himself acknowledges, from a letter Guarino Veronese wrote to Marcello in 1458, the eloquent first of a tradition of panegyrics for that warrior patron.[148]

This *Dialogus consolatorius* is the second of three small works under Mascarello's name clustered after Fortebraccio's consolation in the Glasgow collection. The circumstances of Mascarello's works are, like their author, obscure. In spite of their late placement in the codex, they could be rather early phenomena in the Marcello episode: Mascarello does not mention consolations written by any other authors (as most of the authors do), nor does he respond to a protracted or excessive grief on Marcello's part. The first work is a brief letter dated from Venice on "1 February," conceivably as early as 1461. Here Mascarello explains that he had heard of and seen Marcello's grief, and offers consolatory arguments: Valerio had suffered no evil, while the great Marcello must quickly return to his responsibilities to his city and his family.

The second work is the *Dialogus* described above. Undated, it opens with a statement that refers to a previous letter: surely the preceding one in the manuscript. "I heard, great Marcello, that you were languishing with sorrow on the death of your little son, and that you were pleased by the letter that I sent to console you." Pleased with the success of that first effort, the author will now attempt "to eradicate completely this grief from your heart by applying the remedies of my medical art."[149] Written after the author had received an expression of thanks from Marcello, the *Dialogus* may have been written in response to that patron's solicitation of a lengthier and more elaborate *consolatoria*. In any case, it was evidently written when Marcello's grief, protracted to a degree considered unusual, had advanced to the stage of a malady requiring treatment.

The third of Mascarello's works is again a consolatory letter, longer than the first, but shorter than the dialogue. Undated like the latter work, it could have been written at any time: perhaps as late as 1463, which circumstance would explain the otherwise odd placement of the Mascarello *opuscula*. It adds to the themes presented in the two earlier works a description of the child Valerio: his virtues, his love for his father; and incidents from his life: the first encounter of father and child, the visit of doctor Gerardus, the deathbed tears and vows. These incidents at least, however vaguely described, must have had their origin in a source close to Marcello himself. By the time of this letter's composition, Mascarello had evidently been provided with copies of other consolations for Marcello (or some other such text) containing the elements of the Valerio story for his imitation. Once again, Marcello may have solicited a continuation of the consolatory effort the author had launched soon after Valerio's death.

The consolatory epistle of Battista Guarini follows Mascarello's works in the Glasgow collection.[150] This humanist pedagogue was son of the famous Guarino Veronese, whose teaching methods he codified in his best-known work, the *De modo et ordine docendi et discendi* (On the method and order of teaching and learning)—dedicated, in that small world, to his student Maffeo Gambara, a nephew of Isotta Nogarola.[151] The great master Guarino would surely have written himself to console Marcello, patron of his Strabo translation, had he still been alive; but he had died on 4 December 1460, less than a month before Valerio. Battista Guarini writes much as his father would have done. Like Mascarello, Guarini is familiar with Marcello's military ventures from his father's famous letter, and perhaps also from his father's conversation. The recitation of these events occupies one-third the brief work, while another third is devoted to ancient examples of moderation in mourning, embellished with references to Greek authors especially. The remainder concerns itself with the boy Valerio.

The focus on Valerio's mind and education is a prominent feature of Guarini's letter. A choice of emphasis not surprising for a teacher (one who had already completed, in 1459, the *De modo dicendi* which would become a fundamental work of Renaissance pedagogy), it is shared with the teacher Perleone and the Anonymous Tutor. Who could not sympathize with a father's grief at having lost a son, Guarini writes, "in whose face there was such grace, in whose speech such pleasantness, so that those who saw and heard him could not fail to admire and praise him? a child who showered forth such sparks of intellect? who demonstrated such a lofty mind and, what seems incredible in one so young, such prudence, so that not only a father but anyone at all would be drawn to love him?"[152] Such statements take the place in Guarini's work of the kind of biography studded with concrete detail and anecdotes more commonly found in the Marcello consolations. While they reveal Guarini's special sensitivity to the intellectual life of the young, they also suggest his remoteness, at the court of Ferrara, from the Marcello household.

Guarini's letter is dated without year, "Ferrara." Most likely he composed it after his colleague in humanist studies at Ferrara, Ludovico Carbone, had recited to an enthusiastic and weeping audience of Este courtiers his Latin translation of Filelfo's Greek elegy for Marcello.[153] This theatrical event must have made the consolations of Marcello a popular Ferrarese genre. Ferrara appears often as one of the satellites in Marcello's universe, linked to him through the figure of Guarino Veronese. It was there that Guarino produced his translation of Strabo under Marcello's patronage, and there that the Veronese pedagogue taught several of the figures in Marcello's circle, as has been noted: in addition to Carbone and Battista Guarini, also Bevilacqua, Carrara, Strozzi, Zovenzoni, Pannonius. Along with Milan (the home of Filelfo and Sforza, Tifernate and Grifo), Udine (the site of the final compilation of the Marcello corpus) and Venice, Ferrara must be seen as one of the foci of the literary endeavors in consolation of Jacopo Antonio Marcello.

The tireless Carbone followed up his verse translation of Filelfo's work, as has been noted, with an original Latin elegy—a not extraordinary feat for the man who claimed that scarcely anyone was married or buried in Ferrara without a literary memorial by his pen.[154] This *Carmen . . . in consolationem de obitu . . . filioli sui Valerii* (Poem in consolation for the death of his son Valerio), not included in the Glasgow collection, presents the usual recitation of Marcello's great deeds and the notable events of Valerio's brief life. It also contains some special features: an extended description of the city of Venice, and a list of some of those writers who had already consoled the grieving father. Those named are George of Trebizond, Niccolò Sagundino (known to have suffered an equally grave loss), Pietro Perleone, Battista Guarini, Isotta Nogarola, Francesco Filelfo (in Greek verse and Latin prose); also Tito Vespasiano Strozzi (wealthy humanist and Este servitor, whose consolatory work for Marcello is otherwise unknown); and now Carbone himself.[155] This list dates the work as no earlier than 1462, after the completion of the latest of the consolations named (Filelfo's) at the end of 1461. Battista Guarini's work may belong to the same era, as has been suggested. So might the epigram (and lost works) on the death of Valerio Marcello composed by Guarino's alumnus Janus Pannonius.[156]

ↄ   ↄ   ↄ

Returning to the Glasgow codex, the sequence of the next five works after Guarini's consolatory epistle is perplexing. These are the works by, respectively, Perleone (written in 1461), the Anonymous Tutor (1463) and Anonymous Venetian (15 July 1463), Orsini (1462) and the Anonymous Student (1 October 1463).[157] This organization reveals the traces of the process of the compilation. The scribe is seen transcribing in turn works received long before and those recently arrived, copying sometimes the dates of composition and applying sometimes the date of transcription, or, as elsewhere, no date at all. Thus the contributions of the Tutor and the Venetian (near contemporaries of the Student's, the last of the set to appear) are incorporated in the text before Orsini's, originally composed at a much earlier May 1462.

Who was the Anonymous Venetian? A writer both informed and eloquent, he does not reveal his identity by any telltale statement. Could his be the consolatory work, subsequently lost, known to have been written by Giovanni Mario Filelfo, stationed in Venice through 1460 as public teacher of rhetoric?[158] Filelfo would have had access to his father's work directly, as well as any information radiating from the Udine group. He was a teacher and highly competent humanist, possessing qualities consistent with the text. Filelfo was not in Venice in 1463, however; if he is the author, the letter bearing the dateline of Venice would have had to be composed in Modena in 1463, or in Venice but at an earlier date. Filelfo's *Consolatio*, moreover, was probably in verse.

The work of the Venetian who must for now remain anonymous contains the usual descriptions of the child, material about Marcello and his family, and consolatory elements.[159] Richly endowed with the details of Valerio's life, it shares with the works of known teachers (Guarini, Perleone, and the Anonymous Tutor) a special interest in the child's education, and a notable enthusiasm for the receptivity of young minds. It contains more than the usual references to Marcello's important role within the city of Venice, and an extended discussion of the putative Roman ancestors of the bereaved nobleman. This author, in sum, seems to stand rather close to the Marcello household. That closeness would explain also his claim to feel grief himself at Valerio's death, which he must stem in order to console the nobleman whose greatness of soul he has observed: "for I could in no way indulge my own grief, if I was to be able to counter yours with sound arguments."[160]

Unlike the Venetian, the Anonymous Student is distant from the Venetian scene and deferential to the nobleman whose grief he proposes to counter. His identity is a a puzzle. For the role of the Student, Giovanni Mario Filelfo and Tito Vespasiano Strozzi (whose consolations of Marcello appear to be lost) are unlikely candidates: both had passed the stage of a university career well before the work was composed; while the younger Janus Pannonius (who also authored a lost consolation) probably wrote in verse.[161] The strongest possibility is Leonello Chiericati, grandson of the humanist Antonio Loschi and future aide to the Venetian cardinal Marco Barbo, papal diplomat and servitor.[162] Born in 1443, and still young at the time of the Marcello tragedy, he was the right age to be a university student. Further, he composed in 1463 (the same year as the consolation for Valerio under a discussion) a consolatory work for the Venetian aristocrat Francesco Diedo. That *Dialogus . . . in quo et consolatio magnifici Francisci Diedi . . .* (Dialogue and consolation for the magnificent Francesco Diedo),[163] written during the author's residence at the university of Padua, is probably the consolation for Diedo that our Student claims also to have written.

The Anonymous Student is an earnest and original author. Strongly identified with the academic community of Padua, his own words describe him. Moved to the task of consoling Marcello "by the enormous love of our order towards you," he will press forward although he knows that "a numberless multitude of writers or I should rather say of books" had been written by famous men, older than he, "from all over Italy." In the execution of that goal, he will be so bold as to attempt arguments from the studies in which he is immersed, metaphysics and theology.[164]

These, and not Valerio or his father, are the main subject of his work. From the perspectives of such authorities as Aristotle (above all), Galen and Isocrates, Avicenna and the jurists, he discusses the nature of a father's love for his child, the distinction between body and soul, the special innocence of those who die young. Such consolatory arguments as these, the unnamed student claims, he had recently discussed with the Venetian nobleman Francesco Diedo, in these years possibly a university student himself.[165] Diedo had suddenly lost his father Ludovico "who so shone, as you know well, in your Senate," and found solace in the appreciation of his mother Creusa's continued well-being.[166] Thus the youthful provincial intellectual displays his credentials as a consoler of the Venetian nobility! But his distance from Venice and the Marcello family is betrayed by his mistaken statement that Valerio was the youngest of Marcello's children.[167] Isolated from the network of scholars linked to Marcello, the Anonymous Student knows little of the nobleman's career and Valerio's life.

The diminutive consolatory *epistola* of the Anonymous Student is the penultimate work of the Marcello compilation. Its closing chapter is the *Excusatio adversus consolatores in obitu Valerii filii* (Apology against the consolers on the death of his son Valerio), ostensibly the work of Marcello himself. Its presence transforms the whole volume (which would otherwise be a miscellany of autonomous works) into a summary dialogue between consolers and unconsoled, and an original statement of a bereaved father's obdurate mourning in defiance of bland convention. This transformation takes place even in the teeth of evidence revealing the work's real author: not, as it seems, Marcello, but rather his ghost, Bevilacqua.

Of Bevilacqua's authorship, there is no clue in the Glasgow codex. Marcello speaks: he calls repeatedly upon his old comrade, René d'Anjou, king (as he still called himself) of Naples, to judge between him and his consolers. They accuse him of weakness; but who would not be weak who had lost a son? They urge upon him reason and forebearance; not these, though, but ceaseless tears are the proper response to the death of a beloved child. Marcello hurls back at the logic of his consolers the simpler logic of intuition and passion, calling their sanity madness, and his own fury, good sense.

Powerful is the impression conveyed of this weeping father who not only gives voice to his sadness but who in doing so, subverts the normal moral order. Again and again he turns on the authors (whose works he has carefully gathered) who have dared to console him. "Marcello" writes that "these would-be consolers have acted without benefit and without effect when they committed so many long nights, such toil, such effort, that in consoling me they have written not only letters but even volumes."[168] What they have written is "conceived with great learning . . . and expounded with abundant arguments and principles . . . from the fountain of indulgent love."[169] Yet though these consolers have written with eloquence unmatched even by Cicero, they have failed to wear down with their arguments my "obstinate soul."[170]

These appeals to René, these outbursts of grief, are interspersed in the fabric of a massive work containing the familiar elements of the post-Filelfian consolation: a biography of the child, a litany of the military achievements of the father, a eulogy of Venice. Those elements emerge in the course of the father's angry dialogue with himself.

"Marcello" reflects on the evils that have long beset his family, tracing these from his supposed Roman ancestors Marcus Claudius Marcellus, opponent of Hannibal, and Marcellus, nephew of the emperor Augustus, to his own grandfather Pietro "il Grande." Valerio's early childhood is sketched, from prenatal omens of greatness through his first encounter with his father. Later the narrator describes the child's growth in strength and spirit, and aptitude for learning both in the schoolroom and in the theater of Venetian civic life. As the loving father relates to his child the history and glories of Venice, so these are related to us, his readers. Then the story of Valerio's death is told, interlaced with reflections on the philosophical schools and their attitude towards grief. That theme in turn is interrupted for a look at Marcello's military career: his consolers had urged that reflection upon his past heroic deeds would distract him from his sorrows. Amid these elements of narrative are scattered examples of fathers (and some mothers)—Greek and Roman, biblical and Venetian—who had suffered the loss of their children, bravely or in tears, and Marcello's own frequent and frenzied laments.

Discussions of these themes are scattered and disjointed, betraying the agony suffered by its presumed author. The *Excusatio* is an incoherent work: deliberately so. It is effective despite its meandering disorder. The preceding consolations, all fourteen of them, are corraled in the first three hundred pages as a foil to the *Excusatio's* angry hundred, rebuking them. The collection is wrought into a dialogue between consoler and consoled, with an appeal to René as judge, projecting in larger scale the microcosm of the culminating *Excusatio*. The whole story is contained inadequately in the individual works themselves; it is found completely only in the book itself. Clumsy when viewed as a single artifact, the *Excusatio* is a brilliant conclusion to the collection and to Marcello's career.

The *Excusatio* was meant to be seen as a *tour de force,* the culminating and coordinating work of the volume that was the product of Marcello's grief. The father's voice explains the genesis of the work. He wishes King René to judge the arguments he presents in favor of his right to grieve, "which I have had written down in this letter, not so that I might show myself ungrateful for the multitude of elegant books on the death of my dearest son written to console my sorrows (for they are composed with such elegance of diction, such refinement of most eloquent beauty, such gravity of sentiment, such an abundance of examples, such apt use of words as though wrought by an artist, that they could be numbered among the famous works written by our ancestors and the earliest orators) but so that I might not appear disgraceful if I present myself as I am, the torrents of my tears still unstaunched."[171]

For this purpose, the still-weeping father has gathered up the works into a volume for his friend's consideration: "These consolatory books, . . . if I may now so name them, I now send to you ordered as they were written and sent to me and bound together in this volume. I beg your majesty to read and thoroughly peruse them."[172] It is that very volume that survives today, marked by its author's death, not quite finished and never sent.

The compelling *Excusatio* is not, as it claims to be, Marcello's. The origin of the work is betrayed by the autograph original, preserved today in the real author's native city of Verona. There the *Excusatio* is preceded by a telltale letter, dated from Udine ten days before the companion work which purports to have been composed before the walls of besieged Trieste.[173] Tactfully, its author describes his anger for Marcello's sake. His consolers had charged that the aging soldier's grief ill-suited his dignity and reputation for courage. But Marcello's grief was justified, wrote Bevilacqua, the Venetian's vicar in Udine during the Trieste siege and witness to the mourner's plight during recent months. "I cannot bear your being accused of pusillanimity," he wrote.[174] Even bowed low by grief Marcello was fully worthy of his ancestors. To defend Marcello and silence his well-intentioned accusers, Bevilacqua had written the *Excusatio* (as Marcello had directed) as though that nobleman was the author: "So I have written the letter, as I persuaded you should be done, as though you yourself had composed it in your free evenings, and have addressed it from you to the divine King René. . . . Now I give it to you."[175]

The secret is out. Bevilacqua wrote the *Excusatio*, deliberately and with Marcello's knowledge, as if composed by Marcello amid cannonfire and distraction, "ex foelicibus castris adversus Tergestum," in the camp of a besieging army. The work is a hoax engineered by Marcello and his accomplice. Its inauthenticity supports the theory of the construction of the whole Glasgow volume already presented: that at a certain point, probably after Marcello relocated to Udine, the collection of consolations became a deliberate project, a matter of invitations and rewards, rather than an innocent collection of works spontaneously offered.

Yet if the *Excusatio* is a hoax, and the Glasgow collection a contrivance, still Marcello grieved for Valerio. The elaborate project the father undertook to transform his human pain into undying words—to confer upon it the immortality of letters, as the humanists would have said—does not diminish the reality of that pain. It was entirely consistent with what is known of Marcello's character and past that this book came into being as it did. The man who liked to vacation in a fortress, the man who designed a self-portrait with attendant symbols of exaggerated power, the man who commissioned translators, hired scribes, coddled illustrators, who paid them well, the man who had again and again packaged his messages to his friend in the luxuriant form of an illustrated book, was capable of devising this vast project to be the appropriately bold expression of his heroic despair. The next two chapters look more closely at Jacopo Antonio Marcello.

CHAPTER THREE

Marcello in Word and Image

The Italian wars of the fifteenth century, like our own, were marked by the manipulation of images and words: the glorification of the soldier, the reverence for weapons and tactics, the memory hole of civilian death and suffering, proofs of the inevitability of conflict coupled with claims of preference for peace. Created only to kill, the exquisite sword and embellished cannon both sparkle; the opponent nation disappears behind one single and wholly evil face. Jacopo Antonio Marcello was a participant in those wars and a manipulator of such words and images. Posing as a warrior, he fashioned for himself a heroic guise: that of a *condottiere* always at war, unfettered by any loyalties that might abridge his independence. In fact, Marcello sought peace and served loyally the republic that demanded unselfish obedience of its servitors: a reality more impressive than the carefully wrought image. A patron who commissioned works of art and of letters, and who relished the refined company of the learned, this man of contradictions established himself in a bleak and impregnable fortress miles from the ordered life of republican Venice, and played the role of prince.

Some fifteen miles south of Padua, in the Euganean hills, rises the "hard rock mountain," as it had been called since Roman times: Monselice.[1] From antiquity through the sixteenth century, without interruption, it had been a stronghold. Its heights commanded the intersecting roads leading to Padua and Venice, to Bologna and Florence, to Este and Mantua, to Rovigo and Ferrara. A natural strategic center, it was used by the Romans to hold off the Goths and by the Byzantines to hold off the Lombards. Under Lombard domination, it swelled with refugees from Este and Padua to the dimensions of a city and became the regional center for administration and defense in the tenth and eleventh centuries, in the age of the republics the equal of Canossa.

Monselice was held by the descendants of the Lombards against the forces of the Paduan Republic and by the Paduans against the imperial vicar, Ezzelino da Romano, who won the fortress *per tradimento* (by the treason of its garrison, that is) in 1237. Having rebuilt and strengthened the castle, and extended its walls to join those of the city itself, Ezzelino assailed his enemies from its peak. The Carraresi tyrants of Padua, who like their predecessor won Monselice by treachery in 1259, held it against the Scaligeri tyrants of Verona. The Scaligeri eventually took possession by the same method from 1317 through 1338. The Carraresi reconquered their stronghold, and remodeled it to suit fourteenth-century military needs only to lose it again to the Visconti briefly (1388–90) and to the Venetians finally. The Venetians acquired the fortress never yet taken by force by the sensible Ezzelinian means of corrupting its defender.

In 1405, the Venetian adventurer and hero Carlo Zeno bribed Luca da Leone, Paduan nobleman and intimate of Francesco Novello da Carrara, to surrender the impregnable *rocca* (fortified tower) at the peak of the mountain and the more extensive complex near its base.[2] Soon afterwards, the last Paduan signore and his sons were strangled in a Venetian dungeon and the *castello* at Monselice was purchased by unnamed members of the Marcello family: certainly by 1441, when the first of Jacopo Antonio's sojourns there is noted. New renovations were undertaken before the midpoint of the century, this time in the Venetian gothic style. The Marcello construction joined the Ezzelinian fortress to the older medieval structure, and the whole complex created for military purposes was redesigned for residential use. If not the purchaser, Jacopo Antonio was the likely renovator: he was present in the area, wealthy, and interested in the arts.

Jacopo Antonio's son Pietro remodeled again, beautifying and further domesticating the martial spaces of the building. He constructed above the Carrara barracks at the base of the tower the *piano nobile* of a grand Venetian palace. Carved here and there in the stone trim of the renovated rooms are his initials, PM, and the Marcello arms.[3] There, too, are engraved the emblem and motto of the Order of the Crescent, in which Marcello was inscribed by René d'Anjou in 1449: *Los en croissant.* In his *Itinerario della terraferma* (Mainland journey) of 1483, the indefatigable diarist Marino Sanuto described the town which could be reached by barge from the center of Venice.[4] En route to nearby Este, he visited the old house of a Sanuto forebear, once *podestà* of Monselice: "Monselice is a castle sitting on a mountain," he wrote. Near the peak stood the official residence that had housed his ancestor, "and opposite it, that of Jacopo Antonio Marcello, knight, deceased, now belonging to his sons."[5]

Devastated during the wars of the League of Cambrai in 1509 to 1514, the *castello* was declared "uninhabitable" in 1520 by Marco and Valerio, two sons of Jacopo Antonio Marcello. They made their statement to the Venetian fiscal magistracy called the Savi alle Decime, claiming that the

Marcello castle in Monselice (Italy), in the Euganean hills south of Padua. View of thirteenth-century tower built by the Carrara family, lords of Padua. From Nino Barbantini, Il castello di Monselice *(Venice: Officine Grafiche Carlo Ferrari, 1940), p. 21 (plate 11). Photograph courtesy of Marino Zorzi, Director, Biblioteca Nazionale Marciana (Venice).*

Marcello castle, view of Jacopo Antonio's fifteenth-century Venetian gothic addition embedded in earlier structure. Barbantini, p. 23 (plate 13). Photograph courtesy of Marino Zorzi, Director, Biblioteca Nazionale Marciana (Venice).

property was now too expensive for them to maintain. The Cambrai wars caused extensive damage to the city itself, sacked by the troops of Alfonso d'Este, and destroyed the communal archives (making more difficult this reconstruction of events). Yet rebuilding ensued and magnificence was restored by 1588, when Marcella, daughter of Pietro Marcello, left by her will to her son Alvise "with the great *rocca* of the castle at Monselice, all her books and especially all her writings of every sort and all the furnishings and adornments of her apartment at Monselice."[6]

The upper part of the hill was sold to Francesco Duodo in 1592; he constructed the handsome villa that still rewards the viewer who has labored to climb beyond the castle and the venerable *duomo* of ancient Monselice. The castle remained the property of the descendants of Marcella Marcello when, in the seventeenth century, it was enhanced by a library containing manuscripts, illuminated manuscripts, and early printed books. The same proprietors arranged for the building of the charming miniature church of Santa Lucia (adjoining the *castello*), declared finished by Vettore Antonio Alvise Marcello in 1740. In 1810, still owned by his descendants, the property had again tumbled to *rovine* (ruins), the condition in which it had stood after Cambrai. By 1840, it had been sold to the Girardi family, and was under their care in 1842 when a contemporary tourbook described the *castello* as "square, massive, dark, adorned with sculptures, but ruined by neglect, by age, by mutilations, additions, and changes."[7]

Early in the twentieth century, the castle at Monselice was inherited by Count Vittorio Cini, founder of the Cini Foundation housed in a Palladian cloister on the island of San Giorgio Maggiore in Venice. In 1935, Cini initiated a total restoration of the *castello* to authentic Renaissance condition. The restored building now houses the most important collection of arms in the Veneto after that in the Doge's Palace. These are Cini's gift of 1972, in which year the property was donated to the foundation created in memory of the philanthropist's son Giorgio.

The late-twentieth-century visitor finds that Monselice bears the marks of long evolution. At the hill's peak, the ancient *rocca*, deprived of further military function, is a ruin. Near the base stands the *castello*, an amalgam of structures of varying age and origin. The ancient *casa romanica* dates from the Middle Ages; its main supporting column, hewn from a whole tree, has hoisted the same burden for close to one thousand years. Nearby stands the *castelletto*, also constructed before the era of Ezzelino. Of more recent fabric is the austere palace built by Ezzelino and improved by his Paduan successors. Of fearsome exterior and equally fearsome interior, equipped with secret passages and dungeons, it is still painted floor to roof with the vast red and black checkerboard pattern boasted by the Carraresi, whose arms are carved on its wall.

These three medieval structures are connected by a fifteenth-century one resembling a Venetian palazzo: delicate trefoil windows are cut into its facade, and an elegant staircase leading to a handsome entrance into the *piano nobile* preempts the doorway used by Carrarese soldiers. Behind it is a cortile (of later construction), in the center of which sits a well, modeled on those found in the *campi* of Venice; and a stone sarcophagus on which prowls a fierce Venetian lion, book closed, perpetually at war. The Venetian additions to the venerable fortress were delicately executed, respectful of the lineaments of the original structure: its "primitive physiognomy and especially its harsh medieval aspect."[8] The thirteenth-century Carrara fireplace was restored and extended in appropriate style, and the red and black Carrara checkerboard, where impinged upon by alterations, was carefully repainted. The *salone* on the first floor, its dimensions grand in Venetian style, nevertheless respected the stark lines of the original building it adjoined, and materials from the older structure were incorporated in its walls. A Venetian presence was added to the ancient fortification, but was not allowed to extinguish the spirit of its martial and signorial past.

The proprietor of the *castello* when these modifications were undertaken was Jacopo Antonio Marcello. To Monselice he resorted whenever he could between bouts of warfare; here he vacationed with his family; here he poured over his books. As elsewhere in Europe, where the nobleman's castle was targeted for destruction by a newly aggressive monarchy, the fortress was a well-nigh illicit symbol of power and status.[9] In Venice, Marcello lived in a tame palace on the Grand Canal, strikingly in contrast to the country residence he had chosen for himself at Monselice: for that republican city did not permit its noblemen to live in buildings that looked like fortresses, and clannish patricians did not cluster in the same neighborhoods for mutual protection as they did elsewhere.[10] By the canals of Venice, Marcello dutifully wore the somber robes of the Venetian nobleman. In the aerie castle of Monselice, he wore armor and issued commands, gathering in the inherited authority of the Roman, Lombard, imperial, della Scala, and Carrara dominators of that frontier. Only a man whose vision of himself had outgrown the limits defined by the self-generated culture of the Venetian aristocracy would have chosen for a second home the indomitable fortress of Monselice. Fittingly, this man who fancied a monument in the stones of Monselice sought also to be celebrated in words.[11]

ↄ҉　　ↄ҉　　ↄ҉

Marcello's grandiose self-concept is nurtured in a number of humanist works written at his prompting. Best known of these is a letter by the humanist and pedagogue Guarino Veronese, dedicating to Marcello in 1458 the translation of Strabo's *Geography,* which Guarino had completed at Marcello's request.[12] After early years in Venice and Constantinople (where he studied with that catalyst of Italian Hellenism, Manuel Chrysoloras), Guarino taught in his native Verona until 1429. In that year he removed to Ferrara where he presided at court and at the reborn *studio,* or university, until his death in 1460. In both locations, he exerted influence on a generation of scholars and of other young men who were to play significant roles in the leadership of cities and institutions of Quattrocento Italy. Marcello's relations with Guarino (which may have begun in the 1430s, when the nobleman was active in the Veronese) had certainly crystallized by late 1455. About that time, Marcello assumed the patronage of the Strabo project.

In the prefatory letter to his translation of Strabo, Guarino describes Marcello's role as *provveditore,* or supervisor, of Venice's armed forces during the last phase of the thirty-year struggle with Milan for control of the Lombard plain. The Venetian was descended, his classicizing biographer claimed, from the Roman Marcellus clan whose illustrious forefather Marcus Claudius Marcellus had withstood the enmity of Hannibal. A "second Hercules," Marcello himself performed deeds worthy of his ancestors. The Roman Marcellus was already in the forefront of Guarino's mind when he lifted his pen in praise of his patron. He had recently completed a translation of Plutarch's *Life* of that Roman hero.[13]

A Venetian replica of ancient Roman virtue, according to Guarino, Marcello defended Casalmaggiore from the unexpected onslaught of the army of Niccolò Piccinino, the *condottiere* general of Filippo Maria Visconti. When the city of Brescia (part of the Venetian mainland empire) was subjected to siege by the same Piccinino, Marcello urged the citizens to resistance, and protected access to the city so that provisions could be supplied. "You, Marcello, most wise of men," rushing to the rescue through "wild forests" and overcoming other "evil obstacles," Guarino wrote, "entered the city and heartened the citizens and soldiers, led the charge on the castle of Roado, the key to the city of Brescia and its pillar, and rescued it from the grasp of the enemy."[14]

With a skeletal force, his panegyrist continued, Marcello then "unvanquished, like a second Hannibal," coursed through the rocky and icy paths of the Alps to the Veronese, and saved the garrison isolated within its walls, securing the entire region on the Venetian side of the river Mincio.[15] This

accomplished, he performed a feat "with a strength more than human and
scarcely credible to posterity."[16] Xerxes had boldly stretched a naval bridge
across the Hellespont to invade Greece; but Marcello equaled and even exceeded the accomplishment of that Persian king. For the Persian, in accord
with nature, had deployed his ships on water, while the Venetian "by the
greatness of [his] soul, sharpness of mind, perspicacity of genius, transported a huge fleet . . . over land."[17] Over the mountains separating the
river Adige from the Lago di Garda, chased the whole time by Piccinino's
forces, he dragged the fleet which, launched on that lake, could defend
Verona and supply Brescia. Daedalus, so bold as to attempt the heavens,
should not be admired more than he!

When Piccinino captured Verona, invaded the Vicentino, and blocked
the advance of Venice's captain general Francesco Sforza, it was Marcello
who "like the dictator of Verona," according to Guarino, saved the day. He
opened a path through the mountains, joined up with Sforza, escorted him
to the Venetian camp, and terrified Piccinino into full retreat.[18] Thereafter,
by Marcello's effort, advice, and quick action (as all know, comments our
chronicler) Verona was rescued from the enemy. The Veronese now credit
the safety of their city to Marcello's swift action.

At the battle fought over the island Mezzano in the river Po near Casalmaggiore, the Venetian army was victorious "under [Marcello's] leadership
and judgment,"[19] Guarino's narrative continued. Following up that victory,
Marcello crossed the Adda, the river marking the outermost frontier of Venetian power. He so terrified the population that they surrendered their
cities; and "mighty and ever imperious Milan beheld the standards of Venice flying at its gates."[20] Outside those gates Marcello was knighted, "as a
monument to his magnanimity and fortitude," by the Venetian captain
general.[21] When Filippo Maria Visconti died soon afterward, "shocked by
the turbulence of these events,"[22] the cities of Lodi and Piacenza gave themselves to Venice. The *Serenissima*, indeed, very nearly gained Milan itself,
to become universal sovereign of land as well as sea. In all of this, Marcello
demonstrated his "continence, integrity, innocence": these virtues of his
particularly conspicuous in the fiscal arena. "Amid such license and abundance of wealth, gold, and spoils, in which you could easily have enriched
yourself, you returned home no richer than before; since as a prudent and
sober administrator of public monies you believed that greater glory lay in
despising than in acquiring wealth."[23]

Such moments of Marcello's career are celebrated also by other panegyrists in works composed from the 1450s through 1463. First among these
are the poets Janus Pannonius and Giovanni Michele Alberto Carrara, at

the time both students of Guarino's at Ferrara. They lionized the Venetian *provveditore* in verses probably written prior to their respective departures from their mentor's school—and not long after Marcello's glorious victory at Casalmaggiore. The Hungarian poet and patriot Pannonius came as little more than a child to Guarino's school in 1447, and proceeded to Padua in 1454 before returning in 1458 to his homeland.[24] Best known outside of Hungary for the *Panegyric* of his teacher Guarino (groundbreaking in its epic portrayal of scholar-as-hero), during his eleven-year stay in Italy Pannonius also wrote several works linked to Marcello, members of the Guarinian and Venetian circles, and the Lombard wars.[25]

Pannonius's *Panegyric* to Marcello is an enormous work of more than two thousand verses, replete with mythological imagery and notably thin in tales of combat, celebrating Marcello as both firm defender of Venice and descendant of ancient Rome: "Now noble Marcello from the race of the toga-clad Roman fathers, strong column of Venetian destiny."[26] It narrates the usual story of Marcello's triumphs from Verona to Ravenna, and from Casalmaggiore to the gates of Milan, while it tactfully distances the hero from Sforza's notorious sack of Piacenza and embarrassing victory (for the Venetians) at Caravaggio.[27] The epigram entitled *Comparatio Marcellorum, Veneti et Romani* (Comparison of the Venetian and Roman Marcellos) sounds in brief the same heroic theme, juxtaposing the ancient Marcus Claudius Marcellus (the same figure Guarino had identified as the Venetian's forebear) with the contemporary Venetian hero. The latter must be considered the greater, he argues: "If you compare the deeds of the two Marcellos, the Venetian son vanquishes in glory his Roman ancestor."[28] The Roman hero had never transported a fleet of ships over the Alps, as had the Venetian. The former won Syracuse in three years; the latter took Verona in three days.[29] The references to the pre-Venetian, Roman greatness of the Marcello issuing from the Guarinian coterie in the 1450s would be resumed by the later panegyrists of the consolatory corpus, as will be seen.

About the same time that Pannonius wrote his *Panegyric* for Jacopo Antonio Marcello, his schoolmate, the Bergamese Giovanni Michele Alberto Carrara composed in verse, either at the Venetian's invitation or the suggestion of his teacher, his *De bello Jacobi Antonii Marcelli in Italia gesto* (On the war fought in Italy by Jacopo Antonio Marcello).[30] The scene there described can be identified as the battle near Casalmaggiore of 1446, followed by the ceremonial knighting of Marcello and other battlefield heroes, and a stab at the gates of Milan. In Carrara's grandiose but distorted rendition, Marcello is featured as "commander" [*dux*] and "king" [*rex*] on the banks of the Adda, urging his soldiers to conquest, his stentorian voice causing the tyrannical duke (Filippo Maria Visconti) to tremble. Having routed the enemy and crossed the river, the Venetian troops devastated the countryside and approached Milan. Visconti summoned his supporters: "Marcello has brought his victorious standards into the heart of our realm, and with impunity invades my territory; he exults in his Empire, and having slaughtered many [of my subjects], raging and armed, he subdues them."[31] Ordering the fortification of Lodi and Piacenza, on the Milanese side of the Adda, the Milanese duke sent his minions forth. Marcello, meanwhile, roused his troops to such fervor that they poured forth roaring like "lions," "tigers," and fierce "bears."[32]

Giorgio Bevilacqua da Lazise (one of those who would later contribute to the corpus of Marcello consolations) also wrote a classicizing history (this one in prose) of the north Italian struggle. His *De bello gallico* (On the Lombard war) was dedicated to the Venetian nobleman Marco Donato, an active politician and humanist amateur.[33] Bevilacqua traced that conflict from 1438 through its temporary resolution by the Treaty of Cavriana, engineered by Francesco Sforza, and the ensuing lavish reception in 1442 of that *condottiere* and his new bride, Bianca Maria Visconti, by the doge and city of Venice.[34] Again, Marcello's role in the Veronese is lauded by another of Guarino's alumni, the older contemporary of Pannonius and Carrara.

୧୨   ୧୨   ୧୨

The most elaborate celebrations of Marcello's *gesta,* however, are not these occasional eulogies and histories. Rather they are the passages embedded in the works described in the previous chapter whose chief purpose was to console a father on the loss of his son. Most of the fifteen works appearing in Marcello's compilation, the codex G, contain material describing the bibliophile's military career. So does the contemporaneous and related elegy by Ludovico Carbone. Some of the accounts, while brief, provide gems of important detail: George of Trebizond's, Isotta Nogarola's, Carlo Fortebraccio's, Montorio Mascarello's, Battista Guarini's, the Anonymous Venetian's, Michele Orsini's, and Carbone's. Substantial narratives appear in Francesco Filelfo's consolation, Perleone's *Laudatio,* and Bevilacqua's *Excusatio.*

Marcello's role as liberator of Verona, protector of nearby Brescia, and preserver of Italy is the subject of Nogarola's brief and rather vague encomium. "Our Verona is witness" to his greatness, she told Marcello, "where you performed many memorable deeds, as at that perilous time when the city was threatened with destruction and you were named as chief among so many worthy generals, and the glorious Venetian senate confirmed that election and committed to you the supreme command." Brescia, likewise, is "witness" to Marcello's greatness, "by whose leadership and advice so many and such things were done, that you are ever called advocate, defender and preserver, and as it were guardian angel." Indeed, she continues, all of Italy attests to his greatness: "All of Italy, finally, is witness, whose imperium, dignity, and majesty you preserved by your singular virtue and magnanimity, to which you restored peace and tranquility, and beyond this, reputation, honor, and liberty."[35]

In other accounts, Marcello's deeds are presented in clearer focus. A few authors record, as did Guarino, Marcello's activity at the first battle of Casalmaggiore in 1438. "Casalmaggiore was so strongly and prudently fortified and defended by your deeds and diligence," wrote Fortebraccio, that Piccinino's assault was rebuffed and supplies were gathered to assist the beleaguered citizens of Brescia.[36] Filelfo especially notes the importance of the location, at the center of the region from which grain and other foodstuffs were gathered to supply the army, the besieged Brescians, and even Venice. It was entirely due to the "wisdom and diligence" of Jacopo Antonio Marcello alone that the opponent army withdrew.[37] Mascarello counts the first Casalmaggiore encounter as one of Marcello's record of "triumphs."[38]

Francesco Filelfo, noting the desperate condition of the besieged citizens of Brescia, names Marcello as the key figure in the city's relief: "you particularly were chosen to take charge, as though another Scipio, of this complex and dangerous mission, as one most sharp in intellect and spirit and unvanquished in great and dangerous deeds."[39] Speaking in Marcello's voice, Bevilacqua describes that nobleman's appointment as *provveditore* assigned to relieve Gattamelata, bottled up in the besieged city. Commanded to lead the whole Venetian army safely from Brescia to the Veronese, across rough terrain, at the same time heartening and supplying the oppressed Brescians, Marcello was awed with the greatness and difficulty of the mission.[40]

Mascarello lists among Marcello's "triumphs" his daring negotiations with Count Parisio da Lodrone: these afforded an open route for the progress of Gattamelata's forces from beleaguered Brescia to vulnerable Verona.[41] Perleone explains more fully the nature of that mission to Parisio, "whose wealth and authority was great amid those mountains," and through whose territory lay the only possible route for Gattamelata's necessary retreat to Verona.[42] It was a dangerous task, for Piccinino's forces held the mountains, and no one was willing to do it. Parisio was officially neutral, but had begun to lean towards Piccinino. Any legate to Parisio, therefore, had no certainty of returning safely. "In such peril therefore, in a matter so doubtful and nearly desperate, it fell to you," Perleone wrote, "since all believed that because of either your virtue or fame or glory or fortune it seemed that nothing was so arduous and so difficult that it could not be accomplished and effected by you."[43] Disguised as a peasant (according to Bevilacqua), Marcello performed the risky mission, securing the desired alliance.[44] The task achieved, riding alongside Gattamelata he led the thirty thousand men of the Venetian forces safely over rough mountain passes to the Veronese, from whence they could defend the Adige and continue to supply Brescia.

Most of the panegyrists highlight especially the daring overland removal of the Venetian fleet from the river Adige to the Lago di Garda, effected in the winter of 1439. Francesco Filelfo, like Guarino before him, summoned up Xerxes' naval bridge as a lesser counterpart of Marcello's feat; but Filelfo also likened the Venetian effort to a more recent world-historical naval assault, the Turkish crossing of the Bosporus which preceded the conquest of Constantinople in 1453, "a catastrophe for all of Christendom."[45] George of Trebizond compared Marcello's deed favorably to Hannibal's: the latter guided merely an army, the former a navy, through Alpine passes.[46] Fortebraccio wondered that the very "order of things," the very "laws of nature" were defied by Marcello's achievement.[47] Mascarello likewise called the deed "an unheard-of thing, and an impossible thing," uniquely accomplished by Marcello's virtue and genius.[48]

In the same way, Perleone attributed the whole scheme to Marcello: "What could I first or more powerfully admire than your sharp mind in conceiving [this feat], your singular industry in accomplishing it, or the unheard-of miracle in seeing it accomplished? For ships were dragged from the base of the mountains by steep and rough paths which could scarcely be traversed by goats to the highest peaks, almost as tall as the heavens, by machines and contraptions, with tremendous shouts and staggering labor on the part of the soldiers."[49] Bevilacqua pictures Marcello as the bold adviser who urged the mission to go forward even after *Nicolaus Sorbolus architectus,* the expert engineer commissioned by the Senate, had declared the task impossible: "You, Marcello, to the admiration and stupefaction of all, convinced the Senate that the thing could be done."[50] It was done in the end, by the labor of men more valiant even than the beasts who towed the warships up and over the cliffs, a deed reminiscent of Hannibal's; and its success was due only to Marcello: "directed and accomplished by you alone, beyond the expectations of all, who had declared it absolutely impossible."[51]

In the spring of 1439, it was Marcello again, writes Filelfo, who facilitated Sforza's arrival at the head of forty thousand soldiers into the Veronese, with its fruitful consequences: "Not less therefore by your own diligence, than by the advent and strength of such a general, we see accomplished both the liberation of Verona from Milanese siege and imminent capture, and the recovery of the whole Vicentine and Veronese territory, and for these owe you undying gratitude."[52] George of Trebizond similarly links Marcello's role with Sforza's, "whose military skill was such that our age may contend with antiquity."[53] It was Marcello's mission (previously noted by Guarino) to open a way for that skilled *condottiere* in his march from Tuscany. He slipped out of besieged Verona ("like a greathearted lion," according to Fortebraccio in a description of the same incident; "like a lion enraged by his chains," according to Mascarello)[54] and forged through enemy territory, joined up with Sforza, and soon with him liberated the threatened city.[55] Twice in years to come, moreover, report George of Trebizond and Mascarello, Marcello's wise counsels would save Sforza's life.[56]

Sforza willingly acknowledged Marcello's key part in the deeds accomplished after the *condottiere's* assumption of command of the Venetian force, principally the dramatic liberation of Verona in the fall of 1439. "Marcello," he said, according to Fortebraccio, "we have won Verona today no less by your deeds than by my strength"; a similar statement is found in Mascarello's account.[57] According to Filelfo, "very often and with many others listening, Francesco [Sforza] frequently spoke in praise of you, and spoke at length and freely."[58] Likewise the Milanese *condottiere,* Niccolò Piccinino, reported to his master Filippo Maria Visconti that he had been driven from Verona by that same Venetian nobleman.[59] The Venetian doge Francesco Foscari had particular confidence in Marcello's skill, as Filelfo notes: "sober judge and connoisseur of your wondrous and divine virtue, [who] approved your appointment and hoped that there would result from it great utility and honor to the republic."[60]

Several panegyrists focus, as did Carrara, on Marcello's role at the second battle of Casalmaggiore in 1446. The captain general Michele Attendolo followed Marcello's advice to pursue the enemy boldly, according to Mascarello, resulting in a Venetian victory.[61] With Michele Attendolo wounded, Marcello took charge there, reads George of Trebizond's alternate account, and was that glorious battle's real hero: "you were the cause of that victory won by the Senate near Casalmaggiore against Filippo Maria [Visconti] when Michele, the army's leader injured his leg and therefore the whole weight of battle fell to you."[62] Francesco Filelfo also places Marcello at the fore. With Michele Attendolo holding the title of "imperator" (captain general), it was Marcello who alone crossed the Adda to invade Visconti lands on the other bank: "there was no one found in so great an army who previously had dared to cross that river."[63] It was winter, and the Adda was high, swollen and dangerous; all the bridges were held by the Milanese; no boats were at hand and it was necessary to move swiftly: "Then you, Marcello, ignoring advice to the contrary, with undismayed and stalwart spirit, swiftly led your horse into the river, calling upon the others to follow you; and never wavering amid the high waves and swift currents, you arrived on the Milanese shore before anyone else out of so great a force of soldiers and generals had even dampened the hooves of their horses."[64]

It was certainly Marcello, Filelfo continues, spelling out what Guarino had delicately hinted, who caused the death of the Duke of Milan not long thereafter: "For you alone, Jacopo Antonio Marcello, . . . were the principal cause of the death of that merciful and excellent prince, who not content to have crossed the Adda and released your soldiers to raid the lovely farms and fields with their abundance of goods . . . , flew the very standards and signs of Venice from the walls of Milan's famous and sublime citadel so that Duke Filippo, when he could suffer his eyes to do so, could look upon them." The sight sickened him; "so that from that cause he contracted a violent illness and a few months later, when his regime faced its greatest crisis, he died."[65] Thus did Marcello bring doom to Venice's archenemy, Filippo Visconti, Duke of Milan.

Several panegyrists comment on Marcello's sober management of money, as had Guarino, including payments of soldiers' wages. Echoing Guarino, Fortebraccio comments that amid such an abundance of spoils, Marcello went home no richer than he had left, in imitation of the elder Cato preferring rather to despise than to crave wealth.[66] Particularly fertile in detail here as elsewhere, Perleone offers the scene of Marcello raising a fortune in private funds to pay the soldiers: "When public funds were not sent to cover the soldiers' stipends, you with personal contacts gathered up in one day from your friends so much gold and silver so that you were able to lead a whole army of soldiers out from their winter camps into the field in arms and ready within a few days."[67]

Our authors compare Marcello to Hannibal, Xerxes, and Scipio (as did Guarino). Several dwell (as did Pannonius) on his relation to Marcus Claudius Marcellus, the Venetian's presumed Roman forebear. Michele Orsini uniquely stresses the parallel courses of the two heroes' careers, separated by more than one and one-half millennia. Marcello opposed Piccinino as his ancestor Marcus Claudius Marcellus opposed Hannibal; he had as colleague the future doge Pasquale Malipiero as the Roman had as his hero

Quintus Fabius Maximus. "For Marcello, of Roman probity, name, and family, illustrious both at home and abroad, both in peace and in war, has brought back to life his ancestors' memorable deeds. It would be proper to say that whatever good fortune, virtue, and excellence once shone among all the Roman Marcellos now blaze forth among the Venetians in the one Jacopo Antonio."[68]

One last contemporary work composed apart from the context of either Guarino's school (in the 1450s) or the consolations for Valerio (1461–63) contributed to the Marcello legend: the unique history by Desiderius Spretus, *De amplitudine, devastatione et instauratione urbis Ravennae* (On the greatness, destruction, and restoration of the city of Ravenna).[69] Written soon after the events it describes, and dedicated to the man who dominates them, it includes a full account of Marcello's activity in that city at the point (in 1440) where its native da Polenta signori yielded to Venetian overlordship.[70] This nobleman of Roman ancestry, according to Spretus, and victor of the Lombard wars, was dispatched by the Senate to Ravenna on a particularly delicate mission: to mediate between Ostasio da Polenta and his citizens while preserving traditional relations with Venice.

This task he brilliantly accomplished: "For by his excellent virtue and supreme integrity he managed all matters both of war and peace so wisely, that the energies of all of our citizens were remarkably aroused to good will and loyalty towards Venice, nor did they wish to be ruled by any *imperium* other than that of the Venetians."[71] Like another Scipio, or Marcus Claudius Marcellus (again!), both opponents of the archetypical tyrant Hannibal, he had freed the citizens from the rule of despots and settled them in the sheltering embrace of Venice.[72] The Venetian so effectively rallied the soldiers and citizens when the city was attacked that "all the citizens gathered around Marcello as around their leader."[73] Ostasio was persuaded to relinquish his rule.

Spretus's cameo portrait of Marcello's activity in Ravenna was unknown to the panegyrists of the Ferrara circle or consolation context, but was eventually grafted on to the tradition constituted by their work. It surfaces in the concise statement of Marcello's achievement found in a 1555 inscription to Marcello in the church on San Cristoforo della Pace. That inscription, which summed up the whole panegyrical tradition, can no longer be read *in situ:* both the church and even the island on which it stood have been demolished.[74] The church had been built in the years after the 1454 peace at Lodi, and commemorates that peace, as the chapel does Marcello's role in its achievement. Nearly a century later, Marcello's son (Valerio) and two grandsons (Niccolò and Pietro) unveiled the hero's epitaph in that chapel.

By Jacopo Antonio Marcello, illustrious knight and senator, the harsh three-year siege of Brescia was lifted; the fleet by wondrous design was transported across the mountains and lowered to the Lake of Garda; Verona was recovered from the forces of Piccinino; Ravenna by his leadership and guidance was added to the empire of Venice; the River Adda having been overcome by him . . . , he had reached the gates of Milan, where he was granted the dignity of knighthood, and commissioned by King René with the admiralship of Naples, and ascribed among the first members of [that king's] sacred society [the Order of the Crescent]; finally, through his most noble efforts [he] brought peace to Italy. His son Valerio [began] . . . and his nephews Niccolò and Pietro, sons of Marco, saw to the completion of this work, 1 December 1555.[75]

Fully in the earlier tradition of panegyrical works, the inscription attributes to Marcello the lifting of the siege of Brescia, the hauling of the fleet over the Alps, the liberation of Verona, the crossing of the Adda, the honor of knighthood, and approach to the gates of Milan. Echoing the report by Spretus, it also notes the acquisition of Ravenna. Further, it reports an honor mentioned by no earlier panegyrist: membership in the "sacred order" (of the Crescent) of the French claimant of the Neapolitan throne, René d'Anjou (of whom more later). And its final claim is implied previously only by Nogarola, when she says that Marcello restored to "all of Italy . . . peace and tranquility . . . reputation, honor, and liberty."[76]

The San Cristoforo inscription is repeated by the genealogists of the seventeenth century, who elaborate somewhat inaccurately on the incidents listed there and in the literary corpus on which it relied. The Belgian abbot Theodorus Damadenus, dedicated chronicler of the Marcello family, points to elements of the Marcello legend in the title itself of his genealogy: *Mare-caelum romano-venetum sive Marcellorum a Romani[s] principibus ad Venetos proceres ab anno u. c. CCXLIX usque ad annum Christi MDCLXXVI per annos MMCXXVII de patre in filium deducta progenies* (Sea-Sky, Roman-Venetian, or the family tree of the Marcellos from Roman princes to their Venetian descendents, from 249 B.C. to 1676 A.D., traced from father to son over 2,127 years). The "Mare-caelum" of this title, a pun on the audible parts of the name "Marcello," also refers to the family's coat of arms which features a golden wave (the "sea") slashing diagonally across a field of blue (the "sky"). The intersection of those two elements echoes the two elements of land and sea featured in the Venetian myth. This theme was highlighted in the fifteenth century as that city's largely maritime empire expanded to encompass much of northern Italy. Damadenus also links Jacopo Antonio Marcello to that powerful Venetian myth in the figure of the city's symbolic lion. His voice ascending to the highest pitch of praise, he writes: "Jacopo Antonio Marcello imitated the Venetian lion, symbol of the *patria;* that winged lion, with one foot on earth, the other reaching to the sea, its head and the rest of its body poised between the two. He imitated the lion in fortitude, its wings in velocity and diligence, . . . [and by] its head, he administered the political affairs of the city, situated between land and sea."[77] In the winged lion unstably perched between land and sea we recognize verbal puffery carried to absurdity. But much of the earlier panegyric tradition is flawed as well. It presents not a portrait of Marcello's deeds, but a myth.

⅋ ⅋ ⅋

Most of the panegyrics of Marcello date from the half-decade of 1458 through 1463. The year in which Guarino composed his prefatory letter to the Strabo is twenty years after the first major event that it records (Casalmaggiore I) and eleven years after the last (the submission to Venice of Lodi and Piacenza in 1447). Ample time had elapsed between the events celebrated and the celebration, allowing for the crystallization of an oral tradition about the Venetian's *gesta.* Not surprisingly, the same events are repeated in most of the panegyrics, including those of Carrara and Pannonius composed some years earlier and the much later 1555 inscription.

As a rule, the key moments of Marcello's career as recorded by the panegyrists include the first Casalmaggiore victory, the rallying of the Brescians, the strategic retreat from Brescia to Verona, the treaty with Parisio da Lodrone, all in 1438; the transport of the Venetian fleet over Alpine foothills to the Lago di Garda, Sforza's advent, and the liberation of Verona, all in 1439; the acquisition of Ravenna in 1440; the battle at the "island in the Po" (Mezzano) near Casalmaggiore (the second and greater Casalmaggiore triumph), Marcello's knighthood, and the dash to Milan, in 1446; the death of Visconti and consequent acquisition of Piacenza and Lodi in 1447.[78] In addition, the panegyrists introduce the same undated themes or topics: Marcello's Roman ancestry; his likeness to Xerxes, Hannibal, or Scipio; his relations with Sforza, especially in preserving that figure's life; his proper management of pecuniary responsibility; his role in securing the peace of Italy; and his membership in the Order of the Crescent.

These are the events normally described (or alluded to) in the fourteen works which document in any detail the career of Jacopo Antonio Marcello. Those fourteen include ten from the consolatory cycle of codex G (works

by George of Trebizond, Francesco Filelfo, Nogarola, Fortebraccio, Mascarello, Guarini, Perleone, the Anonymous Venetian, Orsini, and Bevilacqua). The four not contained in the Glasgow volume are the *Carmen* of
Ludovico Carbone (contemporary with works in G), the earlier *Panegyric*
of Janus Pannonius and *De bello* of Giovanni Carrara, and the epitaph of
1555. This listing makes clear how great was the continuity of purpose in
these numerous works otherwise disparate in purpose, or genre, or extent.
So unified are the works in praise of Marcello that the careful reader recog-
nizes considerable cross-referencing among them. The Marcello panegyrics
not only repeat certain key events, but repeat them in the same pattern,
attributing to certain actions the same importance, and employing similar
language to describe them. Sometimes the same metaphors are used (Marcello's feats are compared to Hannibal's in crossing the Alps, to Xerxes' in
bridging the Hellespont). Sometimes even the very same language leaps
from the page, as when both Fortebraccio and George of Trebizond report
the arrival of Marcello's troops in Verona after an arduous winter journey
looking "dead as marble statues."[79]

The continuity among the panegyrics is so strong as to posit the existence of a "fact sheet," a kind of press release, from Marcello's immediate
circle, used by all subsequent authors: like that deduced in chapter 2 from
the biographies of Valerio Marcello. Guarino's letter may have served in
part as such a fact sheet. His own students (the adolescent poets Pannonius
and Carrara as well as the historian Bevilacqua) had already launched the
process of mythmaking, in works known to their master. Most of the components of the panegyrical material listed above were already present in
Guarino's 1458 letter, which surely circulated in Ferrara among his coterie
and in Venice and Friuli among Marcello's, if only in a single copy at the
direction of its recipient and subject. From these centers, the letter itself or
its epitome could have reached Filelfo in Milan, via Perleone, his former
student and Marcello's intimate, or via Sforza, Marcello's comrade and Filelfo's employer.

That the post-Guarinian authors modeled their own panegyrics on
Guarino's letter, or on a similar script approved by Marcello for his own
glorification, is bolstered by evidence showing that several of the writers
were paid for their work (as Guarino was for the Strabo translation) or had
strong expectation of rich reward (as did Filelfo).[80] But Guarino could not
have been the only source for the later panegyrics: they borrowed from
each other as well, and some supply unique details from quite independent
sources. Probably Guarino's letter served as a springboard for the later
works, which in turn circulated among past and potential authors.

The reports of the events of Marcello's career were more literary fabrications than histories built on eyewitness reports. They range from exaggeration to wholesale misrepresentation. The accounts of that nobleman's deeds offered by humanists, genealogists, and inscription alike do not square with the story told by the chroniclers, as other scholars have shown.[81] According to those authorities, Piccinino did cross the Po and surprise Casalmaggiore in 1438, and resistance was offered by the Venetian forces. The resistance was weak, however, and the commander of the forces was not Marcello but the Serenissima's captain general, Erasmo da Narni, known as Gattamelata ("tabby cat"). The Brescians were rallied by Venetian leaders in the same year; but it was Gattamelata again, and the redoubtable captain and humanist Francesco Barbaro, who waded on horseback amid the throngs of distraught citizens, swords held aloft, and commanded first their respect and then, in consequence, their obedience. Marcello participated in the masterful retreat from Brescia to Verona, still in 1438; it was led, again, by Gattamelata. In the same way, Marcello was with the army when it dashed to Brescia the next year.

Early in 1439, the Venetians accomplished the extraordinary feat hailed by the conquerors: they hoisted an entire armada comprising eighty war galleys over the Alpine foothills to Garda, hauled the heavy load on ox-drawn rollers, and lowered the boats by cables down steep cliffs. The project was designed and directed by two foreign architects, the Cretan Niccolò Sorbolo and Blasio de Arboribus, who had won the approval of the Senate for their plan. The Venetian commander was the nobleman Pietro Zeno, not Marcello. Just as his panegyrists attributed the deed to Marcello, other hired pens ascribed it to their patrons: to Gattemelata himself, or to Stefano Contarini.[82]

Several months later, Gattamelata and Francesco Sforza (who had by now joined the Venetian forces) triumphantly entered and liberated Verona. In 1440, Marcello was sent to Ravenna with a force of two thousand infantry to secure the troubled city for Venice, but can hardly be considered the architect of Ravenna's acquisition. In 1446, Marcello was among the Venetians who won victory at the river battle near Casalmaggiore and pushed close to Milan, but Michele Attendolo da Cotignola was in command. That *condottiere* did knight Marcello after the battle (along with the captains Pietro Avogadro and Antonio di Martinengo). The Adda was crossed, but no mention is made of a near approach to Milan. The resilient old schemer Filippo Maria Visconti died several months later in August, 1447, but probably not from the shock of seeing Venetian standards hoisted outside the gates of his city.

A diminished Marcello emerges from this recital of events from the viewpoint of the more disinterested chronicle tradition. The Venetian was present at or near the events described, but not in the key role that his elogiasts assign him. He could not have been: for they portray Marcello as the winner of battles. Venetians hired generals to war for them; they did not in their own persons lead armies on the *terraferma*. At the side of each hired general stood an official who was part supervisor, part spy, part paymaster—the *provveditore*. It was this unglamorous position that Marcello held almost without interruption for twenty-six years.

The position had real importance. In the course of the fifteenth century, *provveditori* would help mold a professional army that constituted an important development in the military history of Europe.[83] The provveditorial system enabled Venice to tame the notorious figure of the *condottiere*, making that hired commander relatively loyal and efficient. An adviser rather than a fighter (one of his duties was to pay the troops, at any cost, *on time*), the *provveditore* did bear arms and travel with cavalry escort. Most were at heart civilians who dodged the conflict, did their duty, and returned to assume higher magistracies in government. "It was . . . rare," one scholar has observed, "for individual nobles to hold offices that were predominantly military or naval throughout their active careers."[84] Yet a few did, functioning as genuine military specialists, strategists, and combatants. Marcello was one of perhaps the dozen Venetian noblemen in his century whose careers belonged to that group. Still, he was no general. The representation of Marcello in these texts is thus distorted from the outset: as a Venetian nobleman with provveditorial duties, he would not have led armies and won victories.

Some of the panegyrists more intimately related to Marcello (or to the business of war) were aware of the distinction between the roles of general and *provveditore:* Filelfo and Perleone, for instance, specify that it is Marcello's counsel or exhortation rather than active leadership that effects the triumphs described. Yet even they magnify the Venetian's role beyond what was possible for a *provveditore:* that magistrate could advise and urge, offer financial or political incentives to laggard captains, but he was not in command. Certainly Marcello could not have acted like the figure painted by Bevilacqua, who reflected thus on his own splendid achievements: "The whole republic of Venice placed its sure hope of victory in me, in me and in my virtue. As their chosen defender I defeated, conquered, and dispersed the enemy forces by my industry, swiftness, and counsel. How many times did I return home as a victor, covered in glory and made famous by my victorious deeds among friends and allies of the Venetian empire? Gifted with such military skill, enumerated among the worthiest champions, always unvanquished, I was always a victor and my name made illustrious for the fame and excellence of my deeds throughout the earth."[85] This implausible Marcello, like Damadenus's winged lion, was a creation of a crew of humanists who obediently lent their pens to the cause of the Venetian's reputation.

If Marcello hired or persuaded a coterie of humanists to confect a flattering picture of his military exploits, he did no more than other powerful men. The *condottieri*-princes of the Quattrocento commissioned humanists to profile their memorable deeds. The deeds of Braccio da Montone, lord of Perugia, were recorded by the humanist Giovanni Antonio Campano, at the request of that captain's son Carlo Fortebraccio. "I send you your father," wrote the author to his patron, "not his mere image . . . but [him himself] speaking, fighting and indeed brought to life, rising from hell into the light to greet you."[86] The deeds of Federigo da Montefeltre were recorded by Pierantonio Paltroni, while the deeds of his archenemy, Sigismondo Malatesta, were recorded by Tobia Borghi and continuator.[87] The Gonzaga lords of Mantua, who doubled as mercenaries, commissioned native son Bartolomeo Platina to celebrate their greatness.[88] Sforza had his own deeds commemorated and the history of Milan rewritten by his loyal secretaries, the humanists Pier Candido Decembrio, Leodrisio Crivelli, and Giovanni Simonetta.[89] More ambivalent but still appropriately grandiose is the heroic depiction of Sforza in Francesco Filelfo's epic *Sforziad*, begun in 1453, commemorating the capture and sack of Piacenza in 1447.[90] To polish the image of the Aragonese monarchs of Naples, the great histories of Bartolomeo Facio and Panormita were written, while the *Commentaries* of Giannantonio Porcellio de' Pandoni (protegé of the Venetian nobleman Ludovico Foscarini), dedicated to King Alfonso, celebrated the deeds of Jacobo Piccinino, protagonist of the Venetian-Neapolitan struggle of 1452 against Sforza.[91] The genre of the glorification of the militant hero culminates in Niccolò Machiavelli's portrayal of the angry Castruccio Castracane, betrayer and conqueror of Lucca.[92]

The celebration of *condottieri* and heroes, not confined to the formal biography or history, found expression in other genres as well: orations, verse, and the arts. The Sienese artist Simone Martini portrayed the fourteenth-century *condottiere* Guidoriccio da Foligno as a glorious conqueror (which he wasn't).[93] The grateful Florentines, who had already rewarded their mercenary captain Sir John Hawkwood with gifts of cash and castles during his lifetime, celebrated his funeral in 1394 in grand style, and commissioned Paolo Uccello to paint in his honor the groundbreaking

equestrian fresco (1436) in their cathedral.[94] Praised in an oration by Guarino Veronese for his great service to Venice, the captain Carmagnola was
later caught fatally in the intrigues between the two states of Venice and
Milan, which alternately employed him, and was executed at the will of the
Council of Ten.[95] Pier Candido Decembrio wrote the funeral oration for
the Visconti soldier Niccolò Piccinino, while the careers of the Venetian
condottieri Gentile da Leonessa and Bartolomeo Colleoni were celebrated
in orations of the Veneto humanists Montorio Mascarello and Giovanni
Michele Alberto Carrara. Montorio's work was discussed by Francesco
Barbaro and Ludovico Foscarini, two thoughtful architects of *terraferma*
policy, as a monument in words equal to those the ancients wrought in
bronze.[96]

In Venice, where the deeds of great men were not normally celebrated
except as part of the ritual magnification of the city,[97] still the victors of
wars at land and sea received special attention. That statement could be
extended: in Quattrocento Venice (with the exception of doges), *only* military heroes were honored with such public displays as state-sponsored funeral celebrations and monuments bearing erect statues: "Only a dead doge
or a military hero could be shown standing."[98] Standing, on horseback, or
supine, the number of sepulchral monuments to military figures in Venice
is impressive. The patrician admiral Vettore Pisani was honored with a
splendid state funeral, and a monument was erected in the family chapel at
the church of San Antonio da Vienna, later to be admired by the child
Valerio Marcello.[99] The Roman *condottiere* Paolo Savelli, who preceded
Carmagnola, Gattamelata, and Colleoni in Venetian service, was also honored with a state funeral (in 1405), attended by the doge himself, and with
an impressive equestrian monument, carved of wood, in the Frari church—
one of the very earliest of the genre.[100] Also in the Frari are pedestrian statues of Jacopo Marcello (kinsman to our Jacopo Antonio), killed at Gallipoli
in 1484, and the captain Melchiore Trevisan.[101] A pedestrian statue for the
condottiere Bernardo d'Alviano was placed in the church of San Stefano,
and one of the kneeling figure of Vettore Capello, the admiral killed in
1467 at Negroponte, in Sant'Apollinare.[102] The elaborate monument by
the sculptor Antonio Rizzo for Orsato Giustiniani, killed at Modone in
1464, is famed, though all but some fragments have perished: "one of the
greatest losses among the many suffered by Venice's artistic patrimony."[103]

Memorialized in Latin orations by the humanists Lauro Quirini and
Giovanni Pontano, the Venetian commander Gattamelata was buried in a
magnificent tomb in a private chapel of the Basilica del Santo in Padua,
arranged by his heirs according to his request.[104] In the piazza before the

Pedestrian statue in late gothic style of the admiral Vettore Pisani which once stood in the church of San Antonio da Vienna in Venice, where it was admired by the child Valerio. Venice, Church of SS. Giovanni e Paolo. Photograph courtesy of Osvaldo Böhm.

Equestrian statue in early Renaissance style of the condottiere *Paolo Savelli. Venice, Church of the Frari. Alinari/Art Resource, N.Y.*

Donatello's elegant equestrian statue of the condottiere *Gattamelata in full classical style. Padua, Piazza del Santo. Alinari/Art Resource, N.Y.*

(Ed. ^{mo} Alinari) N.º 12541. VENEZIA - Campo S. Giovanni e Paolo. Monumento a generale Colleoni. (A. Verrocchio).

Verrocchio's powerful equestrian statue of the condottiere *Bartolomeo Colleoni. Venice, Campo SS. Giovanni e Paolo. Alinari/Art Resource, N.Y.*

church, arranged again by his heirs and approved (reluctantly) by the Venetian Senate, Donatello's famed equestrian statue commemorates in bronze the *condottiere* in the martial pose he had struck during life.[105] The monument to Gattamelata (executed 1448–50) is the first surviving free-standing equestrian monument since antiquity, whose arrogant images of Roman *imperatores* it echoes.[106] In its century, the Gattamelata statue is challenged only by the bronze statue of another Venetian *condottiere*, Bartolomeo Colleoni.[107] Colleoni rides his horse in his employers' city, as directed in his will, a massive and overpowering presence in the *campo* before the church of Santi Giovanni e Paolo (executed 1483–88). Even before his death, Colleoni took interest in his own memorialization: he refurbished the ancient *castelli* (as Marcello refurbished Monselice!) with which the Venetian Senate rewarded him for his long military service, and supplied them with libraries furnished with exquisite volumes prepared by humanists in his employ.[108]

Monuments were rewards after death. But even during life, military figures were honored in Venice. They were disproportionately granted the title of "nobility"—a status to which even natives could not aspire if it was not theirs by birth. Such grants were purely honorary, and did not permit the holder to participate actively in government, but the honor they conferred was great and cherished. Of forty foreigners elected to the Great Council between 1404 and 1454 (and thus granted nobility), thirteen were *condottieri* rewarded for loyal service.[109] Among the Venetian captains general to appear in this narration, Gattamelata, Sforza, and Michele Attendolo were all granted Venetian noble status, as was the Brescian captain Pietro Avogadro, another hero of these events.[110] More tangible than title of nobility was a fine palace. At any given time, three or four Venetian palaces might be in the hands of cherished *condottieri*. Gianfrancesco Gonzaga, who would later betray his employers, was given a palace bought from the Giustiniani clan for 6,500 ducats. Gattamelata had his, previously the possession of Alvise dal Verme, and later in the century, the Sanseverino clan of military professionals had theirs. Sforza was given several, in succession, the periods of ownership punctuated by periods of enmity with the city hungry for empire.[111]

Works of literature also glorified Venetians renowned in war, and those who fought for them.[112] Early in the fifteenth century, the swashbuckling Carlo Zeno who had warred for Venice on sea and land and passed his last years in the company of his books was celebrated after death by two patrician humanists: Leonardo Giustiniani in a famous funeral oration, and Jacopo Zeno, the hero's grandson, in a full-scale biography.[113] The deaths in

1463 of the hired captain Bertoldo d'Este and native patrician admiral Orsato Giustiniani were celebrated with orations by Bernardo Bembo and Giovanni Caldiera respectively, delivered to vast audiences.[114] The consignment of the *bastone* of command to Bartolomeo Colleoni in 1455 and the death of captain general Bartolomeo d'Alviano in 1515 were marked in orations by Paolo Barbo and Andrea Navagero respectively.[115]

To celebrate Francesco Barbaro's heroic stance at Brescia in 1438, the citizen Evangelista Manelmi, brother of a procurator for the Venetian forces in that region, wrote his *Commentariolus de quibusdam gestis in bello gallico . . . Francisci Barbari* (A little commentary on certain deeds of Francesco Barbaro during the Lombard War . . .).[116] Francesco Contarini, a precocious young patrician, wrote his own history of the Venetian campaign in Tuscany in 1454.[117] A good fraction of the biographical and celebratory writing of the age is in fact, in Venice as in Italy generally, about warriors. Marcello's self-glamorization through the hired pens of the humanists could be seen as a half-sibling of that ordinary literary event of the era: the *condottiere* bio.

That the facts of Marcello's career are distorted in the works that portray him is no surprise; no other work of the genre was reliable in this regard. What is surprising is this: that this proprietor of the dark walls of Monselice chose to be portrayed as a *condottiere,* when he was, in fact, a Venetian nobleman. In Marcello's age, Venetian noblemen did not exalt themselves as individuals, or permit self-serving representations of themselves in art or literature.[118] Whatever might have been the personal ambitions of individual noblemen, patrician culture insisted upon understatement and reserve: the nobleman was presumed to exist for the city, not it for him. In this cultural context, Marcello's self-glorification is extraordinary. It is indeed, within the tradition of Venetian humanist literature examined by scholars, unique in that century.

ဢ   ဢ   ဢ

Nor did Marcello limit himself, in the task of self-advertisement, to the verbal medium. He also commissioned paintings of himself, embedded in the books compiled under his direction to be considered in later chapters. Here he was depicted in poses traditionally used to portray kings (receiving a client's gift) or warriors (the stark profile portrait). Portraits in this age served primarily as documentation. In both types, Marcello has taken steps to record his relations to the world of learning and to the royal court of René d'Anjou, and to assert his authority and power.

The presentation manuscript of the Strabo translated by Guarino and intended for the eyes and the library of René d'Anjou is adorned by two illuminations prepared by a major artist of the north Italian school: possibly even Andrea Mantegna or (more likely) his brother-in-law Giovanni Bellini, as intrigued scholars have proposed.[119] Certainly the styles of the two north Italian masters were closely related: most closely in the period of the 1450s and 1460s, the period when Marcello exercised his patronage. Both had ties, moreover, to Marcello and his circle. That Mantegna executed a project for Marcello around 1458 is securely documented by a letter from Ludovico Gonzaga asking for the artist to be released from his labors on a "small work" to come to Mantua.[120] The "operetta" on which he labored might even have been this one. Precisely in the same year, Mantegna painted portraits of the young humanists Galeotto Marzio and Janus Pannonius, both students of Guarino's known (the latter known well) to Marcello; Pannonius responded with his panegyric for Mantegna.[121] Bellini was linked in similar ways to members of the Marcello circle. He painted a miniature portrait of Raffaele Zovenzoni as an illumination (later detached and lost) of that humanist poet's *Istrias,* which included verses addressed to Marcello. Later he painted a portrait of Jacopo Marcello, described below.[122] His father (Mantegna's father-in-law) Jacopo Bellini was probably a Marcello client as early as the 1440s.[123] Bellini's style, moreover, softer than Mantegna's, and the record of his early activity both lend likelihood to his candidacy. Yet the painter of these illuminations cannot be finally determined.

Though of uncertain genesis, the Strabo miniatures are of great interest to historians of art and society alike. The first of the two portrays Guarino in scholar's robes, centered in the architectural frame of a Roman arch, bowing but not bent (though eighty-eight years old on the book's completion), possessed of full humanistic dignity. He conveys his finished work to Marcello, dressed—not like a Venetian nobleman!—but like a courtier.[124] In the second, costumed as before, Marcello presents the same book to his royal friend. Though shown in the conventional pose assumed by the crowd of scribes or authors or artists who offered their handiwork to princes, Marcello is vigorous as he kneels before the fashionable monarch set in his native Provençal environment, marked by the presence of a palm tree surrounded by a pile of Roman architectural bits constituting "one of the first romantic visions of antiquity in the Renaissance."[125] The intermediary between the author and the king on these two painted pages, Marcello publicly announces his key role in the creation and transmission of culture, at the same time that he declares his independence of the milieu of Venice, where noble patrons struck no poses.

Several years earlier, when he and René were enemies (at least according to the disregarded laws of states), Marcello had sent that would-be king and his canny aide, Giovanni Cossa, another manuscript, containing innocently the life of a saint.[126] Of this *vita* of Saint Maurice more will be said below. For now mention should be made of the famous illuminations that grace the pages of the little book destined, like several others, for readers on the far side of the Alps. Among the earliest exemplars of the art of illumination to make their appearance in full Renaissance style, they have been attributed, as were those in the Strabo manuscript, to Andrea Mantegna or Giovanni Bellini or anonymous others of the north Italian school. The illuminations include (besides two illuminated initials in the foliage of which can be detected the face of the patron) four fascinating documents of the relations between Marcello and René. One depicts the assembly of the Order of the Crescent, founded by René, of which Marcello himself (at the king's invitation) was a member: twenty-five scarlet-robed knights seated in a chapter hall.[127] Another is a full-length image of the patron saint Maurice, the armed Roman soldier and martyr, in charming martial pose bearing marks of the style of Italian Renaissance and northern late gothic. A third is an ideogram of Marcello's design in resplendent color, featuring an elephant laden with emblematic meaning, and a verbal device (like those which so intrigued René) on an unfurled scroll. A fourth illumination adorning the volume is a portrait bust in stark profile of Marcello himself, and executed at an era when only great men were so depicted.[128] He sent it, as was commonly done, to stand in place of his own person at the reunion of knights of the Order—as he was engaged on a battlefield, poised to defend Venice against René's advance.

Set against a featureless background which Marcello's strong uplifted features easily dominate, the portrait possesses, wrote one scholar, who believed he was studying the work of Mantegna, a "grandeur . . . unique in Italian illumination."[129] "Almost shocking in its bold juxtaposition of pink and orange in the costume with an intense blue shadow on the background," it is "a powerfully constructed bust, massive, round, and tense, and a truly noble head, held high, with firmly set jaw and dark steady eyes."[130] Only a miniature, painted on a manuscript page, the representation of the Venetian statesman and patron is reminiscent of the imperial pose found on the face of Roman coins or medals.[131] It seems to make the sort of grand claims for the personality of the sitter that are normally encountered in an autonomous painting.

Marcello's portrait is in fact reminiscent of the epochal one painted in 1474–75 by the master Piero della Francesca of that most beloved of *con-*

Miniature portrait in classical pose of Jacopo Antonio Marcello from a manuscript of the life of St. Maurice that he prepared and sent to King René d'Anjou. Paris, Bibliothèque de l'Arsenal, MS 940, fol. 38v. Photograph provided by the Bibliothèque Nationale, Paris.

Twin portraits by Piero della Francesca of the condottiere *Federigo da Montefeltro, Duke of Urbino, and his consort Battista Sforza, posed against a distant landscape. Florence, Uffizi Galleries. Alinari/Art Resource, N.Y.*

dottiere princes and patrons, Francesco da Montefeltro, Duke of Urbino, and his consort.[132] In the twin portraits joined in one frame, the soldier drawn in bold lines, broken nose prominent as a witness to battles past, faces Battista Sforza, who wears the headdress, necklace, and embroidered brocades that proclaim her status and gender. Behind them lies the still landscape, the dominated macrocosm superimposed by the microcosmic dominators of nature and of Urbino. Painted a generation after the miniature of Marcello, these paintings announce a proud imposition of torso, neck, and profile over a submissive world, an image amounting to "visual panegyric."[133]

A few years later, the type is found in Venice in two portraits of noble military leaders whose roles resembled that played by Marcello as much as the full-scale paintings mimic the earlier figure's miniature.[134] One of these, portraying Giovanni Emo (dead in 1483), has been mistakenly attributed to the master Giovanni Bellini. The other, now lost, was certainly by Bellini, and portrayed none other than Jacopo di Cristoforo Marcello (dead in 1484), our Jacopo Antonio's younger kinsman. Describing the earlier and still extant portrait, one scholar highlights the essential features of the visual representation of a military man: she notes the illustration of "appropriate pugnacity in his 'leonine' features, in the thick cylinder of his neck, and even in the convolutions of his cap."[135] The same descriptors would fit the Marcello miniature, completed a generation earlier, commissioned by the soldier himself. The Renaissance portrait distinguishes itself from classical and medieval forebears in that it celebrates a personality, a unique individual more than a clan or a class. Marcello chose at the early date of 1453 to project in this way his own personhood.[136]

Marcello's audacity here is unparalleled, exceeding even the boldness ascribed to him in the poetry of the battlefield prepared by his humanist friends. In the panegyrical works he sponsored and the images he wrought at his dictation, Marcello fashioned a self-image both aggressive and unique, like one of those modern individuals with whom Burckhardt populated the age of the Renaissance. Claiming in words and images to be more than he was and more than he was allowed to be, Marcello played a game that was not without risk. The lord of Monselice was quite as daring as his mountain bastion proclaimed.

CHAPTER FOUR

Marcello in War and Peace

⅋

The portrait of Jacopo Antonio Marcello projected in words and forms and arranged at his bidding was incongruous, inconceivable even, in the context of Venetian culture. It was a myth of his creation, not unlike the city's own myth so carefully constructed by generations of writers, artists, and diplomats, and equally far from the truth.[1] The victories for which he was celebrated he did not win, and the heroic posture that he selected for himself in verbal and visual representations was a fiction. The nobleman who posed as a glorious leader of men was in fact an obedient servant of Venetian policy both in war and peace. In that occupation he accomplished many great deeds, even if they were not those witnessed in the eulogies he commissioned. And his face, had it been faithfully recorded, would have reflected an experience as rich in danger and challenge, disappointment and resolve, as does the one that jumps from the page with its boastful claim of sovereignty. The previous chapter described the hero that Marcello chose to be. This one describes the capable man that he was.

Marcello's warrior ancestors bestowed upon him a heritage of action.[2] His grandfather Pietro "il Grande" (the Great) was murdered on his return from a dangerous assignment in Egypt. Pietro's brothers (Jacopo Antonio's great uncles) had both fought at sea (as had their father Gazano), in the Trecento struggle against Genoa. Pietro's son Francesco (Jacopo Antonio's father) dedicated himself to military ventures: "he excelled in military virtue, and gave birth to no son whose spirit did not crave war."[3] His bellicose father Francesco was still alive when Jacopo Antonio, at age nineteen, reached the threshold of manhood in 1417. Already at that time, and probably more so after Francesco's death, he was influenced in quite a different way by his elder brother Pietro.

Bishop of the university city of Padua from 1409, Pietro Marcello was an early Venetian enthusiast of humanist studies. His episcopal court was a focus of new cultural interests. Those interests extended even to music, for a motet survives, composed by the pioneering polyphonist Joannes Ciconia, sung in honor of Marcello, "the Venetian born of Roman blood."[4]

That prelate must also have hosted Gasparino Barzizza, one of the pioneer pedagogues of the Renaissance, who in 1412 came to Padua from Venice, where he had gathered around him the patrician amateur humanists Valerio Marcello (brother to both Pietro and Jacopo Antonio) and Daniele Vitturi.[5] On the death of another brother, Girolamo Marcello, not long after the demise of the patriarch Francesco, Barzizza addressed to Bishop Pietro one of those consolations the form of which he helped establish: empathetic in tone, Stoic in concept.[6] Meanwhile, soon after his installation in the Paduan see, Pietro took up the study of law at the university and (at the age of thirty-seven) won the doctorate in 1413.[7] The patrician humanist Zaccaria Trevisan the Elder, a relative by marriage, delivered the oration celebrating the degree conferred when the bishop's young brother, Jacopo Antonio, was fifteen years old.

Jacopo Antonio was a member of Pietro's circle when in 1418 he married Fiordelise, the daughter of Pietro Miani.[8] The latter was the bishop of Vicenza, Venetian nobleman, friend and colleague of Pietro Marcello. Still in Padua in 1428, Jacopo Antonio stood at the deathbed of the man whom he loved like "a second father," as Pietro Perleone wrote: "You were present at the death of your brother Pietro, bishop of Padua, a great man by reason of his honor, authority, virtue, wisdom, righteousness, and knowledge of important matters, truly a second father to you by virtue of his benevolence and love. No one else's death ever appeared to you so bitter, so tragic, than was this which you bore with broken and distracted spirit."[9] Pietro died one year after his retirement to a Camaldulensian monastery, but not before he had the opportunity to help mold the intellectual life of his younger brother. In the entourage of this determinedly learned prelate, whose beneficence extended to many literati, Jacopo Antonio developed the love of learning that he exhibited in later years.

The learned bishop of Padua was no warrior. He was an agent nevertheless of Venetian expansion onto the Italian mainland which entered its final and decisive stage in 1405 with the conquest of Padua, along with wealthy Verona and Vicenza. At Marcello's birth in 1398, Venice was a maritime state. This had been her role for centuries; just about a millennium, as myth had it. By his death, the city in the water had established a dominion on the *terraferma*. One by one, Venice absorbed the cities of the northeast that had been previously free, then subject to *signori,* then to the great duke of Milan, Giangaleazzo Visconti, whose short-lived empire reached for the Adriatic coast to the terror of the Serenissima.

Advancing through political maneuver and military pressure, Venice bound her subject cities by other means as well. She took under her control the larger ecclesiastical benefices, which had for centuries played a mighty part in the organization of power in northern Italy. From the early fifteenth century, the bishops of the Veneto cities were almost without exception nobles of Venice, and for most of the century elected in the Senate by members of the same ruling class.[10] Among the first rank of such benefices was the bishopric of Padua, held in the first century of Venice's *terraferma* rule by a succession of first-rank patricians also distinguished for their learning.[11] One of the most important bishoprics that was Venice's to dispose, it was seated in the home of the university that became in this century the university of Venice. As at Padua, also at Verona, Vicenza, and other major Veneto sees, ecclesiastical administration was placed in the hands of noblemen of Venice renowned for their learning: like Pietro Miani, Jacopo Antonio's father-in-law, who presided at Vicenza from 1409 to 1433, and the busy author Ermolao Barbaro the Elder who reigned in at Verona from 1453 to 1474.[12] In this way, at the same time that Venice bolstered its political and military triumph with ecclesiastical control, it reached also for cultural hegemony.

When the city that had always looked to the sea whirled around to lust for dominion on the land, she devised a new politics and a new military to do so—and in accord with these, a new culture.[13] The culture of Venetian humanism and the Venetian thrust to the west are coincident. As the Serenissima sent out her *podestà* and *capitani,* her ambassadors and secretaries, her *condottieri* and *provveditori* to effect the domination of the land that lay beyond the river Adige, then beyond the Mincio, then beyond the Oglio, beyond even the Adda, she also effected the cultural domination of those regions. Her agents in that conquest were the very same patricians who laid down laws and lifted swords. If the bishops of Padua acted as emissaries of Venice's new humanist message, so did the magistrates who supervised the local administration of newly conquered cities. Francesco Barbaro, Ludovico Foscarini, Francesco Diedo, Bernardo Bembo among others, representatives of the Republic from among whose inner elite they derived, were both effective rulers and participants in the colloquy of the learned.[14] Around them flocked humanists in search of patronage, while they themselves wrote works for and to their provincial friends and were enlivened by the intellectual discourse in which they engaged while abroad.

Like these patrician humanists, Jacopo Antonio Marcello participated in both the military and the cultural invasion of lands of northern Italy. In his story we see traced in small compass the shape of Venice's total conquest of the *terraferma,* and its human cost. Although he cannot take primary credit for the victories his panegyrists ascribe to him in their false script,

Marcello was nevertheless a key actor in the wars between Milan and Venice that spelled the transformation of Venice from a maritime to a mainland empire. Not from the humanists whom he commissioned to write his story, but from the records of the Venetian Senate and other sources independent of a patron's dictate, a different and more compelling image emerges of the man who remodeled Monselice and mourned for the death of a child.

ℰℬ   ℰℬ   ℰℬ

Jacopo Antonio Marcello first enters the history of the Lombard wars in the fall of 1437.[15] Before that moment lay the first markers of *terraferma* expansion: the initial 1405 conquests of Padua, Vicenza, and Verona. There followed the acquisition of Brescia and Bergamo in 1428; the execution of the treacherous *condottiere* Carmagnola in 1432, admonishment to all his successors; the peace of 1433; the imperial grant to Venice in August 1437 of "Treviso, Feltre, Belluno, Ceneda, Padua, Brescia, Bergamo, Casalmaggiore, Soncino, Platina, San Giovanni a Croce, and all the castles and places in the Cremonese territory and in the rest of Lombardy on this [the Venetian] side of the Adda."[16] Now Filippo Maria Visconti launched an assault on Venetian territories only recently acquired: on Brescia, between the Mincio and the Oglio, and Verona, on the Adige. His agent was Niccolò Piccinino, heir to the troops and the tactics of Braccio da Montone. As Piccinino approached Brescia on 30 September 1437, Leonardo Giustiniani wrote his friend Francesco Barbaro (both Venetian patricians and humanists) with good news: help was on the way at last, and one of the helpers was Jacopo Antonio Marcello—a real man.[17]

Of Marcello's arrival and activity there, nothing more is heard. But he emerges as a full participant in the struggle with Milan soon thereafter. A first phase of that participation may be defined from the spring of 1438 through the summer of 1440, when Marcello, entitled *provveditore*, followed first Gattamelata and then Francesco Sforza, respectively governor of the Venetian army and captain general of the Florentine-Venetian League arrayed against Piccinino and his devious Visconti master.

In June, 1438, Piccinino besieged and took Casalmaggiore, a critical outpost guarding the river Po at the boundary between Milan and Venice. In July, he crossed the Oglio and swept into the Bresciano with such fury that, as the chronicler da Soldo reports, "in three days, in the whole territory of Brescia, of eight thousand dogs there remained not even one."[18] Gattamelata had resisted him; but there was no victory won, by that *condottiere* or by the Venetian *provveditore* either. Yet in the first of a long series of achievements noted in the records of the Venetian Senate, Marcello performed an important service for his Republic. He persuaded the citizens of the region to remain loyal to Venice, promising in exchange compensation for their ravaged crops, and arranged for the gathering from their fields what had survived for the relief of Brescia, the targeted victim of Piccinino's rampage.[19]

By the following September, Marcello had left Casalmaggiore for Brescia where (consistent with the panegyrical literature) with Gattamelata, the city's rectors of that city, and other *provveditori*, he saw to the city's defense and relief. The Senate ordered those leaders to approach the feudatory Parisio da Lodrone to secure a route for the strategic relief of Gattamelata's seriously overextended army. Marcello was chosen for the mission requiring both personal courage and dexterous diplomacy, quite as his eulogists claim. His agreements with Parisio were subsequently confirmed by the Senate, and he himself was commended for his achievement.[20] The army's withdrawal (brilliantly executed by Gattamelata later that month, Marcello among his company) was similarly commended by the Senate. Both Gattamelata and a Brescian captain were rewarded with the particular prizes that Venice gave its loyal mercenaries: among those, grants of nobility and citizenship respectively.[21] They and not Marcello, *pace* that nobleman's eulogists, were the engineers of the swift retreat.

From December 1438 through February 1439, accompanied by Marcello who communicated frequently with the Senate, Gattamelata labored to keep open a supply route to Brescia.[22] It was during this time that the Senate ordered the Venetian river fleet to be moved from the Adige, where it was trapped, to the Lago di Garda. The only route was over a range of Alpine foothills. Over the mountains it went, a fleet of some eighty ships, "grossissima,"[23] galley by galley, transported by oxen, machines, and men in the February ice, to the northern bays of the giant lake. The true heroes of this enterprise may have been the army engineers who planned it, although his panegyrists give Marcello a strong advisory role. Gattamelata, Marcello with him, provided cover with diversionary raids into the *mantovano*. But the sixteenth-century depiction of the famous naval maneuver on the ceiling of the Great Council in the Doge's Palace in Venice displays on the flank of a war galley the arms of the fleet's captain, Pietro Zeno, and the *provveditore* with the army, Jacopo Antonio Marcello.[24]

In June 1439, Francesco Sforza's army joined with Gattamelata's, who politely deferred to become second-in-command to the more famous *condottiere*. Senate records do not support the panegyrists of Marcello who represented the Venetian as escorting Sforza from the Po border. Two months earlier, however, Marcello (bearing the necessary funds) indisputably traveled with the captains Avogadro and Colleoni on a special mission to Brescia, an event the humanists leave unrecorded.[25] Once Sforza took command, it is he whom Marcello follows. With Sforza and Gattamelata, he crossed the Adige in July 1439, and was at the *condottiere's* side in September through October, perpetually concerned with the relief of Brescia and now endangered Verona. On the last day of that last month, the Senate conferred upon the nobleman a prize of three hundred ducats in recognition of his long and arduous service in the field.[26]

Marcello was with Sforza on 9 November when Venetian forces won an important victory at Tenna. Piccinino was nearly captured, but escaped (hidden in a sack slung over a subordinate's shoulders), and retaliated swiftly by capturing Verona. On 20 November, Sforza and Gattamelata liberated that city, with Marcello (for whom his panegyrists had claimed the victory) in their company. Marcello's letter, describing the victory, was read in the Senate on 22 November. The delighted fathers rewarded Gattamelata and Sforza promptly (a grant of nobility, a palace), and commissioned Marcello to distribute gratuities to the soldiers.[27] The glow of victory forgotten, the original task of relieving Brescia was resumed: perhaps Marcello's conscience was pricked a little by the desperate letter sent him by the Brescian citizen Pietro Rondo on 1 December 1439.[28] The relief of Brescia was the subject of frequent communication between the Senate and Marcello, at Sforza's side, during the period November 1439 to January 1440.[29] In February, two other noblemen were charged to go to Sforza's camp to commend Marcello "who has behaved and is behaving like a true son both in the mountains and elsewhere for the preservation and restoration of our state, sparing himself neither labor nor danger"; and to caution him to watch Sforza's expenditures.[30]

In March 1440, Marcello announced his own desire to be relieved of office and Sforza's intention to return to the Marche to tend to his own domains.[31] But both remained in the field. Marcello was still in Sforza's company in April, and Sforza was still in the Veneto in June, when he decisively defeated Piccinino and relieved pressure on Brescia after a three-year siege. Thereafter, Sforza drifted south as he had yearned to do; by August, Marcello had surfaced in the same region.[32] From this point, Marcello's career has entered a second stage: the period from summer 1440 through spring 1446. In these rather shapeless years (ignored by most of the panegyrists), the war with Milan abates. When he does not drop out of sight altogether, Marcello engages in a sporadic series of military and quasi-military ventures, sometimes involving contacts with Sforza or other *condottieri*. The most notable of these actions occurred at the start. Marcello was summoned to Ravenna by the Senate and became involved in the transfer of power described by his encomiast Spretus.[33]

What Spretus so fulsomely described, Marcello really did do, according to Senate records. These ordered him to return to Venice in September 1440 to set out from there on his assigned mission to Ravenna that was now in grave danger.[34] The Venetian captain Michele Attendolo (Gattamelata was ill, and Sforza engaged in the Marche) released two thousand infantry to Marcello. The *provveditore* marched to Ravenna at their head charged to defend the city and maintain civic peace. His mission required diplomatic skill: he was to determine "by such prudent and cautious means as seem appropriate" what was the mood of the citizens.[35] If they wished to be rid of their signore Ostasio da Polenta, he was to arrange that figure's deposition; if not, Ostasio could stay. In any case, Ravenna was to be kept in allegiance to Venice.[36] These missions he accomplished in October through December of 1440. The da Polenta were deposed, and having taken refuge in Venice were exiled to Candia early in 1441.[37]

Meanwhile, Marcello had returned to Venice, where he probably participated in the gala celebration of the marriage of Jacopo Foscari, son of Doge Francesco, with Lucrezia Contarini, daughter of Leonardo.[38] Certainly Francesco Sforza was there, honorably received by doge and Senate and lodged in the palace of Gattamelata while his own underwent repairs. The companies of Sforza, Gattamelata, and Taddeo d'Este (Venetian captain from the ruling house of Ferrara) competed in elaborate tournaments in the Piazza San Marco for magnificent prizes. This enactment of the classic event of late-medieval chivalry would have appealed mightily to the proprietor of Monselice.

But Marcello's actual whereabouts are unknown until the summer of 1441 when he was at Monselice, where the reconstruction of his castle must have been nearing completion.[39] Though he was elected to the Senate in September for a term of one year, there is no evidence that he served, or returned to Venice.[40] In April 1442, similarly, he was elected *podestà* of Padua; but his name having been canceled in the Senate document, it may be presumed he never assumed that office.[41] Marcello's next official role was as "ambassador" to Sforza, to which position he was elected in May 1442. The Senate wrote Sforza to announce that Marcello had been chosen as he had requested, as a sign of their paternal love for him "which is known to the whole world."[42]

A comradeship had evidently been forged in the year of struggle to raise the siege of Brescia 1439 to 1440, when Marcello and Sforza were in nearly daily contact. That comradeship may have been renewed in 1441 and

1442, when Sforza was in Venice on at least five separate occasions to transact public business, and Marcello was perhaps not far away.[43] It was a senti-
mental tie the Senate was willing to respect in May 1442. These are the
peak years of Venice's engagement with Sforza. During this period, that
condottiere successfully negotiated the peace with Milan established by the
Treaty of Cavriana (the more remarkable because negotiating with the enemy, after the fall of Carmagnola, was not something a hired general undertook without risk).[44] Included in the peace terms were the terms of his
own long-planned marriage to the elusive Visconti's illegitimate daughter,
Bianca Maria Visconti, and acquisition of the long-craved Cremona as her
dowry. The marriage itself had taken place the previous 24 October outside
Cremona, and the new bride was feted and richly endowed in Venice in
May 1442.[45]

By that date, with the Signoria's approval, Sforza had contracted to lend
his sword to the aid of the French royal personage, René Duke of Anjou,
Count of Provence.[46] As designated heir of Giovanna II of Naples, this René
was properly king of that realm, and was seeking to make what was true in
principle true in fact. From April 1438, René had struggled with Alfonso
of Aragon to gain effective rule over the kingdom to which he had clear
title. Before entering Lombardy for the first time in the spring of 1439,
Sforza had assisted the Angevin lords of Naples (as had his father before
him), in which court he spent his adolescence.[47] He was engaged in Angevin service in August 1438, when Alfonso invited him to switch alle-
giances, proferring three horses and some fine clothing: "Tell your prince
that I have more horses than he does, and that I am his enemy," the emissary was answered by the proud *condottiere,* loyal to René.[48] From the fall
of 1440, René again sought the aid of Sforza's arm in the battle with the Aragonese.

But Sforza was mired in the conflicts in the Veneto and the Marche,
under previous contracts with Venice and Florence; and more recently focused on his dominion in Cremona. By the time he was able to come to
terms with René, his old enemy Niccolò Piccinino had been hired by the
pope to contest his claims in the Marche. There detained, he never left for
Naples. On 2 June 1442, René lost his kingdom.[49] He lost it, according to
the Venetian diarist Sanuto, because Sforza (with Marcello) never came:
"And for this reason [Piccinino's presence in the Marche] Count Francesco
could not go to Apulia and aid [René] against the said King Alfonso, and
thus Apulia was taken and Naples lost."[50]

But Sforza had intended to go. Soon after he agreed to do so, evidently
he petitioned the Senate to send to him as ambassador (not *provveditore,*

presumably, since no Venetian military operation was involved) the noble-man who had been his companion in the campaign for Brescia: Jacopo Antonio Marcello. This is the first moment at which the three men whose faces shape this chapter come into focus, though they may never have all met together: the king, the *condottiere*, the nobleman of Venice.[51] After René's defeat, subsequent humiliation, and return to France, the need for Marcello's embassy disappeared. That nobleman was released from his as-signment by Senate order in August.[52] At the time, he was sojourning at Monselice.

Marcello held no other official Venetian magistracy until May 1446: a gap of nearly four years.[53] Nor, with the one exception to be noted in a moment, is there any trace of his other activity during this period. Mean-while, Sforza labored for dominion in the Marche. Unreceptive to Venice's invitation to serve as captain general for the Republic, that *condottiere* saw his cousin Michele Attendolo da Cotignola accept the *bastone* of command instead.[54] Venice's former captain general, Gattamelata, had suffered a stroke in 1440 and died early in 1443, having received every consideration and honor (subsequently expressed in the equestrian monument executed by Donatello) from the state that he had long defended.[55] Gattamelata was dead, and the Venetian forces were established under Attendolo; but where was the *provveditore* whom the Senate had on call from 1438 through 1442? Could Marcello have joined Sforza in that general's struggle to establish a secure base of power and join the company not of hirelings but of those who hired *condottieri*? Nothing in the record denies that possibility; the later links between the two figures (for which their contact in 1439–42 could still be sufficient foundation) makes it plausible.

Certainly Marcello's 1443 marriage reveals a man whose stance was more that of *condottiere* than leisured aristocrat.[56] This second wedding was to a member of a noble Paduan family that boasted military and political achievements similar to those of the Marcellos: Luca, daughter of Bartolo-meo da Leone. Intimates of the Carraresi, the da Leone family transferred its loyalty to Venice at the time of the conquest and would later thrive in the church, the university, and the legal profession under Venetian domination. Marcello's bride Luca ("Luke," that is, not "Lucy") da Leone bore the name of her grandfather: that Luca da Leone who had surrendered Monselice to Venice (at a price) in 1405. The marriage alliance involved reminiscences of a building and a war as well as the launching of a new conjugal unit. It was a double wedding: the second bride was Luca's sister Anna da Leone; the other groom was Marcello's own son Francesco by his marriage to Fior-delise di Pietro Miani. Father and son married two sisters in an alliance constituting a double commitment to the soldier lineage from which the sisters descended.

Marcello's marriage alliance was unusual for a Venetian nobleman. Those proud dynasts occasionally married women not of the nobility, and often married prominent women of non-Venetian cities (especially Padua).[57] Yet the choice for someone of Marcello's stature of the daughter (more, two daughters) of a mainland warrior clan is striking. It is the more so if the marriage habits of Marcello's associates among *condottiere* society are considered. They frequently married among each other and into the lesser ranks of the signorial class.[58] Sforza's wedding to a Visconti bastard is well known. Carlo Fortebraccio, son of Braccio, married a daughter of the ruler of Rimini and soldier of fortune Sigismondo Malatesta.[59] Closer to the point, Gattamelata married Giacoma, the sister of Gentile da Leonessa who would inherit (by Senate order) the company of the elder *condottiere* and serve Venice for a generation thereafter.[60] Two daughters of Gattamelata and Giacoma married the military captains Antonio da Marsciano and Tiberto Brandolini.[61] In turn, Gentile's daughter Giacoma married Bertoldo d'Este of the ruling Ferrarese dynasty, and three unnamed daughters married three sons of Leonello da Leone, second cousin to the Marcello brides.[62] By his 1443 nuptial agreement, Marcello entered the family of the former enemies, present subjects, and hired swords of the Serenissima. The stalwart Luca, of whom we know nothing but her masculine name, would become mother of the child Valerio.

His marriage is the only known event of Marcello's *curriculum vitae* for the period from summer 1442 to spring 1446. The silence of those years contrasts with the uninterrupted sequence of missions performed by that nobleman from 1446 to 1454. During the latter period, his military career peaked and his personal relations climaxed both with Sforza and the distant King René. By 1454, personal concerns had begun to overtake public ones. Of this most fruitful, most complex, and most tormented phase of Marcello's life, the panegyrical tradition (the triumphs of late 1446 aside) makes little mention.

❧   ❧   ❧

When Visconti launched a new offensive on the lands of the Cremonese east of the Adda in May 1446, Jacopo Antonio Marcello was summoned up from vacancy and named *provveditore* to Sforza's cousin Michele Attendolo, Venetian captain general since June 1443.[63] By 20 August, with Marcello at his side, Attendolo had secured Cremona: that move taken to protect Sforza's interest, who held title to the city by virtue of Bianca Maria's dowry.[64] In September, Marcello was busy with provveditorial duties: finding a doctor for Attendolo, wounded in the chest, and renegotiating contracts with *condottieri*.[65] Commending their *provveditore*, who was communicating almost daily, for his "prudence and diligence," the Senate issued instructions for the defense of Cremona and the disposition of troops and urged an immediate foray across the Po, into Milanese territory.

On 28 September, a little more than two weeks after the Senate's last missive, Venetian troops routed the Milanese at the Po island of Mezzano near Casalmaggiore in the Cremonese. This is the victory so celebrated by the panegyrists of Marcello, and considered by Sanuto to be "the finest display of fighting seen in Italy for many years."[66] Marcello's humanists portrayed that nobleman as the critical battle's hero, the first horseman to venture into the dangerous waters, the leader of the advance. The claim was implausible. Yet just how exaggerated was their account? With Attendolo weak and Marcello the trustee of the Senate's counsel to do exactly what was accomplished, the cagey and battle-hardened *provveditore* could have rallied the troops and led the charge into the waters of the Po, onto the island defended by the enemy, securing the bridge to the other bank. Such a reading of events is implied by Francesco Bassano's sixteenth-century depiction of the battle on the ceiling of the Maggior Consiglio in the Doge's Palace: it is Marcello's personal emblem that rises victorious amid a crowd of captured Visconti standards.[67]

Indisputably, Marcello was engaged at the center of that battle. Still on horseback, he dispatched two letters to his colleagues in the Senate, an hour apart, reporting the victory "to your joy": "This is the most glorious victory ever won by Your Signoria, to whose grace I recommend myself. . . . [You] may rejoice down to the vitals."[68] The Senate congratulated the captain general and Marcello and "all our splendid captains and brave *condottieri*." They were to forge on, however; Marcello was to urge Attendolo to press on across the river Adda, gateway to Milan.[69] The next day, perhaps in recognition of the victory, Marcello was elected in Venice to the office of *savio di terraferma*, which would have positioned him in the Collegio, the inner circle of Venetian policymakers.[70] He was not to serve in this office at this time, or indeed at any time in this decade. For he never left the provveditoriate.

Still with the army in October, Marcello negotiated agreements with the localities overrun by the Venetian advance.[71] On 5 November, the Senate again instructed Marcello to prod Attendolo onward, across the stubborn boundary of the Adda. On 6 and 7 November, the captain general led the Venetian troops across that river in a rush on Milan (quite as the panegyrists had claimed): "and our men charged through the Milanese," wrote Sanuto proudly, "putting everything to sack, and taking prisoners."[72] The Senate congratulated the *condottieri*, awarded Attendolo the castle of Castelfranco in fief (in addition to the honorary nobility already granted soon after the victory at Casalmaggiore)[73] and expressed pleasure at "the auspicious crossing of the Adda, and the prosperous progress of our army."[74] On 7 November, Marcello was knighted by Attendolo on the Adda's bank.[75]

Having added (in December 1446) the title of captain of Verona to that of *provveditore* with the army, Marcello spent the ensuing winter executing Senate instructions.[76] He found campsites and provisions for the soldiers, did the bookkeeping, renegotiated *condottiere* contracts, and settled disputes. He returned to Venice on private business briefly in February and April.[77] By the time he returned to the field in May, his old companion Sforza had been outlawed.[78] Niccolò Piccinino dead and Milan vulnerable,[79] Visconti had persuaded that captain to leave the Marche (where he was losing ground) and fight for an inheritance in Lombardy.[80]

By July, the Senate warned their ambassadors and *provveditori* of Sforza's advance. In August, with Sforza not yet in sight of Milan, the inscrutable Filippo Maria Visconti died and left his duchy up for grabs. Among the contenders would be the determined son-in-law of the deceased and the citizens of Milan, who declared the Republic of Saint Ambrose two days after his death.[81] Recognizing the Ambrosian Republic and ready to oppose Sforza, Venice moved to grab Lodi and Piacenza, two cities deep into Milanese territory beyond the Adda. Marcello acted immediately: he established terms, as instructed by the Senate, for the former city's surrender to the Serenissima, and soon arranged the capitulation of the latter. Fearing Venice more than Sforza, the citizens of the new Milanese republic invited that *condottiere* to defend them. Sforza now burst into Lombardy, ally turned enemy of his old master the Senate, and of Marcello, his old friend.

Thus far do Marcello's panegyrists track his adventures. Hereafter, other documents must be relied upon, and they are ample: for the tireless *provveditore* did not cease to labor when his eulogists ceased to write. Indeed, some of Marcello's most critical services to his *patria* are rendered after this date. But regarding them, when his intimates compiled their stories more than a decade later, he must have given the command to say nothing. The silence is curious and instructive. While the aging Marcello claimed to have done things he hadn't in 1438–39 and 1446, he also suppressed discussion of the important things he did in the years after Casalmaggiore. What he suppressed was the story of his deep relationship with Sforza, as it strained but did not break when threatened by the overmastering force of competition between states.

Venice's lust for dominion in Lombardy was now palpable. The sparse language of the Senate records evinces a new ruthlessness: "for the more solicitously measures are taken to crush the enemy and his state," Marcello was advised, "the more we rejoice."[82] Chronicler Zorzi Dolfin, loyal champion of Venice, alluded to intentions now no longer concealed: Milan's ambassadors had walked out on peace negotiations, he reports, "because [they] understood Venice's greed for dominion over the whole of Lombardy."[83] Her former ally Florence in the lead, the other states of Italy feared Venice and condemned her territorial reach. From 1447 an anti-Venetian rhetoric develops, shared by Machiavelli, among others, and culminating in the peninsula-wide League of 1509 to humble the city known for ambition and greed.[84]

Venice reached, but Sforza was implacable: he craved dominion in Milan as much as Venice ached for power in Lombardy. In September 1447, Sforza positioned himself to take Piacenza (on the Milanese side of the Adda) back from Venice. Marcello should urge Attendolo to take Crema, the Senate ordered, in compensation as it were, on the Venetian side of the river. Such action would permit Venice to secure the zone between the Adda and the Oglio and protect lines of communications.[85] If possible, the army should also launch a raid against Pavia, beyond the Adda, to forestall the enemy. Sforza soon after took Piacenza by storm, subjecting it to a merciless forty-day sack: an exhibit of "whatever greed, whatever violence, whatever foul lust can wreak," observed the epic poet Janus Pannonius.[86]

The cycle of point and counterpoint continued over the next several months: Sforza menaced Lodi on the Adda's western bank, while the Venetians based at Caravaggio threatened Cremona and yearned for Crema, all three cities in the zone just east of the Adda. The citizens of the Ambrosian Republic became disaffected with Sforza, fearing from the ruthlessness of his advance, perhaps, a new master as harsh as the Visconti lord they had buried. Beginning in the spring of 1448, Sforza operated alone in his quest for the lordship of Milan, as that quest entered its culminating phase.[87]

In July 1448, Sforza surrounded the Venetian river fleet on the Po near Casalmaggiore—the third time an important battle occurred at that crossroads between Romagna, the Milanese, and the Veneto.[88] Finding himself unsupported by the army under Michele Attendolo, the admiral Andrea Quirini burned the fleet to prevent its capture. Within days, Marcello was summoned from the tranquility of Verona (where he was captain) to proceed "with all possible swiftness" to join the army: as in May 1446, the Senate remembered Marcello when a military crisis presented itself. But he did not join Attendolo. In August, the Senate named three other *provveditori* (three! a measure of the perceived gravity of the situation) to join the captain general in Caravaggio, now threatened by Sforza.[89]

On September 15, nearly two years after the climactic victory at Casalmaggiore in which Marcello had played a key part, the Venetians suffered at Caravaggio the worst disaster of the war.[90] They were completely routed. All but a handful of soldiers and captains were taken prisoner. Valiantly, Ermolao Donato and Gerardo Dandolo (two of those three *provveditori* sent to bolster Attendolo) defended the Venetian standards. They stood firm but they stood alone amid the torrent of retreat. Told to flee, they replied "that they would rather die guarding the public standards than shamefully abandon them to save themselves."[91] Eventually men and emblems were captured at one blow, seized by Sforza and cherished until that day when, lord of Milan, he could display that memento of Venice's humiliation in the cathedral of his city.

When Sforza and the Venetians clashed fatefully at Caravaggio (*sforzeschi* against *sforzeschi,* the nephew against the son of the patriarch Muzio Attendolo), Marcello was nowhere in the vicinity. Having borne no responsibility for the defeat, he was assigned the burden of rescue. Within days after the battle, he was ordered to secure a fund of thirty thousand ducats to be used to ransom the prisoners of Caravaggio. At the same time, he was sent from Verona to Brescia to defend the region between the Oglio and Mincio (the east bank of the Adda now lost) from an advance into Venetian territory opened up by Sforza's victory.[92] Sforza stormed the Bergamasco north of Caravaggio, and crossing to the east bank of the Oglio, ravaged the Bresciano as well, to the gates of the city of Brescia. He got no further. There "Jacopo Antonio Marcello was *provveditore*," according to the contemporary historian Andrea Navagero, "and not being able to conquer it, [Sforza] besieged it."[93]

In the meantime, under cover of war, machinations of peace had begun. Immediately following the battle, Clemente Tealdino, captured secretary of the captured *provveditore* Ermolao Donato, greeted his old friend Angelo Simonetta, Sforza's cagey secretary.[94] Already Sforza's secretary in 1437 (when on 10 November he was granted "original citizen" status in Venice), the loyal Simonetta performed many and sometimes dangerous missions for his employer. Only months before, he had gone secretly to Venice to intrigue with Sforza supporters. Arrested and exiled to Candia (Crete), he soon reappeared at Sforza's side in the wake of the Caravaggio victory. For years to come, he and his nephews continued to orbit around Sforza: among them Cicco, organizer of the new duke's chancery, the best in Italy, and Giovanni, whose account memorialized the *condottiere's* deeds.[95]

Angelo told Tealdino that Sforza wanted to talk peace terms.[96] To that purpose, Venice should send to him either one of two men he trusted: Marcello ("well known to the Count," commented Sanuto) or Pasquale Malipiero (frequently Marcello's provveditorial colleague over the next five years). As Marcello was engaged in Verona and Brescia, Malipiero was sent together with the nobleman Ludovico Loredan. Both were men of the highest rank, having achieved the life-term dignity of Procurator of Saint Mark. Malipiero was later to gain the still higher rank of Doge of Venice.

Still stationed in Brescia, Marcello learned only in mid-November that Sforza was now Venice's ally—peace having been arranged, as the victor had invited, through Malipiero's agency.[97] The Treaty of Rivoltella of October 1448 arranged for Venice to assist Sforza in his designs on Milan, and for Sforza to assist the Republic in hers on Crema and the Ghiaradadda, the localities on the east bank of the Adda. Sforza was also to be well rewarded. He would receive the extraordinary sum of thirteen thousand ducats per month (an allowance which would dangerously strain the Venetian treasury). Further, he would regain a prized possession taken from him in 1447: his palace on the Grand Canal.

Praised for his "prudence and diligence" in securing Brescia against Sforza, Marcello was now sent to meet his former enemy and former friend in the old familiar role as *provveditore*. His responsibility in that post was enormous, as he had authority over the Venetian component of the force Sforza led in the reconquest of Lombardy. "You will be the governor of our men," wrote the Senate to Marcello, in tandem with Sforza and his, "according to the terms of the treaty" (a copy of which was enclosed); "and of whatever happens you should inform us by letter."[98] For the next year Marcello was Venice's main agent in assisting that master soldier and strategist to win the prize of Milan.[99]

Together they prowled the precincts of Milan in January 1449: "Francesco Sforza and his men stood in the Milanese," wrote the chronicler called Anonimo Veronese, "and with him was Jacopo Antonio Marcello, governor of the troops given him by the Venetians for the acquisition of Milan according to the terms of the alliance."[100] From February to March, they won Tortona, Novara, Alessandria, and Parma: "when the news arrived in Venice all rejoiced," wrote the chronicler Zorzi Dolfin, "especially since the victory was won by Jacopo Antonio Marcello."[101] Leading a small force, Marcello with the captain Bartolomeo Colleoni penetrated further west to meet the Savoyards who had presented a new menace.[102]

Meanwhile, the two men who had once intended to journey together to Apulia in support of the beleaguered René d'Anjou opened a new phase of their relations with that French potentate. On 24 February, Sforza wrote René, still self-styled king of the realm he had lost seven years before. The *condottiere* hinted at the possibility of Venetian support for his plan to re-take Naples; plausibly, since at this very time the Florentine humanist and diplomat Giannozzo Manetti was in Venice, working with his unique skill and eloquence for a French alliance.[103] Sforza assured René of his own good will towards the would-be king whom he, in his father's train, had served loyally in his youth. He further noted the good will of Jacopo Antonio Marcello, there with him at his camp in Milan: "He is affectionately dis-posed to your Majesty, and enjoys great respect in all the Councils of Ven-ice."[104] In these months, together with René's intimate, the Neapolitan Gi-ovanni Cossa (who had been pursuing the King's interests in Italy since 1447),[105] Marcello and Sforza stood outside Milan. Apparently they suc-ceeded in raiding that city, or at least in procuring through willing interme-diaries from among the Visconti spoils a set of illuminated playing cards which Marcello dispatched to Isabelle of Lorraine, wife of the Angevin king.[106] René, in turn, looked to Marcello and Sforza for Venetian support in his quest to regain the Neapolitan throne.

The king without a kingdom rewarded his supporters grandly: on 26 August 1449, Sforza and Marcello were named respectively the seventeenth and eighteenth knights of the Order of the Crescent.[107] That company was founded by René on 11 August 1448, shortly before the debacle at Cara-vaggio. Alongside the Orders of the Garter and the Golden Fleece, the Cres-cent was among the most famous (although it was the shortest-lived) of those phenomena of late medieval chivalry. The two Italians were in fact inscribed in the rolls of the Crescent, which survive to bear witness. In 1471, some years after his death, an inventory of the crimson robes and cushions (*carreaux*) which were the prescribed accoutrements of the sworn knights of the order included those labeled with the names of Sforza and Marcello—the latter's *carreau* embroidered with the motto "alta vita" inter-twined with vines.[108] It was probably also in 1449 that René awarded Mar-cello the empty title of the *praefectura maritima:* command of the naval forces the Frenchman felt it would soon be his to command again.[109] Dur-ing the tortuous and triumphal march toward the trophy of Milan, this odd trio of warriors—Sforza, René, Marcello—joined forces. The personal links forged in 1449 were to survive the dissolution, yet to come, of their alliance.

No sooner had the two Italians been received into the Crescent but the league between Sforza and Venice faltered.[110] On 15 September, having learned of Sforza's conquests of Lodi (beyond the Adda) and Crema (between the Adda and the Oglio, long desired to secure Venetian power in that zone), the Senate "from the heart" congratulated Sforza "with paternal affection." At the same time, via the two ambassadors then appointed to the conqueror (Pasquale Malipiero and Orsato Giustiniani) and their *provveditore* (Jacopo Antonio Marcello), that congress of Venetian rulers demanded that Crema be surrendered to them immediately. Nine days later, the paternally minded Senate negotiated a new alliance with the Ambrosian Republic. The Republic would get Lodi and Como; Venice would get Crema and the Ghiaradadda; Sforza, should he choose to join the league, would get Piacenza, Pavia, Parma, and Cremona, on condition that he vacate the region within three weeks.

The next day, Giustiniani, Malipiero, and Marcello were ordered to present this offer of reduced rations to the *condottiere,* whose stomach was pining for the larger morsel of Milan.[111] Marcello was specifically informed by separate letter (the Senate being well aware of his strong link to Sforza) that his comrade was included in the proposed peace terms. But the *provveditore* was also instructed (along with the captain Colleoni) swiftly to remove the troops he had directed since late 1448 to the Venetian side of the Adda. Malipiero was to await Sforza's response; if it was negative, to position himself in Crema, now the pivot of Venetian ambition. When Sforza (predictably) failed to accede to the offered terms, at the end of September Marcello dutifully led the Venetian forces from the camp of his partner in battle: "placing public duty over a private bond," observed Pannonius.[112]

Learning that his comrade had removed to the other camp, Sforza was regretful but understood that duty to Venice had compelled Marcello to desert him.[113] Marcello declared his own feelings with his feet: he vanished from the front, withdrew via Brescia, and without a word to the Senate, took refuge in his fortress-villa at Monselice. The Senate instructed the rectors of Padua to go and find him: he was needed in Venice to report on conditions in Lombardy. Marcello ignored the summons. He was still in Monselice in November contemplating the view from the battlements, perhaps, as Sforza planned his lunge for Milan. The supposition that both battle-hardened veterans felt regret when the business of states compelled them to rupture a ten-year friendship, implicit here, will be supported by further events.[114]

Sforza's rupture with Marcello and Venice alike occurred in October 1449. Now he moved forcefully; with some justice the Venetian apologist Marcantonio Sabellico wrote that if any general of the age deserved to be compared to Julius Caesar, "for greatness of soul, or grandness of fortune, or for any other reason," it was Sforza, "and none other."[115] Within the next four months, he had encircled Milan, starved it, and compelled its capitulation: the craved victory at last, after so long a wait. "Great was his constancy," marveled the enemy chronicler Zorzi Dolfin, "even though the Venetians, the Milanese, and King Alfonso [of Aragon] were all leagued against him, yet he stood constant at the siege of Milan."[116]

Meanwhile, Venice latched on to Crema and would not let it go. To secure its treasure, the Senate appointed that one of their number whose military capacity and loyalty were undoubted, in spite of his known relationship with Milan's new master: Jacopo Antonio Marcello, elected *provveditore* in Crema barely a month after he had left Sforza's side.[117] While his name was proposed in the Senate, Marcello sat in Monselice. He did not respond to the notice of election; an extension was granted. He did not proceed to his embassy as required: an extension was again bestowed. To Crema he went at last in February 1450. There he remained until danger had abated towards the middle of 1452, an armed mother hen nurturing the one chick Venice had plucked from the expense and turmoil of the Lombard wars: which it would still hold secure, when the dust settled, after the final peace of 1454.

Marcello took charge in Crema, and Sforza won Milan.[118] On 26 February, he was acclaimed duke by the assembled *popolo*. On that very day, and a full month before his formal investiture, he sent an emissary secretly to Marcello to open the discussion of peace. The negotiations continued for six months. Sforza would deal only with Marcello. Marcello complained repeatedly to the Senate that he did not wish to be ground between the mills of Venice and Milan. The Senate as often enjoined him to persevere. "We fully understand," it wrote once of many times on 13 March, "how, fearfully, you distance yourself from these procedures, which exceed anything we had anticipated or planned; but since you are a noble citizen of Venice, and we have complete faith and confidence in you, we prefer that this matter proceed by your hands rather than by any other means." Let us know whatever happens: "by letter, immediately, conveyed by the swiftest of horses."[119] On 14 April, after several cycles of persuasion and resistance, the Senate admonished Marcello sharply: "Therefore we command you that you make no further protests to us; this matter will be managed for us by your hands."[120]

Peace negotiations were tortuous processes. The unlucky *condottiere* Carmagnola had been executed in 1432 in part because he listened too eagerly to peace terms offered by the enemy of his employer. Sforza himself had succeeded, in contrast, master operator that he was, in arranging the 1441 peace between the same two adversaries.[121] From December 1453 to April 1454, Fra Simone da Camerino would travel tirelessly between the two capitals to arrange the terms of the eventual and monumental settlement at Lodi: perhaps the grandest treaty of a century that knew many, arranged by a reform-minded Augustinian canon with no diplomatic experience.[122] Marcello's 1450 negotiations with the emissaries of his old friend on behalf of the city to which he remained fixedly loyal forms part of this sequence. But those negotiations failed (although one chronicler reports momentary success)—having reached a lowpoint when the Council of Ten contemplated hiring an assassin to deal with the recalcitrant duke.[123] Neither Venice nor Milan would yield on the stumbling block of turf.[124] Venice wanted Crema, where Marcello sat uncomfortably but watchful, a human rock. Sforza wanted all the territory in the precincts of the Adda. Peace was not achieved, but war was only languidly pursued, until the ultimate settlement at Lodi.

War flared up in the spring of 1452, Venice taking the initiative in an aggressive "sorpresa" that set even the wily Sforza off balance.[125] Leagued with Alfonso of Aragon, Venice faced her formidable enemy, now allied with Florence and France.[126] (The Florentines had engineered a promise from the French king Charles VII, brother-in-law of René d'Anjou, for military support; but it would be a full year and more before the promised troops arrived.) As these events transpired, Marcello completed his term as *provveditore* in Crema.[127] He reappeared briefly in the field as *provveditore* assigned to the new captain general Gentile da Leonessa with Tommaso Duodo as colleague, Pasquale Malipiero, having been elected to so serve, being abroad.

Milanese and Venetian armies were in the field through the fall, but made little contact. Still tension was high. In October, Sforza hurled a furious letter against Venice, declaring renewed hostilities; and worse, a bloodied gauntlet, signifying his fierce challenge to battle.[128] The Senate replied, threatening reprisals against Sforza who had "at our expense . . . won for himself a wife and an empire."[129] In Venice, the palace that had been given to Sforza in 1439 and confiscated in 1447, purchased by Doge Francesco Foscari and restored to the *condottiere* in 1448, was purchased again by Foscari, to be demolished and rebuilt more splendidly.[130] Marcello was in Venice, too, sitting out this penultimate phase of the war that had engaged him for much of his career. From late May through December, he made no appearance in reports of the campaign. On the last day of the last month of the year, he was elected ducal counsellor (*consigliere*). This was the first sedentary office Marcello ever actually performed for the city he had served armed and on horseback for fourteen years.[131]

He remained thus occupied for nearly four months, until he was dispatched, in April 1453, on a final Lombard mission.[132] With Pasquale Malipiero again as colleague, Marcello was instructed to reorganize the army in preparation for a new threat. Gentile da Leonessa had just died ("so much to be mourned," moaned the Senate), and the new captain general was to be installed. This was Jacopo Piccinino, son of Marcello's old adversary Niccolò, the fifth army commander Marcello monitored in the course of the Lombard wars. Sforza had activated against Venice the French alliance arranged by Florence early in 1453, and was expecting the arrival of a French army of 2,400 horse under the leadership of a prince of the blood.[133] That prince was the same René d'Anjou who had enrolled Marcello and Sforza jointly into the chivalric Order of the Crescent which required as conditions of membership absolute fidelity to earthly rulers and daily attendance at mass.[134]

René was no match for the canny rulers of Milan and Florence: who deceived him, according to French historians; who outpaced him, diplomatically and militarily, according to the Italian school.[135] He was slow to gather his army and set out for Italy. He was still in Provence throughout June, although he had promised he would arrive in Italy on the fifteenth of that month. Sforza's letter of the second prodded him to action: "since things are as well set up and disposed as they can be, come now to win glory, fame, and immortal honor."[136] In Lombardy in late August, the royal mercenary continued to make only slow progress—for wages of ten thousand florins per month he was in effect a high-status employee of the unarmed Florentines.[137]

By September, he had reached Pavia, where he was welcomed with a lavish reception and Latin oration. Only in October, nagged by Colleoni (who had deserted to Milan in 1451), did he join up with the main body of Sforza's army. Once united with those forces, he was assigned to the last place in the lineup (a deep humiliation) behind the captains Ludovico

Gonzaga, Colleoni, and Tiberto Brandolini, with Sforza himself at the head.[138] On 10 October, René and his lieutenant Cossa (whose peace initiative of the previous week had been rejected by Venice) sent heralds with full chivalric paraphernalia to present a formal declaration of war to the two Venetian *provveditori* Marcello and Malipiero.[139] "Justly have we come to Italy bearing arms . . . ," read the statement.[140] The cautious Venetians referred the matter to the Senate.

War declared, a brief campaign followed in October and November. Milanese forces bolstered by René's reinforcements overran the area so much contended along the banks of the river Oglio.[141] By early December, Sforza and René moved separately into winter quarters: Sforza impatient and ready to settle the peace (as he had been since 1450, on the right terms); René nursing his humiliations. The latter left Italy for the last time in the early days of 1454, making courtly excuses for his departure, so much more swiftly executed than his advent, and promising a prompt return.[142] Marcello and Malipiero were still in the field through December when, at the Senate's command, they drew lots to see which of them would return to Venice.[143] Marcello lost, and stayed (without salary) until he was finally released from all duties the following February. It was the winter of 1454, and Fra Simone da Camerino had already begun to build the peace that would put an end to thirty years of struggle for the mastery of Lombardy, and a year in which Marcello had faced two old allies on the field of battle.

c/೨   c/೨   c/೨

Back in Venice, Marcello did not immediately assume high office; nor did he ever accumulate the continuous record of such offices that mark the careers of others of his class who inhabited the inner circle of power.[144] A specialist in military missions, he either did not choose or was not quickly placed in civil ones. Perhaps he was at odds with the administration in power: that of Doge Francesco Foscari, whose policy of mainland expansion from his election in 1423 rendered his reign "gloomy with pestilence and war."[145] He may have been linked with Pasquale Malipiero in opposition to the Foscari regime in the years after Lodi. Malipiero, who had been Marcello's companion on many military and diplomatic missions in the last years of the Lombard conflict, was a known Foscari opponent, and "very friendly" with Sforza.[146] In 1457, he would replace the still-living doge. If Marcello voiced criticism of Foscari, in fact, in the years following 1454, he was one of a growing chorus. In any case, the relation between political success and proximity to the doge are unclear. One would have to assume both that such links existed and that Marcello fell from grace to find here an explanation for the quietude of that nobleman's political record in the middle 1450s.

The contrary argument is posed by other evidence. Malipiero succeeded Foscari in 1457, and his five-year reign includes most of those years when Marcello was available for political assignments.[147] It would be difficult to suggest in his case the impediment of dogal antipathy. Nor is the suggestion of poor relations with Foscari persuasive. Prominent members of both doges' families participated as witnesses in the registration with the Avogaria di Comun of Marcello's children or grandchildren: a presence suggesting the strongest links to dogal favor. On 31 July 1465, Pietro di Maffeo Malipiero witnessed the ascriptions of Girolamo Marcello (grandson of Jacopo Antonio by his son Francesco) and Pietro Marcello (the patriarch's son). On 2 December 1474, Ludovico di Marco Foscari, nephew of the deceased Francesco Foscari, witnessed that of Jacopo Antonio's son Lorenzo.[148] If he was not out of favor with either Foscari or Malipiero, Marcello's absence from office in these years must be otherwise explained: perhaps he did not seek such responsibility. That hypothesis is consistent with the record of his literary activities in this decade, to be examined shortly. In any case, in 1458, four years after Lodi, Marcello begins to appear in government magistracies at the very highest levels, but only briefly.

From October 1458 through June 1459, Marcello was a member of the Council of Ten, and several times served (for the normal one-month term) as *capo* of that elite body.[149] From 31 October of 1459 through 31 May of the following year, he served as *consigliere*. On 9 and 11 May 1462, he participated in the third, fourth, and final "hands" of the election of Doge Cristoforo Moro. Later that month and through the following July, he again held the title of *consigliere*. On 19 May, as an official supervisor of the planned tournament, he was sent forth to buy necessary equipment "with cash in hand." These are the brief traces of Marcello's civil career.

By summer 1462, again the smell of war was blowing in the wind.[150] Venice would shortly launch an offensive to the East, as serious as the thirty-year struggle for Lombardy that had engaged Marcello's youth. Her war against the Turkish advance in 1463–79 was quite as important for the future of her polity. During the first year of that sixteen-year war, Venice was distracted by a problem at the northeasternmost extremity of Venice's dominion.[151] The autonomous city of Trieste was interfering with the trade of Istrian cities within the Venetian orbit, and flirting with the Emperor Frederick III and his agents. Hardly had difficulties begun to arise than Marcello was dispatched, now a man of sixty-four years, to be *luogotenente* (governor) of Friuli, stationed in that region's capital of Udine. He was already there in October 1462, when the Senate granted him funds for the repair of the official palace.[152] In Udine, within easy reach of the trouble spot in Trieste, he awaited the Senate's further instructions.

From July through November of 1463, Venetian forces surrounded Trieste. Initially, the loyal captain Antonio da Marsciano led the besieging forces, while the Senate placed the disposition of equipment and supplies under the authority of the nobleman Vitale Lando, *provveditore in campo*.[153] On 24 September, Marcello was ordered to proceed immediately to the siege to join forces with Carlo Fortebraccio (Marcello's old companion from the Lombard campaign): "as soon as you receive these instructions you should get on your horse . . . , and go as swiftly as possible to the siege at Trieste, assisting and speeding operations there as best you can, until Count Carlo Fortebraccio arrives."[154] Three days later he was enjoined again to go immediately and bring the "pertinacious" city to obedience, "and by warlike interventions boldly and bravely defeat it." If the Triestini sue for peace, he might negotiate with full authority. The Senate relied on him: "We have faith in your customary prudence and experience for bringing this city back under our jurisdiction."[155]

Arrived at the siege, Marcello's role was to direct the bombardment of the walls and gates from one of the hilltop positions on the perimeter.[156] There he labored during October and November. The terrible bombardment locked up the starving citizens—all but the undaunted brave who sortied repeatedly, even in the face of their assailants' fire, to harry their attackers and bring home provisions. Their tremendous suffering is recorded by one of Marcello's humanist clients, Raffaele Zovenzoni, in his powerful verse sequence *Istrias*.[157] Meanwhile, the noble colleagues of the two *provveditori* hammered out a peace settlement (Pope Pius II intervening) with the Triestines, assuring territorial gains and restitution for losses suffered. Upon their agreement to these harsh terms, Venetian ambassadors in Rome proceeded to arrange a treaty with Burgundy and the pope for coordinated efforts against the Turks. Both of these agreements were in place by December 1463, when the *provveditore* Lando (who had been wounded and replaced) was back in Venice.

The man who directed the siege at Trieste was sixty-five years old: back in the field, after an apparent retirement from things military in 1454. Sixty-five was not old for a Venetian nobleman. The gerontocrats of Venice often engaged in military action.[158] But Marcello's career in the field was nearly over. A manuscript note suggests he was alive on 15 December. After that date, the record is silent. Marcello died not long afterwards, probably by the following March.[159] With the exception of his last flourish in 1463,

Marcello's public profile between February 1454 (when he returned from the Lombard wars at the moment of their pacification) until 1462 (when he embarked for the Friuli) was remarkably retiring; especially for a man who, as has been seen, approved and promoted the literary celebration of his military triumphs and housed himself in a castle that was itself a statement of aggressive force. Possible explanations of Marcello's avoidance of or exclusion from public office have been presented above. Of these, the most likely is that his retirement was the result of a deliberate choice. He was plotting a new course. Turning inward from the idols of the court and temple, he nurtured the relationships with the friends he most valued in the rediscovered medium of words.[160]

After 1450, the adventures that preoccupied Marcello were literary. Following the death of his son Valerio on the first day of 1461, that preoccupation turned to obsession. The basis for those intellectual interests had been laid in youth, when he dwelled in the circle of his humanist brother, bishop of the university city of Padua. But it was not until the midpoint of the century, when Marcello himself passed fifty, that he began to cultivate writers and artists, collect texts, and create books. The stimulus for this late-blooming literary career was disillusionment with his first-chosen military one: for in 1449, he had been compelled to turn against a comrade, and in 1453 against an admired king. Marcello's interests shifted from battle to books. The strain of the rupture with Sforza in 1449, the unsuccessful peace process of 1450, the French alliance with Sforza against Venice in 1452–53, encouraged his new orientation.

Two bodies of evidence support the hypothesis here proposed. The first witness is the sequence of panegyrical works analyzed earlier in the previous chapter: they hailed Marcello for victories that were not wholly his in the period 1438–39 and 1446, while they wilfully neglected Marcello's critical role in the period after August 1447, when Visconti died and Sforza burst into Lombardy. The humanists did what they were told. Marcello evidently did not wish to publicize his role on Venice's western frontier, either as Sforza's friend or his enemy, in the seven years before the settlement at Lodi. The silence of the panegyrists bespeaks Marcello's rejection of a difficult phase of his active life, and coincides with his turning to the sanctum of a private one.

The second witness to Marcello's state of mind in his conversion to cultural pursuits is the nature of the projects undertaken after 1450. The books that Marcello composed were all of one type. He located a text or texts of interest (in Greek or Latin, geographical, historical, philosophical, or hagiographical), arranged for attractive transcription and illumination, and added a prefatory letter of his own. The letters were addressed in every single case to René, Duke of Anjou, Count of Provence, brother-in-law of Charles VII, would-be king, master of tournaments, painter and poet, bibliophile and patron of arts and letters, founder of the Order of the Crescent.

This scion of the second French royal house of Anjou had inherited the claims of the first to the throne of Naples, the remnant of the ancient Kingdom of the Two Sicilies won by Norman predecessors.[161] His grandfather Louis I had reigned there in 1382–84 alongside the principal heir Giovanna I, before losing his throne to Charles of Durazzo. His father Louis II won the throne back briefly from Charles's successor Ladislas in 1410, just a year after René's birth. For fourteen years after 1420, René's elder brother Louis III struggled for the same throne; after 1423, he was adopted heir of Giovanna II, successor to his Angevin foe Ladislas. The third Louis died in 1434, and Giovanna herself died in 1435, leaving to Louis's heir René—who already held title to Bar and Lorraine—Provence and Anjou, and the kingdom of Naples ("Sicily"). For the rest of René's life he would bear on his many-sectioned coat of arms the signs of these possessions. It was the one kingdom in Italy that caused him the most distress.

Imprisoned in Burgundy, René was unable to proceed immediately to Naples in the winter of 1435. His wife, the redoubtable Isabelle of Lorraine, went as his surrogate. Raised in the tradition of feudal monarchy, one of her first acts on Italian soil was to confirm the pledged allegiance of the Neapolitan barons, many of whom remained loyal to René years after his departure from their midst. Among them was Giovanni Cossa, whose unfailing loyalty matched his extraordinary diplomatic and military capacity. Cossa would serve René until his death in 1476, "the most precious conquest King René ever made in Italy."[162] At that time he bore, in addition to the title of Count of Troia which was his by birthright, that of Grand Seneschal of Provence.

René himself arrived in the spring of 1438, expecting an easy triumph for the cause he believed just: "but his naiveté was as great as his valor."[163] He wrestled through 1442 with Alfonso of Aragon, the eventual victor, as has been seen. Then, dislodged from his capital, mocked by his opponent, deserted by his allies, poorer by twenty thousand florins, he returned to France. For the next decade, he awaited an opportunity to return to Italy, sending Cossa there as diplomat to discover an ally among the contending states of the north of Italy. Milan and Florence finally presented themselves as allies in 1452, and René descended to Italy a second time in 1453, with the poor results that have been seen.[164] He had provided Florence with a mercenary force, but received from that city in return no assistance (none had been specifically included in the terms of the league) in his primary goal of recovering Naples.

One last time René sailed to Italy to fulfill his regal ambitions.[165] In 1458, his son Jean d'Anjou seized possession of Genoa (a prize sporadically in French hands throughout the century). That action was part of a campaign aimed, once again, at Naples that Jean waged from 1459 to 1464, Cossa at his side, with a French army displaying the latest in organization and equipment. In 1461, the Milanese assisted the Genoese to isolate and disperse the French garrison. Some of those soldiers fled to the ships waiting none too patiently in the harbor under the command of René d'Anjou. After this third humiliation, René left Italy for good. He never abandoned his pretension to the throne of Naples, proudly claimed in his testament of 1471, and presumably nurtured until his death in 1480.[166]

An almost comical player among the cynical potentates on the Italian stage, the chivalrous René saw his military ventures descend to failure. His career as a patron and practitioner of letters and the arts was more successful. His court at Anjou and Provence was a center of civility and conversation of European importance, rival to those of his cousin Charles d'Orleans and his uncle, the duke of Burgundy, Philip the Bold. To that court he invited the Neapolitan humanist Giuniano Maio and the wandering son of Francesco Filelfo, Giovanni Mario, as official librarian and teacher of Greek.[167] Gathered in Angers were also painters, architects, and musicians from Flanders and Italy, who adorned René's palace, filled his wardrobes with *objets* of notable workmanship, illuminated his books, created the celebrations of birth, marriage, death, and victory that were staged on the grand scale befitting a member of the French royal house.

Also in his entourage were scribes who composed works on commission, sometimes in his name, sometimes at his direction: for "he had around him scribes or secretaries, to whom he sketched out what they should write, if he did not actually dictate it."[168] The monarch himself wrote books (and painted pictures) for circulation at his court: love poetry, occasional verse, a dialogue on the art of dying, a treatise on the proper way to run a tournament—a standard text for that century.[169] These books and others he housed in a fine library containing volumes in Hebrew and Arabic, Latin and Greek, French, Italian, and German, ranging in content from theology and law to history and geography, and literature ancient and modern.[170]

Among René's projects was the beautification of the cathedral at Angers, where the members of his family had long been buried. The cathedral was dedicated to Saint Maurice, the warrior saint who was also the patron of the Order of the Crescent founded by the would-be king in 1448. The meetings of the knights of that order were held in the cathedral's chapter hall, and its canons were curators of the order's books and possessions. The cathedral was adorned with a special chapel dedicated to the Sienese preacher Bernardino (who had been promptly canonized after his death in 1444), built by René to commemorate the effect wrought upon him by the saint's stirring sermons in Aquila in 1438.[171] In the principal chapel, René ordered built the remarkable mausoleum where he would be buried along-side his first wife, Isabelle of Lorraine (dead in 1453).[172] Begun in 1445 or 1446 after his return from Italy, its classical forms were in the style of Italian masters that the French prince had admired in Naples.

René's literary and artistic interests, or perhaps his model of chivalrous knighthood (so unlike the pattern of Venetian nobleman!), or perhaps the pathos of his failed quest for kingship, sparked the imagination of Jacopo Antonio Marcello.[173] The latter expressed his admiration for that connoisseur by dispatching small but elegant volumes for the Frenchman's perusal and the enrichment of his library (poor in classical and especially Greek materials). Gift-giving was and is a familiar mode of securing relationships, and especially with the powerful. The giving of books, in particular, among that limited circle for whom books mattered, was a behavior also characteristic of the period.[174] But Marcello was perhaps exceptional in the steadiness of his giving: a stream of ornate manuscript treasures over a little more than a decade, all directed to the absent king.

The first of these dates from April 1452, when Marcello had come to the end of his two and one-half year term as *provveditore* of Crema, at the westernmost point of Venetian domination.[175] The learned *provveditore* had some time earlier sent to the Venetian patrician humanist Lauro Quirini the Greek text (excerpted from the lexicon attributed to Suidas) of a pious legend entitled *De sacerdotio Jesu Christi* (On the priesthood of Jesus Christ).[176] Quirini soon translated the diminutive work. The commissioned translation back in his hands, Marcello dispatched Greek and Latin texts together in a manuscript headed by his own prefatory letter to René. Later that month or during the next, Marcello dispatched a second version of the same work to René: this one translated by an unnamed "learned friend" who had derogated Quirini's effort. It was headed by a new letter referring to the illness of the queen, Isabelle of Lorraine, proof of Marcello's access to sources of information at the Angevin court.

Early in 1453, Isabelle died, and René d'Anjou grieved, inventing the device of a bow with broken string as emblem of his despair.[177] Marcello wrote the king a letter of consolation, followed up not long after by another manuscript gift aiming to comfort the learned and desolate Frenchman. That manuscript contained a homily of Chrysostom's on mourning in Greek and Latin (translated by the same fastidious but anonymous scholar who had corrected Quirini), and the usual prefatory letter by the man who had arranged for the transcription and translation.

Soon thereafter, Marcello composed and sent to King René a gift of an extraordinary nature: an elegant package between two covers containing a manuscript, a dedication, some verse, a portrait, and a puzzle.[178] Here the life of St. Maurice, patron of the King's Angevin ancestors and of the knightly Order of the Crescent, is sandwiched between Marcello's own prefatory letter to Giovanni Cossa, then Senator of the Order, and a concluding epigram. Interspersed are the brilliant illuminations of the fifteenth-century north Italian school already described, climaxed by the bold image of the author of the manuscript. Bold as that image is, it is not so bold as the message residing in the text.

This manuscript book was in fact no courtly token. The prefatory and illustrative and concluding material were more important than the pious *vita* they enclosed. Ostensibly a courtly apology for his failure to attend the annual convention of the Order of the Crescent (of which Cossa was that year president), Marcello's letter pointedly omits the reason for his non-attendance: that fully armed and with the Venetian forces, he was awaiting the invasion of the Veneto planned by the king and his lieutenant. For while Marcello was preparing to send to René the life of a saint, René was preparing to cross the Alps at the head of an army bent on war.

More eloquent than the letter is the elephant fantasy on the last page of the manuscript.[179] This is an "utterly phantasmagoric" vision that looks like "some sort of outlandish wedding cake done up in a great white ribbon." "A grayish elephant stands on a patch of bare brown earth between two hillocks" spotted with grass. "Blue water fringed with grasses spreads over his back like a cushion," upon which perch two ducks, three dolphins, and a heron. Atop the water pooled on the elephant's back sits a replica of Venice's Ducal Palace, with various other Venetian emblems: the enthroned figure of *Venezia Magna*, borrowed from various representations in that building, two Furies, the scales of justice. Unfurled over the beast's head is a banner with inscription, blazoned in enigmatic golden words. Venice says to the beast: "I acknowledge that you sustained me when I was falling." The animal (a stand-in for Marcello himself, hero and maker of books) responds modestly: "I deny this for it is by divine power that you escaped." Who was this courteous elephant? As the vehicle favored by Hannibal (once defeated by a Marcello forebear), that beast served as a symbol of military

The knights of the Order of the Crescent in session, illumination in the St. Maurice manuscript. Paris, Bibliothèque de l'Arsenal, MS 940, facing fol. 1. Photograph provided by the Bibliothèque Nationale, Paris.

FATEOR ME

VIRTVTE EVASISTI

PRECIPITANTEM SVSTINVISTI°

INFICIOR NAM DIVINA

*Illumination in the St. Maurice manuscript, an intricate pictorial puzzle prepared by Mar-
cello to deter King Renè and his general Giovanni Cossa from their planned offensive against
Venice. Paris, Bibliothèque de l'Arsenal, MS 940, facing fol. 39. Photograph provided by
the Bibliothèque Nationale, Paris.*

triumph—that of Venice, and Marcello, presumably, over any French interlopers! Venice expresses its gratitude to Marcello, as Marcello, in the image to be considered, announces a warning to René's lieutenant, the Italian Cossa.

Facing the elephant image is the portrait of Marcello that has already summoned our attention, a bust rising from a massive parapet upon which is written another inscription, in strange figures: in fact, in cipher, a resistant code known to the author and his addressee.[180] Decoded it reads: "Se mia speranza non dixe bugia / Non farai ingrata patria Cossa mia" ("If my hopes do not deceive me / You, Cossa, will not make my country ungrateful to you"). The untangled message urges Cossa to reconsider his alliance with Sforza and hostile intent against Venice. The sum of the messages enclosed in the pretty manuscript book amount to a last-chance diplomatic plea by Marcello to his French friends not to open hostilities against Venice: "Marcello has scarcely veiled a bribe."[181] Even Marcello's earlier manuscript gifts to René in 1452 and 1453 had been sent after the enemies of Venice had negotiated an alliance with the French king Charles VII, the Angevin's brother-in-law; and René from the first had been that "prince of the blood" that Florentines expected to fight their battles for them.[182] But now René had an army assembled to execute that purpose.

Marcello's book and its hidden message were dispatched just as René and Cossa were setting out for Italy to join Sforza and the Florentines in the struggle against their rival. Its dateline was a battlefield, the Venetian army camp lying between two of the towns over which the Lombard conflict had hovered for nearly thirty years, on the west bank of the river Oglio: "1 June 1453, from the most auspicious camp of the Venetians after the victories at Quinzano and Pontevico."[183] Thus audaciously does the volume close in which intersect the military, the learned, the artistic, and the diplomatic vectors of Renaissance culture. Marcello positions himself within that tradition of soldier-scholars marked by the example of Julius Caesar who both fought and wrote about the war for Gaul, and the more recent one of Jacopo dal Verme, Giangaleazzo Visconti's general: the "glory of knighthood and light of Latinity," both.[184]

As if the St. Maurice codex were not extraordinary enough, an enigmatic gift with its hidden warning dispatched by the Venetian to his country's enemy, Marcello also commissioned at about the same time a panegyric of the would-be king of Naples. The author was the precocious foreigner Janus Pannonius, already encountered as a eulogist of his teacher Guarino and, at great length, his patron Marcello. The previous year, at René's behest, the prodigy had composed the *Carmen pro pacanda Italia* (Song for the peace of Italy), dedicated to the Emperor Frederick III on the occasion of an imminent imperial visit that posed some challenge to that peace. Now he composed the *Panegiricus ad Renatum,* written for and to his patron as its subject stood poised to descend into Italy at the head of an army.[185] "Receive, Jacopo, this eulogy of great Renato," the poet invited in the dedicatory preface, "Receive the verses sung at your command!"[186] Of the many mysteries that linger in Marcello's story, surely conspicuous is that of the Venetian's stance with regard to his country's enemy, in whose honor he commissions a eulogy from his poet protégé. In 1449, Marcello had in obedience to the Senate led his troops from Sforza's camp without muting his love for that comrade. In 1453, equally, while the Venetian defended the interests of his city, he did not allow the advent of war to interrupt his relationship with his literary friend.

While Pannonius honored René with verse, Marcello was armed and ready for his advent. But the winter of 1453–54 descended to interrupt hostilities, and demobilization ensued soon thereafter with the final signing of the Peace of Lodi. Marcello was now freed from immediate military assignments to pursue his new interests. For the next several years, he is found most often in Monselice, in close contact with the cultural life of nearby Padua. He was in contact with several of the literati of that city, including Onofrio Strozzi (son of the Florentine exile and bibliophile Palla), from whom he procured the *mappamondo* to be described in due course; with the eminent doctor Matteolo, "prince of physicians," who attended the family; and with the cleric Maffeo Vallaresso whose earlier relations with the Venetian are referred to in a letter dated from Padua in 1460.[187]

During these years, too, his relationship deepened with the brilliant Pannonius, who a few years later from that other world north of the Alps would send verses mourning the death of the child Valerio.[188] Pannonius had moved from Guarino's school at Ferrara to study law at Padua, where he resided from 1454 to 1458. There established, Pannonius not only continued to compose verse for Marcello, but dined often at his patron's table, and shared intensely in his experiences, as epigrams written in these years disclose. "Marcello is to me what Pollio, Maecenas, and Proculeius were to poets of a sacred age," wrote the young man in one of his fine Latin epigrams. "I am to Marcello what Choerilus once was to Xerxes."[189] In another, he offers qualified praise of Marcello's own vernacular poetry: "I would not deny you're a poet, Marcello," he grants, "because your muse creates verses in a vulgar tongue." Even in Italian, the poems are worthy: "We praise the speechless bird, if the songs are sweet."[190]

More startling than this clue that Marcello filled his quiet moments with versification is the revelation that he hired Pannonius to translate his efforts into Latin; more, that they were love poems! That announcement is made in an epigram entitled *De versibus Marcelli a se latine expressis* (On verses of Marcello, translated by him into Latin) that must have closed Pannonius's book of translations of his patron's work. "Often the poets of old lamented their own passions," Pannonius complains. But he as client must turn his talents to another man's needs: "I sing Marcello's flames of youthful passion, / passion that he lately sang in his native metre."[191] (At nearly sixty, Marcello was hardly youthful, though his real or imagined passion may have had that wonderful quality.) Pannonius, on the other hand, was still quite young. He points this out himself, in a verse paired with his claim of greatness: "I, unschooled in love, have written of Marcello's fiery passion, / I, the outstanding glory of my native Pannonia."[192] Of Marcello's career as a vernacular poet there is only this slight evidence. Was he incapable of Latin composition? If not, were all the letters dedicating works to King René written by someone else, at dictation, or translated from Marcello's draft? These questions cannot be settled. Though he could not himself write Latin verse, Marcello may have been capable of writing Latin prose (as his literary tastes imply), and may retain full title to the letters.

Pannonius's epigrams provide one further piece in the puzzle of Marcello's private life, illuminating his relationship with René d'Anjou. In one verse, he likens the Venetian to sixteen different Greek and Roman heroes (a series featuring such as Diomedes and Ulysses, Heracles and Achilles, Theseus and Augustus), and concludes: "just so are you, Marcello, and noble Renato; / blessed Marcello, you are worthy of the love of kings."[193] A relationship is witnessed here between the French royal figure and the Venetian nobleman that emerges from no other document.

ℰℱ   ℰℱ   ℰℱ

Pannonius is the link to another dimension of Marcello's cultural activity in the mid-1450s. Before he departed Italy in 1458, having completed his degree in canon law, the poet wrote an elegy to Andrea Mantegna. The artist had just painted a portrait of Pannonius and fellow-student Galeotto Marzio da Narni, countryman of Marcello's *condottiere* friend Gattamelata and future target of the rage of Giovanni Mario Filelfo. The painter whose inspired hand commemorated these two alumni of Guarino's school was also a traveler in Marcello's circle.[194] In this very year, as has been noted, Mantegna was working on an unnamed "operetta" for Marcello: an undertaking that delayed the artist's move to Mantua where his most important work would be completed. What was that little job? One of Marcello's manuscripts for René? The massive *Agony in the Garden* now in London has been suggested, but is ruled out by size. The best possibility is the painting of *Saint Sebastian,* stabbed with arrows and lashed to a column that stands amid some remnants of Roman architecture. Sebastian was a plague saint, and in 1456–57, when the painting could have been commissioned, Padua was struck by plague. The university setting, and a link to the humanist patron is implied by the Greek signature incorporated in the painting: *To ergon tou Andreou,* "This is the work of Andrea [Mantegna]."[195] The Greek tag, the heroic and solitary pose of the subject, the classical ruins, mark this painting as one that would have found favor in the eyes of the soldier and patron Jacopo Antonio Marcello.

Mantegna was not the only artist whom Marcello cultivated during his respite in the Veneto in the 1450s. He was probably the major patron of Jacopo Bellini, pioneer of the Renaissance tradition of Venetian painting, through the end of the decade.[196] The best evidence for Bellini's connection to Marcello is provided by that artist's studies of Roman monuments based on reliefs located in the churches of Monselice—Marcello's personal mountain at this juncture, from the newly remodeled castle guarding its base to the lordly *rocca* at its peak.[197] Among those sketches is one of a monument bearing Marcello's name. These, and the format of the pages adorned by the drawings, suggest that they are studies for a grand project to be constructed in honor of that patron. One of Bellini's planned panels of St. George may also have been destined for Marcello's delectation in the Monselice church of San Jacopo which purportedly housed the body of the militant saint.[198] From a slightly later period (more precisely from early 1462, if these suppositions are correct) dates Bellini's swift and elegant drawing of a decorative basin: possibly the plan for the one Marcello commissioned and bestowed upon Francesco Filelfo, the handsome reward for that scholar's *Consolatio* for the child Valerio.

Less speculative is Marcello's involvement in the planning of the Gattamelata chapel in the church dedicated to Sant'Antonio da Vienna in Padua ("the Santo"), before which stands Donatello's more secular monument. As he had been companion to the *condottiere,* Marcello was the counseler of his widow, who commissioned Jacopo Bellini and his sons Giovanni and Gentile to paint the altarpiece for the first nave chapel on the right from the entrance of that church.[199] Also undisputed is the master artist's role as programmer of the lavish tournaments frequently celebrated in the Piazza San Marco during these years of Venetian militancy on the mainland, when these sports "took on a revived sense of official mission."[200] Just as Marcello had a taste for art, the tastes of his favorite artist inclined to the passions and paraphernalia of battle. Not only was Bellini the architect of the grand jousts of 1441 (for the marriage of Jacopo Foscari) and 1458 (for the ceremonial conferral of the baton of command to the *condottiere* Colleoni) among many others, but military figures and events are a major theme of his art.

That bent for martial themes most certainly does not characterize the work of Jacopo Bellini's son Giovanni, a key figure in the transition of Venetian style toward the softer and more coloristic mode of its climactic phase. Yet Giovanni could also have found employment with Jacopo Antonio Marcello. In a brief detour from his career as a painter, he may have worked as an illuminator for the Venetian patron, adorning two of the books which Marcello had made for the library of René d'Anjou: the St. Maurice *vita* and Strabo's *Geography*.[201]

Four years after the first of these was dispatched to René, after the war and after the peace, the string of Marcello's recondite literary messages resumed in 1457.[202] René's agent Ludovico Martelli had been searching for a suitable world map (*mappamondo*) for his master's collection: René had a particular interest in geography. Marcello obtained one from Onofrio Strozzi, which was nearly complete and ready to dedicate to Marcello with his arms, as Marcello explains in his dedicatory letter. Marcello had it finished and shipped, cut in two sections and folded inside a volume to René containing the Greek text of Ptolemy's *Cosmography* (with Latin translation by George of Trebizond), a work whose Renaissance vogue had only recently begun. At the front is the dedicatory letter dated 1 March of that year, from Monselice.

Between 1455 and 1459, Marcello conceived and supervised a project of greater magnitude: the Latin translation of Strabo's *Geography*.[203] Guarino Veronese had undertaken that task for Pope Nicholas V in 1453, but it was still unfinished in the spring of 1455 when that pontiff and patron unkindly died—Guarino's reward of five hundred *scudi* probably uncollected. Having tried without success to win Medici patronage for the toilsome project, Guarino then offered it "to a Venetian gentleman of a most generous spirit, willing to compensate him for his labour," reported the contemporary biographer Vespasiano da Bisticci.[204] Marcello was that philanthropic gentleman. At about the same time, as has been previously noted, that Marcello undertook to support Guarino's efforts, Francesco Sforza was supporting Gregorio Tifernate's translation of the same work. Thus the old companions and adversaries, freed from military occupations by the Lodi settlement of 1454, engaged during the late 1450s in a new form of contest: a race to translate the Greek geographer.

By 13 July 1458, Guarino had finished. His own version of the work was sent to Marcello, who then supervised the creation of an elegant presentation copy. During the next fourteen months were accomplished the tasks still required to prepare a suitable work for René's growing library. A scribe copied the text itself and the introductory letters composed by Guarino (to Pope Nicholas and Marcello) and his patron (to René). And once again Marcello hired an artist to paint rare portraits to illustrate the dedicatory letters. The first portrays the austere Guarino offering his book to a courtly but aged Marcello. The second miniature depicts Marcello, on bended knee, offering the book in turn to the Angevin king. Marcello and the king are locked together by the gesture of their hands and the deep yearning of their eyes, the communion between them palpable and gripping; and all the more surprising since, except on this page, they may never have met. On 13 September 1459, in Venice, the work was signed in Marcello's name and sent to France: "one of the supreme accomplishments of the Quattrocento in the sphere of the book." [205]

These works composed in the period after 1452 (with the exception of the battlefield St. Maurice codex) punctuate the one decade of Marcello's maturity when he pushed aside the business of war and sought renewal in literary pursuits. The monuments of this literary career are his own works and those addressed to him by Carrara and Pannonius, Guarino and George of Trebizond. In addition, contacts with literary friends are witnessed by occasional letters (one each from Maffeo Vallaresso and Francesco Filelfo) and records of conversation: at the church of San Antonio, at Marcello's palace in Venice on the Grand Canal, at Monselice. [206] In 1460, he summered at that fortress-villa. Only a few months after his return to Venice, his son Valerio died. Born in the last months of Marcello's provveditoriate in Crema, the boundaries of that child's brief lifetime correspond almost exactly to the period of his father's literary fruitfulness. It was during these years that Marcello forged that profound relationship with his son Valerio, ended by the latter's death on the first day of 1461. Thereafter, Marcello's literary life merged with his sorrow, and his patronage activities focused exclusively on the mighty task of soothing his own grief. That grief was to find literary expression in the funerary volume, destined for the eyes of René d'Anjou, that rests today in Glasgow. As unfinished as the father's grief, this one volume was never sent.

While Marcello's relationship with René was left as unfinished as the consolation volume, his relationship with Sforza achieved resolution. That ex-*condottiere* never forgot, when he became duke of Milan, that adornment to reputation afforded by a palace on the Grand Canal of Venice. [207]

He had been granted by the Senate in 1439 a palace with two towers (reminiscent of mainland castles) in the parish of San Pantaleone as a "monument of perpetual love"; it had previously belonged to Gianfrancesco Gonzaga, marquis of Mantua, the Venetian captain who deserted to the Visconti in 1438.[208] In 1447, the palace with two towers was confiscated by the Serenissima when their captain general became their enemy and was sold to the family of Doge Francesco Foscari.[209] Its restoration to Sforza was a condition of the renewed alliance of 1448; but when a year later Venice abandoned Sforza (who held out for better terms than could be won), the property was reclaimed by the Foscari who built on its ruins the present Ca' Foscari, seat of the University of Venice.[210]

Its loss was not to be suffered, and a remedy was soon obtained. According to the arrangements of the Italian League in 1455, Sforza was once again a Venetian ally and, by Senate decree, the possessor of a palace: this time in Campo San Polo.[211] But he wished a grander one: one on the Grand Canal. In 1461, he exchanged the San Polo building for one near San Samuele (the property of the exceedingly wealthy Marco di Giorgio Corner), closer to the center of the city, and squarely facing the coveted Canal.[212] The structure had only recently been begun, in 1457, by Bartolomeo Buon, when Sforza took it over. He planned its completion and remodeling, in the Venetian style but uniquely marked by the rusticated surface of a mainland *castello*. Had Sforza's designs been realized, the building would have been "the largest private palace in Venice at the time, and one of the biggest ever built."[213] Today a corner finished with rusticated stone is still visible, and the building is called the "Ca' del Duca." Before the stonework could be completed, however, and the "Duke's House" occupied by the one to whom its possession meant so much, Sforza died, and the building reverted to the Republic. But Sforza was to find a place in another Venetian monument, where his memorial would be linked with Marcello's.

Having through many attempts established the terms upon which the Peace of Lodi was concluded on April 9, 1454, Fra Simone da Camerino received concessions from the Senate in recognition of his peerless service to Venice.[214] Among other items, he was granted funds to augment and complete the church and monastery on the tiny island of San Cristoforo, lying between Venice and Murano, and belonging to the Augustinian congregation of Monte Ortone that he had founded.[215] Upon Fra Simone's request, the island was renamed San Cristoforo della Pace, commemorating that peace which the friar was pleased to recognize as his greatest achievement.

Who was this friar, from the Marche as his name suggests, according to

*Positioned under a Roman arch, the scholar Guarino Veronese offers to Marcello his transla-
tion of Strabo. Manuscript illumination. Albi (France), Bibliothèque Municipale, MS 77
(formerly Bibliothèque Rochegude, MS 4), fol. 3v. With the permission of Dr. Jacques
Pons, Director.*

In a fantastic antique setting, Marcello offers Guarino's Strabo to King Renè. Manuscript illumination. Albi (France), Bibliothèque Municipale, MS 77 (formerly Bibliothèque Rochegude, MS 4), fol. 4. With the permission of Dr. Jacques Pons, Director.

Sanuto "a great preacher, and a man of holy life," who extracted from the Venetian Senate the extraordinary prize of a perpetual monument to peace?[216] A familiar of Doge Francesco Foscari, who had granted the earnest reformer the right to build his monastery on that Venetian island as early as 1436,[217] Simone also had ties to Sforza. He may have been Sforza's (or his wife's) confessor, as the chronicler Dolfin states, who had in 1453 preached "in the Duke's court, inspired by God" a series of Lenten sermons. Perhaps he had known Sforza even earlier: during the years the latter spent in the Marche, where stands Simone's natal city Camerino, from whence the friar migrated to the Veneto.[218] His later behavior certainly testifies to the deep commitment of this nonpolitical Augustinian to the welfare of Sforza and his kin.

From the Lodi settlement of 1454 until his retirement to the Paduan foundation of Monte Ortone in 1468 (ten years before his death and burial there), while presiding over the little island of San Cristoforo pledged to the peace of Italy, Fra Simone worked for Sforza's interests in Venice.[219] Letters to Simone from Sforza, adorned with friendly sentiments towards the Serenissima, the friar read aloud in the Senate, expressively, to an audience of stone-faced patricians once fired with hatred for the sender. In his own letters to Sforza, he described the effect wrought on his hearers by the duke's words. He won from the Senate the assurance that it would take under its protection Sforza, his sons, and the sons of his sons, and arranged for the grand reception in Venice of one of that progeny: Galeazzo Maria Sforza, at the time (1454) a youth of thirteen. It was Fra Simone who directed the artistic program at San Cristoforo, described below, where the newborn amity between Sforza and Venice was carved in stone. And it was Simone who extracted from the same oddly pliable Senate yet another palace for the *romagnol condottiere* now lord of Milan. As soon as he received word of the Senate's act of donation, he hastened to write Sforza: "O what honor, O what fame will this grant bring Your Excellency, because it is a sign of great friendship and love."[220]

The prince who inspired the devotion of this Christian laborer (and who won Machiavelli's lively attention) has been until recently underestimated by historians.[221] The only one of Italy's mercenary captains to win a domain and establish a dynasty, he was surely the finest *condottiere* of the age. More, Sforza was a diplomat and politician of great acuity: whose vision for Milan centered on but also transcended his own aspirations, who nurtured early hopes for Italy as a nation at the same time as he participated in opening its gates to the foreign princes who would in time consume it. By 1454, the warrior Sforza desired peace, encouraging secret negotiations with Venice and conceding much to gain it. His agent (as it seems) Simone da Camerino encouraged and assisted him, and his friend (as it seems) Jacopo Antonio Marcello associated himself with those ambitions in the final intimacy of the tomb.

The church on San Cristoforo was not completed until late in the century of its founding (with facade by Pietro Lombardo), and the telltale inscriptions and insignia not carved until the next. But the program was settled under Fra Simone's supervision in the years immediately following Lodi, before the deaths either of Marcello in 1463–64 or of Sforza in 1466. The architect of the peace, Fra Simone would be buried in his church of Santa Maria de Ortone (mother church of the same congregation) before the main altar, with an inscription noting his achievement of that settlement. Jacopo Antonio Marcello was buried in the *capella maggiore* at San Cristoforo. The choice is significant: in Marcello's culture, where one's burial was linked to a sense of "sacred geography," place counted even more than the cost or ornament of the tomb.[222] Our Venetian chose to be buried not with other members of his family—not even with the precious Valerio—but rather with the place that monumentalized his "ritual brothers": the victors of the peace, the architects of Lodi.

By 1555, inscriptions to both Jacopo Antonio and his son Pietro were added to the walls of that chapel. In the nave of the church were hung Sforza's battle standards, their presence in Venice not (as was usual) a token of surrender but rather of reconciliation, laid to rest in a holy place near the center of Venice, alternately ally and enemy. On the exterior walls was carved a device, consisting of the interlaced arms of Sforza and Foscari, the regnant doge for the whole term of the battle for the Lombard plain, joined by an iron chain, and inscribed with the words "PAX—quis nos separabit?" ("Peace—who will separate us?").[223] In this one small church on its diminutive island there were melded commemorations of Marcello and Sforza, the friar who achieved the peace, and the doge who had launched the war.

Marcello remained a soldier until the end of his life, bearing arms at the Senate's command in his sixty-fifth year. But in the last fifteen years of his life, he ceased to glory in war. He acted through his coterie of humanist and artists to reconstruct his past, and commemorate his relations to the three persons whom he loved more, even, than Venice: his comrade in arms Francesco Sforza, now duke of Milan; René d'Anjou, romantic dilettante, quixotic adventurer, failed king; and Valerio, dead at age eight, upon whom Marcello had fixed all his hope.

CHAPTER FIVE

Father and Son

ᡒᡑ

Victor of Casalmaggiore, protector of Ravenna, companion of Sforza, proprietor of Monselice's grim walls, Jacopo Antonio Marcello yielded to grief in January 1461. Among the motives that spurred his consolers to wield their pens, this one was foremost: the unusual and unseemly spectacle of a proud nobleman, a veteran of battle, a rational and cultivated man, sunk in prolonged and excessive mourning. A man of the "greatest soul" and "most prudent," it was more credible "that sorrow should be conquered by you, than you by sorrow," wrote Gregorio Tifernate.[1] The vulnerability to sorrow of this effective and experienced man is a measure of the profundity of his love for his child. The frustration of his consolers with his inconsolability is a measure of the rarity and mystery of that love. This chapter explores the unusual depth of the father's relationship with his son and, consequent upon it, the extraordinary quality of his grief.

Tifernate's pointed statement expresses in brief the consolers' responses to Marcello's grief. In one of the earliest consolations, Sagundino is more discursive. It is right to mourn, the humanist admonished "but not unrestrainedly or without limit, not in a weak or womanish way, not at length or forever, not always with the same force." If such restraint befits the ordinary man, how much more is it required of Marcello, brave and illustrious, glorious in the record of great deeds accomplished?[2] "Collect yourself then, dry now your tears, quiet your sighing. . . . Look about you and reflect on who you are, how much you are, where you are, what it behooves you to do and not to do, what men should hear about you and expect of you, consider your age. Do not so indulge your sorrow and tears that, while you feed this sickness of yours, you neglect your duty to yourself and to those who depend upon you." Given his wisdom, valor and bodily strength, his record of glorious deeds at home and abroad, it is disgraceful for him to be cast down by so small a tragedy.[3]

Look at Marcello's city, flourishing, wealthy, powerful on land and sea: "It is shameful . . . to find among the first men of the city, amid the senatorial class, one so cast down by personal cares." Look at the Marcello family, descended from the ancient Romans. Should not a scion of that glorious line not only show no weakness, but not even be suspected of weakness?[4] Grief of this magnitude is suitable for women, not men: Roman law forbade men to mourn unless they removed their *toga virilis,* the very sign of manhood, and dressed as women.[5] Marcello should recall his duty to others for the sake of his wife, of his now beatified Valerio, of his other sons, "who depend on you, who form and mold themselves to your mood and will, who cannot exist unless you are whole and robust; remember that you are not born for yourself alone, but for your country, your spouse, your children, your neighbors, your friends, your clients, for whom you should be not only a consoler in difficult times, but also a solace."[6]

In this manner the first known of Marcello's consolers rebukes him, the victim, for too great an indulgence in sorrow. Three injunctions are stated in these passages that will reappear in different form throughout the consolationary corpus. Marcello must recall himself from shame to honor, from self to society, from womanliness to masculinity. His power of body and loftiness of mind, his illustrious deeds, his city's eminence, his family's glory, win him honor. Sorrow dishonors him. Thus shamed, he cannot effectively protect his family, his friends, his clients, who rely on his reputation as much as his actions. Having allowed his honor to give way to shame, he has turned his face on society, and thinks only and endlessly of himself. This is not the posture of a man; it is explicitly (in the two instances cited) that of a woman. It is not merely unusual for Marcello to behave the way he does: it is uncivil, it is immoral, for he has upset the social order, and reversed the natural one.

These concerns about excessive grief are pre-modern. The concept of honor itself peaked in the early modern period, as social elites developed codes and customs to protect their authority in settings where status could not reliably be conferred by the state.[7] As a Venetian nobleman, Marcello belonged to one of the few elites of his age whose members derived their authority from a rational political order. Yet even from that privileged stance, he both deliberately cultivated his own reputation, as has been seen, and was urged to do so by others in a quest for honor. Only a man with honor intact (a woman's honor had none of these public qualities) could operate effectively in the world. He must mourn, as he did all other things, in a manner appropriate to status. In the fifteenth century, Marcello's supererogatory mourning concerned the whole community. It was a violation of social order so radical as to amount to an inversion of sexual roles: an abomination.

Such admonitions are heard also from later consolers in the first year of

Marcello's mourning. George of Trebizond was struck, four months after the death, that Marcello was still grieving: "by a bitter sorrow you are bitterly tormented." He had faith that the nobleman was governed by reason, and would not persist in irrational mourning.[8] Yet he was concerned: would Marcello forget his place in the world, and give in to the passion of despair? In the face of the requirements of prudence, modesty, fortitude, and other such virtues,

> are you one who alone and wrapped in sorrow will desert yourself? Did your child Valerio, seeing you weeping as he lay dying, lest he indeed be overcome by the harshness and fear of death, greater than all others, summon you to reflection on yourself? Did he not judge that it would be shameful if you were to degenerate from the standard you set by your great deeds and gravity? And you, a man now old and hoary, will you not review in your memory who you were, who you are, what deeds you accomplished and how many, and how much honor and glory did that child in his dying moments show in his great soul so worthy of the Marcello family? And you, a man great in the arts of war and peace, proven on the sea and on the land, famous at home and abroad, conspicuous in the Venetian Senate for prudence, eloquence, and gravity, will you allow yourself to be defeated by this perturbation of soul? This I know you will not do.[9]

Despite this pronouncement, George was not convinced that Marcello would not linger in sorrow. He has won great glory; he must beware lest he lose it. "I see this glory flower in you, and it will flourish there in the future . . . unless you yourself forget yourself, unless you desert yourself. For truly you desert yourself if you dwell not on who you were, who you are, what behavior befits you, what is shameful for you, if conquered by sorrow you are consumed in tears."[10] Honor could be consumed by shame. Marcello must bear his sorrows bravely if he wishes to be numbered among the great,

> and confirm your past glory and render your future glory perpetual; but if on the other hand you bow down to sorrow . . . , you will win no further glory in the future, and even that glory established by your past deeds will be undone. For many (forgive me for speaking freely) will believe that you achieved those great deeds by chance rather than by reason and unvanquished strength of soul. Rely, therefore, not on anyone else but on yourself, as you have done in the past. Set yourself as your model for yourself. Imitate yourself, speak with yourself, struggle with yourself. Vanquish yourself and

do not doubt that it is to your glory if as you grow greater in age, so also you grow daily more splendid in virtue.[11]

Centrally concerned with the issue of honor, George of Trebizond spurs Marcello to save his reputation before it is dissipated by the sight of the mourner's great despair. Nogarola echoes George in her consolatory letter of the following summer. Writing to lighten the Venetian's excessive grief, she also empathizes with him. She herself had recently lost her mother, from whose death "I have suffered incredible grief and more serious than I ever would have thought possible." Now "sorrow and sadness . . . lead me captive."[12] Together we must apply "the reins of reason and not allow our sorrow to wander, unrestrained, too long." This restraint is especially necessary for Marcello, who must guard his reputation: "And you first of all, most illustrious man, since it is a source of great and admirable glory to have wisely borne calamities, to have withstood the force of fortune, to have remained dignified amid great difficulties."[13] As a woman, she acknowledges the depth of sorrow they share; but she recalls his attention to his masculine duty: the preservation of honor.

In the fall of 1461, Perleone remarked on his patron's prolonged mourning: "Often I have marveled that you, Jacopo Antonio Marcello, of soul so great and grave, who have always withstood bravely and soberly the effects of both good and bad fortune, should now so painfully bear the loss of your son Valerio."[14] He reminded Marcello (both in his brief consolatory letter and larger *Laudatio*) of his stature and his responsibilities. "This I implore you: remember that you are Jacopo Antonio, who was never defeated by adversities, nor enemies, nor fortune." Great in both war and peace, renowned as much for justice at home as for courage in the field, now you must cast out the sorrow from your soul. "Respect, then, your dignity and honor; respect Valerio, who does not want you to mourn; respect, finally, your other children and all your friends, in whom your sadness has caused a double grief, both because you have lost a son, and because they see you weep."[15] Marcello's grief not only dishonors him, but it threatens (as Sagundino had warned) the welfare of his friends.

By December of the first year of Marcello's orphanage from his son, the abundance of the father's mourning was indeed a *cause célèbre*. Writing a few days before the anniversary of Valerio's death, Francesco Filelfo (who had recently lost his own son) exhorted the bereaved father to put his grief aside: "For whoever adds greater anxieties to a recent wound exacerbates the pain, and does not lessen it. But now a year has passed during which you have mourned! Enough has been allowed to the weakness of nature, enough to common opinion, enough to duty. Now it befits us to accede to reason." His friends depend upon his acting with his well-known and much-praised liberality in order to free them from grief: "For all those of us to whom you are dear grieve for your sake."

A year had been allowed to grief; now Filelfo summoned the nobleman, much as had George of Trebizond, to return to himself. "Upon you are directed the eyes of the flourishing Senate and of all good and responsible men," he warned; take care that you bear yourself well.[16] "Or," implying (as had Sagundino) that the Venetian's manliness was undermined by his excess of passion, "are we more weak-spirited than women? For how often do we read of women who bear the death of their children with a firm and unyielding spirit?"[17] Indeed, Marcello's own wife Luca had ceased to mourn: she has been "much longer afflicted by your mourning than by the death you both suffered of your most lovely child."[18]

All writing after the first anniversary of Valerio's death, Orsini (in a hasty aside),[19] Guarini, and Mascarello made note of Marcello's conspicuous grief. When Valerio died, wrote Guarini, not only his father but the whole of Venice mourned. But now mourning must cease. Soft, effeminate, un-philosophical and unchristian, it was not to be indulged in a man of Mar-cello's stature.[20] Struck by the intensity of Marcello's grief (for the author had heard he was still "languishing with sorrow on the death of [his] little son"),[21] Mascarello is determined to change his attitude by enumerating the hero's "triumphs": each one an argument for fortitude in adversity and the cessation of grief. Consciousness of these should persuade the noble-man whose welfare was so vital to the republic to act reasonably. To this contemporary, a soldier of Marcello's magnitude and an excessively grieving parent could not coexist in one person.

In the period July through October, 1463 (at a distance now of more than thirty months from the little boy's death) two anonymous authors and the soldier Fortebraccio echo earlier judgments about the Venetian's imponderable grief. Fortebraccio repeats the complaint earlier heard from Sagundino and Filelfo: rather than a protector, in his unattractive despair Marcello is a burden to his friends and family. "Free your friends of this burden who day and night sorrow with your sorrow."[22] A man of his mili-tary stature (well known to the *condottiere*-author) should fight off adver-sity, not submit to it. Reciting the litany of Marcello's accomplishments, Fortebraccio concludes by calling the man to himself, "so that you might see yourself in proportion to your amplitude, regain the semblance of your-self in so many deeds, and likewise exhibit prudence in your bitter mourn-ing for your child Valerio. . . . How does it profit you if by overcoming the enemy you seized such great glory by your energy and magnitude of soul and judgment, when at home you are vanquished by sorrow?"[23]

The Anonymous Venetian likewise appeals to Marcello's conception of civic role and responsibility. Fired by your love for your country, your friends, your family, he reminds the nobleman, you always placed public concerns before private ones, whether clad in senatorial toga or martial armor sustaining the republic with all your strength of mind and muscle; you held your fellow citizens in your embrace, and raised your children, "born not merely for you but through you for the *patria.*"[24] A man in Marcello's position could not be permitted to dissolve in personal sorrow, but must accommodate himself to the requirements of reason.

The Anonymous Student extolls Marcello's excellence in all of the four virtues defined by the Stoics (prudence, fortitude, justice, and temperance) and calls upon him to dismiss his sorrow. "Adorned with the grace of so many virtues, you must not fail to show in the face of the most bitter death of your son your usual strength of courage and constancy, but rather the intensity of your sorrow should be moderated." Marcello is old now, and from experience should be ready to withstand adversities of this sort with the courage that the examples of the great men of antiquity inspire. These bore with equanimity notice of the death of their sons. Like them, Marcello must acknowledge that the child he bore was mortal.[25]

The Student thereupon presents Pericles, Xenophon, and Lucius Aemilius Paullus from among the Greeks and Romans as models of such forbearance, followed by Job and Abraham, Stephen the Protomartyr and Jeptha, from Scripture. Other consolers of Marcello also produce a roster of classical and Christian exemplars of paternal and even maternal fortitude in the face of child death.[26] From the Greeks, in addition to Pericles and Xenophon, there are also Dion of Syracuse and Anaxagoras, Priam, the father of Hector, and the Lacedaemonian mother who cheerfully bore the death of the son she had raised to meet death for his country.[27] From the Romans, there are in addition to Paullus the clans of the Cornelii and Fabii, Marcus Cato and Quintus Fabius Maximus, and the elder Marcus Claudius Marcellus, presumed ancestor of the Venetian clan.

Other examples noted from Scripture were David who mourned for Absalon, Jesus who mourned for Lazarus, and the Virgin Mary who mourned for the Son who had been sacrificed by his Father. From Venice's own history were proferred as models the patricians Pasquale Malipiero, Francesco Foscari, and Niccolò Tron (all doges), as well as Francesco Barbaro, Leonardo Giustiniani, Carlo Marino, and Paolo Morosini.[28] While the classical and Christian exemplars of forbearance are all conventional devices of workers in the consolatory tradition, the Venetian models were new elements in the legend of heroic resistance to grief.

Neither the salutary example of this procession of heroic mourners, nor the hortatory arguments of his consolers, could soothe Marcello's grief. His despair, but even more his resistance to those who would counsel moderation in sorrow, is fully recorded in the capstone work of the Marcello corpus, Giorgio Bevilacqua's *Excusatio.* The object of this work is to defend Marcello against the charge of inapppropriate mourning: the bereaved will himself justify his own grief. The norms announced in the first of the consolations by Niccolò Sagundino, and echoed in all that followed, he will defy. He will not collect himself and be strong, as honor demands. He will not subordinate his own needs to those of country, friends, and family, as his social standing requires. He will not be "manly" when depth of feeling makes him "womanly."

ロ   ロ   ロ

In the panegyrics which lauded his military exploits, Marcello had permitted himself to be portrayed as *condottiere* and conqueror, defying the boundary lines of self-definition that encircled the noblemen of Venice. There he assumed a posture of greater authority than was real, and left unsaid what was not congruent with his preferred self-image. Now in the consolations for his lost child (written by others, but approved by the father) he issued a radically different self-portrait, but one equally far from that authorized by the norms of Venetian culture. He displayed himself in public as weeping, self-indulgent, effeminate, a rebel against tradition and obligation. The representation of a melancholic hero that emerges from Bevilacqua's *Excusatio* was the chosen mask of the patron who commissioned it.

The *Excusatio,* as has been seen, takes the form of a letter petitioning René d'Anjou to judge between himself and his consolers: between his grief and the rules of reason and propriety. After presenting all the consolations he has received to René, Marcello will present his own case. He had not written earlier, as he should have, to ask the Frenchman's aid: "For such sorrow afflicted me, I was paralyzed by such a flood of passion, that I was unable to do it, and always tormented by anguish and pain, it was never possible to suppress either grief or groans. I was never able to rouse you with a letter to the task of consoling me, although from you I could have hoped for healing remedies from the hurtful wound."[29]

In time, he was able to write in justification of his cancerous grief: "At last I have succeeded in writing you, and to demonstrate the causes of the sorrow by which I am oppressed." He has had all the consolatory works addressed to him copied and gathered in the volume which accompanies his letter, so that René may consider them. "And by this letter I appoint you arbiter and judge between me and my accusers."[30] You will tell me which course I must take, Marcello continues: whether I continue to "burn" with the "flames of sorrow," or whether, cold-hearted, I must put aside my grief as I have had to bury my child. "Alas! my noble son snatched from his father's breast, from his mother's embrace, and flung into the abyss of death, and I am permitted neither to weep nor to mourn."[31] Directed at first against those who would dare to remove from him the capacity to express grief, Marcello's anger turns to Death itself:

> O death impure and savage, . . . why did you wish to hurl this unleashed violence in the death of so sweet a child? O stealthy and execrable death, why did you want with your firebrand upraised, with incensed rage, to assail such a spirit, which presaged the development of so fine a man? O death entangled in viperous knot, with what wild fury, with what pestiferous poison did you consume so noble a son? How did it enter your mind to devote yourself to the undoing of such a boy, as if you would win a glorious prize for his entombment? . . . Why could you not preserve my child for me, so that you could declare the end of his days at some later time when he had reached a more mature age?[32]

Marcello's martial past expresses itself, it seems, in the drama of paternal grief. His posture is agonistic. The grieving father wrestles with death, he defies nature, he resists those who attempt to console him. They act badly! he argues. "These eloquent men who have set out to perform the friends' office of consoling me in so tragic, so heartbreaking a loss, if they had wished truly to heal and calm my misery and wretchedness, they would not have been such harsh, not such severe consolers, not such accusers of my sunken spirit, but they would have in the face of so horrible a tragedy acted more indulgently and leniently." How am I to respond to such learned men, wise, and eloquent men? If I answer them, as I must, without eloquence, I shall be thought boorish or stupid. Let them come and see for themselves the much more eloquent spectacle of me "in this perpetual mourning, in this protracted lethargy and constant sorrow, whose eyes are flooded with relentless tears."[33]

He had been a hero, opponent of Piccinino, comrade of Gattamelata, *provveditor* of Brescia, architect of the naval withdrawal from the Adige to the Lago di Garda; now all are astonished to see him reduced to weakness:

"all clamor that now I am weak, lax, humbled, defeated, overcome by sorrow, a thing incongruous in a man of my stature to be so struck with sorrow by the death of a child, to surrender his soul to fortune."[34] Born to the senatorial order, splendid in noble heritage, greatness of soul, military successes, to the amazement of all he has "succumbed to the death of one little child."[35]

If "all" are surprised to find Marcello react in this way to so commonplace an occurrence as the death of a child, so is the gentleman himself: "Never would I have thought that I would grieve so profoundly his death at so tender an age, that it would afflict me so painfully, so savagely."[36] Fortune has defeated him in his old age: "which if she once smiled on me and made me happy, proud with offspring, rich with glory, yet thereafter she brought calamity upon me, so that by the death of my one dearest son she has left me, at the last instant of my lifetime, destitute of all these goods."[37]

How can I not grieve?[38] Marcello hurls the question like a challenge to those who would assail him with consolations. They have not succeeded in their crusade, despite all their labors and efforts, despite their letters and their books.[39] "I say I have received no solace for my tears, no remedy to date for the sorrow and the pain I suffer because of the death of my sweetest son Valerio; and more easily could Orpheus move and sway the dead with his lyre, . . . much more could Cicero's words change Caesar's will, than I could be relieved of my despair by the excellent and incredible richness and abundance of the speech of those eloquent men. For I shall not deny my sorrow, even if orations wondrously encompass me with sweetness."[40] Their splendid words, their more than Ciceronian eloquence, still could not dry up the river of his tears.[41]

Why should tears be denied to fathers? These would-be consolers "dare condemn me, and say that I must suppress this duty that I owe to my much-beloved son. If other fathers of sons have wept at their funerals immoderately, . . . why should the flow of tears, which sorrow and grief press from the eyes, impelled by nature, for the preservation of the child's memory, be forbidden me?"[42] If any of them had lost a child whom he loved, he too would have wept.[43] My consolers have demanded an impossible thing, that I should view without feeling my dead son, whom I loved more than my own soul. "Is this what it is to be a father? Is this what it is to be human? Is this what it is to be pious? If these things are to be praised in another man, they must be allowed to a parent and father. . . . He who loves himself, must also love his son. If anyone grieves for himself, when touched by any misfortune, he must also grieve for his child."[44] "If you ripped out part of my soul, should I not grieve?" My son has died; should I become a stone? "Should I lack all sensation? Should there be no difference between me and a brute? Should they rather not accuse God, who did not give me an adamantine heart?"[45] "They are inhuman, they are impious, they are cruel, who insist that we view with dry eyes the burial of our sons!"[46] The burial accomplished, the tears continue to flow, Marcello marvels in Bevilacqua's account. Sorrow for the child gives way to the self-pity of a father for the loss he has suffered.

> I am choked by tears, and afflicted with anguish, when I realize that I have lost my son forever, that the spirit of such a child has to be ripped away from me. However much I reflect upon it, yet never do I come to the end of my reflection. Nor can I come to the end of lamenting that this great hope of my family has been forever snatched away, for which he would have shown himself in the future a praiseworthy man, and the equal or surpasser of the examples of his ancestors, whoever they might have been. I try valiantly to cast from me these troubles. The wonder is that these pangs, which in others normally diminish with time, in me increase, and the bitterness of despair constantly presses me; and that despair in this desolation accumulates rather than recedes.[47]

This condition of unrelenting despair was wrong, Marcello knew. Like the authors who wrote to console the bereaved father, Bevilacqua (writing in the father's name) offers examples of those who righteously withstood despair in mourning the death of loved ones. The names of those exemplars of fortitude are already familiar: Pericles and Xenophon, Aemilius Paullus and the senior Marcus Claudius Marcellus, David, Jesus, and Francesco Foscari. To these Bevilacqua adds other ancients who bore the Marcellus cognomen, all presumed ancestors of Jacopo Antonio Marcello: among them the junior Marcus Claudius Marcellus, defended before Caesar by Cicero, and the youthful Marcellus, son of Octavia, nephew of Augustus, mourned unforgettably by Vergil.[48] Yet the models of correct grieving are presented differently by Bevilacqua than they were by the other consolers. Their stoic strength is resisted or minimized, their grief is emphasized and indulged, the tragedy of life lost is highlighted.

The portrayal of the sufferings of Doge Francesco Foscari may serve as an example: he was the Venetian doge whose beloved son Jacopo was prosecuted and punished by the Council of Ten for crimes against the state.[49] As Francesco Filelfo describes that father's plight, Foscari never quailed even when he heard the screams of his son, under torture, in the next room at the ducal palace: "Nor did the Doge Francesco either change the expression of his face, nor utter so much as a word, at the unspeakably horrible calamity that befell his son."[50] In Bevilacqua's portrayal, Marcello admits that Foscari should be his model. Handsome and wise, great in war and peace, blessed by fortune, of the three sons born to him before he ascended to the *dogado,* two died of illness while still young. "The third, whom he raised to a greater age, and whom he lavished, as the one left to him, with delights and the ornaments of pleasure, he saw when grown tortured by the most horrible torments, and his body mutilated by cruel punishments, and heard his voice thinned to voicelessness, weakened by the exhaustion of his body." Yet that "robust" father never submitted to fortune, but maintained his strength and dignity. Weakened, nevertheless, by illness and old age, he was removed from the supreme office he held. That final blow he could not withstand, and he yielded to despair: "He could not forebear so great a calamity, he could not but deplore his fate, he could not but bemoan the wretchedness of his condition, in great torment of soul."[51]

Bevilacqua offers here and elsewhere, as Marcello's self-justification, examples of the strong who were touched in the end by irresistible pain. Further, he presents laudatory examples of those who grieved. Cicero lapsed into despair at the loss of his daughter, Marcus Cato at that of his brother.[52] Adam grieved for Abel, Abraham for Sarah, Jacob for Joseph (whom he thought killed). Rachel grieved for her children, as did the mothers of the innocents, victims of Herod, for theirs; and Mary, the mother of Jesus, "shed for a long time most bitter tears."[53]

No scriptural patriarch or matron exceeded Augustine in the passion of grief. Veteran of the loss of the friend of his youth and his own son Adeodatus, that saint's profound mourning for his mother Monica occupies many pages and a critical moment in the record of his *Confessions*—and many folios of Bevilacqua's *Excusatio.*[54] "If it was not possible for Augustine," Marcello concludes the narration of that event, "to contain his tears at the death of his mother; if sorrow and distress so confounded him at the death of the one who had given him birth that this holy man spent himself in anguish and tears, why do these learned consolers wag their fingers at me . . . because a flood of tears overcomes me and reduces me to faintness and trembling?"[55]

The description of the despair Bevilacqua approves for Marcello through the manipulation of classical and Christian exempla of forbearance and surrender reaches a climax in a discussion of suicide.[56] Death would be better than life without my child, Marcello argues. "If in the end I must live a meaningless life without Valerio my son, I would rather exchange life for death, and go to that place where either I could see him, or if the sight of him were denied me, at least I would rejoice in not being here, where I have suffered such bitterness."[57] His consolers are wrong when they accuse him of indulging in grief: he would rather be freed from grief by death. "Let not those eloquent consolers hurl this wicked charge against me," Marcello responds in Bevilacqua's words, "by which they increase my sorrows with a more painful torment, that I would prefer eternal grief and ceaseless tears to death, by which I could cast off these woes and daily ills. For if I died, I would be freed from the cruel burden of this despair."[58]

Among our ancestors were many who assuaged their pain by choosing death; and not only men, for Lucretia died a suicide to preserve her honor. But in Cato of Utica, Marcello finds the peerless exemplar of the suicide, just as he had seen in Augustine an irreproachable model for limitless grief.[59] Several laudatory pages relate the story of Cato's death, which followed that hero's thoughtful rereading of Plato's *Phaedo,* and report the admiration of the ancients for that stoical hero. In the end, Marcello prudently distances himself from the remedy of suicide, freeing himself from any imputation of disobedience to the will of God. Cato's suicide demonstrated his courage rather than his wisdom, declares the Venetian: "For all those who kill themselves, who cannot endure their own harsh or evil destinies, are greatly to be condemned, and not forgiven." It behooves human beings to show moderation in the face of adversity.[60] He himself had never considered suicide, Marcello assures his readers: "For my own part I can state that never have I been so imprudent, or I should say so crazed, as to consider putting an end to my life. For I have always thought it was the manner of beasts to hate this life, and to love death. . . . Truly I have never praised death, I have never asked whether I had already lived enough, nor have I ever forgotten for what purpose I was born."[61] Let them (his consolers?) not reproach him if he chooses to live, and suffer: he has pledged himself "not only to respect the will of God, unbidden by whom we are not to exit this life, but also to follow nature, which teaches by the example of wild beasts what it is we should do."[62]

The entire section of Bevilacqua's *Excusatio* discussing Marcello's repudiation of the attractive option of suicide is excised from the version of the work copied, under Marcello's direction, in the manuscript now in Glasgow.[63] Bevilacqua was careful to balance his presentation of Marcello's fascination for suicide with his clear rejection of it, accompanied by protests of obedience to divine and natural law. But his sleight of hand was evidently too subtle for Marcello's taste. The Venetian apparently wished to avoid even the slightest opportunity for others to suspect him of suicidal inclinations and the taint of mortal sin. At the same time, he did not hesitate to reveal publicly the extent of his despair. In the original version of the *Excusatio,* musings that include the remedy of suicide as a possibility only deepen the impression of irremediable grief.

☙   ☙   ☙

Marcello's behavior, indeed, as evident in his actions and presented in the *Excusatio,* displays a pattern of grief so profound that it may reach what present-day psychologists would consider abnormal.[64] Grieving for these experts has an expected course. The intensity of sorrow ebbs and its duration has limits: a week, a month, a year. The mourner normally first experiences an initial phase of numbness (lasting from a few hours to a week) punctuated by outbursts of anger. That brief phase yields to a prolonged one of yearning or searching for the lost person, interrupted again by periods of intense distress or anger (often against the clergy, doctors, or officials who offer counsel). Yearning gives way to despair, and despair eventually matures to detachment as the bereaved adjusts to the absence of the beloved. To achieve that liberation from despair, the bereaved must engage earnestly in "grief work." If his efforts are halfhearted or incomplete, he remains suspended in time, a captive of loss. If pain does not abate, and if the bereaved does not cease his attempt to recover the person who is lost, he becomes "locked in the service of a hopeless cause."[65] He is "fighting fate, trying desperately to turn back the wheel of time. . . . locked in a struggle with the past."[66] Such grief is "pathological": it is viewed not as an impropriety, that is, a cause for shame, but a disease.

Excessive grief in a twentieth-century man would concern his family, his employer, and his physician. In the fifteenth century, it concerned his friends who feared to be dishonored by his immoderate expression of sorrow. They themselves had struggled with loss and overcome despair. Several of Marcello's consolers had recently encountered death in their own families. Sagundino saw his wife and three children swept overboard in a shipwreck in 1460 (and was consoled by Perleone, a Marcello familiar). Isotta Nogarola had lost her mother in 1461, and Battista Guarini his father at the end of 1460. Francesco Filelfo had buried his son Olimpio just two months after Marcello buried his Valerio. Fortebraccio described the loss years earlier, when he was still a child, of his notorious father Braccio da Montone.[67] All of these, while admitting to great pain at the death of loved ones, still had grieved and passed on to the continuation of their own lives. Marcello did not. Though he had been active in either literary or military or political affairs from 1438 through 1460, Marcello disappears from late

Column capital by an anonymous fifteenth-century sculptor, showing parental reactions to the death of a child. Venice, piazzetta *facade of the doge's palace.*

1460 through mid-1462: he fights no wars, sends no books, walks no corridor of power. In the space of this conspicuous silence Valerio dies and Marcello mourns: these seventeen months mark the span of Marcello's uncontrolled sorrow. Long after the child's death, the Venetian was still clad in black and wore his beard still uncut.[68] With Petrarch, writing a century earlier, he might have lamented "that I so feed upon my tears and sufferings with a morbid attraction that I can only be rescued from it by main force and in despite of myself."[69] Not only to his consolers, but to most observers in the social universe of Renaissance Europe, Marcello would have presented a peculiar spectacle: a father incapacitated by grief for his son. Even in the twentieth century (though grief for the death of a grown child is known to be sorrow most distressing and enduring), fathers are thought to be less affected than mothers by the death of a child. In pre-modern Europe, the great majority of the parents who grieved were mothers.[70] The greater involvement of the mother is silently witnessed by the compact sculptural program on one capital of the loggia of the Doge's Palace in Marcello's city, along the Piazzetta. Here an anonymous fifteenth-century artist displays the course of human life: a courting couple, a couple in bed, a new infant, the child's death, the mother's anguished tears, the father's prayerful forbearance.[71] The Stoic Seneca expressed the conventional view of the mother's greater vulnerability to sorrow in the consolation he addressed to the widow Marcia after three years of desolation over the loss of her son Metilius: "though they suffer the same bereavement, women are wounded more deeply than men, savage peoples more deeply than the peaceful and civilized, the uneducated, than the educated."[72] Mary wept for the child she had borne and buried; the *pater dolorosus* was anomalous. If that was the case, it stemmed surely from the exclusion of the father from the child's social world in his earliest years.

Mothers' vulnerability to grief was perhaps proportional to their involvement with child life. Early nurturance, and the emotional investments it required, was largely left to mothers.[73] That nurturance began with the biological function of breastfeeding, which only mothers were equipped to perform. They shaped the moral character of their infants, it was thought, through the magic substance of their milk, and through their admonitions. The Venetian Francesco Barbaro's treatise *De re uxoria* (On marriage), written at about the time of Marcello's own first wedding to Fiordelise di Pietro Miani, emphasizes the mother's contribution to the noble male child. Her nobility ensures his. The best fruit produces the best seed: "For all men agree, that they may expect from excellent wives even more excellent offspring."[74] A mother transmits her character to the fetus by her blood in the womb, and after birth, to the infant at her breast by her milk. "It is very important that an infant should be nourished by the same mother in whose womb and by whose blood he was conceived. . . . The power of the mother's food most effectively lends itself to shaping the properties of body and mind to the character of the seed."[75]

After the phase of infancy passed, mothers were still considered responsible for the child's early education to the age of seven. The mother's primary responsibility for care of children from conception through the early years of life was highlighted by the contemporary physician and antiquarian, Michele Savonarola. His treatise on gynecology and pediatrics, the first in the modern west, was directed especially to women and was for their sake (since they had no access to Latin, the language of scholarship and science) written in the vernacular: *Il trattato ginecologico-pediatrico in volgare: Ad mulieres ferrarienses de regimine pregnantium et noviter natorum usque ad septennium* (To the women of Ferrara on the management of pregnancy and the newborn up to age seven).[76] Only after that threshhold of seven years was passed was it expected that fathers should participate in the education of their sons; for daughters remained the province of the mother. The humanist Leon Battista Alberti (in his *Della famiglia* [On the family]) makes a clear distinction between maternal and paternal roles in an elite family of the Italian Renaissance. The father should not "concern himself at all" with those things "which are women's domain and properly fall to the nurse and the mother."[77] The "whole tender age" of early childhood "is more properly assigned to women's quiet care than to the active attention of men," lest the baby suffer "in his father's hard hands." "So let that earliest period be spent entirely outside the father's arms. Let the child rest, let him sleep in his mother's lap."[78] The mother loved, and the mother wept.

It was the father's role to prepare the child to fulfill the responsibilities of class and rank. As the bearer of patrilineal authority, honor and wealth, more striking than his love was his power.[79] The father's posture was likened not only to the ruler of the state, but even to the ruler of the universe: God the father.[80] Fathers demanded obedience from their sons and anxiously guarded the patrimony for transmission to legal heirs in the male line. They supervised the education of boys for their greater honor and success in what Alberti likened to a race. Fathers must draw the young to virtue, he advised, "and make them every day more learned and more charming, more loved and more valued . . . keep them to the study of the best things and those of highest esteem . . . fill them with good counsel and lessons."[81] Fathers even took a hand in infant nurture by supervising the nursing and wetnursing of their infants.[82] Primarily concerned for the continuation of their biological lineage and social standing, fathers were sometimes emotionally detached from children not yet old enough for paternal instruction.

Parents in general in the pre-modern era, it has been suggested, may have forged ties with their children more tentative, more cautious, even more shallow than they do in the modern world.[83] The children they conceived often knew difficult births, often died in infancy, often lived apart from one or both parents; the parents in turn often fell prey to death in childbirth or war, often sent their newborns away to wetnurses and their adolescents away to employers or mentors or schools. In all, it was a common experience for a child to be raised by someone other than his own mother or father. And it was a common experience for a parent to have lost several children to death. Child mortality was carried inexorably by epidemic disease, chronic malnutrition, and unrelieved filth. Infants, children, and adolescents succumbed to the plague at a higher rate than adults; and to diarrhea, flu, catarrh, tuberculosis, starvation. The banality of child death was everywhere evident in the Renaissance epoch, when only 1/4 to 1/3 of western Europeans survived childhood, and children formed a frightening proportion each year of those who died.[84] A father of Marcello's stature could be expected to concern himself with his own reputation, the honor of his family, and the survival of his lineage—not the death of one individual child.

Yet the grieving father was not unknown. Melancholic but stoic, Francis Petrarch expressed shock at the case of Paolo Annibaldeschi: that doting father had died of grief upon viewing the mutilated body of his son, killed in battle.[85] The more moderate grief of his friend Donato Albanzani (for the death of his son Solone) Petrarch soothed in a masterly letter also meant to comfort himself on the loss of his own grandson Franceschino, "little Francis."[86] "My love for that child so filled my breast," wrote the poet and humanist, "that I cannot think that I ever loved anything else on earth so much."[87] Overwhelmed with guilt for his neglect of a son who died, the Florentine merchant Giovanni Morelli engaged in elaborate rituals of penitence or restitution, payments of the love unexpressed during life.[88] In a letter to his confidant, the merchant Francesco Datini, the notary Lapo Mazzei spoke of his love for two young children he had lost to the plague. "It is now the third day since I saw two of my sons die . . . , in my arms, in a few hours. God knows how much hope I nurtured for the elder, who was already a companion to me, and with me, the father of the others."[89]

With similar sentiment, although in the stiffer prose of a Latin epistle, the humanist Gasparino Barzizza poured forth to Valerio Marcello (Jacopo Antonio's elder brother) his sorrow at the loss of "several" sons in the space of a few days: one of these the beloved Niccolò, from whom after an investment of effort and energy he had expected much fruit, and had just begun to glimpse signs of wisdom and honor.[90] A humanist who handed out sober advice to others about self-control in the face of adversity, Barzizza himself succumbed in the case of a personal tragedy. Perleone rebuked his friend Niccolò Sagundino for irrational grief at the loss of his wife, a daughter, and two sons to a storm in the Venetian harbor: why mourn for these small children, who had scarcely declared their existence or promise, when some months earlier the father had borne with fortitude the death of an older son, full of promise? "Why . . . are you now struck with grief for the death of one woman, of the weaker sex and already old, and one girl and two little boys?"[91]

Such pain reached even those in highest places: the portrait of Venetian doge Niccolò Tron, emblazoned on the silver coin named after him the "Trono," displays the beard that he left untrimmed as a sign of continued mourning for his adult son Giovanni, killed two years before his own death at the disastrous battle of Negropont.[92] In the sixteenth century, Benvenuto Cellini was devastated by the loss of his son, as was the Jewish scholar Leon Modena in the seventeenth.[93] The latter's child was seized from his arms, a prize of the Inquisition, lost not only to his parents but to the heritage of thousands of years. Later, the unlimited grief he experienced consequent upon the death of his sons impelled Modena to write his autobiography, one of the first of the modern world. Already in certain circles—rarified circles, perhaps—as early as the Trecento in Italy, certain children and certain symbols of childhood profoundly affected some fathers.[94]

North of the Alps there can be found disconsolate fathers as well. Grief hounded Martin Luther upon the death of his children, and the patrician Paumgartners forever mourned the loss of their one son.[95] The contemporary Englishman William Brownlow, seven of whose children would die in the course of eight years, described his condition: "I was at ease but Thou O God hast broken me asunder and shaken me to pieces."[96] Soon Ben Jonson would write "On My First Sonne," lent to the grieving father for only seven years: "Rest in soft peace, and, ask'd, say here doth lye / *Ben. Jonson* his best piece of *poetrie.*"[97] In these later centuries, at least, and at least among an elite, an interest is taken in the child as important to adults, and in childhood as a special phase of life.[98] The essayist Michel de Montaigne remarked that next to the love each creature has for himself, "the affection that the begetter has for his begotten ranks second."[99]

Other traces survive of the affection fathers felt towards sons still living. Tones of deep paternal involvement in the lives of children are heard in some of the diaries and *ricordanze* (books of paternal advice to heirs) that abounded in the Renaissance, especially in Florence. Prominent in these is the theme of the father-son bond as the root of familial and social life. *Ricordanza* authors Giovanni Rucellai, Donato Veluti, Cappone Capponi, and Giovanni Morelli all dwelled on this theme.[100] It was articulated also by none less than Marsilio Ficino, founder of modern Platonism, and the historians Francesco Guicciardini and Niccolò Machiavelli. Ficino instructed his brothers that a father loves his children more than he loves himself, and that paternal love "is the greatest love that can be imagined between all mortal creatures here below."[101] Guicciardini learned his first lessons from his father, whom he loved "more dearly than men usually love their fathers," while Machiavelli, that ruthless realist, wrote from abroad comforting letters to his children.[102]

Among the humanists, the father-son relation is the central theme of two major works of an author whose own secure place in the domestic unit was shaken by both illegitimacy and exile: Leon Battista Alberti. His formal *De iciarchia* (On the householder) exalts the authority of the father, while the more widely known *Della famiglia* features elder males pleading and persuading younger ones to assume actively the responsibilities of domesticity.[103] The German humanist canon Albrecht von Eyb ascribed special importance to the relation between father and son: "A father holds his son more dear than his own life and suffers more in his son than in himself. He sees himself and his son as one person and one flesh. For a son is part of his father's body, and after his death the father lives on in the person of his son."[104] Von Eyb's vision is a conspicuous reversal of the more common understanding of the relation of mother and child: the son is seen as bodily related not to mother, but father.

The moral responsibilities of fathers to sons and sons to fathers are outlined in the classics of Renaissance pedagogy (principally those of Pier Paolo Vergerio and Maffeo Vegio) and in the ancient works which informed them, particularly those of Plutarch and Quintilian.[105] In Venice (where the *ricordanza* tradition is notably absent), letters of humanist fathers and uncles attest to paternal involvement in the careers of sons and nephews.[106] Such father-son or uncle-nephew pairs as Leonardo and Bernardo Giustiniani, Francesco and Zaccaria or Ermolao Barbaro (the Elder), and Candiano and Domenico Bollani give striking evidence of tenderness or intimacy, especially where there is a common interest in studies. Some generations later, the noble mathematician and humanist Francesco Barozzi expresses a yearning for a deep relationship with his nephew based on such commonalty of interests, his own "carnal sons" having failed him in this respect.[107] It had been his wish, he explains, to have raised his own son, who having been "nobly born, and from a wise and diligent father, and taught by learned teachers" would have become "a man perfected in virtue." Not only were his two sons differently inclined, so that they turned out to be not only "the contary of what I had wished," but "the foremost enemies and most cruel subverters of the life of me, their wretched and unhappy father."[108] Barozzi has now focused all his hope on his adoptive son, born of his brother, deeply engaged in studies at Padua.

The cases of paternal love for sons best known to us in the Italian Renaissance are those of four humanists: Giovanni Conversini da Ravenna, student and heir to Petrarch's early humanism; Coluccio Salutati, the first humanist chancellor of Florence; Gianozzo Manetti, Florentine scholar and diplomat; and Francesco Filelfo, client to Sforza and, in this instance, to Marcello.[109] When Conversini's deep grief for the loss of son Israele did not go away, he sought resolution in composing a dialogue between "The Mourner" and "The Consoler." Coluccio Salutati, who proudly asserted that he bestowed a last blessing on his dying son Pietro without a tear, and followed him to the grave without a sigh, succumbed soon after his death (on 31 May 1400) and that of a second son (two months later) to deep grief, despite earnest reflection on the consolatory principles of the philosophers.[110] Francesco Filelfo's still-fresh grief for the recent loss of his son

Olimpio is expressed in his consolation to the Venetian Marcello. Gianozzo Manetti, best known for his defense of the "dignity of man" in response to Pope Innocent III's treatise on human misery, asserted in his self-consolation that paternal love is a component of humanity itself.[111] Rejecting the ideal of the denial of human emotionality, Manetti may be an early witness to the modern "apotheosis" of the child.[112] As the father loved his child, that young creature also conferred benefits upon the father. Manetti's willingness to acknowledge dependency and grief, as one scholar has commented, "denotes a radical transformation of the place of emotions in the family."[113]

The abundant grief of these humanist fathers tells us little, in itself, about the general condition of paternal involvement in the lives of their children, or of parental feeling for those who died young. It may bespeak only the particular sensitivity of men of letters to their human relationships. These were men who had in the first place valued ideas over money or power, and were perhaps more open than others to the experience of parental love. They were uniquely equipped, moreover, with the linguistic skills to describe their feelings and publicize their grief. Yet the depth of their feeling does seem to point to a deepening of concern for the children of some families, measured by the depth of their mourning.

In time, mourning for a child became more understandable, and even acceptable, for large numbers not of the exceptional, but of the ordinary, class of parents.[114] Portraits of dead children, increasingly common, bespeak the need felt by parents to remember the originals. Grieving parents testified to the "resurrection" of their unbaptized infants buried in unhallowed ground so that these could be baptized and reburied within the precincts of the holy. Formal tombs for children (such as Marcello must have had erected for Valerio) were rare before the fifteenth century, but became more frequent thereafter. In early modern England, grieving parents often planned elaborate funerals for children. From the seventeenth century, bereavement particularly for young children is mentioned as the cause of deep melancholia. By the nineteenth century, the graves of little ones filled the cemeteries, and their deaths were most often recalled in objects gathered or created *in memoriam*. The deaths of those who had lived too few years became, in the modern west, "the first deaths that could not be tolerated."[115]

∽   ∽   ∽

Though parents grieved, others were slow to accommodate their despair. Young children had lived so few years, and left so slight a mark, friends and strangers were impatient with the persistent melancholy of the bereaved parent. If such frustration with the bereaved continued even into fairly recent years, it is no wonder that the humanist coterie surrounding Jacopo Antonio Marcello, trained in resignation both Stoic and Christian, clamorously urged him to move on. Dismayed by the intensity of his grief which continued, unabated, as month followed month, their consolatory letters gave way to consolatory dialogues and treatises and first-person apologies. Occasionally, they ask why: why did Marcello's grief so exceed the bounds of convention? The modern reader might well ask the same question. In attempting to answer, the questioner will become enmeshed in "what is perhaps the most difficult of all branches of history—the history of emotion."[116]

Was it because the child was unusually beautiful, or skilled, or precocious?[117] "Never will I cease to wonder," wrote Battista Guarini, "that at so early an age [Valerio] radiated his father's greatness of soul."[118] For Perleone, Valerio had qualities "beyond the standard of his age, and beyond the character and nature of other infants." It must be admitted "that either something great and excellent resided in that infant, or that a divine power rather than a human one was expressed in him, for not without the great grace of God do such great signs appear in human things, exceeding their nature."[119] Valerio was an "extraordinary" child, observed the Anonymous Venetian, who cast glory on his father; God wished, it appears, to place the finest of children in the Marcello family.[120]

Could the prematurity of Valerio's death explain Marcello's excessive mourning? Often young persons of truly luminous qualities do not reach an advanced age, observed George of Trebizond: "For if anyone will diligently consider the history of the Greeks and the Romans (I will not mention other peoples) he will discover very few who, if they are great of soul and show wondrous signs of the hope of achieving great things, fully reach the age of manhood."[121] Of the same sort was your Valerio, George explains to Marcello. "For your Valerio . . . , in whom it was clearly seen that the seed of all the virtues was to find a place, before he had reached nine years of age was ripped from your hands, was snatched from the embrace of his dear mother, was removed from the sight of all his friends, and brought sorrow to all those who either love you, or should. . . . For as we are accustomed commonly to perceive in boys the image of a future virtue, in him there shone very certain signs of singular virtues of mind or, more precisely, of a certain wondrous intelligence."[122]

Was it because Valerio resembled Marcello so nearly, as the Anonymous Student speculates? It is no wonder that you grieve for this child, writes that author, "since nature so formed him as to be in every way in your likeness, and the exact image of Jacopo Antonio Marcello, as many said."[123] Fortebraccio added, observing Valerio's fine proportions of body, grace of posture, and quickness of intelligence, that he was "just like you."[124] Did Marcello mourn for himself in mourning for Valerio, for the fate that he was born for? Bevilacqua, speaking as Marcello, points to the unfair *violence* of the death (in a passage cited earlier), its frenzied and unleashed fury.

This last complaint may have been a profound and especially severe one. In the consolatory letter that was never included in the Glasgow collection, Perleone alludes to this theme in the earliest days of the father's mourning. Marcello grieved not so much because he had lost a child, Perleone surmises, "but that you lost him to a premature and sudden death."[125] The humanist destroys that argument: no death is premature, since each being achieves its end in its own time and at God's being. How can a death be considered violent or sudden if it is propelled by a natural force—such as sickness—and is a mere fulfillment of a predestined plan? But Marcello protests still that Valerio was snatched from life: "But you say, 'My Valerio went unwilling to his death.'"[126]

Although the father has made his feelings clear, Perleone is not satisfied with the hypothesis that a "violent" death provoked undue grief. Several months later, in his *Laudatio,* Perleone still seeks an explanation for Marcello's unbounded despair. Marcello had known so much death among those closest to him. Could it be that in Valerio's death there accumulated all of Marcello's unexpressed sorrow? That in that one death were gathered all their deaths? All of these earlier deaths he had borne with wisdom and moderation:

> For you lost your splendid father Francesco, gifted with the magnitude of a rare soul, liberality, counsel, authority, military skill, and learning, whom you loved no less than your children—indeed, who was always dearer than life to you. . . . You bore modestly and moderately the death of your mother Magdalucia, whose reputation is known to all, an excellent and rare example for her time of chastity and domestic administration. . . . You stood at the deathbed of your brother Pietro, bishop of Padua, a man luminous with honor, authority, virtue, counsel, morals, and deep learning, and to you truly in benevolence and charity a second parent. . . . What of Girolamo, a man of rare excellence; what of Valerio resplendent with excellent mind, prudence, and the studies of the good arts; what of your brothers Lorenzo and Giovanni, men I consider worthy of every

praise on account of their many and great virtues, with what strength of soul did you withstand their deaths? What of the deaths of your sisters Maria, Bianca, Chiara, Taddea, Margarita, Agnes? What shall I say now concerning the death of your dearest daughter Taddea, a woman truly chaste, and married to an excellent husband most fertile with offspring, who unless I am mistaken now five months ago was taken away by bitter death? The death and tragic loss of all of these of your family, then, you bore with a greatness of soul and restraint of speech that was surely admired by all. In the death of all your other children, moreover, whom you considered most close and dear, all who attended you at these tragic moments are witnesses of the fortitude and wisdom you displayed.[127]

As this recitation of the deaths experienced in Marcello's immediate family amply demonstrates, Marcello had many siblings and many children, of whom many predeceased him. A Venetian noble clan is a vast octopus, and Marcello's is no exception. The constellation of that family is pertinent here: Marcello's special grief for Valerio is all the more striking when one considers the vastness of the family circle at the center of which he resided.

Marcello's great-grandfather and grandfather had been men of wealth and power: Girolamo (called "Gazano") of San Vitale and Pietro "il Grande."[128] Their military ventures have been noted in the previous chapter. In addition, they served at the highest levels in the government of the Signoria, including in the role of ducal elector. Girolamo played a role in the deliberations that accomplished the suppression of the conspiracy against Marino Falier in 1355. In the great fund drive of 1379–80 when, in its greatest extremity, Venice prosecuted the Chioggian war, Girolamo was a contributor (along with several other Marcello patriarchs, including four co-residents of the parish of San Vitale). Pietro shone in several embassies, including the most important and also final one of 1368, when he and a colleague were charged to recover in Egypt the persons and property of some Venetian merchants—a delicate and dangerous mission. Murdered on the return journey, he was magnificently buried on the Venetian subject island of Crete.[129]

Pietro had at least two brothers (Marco and Bernardo, who also pursued active political and naval careers), and three sons. One of those sons, Francesco, was the father of Jacopo Antonio. In 1383, Francesco married Magdalucia, daughter of Paolo (son of Giovanni) Trevisan, of a family ennobled only recently as a result of their contributions to the Chioggian struggle.

Magdalucia's extraordinary fertility ensured that Jacopo Antonio was raised in a large and busy household. She gave birth to twenty-six children, thirteen of whom survived childhood (six males, seven females). Some of these might have been older than Jacopo Antonio, but some were certainly younger. Magdalucia could have borne no more than fifteen children prior to our subject's own birth. In the next nineteen years, she gave birth to at least eleven more.

Both the mother and father of this mammoth brood were alive in 1417 (3 December), when they presented Jacopo Antonio for ascription to the Balla d'Oro before the Avogaria di Comun in Venice. At his entrance to adulthood, Marcello still knew both parents, including a father who had lived to an advanced age. But Marcello's father predeceased his much-elder brother Pietro (whose own death occurred in 1428), who performed a key role in the young man's rearing. In addition, according to Perleone (in the passage quoted above), six sisters and five brothers predeceased Jacopo Antonio. Jacopo Antonio Marcello was raised in a family replete with children (of whom he was neither the youngest nor eldest) marked by frequent death, frequent new births, frequent marriages, many transitions.

Although his own wives were not so prolific as his formidable mother, they were scarcely infertile: the household he would himself head had contours similar to the parental household in which he was reared. Jacopo Antonio Marcello married twice, as has been seen, and had children by both marriages. The first marriage, in 1418, was to Fiordelise di Pietro Miani, whose father was a colleague and friend to Jacopo Antonio's brother Pietro. Jacopo Antonio was a mere twenty years old at the time of this marriage, and his son Francesco, born before 1425, knew a father not distant in age or interests from himself. In addition to his son Francesco (and any other children who might have predeceased his wife), two daughters, Taddea and Serena, were born to Marcello and Fiordelise by the same terminal date. A year later their mother died, perhaps pregnant with a fourth. The known children of Jacopo Antonio by Fiordelise Miani, Serena, Taddea, and Francesco, died respectively in 1490, 1494, and between 1473 and 1494.

Jacopo Antonio Marcello married a second time in 1443. It was a double wedding: father and son simultaneously married two sisters, both daughters of Bartolomeo da Leone of the noble Paduan family introduced in the previous chapter.[130] Jacopo Antonio's wife Luca would bear at least ten children in the twenty years between her wedding and her husband's death. Francesco married Anna, who would bear at least three. Francesco's children were raised in the same household with Jacopo Antonio's own children, some of whom were a full generation younger than his eldest child. Contemporaries raised together, the children of Jacopo Antonio and Francesco included aunts and uncles, nieces and nephews, to a total of at least thirteen.

The children of Jacopo Antonio by Luca da Leone were eleven (possibly ten): the males were Pietro (born 1447), the exact contemporary of his nephew Girolamo (Francesco's son); Valerio, the subject of the Marcello consolations (born 1452); Lorenzo (born 1456), the youngest son alive at Valerio's death in 1461; Valerio, named to take the place of his elder and predeceased brother (born 1463); Marco (birthdate unknown); Bernardino (birthdate unknown, and possibly conflated with Francesco's son Bernardo, Jacopo Antonio's grandson); the females, Maddaluza, Bianca, Agnesina, Pasqua, and a second Taddea, who died in 1461, namesake of her still-thriving half-sister, the daughter of Fiordelise. Luke, the mother of these named, had amply performed her duty to give birth to noble citizens of Venice.

The children of Francesco di Jacopo Antonio Marcello and Anna di Bartolomeo da Leone were at least three: Girolamo (born 1447); Bernardo or Bernardino (born 1451); and Andrea (born 1455). If to Jacopo Antonio's eleven (or ten) or more children by Luca are added (at least) three children by Fiordelise and (at least) three children of Francesco, over the forty-five years from 1418 to 1463, the Marcello household included some seventeen children, of whom the eldest was some forty years older than the youngest. Of these two are known to have died. The mixed household is characteristic for this period, and the record of child deaths, if anything, small—possibly concealing the deaths of infants whose names do not even enter the record. This abundance and variety of child life surely makes the patriarch's attachment to the one Valerio the more conspicuous.

This reconstruction of Jacopo Antonio's immediate family shows him with perhaps five surviving sons after the death of the first Valerio in 1461 and before the birth of the second in 1463: Francesco (by Fiordelise) and (by Luca) Pietro, Lorenzo, Marco, and (possibly) Bernardino. The figure five is consistent with the account of the Anonymous Tutor, which has Valerio remind his father from heaven to tend to those other claimants for his love: "May my surviving brothers and nephews receive in their embraces your lengthening years; and if you are a Christian, a lover of God, no less joyfully should you as father celebrate that one angel has prepared for you a way to heaven than that you have left those other five as leading citizens to the republic."[131]

Otherwise, no numbers are named, but the survival of "several" children is amply witnessed. Perleone reminds his patron of his "many and excellent children," while Guarini urges him to seek consolation in the sight of his other remaining sons.[132] Sagundino chides Marcello about his responsibility to those others for whom he should be consoler and not consoled: friends and clients, wife and children, "who depend on you, who form and mold themselves to your mood and will."[133] Marcello should recall his duty to his republic, his friends, and his children, echoes the Anonymous Venetian, "born not merely for you but, together with you, for the *patria,* whom you reared to manly character and to the ancient virtue of the Marcello family, whom you have always held to be dear above all other goods of fortune."[134] In his consolatory oration, mentioning the presence of other children, Tifernate summons Marcello to turn his hopes to the already mature Francesco, "who in modesty and prudence aspires to equal his father's dignity."[135] Filelfo asks why Marcello should so grieve for one child, when he has several, and one in particular—the same Francesco—whom he should cherish:

> How can you consider yourself badly off in the goods of soul and body and fortune, when from so many children God recalled to himself only one of your sons? How can God be unjust if from so many children whom he lent us for a time, he has demanded one for himself? You have many daughters and sons, big and small, of excellent mind and character, by whom you can not only be consoled, but also truly delight your soul. Passing by others, how much solace, how much joy and pleasure should your Francesco be to you, a man of such mind, fine character, and probity? Do you not already possess all that you might desire for the height of felicity when you turn your mind and eyes to that one Francesco? Does he not resemble you in all regards? Will the memory of a child torment you more than the presence and sight of an adult son delight you? It is my hope that what you once hoped for in Valerio, you should now look for in Francesco."[136]

It was not for this man, however, but for his brother Valerio that Jacopo Antonio cherished hopes of a brilliant career in the eight years of his earthly existence. Younger than his eldest brother Francesco by some thirty years, Valerio held no special place among Marcello's children. He was not the last-born of Marcello's brood, as the Anonymous Student claimed: "The youngest and noblest of all your other children."[137] Nor was Valerio's death the only one Marcello experienced; it was not even the most recent. According to George of Trebizond, the death of Marcello's daughter Taddea followed Valerio's by three months.[138] Perleone notes its fresh occurrence in the passage quoted above.

Yet her recent loss could not compare in her father's mind with Valerio's more distant demise, which alone rendered their father distracted and ineffective. Not the youngest, nor the eldest, not the sole child, not the only one to die, Valerio's power to provoke in death that patriarch's violent grief remains a puzzle. The consolers of Jacopo Antonio Marcello, frustrated by their patron's immodest grief and imminent dishonor, however inadequate their answers, asked the right question. Why was Valerio's death particularly mourned? Valerio's death uniquely, of a vast family, penetrated the stoic armor that protected the nobleman from too great an intrusion of the passions. The explanation lies not with the child's death but with his life: with the nature of the special relationship forged between father and son. The profundity of that bond determined the profundity of the father's grief.

෨ ෨ ෨

Amid the cacophonous Marcello household, filled with children of at least three sets of parents and a full spectrum of ages, as well as family friends, clients, and servants, father and son formed an exclusive dyad. Or so it appeared to the authors who wrote to console Marcello on his loss. Their depictions of the household, like their depictions of the father-son pair, or of the heroic father himself, or of his city, surely met with the approval of the patron and collector of their works. While no objective documentary evidence exists to tell us of the relationship of Marcello to Valerio, at least the literary evidence before us reflects what the father believed and wished to have believed about his life with his child. What emerges is the spectacle of an aging father a full two "generations" older than the son with whom in early infancy he forms a deep bond that preempts other relationships, whether with contemporaries or other children.[139] As other persons are excluded from the closed society of father and son, Marcello takes on the roles of the would-be intruders. Unusual in an age of stern or distant or moralistic fathers, Marcello himself becomes mother, teacher, and child of his child.[140]

The drama which epitomizes the father-son relationship is described by seven of sixteen consolers, who more or less share the same script.[141] The moment is the summer of 1452, when Marcello returns from the field to greet for the first time his three-month-old son. The scene that occurred is striking: the father fully equipped with the apparatus of the world gazes upon an infant wrapped in softness, tended by a nurse, in the company of his mother, and falls in love. The child reciprocates, and will not remove his eyes from the father. The nurse attempts to recall the infant to the world appropriately his at this age: a world of women, of gentleness, of nourishment. But the child rejects the breast. From this moment he is wholly his father's. And indeed, that patriarch at his homecoming has seized the power to nurture from the female forces who claimed and lost it.

How much Greek did Jacopo Antonio Marcello know? Enough to love Greek texts and order them translated into familiar Latin; surely not enough to read Homer. But among the consolers reporting this incident were four whose knowledge of Greek literature was excellent: the Greek-born Sagundino and George of Trebizond; Francesco Filelfo, who had studied with Manuel Chrysoloras in Constantinople; and Filelfo's student, Pietro Perleone. All were familiar with the Greek poet. Sagundino had inscribed lines from Homer in the notebook of that zealous antiquarian Ciriaco d'Ancona, on a jaunt through Greece. Filelfo incorporated in his *Consolatio* passages translated from Homer, while Perleone translated the pseudo-Plutarchan *Vita Homeris* (Life of Homer).[142] Inevitably, as the passages were composed that describe the meeting of father and son, they thought of *Iliad* 6.466–81.

There the war-helmeted Hector has come home from the desperate battle waged outside the city's walls to encounter his wife, Andromache, with their infant son, Astyanax, held in his nurse's arms. He reaches out to embrace the child: the child shrinks away, alarmed by the bronze mask and plumage. Hector and Andromache laugh, as Hector removes the fearful helmet, in shared understanding of the child's isolation from the world of war and men. In both episodes, the players are warrior-father, child, mother, and nurse. But in the Homeric drama, the adult spouses together relate to their child, accepting his preference, appropriate to his infancy, for the warmth and comfort offered by his nurse. In the Renaissance rewrite, wife is ignored by husband, mother and nurse alike rejected by child: that child showing no fear but only the abandon of love for the awesome father who has suddenly sprung into his life.

At three months the infant Valerio fully entered the male society of his father, while his father mothered his precocious child. That mothering, according to Bevilacqua, began even before birth. Marcello was on campaign during his wife's pregnancy, and had a vision of the child who would be born to him:

> While I performed that magistracy [as *provveditore* in Crema], my wife, whom I had left in Venice, was pregnant with a child. But before the news of the birth of that child reached me, O! how many

and wondrously varied dreams foretold to me, while I lay alone sleeping in my room, that there would be born to me a male child splendid with most elegant form and every kind of virtue! O! how many nights did I embrace in my dreams the vision of that beautiful child, smell the fragrance of that infant, delight in his kisses![143]

Bevilacqua is the unique witness for Marcello's prenatal visions of his child. The genuineness of this incident is consequently suspect, especially in view of Bevilacqua's apparently unfocused interest in the matter of visions; upon which he divagates for some pages.[144] Yet if the dream visions are an invention, they are a telling invention. For there is a strong precedent in western literature for prenatal visions of exceptional children: it is found in the hagiographical tradition.[145] The extraordinary virtue of future saints was made known even before birth (as Jesus' special destiny was announced to his mother Mary by a heavenly messenger). The future Franciscan saint Francesco Venimbene was weightless in his mother's womb, while the mother of the later Saint Dominic (that "dog of the Lord") dreamed that she bore within her a little dog.[146] In these examples is observed the difference between the literary tradition and the Marcello incident. Such visions came to mothers of future saints, not fathers. Mothers were the powerful agents in the shaping of these holy prodigies, while the father, more often, was "invisible in the prenatal events."[147] Placing Marcello with his highly masculine profile in the frame of this hagiographical topos, Bevilacqua robs Luca da Leone of her own pregnancy—it is a biological fact, but not a moral one—and makes Marcello the mother of the preternaturally splendid child in the making.

Other passing references point to the continuation of Marcello's mothering role during Valerio's childhood. The child would not leave him alone, Marcello complained in Bevilacqua's *Excusatio,* even at night! As an infant, he clung always to his father's side, bemoaned each separation, yearned to be picked up. But as Valerio aged, mothering was transformed into another kind of nurture: that performed in education. The transition is consistent with the assumptions of contemporary thought, already encountered, by which the father took over responsibility for a child's education at age seven. Perhaps it was at this critical juncture that Marcello began to feed Valerio with information about the history and public affairs, the conduct of war, and the values that formed a nobleman of Venice.

Two episodes that bespeak this new relationship occurred when father and son had taken refuge from the plague in the monastery of San Antonio da Vienna. The abbot of that monastery was the same Michele Orsini who authored the *Opinio de summa venetorum origine* in which the episode is reported: he was an eyewitness. Marcello explained to his constant companion who Vettore Pisani was, the hero of the not long-distant battle of Chioggia whose statue adorned the church of San Antonio. On another occasion, Valerio gazed admiringly at Donatello's monument for Gattamelata, that loyal servant of the Venetian empire. Valerio yearned to equal the men who, like his father, were exemplars of the aristocratic ethos. On both occasions, resting comfortably in the embrace of his father's love, Valerio learns to cherish the values that permeate his parent's culture.

At other times, the child asked his father about the ships that graced the Venetian lagoon; or from his father and his father's friends he gathered data on the cities of the *terraferma* or animal husbandry, celestial events or news of the city.[148] In this manner Valerio absorbed the messages derived from knowledge and experience and social position that his father conveyed uniquely and exclusively to him. Not only did Valerio learn eagerly from his gifted father, but he wished to imitate him in all ways—as he did in his childish encounter with enemies of the *calli* of Venice, when he executed a skilled retreat while holding off a gang of bullies with stones.[149] Why didn't he just run, his father asked? Because I wished, responded the child, "to imitate your deeds and obey your words." The battlefield veteran, all empathy, comforts his son while cautioning him against excessive boldness.

If the incident of the neighborhood toughs shows Marcello's empathy with his child, at other times Valerio is supersensitive to his father's position, wishes, even moods. He accompanied his senior constantly, scrutinizing his face for telltale signs of anxiety or pleasure, and consulted with other family members about the patriarch's state of mind. Such interactions between father and son to which we are admitted by the pens of Filelfo, Bevilacqua, Perleone, and others, show the couple absorbed with each other and detached from other members of the household. As the child grows, Marcello nurtures Valerio first in a maternal, then a paternal mode, but with no trace of that preachifying sternness that is so often a part of a father's stock in trade. Even in training his son for the corridors of power, Marcello nurtures. A reflection in art of the kind of paternal affection felt by the aging Marcello and the young Valerio could perhaps be seen in Ghirlandaio's portrait of an old man (perhaps a grandfather) with a child. Another is found, perhaps, in the portrait of Federigo da Montefeltro, Duke of Urbino, in his library with his son Guidobaldo: a depiction focused on the father's educative role. For in the exceptionally important area of education (that of training in the *studia humanitatis,* the humanist disciplines) Marcello demonstrates the same nurturing concern. He seems to have

Domenico del Ghirlandaio's portrayal of an old man and a boy at about the ages of Marcello and Valerio before the latter's death. Paris, Louvre. Alinari/Art Resource, N.Y.

Pedro Berruguete's portrait of Federigo da Montefeltro, Duke of Urbino, with his son Gui-dobaldo. Urbino, Ducal Palace. Alinari/Art Resource, N.Y.

worked directly with Valerio in his studies: on Latin and Greek the child worked eagerly with "his father or his tutor."

Certainly Marcello established in his own household a school for the education of its youth.[150] There Valerio shone among the other students (Marcello's other children and grandchildren?) like "the golden sun," winning races, settling disputes, and tutoring a slower sibling. Perhaps Valerio excelled to such a degree in the household school that Marcello saw the need for that one child's particularly intense education in the humanistic disciplines. He appointed a tutor for Valerio, not yet six, whose efforts seem devoted especially to this one child.[151]

The Renaissance provides many examples of fathers who took special interest in the education of their sons. The father of the French Calvinist Agrippa d'Aubigné brought from Paris for him, then aged four, a tutor to teach Latin, Greek, and Hebrew. Under his harsh tuition, the child became an accomplished linguist, but a gentler master was soon found for him.[152] The father of Girolamo Cardano himself tutored his son, the future physician, from his earliest years in arithmetic, astrology, and geometry.[153] Richard Evelyn "was already developing into one of those child prodigies so admired by the age, and who therefore delighted his pedantic father" when he died in 1658, not yet six; he could read, had nearly mastered English grammar, and possessed some French.[154] A painting by Benozzo Gozzoli of the first day in school for little Saint Augustine provides a touching image of the continuity of care from father to tutor.[155] In the father's own tutelage of the son, and even in his assignment of another person under his authority to assume that burden, is expressed much love.

Perleone praises Marcello for the attention he gives to his son's education, comparing him favorably with other, more neglectful, fathers. The Anonymous Tutor, a surrogate father, devotes himself fully to the child's needs, as when at Easter of 1460 the scholar accompanies the child on a vacation journey to Monselice. The child was commended to the tutor's care when he was six, and they were companions until the young charge died. Even under his tutor's care, though, Valerio is his father's son. Far from distancing the child from the father, humanistic learning must have brought them closer together. A similar interaction can be observed two generations earlier, in Florence, where the humanist chancellor Coluccio Salutati felt a special bond to the child with the most compelling intelligence: the very son, Piero, who would fall victim to the plague in 1400.[156]

Yet though other humanist fathers responded with love to the signs of intelligence noted in their sons, none grieved so desperately, so publicly, or

31408 - SAN GIMIGNANO - Chiesa di S. Agostino - S. Agostino condotto dal maestro di grammatica - B. Gozzoli - (Stab. D. Anderson 1932).

Detail from Benozzo Gozzoli's fresco sequence of the life of St. Augustine, showing the saint as a child being given to the grammar master. San Gimignano, Church of S. Agostino. Alinari/Art Resource, N.Y.

so long as did Jacopo Antonio Marcello. To the bonding capacity of shared intellectual interests, to the spiritual capacity of this career warrior for gentleness and nurturance, must be added another explanation of the unusual profundity of feeling he experienced. That explanation must lie in the web of circumstances that made Marcello uniquely available to this, as he was to no other, child. Valerio was born in April (probably) 1452, nearly at the moment when Marcello interrupted a six-year tour of duty with the Venetian armies in Lombardy. He returned to Venice the following summer, as has been seen, to greet for the first time the child conceived in the frontier outpost of Crema, the furthest point of his military action, but born in Venice, the place of his retreat from that involvement. Valerio's life coincides, therefore, with Marcello's first withdrawal from an intense career of military aggression.

It coincides as well with Marcello's disillusionment, or at least frustration, with Venice's military ventures. That distancing from his city's expansive efforts is witnessed by the launching of a literary friendship with Venice's opponent, René d'Anjou, and by the reluctant interruption of a friendship built on the granitic foundation of shared experience with Francesco Sforza. The changes in Marcello's behavior and career pattern at this juncture have already been noted in chapter 4. They opened a space in his heart and a vacancy in his agenda aptly filled by the innocence, charm, and intelligence of young life concretized in the newborn Valerio. Valerio did not win Marcello's heart because he was the youngest or the eldest or the only son, but because he was the son born at the moment of the father's spiritual death and rebirth—gifted, *per accidens*, with the capacity to respond to the father's needs. Marcello did not love Valerio with a unique passion because he was old and tired, but because years and expense of spirit had purchased wisdom without dampening fire.

Valerio thrived with the nurturance provided by his father's love in the eight years of his life. Marcello thrived, too, enriched by the relationship with a child whose existence met his needs at the midpoint of his life, rimmed with crisis. The loss of that relationship was more than the loss of one of a cluster of children: it was the loss of a dimension of Marcello's own existence, recently discovered by a man too seasoned to expect that it could be replaced, and too self-centered to accept its loss. As the humanist Alberti knew, the desire to mold a child to express one's "very image and likeness" was overwhelmingly powerful.[157] Could not God recall just one of his own? asked Marcello's consolers. Not even God; Marcello would wrestle with God, as he had wrestled with Milan, for the richness of life he had cultivated and won.

But if Marcello would not relinquish Valerio, the child Valerio could surrender himself to God and for his father. Unlike his obdurate father, Valerio was the ideal practitioner of the *ars moriendi:* the method of dying well, which nourished an abundant advice literature in this very century.[158] Valerio prepared for his certain future joyfully and confidently. He performed all the duties required for the last rites, bathing the proffered crucifix with penitential tears. Twice on his deathbed he offered to make sacrifices, we are told, relieving his father of the burden. Twice he commanded his father to check his tears. Where the father, reduced by grief, was unable to care for his other children, his family, his friends, his son took responsibility for a sister, commending her to his father's attention in a deathbed request. It is scarcely credible that a child could behave in this way.[159] Like the prenatal visions that promised a splendid birth, this deathbed scene could be found in many a saint's *vita*. But whether the child's deep empathy with his elderly and overwrought parent was real or imagined, surely in

Marcello's mind the roles of father and son have been inverted. His dying son nurtures him; the vanquished father can do nothing but weep.

To the degree that hope is centered in another, experts inform us, grief extends.[160] At a turning point in his life, much nearer the end than the middle of that journey, Marcello had removed his heart from the field of battle and invested it in his friends and his books, in thoughts of peace, and in the future of one special child. The death of that child attacked the very center of the newly enriched spiritual life that the aging soldier had experienced. No wonder he sought consolation from the child who had nurtured his soul as he had nurtured the child's infancy; and he sought it from none other, certainly not from his consolers who believed in the capacity of reasonable words and cogent argument to solace. Marcello must work through his grief and move on, they advised. That is what Filelfo did, he explains to Marcello, when he lost his son:

> You will easily throw off your grief once you have resolved to use in your situation the same remedies that I myself used on the death of my Olimpio. . . . Greatly will it benefit you not only in alleviating your pain, but in adding sweetness to your life, if you make yourself review in your mind the babyhood of your son Valerio, his charm, his wit, the form of his body, the uprightness and dignity of his character, his studies of the arts and of eloquence. . . . Nor must you forget how Valerio hung from your neck, how he kissed you, how he melted in your arms, how he mangled words when he babbled, yet made them lovely to hear.[161]

Other humanist fathers who had suffered the loss of children must have done the same: freed themselves by reliving the past, and recreating it in words. They applied "logotherapy" to their injuries, and in the verbal expression of their pain found surcease.[162] Work itself, for these intellectuals, was the "griefwork" that Sigmund Freud defined in the twentieth century as the remedy for exaggerated grief.

Marcello refused to battle grief with the soft weapons of words, preferring to battle death with the full armament of his anger. As he had stood firm on the battlefield, Marcello stood firm in tragedy. He would not surrender to the enemy: those consolers who offered him the cheap coin of reason to pay the limitless cost of passion. For his despair there was no compensation available in words, although words could be employed to exalt the justice of his cause. To René, then, he turns, to judge the case between the inconsolable father and the consolers who, however they struggled to do so, failed to understand the mystery of that father's love. Heroic in action, heroic in friendship, heroic in despair, Marcello did not surrender, but died before he yielded to the false play of words that mixed the flawed drug of consolation.

CHAPTER SIX

In Sympathy

The father clothed in black bore his child clad in white to the funeral of an angel: "an angel, Valerio enters heaven in triumph."[1] The innocence of children dead before the age of ten, contemporaries believed, won them that special place in heaven. "They are like angels of God," wrote the Anonymous Student, "and crowned by the splendid glory of their innocence they ascend to the throne of celestial majesty. To which state it can scarcely be doubted that the noble spirit of your Valerio was appointed, as he was taken when he was not yet ten years old."[2] We mustn't grieve when our little ones are taken from us, for they are blameless, as yet unstained by vice. "They have avoided the arrows of adverse fortune, the harsh pains of this world, the infinite variety of evils and many tragedies to which childhood is prone."[3] In all things—his parentage, his rearing, his city, and his early death—Valerio was fortunate: "[Untouched] by any blemish of vice, [raised] not among barbarians or amid catastrophes, but in a worthy home adorned with all the virtues, under the authority of the Venetian empire, by you, honored with the well-deserved magistracies of your republic and resplendent with the glory of great deeds, . . . in innocence of heart and with the finest moral training, from the shadows of this world [he] escaped to the stars."[4]

Why should Marcello grieve, when his son has attained the beatitude for which all strive? His consolers summon before him the image of the angelic Valerio. "No more excellent reward can be named or thought," wrote Carlo Fortebraccio, "than to be with Christ, with the blessed spirits to witness the glory of the Creator, to behold the face of God, to apprehend that inner precinct of light, free of all fear of death to enjoy the blessing of eternal incorruption. Wherefore if we put aside the obstacle of our sorrow and faithfully and bravely reflect, we must rejoice rather than grieve for the death of your son Valerio, whose soul has been liberated from this dungeon . . . of the flesh, and has fled, sanctified, to its heavenly homeland."[5]

Even a fool should recognize, wrote Isotta Nogarola in the same key, that when it strikes so splendid a soul, death is not to be regretted but welcomed: "For he knew that [Valerio] would go to a better life, where there shall be no more death nor crying nor sorrow; and that though he was in this life a wayfarer and pilgrim, he has returned from exile to his fatherland, from wretchedness to glory, from mortality to immortality."[6] How can you doubt, chided Niccolò Sagundino, "that your Valerio is not lost in darkness, but has ascended to a truer and brighter light, from a low and squalid existence has attained heaven, has migrated to the holy city . . . which is sacrosanct, immune, unblemished, safe, impregnable, vibrant with concord, peace and tranquility."[7]

There the child becomes the protector of those he loved and who were left behind, continued Sagundino: "He has not deserted you, nor has he abandoned his dear mother, nor his sweet brothers, but the blessed boy has preceded you all to prepare your way."[8] "Wrapped in the splendor of the divine presence," added the Anonymous Student, "he [with all the other children who have become angels] pours forth incessant prayers for us who gave him birth and who remain in this wretched vale of tears."[9] It should be a joy to you as a father, wrote Mascarello, "that you have a son who attends the highest King, who has loved you and will love you with a wondrous love, who beloved by that King and a participant in His reign unceasingly prays for his dear parent that your sorrow upon his death may turn to joy, and that all things that you might rightly wish for in this life may be granted."[10] As Valerio lay dying, wrote Giorgio Bevilacqua in Marcello's voice, he already anticipated his intercessory role in heaven. "At times he tried to soothe me, saying I should quiet all my sorrows, and trust that I would have a son in paradise who had attained a more glorious rank than any which could ever have been conferred on him by the Venetian senate." He promised further "that he would diligently entreat the Savior for my salvation, and for his dear mother, and sweet brothers."[11]

From his seat in the ranks of angels, his unnamed tutor imagined, Valerio continues to speak to his father, rebuking him for his unkempt hair and black garb that were the signs of protracted mourning. "Only an impious father would value his own small pleasure above the greatest happiness of his children." Does he grieve for an heir? he has other children and grandchildren. As a Christian, Marcello should rejoice as much in having given birth to one angel in heaven as to all those other future citizens of Venice.[12] "And you, great man that you are," the Tutor interjected to address his patron, "how will you answer this angel?" At the thought of Valerio's present state my own grief gives way to joy, and so must yours: "Now I want to rejoice in the felicity of our Valerio, I want to delight in his good which is also mine." Marcello's unremitting grief mocks his child, who should be free to dwell in grace: "Do you still let hair and beard grow wild and swathing yourself in black do you flee from the light? Will you as a father thus injure your son?" Indeed, he mocks the Almighty, whose will he continues to defy: "Wisest of men, put away this unrelenting grief of yours, and show yourself no longer to be a rebel against the will of God."[13]

What if Christ himself were to speak thus to Marcello from heaven, asks Fortebraccio, to rebuke the father for his selfish grief? "Why do you weep, Jacopo Antonio, why do you indulge yourself with tears, why do you groan aloud with such sighs, why do you quarrel with what I have decreed?" I have given you many goods, Jesus reminds him: high birth, nobility, honors, wealth, glory, first place in the finest of cities; wife, children, relatives, friends. "Recently from among your children I have chosen to recall one, and borne him from the mortal glory and greatness that you hoped for him to certain immortality and blessedness; and he who was called your son on earth, I have chosen now to be and to be called my true son, and heir to my heavenly kingdom." Will Marcello defy what Christ has ordained since before the foundation of the world? "You complain that your son Valerio has been made mine, I who rule the things of men and God and the realms of the divine."[14]

The angel Valerio is evoked by Francesco Filelfo in all the postures outlined by these other consolers of Marcello. He is the guiltless child who was rescued by a loving and providential God from the evils of the world: "For how many sad and wretched and horrible things occur daily in this life, which are evaded only by death?" His short lifetime permitted him neither to understand nor commit evil. "The faster your Valerio sped from the living, therefore, that much more must his death be judged desirable."[15] Since Valerio's life was untouched—"not even a little"—by any contagion of vice, Marcello must not mourn his son as lost.[16] Valerio is not dead, but he is changed: "he who was mortal, has been made immortal." Now with the angels, "to whom he was created most similar in grace and beauty and splendor," he rejoices in the ineffable vision of God.[17] Rather than lament, Marcello should thank Jesus Christ for making him the father of the boy who would now, as a patron, intercede for his own parent's eternal welfare.[18] "Now indeed you, who were before only a Venetian citizen, by Valerio's intercession have been made a citizen of the celestial fatherland," where harmony reigns, not discord. The child can give heaven to his father, as the father had given life to the son.[19] Exultant amid the angelic chorus, Valerio is preparing for his father ("than whom, while he lived on earth, nothing was more dear, more delightful") a place in heaven.[20] "Why then do you pour forth such a flood of tears? Why do you still moan, why do you longer grieve?"[21]

With Valerio in heaven is another angel, who waits also for his father: Olimpio Gellio, Filelfo's own son, who had also died at age eight only a few months after Valerio.[22] We shall see them again, "both you your Valerio and I my Olimpio," two children of the same age born to two fathers of the same advanced age, before whom death loomed close. "Wherefore the divorce between us and the sons we have lost will not be long."[23] You will rejoin Valerio in that home he has prepared for you, "where soon at his side you will live a tranquil and lovely life forever."[24]

స౧ స౧ స౧

The drama of father-son reunion sketched by Filelfo depends for its realization on the truth of a single doctrine, one not yet (in 1461) official dogma of the Roman Catholic Church: that of immortality.[25] Filelfo's words here introduce the discussion of the doctrine of immortality in his *Consolatio* for Marcello, one-third of which is dedicated to that issue. If souls are immortal, then Valerio as well as Olimpio) is an angel. If souls are immortal, then Valerio is not dead, and his father can expect reunion with him. If souls are immortal, then Marcello must not grieve, but rejoice: he must accept consolation. To do otherwise is to spurn the divine will, to prefer life in the fallen world to life everlasting.

It is Francesco Filelfo's special mission to recall the defiant nobleman to due obedience to the divine. More than any other of Marcello's consolers, Filelfo is equipped to explore the philosophical questions of the nature of soul and the reality of the afterlife. These are the twin purposes of the central part of Filelfo's text: the section which identifies the *Consolatio* as one of the most original moral philosophical statements to emerge from Italian humanism. First, there is the philosophical goal of unfolding proofs of the hypothesis of immortality. Second, there is the rhetorical goal of persuading Marcello to accept the consolation he so staunchly resisted.

Filelfo provides three proofs for the immortality of the soul. The first, for which the evidence is literary or anecdotal, is that human beings have perceived souls apart from bodies. The second, for which the evidence is the assembled argumentation of the philosophers beginning with Plato, is the necessary separateness of soul and body, of eternal and mortal substances. The third, for which the evidence is theological and legal, is that the requirement of justice, implicit in God's existence, can only be fulfilled if lives are judged at the threshold of death and reward or punishment assigned to never-dying souls.

There has never been a human community, Filelfo opens his first proof, which does not honor its dead with poets' celebrations and priestly rites.[26] These observances are offered because survivors believe that those who have died still continue to live. What all believe is probably the case: even more so if the leaders of the community share in the consensus. "And that which all nations commonly believe, exists in fact by a certain law of nature. Indeed, the general consensus concerning the immortality of souls is also confirmed by all those who have been judged great because of the quality of their spirit or brilliance of their mind." Only if they believed in a future life would the Athenian king Codrus, or the Roman consul Decius, offer up their lives in acts of "self-devotion"; or Theombrotus leap from the top of a wall, or Empedocles launch himself into eternity. From these examples it is seen "that the soul is not only not buried with the body, but freed from its chains, it enjoys a better existence by far."[27]

Witnesses to that truth are the Greek poets, most notably Homer and Euripides, from whom lengthy passages are quoted reporting visits of the spirits of the dead to those still living.[28] Speaking of Homer, whose dead Patroclus addresses Achilles, Filelfo asks: "Now would that ancient and divine poet ever have created this scene if he had not been persuaded by the soundest arguments that the souls of men when they have left the body exist in and of themselves, untouched in any way by death?"[29] And if the dogmas of the pagans are unpersuasive, the humanist continues, the same assumption is found in Christian authors. Consider the stories told by Saint Augustine to Bishop Paulinus of Nola about spirits of absent persons, dead and alive, who appeared to those sleeping: "and that serious man would not have reported such things if he did not know for sure that they were true." Jerome, "as a man learned in three languages unsurpassed by any in understanding and holiness," described even more astonishing happenings to Eustochium and her virginal companions. Still alive, he had been lifted up out of his body to join the angelic choirs, behold the vision of God in the form of the divine Trinity. The Apostle Paul reported similar cases.[30]

Such experiences occurred to contemporaries as well as to ancients, Filelfo argued.[31] The Venetian cardinal Gabriele Condulmier had fallen sick and was on the point of death when the apostles Peter and Paul appeared to him, promising that he would regain his health and be named pope. Both promises were realized, and he ascended the papal throne as Eugenius IV. The Cardinal Niccolò Albergati appeared to Tommaso Parentucelli (later Pope Nicholas V) and some such vision must have moved Eneo Silvio Piccolomini to foresee his own papacy as Pius II. These *phantasmata*, as the Greeks called them, are for Filelfo proof of the separability of soul from body and its potential for immortal life. "Thus your son Valerio lives, I say, Jacopo Antonio Marcello," Filelfo says in concluding his first argument, "and he lives indeed a life which is subject to no mutability, but one which is enduring and forever blessed."[32]

Filelfo's second proof of the immortality of the soul (considerably longer than the first) consists of an exposition of the views of the philosophers, from the earliest pre-Socratics through the most famous of the Arabs; but not, conspicuously, the scholastics.[33] The list (demonstrating the Hellenist Filelfo's considerable range) includes Thales, Anaximenes, and Anaxagoras; Aristoxenus, Dicearchus, and Critolaus; Epicurus, Democritus, and Leucippus; Heraclitus and Xenophanes, Parmenides and Empedocles; Xenocrates and Arcesilaus, Critias and Hippon, Crantor and Posidonius; Zeno, Chrysippus, and Diogenes; Boethius and Averroes. The views of Plato and Aristotle dominate. In their explication Filelfo repeats much of the standard philosophical discourse of the day.

For Aristotle, the soul is separate from body and superior to it; separate from the vegetative and sensitive parts of the soul, it is one with mind and virtue and imagination and, like them, incorruptible. Some of his successors, both in Greece and in the universities of Italy, posed alternate views of the soul (viewing it as part of the body, and corruptible). Such interpretations Filelfo dismisses. For Pythagoras, soul has the perfection of number, but is more than number: it is the *monad,* or fount and origin of number itself, perfect unity, beginning and end. The great Plato, in matters theological and metaphysical, followed Pythagoras. Pure mind, the rational part of the soul, is perfectly separate from body. It moves itself, and is thus life itself, never ceasing to move, and immortal. "Our soul contains in itself nothing mixed, . . . nothing concrete, nothing corporeal, nothing external, but by its own particular nature exists of its own force, by which it senses, by which it knows, by which it lives and thrives, by which it is perfectly similar to God; by Whom it is made so that it can never be dissolved, nor ruptured nor destroyed, but rather, self-evidently, it is immortal and sempiternal." Since this is so, Filelfo concludes his vast encyclopedia of the science of the soul, "Why then do we mourn, Jacopo Antonio Marcello, for the sons taken from us? Why do we still weep, why lament?"[34]

If the soul is not immortal, then human beings are not accountable for their sins, argues Filelfo in his third and final proof of the soul's immortality: then injustice reigns. But justice is most precious of the virtues: "For neither the household nor the republic nor the whole human race can survive without it."[35] Now this world is abandoned to injustice: "Those who are inferior in every virtue rule good men and crush them; the impious are honored, the pious scorned; those who excel in learning and seriousness are ridiculed, while ignorant hypocrites are revered. . . . The just are afflicted by the impious, and for the whole course of their lives up until death they are horribly tormented. Those who abuse and assail and abase them, meanwhile, not only go unpunished for their wickedness, but even thrive amid delights and pleasures."[36] Given this state of affairs, where would be God's justice if the soul were not immortal? But God is just, for that is His nature, and immortal souls are rewarded for virtue and punished for vice. As a Venetian, Marcello must especially recognize this truth: "Have you alone of all the noblemen of Venice decided not to believe in divine justice? For this is the special glory of Venice, for you were the first of all mortals to cultivate and revere justice. Can it be that Venetians are just, but God is unjust?"[37]

His threefold proof of the immortality of the soul complete, Filelfo asserts that Marcello has no further cause for grief: "there is no necessary nor honorable cause for the great duration or great depth of your sorrow."[38] Here ends the consolatory section of Filelfo's work, which presents at unusual length and with unique sophistication the doctrine of immortality. Two other authors writing respectively before and after Filelfo also posit the immortality of the soul as part of their consolatory strategy: Sagundino and the Anonymous Student. For Sagundino the soul, or mind, is "absolute and simple force . . . , distinct and separate from any spot or stain, from all contagion of body." Formed by God (who receives scarcely a nod from Filelfo!) in His image, it is lodged in a body made of earth and subject to death. "The soul, or mind, on the contrary, entirely simple and immortal, continues to live and move when the body perishes and dies, and seeks its place in heaven by its own force, overcoming all obstacles, there beholding and contemplating the creator and lord of all . . . , [and] having achieved its final end, rests and is forever blessed."[39] If in its life in the body, however, the soul has been weighted down with sin, it will be rightly deprived of heaven and suffer due punishment eternally; or it will be sent to Purgatory until, cleansed, it can join the blessed in paradise.

The Anonymous Student argues the same point from the same philosophical tradition known to Filelfo and Sagundino.[40] Possessing neither the former's erudition nor the latter's eloquence, he shows a keener awareness of the conflict between the views of some philosophical schools and Christian doctrine. Human bodies, which are corruptible, are born with an immortal form separable from them and subject to no corruption: this form is what was named soul by the ancients. After the death of the body, the soul continues to live: according to the gentiles in the Elysian fields, but more truly (our author believes) and as "the divine authority of our faith confirms, in sempiternal glory and in the triumphal realm of paradise, prepared for all the elect from the foundation of the world."[41]

The concept of the immortality of the soul is one of two sets of arguments employed by Marcello's consolers to lighten the anguish of the bereaved father. Based partly on Cicero's *Tusculan Disputations,* a repository of Greek thought, they draw also on Plato and Plutarch and other authors of the Greek philosophical tradition available with new richness only in the century of Marcello's loss. The attention to the Greek heritage is characteristic of the Venetian milieu, and inevitable given the backgrounds of these authors: Filelfo, trained in Constantinople; Sagundino, born in Euboea; the Student from Padua, where the arts curriculum was shaped by the discussion of Aristotle and his commentators. Yet this body of Greek thought is grafted upon the Christian tradition of consolation. So is the heritage of Roman thought. From the Greek through the Roman and the Christian heritage derives the other main set of arguments applied to heal Marcello's wounds: those calling for Stoic calm and Christian forbearance. Death is part of the human condition, proclaim Marcello's friends, and the wise man must accept what is decreed by nature.

"When you first saw the son to whom you had given birth, did you not know that he was mortal?" asked Carlo Fortebraccio. Every particle of nature must perish. "Look about you at the whole orb of the earth and all the expanse of the sea and all the depth of the heavens, do they not all admit that they must die? Heaven itself, so great, so splendid, so noble, will one day disappear; sun, moon, and all the other stars will not endure; all animals that crawl or swim or fly, every creature and the earth itself, all will soon cease to be."[42] The length of life is in the hands of God. None die prematurely, for all die at the same moment of fulfillment: when God decrees that life has reached its limit. "No one's death has been premature, therefore, when the immoveable sentence of the divine decree has declared it mature."[43] If the doctors at his bedside had told you Valerio would not die, would you have believed them? Faith should not be placed in doctors, but in Christ: "He is not to be mourned whom Christ, our God and lord, has promised to resurrect."[44]

In a funeral oration quite distinct in genre from the consolations of the Glasgow codex, Gregorio Tifernate offers a similar message. All things die, nothing exists without change. "We see that not only individuals have the briefest of lives, but also famous cities and great nations, whose names were, it was hoped, eternal, of which nothing is left but their memory." The catastrophes that befell the Romans are well known, "although by themselves they were the equals of any on the rest of the globe. There is no one who does not see the ruin that Greece has become, which causes me to think that our life is but a dream and a shadow. Where are all those great minds, such fine intellects of the Greeks? Where are their splendid cities? Have they all been uprooted and destroyed?" If destruction comes to these, why do we wonder at the death of such as ourselves? "Why do we suffer so much sorrow and pain at the loss of just one child? It is as though we thought that we were not beset by infinite dangers, that we were not mortal. We are not made of such fine stuff; we humor ourselves too much."[45] We must realize, Isotta Nogarola echoes, "that we are born in that condition which is subject to death, and that he who tries to withstand death attempts to defy the will of God, which it is impossible to oppose and wrong to want to."[46]

The theme of the inevitability of death is most fully developed by the Greek-born Sagundino. You are right to lament the horrible blow that fortune has dealt you, he writes, and we join you in your sorrow.[47] It would be wrong, though, to allow a flood of passions to overwhelm us. "Must we allow passion and feeling to lead us here, pull and drag us there, someone will ask, so that having lost our hold over appetite we are a slave to it like wild beasts?" Rather, we must take control of "the ship of our life" and govern it firmly. "This is a task proper to man, in this a man differs from a beast, by this capacity he in some way participates in divinity."[48] You must take charge of yourself, therefore, and take direction of your own existence: "You yourself can be in such a way your own guide and instructor, that you would appear to all onlookers to be the brave and effective creator and lord of your own life."[49] To do so, you must first understand the nature of death, and know that it is foolish to nurse "eternal and immortal grief" for a being which is "perishable, transitory, weak, and by its very nature mortal."[50]

Everything in nature that begins has an end, Sagundino explains. If you resent the end that must come, why do you not equally resent the beginning? Death is the companion of life from its beginnings, and "by day and at night both at home and abroad it is always with us . . . , until it reaches its sign and measure, and offers itself and appears to us, and at the same moment and point in time it at once extinguishes and is extinguished, so that it deserts us no more than it seems to be deserted by us."[51] Life and death are consequent upon each other, and both form part of nature's unchangeable law. "Now if you were born in Athens, or Thebes, or Lacedaemonia, you could not decline to obey the laws and institutions of the city and people where you were born. . . . Born in the common city of the universe, drawing your life from the sacred springs of nature, do you dare to defy its laws and institutions, and do you try to change the conditions upon which you were brought forth into this life?"[52]

The end of life is no more awesome than its beginning, as a stream of ancient philosophers attest. From them we learn not only not to fear death, but to despise it: "that which comes in any case, that you can halt by no argument or counsel, that by the nature, order, and course of things will necessarily come, that when it comes seems to bring no evil nor discomfort." The fear of death having no basis, it must derive from an error insinuated in the mind which the wise and brave man will "correct, eliminate, and entirely destroy."[53] He should neither tremble before death because he so much loves life, nor hating life, seek its end. Rather he will "like a mortal, modestly enjoy his comforts, and face death calmly according to the decree of the laws of nature and the will of greatest ruler of all things, God the creator."[54] And so must you, Sagundino turns to address his patron Marcello: "Now I turn myself to you, I speak to you, I present before you my case, since you now easily understand all these words I have spoken about life, about death, about the law of nature and the human condition. What do you say, splendid Jacopo Antonio, what do you think, what is your response?"[55]

The response Sagundino elicits is provided by Giorgio Bevilacqua in words crafted to express Marcello's thoughts. Those who urge him to moderate his grief want him to choke off feeling and strangle love. This he will not do. Where they present the arguments of the Stoics, he will answer with those of the Peripatetics, who permit human beings to be human. The father's grief and despair seen in the previous chapter as the counterpart to the father's profound love for his child emerges here as the counterpoint in the philosophical discussion of death.

Emotions are natural, indeed essential to human beings, Marcello argues in Bevilacqua's script. It would be easier to kill a man than to root these out and change what is essential to his nature. All beings that enjoy life are determined by the nature that is given to them: trees are evergreen or deciduous, animals are destined to fly or swim or crawl. What nature has created or "mixed" with all these creatures, as with the human being, cannot be changed: "[this natural force] compels him so that however hard he struggles against it, he is wholly vanquished by that which has been fixed and rooted in him by nature."[56] Where the Stoics insist that human beings should rise above passions, Marcello insists that they are naturally subject to these movements of the soul. "There has never been a man endowed by nature with sense and intellect . . . who could escape these passions of the soul and not suffer them, or not feel pain."[57] So much the better, he feels (concurring with the Attic opponent of the Stoics unimpressed by the sage who had achieved *apatheia,* the passionless state sought by followers of that school): "Those who wish to be seen as tranquil, untroubled, and immobile, and since they desire nothing, grieve for nothing, are aroused by nothing, delight in nothing, with all the functions of the impassioned soul cut off, grow senile in a body, torpid and void of life."[58]

These bloodless Stoics forbid a wise man to grieve, for virtue, they believe, cannot coexist with sorrow. Sorrow is a "sickness of the soul," hostile to virtue.[59] To their reasoning the Peripatetics respond in turn: "For since man is a composite of body and soul, that which favors the conservation of human life is some kind of good for man, even if not the greatest good." Moderate sorrow will not greatly injure the wise man, who cannot after all, though he lives his life without serious error, live a totally perfect life.[60] Great men have known sorrow: witness John the Evangelist and the Apostle Paul, and Jesus himself, perfect in virtue, who wept at Gethsemane. A wise man can shed tears, therefore, and even find in them relief for his sorrows. "Next there arises this problem, whether weeping or tears could be a remedy for the mitigation and amelioration of sorrow and sadness. Many see this as absurd, and especially those who have tried to console me with such eloquence find my weeping absurd, to which the whole force of nature compels me. They say that no effect can cause the lessening of its own cause."[61]

Though Marcello's consolers deny that claim, he will defend it. Crying is itself a pleasure, he insists, and relieves sorrow. Why do these intelligent men condemn me for a behavior to which nature forces me? "If other fathers have arranged sumptuous and elaborate funerals to celebrate the lives of their dead sons, . . . why should the flow of tears . . . be forbidden me?"[62] With those forbidden tears we reverence the dead, and preserve their memory forever: "The one we have cherished, loved, and nurtured, let us now remember him forever, let us recall him who is gone and keep alive with tears that [grief] which is a sign of mercy and humanity."[63] Nature forces him to weep tears which defeat death, as Marcello argues the Peripatetic case in Bevilacqua's words. These are life-giving tears that his Stoic opponents would deny.

℘   ℘   ℘

Marcello's defense against his consolers rests on the opposition of Stoic and Peripatetic schools, a common theme of contemporary moral thought.[64] Francesco Filelfo regularly distinguished between the two schools in his philosophical works, most notably in his important *De morali disciplina*

(On moral thought)—just as he and contemporaries regularly discussed the relative virtues of Plato and Aristotle. It was as part of this war of the schools that Lorenzo Valla composed his *De voluptate* (On pleasure), challenging the Stoic by elevating (in this case, and provocatively) Epicurean values.[65] Earliest of all of these, Coluccio Salutati had debated the strengths of Stoic and Peripatetic views in both his treatises and his letters, and especially on the issue of the nature of death.[66] Although it was certainly not the only theater in which such ideas were discussed, the Marcello corpus is notable for its wrestling with these philosophical themes—both the individual parts of the corpus, and even more curiously, the whole, as the army of Stoic consolations marshaled in the Glasgow codex are met and challenged by one immoveable Peripatetic response.

Distinguished (especially through the vehicle of Filelfo's *Consolatio*) for its highlighting of the issue of immortality, and, in many of its voices, for its staging of the tension between Stoic and Peripatetic poles of classical moral thought, the Marcello corpus is firmly rooted in a tradition. Bound up in the arguments, consolatory and anti-consolatory, that emerge from the Marcello texts are several strands of contemporary thought: Christian commonplaces, arguments from a consolatory tradition crystallized in antiquity by Cicero and Seneca, and arguments from the moral philosophical tradition of greatest interest especially to those humanists with some access to Greek. Just as there is a mixture of ideas in the Marcello consolations, so also is there a mix of genres. Among them are works which mimic the consolatory *epistola* and longer *consolatio,* the manuals on pious death and the legends of saints and martyrs, the philosophical treatise and the oration, main instrument of the rhetoricians. The variety of style and form and the richness of argument make them in the composite a unique source for the history of Renaissance consolation. To that tradition discussion now turns.[67]

Ancient authors both Greek and Roman (Plato, Diogenes, Carneades, Clitomachus, Cicero, Seneca, Plutarch) bequeathed to western civilization high models of consolatory writing. The earliest examples of ancient poetry include elegies for the dead or epigrams to be inscribed on tombs. From the classical period derive the funeral oration, reciting the accomplishments of the deceased and of his family, the formal letter of sympathy, and the consolatory treatise proper (often concerned with death, though sometimes with other calamities such as exile or imprisonment). Based on the models of ancient authors, the consolatory tradition was augmented even before the close of antiquity by the influential writings of the saints Jerome and Basil, Ambrose and Augustine, and the philosopher Boethius.

Subsequently, a considerable consolatory literature emerged during the Middle Ages and underwent distinctive evolution during the Renaissance when the classical models were vigorously imitated. Early in the latter period, the humanist and poet Francis Petrarch's *De remediis utriusque fortunarum* (On the remedies for both kinds of fortune) won a vast readership in the European nations. Concerned not only with bad fortune but also good, and in the former category not only with death but also with other adversities, the *De remediis* is an encyclopedia of Christian moral thought, laced with classical (especially Senecan) and medieval elements. More strictly classical in genre and message are the many consolatory letters penned by Petrarch over a lifetime to his friends on the deaths of their brothers, parents, children, and familiars. Within a generation, the form of the literary consolation—whether letter, oration or treatise—had become thoroughly classicized.

Characteristic of the classical consolation and its progeny are two components. The first includes the praise of things past (the victim's or mourner's character, deeds, virtues, family, and country). The second comprises an array of rational arguments for the cessation of grief (the need for moderation, the dangers and pains of living, the understanding of death as a change for the better and an occasion of joy). These elements typically displayed in most works of the consolatory tradition are found, too, in the consolations for Marcello. Much of what the authors write to that bereaved nobleman is pure convention. Inherited from the ancient and medieval past, those conventions were reshaped and repolished by the early humanists of the Renaissance. Among the architects of that revivified tradition was a writer centrally involved in the molding of Venetian culture.

Venetian neither by birth nor residence, Gasparino Barzizza was a frequent guest in the patrician palaces of Venice, and spent much of his career at Padua in the orbit of Venetian power. Two Venetian noblemen with whom he conversed as companion, as teacher, as client, were the friends Daniele Vitturi and Valerio Marcello. Vitturi, already adult in the early years of the century when Barzizza came to Venice (and distantly linked by marriage to the Marcello clan), was a leader of the first generation of humanism in that city.[68] A bibliophile and patron, he was a correspondent of the humanists Guarino Veronese, Francesco Filelfo, and Antonio Panormita outside of Venice, as well as of Barzizza (who dedicated to Vitturi's young sons in 1418 his work *De orthographia,* a manual of spelling rules), and the patrician Francesco Barbaro. Valerio Marcello, brother of the bishop Pietro and our Jacopo Antonio, the uncle for whom the child Valerio was named, is not known as a participant in intellectual circles other than through his correspondence with Barzizza. Around the year 1412, the experiences of these figures intersected and are recorded in Barzizza's works.

On 22 February of that year, Barzizza wrote to his two Venetian friends jointly.[69] He had just returned to Padua, the city of studies, after visiting them, and confessed that the delights of Venice, its wealth, their friendship, had almost held him back. The next day, he wrote to Valerio alone.[70] Soon after he had finished the previous letter, Girolamo Marcello, Valerio's brother, had come to see him. Barzizza required money from the Venetian *questor*s of the city, and Girolamo had munificently interceded to resolve the matter. Barzizza fulsomely thanked Valerio for having spurred his brother to assist the penurious scholar. Not long afterwards, Girolamo Marcello died. That event is known from the "oratio" Barzizza wrote (a piece more formal than a letter, not delivered orally) to console the grieving bishop of Padua, his brother, for the death.[71]

Its message is Stoic: it calls upon the bereaved's resources of wisdom and moderation in tolerating the pain of loss. "Recently" orphaned of his father Francesco, now the "sudden news" of the death of his beloved brother would surely have defeated Pietro were it not for "his incredible, indeed almost divine strength of spirit." No evil could be so great that his wisdom could not either diminish, or indeed totally vanquish it.[72] That spirit had already endured many losses: two sisters and a sister-in-law, another brother Lorenzo, and his nephew, the infant son of Valerio. Faced with such tragedies, Pietro would necessarily mourn. "I don't dare to ask this, that you not grieve," coaxed Barzizza, "but this I urge, that you grieve moderately; for not to grieve would be alien to your humanity, while to grieve too much would be alien, I believe, to your wisdom."[73]

Barzizza, a polished practitioner of the consolatory genre, exerted much influence on the first generation of Venetian humanism. That city's humanists themselves produced a body of consolations as the century unfolded. The writer who launched the tradition was the same Bishop Pietro—brother of Jacopo Antonio—whom Barzizza would later console. In January 1405, he addressed to the bishop and humanist Fantino Dandolo a letter which launched the humanist genre of consolation in Venice on the death (on 16 January 1405) of Dandolo's father, Leonardo.[74] A brief work, it signaled nevertheless the usual Stoic message; an odd one for a Christian professional, one might think, but it is to be remembered how this Marcello, at an advanced age, embraced the new classical studies. He will not condemn his friend, wrote the bishop, since it is human to grieve. Still, to lose a father is a natural and expected event, and the son must find comfort in the thought of the life eternal now enjoyed by his parent, and purpose in a new dedication to the service of his city.

Later in the century there began to appear in the Venetian milieu full-scale works of consolation. The works of three authors (a noble amateur, an immigrant professional, a high-placed prelate) will be examined here for their relations with the works of the Marcello corpus: the extensive consolatory letter by Francesco Barbaro (Venice's "archhumanist") to his daughter; a treatise by one Marcello client (Pietro Perleone) to another (Niccolò Sagundino); and the consolations of Pietro Barozzi, another humanist-bishop of Padua, who brought in his elegant and comprehensive works a new standard to both dying and grieving.

Written to a woman about the death of a woman, Francesco Barbaro's 1447 letter of consolation to Costanza Barbaro (the author's daughter) does not noticeably depart from the normal boundaries of the genre.[75] Just as he would a man, Barbaro exhorts his daughter, a nun, for the sake of her family name and her duty to her convent, to "preserve with dignity a grave manner."[76] The brief work is replete with examples of stoical forbearance, ranging from Scripture (Job), to the ancients (Quintus Fabius Maximus) and recent dignitaries (King Robert of Sicily), and including even a sprinkling of contemporary Venetians (Federico Contarini and Francesco Foscari, the brothers of Lorenzo Giustiniani on the occasion of that saint's death, and Barbaro's nephew Ermolao on the death of his sister). The drama of the dying woman is also conventional (she withstood great pain, received the sacraments of the church humbly) although colored by gender difference: she thinks of her children, is particularly commended for chastity, and at the moment of death glows with beauty and is fragrant with the odor of sanctity.

The letter of consolation written to Niccolò Sagundino by Pietro Perleone, both subsequently consolers of Marcello's, is notable for being addressed by one employee of the Venetian state to another.[77] In July, 1460, he had boarded the ship that was to take him and his family to Crete where he was slated to assume the new and prestigious position of chancellor, when his vessel was struck by a sudden and inexplicable storm right in the Venetian harbor.[78] In the course of the furious shipwreck that it occasioned, the humanist lost his wife, two daughters and a son, his fortune, and his books. He grieved enormously for his lost books, and faced bleakly the prospect, all assets lost, of raising an adolescent son and dowering five daughters from his meager income.

The pain of these losses Perleone soothed by pointing to the survivor's benefits. He could still read (while others, in old age, had been afflicted with blindness), and Venice was full of libraries. Moreover, Perleone reasoned, Sagundino still enjoyed the munificence of Venetian patricians to men of letters that he had known in the past and would in the future enjoy. You should not forget "your patrician friends," Perleone warned Sagundino, "the princes of the earth and the protectors of all things," whose friendship was "a fine and precious inheritance, indeed, for parents to bestow upon children, first after virtue."[79] His lost fortune, furthermore, had been more than compensated by action of the Venetian Senate. Noting his hardship and loyal service, that body awarded him a cash gift—six hundred ducats!—guaranteed employment for himself, dowries for his motherless daughters, and a promise of a secretarial career for his son.[80] What were his misfortunes when compared with the benevolence of the city? "Now compare those goods and possessions that were lost by nature's law to the shipwreck, compare them . . . to the most precious treasure of the kindness and benevolence of the Senate and Republic of Venice."[81] Enough said: the servant of Venice having lost those possessions that were properly his is to content himself with his condition of servitude and the charity of his masters. Perleone's message of consolation here, though adjusted to the social universe of consoler and consoled, is typical of the genre in that it urges fortitude as the remedy for loss, and promotes no indulgence in grief.

The cleric and humanist Pietro Barozzi, one of the successors to Marcello's own brother Pietro as bishop of Padua, is perhaps the best known of Venetian authors who assumed the task of consolation. In 1531 there were printed his three consolations (composed around 1480) bound with his manual *De modo bene moriendi* (On the art of dying well).[82] The latter treatise holds pride of place among Renaissance treatises on the *ars moriendi,* a genre that was recent when Barozzi made his own sophisticated contribution to it. Like his colleagues, he described a method of approaching death which required of the fated patient a pristine conscience and cheerful readiness: precisely the same attitudes Barozzi requires of those whom he consoles for the death of loved ones.

In both literary genres, his work epitomizes the message and form of the Renaissance approach to death. The first of the consolations is directed to the cardinal and bishop of Verona Giovanni Michiel, who had lost the younger brother he had nurtured to the threshold of maturity. Here Barozzi examines the reasons why Michiel might reasonably sorrow: if his brother had not possessed "external goods" (wealth, pleasure, honor)—but he did; or if he had not had adequate time to prepare for death—but he had. Now Vettore Michiel, Giovanni's brother, has attained the peace of heaven, where he enjoys the vision of God, good friends, and the continued delights of knowledge. The learned Barozzi argues that men attain the knowledge of civil and canon law, or philosophy, or theology, only with great difficulty, and must labor long years at Padua or Bologna or even make perilous journeys to universities beyond the Alps; but Michiel's brother Vettore "without toil, without cost, without discomfort, having ascended from the exile of this present life to the heavenly homeland, has learned and now possesses firmly all those things which it is possible for our intelligence to know."[83]

Unlike the young Vettore, who had died (as the text reveals) before the completion of his advanced education, Pietro Foscari's brother Ludovico died a mature man. Pietro, nephew of the former doge Francesco Foscari and a cardinal and bishop of Padua (Barozzi at this time held the see of Belluno) had lost a brother; that brother's family, a father and husband; and Venice, a citizen. But Foscari must not grieve. His brother Ludovico, in dying, escaped not only his burdensome illness but the ills that beset Italy: especially the terrible threat of Turkish invasion. His services to the republic will be missed; but Pietro, who survives him, as a cleric occupying the highest positions in the hierarchy of the Church, benefits his *patria* just as importantly.[84] Similarly, Ludovico's paternal role is easily filled by Pietro. The surviving sons are left well-provided and in good health, safely past infancy and competently advanced in their studies. As long as Pietro is alive to serve as "tutor, protector, adviser, teacher, father," they will lack nothing.[85] He must be mindful of the human condition, and recognize that leagued about him are his "dutiful consolers," eyes fixed intently on him, expecting him to show in misfortune the same constancy he has shown when fortune was favorable.[86] Thus Barozzi profers Foscari the same advice that his consolers proferred Jacopo Antonio Marcello; but without the same unwilling response.

More numerous in the Venetian tradition than the *consolatio* for the dead was the *oratio,* the funeral oration which developed so richly in the Quattrocento in ways distinctive to its humanist culture.[87] The humanists of Venice, dominated by members of the patriciate who were both patrons and participants in the movement, inclined to celebrations of public, more than reflections on private, issues. The very earliest product of this city's humanism was the oration delivered in 1415 by the young nobleman Andrea Giuliani for the Greek diplomat and teacher, Manuel Chrysoloras, whose work so inspired the development of Hellenism in Italian literary circles.[88] In 1418, Leonardo Giustiniani celebrated the devotion to studies and military feats of the admiral and adventurer Carlo Zeno.[89] In the years to come, doges and statesmen, heroes and clerics were honored with orations, as was the doge Francesco Foscari by Francesco Barbaro, Barbaro himself by Filippo Morandi da Rimini, Pietro Barozzi by Cristoforo Marcello, invariably according to the same principles of composition.

The consolations of the Marcello corpus are, with one exception, not orations. The exception is Tifernate's work (one not included in the Glasgow codex), which bears the title "oratio": yet is more truly an *opusculum*, a small work meant only to be read, not delivered. Other of the consolatory works for Marcello, however, share features common to the genre of the funeral oration, and rare for that of the consolation. A funeral oration commonly praised the subject's family, the subject himself (with a narration of that figure's career, particularly if he had a distinguished record of public service), and the city from which he came. Just as the contemporary funeral oration lauded the individual who had died, his family, and his *patria*, so the Marcello consolations contained within their fabric the same elements of celebration. They serve, therefore, a complex of purposes in addition to the primary one of consoling the bereaved: to honor the dead child, to describe the father's love, to celebrate the glories of that heroic mourner, his clan, and his country, so contrasting in their pride and posture to his heroic grief.

The three elements of the oration are found in some, not all of the consolations, and not all three appear necessarily at once. Several authors provide summaries of Marcello's career (studied in chapter 3 above): Filelfo, Perleone, and Bevilacqua at great length. Even a consolatory work would provide a portrait of the deceased, but the celebratory tone of the panegyric passages studied here resemble that of the funeral oration more than the consolation. In any case, the deceased was Valerio, whose story is told in briefer or larger compass by all the consolers, with the effect that the biographies of his father are more conspicuously attached to another genre. More, several authors (Orsini, Perleone, and Bevilacqua most extensively, all Marcello familiars) describe the history of the Marcello family, while Perleone supplies the history of the da Leone family as well, that of young Valerio's mother. Finally, three consolers (Filelfo, Orsini, and Bevilacqua, especially the latter two) dwell on the origins, the nature, the greatness, the uniqueness of Venice: a focus unusual for the genre of consolation, but not, in the setting of this aristocratic republic, for that of the funeral oration. In Orsini's *Opinio*, indeed, the celebration of Jacopo Antonio and his son are subordinated to the preeminent theme of the celebration of Venice. Filelfo, whose career developed on the periphery of Venice, had introduced a reading of that city's past unacceptable to the adamantine self-conception of the humanists who were guardians of her pride. Orsini defends it, and is followed by Bevilacqua. The two trot out the usual elements of the Venetian myth: the uniqueness of the city's site, its role as a world center of commerce, its vast empire, organized for the freedom and benefit of its subjects, its pure and benevolent nobility, its original and enduring liberty: odd materials for the therapy of grief.[90]

If the Marcello consolations can be seen as borrowing from the genre of the oration, they incline also at times to those of biography and hagiography. Venetian humanism produced two massive exemplars of those genres: Jacopo Zeno's biography of his lionized and disgraced grandfather, the buccaneering Carlo Zeno, and Bernardo Giustiniani's of his holy uncle, the first patriarch of Venice and official saint Lorenzo Giustiniani.[91] The subject of the former is a figure (one whom Marcello rather resembles) who combined military and literary interests and, more, struck a surprisingly assertive stance within the restrained polity of Venice. The authors of both works celebrate an ancestor in the male line renowned for great deeds and especially service to the *patria*. Here they approximate the works of the Marcello corpus which praise both the hero's family and his own achievements. The Marcello eulogies are closer to those of Zeno and Giustiniani than to other biographies of Venetian figures, mostly written by professional humanists of the Veneto to celebrate professional soldiers or rulers.[92]

The Marcello corpus (and more particularly, Marcello's capstone *Excusatio* for his grief composed by Bevilacqua) shares a family likeness with autobiography, focusing strongly as it does upon the psychological life of the chief mourner. Utilizing perspectives both classical and Christian available only after the contributions of Petrarch, autobiography was a genre scarcely emergent in the fifteenth century. Speaking in Bevilacqua's words, Marcello poses much as the modern subject of an autobiography, recalling the past, examining his emotions, searching for meaning, making public his quest—a real predecessor of Agrippa d'Aubigné or Leon Modena, if not the boastful Cellini.[93]

The hagiographical tradition, often medieval or even ancient in origin, includes vernacular more than humanist texts. Thus it seems less directly related to the Marcello consolations than other literary strands. Yet there are points of intersection, notably in the portrayal of a young child—for such a figure would scarcely have entered the literature of this age except as the figure of a future saint. Much-read lives of the saints abounded with cases of children perceived, like Valerio, as old before their time (the type of the *senex puer,* also found in antiquity), preternaturally prudent, inclined to ascetic behavior.[94] All over late-medieval Europe, little saints hated to play and loitered around holy places (like Antonio Manzoni of Padua,

Richard of Chichester, Hedwig of Poland). Herman Joseph of Steinfeld, like Valerio, neither uttered unseemly words nor "thrust his arms and legs about too much, practices which generally mar the majority of infants in our day."[95] Like Valerio, too, saintly infants often turned from the breast;[96] but they did so with thoughts of God, Valerio to seek the companionship of his father. Their subsequent development, unlike that of other infants, was untroubled and smooth, and they inclined equally, like Valerio, to learning and virtue.

∾ ∾ ∾

The closest cousins of the Marcello consolations are not these shadowy narratives of precocious saints, however, but other works directed to a bereaved father on the loss of a beloved son. These are numerous. Scripture itself invites such works in its sympathetic portrayal of father Abraham, compelled to offer his son in sacrifice; of Jacob, father of Joseph; of the inconsolable Job; of the Almighty, who so loved the world that he sent for its redemption his only-begotten son. Later literature features such fathers as well. Since those who grieved mightily were normally the close intimates of those who died, it is no surprise that consolations are often addressed to the relatives (rather than friends) of the dead: and notably among them, the fathers of sons. Fathers, rather than mothers. Even if women more often or more powerfully grieved the loss of their children, they were largely excluded from the networks of the learned: few except among the elites were literate, and even among these, few had access to Latin, the language in which consolations both medieval and Renaissance were written. Fathers bereft of sons, therefore, figure more prominently than mothers in the literature of consolation.

The literary tradition of the grieving father begins as early as the lost *On Grief* of the Academic Crantor (third century B.C.). That philosopher's work consoling his friend Hippocles on the death of his children inspired other ancient authors of consolations: notably Cicero and Plutarch.[97] The tradition reaches a climax in antiquity with Cicero, whose lost *Consolatio* lamented the death of his beloved daughter, Tullia.[98] Based on this earlier work, Cicero's consolatory thought is further developed in his *Tusculan Disputations*. A little more than a century later, the late Greek author Plutarch added to his many works on marriage, family, and childrearing his consolation *Ad uxorem* (To my wife), on the death of their two-year-old daughter Timoxena. He or an anonymous contemporary authored another much-read example of the classical consolation on the death of a child, that *Ad Apollonium* (To Apollonius).

Not so desperately as he later mourned his mother, the Latin father of the Church Augustine grieved over Adeodatus, "given by God," the illegitimate and unsought son of his African concubine who, he admitted, compelled his love.[99] His younger contemporary and correspondent Paulinus of Nola was the earliest Christian author to devote a full-scale work to the mourning of a son: his Poem #31, *De obitu Celsi pueri panegyricus* (Panegyric on the death of the child Celsus).[100] The poem was written (probably in the late 390s) to console his close kinsmen, the Aquitanian magnate Pneumaticus and wife Fidelis on the loss of their infant son Celsus. The arguments are theological.[101] The hearts of the inconsolate suffer an "inner numbness" because they are "forsaken by the truth." They must make haste to repent, to weep not the fruitless tears of mourning but "tears that profit us" for salvation. If the sorrowing parents wish to join their son and enjoy him forever, they must ensure by their conversion to God that they gain entry to the court of heaven where he forever dwells.

Paulinus's own son, also named Celsus, had died eight days after birth.[102] That loss was one of a series of traumatic events which propelled this late-Roman aristocrat to retreat from the world, an act that proved so fruitful for later generations which bestowed upon him the name of saint. Pontius Merpius Paulinus was a pioneer even in the burial of his child. At the dawn of the worship of the material remains of the holy dead, Paulinus had the boy's body carried to a site in Spain near the martyrs of Alcala, so that his soul might gain power "from the nearby blood of the saints."[103]

Few children are mourned in written words by medieval authors, but by the time of the Renaissance, fathers express their grief.[104] The profound love for their sons of the humanist fathers Giovanni Conversini, Coluccio Salutati, and Gianozzo Manetti has already called for attention, and was revealed in their powerful grief on the death of those children. They eloquently voice the despair sounded also by Marcello at loss felt as unjust and inexplicable. Like the Venetian, they are dissolved in sorrow and fail at first to find consolation.[105] But in time they do, while Marcello does not.

In his *De consolatione de obitu filii* (On consolation on the death of his son), Conversini's "Mestus" (Sorrow) describes his pain to his interlocutor "Solator" (Solace), and in the end accepts the will of God and finds comfort in the thought of heaven. Salutati will find the same peace. The resolution of Salutati's grief on the deaths of his two eldest sons, Piero and Andrea, in the summer of 1400, is recorded in two letters to his friend Francesco Zabarella.[106] In a first letter, soon after the first death, he described his patient surrender to the will of God. Addressing the Lord, he calls himself "mere ashes and your figment," willing to accept "whatever your wisdom, goodness and omnipotence has wished."[107] That surrender to the will of God was not unconditional, however, for several months later Salutati wrote again to Zabarella, in different terms. Now he was unwilling to accept Stoic counsel of submission to reason, arguing instead the Peripatetic counsel of the naturalness of human emotion. The cold Stoics could offer him no solace. Yet, in Christian humility, he would find it in contemplation of the infinite mystery of the divine will.

The humanist father whose grief for a lost child most closely approximates the experience of Jacopo Antonio Marcello is the Florentine Gianozzo Manetti.[108] Fifth of his father's seven sons (as in the case of Valerio Marcello, neither the youngest nor the eldest), Antonino died at the age of four during Holy Week of 1438. To console himself (as he himself defines the goal of his study of classic works of consolation)[109] Manetti constructed a Latin dialogue soon after the death, and dictated a vernacular translation of the work to a scribe in 1439. In both versions, the work circulated widely, suggesting a lively interest among two strata of Renaissance readers in the experience of a bereaved father.

The dialogue presents Manetti himself, defending the intensity of his sorrow, and two contemporaries.[110] In the first part of three, the Florentine patrician Angelo Acciaiuoli urges restraint of grief. Spokesperson for the Stoic tradition, Acciaiuoli, scholar and diplomat, draws from Seneca's three consolations (particularly that for Marcia) and Cicero's *Tusculan Disputations* (thought to contain material similar to that in the author's lost consolation for his daughter Tullia) to argue that while destiny is unavoidable and often cruel, it is the task of the human being, gifted with reason, to struggle against and conquer both tragic circumstances and the emotional tumult they cause. Manetti responds in the second part of the dialogue, drawing especially on Cicero and Aristotle, by urging the legitimacy of human emotions and the need for their expression. To the Stoic Acciaiuoli, Manetti remarks: "I follow the views of the Peripatetics as more suited to human nature."[111] In the third part of the dialogue, the cleric Niccolò da Cortona presents the views of the Fathers of the church (Augustine, Ambrose, Jerome, Gregory the Great) and the medieval Saint Bernard of Clairvaux, which permit human grief but urge Christian forbearance and transcendence.

Of the three, the original voice is Manetti's, and it rejects the conventional message of consolation, both Christian and Stoic. In this early dialogue, he foreshadows his later work in exalting the multidimensional human being, capable at once of sorrow and of greatness. Yet Manetti's sorrow as expressed in the words of the *Dialogue*, however genuine, is muted compared to Marcello's later raging expressions of grief. The loss of a child whose full maturity they had hoped to see, he writes, "cannot be borne [by parents] without a certain disturbance of spirit."[112] Or again, "it is not possible," as if we were made "of stone," that parents "should not be moved more than a little" by the death of little ones barely begun on the harsh passage of life.[113]

Though Manetti challenges his consolers, moreover, by presenting an alternative vision of a feeling and passionate humanity (a vision as persuasive and authoritative as theirs) his arguments are not allowed to dominate. They are the views of one of three interlocutors, whose message, in the classic balance of the humanist dialogue, is also communicated with authority. Indeed (as was conventional), the Christian argument is saved for the final and triumphant place. That argument is sufficient, in fact, to bring resolution to Manetti's grief. He turns to his companions, in the closing pages of the *Dialogue,* with these words: "Having now indulged a little in tears, wise gentlemen, restrained by your counsel, what remains is that we bravely accede to the wish of our son and give thanks to immortal God, even if the death of our children can torment us more bitterly than any other calamity."[114] Manetti's work offers the entire process of grieving: pain, but also its resolution. The author's modest statement of grief and acceptance of solace contrasts with the message of the Marcello corpus, where the bereaved wildly assails his consolers and flings back in the teeth of their counsels of moderation the raw fact of inconsolability.

The intensity with which Marcello refuses consolation, the terrible rationality of his rejection of the traditional arguments, his angry duel with his well-meaning consolers, the determination to leave anguish unresolved, is uniquely compelling. His repudiation of consolation measures his defiance of the psychological limits imposed by classical, by Christian, and contemporary moral thought. The proprietor of Monselice claimed full ownership of his mental world. When death came, his spirit remained unconsoled, unvanquished, unreconciled to the divine will. His defiance may mark him, at least—whether or not any others can be named—as one of the firstborn sons of the modern world.[115]

e⁄ɔ   e⁄ɔ   e⁄ɔ

Did Marcello refuse to become reconciled to his son's death because he feared his own? His contemporaries did. The Renaissance era is one of heightened awareness of death.[116] The men and women of the age tell us of their feelings about death by their mourning costume and their ornament, their elaborate funeral processions, the books and pictures which record them, the tombs that they built. These rich communications from the fourteenth through the sixteenth century reveal an age characterized by the increasingly flamboyant depiction of death, its celebration and its discussion—an obsession, in fact, with the tomb and decay and the loss of self.

Not all the monuments created to commemorate forever the lives of those lost to the other world have survived. In their attempt to record their own footsteps on this earth, Marcello and his friends were especially unfortunate. They have left behind ruins and traces, a tremendous legacy of loss scarcely legible today but worth a few last pages in the attempt.

René d'Anjou, Marcello's chosen literary friend, was fascinated with death, as he was with war, chivalry, and honor: the very themes that also spiral around our Venetian. About 1445, five years before he composed his manual on tournaments, René had written a treatise of the type of the *ars moriendi* (the "art of dying") characteristic of the century.[117] Death is terrible, according to René, because we do not know the hour of our death and might die in sin, to be taken captive by the devil and led to the kingdom of the damned: "In the pit of hell, there where he will have you suffer horrible torment, forever."[118] Another *memento mori,* the visual equivalent of his treatise, is found in Avignon, in the monastery of the Celestines. There a painting perhaps by René himself projects a ghastly image: "the body of a dead woman, standing enveloped in a shroud, with her head dressed and worms gnawing her bowels." The long inscription below begins with these words: "Once I was beautiful above all women / But by death I became like this, / My flesh was very beautiful, fresh and soft, / Now it is altogether turned to ashes."[119] Death was on the mind of this king, and it surrounded him.

Elsewhere he commemorated his own nurse with a mortuary monument, and the cathedral church of St. Maurice in Angers was studded with the tombs of his family: Louis I and Marie de Blois; his parents Louis II and Yolande of Aragon; his second wife Jeanne de Laval; his daughter Margaret of Anjou, ousted queen of Henry VI of England. All predeceased him, as did his other children. His first wife Isabelle of Lorraine had already lost six of her offspring "in their blond childhood" when she died in 1453.[120] Three survived their mother, but not their father: Jean, the duke of Calabria, Yolande, and the unfortunate Marguerite. She had spent her bitter years of retirement in her father's castle where she daily read the early French manual of consolation composed in 1471 at her request.[121] Of all his immediate descendents, only the children of his daughter Yolande survived René: none in the male line. The second house of Anjou was extinguished a year after his death, and René's feudal possessions were lost: the titles to Anjou and Provence, Jerusalem and Naples all passed to the crown.

René's sepulchral monument in the cathedral dedicated to Saint Maurice in Angers was designed by that prince for his own body and that of his first consort.[122] Memorable as the first exemplar of monumental tomb sculpture among the Angevins (the kings of France and dukes of Burgundy had already launched that artistic tradition in their families), it is especially notable for its aesthetic qualities. A mass of black marble more than four feet high and nearly six wide, it was adorned with finely sculpted statues of the monarchs in contrasting white stone, accompanied respectively by a lion (signifying courage) and two greyhounds (emblematic of conjugal fidelity), and in an assertion of royal personality, displaying the arms of Anjou and Lorraine. Surmounting the tombs were vaults painted in blue with gold fleurs-de-lis, and a sculptural group showing the crucifixion with René and Isabelle on either side of the cross.

On the wall above the tombs was painted a fresco, apocalpytic in theme and traditional in style, emblematic of an obscure message. Executed by an artist unknown, it was once said to be by René himself; that sovereign surely played a role in its design. In two books of hours once in René's possession (and now in the national collections of libraries in Paris and London), are seen the same image of the "roi mort" that once surmounted his tomb.[123] This pictorial puzzle on the theme of death—or better, hell—featured a spectral king, a cadaver wrapped in a long robe, upon a glittering throne, about whose feet were scattered crowns and tiaras, globes and books. These represented all the objects and even the knowledge by which the human creature sought, futilely, to make himself immortal: the "flowers, trophies and honors of the world, meaningless fame, foolish ceremonies" specified in the epigram (composed perhaps by the poet-king) that was inscribed beneath the fresco on an azure band. "Death levels master and servant, base and honest men; / The same tomb encloses king, shepherd, and vain scholar." Thus did the royal artist and poet, haunted as he was by the image of the "roi mort," comment upon his own destiny.[124]

René's tomb is no more. Begun in 1447, it was still unfinished when there were placed there the bodies of Isabelle (in 1453) and René (in 1480). Brought to completion in 1540, it was destroyed utterly in 1793, another victim of Revolution. The black marble structure was "reduced to shapeless rubble and thrown pell-mell in a heap in front of the church until unknowing workers . . . made of the remnants their chests, their mantelpieces, and their knick-knacks."[125]

René's sometime ally Francesco Sforza was also concerned with monuments. As soon as he arrived at the pinnacle of his aspirations in 1450, he authorized the many projects which long survived him: the building or rebuilding of the *castello sforzesco,* the Certosa in Pavia, the city's famed *ospedale,* the largest then in Europe. His palace in Venice, as has been seen, met with a less happy fate: only one mere corner of the building, full of promise for late architectural style in that city, and the name of "Duke" remain.[126]

Another monument, once famous, to the person and spirit of this most determined and successful of *condottieri,* has been destroyed.[127] Francesco's son and heir Galeazzo Maria commissioned two sculptors, the brothers Cristoforo and Antonio Mantegazza, to erect in honor of the first Sforza dynast a grand equestrian monument to stand before the main entrance of the Castello. Before the work began, the patron died, and his brother Ludovico, then regent though later murderer of the unlucky Giangaleazzo, did not rush to execute the project. Some years later Leonardo da Vinci, having newly arrived at the Milanese court, offered, among a host of other enterprises, to undertake the monument to Francesco Sforza—expressing rather greater interest in the horse than in the rider. By this time, in addition to the models offered by the ancient statue of Marcus Aurelius in Rome and Donatello's Gattamelata in Padua, Verrocchio's Colleoni was available for study. Ludovico commissioned the great artist to proceed with a plaster model for an eventual bronze sculpture. An extant study shows that Leonardo referred to the Colleoni, but planned to introduce the novel and potent element of motion: the horse rears, the rider thrusts out his sword, a man is trampled underfoot by raging hoofs.[128]

After several years of the usual da Vinci prevarication, on 30 November 1493 (on the occasion of the marriage of Bianca Maria Sforza to the emperor Maximilian), the temporary monument was displayed under a triumphal arch in its fitting and long-intended position outside the gate of the Castello.[129] Known as the "Colossus," the statue soared atop its base to a height of twelve *braccie* (more than twenty feet) according to the mathematician Fra Luca Pacioli, whose measurements should be credible. But the temporary creation was never cast in the durable bronze for which it was intended, and stood unprotected in the open air, deteriorating. In 1501, Duke Ercole d'Este of Ferrara, who wished to memorialize himself in an equestrian pose, thought da Vinci's model would serve for his own artists and offered to buy it, without success. The Colossus remained in Milan, and the man who had relentlessly toiled to have in Venice a monument in stone was to receive no more solid commemoration at home than a fragile

A hint of the style of the equestrian statue Leonardo da Vinci crafted in wax of Francesco Sforza and planned to execute in bronze is provided by the artist's silverpoint drawing entitled Horseman Trampling on Foe. *Windsor, Royal Library. Foto Marburg/Art Resource, N.Y.*

plaster ghost. Torn down in the French invasion of Milan in 1502, it is no more.

Also destroyed are many of the monuments (the castle at Monselice a notable exception) associated with Marcello. His palace on the Grand Canal, to which little Valerio fled for refuge from the menacing jeers of the boys of his quarter, once graced today's Corte dell'Albero.[130] It stood adjacent to the surviving Palazzo Corner-Spinelli which, when last seen by this author, housed the municipal office where applicants purchased transportation passes for the city's *vaporetti*. Marcello's heirs lived there still when the *condottiere* Tuzio Costanzo visited in 1509, by testimony of the omnipresent gossip Marino Sanuto. In 1676, the palaces of Marcello's descendants and their neighbors of the Cappello family were razed to make way for the Teatro Sant'Angelo, which they jointly owned. Frequented by Casanova in

The Ca' del Duca, or "Duke's Palace," begun by Francesco Sforza, Duke of Milan, showing a section of rusticated stone in the lower right corner of the façade which introduced to Venice the pattern of a more militant style of terraferma *architecture. Venice, Grand Canal. Photograph courtesy of Osvaldo Böhm.*

the following century, the theater was famed in its heyday for its productions of the native playwright Carlo Goldoni. It was closed and torn down in 1803, to be replaced by an ordinary warehouse.

Also obliterated in the same era of Napoleonic housecleaning were the monastery and church of San Antonio da Vienna where the statue of Vettore Pisani inspired the child Valerio to heroic achievement he was never to know. The tomb of Jacopo Antonio Marcello and his son Pietro in the church of San Cristoforo—the church that bore also the mark of Sforza—

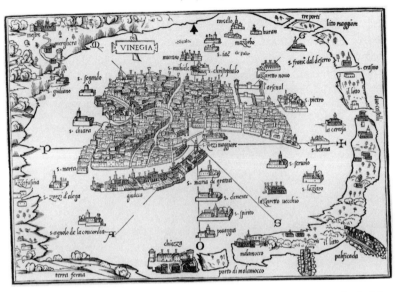

This 1534 map of Venice by Benedetto Bordone shows the location of the island of San Cristoforo della Pace, later destroyed, on which stood the church of San Cristoforo containing an inscription to Marcello and memorabilia of Francesco Sforza. Venice, Museo Correr, with permission. Photograph courtesy of Osvaldo Böhm.

was yet another victim of Napoleon. Even the island itself on which it stood, commemorated to the peace that was to last forever, disappeared. The channel which separated it from the nearby island of San Michele was filled in, and the enlarged site was converted to use as the cemetery where today tourists take in the stone that honors Stravinsky. Valerio's tomb in San Giorgio Maggiore, that ancient and sacred Venetian site, was likewise demolished when the church was rebuilt to Palladio's design a little more than a century after the child's death. On the diminutive island of San Giorgio today is housed a school for young boys and a foundation for scholarly studies created five centuries after Valerio's death by another grieving father in memory of his son, Giorgio Cini, prematurely deceased. And it is that same bereaved father who today holds title to the castle at Monselice where Valerio frolicked in the speck of time allotted him.

Not one stone is left today commemorating the lives of Jacopo Antonio Marcello and the child Valerio. What has survived is a book, provocatively unfinished, never read by the chosen arbiter, René d'Anjou, never placed alongside the others Marcello had dispatched over the Alps to that royal bibliophile. It is finished here by a stranger locked in another century. Her task has been to publish at last the message the bereaved father wished spread abroad, the final and most important message he chose to send to posterity before his own exit to rejoin the angel who awaited him in heaven. The loss of a child is irreparable loss, its sorrow inconsolable sorrow, the door to the future doubly sealed.

APPENDIX ONE

Marcello Family and Monuments

❦

I. THE MARCELLO FAMILY

A. The Lineage of Jacopo Antonio Marcello

1. A Venetian noble clan could have many branches possessing different characteristics and specializing in different activities (see esp. Chojnacki 1973, 1985, and 1986; J. C. Davis 1962; J. C. Davis 1975). Such is the case with the Marcello family.

2. The ancestor from whom Jacopo Antonio's branch of the family descends is identified by the nineteenth-century biographer Emmanuele Cicogna as Girolamo, also called Gazano, son of Andrea, resident at San Vitale (Cicogna 1841, 14–15). This figure was active in political life from at least 1331, when he appeared in the Senate. In 1354, he was one of several counselors assigned to assist the admiral Paolo Loredan in the naval defense of Venice against the Genoese. He was part of the *zonta* that consulted with the Council of Ten at the time of the suppression of the conspiracy of Marino Falier in 1355, and was an elector of the Doge Andrea Contarini in 1367. In 1373, he made his will.

3. Yet Gazano was still alive in 1379–80 when along with four other male Marcello noblemen resident in San Vitale, he contributed to the funding of the Chioggian war effort. The others were Bortolomio, Marcellino, Nicoletto, and Vettore. In addition to these residents of San Vitale, probably close relatives of Gazano's, three Marcellos resident at San Michele Arcangelo (Andrea, Fantino, and Mario) and one each at San Basilio and San Samuele (Marco and Paolo) are noted by the chronicles (Cicogna 1841, 14–15). The Marcello family overall, in the 1379 *estimo*, ranked fifty-first among noble families—wealthy, but not the wealthiest. During the fourteenth century, it ranked nineteenth among noble families in the number of major offices held (Chojnacki 1973, 74–75).

4. Gazano's son Pietro, called "Il Grande," is identified by Cicogna as Jacopo Antonio's grandfather. Like his father, Pietro was noted for his political role. In 1361 he was one of the forty-one electors (the final "hand" in

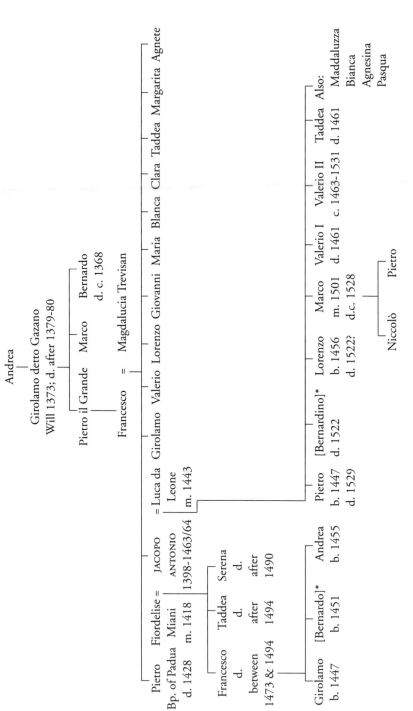

*Bernardino di Jacopo Antonio and Bernardo di Francesco may be only one figure

Marcello family: resident at San Vitale, later Sant'Angelo (San Marco)

that complicated electoral process) of the Doge Lorenzo Celsi (Cicogna 1841, 14), and from 1357, he served in important embassies (ibid., 12). Among these was the mission in 1368 to Egypt, when Pietro Marcello and a colleague were charged to recover the persons and property of some Venetian merchants.

5.   It is this last adventure that is described in Bevilacqua's *Excusatio* (IV.2 below). Here Jacopo Antonio's grandfather Pietro is said to have been sent as ambassador "to the king of the Moors," and his reception is compared to that of Lucullus by the Egyptian ruler Ptolemy. On the return journey, the writer continues, he was murdered, and buried in great magnificence on the island of Crete, part of the Venetian domain.

6.   Jacopo Antonio's relationship to Pietro "il Grande" di Gazano is thus confirmed by the consoler Giorgio Bevilacqua, a knowledgeable contemporary. Three seventeenth-century genealogists offer alternative trees which must be rejected: two identify the grandfather of Jacopo Antonio as Pietro of Sant'Angelo, the son of Francesco, the son of Giovanni, the son of Pietro (Barbaro, *Arbori,* 4:461; Cappellari, *Campidoglio veneto,* 3:38v), while a third places Pietro in San Maurizio (Damadenus, *De origine,* fol. 303). A confusion between the San Vitale and Sant'Angelo branches may be partly accounted for in this way. The San Vitale branch of the Marcello clan, to which Gazano and at least four other adult males belonged in the late years of the Trecento, moved when the Pisani family purchased the properties (Gallo 1944, 87). Perhaps they moved immediately to Sant'Angelo, where Jacopo Antonio's household is located in the mid-fifteenth century.

7.   Jacopo Antonio's illustrious forebear Pietro di Gazano was the brother of Marco and Bernardo, sons of the same Gazano, both active in naval roles and prominent in political life (Cicogna 1841, 12, 14, 16). He is the father of Francesco (named "di Pietro" in ASV, AC-BO 162/I, fol. 99v) and possibly also of Fantino and Marcello, denoted as sons of "Pietro" (Cicogna 1841, 14, 16).

8.   Like his father and grandfather, Francesco was known for his military activity: "cum bellica virtute excelleret, et non nisi bella spirantem filium procreaverit" (Damadenus, *De origine,* fol. 303). In 1383, he married Magdalucia (quondam Paolo quondam Giovanni) Trevisan (Barbaro, *Arbori,* 4:461), the mother of Jacopo Antonio. The genealogist Damadenus (loc. cit.) names the daughter of Paolo Trevisan "Maria"; but Magdalucia is confirmed by other evidence. At the presentation of Jacopo Antonio to the Avogaria di Comun for ascription to the Balla d'Oro (ASV, AC-BO 162/I, fol. 99v), the young man's father Francesco is accompanied by Alessandro

di Vittore Marcello as well as by his wife Magdalucia, the subject's mother. Alessandro di Vittore might be the son of that Vittore (Vettore) recorded as resident at San Vitale and, with Gazano and others, a contributor to the Chioggian war effort in 1379–80. The Trevisan family had recently been ennobled for exceptional service during the same Chioggian struggle. The alliance between Pietro and Magdalucia was between two families who shared a political role at that critical moment in Venetian history.

9. Francesco and Magdalucia had a large family: twenty-six children, according to Perleone, of whom thirteen survived childhood: six males and seven females, the latter all successfully wed to patricians (IV.1.a below). The same passage names six of Jacopo Antonio's seven sisters, who predeceased him: Maria, Bianca (lat., Blanca), Clara, Taddea, Margarita, Agnete. Perhaps the seventh, unnamed, was still living. It refers to five brothers, also predeceased: Giovanni, Girolamo, Lorenzo, Pietro, and Valerio. The genealogist Marco Barbaro (*Arbori,* 4:461) lists all of these but Pietro (perhaps because he early entered upon an ecclesiastical career), noting the marriages in 1400 and 1408 respectively of Giovanni and Girolamo to (noble) daughters of an unnamed Quirini and Matteo Barbaro. Jacopo Antonio's brother Valerio was demonstrably that Valerio Marcello who, together with Daniele Vitturi (see below I.A.31), had relations in 1412 with the humanist pedagogue Gasparino Barzizza (Barzizza 1723, 141–43, also letters to Valerio alone at 145, 186–87; see C. Colombo 1969, 13–14).

10. Pietro di Francesco (named after his grandfather Pietro il Grande) was himself a noted figure (Cicogna 1841, 24, 29; King 1986, 397–98). Born in 1376 (and thus more than twenty years older than Jacopo Antonio), he was made bishop of Ceneda in 1399, and bishop of Padua in 1409. In Padua, he became an early Venetian enthusiast of the humanist studies that also drew his younger brother probably soon after the death of their father Francesco in 1411 in the war against King Ladislas of Hungary.

11. Already mature, Pietro di Francesco studied law at the university and won the doctorate in 1413. At the conferral of that degree, he was honored with an oration by another early Venetian humanist and relative by marriage, Zaccaria Trevisan the Elder. He died in 1428, one year after his retirement to Camaldulensian monastery, not before he had opportunity to exert considerable influence on the intellectual life of Jacopo Antonio, then perhaps thirty years old. Girolamo had died earlier; upon his death, Gasparino Barzizza (one of the prominent humanists in the Paduan bishop's circle) had written to Pietro Marcello in consolation (Barzizza 1723, 85–87; King 1986, 397–98).

12. Jacopo Antonio also had a sizable family; but nowhere in the consolatory literature (composed 1461–63) is found a precise accounting of it. Several references are made to the fact that he had "other children" than the Valerio who figures at the center of this study (IV.6–19 below). One comment notes five children, unnamed—all these necessarily male because of the reference to citizenship responsibility (IV.11 below). There are two specific references to a promising boy, Francesco, apparently already mature—as he must have been if he himself married in 1443! (IV.15, 16 below). There is also a specific reference to a younger brother Lorenzo (IV.14 below).

13. Francesco in turn had at least three sons, old enough to have formed part of the patriarch's household. On 31 July 1465 Girolamo, son of Francesco (himself son of the then deceased Jacopo Antonio) by legitimate marriage with Anna da Leone, was presented to the Avogaria di Comun for ascription to the Balla d'Oro by his grandfather's widow, Luca da Leone (ASV, AC-BO, 164/III, fol. 261). Attesting with her to the child's legitimate birth was Giovanni da Leone, "egregius legum doctor et miles," kinsman to both da Leone women. This Girolamo, born in 1447, would have been older than Valerio, our subject and his uncle, born in 1452. This grandson of Jacopo Antonio's, but elder than Valerio, is recalled by the young boy according to the account of Pietro Perleone (IV.13 below).

14. On 2 December 1469, Francesco himself presented a son Bernardo, born accordingly in 1451 and our Valerio's senior, who was also the fruit of his father's sole known marriage to Anna da Leone (ASV, AC-BO, 164/III, fol. 261v). On 3 December 1473, Pietro di Jacopo Loredan (whose deceased father had been Procuratore di San Marco) presented to the same tribunal Andrea Marcello, son of Francesco and grandson of Jacopo Antonio (ASV, AC-BO, 164/III, fol. 262). Francesco's third child would have been born in about 1455. His father, not noted as "quondam," must have been still alive although absent from Venice on this date (as is also confirmed by the consolatory tradition in which Francesco is still alive in 1461). Bernardo ("Bernardino") and Andrea are also listed in the will of Taddea di Jacopo Antonio Marcello (of whom more below) of 12 January 1494 (Girgensohn 1989, 26 and n121). At the time of testation, Taddea's brother Francesco was already dead.

15. Such is the heritage of Valerio's elder brother Francesco. His younger brother Lorenzo was born around 1456, and presented to the Avogaria di Comun as the legitimate offspring of Jacopo Antonio Marcello and his wife Luca da Leone on 2 December 1474 (ASV, AC-BO, 164/III, fol. 262v) by

the sons of Francesco, the two brothers Girolamo and Bernardino. The genealogist Barbaro (*Arbori,* 4:461) gives the year of Lorenzo's death as 1522.

16. Other sources attest to four sons of Jacopo Antonio not named in the consolatory literature: (1) Pietro, a famous military figure on the pattern of his father; (2) a second Valerio, born posthumously after our Valerio died and baptized with the name of the child forever lost; (3) Marco; (4) Bernardino. Thus Valerio may have had both a brother and a nephew named Bernardino, an uncle and *two* nephews named Girolamo (one the son of Francesco, one of Serena), and two sisters named Taddea.

17. Pietro di Jacopo Antonio, so oddly ignored by his father's consolers, forged a career like that patriarch's (see Cicogna 1841, 13, 15, 18, 20; also Barbaro, *Arbori,* 4:461; Sanuto 1879–1903, ad indicem; Sanuto 1980, 186–87). Presented by his widowed mother Luca da Leone for ascription to the Balla d'Oro on 31 July 1465 (ASV, AC-BO, 164/III, c. 261; Fabbri 1983, 246), he was born in 1447. He held government positions from at least 1480: ambassador in 1495, ducal elector (of Leonardo Loredan) in 1501; *savio di terra ferma* in the same year; *avogador* in 1504; *podestà* of Padua in 1506. But like his parent he specialized in the *provveditoriate.*

18. In that title Pietro Marcello participated in wars with Ferrara (1482), against the advance of King Charles VIII (1495), in Tuscany (1498), against the League of Cambrai (1508–9), and in Friuli (1514), but died an octogenarian and apparently at peace in 1529, to be buried in the same chapel where his father lay in San Cristoforo della Pace. On the wall of that building could once be read an inscription recording his deeds (below, III.C.6). He employed the unique variation of the family coat of arms that his father had first adopted, and had them carved on many surfaces of the Monselice castle/palace, the renovation of which, initiated by his father, he brought to completion.

19. The younger Valerio was presented for ascription to the Balla d'Oro in 1481, having thus been born in 1463 (Fabbri 1983, 231n10), and died in 1531. Married to a daughter of Andrea di Marco Corner, he held naval and *terraferma* positions, including count of Zara and *podestà* of Rovigo. He participated in the design of the sepulchral inscription found at one time in the Church of San Cristoforo della Pace, which was more likely completed (in 1555) under the supervision of Niccolò and Pietro, apparently Jacopo Antonio's grandchildren and Valerio's nephews by the obscure Marco (below III.C.5).

20. This Marco, who married a daughter of Niccolò di Domenico Michiel in 1501, as *podestà* (and castle proprietor) defended Monselice against the French in 1510, and died after 1528 (Barbaro, *Arbori,* 4:461). Of Bernardino, an ecclesiastic, we have the testimony of the nineteenth-century biographer Cicogna (Cicogna 1841, 30); this Bernardino may possibly be conflated with Bernardino, Francesco's son, born in 1451 (see above).

21. As reconstructed here, the sons of Jacopo Antonio were seven (perhaps six): Francesco (d. after 3 December 1473 but before 12 January 1494), Pietro (d. 1529), Lorenzo (d. 1522?), Marco (d. after 1528), Bernardino perhaps (d. 1522), one Valerio (d. 1461), and a second "remade" Valerio (d. 1531). With the inclusion of Bernardino and the omission of Valerio I (prematurely dead) and Valerio II (born after the composition of the Marcello consolations), this accounting squares with the report made there of five sons still living.

22. To these sons of Jacopo Antonio Marcello's may be added seven (or perhaps eight) daughters. Two are mentioned in the consolatory corpus. A daughter Taddea, already mature, died soon after Valerio, as noted in two passages (IV.17, 18 below). A second, unnamed daughter is also noted in those texts (IV.19 below) as particularly loved by that unfortunate child, and commended on his deathbed to his father's attention.

23. Sources outside the consolatory corpus attest to six daughters. (Of these, one may correspond to Valerio's favored but unidentified sister therein mentioned. If so, the total of seven daughters of Jacopo Antonio Marcello is attained; if not, the young sister reported in the consolations is an eighth female child.) Two of the six are Taddea (a second of that name, the Taddea named in the consolations dying in 1461) and Serena. These sisters died after 12 January 1494 and 18 May 1490, when respectively they made their testaments (Girgensohn 1989, 26 and nn121, 122). Taddea's will notes younger sisters Maddaluza, Bianca, Agnesina, and Pasqua—these are the remaining daughters of Jacopo Antonio Marcello. Serena names in her will her own children Filippo, Girolamo, Marco, Paolo, Loredano, and Angela.

24. The fourteen (or thirteen or fifteen) children of Jacopo Antonio were the fruit of two marriages. The first was to Fiordelise in 1418, when Marcello was an unusually youthful groom of twenty. The bride was daughter of the wealthy Venetian nobleman and bishop of Vicenza, Pietro Miani, who fathered four legitimate children before assuming a clerical calling in 1407 (Barbaro, *Arbori,* 4:461; Cappellari, *Campidoglio,* 3:38v; Fabbri

1983, 246; Girgensohn 1989; also private communications from Dr. Margaret Bent, to whom I am most grateful, and who also supplied me with a copy of Fiordelise's manuscript will). From this union were born before 10 October 1425 (when Fiordelise made testament and enumerated these offspring) one son Francesco and two daughters Taddea and Serena. Possibly pregnant with a fourth child at this time, the testatrix had died by 25 September 1426 (Girgensohn 1989, 26 and n123). She predeceased her father Pietro Miani, who died 4 May 1433, and whose splendid tomb would be built in the Frari church in Venice as stipulated by his testament of 2 April 1429 (Girgensohn 1989, 42).

25. The second marriage was in 1443 to Luca da Leone (Giomo, *Indice,* 1:340). The consecutive marriages in 1442 and 1443 (noted by Fabbri 1983, 246, and King 1986, 394) to daughters respectively of Cao de Vacca of Padua and Bartolomeo Lion of Padua must be reduced to one: Bartolomeo da Leone bore the surname "Cao de Vacca," and is one and the same person; for this clan, see below, I. C. The extreme youth of Jacopo Antonio at his first marriage to Fiordelise di Pietro Miani, and resulting closeness of his age to Francesco's, is underscored by the double wedding of 1443, when father and son together married two sisters, Luca and Anna, daughters of Bartolomeo da Leone.

26. That relationship is known from ASV, AC-BO, 164/III, fol. 261, where on the same day (31 July 1465) the widowed Luca da Leone presented for ascription to the Balla d'Oro her son and her nephew: respectively Pietro (son of Jacopo Antonio) and Girolamo (son of Francesco di Jacopo Antonio and Anna di Bartolomeo da Leone). She and Giovanni da Leone, a Paduan jurist and cousin of Luca's father Bartolomeo, attested to the legitimacy of Anna's marriage. Father and son married sisters, whose firstborn sons first saw the day in the same year of 1447.

27. Marcello's children by Luca da Leone were thus born between 1447 and 1463. They numbered at least eleven (ten if Bernardino is excluded; twelve if both Bernardino and an unnamed sixth daughter of Luca da Leone are included). These included a maximum of six sons (Pietro in 1447, Valerio I in 1452, Lorenzo in 1456, Bernardino and Marco, with unknown birthdates, Valerio II in 1463), and a minimum of five daughters (Taddea II, known from the consolatory literature, and Maddalena, Bianca, Agnesina, and Pasqua, named in the will of the elder Taddea I, Marcello's daughter by Fiordelise di Pietro Miani). Of these, all but Valerio I and Taddea II were alive in 1461–63, together with Jacopo Antonio's three children by his first marriage (Francesco, Taddea I, and Serena).

28. A note on names: these tended to run over centuries in this Marcello clan. Already in the cohort of Jacopo Antonio's brothers, the names Giovanni and Pietro were commonplaces of earlier generations. Girolamo, Lorenzo, Valerio, and Jacopo Antonio were, however, new. Of these, Lorenzo and Valerio will appear among Jacopo Antonio's sons, Girolamo among his grandsons, and the venerable Francesco and Pietro will recur; Marco and Bernardo will resurrect the names of the brothers of Jacopo Antonio's grandfather, Pietro il Grande. Jacopo Antonio itself is unique; but Jacopo is found in other branches of the family.

29. Among Jacopo Antonio's grandsons, Andrea (son of Francesco) and Niccolò (son of Marco) have novel names—the name Niccolò, however, was common in other branches of the clan and was borne in 1473–74 by a doge of Venice. Among females, the names of Marcello's mother (Magdalucia, or Maddalena) and some sisters (Bianca, Agnete, Taddea) are repeated among his daughters; Taddea appears twice, one for each wife of the patriarch!

30. Relations between the lineage of Jacopo Antonio Marcello and other important families can be detected from marriages, where known, and from the names of witnesses to Balla d'Oro documents recording the ascriptions of some male members. The Trevisan lineage of Jacopo Antonio's fertile mother Magdalucia has been noted (above, I.A.8) so inquiry may turn to his own spouses.

31. Fiordelise, the first of these, has already been introduced as the legitimate daughter of Pietro Miani (who called himself Emilianus, alluding to Roman origins), of a family of exceedingly great wealth (Girgensohn 1989, 13, 31–38 and passim for what follows). Miani was through his mother related to the noble Barbarigo clan, through his wife to the Contarini. Miani's wife Contarina di Giacomo Contarini was able to bequeathe 600 ducats of her own dowry wealth to her daughters Fiordelise and Camilla, in addition to dowry grants made by their father. Besides the link to the Marcello clan made through Fiordelise, Miani was joined to the Vitturi by the marriage of his son Giovannino to Margherita di Niccolò, brother of the learned Daniele Vitturi (see King 1986, 445–46).

32. Jacopo Antonio and his son both married into the noble Paduan da Leone family in 1443 (see above, I.A.25–26; below, I.C). This alliance forged no friendships for them within Venice, but it linked them to a high-profile *terraferma* clan known for its generals, prelates, and jurists. Two of Marcello's other sons (Lorenzo and Marco respectively) married daughters of the noble Corner (of notable wealth) and Michiel lineages, while daugh-

ter Serena married Francesco, a son of the distinguished Ludovico Loredan, who held that title second in Venice only to the *dogado:* Procuratore di San Marco.

33. Appearing in the Balla d'Oro documents, aside from members of the Marcello or da Leone clans, are these patricians: Francesco Loredan, son of the Procuratore Ludovico, and Marcello's son-in-law, as has been noted (ASV, AC-BO, 164/III, fol. 261; 31 July 1465); Pietro Loredan, son of Jacopo, also Procuratore di San Marco, of the same family (ASV, AC-BO, 164/III, fol. 261; 3 December 1473); Pietro di Maffeo Malipiero (31 July 1465, as above), of the Malipiero family honored by the *dogado* in the person of Marcello's old comrade Pasquale Malipiero (1457–62); and Ludovico Foscari, son of Marco, the Procuratore di San Marco and brother of deposed doge and architect of Venetian expansion Francesco Foscari (1423–57). The associates of the immediate line of Jacopo Antonio Marcello included members of some of the wealthiest and most powerful clans among the Venetian patriciate.

B. Other Branches of the Marcello Clan

1. The most famous branch of the Marcello family is that resident in Santa Marina, from which derived Niccolò di Giovanni, a contemporary of Jacopo Antonio. Renowned for his great philanthropic activity while procurator, he was elected doge of Venice in 1473 and died the following year. (Malipiero 1843–44, 662–63; Sanuto, *Cronica sanuda,* fol. 241; Cicogna 1841, 11, 13; his funeral oration by Ermolao Barbaro Giovane, see E. Barbaro 1559). For their palace, see below, III.A.1.

2. Also wealthy and illustrious was the branch of the Marcello clan resident in San Tomà, of which the fifteenth- and sixteenth-century figures are well known. Jacopo di Cristoforo was one of those Marcellos who, like Jacopo Antonio and his son Pietro, excelled in a military career. He was born some fifteen years later than his near-namesake Jacopo Antonio with whom he is often confused, having been presented to the Avogaria di Comun on 27 November 1432 by his father Cristoforo di Vittore (ASV, AC-BO, 162/I, fol. 100v; see also Fabbri 1983, 250).

3. Jacopo Marcello died heroically in the high tradition of his clan while admiral of the Venetian fleet opposing Gallipoli in 1484. His monument is still seen in the church of Santa Maria Gloriosa de' Frari, not far from the family residence. One passes today in walking from San Tomà to the Frari a narrow *calle* named *gli stretti di Gallipoli* ("the straits of Gallipoli")— a memory surely of the famous admiral and hero. Jacopo's portrait by Gio-

vanni Bellini, now lost, was treasured by his descendants (Cicogna 1841, 17–20; Goffen 1989, 192–93). For the palace at San Tomà, see below III.A.2.

4. Antonio, son of Jacopo di Cristoforo Marcello, predeceased him. Jacopo's unnamed grandchildren by Antonio were granted special privileges in recognition of their ancestor's sacrifice (King 1986, 398). Those grandchildren are not specified in the Senate act, but they may have included the following three sons of Antonio's, of whom the first is identified as belonging to the Marcellos of San Tomà. That figure is the famed churchman and writer Cristoforo, archbishop of Corfu from 1514, papal favorite, and victim in 1527 of the sack of Rome (Cicogna 1841, 25, 30; Cicogna 1824–53, 2:79–84, 421–22; 4:630; 6:775).

5. Cristoforo's brother Girolamo, the second of these three, was a collector, possessing pictures by Giorgione, Titian, Palma Vecchio, and Giovanni Bellini, including the latter's portrait of his grandfather Jacopo, mentioned above (Cicogna 1841, 20, 28; for the relationship, Goffen 1989, 317n3). The third, Pietro, was a minor humanist whose works probably included an oration for the same Jacopo (Cicogna 1841, 25; King 1986, 398–99; *Iter* 2:578).

6. At the time that Cicogna wrote the history of the Marcello family (before 1841), an Alessandro Marcello of San Tomà was in possession of the manuscript *Mare-caelum romano-venetum sive Marcellorum a Romani[s] principibus ad Venetos proceres* by Amaden or Damadenus (Abbot Theodorus) presented to Federico di Andrea of the same family (and possibly of the same residence, but that is not specified) in 1676 (Cicogna 1841, 9, 29, 35n1). One of two manuscript copies of that work (probably the original) was consulted by Fabbri prior to 1983 at the family library of Dottore Girolamo Marcello, resident near Campo Sant'Angelo (Fabbri 1983, 231n10). This was a seventeenth-century Latin manuscript (1676) which, along with an eighteenth-century Italian translation by Vettore Marcello, also in manuscript, was seen by me at the kind invitation of Dott. Marcello, in July 1990. Another Latin version is in Paris, Bibliothèque de l'Arsenal, ms. 1211.

7. Not far from San Tomà, at San Polo, dwelled Pietro di Andrea Marcello, a sixteenth-century collector of precious medals (Cicogna 1841, 29; perhaps it is his palace discussed below, III.A.3). In the seventeenth and eighteenth centuries, there flourished at Santa Maria Maddalena four learned and politically prominent members of the family. Three were brothers (all sons of Agostino): Alessandro (1684–1750), Girolamo (d.

1742), and Benedetto (1686–1739); the fourth, of the same line, was Lorenzo Alessandro. All were *letterati* of considerable refinement, and Alessandro and Benedetto (especially the latter) enjoyed considerable fame as musical theorists and composers (Arnold 1983; Cicogna 1841, 27; Fontana 1865, 317–20; Talbot 1980). For their palace, see below, III.A.4.

8. In the Trecento, in addition to the Marcellos of San Vitale (or San Maurizio, for Damadenus, *De origine,* fol. 303; or Sant'Angelo, for Barbaro, *Arbori,* 4:461, and Cappellari, *Campidoglio,* 3:38v) from whom Jacopo Antonio descended, Cicogna notes Marcello contributors to the Chioggian war effort (1379–80) resident in San Michele Arcangelo, San Samuele, and San Basilio (Cicogna 1841, 15). The genealogist Marco Barbaro (*Arbori,* 4:455–92) notes in addition to those at Sant'Angelo, San Tomà, Santa Marina, San Polo, and Santa Maria Maddalena, branches of the Marcello clan at San Trovaso, the Riva de Biasio, and in Candia.

9. In the fifteenth century, spurred by the humanist taste for antiquity, the Marcello family traced its origins to ancient Rome: especially to three figures named repeatedly as forebears of Jacopo Antonio Marcello in the consolatory corpus, all bearing the name Marcus Claudius Marcellus. The most senior of these (c.268–208 B.C.) was the consul and colleague of Fabius Maximus, who besieged and won Syracuse in the Second Punic War, and confronted Hannibal (see Livy 23:16 and Plutarch's life of this figure). The second (died 45 B.C.) was the friend of Cicero who opposed Julius Caesar in the civil war. The third (43?–23 B.C.), was the son of Augustus's sister Octavia, married to the emperor's daughter Julia, and mourned by Vergil (*Aeneid* 6.860–85) and Propertius (3.18). The Vergilian phrase "Tu Marcellus eris" (6.883), used of this youthful Marcellus, was adopted as the motto of that branch of the Venetian clan (contemporary with our Jacopo Antonio) from which stemmed the doge Niccolò. The contemporary chronicler Zorzi Dolfin already refers to these Roman ancestors in c. 1458, saying "questi venevo antigamente da roma, i furno tribuni antichi ma busar di altra modo i erano homini di bataglia, e spesse volte i fevano brige" (*Cronaca,* fol. 54 [22]). Two centuries later, Damadenus traces the Marcello family "a romani[s] principibus ad venetos proceres, ab anno u. c. [249] usque ad annum Christi [1676] per annos [2,127] de patre in fiium deducta progenies" (*De origine,* 1:title page).

C. The Da Leone Family of Padua

1. This eminent noble Paduan family with a history of Carrara service in the Trecento and Venetian cooperation after the 1405 conquest is eulogized

by Perleone (IV.3 below); see also references of Filelfo and the Anonymous Tutor (IV.4, 5). It was Luca da Leone, father of Bartolomeo, and grandfather of Jacopo Antonio's second wife (Valerio's mother), who yielded the bastion of Monselice (see below) to the Venetian nobleman, adventurer, and soldier Carlo Zeno in 1405 (see III.D, below, for Monselice; for Luca also Scardeone 1560, 319). This step in the city's acquisition of the *terraferma* was won *per tradimento,* and for a price: the fortress was by other means, to that date, impregnable. Jacopo Antonio's wife Luca (not Lucia) di Bartolomeo was named after her warlike and practical grandfather. (Father Bartolomeo led a quieter life that leaves few other traces than his attendance at the granting of various degrees in Padua, 1414–15; Zonta & Brotto 1970, 1:130–32, 135–36, 139, 140; docs. ##317, 319, 328, 335, 338). Luca's brother, Paolo da Leone, a former Carrara adviser, became a trusted Venetian servant as a military consultant (Savonarola 1902, 43n4; Scardeone 1560, 320). Even prior to his capture while fighting for the Carraresi in 1405, he had married into the Venetian noble Soranzo family (Mallett and Hale 1984, 101n1); he stood among the honored guests as Pietro Marcello, bishop of Padua and brother of Jacopo Antonio, was examined for his license in both laws (Zonta & Brotto 1970, 1:125, #303; 16 October 1413); and he was eulogized on his death in 1431 by the loyal Venetian *cittadino* Pietro del Monte (McManamon 1989, 281; Savonarola 1902, loc. cit.).

2.   Among Paolo's sons (nephews of the one Luca, cousins of Bartolomeo, the second's father) were Giovanni, Cecco, and Leonello da Leone. The first of these was an eminent doctor of laws and professor of jurisprudence at the university in Padua (Facciolati 1757, 1.2:34–35; Zonta & Brotto 1970, 1:234, #741 for degree granted 9 November 1429, and further appearances through 1434, ad indices). He was the kinsman of the sisters Luca da Leone, widow of Jacopo Antonio, and Anna da Leone, wife of Francesco Marcello, and was present at the ascription to the Balla d'Oro of Girolamo Marcello, fruit of the union between Anna and Francesco (see I.A.13 above; ASV, AC-BO, 164/III, fol. 261; 31 July 1465). Cecco also studied law, receiving his doctorate in civil law on 29 January 1432 (Zonto & Brotto 1970, 1:278, doc. #870) and making later appearances in that capacity through 1450 (ibid., ad indices). Leonello, entitled *miles,* had at least three sons each of whom was married to a daughter of the respected Venetian *condottiere* Gentile da Leonessa (Eroli 1876, 156–57; the daughters were named Milea, Battista, and Tarsia). Later da Leone descendents bearing the title of Counts of Sanguineto added in 1651 to the

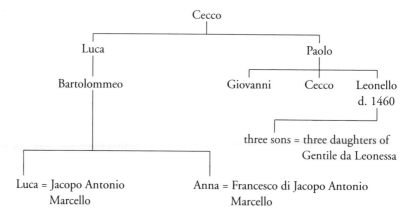

Da Leone family of Padua

monuments in the church of San Antonio, Padua, to their ancestor Gattamelata (Salomonius 1701, 356–57, ##23, 24, 26). Giacoma, a fourth daughter of Gentile's (to indicate in what circles that warrior could establish marital ties), was married to Bertoldo d'Este of the reigning Ferrarese dynasty. For these relationships, see da Leone genealogy; also IV.3–4.

3. As many as nine members of the family are listed among the professors of jurisprudence at the University of Padua in the fifteenth century (Belloni 1986, ad indices; also Facciolati 1757, 1.2, ad indices; Scardeone 1560, 182; Zonta & Brotto 1970, ad indices), and da Leone men continued to shine in that profession in later centuries. Ten others (the name in the form "Lion," often with *nobile* ascribed) are listed as canons of the cathedral of Padua between 1369 and 1761 (Orologio 1805, 107–8). In the sixteenth century, the physician Battista Leone belonged to the circles of Cardinal Pole and Pietro Bembo (Scardeone 1560, 219). The family remained prominent in Padua well into the nineteenth century: male descendants (the name in the form "Leoni") bearing clerical titles or the descriptor *nobile* still belonged to the prestigious Accademia Patavina (founded 1599), in which they were enrolled from the first generation of its existence (Maggiolo 1983, 168–69).

II. THE BIRTH AND DEATH OF JACOPO ANTONIO AND VALERIO MARCELLO

A. *Jacopo Antonio's Birth*

Francesco Filelfo is the sole source of a precise date for the birth of Jacopo Antonio Marcello: 17 January (XVI kalendis febr.) 1398 (IV.21.c below), counting 64 years back from 1462 (in late 1461 when Filelfo writes, Marcello had already *entered upon* his sixty-fourth year, which he would have *completed* in 1462). The year 1398 is, moreover, identical to the independently established year of Filelfo's birth. Birth in that year is also consistent with the record of Marcello's activities. But the date is not certain. Marcello was presented for ascription in the Balla d'Oro on 3 December 1417 (ASV, AC-BO 162/I, fol. 99v; by his father, identified as Francesco Marcello di Pietro, a relative, Alessandro Marcello di Vittore, and his mother Magdalucia, without surname), a step usually taken when a candidate had reached the age of eighteen; if it was thus in this case, Marcello was born in 1399. Meiss 1957, 86n21, puts Marcello's birth at about 1400.

B. *Jacopo Antonio's Death*

1. Jacopo Antonio was still alive in December, 1463, when Giorgio Bevilacqua addressed to him a last laudatory work on his participation in the siege of Trieste (see Chron.). But he died not long afterwards. No trace of his career after these dates is known to this author, and it seems otherwise inexplicable that so active servant of Venice should vanish from official records. In those documents, his last recorded office is *luogotenente* in Friuli. It is striking that a member of his own clan, Niccolò Marcello, was sent to Friuli with that title on 21 March 1464 (ASV, CLN 10, fol. 96). A persuasive hypothesis is that Marcello died in that office between November 1463 and March 1464, and was replaced by a figure seen by the Venetian Collegio as comparable in quality and competence.

2. Two letters could point to Marcello's survival into the fall of 1464, but their testimony is weak. The evidence presented by Monfasani 1984, 176n203, does not in itself establish a late date of death for the Venetian. He points out that Marcello's death was not known to Francesco Filelfo when in a letter of 3 November 1464 that humanist asked Giovanni Diedo whether Marcello had yet returned to Venice. Filelfo's letter need not be read as evidence that Marcello was still alive (as Fabbri does: 1983, 246). No more persuasive is the letter of Giovanni Mario Filelfo to Marcello from Verona on "Kal. Sept." (cod. Vat. J.VIII.124, fol. 125v). No year is given, but it might have been 1464, when the younger Filelfo moved from Milan

to Verona (Favre 1856, 102). Even if he did write Marcello on that date, he might not have known of Marcello's prior decease.

3.   Francesco Filelfo's letters to Michele Orsini of 16 March and 23 August 1464 make no mention of Marcello as alive or dead, but they lend plausibility to the argument that Marcello had already died before the earlier date (Filelfo 1502, 149, 155v). Filelfo rebukes Orsini in the first of these for his long silence—a silence that could correspond to the period of Orsini's last involvement with his patron. In the second, again, Marcello is not named. Marcello had certainly died by 31 July 1465, when in presenting her son Pietro for ascription to the Balla d'Oro, his wife declared that she was a widow (ASV, AC-BO, 162/I, fol. 261). He was buried in the church of San Cristoforo della Pace on the island of that name, reestablished by Fra Simone da Camerino as perpetual memorial to the Peace of Lodi that put an end to the wars in which the nobleman had labored (Barbaro, *Arbori*, 4:461; see also below, III.C.3).

C. Death of Valerio Marcello

1.   Valerio Marcello died on 1 January 1461 (our calendar; 1460 *modo veneto*, by which the year began on March 1) according to the witnesses George of Trebizond and Francesco Filelfo (IV.30, 21.d). George's consolatory work, written only a few months later (see Texts II.C.2), gives an additional confirming *terminus ante quem*. Filelfo also provides such a terminus when he states, writing at Christmas time, 1461, that Marcello had been grieving nearly a year (IV.21.d below).

2.   Filelfo's own son had died on 8 March 1461, some weeks after Valerio, but still "recently" at the time that Filelfo wrote in consolation. If the passages noted at IV.21.c and 31–33 are interpreted in the most obvious way, they point to the conclusion that Valerio died when he was eight years old—that is, he had completed his eighth year, and had entered upon his ninth, but had not yet reached his ninth birthday.

3.   The dates of death given by Millard Meiss, Emmanuele Cicogna, and Apostolo Zeno may be discarded. The former states (Meiss 1957, 35–36, and 89n19) that Valerio died in 1460 at age eleven. Guarino Veronese, he further states, wrote to Jacopo Antonio Marcello in consolation just before his own death (on 4 December 1460). Remigio Sabbadini, Guarino's biographer, presents a different case in his "Traduzione guariniana" (Sabbadini 1909, 13n1), which Meiss judges "apparently incorrect." In fact, it was Battista Guarini, and not Guarino, who wrote in consolation and after his

father's death; see Texts II.C.9, with further discussion in chap. 2. Cicogna gives the date of Valerio's death as 1464 (Cicogna 1841, 24, 42, n87; Cicogna 1824–53, 5:671); perhaps he followed Apostolo Zeno (Zeno 1752–53, 1:297).

D. Birth of Valerio Marcello

1. If Valerio's ninth birthday was to have been reached after the January 1 date of death, as seen in section C above, he was born in 1452. Francesco Filelfo gives the month and day as 24 April (close to Olimpio's birthdate of 11 April), and the year as 1453 (see IV.21.a–c; Martin 1898 gives 27 April). In so doing, he contradicts his own statement (IV.21.c) that, before he died not long after Valerio Marcello, his son Olimpio had completed his eighth year; at IV.21.a, however, he gives the apparently correct information that his son had not yet completed his eighth year—which would have been the case had Olimpio been born in 1453. But Valerio died at age eight, as has been seen, and must have been born in 1452.

2. Sealing the case for that birth year is the fact that Marcello was in the early part of that year in Crema, serving as Venetian governor of that city: a position that, as several authors state, he held at the time of Valerio's birth (see IV.23, 24, 26, 27 below). By 1453, he had been replaced in Crema, and had moved on to other missions. See Chron. at 1449–53 for Marcello's career at these points.

3. The month and day given by Filelfo may be correct even if the year is not. It seems to be consistent with the information given by several authors about Marcello's return from Crema or from "abroad." Marcello was in Crema from early 1450 until mid 1452 (see Chron. at these dates for what follows). The date of his return to Venice is difficult to fix. On 9 February 1452, he was still in Crema. On 10 April, the Senate replaced him as *provveditore* (by which date he may have still been in Crema, or already back in in Venice for some time), while on 5 April, a letter he wrote to René d'Anjou was addressed from Venice (suggesting but not proving his presence in the city, since the letter could have been so closed by a scribe). Before 27 April he was elected *provveditore,* and must have been already in the field, because Senate notes assume he had joined the Venetian *condottieri* Gentile da Leonessa and Jacopo Piccinino by 28 April. On 19 May, he was still in the field, in the vicinity of Cremona, but then disappears from Senate documents until 31 December 1452, when he was elected to be a stay-at-home *consigliere;* a position he never assumed. Before the end of 1452 but after 19 May, in short, he returned to Venice to see his young son Valerio for the first time.

4. At his return, Valerio was already three months old (see IV.22, 25–27); or he returned four months after Valerio's birth (IV.29); or four months before the end of the year in which Marcello was to lay down his office (IV.23). If Valerio was born on 24 April (as Filelfo says) 1452 (the year necessarily established), and Jacopo Antonio returned to Venice to see him for the first time three to four months later, the homecoming would have occurred between 24 July and 24 August—or very likely in August, four months and a fraction before the end of the calendar year (the standard one, that is, not the peculiar Venetian one which ended in February). Here the separate witnesses at IV.22–29 appear to concur. In any case, Valerio's birth must have occurred after 1 January 1452, or Valerio would have completed his ninth year (against all testimony) before he died on that date in 1461. The birthdate of 24 April 1452 seems best to accord with the evidence.

E. Valerio's Illness

Of what illness did Valerio die at age eight? Plague is ruled out: none of the characteristic signs of plague are noticed. The illness, indeed, appears to be very much without symptoms: no rash, no cough, no disability, except vague mentions of fatigue. (See chap. 1, at nn96–113 for descriptions of the illness and treatment.) Aside from the plague (for which see Carmichael 1986: for child deaths in Florence, esp. 92, table 4.2), the most common causes of childhood (post-infantile) deaths were fistulae and ulcers, gastrointestinal disorders often blamed on "worms," dropsy, and tuberculosis (see Herlihy & Klapisch-Zuber 1985, 274–79). Tuberculosis is consistent with the evidence as given, and is a likely cause of death.

III. BUILDINGS AND MONUMENTS

A. Palaces

1. The Marcello clan possessed several residences in Venice. The following ten associated with the clan are known to this author. The first is the lavish Marcello palace at Santa Marina in Castello (for which Bassi 1976, 238–41, with photograph at fig. 299; Fontana 1865, 221–24; Tassini 1933, 408–9). Originally built by the Anzelieri merchant family, immigrants from Lucca, it was purchased with surrounding gardens, for 1,623 ducats in 1474 by Doge Niccolò Marcello (Bassi, Fontana), or possibly for 800 ducats by his father Giovanni (Tassini), and refurbished at a cost of 14,610 ducats (Fontana). It was modernized in the seventeenth century by Longhena, enlarged again after being sold to the Pindemonte family of Verona in 1701, and restored after passing to the Papadopoli family in 1808. In the same area,

but not the same building, was born the Niccolò who became doge (1473–74) (Fontana 1865, 221–24; Tassini 1933, 229), celebrated on his death by the famed humanist Ermolao Barbaro the Younger (E. Barbaro 1943).

2. The second, "dei Leoni," on the Grand Canal at Fondamenta del Traghetto, 2810, at San Tomà, belonged in the sixteenth century to Girolamo Marcello—"di Giorgione," according to Tassini (Tassini 1879, 281), but evidently "di Antonio" (because of the information that follows and that presented above, I.B.2–6). In it were seen portraits of the owner, of his brother the Archibishop Cristoforo Marcello (by Titian), and of Jacopo Marcello (the military hero killed in 1484), Girolamo's grandfather (by Giovanni Bellini), as well as other treasures. Marino Sanuto describes the celebration in this palace on 23 May 1530 given by Girolamo's son, Antonio, for the marriage of his granddaughter to Pietro Diedo (Tassini).

3. The third, in the Calle della Testa, was built in the fifteenth century by the Marcello family, sold in 1474 to the Contarini when the Marcellos moved to Santa Marina, and remodeled in the sixteenth century (Bassi 1976, 490ff.). The fourth, called the Toffetti palace, at Fondamenta Sangiantoffetti, 1075, at San Trovaso (Dorsoduro), originally a Marcello palace, is now used by the University of Venice (Bassi 1976, 507ff.) The fifth, constructed in the sixteenth century on a twelfth-century skeleton, is in San Polo. Although it is presently named for Grimani proprietors, the Marcello family was one of the original owners (Bassi 1976, 418ff.) This may have been the residence of the collector Pietro di Andrea Marcello mentioned above (I.B.7).

4. A sixth, the gothic Palazzo Michiel (at the Ponte Marcello), at Fondamenta Minotta, 134, was a Marcello residence also as early as the fourteenth century (Tassini 1879, 286; Tassini 1933, 407–8). The seventh (at Santa Maria Maddalena), a late construction, was associated with Marcello patrons and practitioners of music (Fontana 1865, 317–20; Tassini 1879, 286). These may be identified as the four *letterati* (two of them also musicologists) noted above as residing in that district (I.B.7). Two other palaces were also latecomers to the Marcello clan (Lorenzetti 1926, 449, 481): one a seventeenth-century construction near San Giovanni Degolà and the Fondaco dei Turchi, the other a fifteenth-century gothic structure near San Fantin once the property of the Moro family but now, to this day, in Marcello ownership. The tenth palace, no longer standing, is the one once occupied by Jacopo Antonio Marcello and his descendants.

5. Internal evidence tells us that this last palace was located near the Campo Sant'Angelo in San Marco (see the account of Valerio's encounter

with neighborhood children described in chap. 1, at nn82–84). Although there is no palace now standing in that area that may be identified with that of the Marcello family, there was one once. The Marcello palace, standing in the Corte dell'Albero near Sant'Angelo and overlooking the Grand Canal (Tassini 1885, 47), was built in the fifteenth century, possibly by the Marcello family. It must have been adjacent to the still visible Palazzo Corner-Spinelli (Campiello del Teatro 3877), dating from 1485–90, designed by Codussi, with paintings by Vasari (Bassi 1976, 386–99; Lieberman 1982, plate 63).

6. Marino Sanuto reports the visit of the Venetian *condottiere* Tuzio Costanzo to the palace, with his wife and children, on 11 August 1509 (Tassini 1885, 47–48), indicating the ongoing contacts that Jacopo Antonio's branch of the family had with military servants of the republic. The Marcello family owned the palace still when it was sold in the seventeenth century and razed, so that on its plot and the neighboring one (belonging to the Cappello family) there could be constructed the Teatro Sant'Angelo. That theater was built in 1676, funded by Francesco Santorini, but passed to the ownership of the Marcello and Cappello families. Famed for its associations with Vivaldi, Casanova, and Goldoni, the theater thrived until 1803, when after a last performance, it too was razed or converted—into a warehouse (Bassi 1976, 395, at fig. 536; Tassini 1885, 48).

7. Although we cannot reconstruct the domestic circumstances of the Marcello family in their Sant'Angelo palace in the mid-fifteenth century, the excellent descriptions available of palazzo origin, layout, and management available may partially supply the lack (see Howard 1975, 120ff.; Howard 1980, 85–97; Huse & Wolters 1990, 16–26; McAndrew 1980, 194–211).

B. *Church of San Antonio Abate and the Pisani Monument*

1. Jacopo Antonio and his son apparently frequented the church and monastery of San Antonio Abbate (da Vienna), or San Antonio di Castello, in the care of regular canons of that saint who had left Vienna for France in 1095. The prior from 1449 until about 1475 (and thus during the whole of Valerio's lifetime) was the Marcello family friend and eventual consoler Michele Orsini. In that church, father and son viewed a pedestrian statue of the naval hero Vettore Pisani (see chap. 1 at n78; for the statue, see below, III.B.3–4).

2. The land "in extrema illa Urbis parte quae Orientem inter et Austrum in angulum procurrit et desinit, portum Littoris Majoris respiciens" was

granted by the Maggior Consiglio to two individuals in 1334, by whom it passed in 1346 to Fra Giotto degli Abati (Goto de Abbatibus, of Florence), prior of the regular canons of San Antonio da Vienna (Cornelius 1749, 6:294–312; Da Mosto 1937–40, 2:125; Tassini 1933, 30–31; Zangirolami 1962, 108–10; Zorzi 1972, 2:312–17 for what follows). Under Fra Giotto's supervision, the buildings were erected beginning on 1 November of the same year, as a cornerstone inscription once testified (Cornelius 1749, 6:295–96). More property was obtained in 1360, and further construction was completed by the Leone, Pisani (see also Gallo 1944, 66–67), and Grimani families in ensuing years. A sacred site indeed, the building housed (among other relics) three hundred relics of the armbones of the apostle Saint Bartholomew, two of the heads of the martyred companions of Saint Ursula, two teeth of Saint Mercurius, and a finger joint of Saint Bernard.

3. It also housed the tombs of two Venetian doges and other prominent heroes of the Venetian past: most notably, Vettore Pisani (1324–80) (Lazzarini 1896; Molmenti 1919; for some unheroic behavior by the hero, Queller 1986, 163–64, 236–37). That hero, mortally wounded, had triumphed over the Genoese during the Chioggian war; he was honored with a magnificent state burial, attended by Senate and doge, and a memorial statue erected in the *capella maggiore,* alongside the altar: "ejus autem corpus magnifico funere elatum principe et senatu comitantibus totius urbis cum moerore ad D. Antonii Aedem delatum est, statuta proinde ad perennem maximi viri gloriam Imperatoria statua, quae ad ejus conspicui sepulcri ornatum in sacello maximo collocata est hac subjecta epigraphe: Inclytus hic Victor Pisanae stirpis alumnus / Janorum hostilem Venetum caput aequore classem / Tireno stravit, hunc Patria claudit; at ille / Egreditur clausam referans ubi Brundulus altis / Stragibus insignis deduxit in aequore Brintam / Mors heu magna vetat tunc cum mare classibus implet" (Cornelius 1749, 6:303–304; also Cicogna 1824–53, 1:180).

4. Sanuto confirms the presence of a Pisani monument in this church, reporting that the naval hero, who died on 14 August 1380, was buried in San Antonio, and also published the epitaph (Sanuto 1733, 715). The statue of Pisani was among the items dispersed when the church of his burial was destroyed. Removed to the Museo dell'Arsenale, it was finally re-erected in the church of Santi Giovanni e Paolo in Venice (Lorenzetti 1926, 330), not far from that other military memorial outside the building in honor of Bartolommeo Colleoni. The hero's remains, housed in the interim in a chapel in a villa belonging to the Pisani Zusto family, were reunited with statue and inscription in that church as well.

5. The convent of San Antonio was notorious for its peculiar custom. In honor of their patron, the canons set pigs loose to wander the city and grow fat on the alms of the faithful. Rounded up and returned to the monastery, they would serve as the prior's dinner. The practice was halted by a decree of the Maggior Consiglio on 10 October 1409. In 1471, by papal request, the property was sold by the canons of San Antonio to those of San Salvatore, who held it until the convent was suppressed by a law of 7 September 1768. The buildings were then put to other uses. In 1787, they housed an institute for the instruction of seventy poor Venetian girls in the arts of embroidery, and thereafter until 1806 a hospital for wounded soldiers, when they were occupied by Austrian marines. Like the Marcello palace near Campo Sant'Angelo, the church and monastery of San Antonio da Vienna were destroyed by order of Napoleon (7 December 1807, executed 1809; Da Mosto 1937–40, 2:125). They were razed to make way for the spacious public gardens at the tip of the Castello, opposite the island of Sant'Elena, where today visitors flock to the *Biennale d'arte moderna.*

C. Church of San Cristoforo della Pace

1. Jacopo Antonio Marcello was buried in the great chapel of the church of San Cristoforo della Pace on the small island of that name located off Venice near Murano. (For the following, ASV, ST 3, fol. 114; Predelli 1876–1914, 4:210–11 [XIII, 20]; Cornelius 1749, 1:253–78; Da Mosto 1937–40, 2:128; Romanin 1853–61, 4:225n2; Zangirolami 1962, 169–71; Zorzi 1972, 2:401–3; among many plans and views of Venice showing the island in its Renaissance condition, see that of Benedetto Bordone [1534], in Romanelli & Biadene 1982, 26, #7.) A church had stood on that site since 1353. Having passed to the Friars of Saint Bridget on 21 May 1424 by dogal grant, it was transferred again on 25 November 1436 as part of a reform movement to Fra Simone da Camerino, founder and general of the order of Augustinian canons of Monte Ortone, as recognized by papal decree (Walsh 1977; Walsh 1989, for the congregation of Monte Ortone). Building of a church with one nave and seven lateral chapels (in addition to an absidal chapel) began late in 1439 (Dolfin, *Cronaca,* 376v [265v]; Sanuto 1733, 1045). Construction (probably by the architect Pietro Lombardo) was completed after 1454 under the direction of Fra Simone, to whom the Senate had granted funds for renovation and amplification, as well as immunity from all fees, in recognition of Simone's services in negotiating the Peace of Lodi (for documents, Walsh 1977, 62 and n64). Simone's identification with these negotiations explains the island's new name, bestowed in celebration of the conclusion of that peace. It also ex-

plains Jacopo Antonio Marcello's association with San Cristoforo, for he was involved in the war and the peace alike.

2. An inscription in the church of Santa Maria di Monte Ortone in Padua, under the protection of his congregation of Augustinian friars, commemorated Fra Simone's role in the peace (Cornelius 1749, 1:257), reading at the end: "Senatus beneficii non imemmor, Insulam prope Murianum, ibique Templum tunc exstructum, ac eo nomine Divo Christophoro a Pace dicatam, Congregationi donavit, omnique prorsus immunitate, in honorem Dei, et ex conto, eam liberalissime auxit, suamque in tutelam recepit." The friar ("gran predicatore, e uomo di santa vita") was himself buried in Santa Maria in front of the altar (Sanuto 1733, 1045, 1152). A similar inscription to Fra Simone appeared in another church the Augustinian had founded in Cittadella near Padua, that of Santa Maria del Camposanto (Cornelius 1749, 1:258).

3. In the great chapel of the church of San Cristoforo, Jacopo Antonio Marcello himself was buried. On one wall of the chapel there was engraved nearly a century after his death an epitaph to Marcello with unusually discursive text. It is reported by Cappellari, *Campidoglio*, 3:31; by Damadenus, *De origine*, 2:303 (for which see Cicogna 1841, 9 and n, and Fabbri 1983, 231n10); by Sansovino 1968, 1:234–35; by Cornelius 1749, 1:267; by Fabbri 1983, 248; by Martin 1898, 254n1; by Monfasani 1984, 235–36; and here below (Fabbri's text). The inscription records Marcello's most conspicuous military achievements and the honors bestowed on him by René d'Anjou, and concludes by noting his role in securing the peace:

4. Iacobo Antonio Marcello Equiti Senatori clarissimo Brixia dura triennii obsidione levata, Benaco lacui admirabili invento classi per montes immissa, Verona e Picinini faucibus erepta, Ravenna eius ductu auspiciisque imperio Veneto adiecta, Abdua amne primum ab eo superato, cum ad Mediolani usque portas insultatum esset, ubi illi aequestris dignitas virtutis ergo parta ac Regni Neapolitani maritima praefectura a Rege Renato commissa, cuius et sacrae societati inter primos adscriptus est, pace demum honestissima eius opera universae Italiae data. Valerius eius filius P.M.P. Nicolaus et Petrus Nepotes ex Marco extremam operi manum imponi curaverunt MDLV K D.

5. The inscription was arranged by Valerio, the hero's second son of that name, but was only completed by two grandsons Niccolò and Pietro (sons of Marco) in 1555 (it bears the date 1 December of that year); see above, I.A.19. On the other wall of the chapel could be read the memorial to

Jacopo Antonio's son Pietro, also buried in San Cristoforo (Sansovino 1968, 1:235; Cornelius 1749, 1:267):

6. Petro Marcello Jacobi Antonii filio Equiti, qui paternae virtutis ae-mulator, Rhodiginam Pollynessum patriae primus subdit, Marti-nengium adversus hostes acerimos servavit; Cassentinatem saltum et Bibienam coepit, durissimam omnium obsidionem ab hoste pas-sus; unde Pisi Libertas incolumis mansit, Amplissimis honoribus functo, summa semper in patriam, in Deum pietate Valerius Frater Clariss. Marcellae familiae testimonium posuit. Nicolaus et Petrus fratres fecerunt. Extremum operi manum imponi curarunt.

7. Yet another figure was commemorated in stone at the church of San Cristoforo della Pace: Francesco Sforza, Marcello's friend, and Venice's one-time enemy. A marble memorial to the peace at the western corner (*angu-lum occidentale*) of the extinct church bore an image of the entwined arms of Sforza and the Venetian Republic (according to this witness), linked by an iron chain (Cornelius 1749, 1:259): "Venetae Reipublicae, et Mediola-nensis Ducis insignia ferreo vinculo arcte colligata visuntur, quasi fausto omine de nunquam solvendo ignotae reconciliationis foedere." The arms, however, were those of Sforza and Foscari (Fontana 1870–71, 1:786): "l'arma del doge Foscari, congiunto per un anello di ferro a quello dello Sforza, con sotto l'anno del fatto." The device had been planned by Fra Simone, who enthusiastically described in letters to Sforza its veiled mean-ing, and reported the words that were to be carved thereon: "PAX—quis nos separabit?" (Greppi 1913, 336). In the 1660s, Giustiniano Martinioni, editor and amplifier of Sansovino, described Sforza's standards which were still displayed in the church, though decayed—"benche corrosi dal tempo"; they had been given by that duke of Milan to Fra Simone in honor of the peace (Sansovino 1968, 1:235).

8. Martinioni also described several fine paintings that adorned the church, including one by Bellini completed in 1505 (and from a later pe-riod, a Canaletto and Giacomo Guardi), all alike destroyed along with the monuments to Marcello, to Sforza, and to the peace. The church and con-vent were suppressed and ordered razed by Napoleonic decree of 8 June 1805, to make way for a public cemetery ordered on 7 December 1807. Excavations began in 1813, and the islands were artificially united (by ar-chitect Giuseppe Salvadori) to form the requisite expanse of land in 1817. The project was completed only after 1870, by Annibale Forcellini (Bassi 1936, 77–78; Da Mosto 1937–40, 2:128). According to Fontana, the channel separating San Michele and San Cristoforo was filled in "colle mac-

erie tolte alle rovine di Venezia," so that Venice gained a cemetery "col discapito delle arti" (Fontana 1870–71, 2:1121).

D. Monselice

1. For Monselice, see in general Barbantini 1940, esp. 5–50; Gloria 1862–65, 3:126–63; Hayward and Antoniazzi Rossi 1980; Mazzarolli 1940; *Monselice*, 1956. Nino Barbantini participated in the Cini restoration and is the authoritative source for the structure and evolution of the *castello*. The collections of manuscripts and printed books date from a generation after Jacopo Antonio Marcello, and have modern catalogues (cited by Barbantini, 288). Hayward catalogues the weapons collection and Antoniazzi Rossi provides a brief chronological survey (Hayward and Antoniazzi Rossi, 25–30.) The town is fifteen miles south of Padua, between Abano and Este, in the Euganean hills.

2. Marcello's consoler the Anonymous Tutor describes a visit to Monselice (1460), where the family was accustomed to vacation. He and several consolers refer to an earlier visit to Monselice where Valerio, then three, witnessed a young nephew's treatment (in 1455) by the doctor Gerardo. Senate documents and other sources also refer to Marcello's visits to Monselice (see Chron. at 1441: 6 July; 1442: 4 August; 1449: 15 October and 8 November; 1457: 1 March).

E. The Church of San Giorgio Maggiore

1. The same Count Cini who restored the castello at Monselice was the creator of the school and Fondazione Giorgio Cini, located on the island of San Giorgio Maggiore in Venice. That little island is the home of the splendid Palladian church of San Giorgio (built in 1556) and the adjoining monastery that houses the institutions just named. There is more than a little irony here. The Cini legacy is named after Count Vittorio's son Giorgio, who died in adolescence. It is in an older church of that name, built in 1419 (on the same site) that Valerio Marcello was buried in 1461 (see IV.33 below). The shadows of two boys prematurely deceased join hands in the same city that, centuries apart, gave them birth.

2. Valerio's tomb no longer survives: its place was taken by those of the Palladian structure, just as his may have displaced an older monument in the prior construction of 982. Even that ancient structure was not untouched by Marcello associations. At that distant year, when the Maggior Consiglio first granted to Benedictine monks the island opposite the city center, Domenico Marcello *presbiter* and Pietro Marcello were among the signatories of the act of donation; the latter, a layman and illiterate, applied

his *signum manus* (Lanfranchi 1968, 2:21). Earlier still, the original church and monastery first rose on the lagoons in 790 under the patronage of the Partecipazio family.

F. Verona, Piazza dell'Erbe

Marcello may have left his mark in Verona as well, where a column in the Piazza dell'Erbe is inscribed with Marcello arms, surrounded by, on the left, *IAC* (Iacopo), and on the right, *MAR* (Marcello). If the Marcello commemorated is Jacopo Antonio and not another member of the family (perfectly plausible; Nogarola sees Marcello as the savior of her city; see chap. 2, at n64), the association may date from his captaincy of Verona in 1448, or from his role in the liberation of Verona on 20 November 1439. (My thanks to Dott. Girolamo Marcello for pointing out to me contemporary photographs of the column inscribed as noted.)

IV. EXCERPTS

1. Perleone, G, 190–91 (B, fols. 4–6): Marcello's father, mother, brothers, sisters, children.

> a. Amisisti enim Franciscum patrem tuum virum clarissimum, ac singulari animi magnitudine, liberalitate, consilio, auctoritate, multamque {B militarumque} rerum cognitione atque doctrina preditum, quem non minus quam filios dilexisti, imo quem semper habuisti vita tua cariorem, atque eo tempore quam omnia in te fuerint pietatis et offitii plena quam nihil nisi magno et sapienti animo dignum, omnes profecto intelligunt. Matris vero tuae Magdalutie mortem de qua omnium est fama consentiens, fuisse illam singulare atque precipuum forme pudicitie, ac rei domestice administrande sui temporis exemplum, modice certe moderateque tulisti. Cuius quidem desiderio vel nos qui nunquam illam vidimus sepe commovemur cum multas eius magnasque virtutes, tum fecunditatem tantam tamque uberem gignendi felicitatem admirantes. Sex enim et viginti filios ex Francisco digno coniuncta viro peperit, ex quibus tredecim sex mares et septem feminas robuste etatis, has quidem summis clarissimisque patriciis nuptas. Illos vero singulari innocentia integritate et multis magnisque ornamentis preditos, ambo parentes ultimo senio morientes patrie reliquerunt.
>
> b. Hanc tantam domum, tantam sobolem, tantam nepotum spem optima et prestantissima femina mira diligentia regebat. Fratrem tuum Petrum patavinum pontificem honore, auctoritate, virtute,

consilio moribus, et magnarum rerum disciplina praestantissimum virum tibi vero benivolentia et caritate parentem alterum morientem vidisti. Nemo in fortuna illa tam accerba, tamque luctuosa quicquam in te animadvertit, quod fracti et demissi animi foret.

c. Quid Hieronymum singulari prestantia virum, quid Valerium excellenti ingenio et prudentia et bonarum artium studiis ornatissimum, quid Laurentium et Iohannem fratres tuos, viros ob multas magnasque virtutes omni laude dignissimos commemorem, qua fortitudine animi extuleris? Quid obitum sororum tuarum, Marie, Blance, Clare, Thaddee, Margarite, Agnetis referam? Quid Thaddee filie tue carissime mortem nunc explicem, femine quidem pudicissime, ac genero primario nupte filiorumque sobole fecundissimae, que ni fallor nunc quinto mense acerba morte subrepta est? Horum igitur omnium interitum et gravem familie tue stragem mirati certe sunt omnes quo oris habitu, ac animi magnitudine tuleris. In aliorum preterea filiorum tuorum ceterorumque omnium morte, quos coniunctissimos et carissimos habuisti, quam fortitudinem et sapientiam ostenderis, testes sunt omnes, qui in ipsis gravissimis casibus tuis adfuerunt.

2. Bevilacqua, G, 319–20 (V, fols. 20–21): Marcello's ancestor Pietro, dead while in Venetian service, is buried in Crete.

a. Non contentem his tam illustribus viris inexorabile fatorum numen, quasi plurima tempora praeterissent, quibus aliquem Marcellorum nostrorum in interitus praecipicium minime dedisset, in Petrum attavum meum crudeles manus furiale parcarum venenum iniecit {G inictit}. Nam is a Senatu nostro venetorum ad Maurorum regem legatus creatus, paratissima trireme pro summa rei publicae salute adnavigavit, ubi ab rege et Babiloniorum principe tam honorificentissime fuit acceptus et habitus celeberrime, ut propter eius eximiam sapientiam, moderationem, modestiam, magnanimitatem, munificenciam, et hominis dignitatem fuerit honorificis muneribus a rege donatus, ab omnibusque provincialibus laudatus, adeo ut L. Lucullum apud Ptholomeum Aegyptiorum regem honoratum satis in Petro attavo legere videar, in quem singulae ac inusitatum humanissimae benivolentiae studium declaravit.

b. Nam intra regiam eam cum familiariter tum splendidissime hospitatus est, quo nemo ante Lucullum superiorum ducum honore a Ptholomeo donatus fuerit. Cibariorum vero non quantum parari caeteris consueverat, sed quadruplum Lucullo dabatur; tam et si nihil amplius ipse, quam quod modestissimo viro dignum esset, acciperet. Sic apud quos Petrus is diutius commorabatur, tanquam in eo imperatoriae virtutes apparerent, illum cuncti benignissime excipiebant, honorabant, admirabantur faciem corporis decoram, mansuetudine humanitateque ornatam videre, atque istius sapientiam audire desiderabant.

c. Eo igitur legatione summis suis cum laudibus functo {functu}, hei mihi! qui ab insidiis et huius mortis immanitate {G immanitate huius mortis} cavere se genus hoc nostrum minime potest. Nam antequam is hoc legationis munus obiret, nescio quae fatorum atrocitas illum adnavigantem interemit, et in Cretam insulam delatus, comitantibus civibus bonis omnibus et maxima vulgi frequentia in basilica maiori sepultus fuit. Ad cuius memoriae immortalitatem vexilla prosapiae Marcellorum signis insignita iisdem temporibus affixa, in hos usquam dies ornatissima spectantur.

3. Perleone, G, 194–96 (B, fols. 11–16v): Valerio's maternal family, the Paduan da Leone clan.

a. Leonum vero familia Patavium incolentes urbem quondam populosissimam, et Venetie provintie caput marique ac terra inclitam singulis etatibus maximos et excellentes in omni virtutum genere, et amplissimis ordinibus viros in lucem eduxit. Verum ut humanarum rerum conditio est, que fragilis et caduca, non homines modo et domos atque familias sed urbes etiam et populos deijcit opprimit ac funditus evertit, genus illud quondam clarum et illustre simul cum imperio patavino cadens aliquot etates latuit obscurum. Rursus vero fortuna que semper instabili rerum motu summa infimis, et infima summis nullo discrimine permiscet, generosos homines quanquam temporum calamitate obscuros, pristinam tamen sponte repetentes naturam, iam Patavino regno ad Carrarienses delato in veterem dignitatem atque splendorem revocavit.

b. Itaque memoria patrum nostrorum ceteris egregiis et prestantibus huius familie viris silentio pretermissis accepimus fuisse Ceccum virum integritate, prudentia et rerum humanarum usu excellentem, qui apud Cararienses principes ea semper gratia et auctoritate fuit, ut nihil omnino publicum aut privatum, sine huius consilio et sententia gereretur, humanitate vero tanta et benignitate in plebem populumque fuisse, ut cognomento pater pauperum sit appellatus, non studio, modo consilio, opera, fide atque auctoritate, sed opibus etiam atque fortunis benefitia ubi opus esset conferendo.

Itaque quantum benivolentie et cultus erga se vivens ab omnibus excitavit, tantum moeroris attulit mortuus patriae lugenti, et suo tamquam parente ac patrono in dubiis et afflictis rebus orbate.

c. Hunc autem genuisse Lucam et Paulum dignos patre viros, qui arbitrantes precipuum filiorum munus esse non patris modo rerum atque fortunarum, sed benivolentie quoque amicorum hereditatem adire. Virtutem patris imitari non minorem apud reges auctoritatem sunt assecuti, quam antea pater habuisset. Ambo equites, ambo domi ac floris clari, ambo cum ceteris obsequio fide atque observantia in regus cum regibus vero liberalitate ac benignitate in ceteros contendentes. Itaque brevi factum est ut omnes non solum vivere Ceccum sed geminatum etiam crederent, utque nec reges in consultatione vetus consilium et sententiam, nec cives in rebus dubiis presidium sibi deesse arbitrarentur. Quod nisi virtus in his viris egregia in Paulo etiam singulari admirandaque fuisset, nunquam profecto senatus Venetus Paulum fratri superstitem, et Galeatius Vicecomes Mediolanensium dux, multis ante annis longe maximo honore atque benivolentia dignum iudicassent.

d. Urbe vi capta et de rege sumpto supplitio senatus rebus nondum confirmatis, et regni novitate, non modo Paulum suspectum non habuit, sed honore gratiaque complectens, domi semper apud suos ea dignitate et auctoritate esse voluit, quibus prius apud reges Cararienses fuisset, eam in illo viro integritatem esse cognoscens, ut qui fidem semper omnibus sanctam habuisset, eandem quoque inviolatam rei publicae observaturum crederet. Bello quoque quod adversus Panonios gestum est in castris Paulum legatum patres decreverunt, quod munus ut maximum et amplissimum, ita et primoribus patriciis consilio, auctoritate ac plurimarum rerum usu atque experientia excellentissimis demandari solitum est. Quibus ex rebus intelligere possumus, quanta non solum fidei sanctitate verum etiam bellicarum rerum scientia Paulus excelluerit, quem senatus tanto domi honore et gratia ac auctoritate, foris autem etiam imperio militari, et dignitate patritia exornaverit.

e. Ex hoc prestantissimo patre Paulo sunt excellentes filii Joannes et Ceccus, alium hic quidem etiam nomine, ambo virtute atque gloria referentes. Nam cum sint iuris civilis interpretes, et equestri dignitate insigniti, quantum ex doctrina ornamenti afferunt ordini litterario, tanto splendore dignitatem equestrem illustrant, ob singularem in bonos, munificentiam, in egeosque presidium. Preter-mitto Leonellum horum fratrem equestri ordinis virum, ac multis magnisque virtutibus excellentem, quem superiore anno cum incredibili omnium merore atque iactura ex morbo amissimus.

f. Ex Luca Pauli fratre natus est Bartholomeus, vir sane modestus et egregia integritate preditus, de quo Luca est Valerii mater femina quidem ut pudica et optima, sic in feminino sexu avitum et virile nomen ob prestantiam habens. Verum his contenti ceteros egregios ex hac familia viros pretereamus, ne rerum multitudine nimium oratio nostra protrahatur. Scio tempus et rem ipsam hoc me loco admonere ut quemadmodum Valerii quosdam materni generis illustres viros commemoramus, ita et paterni quoque illos saltem oratione nostra complectamur, qui virtute atque gloria meruerunt, ut eorum mentio cum illustri laude et predicatione rerum gestarum habeatur.

4. F. Filelfo, G, 123 (ed. fol. 44): Valerio's mother and the da Leone family.

Quod si neque tua neque nostra etiam causa, ut tibi tueque etati parcas, potes adduci, moveant te saltem reliqui tui liberi, quos tuus meror tenet in lachrimis, moveat Luca uxor nobilissima prudentissimaque virago, quam longe magis tantus dolor tuus affligit, quam comunis iucundissimique filii mors commoverit. Quam eius ingenium, eius moderatio me delectat, quam {ed. que} se maiorum suorum similem quam se ostendit illustrem. Est uxor ista tua patavina {ed. patavia} et ex Leonibus quidem patavina. Fertur autem Leon {ed. Leo} inter Antenoris proceres clarissimus extitisse. Ex illo autem auctore Leonum familiam Patavii emanasse.

5. Anon. Tut. G, 244: Valerio's mother Luca with family at Monselice. Exorasti vir optime, nam paucis admodum diebus elapsis [after Easter] animi laxandi gratia Veneciis soluimus et universa familia Montem Sylicem versus navigamus. . . . Portus oppiduli tandem intramus, ubi mox cives primarii nobis obviam fiunt, ut una matronae cum coronatis de more virginibus aderat, enim et Luca Leona coniux tua femina spectatissima, quae eadem in navi devecta erat. Hic omnes in Valerium oculos coniciunt, omnes salutant, omnes amplectuntur et stupent.

6. Sagundino, G, 24–25 (F, fol. 105; VatS, fol. 12v): Marcello's responsibility to surviving wife and children.

Easobres, dolorem amittere te oportet, moerorem ponere omnem

animo molestiam depellere, consolere te tum tuo tum Valerii tui
nomine, respice coniugem clarissimam feminam sanctissimamque
matronam {F matrem}, respice reliquos filios, qui de te dependent,
qui ad vultum et nutus {F motus} tuos sese componunt atque infor-
mant, qui non nisi te incolumi et extante consistere queunt, non
tibi soli natum te esse memineris, sed patrie, coniugi, liberis, propinquis, amicis, clientibus, quibus non modo consolator in rebus
adversis, verum etiam solatium esse debes.

7. Perleone (Texts II.D.21), VatP, fol. 104 (F, fols. 106v–107; MU, fol.
96rv): Marcello's wife and other children.

Imo si {VatP,F is} es qui semper fuisti beneficiorum gratus et
memor, debes gratias Deo qui cum multos {VatP,MU et} egregios
tibi filios, pudicam uxorem, patriam excellentem, genus illustre,
opes, honores, dignitates, gloriam dederit, caeteris rebus omnibus
tibi relictis, unum dumtaxat post multos annos repetivit filium
quem, et caetera quae possides bona, iure ipsi {VatP *adds* ea} qua
{MU qui} dedisset hora repetere licuisset.

8. Mascarello, G, 162: Marcello's wife and other children.

Contuli ingenium, cumulavi elloquium, adieci divitias, castissimam
coniugem, numerus liberorum.

9. Anon. Ven. G, 249: Marcello's other children.

Venit in mentem ardor amoris qui te vel pro re publica, vel pro
amicis, vel pro liberis anxium tibi nunquam parcere permittit, quo
publica semper privatis anteponendo, patriae pater tociens illam
tuis humeris, tua cervice, tuis laboribus sustentatam, nunc toga,
nunc armis periculosa, dura et insuperabilia tolerando saepe ab im-
inenti clade ad insperatam gloriam reduxisti. Quo concives tuos vel
bene de re publica meritos, vel aliqua probitate nitentes amplecteris;
quo filios non tibi solum sed tecum patriae natos, in viriles mores
et antiquam Marcellae familiae virtutem educando super omnia
fortunae bona caros habes.

10. Guarini, G, 182 (F, fol. 111): Marcello's other children.

Ille ut pius filius dextra quam deficiente spiritu vix attolere poterat
oculos abstergens te exhortabatur ne casum tuum quem dominus
Deus dedisset iniquo animo ferres potiusque dum liceret ad oscula
suavissimi filii te infugientem {F inclinares et fugientem} animam
prono ore colligeres, ac te ipsum in reliquorum filiorum aspectu
consolareris.

11. Anon. Tut. G, 248: From heaven, Valerio reminds Marcello of five surviving sons.

> Nec si hereditatem querit quem Deus omnipotens adoptavit ingravescentem aetatem tuam reliqui fratres mei, nepotesque suis amplexibus excipient. Et si christianus, si Dei cultor es non minore gaudio pater afficieris unum te caelo angelum peperisse, quam istos quinque rei publicae cives reliquisse primarios.

12. Fortebraccio, G, 144: Valerio in relation with other household children.

> Germanis propinquis ceterisque cognatis ita sese eorum studiis insinuabat, ut facile de se prestaret quanta cum illis etate provectioni concordia, vitam esset acturus maiores vero natu mirum quo honore qua reverentia prosequebatur.

13. Perleone, G, 230 (B, fols. 85v–86v): Valerio recalls in details the illness of his nephew Girolamo at Monselice, when Valerio was three years old.

> Cum hesterna inquit vespera iusisset huc te pater advocari non te noveram, nec quis esses venerat in mentem, ut qui nomine appellatum nunquam audivissem. Nunc vero te inspitiens agnosco. Quippe qui sis ille quem olim Patavio Monsilicem pater accersivit Hieronymo nostro (erat enim is ex fratre maiore filius) gravi morbo laborante. Veneras autem noctu quo tempore castelli portas iussit pater aperiri ocreatus et clamidem pluvialem ac insulam rotundam in capite cum pileo desuper gestans, tunica erat duplex et rubea in pedibus calcaria, cingulum erat nigrum cum fibula et clavis aureis unde gladius demissus capulo ebore atque oricalcho intertexto pendebat; in dextera flagellum gestabas, quo in levam translato cum aliquantulum quievisses; pulsuque Hieronymi explorato, et urina inspecta, parentem ac omnes adstantes bono animo esse iussisti.

14. Anon. Tut. G, 243: Valerio in relation with other children: he assists his younger brother Lorenzo with schoolwork.

> Sudabat interdum adiscendi fervore, cum caeteros condiscipulos hyems exagitaret. Adsidebat una Laurentius maximus frater natu minor, quem modo blandiciis, minis aliquando, nonnunquam et crustulis et muscaciis alliciebat ut disceret. . . . Quare tanta mox benivolentia puerorum mentes allexerat ut eum omnis veneraretur ut dominum, observaret ut patrem, coleret ut animam. Exoriebantur saepenumero lites inter eos de pilla, de carceribus, de meta. Statim hic veluti dictator eas dirrimebat.

15. Tifernate, *Oratio* (Texts II.D.23), fols. 129v–30: Marcello's other children, among whom Francesco, the eldest.

> Manent liberi magnum moeroris tui solamen, in quibus praeclarum et ingenii et virtutis specimen elucet, quorum natu grandior Franciscus modestia ac prudentia ad paternum decus aspirat.

16. F. Filelfo, G, 119 (ed. fol. 43v): Marcello's other children, among them Francesco.

> Num idcirco in tot et animi et corporis ac fortune bonis deterius habes, quid {ed. quod} ex tot liberis puerum unum ad se revocarit Deus? . . . Num Deus iniustus sit, si ex tot liberis, quos nobis mutuo dedit, unum sibi exegerit? Habes tu et filias et filios pluris moribus ingenioque eximios eosque et grandiusculos et minusculos, quibus te potes non consolari solum, verum etiam per omnem animi iucunditate oblectare. Ut enim ceteros preteream, quanto tibi solatio, quanto gaudio voluptatique esse debet Franciscus tuus tanto ingenio, tanta morum elegantia, tanta probitate vir? Num habeas, quod ad tue felicitatis summam tibi sit desiderandum, cum oculos ac mentem in Franciscum unum conieceris? Nonne etiam iste tui est quamsimillimus? Num pueri magis te recordatio torqueat, quam viri filii presentia aspectusque delectet? At de Valerio mihi magna spes erat, quod de Valerio futurum sperabas, id tibi de Francisco prestare licet.

17. George of Trebizond, G, 31, 36 (Mon. ##15, 34): Daughter Taddea, also recently deceased.

> a. Et tamen subdubito ne vulnus ab obitu pueri acceptum recrudescat obitu Tadee, tue carissime filie primarieque, pudicitia femine nuper subsecuta.
> b. Non equidem ipse negaverim idcirco Kalendis Ianuarii filium et confestim Kalendis Aprilis filiam tibi ereptam esse ut sicut argentum atque aurum igni probatur, sic animus tuus dolore ingenti conduplicatoque formatus effulgeat.

18. Perleone, G, 191 (B, fol. 5v): The death five months before of Marcello's daughter Taddea, a mature woman with children, married to a nobleman (was Perleone possibly mistaken as to which Taddea had died?).

> Quid Thaddee filie tue carissime mortem nunc explicem, femine quidem pudicissime, ac genero primario nupte filiorumque sobole fecundissimae, que ni fallor nunc quinto mense acerba morte subrepta est?

19. Anon. Tut. G, 246: The dying Valerio commends his unnamed sister to their father.

At ille sororem quae se singulari cura vel ab ipsis incunabulis educaxerat, unice tibi commendat.

20. Anon. Stu. G, 303–4: Valerio called Marcello's youngest and noblest child.

Hic autem iunior et inter omnes filios tuos nobilissimus . . . ex huius saeculi tenebris migravit ad astra.

21. F. Filelfo: Birthdates and deathdates: Olimpio Gellio, Valerio Marcello, and their fathers.

a. G, 38 (ed. fol. [29]): Olimpio's birth and death (11 April 1453 and 8 March 1461)

Erat enim mihi puer mirabili indole Olympus Gellius, qui natus {ed. nato} tertio idus Apriles anno a natali christiano millesimo quadringentesimo quinquagesimo tertio, cum nondum implesset octavum annum ea et loquebatur et sapiebat que vix adultae aut etiam grandioris etatis solent.

b. G, 67 (ed. fol. 34v): Births of Olimpio and Valerio. Valerio's horoscope; according to Filelfo, born same year and month as Olimpio; 3 idus april (11 April) shortly before sunrise and 8 kal. mai (24 April), second hour after sunrise; astrologers say long life not possible with this horoscope.

Valerius tuus natus est eodem et anno et mense, quo meum Olympum superius natum memineram: verum {ed. iterum} hic ad tertium idus Apriles paulo ante solis ortum, at Valerius post solis ortum circiter horam secundam ad octavum kalendas Maias.

c. G, 55 (ed. fol. 32): Births of Marcello and Filelfo (17 January and 25 July 1398)

Verum ea nobis offertur consolatio, quod non multum abesse possit, ut quos tanto animi ardore desideramus, coram liceat intueri, et tibi Valerium tuum et mihi Olympum meum, equalibus nobis equalis illos. Nam ut illi eodem et anno et mense nati complerant annum octavum neuter, ita nos annum quartum et sexagesimum ingressi uterque sumus, tu ad XVI kal. Februarias, ego vero ad octavum kal. Augustas.

d. G, 119–20 (ed. fol. 43): Valerio's death (1 January 1461)

Quid quod iam annum prope agis in luctu? Hic est natalis christianus. Ad proximum kalendas Ianuarias Valerius tuus reliquit membra mortalia.

22. Anon. Ven. G, 254: The infant Valerio greets his father.

> Pacatis enim rebus apud opidum Cremam recenti victoria tunc sub iuga veneta missum cui Senatus imperio praesidebas publica laude simul et leticia, domum rediens optatum filium nonaginta pene dierum spacia complentem cumulata leticia vidisti.

23. Bevilacqua, G, 330–31 (V, fols. 34v, 35v): Born while Marcello was in Crema, the infant Valerio greets him on his return.

> a. Post bella quae Senatus venetus noster cum Francisco Sfortia nunc Mediolani principe gessit, Creme oppidum amplum inter insubres scitum in foedere pacis imperio senatus accesserat, ut fit in populis recens adeptis, quorum mentes {V merites} mulcendae et ad obedienciam principum illiciendae sunt, ut oppidanorum animi componerentur scierentque se clementissimo atque iustissimo dominio additos. Et ideo ad parendum ultro disponerentur, eo senatusconsulto creatus ut ibi praesiderem profectus eram. Tunc magistratum gerebam cum uxor quam Venetiis reliqueram infantem fuit enixa.
>
> b. Quatuor menses anno defuerant, in cuius exitu magistratus deponendus erat, et Venecias redeundum. Quo ubi applicui, adventui meo Valerius filius adhuc inter crepundia obvolutus mihi oblatus est, quem ubi inter ulnas ad osculum accipio, quem que ut fieri solet, ad novum adventum meum evagire putassem, video istum mihi arridentem, et quo ad ei potis est, risu gestientem.

24. F. Filelfo, G, 41–42 (ed. fol. [29v]): The announcement of Valerio's birth to his father.

> Aberas tu Creme praetor cum tibi nuncius est allatus de infante nato, quod ipse audiens tanta voluptate animi affectus perhiberis, ut ex oris hilaritate admirationem iniiceres circunstantibus. . . . Tantam de illius futura probitate spem conceperas, ut tibi magnum ad felicitatem cumulum additum putares. Nec te tua fallebat opinio. Fertur enim susceptus in lucem infans et cum minimo parturientis brevique labore, et quod mirabile dictum est, non modo non vagiens sed etiam surridens.

25. Sagundino, G, 5 (F, fol. 94; VatS, fol. 2v): The infant Valerio greets his father.

> Illud mihi nequaquam videtur tacendum: aberas forte tu et magistratum foris gerebas, cum tuus tibi Valerius domi tue {F tui} est natus. Trimestre exacto exinde spatio domum rediisti, et quamquam infans non nisi nutricis gestationi atque amplexibus ac-

quiescere consuerat, ut te tamen primum conspexit, tamquam ag-
novisset quem antea nunquam viderat.

26. George of Trebizond, G, 27 (Mon. #6): The infant Valerio greets his
father.

In Valerio autem tuo illud vel divine mentis iudicium vel divina-
tionis quedam species fuit quod te absente (Crema namque, si bene
memini, rem publicam gerebas) natus trimestrisque puer factus re-
deuntem agnovit patrem adeo ut, quod nunquam in alium facere
visus est, nutrice contempta capitis motu manuumque porrectione
te peteret in manibusque tuis sic acquiesceret ut nutricis oblitus fuisse videretur. . . . Mirabilia dictu hec sunt, sed vera. Nam etiam
apud priscos non nihil huiusmodi evenisse legimus.

27. Fortebraccio, G, 144: The infant Valerio greets his father.
Nam forte eo tempore natus est tuus hic Valerius, cum tu in prefec-
ture fascibus Creme ageres. Redeunte te in urbem reipublice causa
iam trimestris puer erat, qui ut priuum te conspexit in oscula in
amplexus tuos natura docente et capitis motu et manum porrectione gestiebat nec acquievisse fertur donec ulnis tuis contempta nutrice fuisset acceptus.

28. Guarini, G, 180 (F, fol. 110): The infant Valerio greets his father.
Cum {G enim} te absente natus esset, et . . . in patriam rediises,
oblatus subito infans risu (*quem nunquam antea ediderat* [emphasis
mine]) paternos excepit amplexus.

29. Perleone, G, 212 (B, fols. 47v–48): The infant Valerio greets his father.
Cum e castris quarto mense post in urbem pater venisset infan-
temque nunquam antea visum a nutrice acceptum substulisset,
blandiens ut fit aliquantulum admiratus infans, ac intentos in parentem tenens oculos statim toto gestire corpore ac ridere cepit, et
quod neque sermone nec offitio poterat parentem risu gestuque
cognovit.

30. George of Trebizond, G, 36 (Mon. #34): Valerio's death.
Non equidem ipse negaverim idcirco Kalendis Ianuarii filium . . .
[ereptum].

31. Perleone (Texts II.D.21), VatP, fol. 103v (F, fol. 106v; MU, fol. 94v):
Valerio died at age eight.
Ita filius tuus qui octavo aetatis anno mortuus est, ultimo senio
mortuus est, si quidem illud erat ipsi ultimum vivendi spatium
praestitutum.

32. Fortebraccio, G, 156: Valerio lived for eight years.

> Qua ratione tu quoque octo annorum spatio Valerium filium tuum, apud te comodati nomine fuisse fatearis oportet.

33. Bevilacqua, G, 377 (V, fol. 95v): Valerio's death in ninth year, burial in San Giorgio Maggiore.

> Qui in nonum annum vita functus, et in aede sacra Sancti Georgii Maioris nuncupati, sepultus.

Chronology

꙰

Sources are noted in parentheses following each event (primary first, secondary following, in alphabetical order). Where none is given, the event is well known and can be established from a range of sources. Where different witnesses give different dates, in the absence of documentary evidence, the most recent authority has been followed. Archival references are to original page numeration wherever that has been legible. Brief summaries of the events of Jacopo Antonio Marcello's career in Fabbri 1983, 246–50; King 1986, 393–98; Mallett 1973, 144n91; Mallett & Hale 1984, 172.

1380: 14 August
Death of Vettore Pisani, who was honorifically buried in San Antonio Abate (da Vienna), with monument and epitaph subsequently admired by Valerio Marcello (Fam. III.B.3–4).

1382–
Louis I d'Anjou, grandfather of René, shares Neapolitan throne with Giovanna I of Sicily, but after her murder (21 September 1384) loses it to Charles of Durazzo (Lecoy 1875, 1:14–15).

1383
Marriage of Francesco Marcello and Magdalucia (di Paolo di Giovanni) Trevisan, parents of Jacopo Antonio (Fam. I.A.8).

1398: 17 January
Birth of Jacopo Antonio Marcello (Fam. II.A, IV.21.c).

1398: 25 July
Birth of Francesco Filelfo, most prominent of Marcello's consolers, and his contemporary (Fam. IV.21.c).

1401: 23 July
Birth of Francesco Sforza, illegitimate son of Muzio Attendolo, future *condottiere,* eventually duke of Milan.

1405
Venice seizes Padua, capturing and executing (early 1406) the last Carrara rulers (Romanin 1853–61, 4:31–38). The Castello of Monselice falls to

Venice on 14 September, betrayed by Luca da Leone—who had been bribed by Carlo Zeno. Soon after, it is sold to a member of the Marcello family, who adds a section joining the ancient *casa romanica* and the Carrara *torre* in the first half of the fifteenth century (Barbantini 1940, 7, 17–18; Gloria 1862–65, 3:134; Hayward 1980, 29; for the bribery see also Queller 1986, 331; Zeno's reputation was defended by the contemporary humanists Leonardo Giustiniani and Jacopo Zeno: L. Giustiniani 1941; J. Zeno 1940).

1406: 12 November
Obizzo da Polenta asks Venice to send a *podestà* to Ravenna each year to defend him and his legitimate male heirs (Barbiani 1927, 27; Pasolini 1881, 67, #12); Venice subsequently complies on 20 November (Pasolini 1881, 73, #13).

1409: 16 January
Birth of René d'Anjou (Lecoy 1875, 1:3).

1410: 19 May
Louis II d'Anjou, father of René, wins naval victory over Ladislas of Durazzo, briefly winning Neapolitan throne, but is forced subsequently to abandon it to Ladislas's reoccupation (Lecoy 1875, 1:28).

1410: 20 June
The will of Obizzo da Polenta (father of Ostasio, who would be the last male descendant), granting Venice right of succession to Ravenna in the absence of male heirs, rendering the city "apertamente vassalla" to the Serenissima (Barbiani 1927, 30–31; Pasolini 1881, 81, #14).

1413: 16 October
Pietro Marcello, brother of Jacopo Antonio Marcello and Bishop of Padua, is examined and receives his license in both laws at Padua (Zonto & Brotto 1970, 1:125, #303).

1417: 3 December
Jacopo Antonio Marcello presented for ascription in the Balla d'oro by Francesco Marcello di Pietro, Alessandro Marcello di Vittore, and his mother Magdalucia (Fam. I.A.7,8).

1418
Jacopo Antonio Marcello marries Fiordelise, legitimate daughter of Pietro Miani, Bishop of Vicenza (Fam. I.A.24).

1420: 23 July
Francesco Filelfo granted Venetian citizenship following two-year residence (Castellani 1896, 369; Fabbri 1983, 234n25).

1420–

Louis III d'Anjou, elder brother of René, struggles for Angevin domination of Naples until his death on 12 November 1434; after 1423, he is the adopted heir of Queen Giovanna II, sister of Ladislas of Durazzo (Lecoy 1875, 1:50, 112).

1424: 2 June

Francesco Sforza wins glory and a heap of gold as victor of the battle of Aquila where Sforza's father, Muzio Attendolo, led the armies of Giovanna II of Naples (last survivor of the dynasty called the "first house" of Anjou) against his old adversary Braccio da Montone. Attendolo having drowned en route, Francesco (given the cognomen of Sforza by Queen Giovanna II) takes command (Peyronnet 1982, 11; Pontieri 1958, 2:846–74; Toderini 1875, 116).

1424: 5 June

Death of Andrea d'Oddo Braccio da Montone, son of Oddo Fortebraccio, father of Carlo Fortebraccio da Montone; buried in unhallowed ground at the command of pope, subsequently buried in Perugia by son Niccolò Fortebraccio (Campano 1731, 620–22; Argegni 1936, 1:404).

1425: 10 October

Testament of Marcello's wife Fiordelise di Pietro Miani when pregnant with last child; Fiordelise will die before 25 September of the following year (Fam. I.A.24).

1428

Death of Pietro Marcello, bishop of Padua, Jacopo Antonio Marcello's elder brother and probable guardian after 1411 (Fam. I.A.10–11).

1428: 26 May

Treaty of Ferrara, settling the war between Milan and the league of Florence and Venice, gives Brescia and Bergamo to Venice (Cognasso 1955, 6:247; Romanin 1853–61, 4:128–30).

1432: 5 May

Execution of the Venetian *condottiere* Carmagnola, sending silent admonitions to Italy's mercenary captains (Romanin 1853–61, 4:161).

1432: 27 November

Cristoforo di Vittore Marcello presents to the Avogaria di Comun his son Jacopo, often confused with Jacopo Antonio (Fam. I.B.2).

1433: 26 April

Peace treaty secures pause in Lombard wars, in which Venice's eventual designs on a frontier well to the west are first outlined (Cognasso 1955, 6:229–30; Romanin 1853–61, 4:164–65).

1433: 7 December
With conquest of Jesi, Francesco Sforza gains foothold in the Marche, where he remains engaged through 1447.

1435: 2 February
Death of Giovanna II d'Anjou, queen of Naples, and titular succession of René d'Anjou; Queen Isabelle of Lorraine, wife of the king then held in a Burgundian prison, proceeds to Naples to secure possession, entering 10 October (Lecoy 1875, 1:112, 144).

1435: 3 April
Taddeo d'Este (who will serve as Venetian *condottiere*) is granted honorary membership in Venetian nobility (ASV, SP 2, fol. 19v).

1436: 31 January
Giorgio Bevilacqua writes encouraging letter to Isotta and Ginevra Nogarola, warns that they face skepticism because of sex, sends a volume of Lactantius (Nogarola 1886, 1:12–17).

1436: 3 April
Giorgio Bevilacqua writes to Isotta and Ginevra Nogarola. Responding to their letters, he compares their mother Bianca to Cornelia, mother of Gracchi (Nogarola 1886, 1:18–24).

1436: 25 November
The island of San Cristoforo near Murano is granted by dogal letter to Fra Simone da Camerino, founder and general of the order of Augustinian canons of Monte Ortone (Fam. III.C).

1437: 22 June (or 1436)
Giorgio Bevilacqua writes letter to Nogarola sisters on learned women, and sends a life of Saint Jerome (Nogarola 1886, 1:25–35).

1437: July (or 1436)
From Verona, Isotta Nogarola writes to thank Giorgio Bevilacqua for the book he sent (Nogarola 1886, 1:36–41).

1437: 16 August (Prague)
Emperor Sigismund formally invests Venice with *terraferma* possessions; declaration in Venice follows 20 November. Venetian doge is now officially "Doge of Treviso, Feltre, Belluno, Ceneda, Padua, Brescia, Bergamo, Casalmaggiore, Soncino, Platina, San Giovanni a Croce, and all the castles and places in the Cremonese territory and in the rest of Lombardy on this (the Venetian) side of the Adda" (Hazlitt 1915, 1:914–15).

1437: 30 September
Leonardo Giustiniani writes Francesco Barbaro, captain of Brescia, an-

nouncing that Jacopo Antonio Marcello among others will shortly arrive to assist (B. Giustiniani 1492, sigs. 62a–62b).

1437: 10 November
Angelo Simonetta de Policastro, Francesco Sforza's secretary, is granted privilege of "original citizenship" in Venice (ASV, SP 2, fol. 22).

1437: 23 December
Gattamelata made captain general of the Venetian forces, following Gianfrancesco Gonzaga's desertion of the previous month; he will receive 300 ducats per month in salary, and the standards and *bastone* of command are to be conferred upon him (Eroli 1876, 97–98; Hazlitt 1915, 1:60–61).

1438: March–September
Ostasio da Polenta surrenders Ravenna to Milanese general Niccolò Piccinino, remaining titular *signore;* citizen uprisings follow (Barbiani 1927, 32ff.).

1438 a few days before Good Friday
Death of Antonino (born 18 January 1434), son of Giannozzo Manetti, at age 4 years 2 months (Manetti 1983, intro. by De Petris, xii), which spurs the composition soon thereafter of Manetti's *Consolatoria.* The following year the work was published in an Italian version written by Tommaso Tani from Manetti's dictation (Manetti 1983, intro. by De Petris, xii–xviii).

1438: 4 April
Jacopo Antonio Marcello is elected *provveditore* of Casalmaggiore for a term of one year with a salary of 40 ducats monthly (ASV, SMI 60, fol. 71v).

1438: April
René d'Anjou, legitimate heir of the first and second houses of Anjou and chosen successor of Giovanna II, sails for Naples via Genoa to launch his struggle for lordship of Naples. Arriving at Genoa on 15 April, he proceeds to Porto Pisano, where he is greeted by Francesco Sforza, who aids him in the early phases of the attempt to retake Naples. The struggle lasts until June 1442, when he sails home to France (Lecoy 1875, 1:136–223; Léonard 1967, 617–19; Peyronnet 1969, chap. 4).

1438: 13 June
Jacopo Antonio Marcello, *provveditore* of Casalmaggiore, reports that Niccolò Piccinino has crossed the Po and menaces Casalmaggiore; Senate orders him to persuade the citizens to participate in its defense, if necessary promising reparations for any damage done to their crops (ASV, SS 14, fol. 116v). Marcello continues to hold the title of *provveditore* of Casalmaggiore through 2 October (at least; SS 14, passim, and dates below). Some authors

attribute to him a major victory during June (da Soldo 1733, 792; see Guarino Veronese 1915–19, 3:487; Meiss 1957, 10).

1438: 30 June
Niccolò Piccinino besieges and takes Casalmaggiore, then proceeds with intent to cross Oglio to invade the Bresciano (Eroli 1876, 109–10; Tarducci 1899, 270; Soranzo 1957, 79); soon after, Venetian captain Gianfrancesco Gonzaga will turn to Milanese alliance (joining his son Ludovico, already in Visconti employ, and hoping for territorial gains).

1438: 2/3 July
Piccinino succeeds in crossing Oglio secretly by naval bridge constructed of Gonzaga's Mantuan boats, outmaneuvering Gattamelata (Tarducci 1899, 276); he explodes in Bresciano, and besieges Brescia which will not be free until the spring of 1440 (Eroli 1876, 122f.; Lane 1973, 230–32; Romanin 1853–61, 4:194ff.).

1438: 29 July
Gattamelata, at head of Venetian army, enters Brescia for its defense; the captain of Brescia Francesco Barbaro will persuade him to go to Verona for supplies and assistance (Eroli 1876, 113ff.).

1438: 2 August
Jacopo Antonio Marcello, *provveditore* in Valle Lagarino, and Leonardo Marcello, *provveditore* in Rovereto, grant exemptions to the residents of the region for the great loyalty shown in the war: "per la fedeltà mostrata nell'ultima guerra"; the act is confirmed 14 January 1441 (Predelli 1876– 1914, 4:241 [xii, 110]).

1438: 12 August
Venetian troops take Roato (Roadum, Rovatum), the key to Brescia (Soranzo 1957, 83, da Soldo 1732, 796–97; see Guarino Veronese 1915–19, 3:488).

1438: 20 August
Still entitled *provveditore* of Casalmaggiore, Jacopo Antonio Marcello is elected *provveditore* with the army (*provisor ad exercitum*) (ASV, SMI 60, 167v).

1438: 11 September
A Senate letter informs Jacopo Antonio Marcello, *provveditore,* and the rectors of Brescia, that needed money has been sent (ASV, SS 14, fol. 149).

1438: 16, 20 September
Senate letters inform Jacopo Antonio Marcello and Federico Contarini, *provveditori,* and the rectors of Brescia, of the need to persuade Count Par-

isio da Lodrone (by means of a promise of up to 20,000 ducats) to open a path to Gattamelata's army, then retreating across Alpine foothills from Brescia to Verona; Jacopo Antonio Marcello will go secretly to do so; an agreement is reached (ASV, SS 14, fols. 151v, 153; Eroli 1876, 118ff.).

1438: 24–28/29 September

Gattamelata retreats hastily from Bresciano to Veronese *contado*—a clever retreat accomplished in spite of impassable mountains and rivers—but the Brescians are left isolated (da Soldo 1732, 798; Guarino Veronese 1915–19, #890, 3:488; Eroli 1876, 116ff.; Hazlitt 1915, 1:919; Soranzo 1957, 85). The retreat "became almost legendary in the annals of Italian warfare" (Mallett 1974, 187).

1438: 1 October

The Senate wishing to honor Gattamelata, captain general of Venetian army ("volentes . . . per aliquod gratitudinis signum eundem ad venture posteritatis memoriam decorare"), grants honorary membership in the Venetian nobility to him and his hereditary descendants in the male line; and to the same, a "magna domus" near the church of San Polo that had previously belonged to the *condottieri* Alvise dal Verme (who had turned to the Visconti standard [Tarducci 1899, 274]; for his activity see Dolfin, *Cronaca,* fol. 405 [294], account of 1446 battle at Casalmaggiore), Jacopo dal Verme (an old lieutenant of Giangaleazzo Visconti and one of the three regents appointed by his testament), and Jacopo da Carrara. He will also receive an augmentation of salary from 300 to 500 ducats per month (ASV, SS 14, 155–56; SP 2, fol. 24 [recorded on 10 July 1439]; Sanuto 1733, 1073; Eroli 1876, 100ff.; Norwich 1982, 321n1).

1438: 2 October

Jacopo Antonio Marcello having gone to Count Parisio da Lodrone and obtained permission for the Venetian army to pass through his territory, the agreements he made are approved and should be honored (ASV, SS 14, fol. 156; Soranzo 1957, 86). Count Parisio is henceforth actively engaged with Venetian forces, and will be rewarded by the Republic on 6 April 1439, shortly before his death five days later (see below at 6 February 1439; and Sanuto 1733, 1068, 1073, 1074).

1438: 8 October

Pietro de' Avogadri (de Advocatis or Avogadro), "commendabilis" citizen of Brescia (who had notably assisted Venetian military campaign), is granted honorary membership in Venetian nobility (ASV, SP 2, fol. 22v).

1438: 19 December

Senate in a letter to Jacopo Antonio Marcello, *provveditore* with Gattamelata, encourages opening up the route from Verona to Brescia for the relief of the latter at all costs, even if the bishop of Trent is attacked (ASV, SS 14, fol. 170; Soranzo 1957, 89–90).

1439: 6 February
A Senate letter to Gattamelata, responding to the communication of his activities by Jacopo Antonio Marcello, urges him to continue to create diversionary trouble in the *mantovano*, to lure its Marquis Gianfrancesco Gonzaga and relieve pressure on Parisio di Lodrone, and to facilitate the safe arrival of the "armata" (see below at 15 February) on the Lago di Garda (ASV, SS 14, fol. 180v).

1439: 15 February
A Venetian river fleet having been transported over Alpine foothills is launched in the Lago di Garda under cover of Gattamelata's army (da Soldo 1938, 30; Sanuto 1733, 1086; Eroli 1876, 126; Hazlitt 1915, 1:921–22; Lane 1973, 230–32; Mallett & Hale 1984, 98; Romanin 1853–61, 4:196–97; Soranzo 1957, 92–93). The scheme had been suggested by two engineers, Blasio de Arboribus and the Cretan architect Nicolò Sorbolo, and Pietro Zeno commanded flotilla of 80 ships, including at least two war galleys from the mouth of the Adige to Roveredo, from whence they would be hauled up and over Monte Baldo (by 120 oxen) to Torbole, the nearest Garda port. The feat is attributed by some to Jacopo Antonio Marcello (see da Soldo 1732, 808; da Soldo 1938, 30; Guarino 1915–19, #890, 3:488; Argegni 1936, 2:201); by the humanist Ludovico Merchenti to Stefano Contarini (Merchenti, *Benachus*); and by many modern scholars to Gattamelata. As represented on the ceiling of the Maggior Consiglio in the Ducal Palace, there are painted on the side of the first galley the arms of Marcello and Stefano Contarini (Franzoi 1982, 233).

1439: 19 February
Venice contracts with Francesco Sforza for payment of 18,000 ducats per month for him and his companies, and promise of Mantua if he conquered the Gonzaga, and Cremona if he didn't; or Milan, if he succeeded in crossing the Adda (Hazlitt 1915, 1:923; Peyronnet 1982, 13; Romanin 1853–61, 4:198; Soranzo 1957, 102).

1439: March
Piccinino ravages the Veronese and Vicentino, March–May (Guarino 1915–19, #890, 3:488; da Soldo 1733, 809; Eroli 1876, 127).

1439: 26 April
The Senate has been informed by Jacopo Antonio Marcello and the rectors and citizens of Brescia of the city's extreme peril. A small force under Jacopo

Antonio Marcello, Petro de Avogadri, and Bartolomeo Colleoni should immediately set out to succor the city, for which purpose funds are sent to Jacopo Antonio Marcello (ASV, SS 14, fol. 197). On the same date, Marcello accepted oaths of loyalty to Venice from representatives of Tierno, Besagno, and Sano, localities in the Valle Lagarina (Predelli 1876–1914, 5:134 [xv.41]).

1439: 20/23 June
Sforza joins Venetian forces; united colors of Venice, Florence, and Genoa sent him as emblem of command (Hazlitt 1915, 1:922; Soranzo 1957, 103). Gattamelata is a willing second-in-command (Eroli 1876, 128ff.).

1439: before 25 July
Jacopo Antonio Marcello, *provveditore* with Sforza and Gattamelata, crosses the Adige after winning a series of victories, and marches to Soave, which is taken 9 August (Guarino 1915–19, #890, 3:488; da Soldo 1733, 811).

1439: 28 July
The Senate decrees that Jacopo Antonio Marcello may return, his long and worthy service in the field being duly noted ("steterit . . . longo tempore in nostris serviciis, laudabiliter se gerens et sine premio aliquo") (ASV, SS 14, fol. 213).

1439: 20 August
Jacopo Antonio Marcello is elected *provveditore* with the army (ASV, SMI 60, fol. 167v).

1439: 8, 15, 20, and 26 September
Senate letters issuing orders, urging vigilance, etc., addressed to the Venetian ambassador to Francesco Sforza and Jacopo Antonio Marcello *provveditore* with Sforza (ASV, SS 14, fols. 218, 222–224, 226rv).

1439: 26 September
Venetian fleet on Garda at Torbole under Pietro Zeno surprised and annihilated (da Soldo 1733, 813; Hazlitt 1915, 1:927; Dolfin, *Cronaca,* fol. 385 [274] gives 16 August); soon replaced by another smaller one of eight galleys and four small ships built on the spot (Mallett & Hale 1984, 99).

1439: 1 and 4 October
Senate letters as in September to Venetian ambassador and Jacopo Antonio Marcello *provveditore* with Francesco Sforza; second letter eloquently stresses need to recover Brescia, and promises a more powerful fleet by which to supply the city (ASV, SS 14, fol. 229v–230v).

1439: 10 October
Stefano Contarini is made captain of the new fleet to be constructed on the Lago di Garda (Dolfin, *Cronaca,* fol. 385v [274v]; Sanuto 1733, 1082).

1439: 13, nd, 30, and 31 October

Senate letters to Jacopo Antonio Marcello, *provveditore* with Francesco Sforza, urging, among other matters, Marcello to persuade Sforza to cooperation with Senate negotiations with pope and arrival of *condottiere* Michele Attendolo (Sforza's kinsman); Marcello granted 300 ducats free of all imposts in recognition of his long and valued service in the field (ASV, SS 14, fol. 231v–232, 234rv).

1439: October

Giorgio Corner, released from Visconti prisons, returns to Venice, a broken man; dies following December (Hazlitt 1915, 1:905–6; Romanin 1853–61, 4:165–68).

1439: 9 November

Sforza's victory over Piccinino at Tenna, assisted by Brescian militia; Carlo Gonzaga taken prisoner, Niccolò Piccinino escapes, to turn and seize Verona, diverting Sforza from progress to Brescia (da Soldo 1733, 814–15; Eroli 1876, 133; Hazlitt 1915, 1:924–25; Soranzo 1957, 107).

1439: 12 November

Senate's letter to Jacopo Antonio Marcello, *provveditore* with Sforza, is delighted with victory just achieved; that victory should be followed up by a swift move to bring aid to Brescia (ASV, SS 14, fol. 236).

1439: 19 November

Senate's letter to Jacopo Antonio Marcello, *provveditore* with Sforza, expresses alarm that Verona has been retaken and urges its prompt recovery (ASV, SS 14, fol. 237v).

1439: 20 November

Sforza and Gattamelata retake Verona, with Jacopo Antonio Marcello in their company; Marcello negotiates with Piccinino the fate of the prisoners (Guarino 1915–19, #890, 3:488; da Soldo 1733, 815–16; Sanuto 1733, 1084; Eroli 1876, 133ff.; Soranzo 1957, 108–9).

1439: 22 November

Jacopo Antonio Marcello's letter from the field is read in the Senate, describing the fruits of victory, including 300 horses and 1,000 prisoners taken (Sanuto 1733, 1086); Senate notices of congratulations are sent to Sforza and Gattamelata (Soranzo 1857, 109).

1439: 23 November

Senate emissaries arrive in Verona to congratulate Sforza on his victory (Sanuto 1733, 1085–86). The Senate grants Francesco Sforza and his legitimate male heirs honorary membership in the Venetian nobility as a sign of its devotion and friendship ("sinceri devotionis ac constantis amicicie signum"), as well as, to give concrete expression to that affection, a palace (distinctive by its two towers, reminiscent of *terraferma* castles) on the Grand Canal ("vos et illustrem domum vestram in civitate nostram venetiarum in amoris perpetui monumentum aliquo notabili munere decorare . . . concedimus . . . domum nostram duarum turrium situatam in civitate nostra venetiarum super canale maius in parochia Sancti Panthaleonis" (ASV, SP 2, fol. 24v; Toderini 1875, 117). The palace had previously belonged to Gianfrancesco Gonzaga, marquis of Mantua, now with the Milanese forces (Sanuto, Toderini, as above; also Greppi 1913, 326–31). Gattamelata is also given land in Montorio by the Senate, and is promised by the Veronese a gift of 3,000 ducats, payment to extend over six years because of their great poverty (Eroli 1876, 140).

1439: 24 November

Senate's letter to Jacopo Antonio Marcello, "orator" ("ambassador") with Sforza, commending recent victory reported by Marcello's letter of 21 November; a bonus to be distributed among the soldiers is authorized (ASV, SS 14, fol. 239v).

1439: 29 November

Senate's letter to Jacopo Antonio Marcello with Andrea Mocenigo and Ludovico Storlado, all entitled "orators" to Sforza, responding to Jacopo Antonio Marcello's letters of 23 and 26 November; need to proceed to relief of Brescia, and promises of eventual readiness of Garda fleet (ASV, SS 14, fol. 241rv).

1439: 1 December

Letter to Marcello from the Brescian Pietro da Rondo describing the desperate plight of the citizens (Texts III.9).

1439: 10 December

Jacopo Antonio Marcello's letters from the field are read in the Senate, reporting on Piccinino's advances and the needs of the Veronese (Sanuto 1733, 1086).

1439: 31 December

Senate instructs its secretary Giovanni de' Reguardati to communicate its commission to Francesco Sforza in the presence of Jacopo Antonio Marcello concerning negotiations with the community of Arco and the bishop of Trent, controlling the arteries to Brescia (ASV, SS 15, fol. 5v).

1439: June

Francesco Filelfo moves to Milan, the center of his career in the service of four administrations through 1476.

1440: 2 January
Gattamelata is struck with apoplexy (Eroli 1876, 141; Soranzo 1957, 110).

1440: January
Carlo Fortebraccio, son of Braccio da Montone, with 200 soldiers, listed among Venetian forces (Sanuto 1733, 1089); hereafter, Carlo Fortebraccio frequently in Venetian service (Argegni 1936, 1:404–5; Mallett 1979, 153).

1440: 9 January
Senate letter to Jacopo Antonio Marcello, ambassador to Sforza, confirming receipt of his letter describing Sforza's negotiations with Carlo Gonzaga (ASV, SS 15, fol. 8).

1440: 11 February
Senate instructs Orsato Giustiniani and Giovanni Pisani to go with greatest possible speed as ambassadors to Sforza, and in the presence of Jacopo Antonio Marcello to congratulate him for all his efforts "ut verus filius se gessit et gerit et in montibus et alibi per conservatione et reintegratione status nostri, nullis parcendo laboribus et periculis." Furthermore, they are to recommend more modest levels of expenditure by Sforza himself and the *condottieri* under him (ASV, SS 15, fol. 10).

1440: 4 March
Jacopo Antonio Marcello having been in service for some time as ambassador to Francesco Sforza, and having written many letters requesting leave to handle business at home, another candidate may be elected to replace him (with monthly salary of 70 ducats) so that he may return (ASV, SMI 60, fol. 199v). Niccolò Piccinino creates diversion in Tuscany, and Sforza wishes to cross the Po southwards against Venetian wishes.

1440: 19 March
Jacopo Antonio Marcello having informed the Senate of Sforza's desire to leave for the Marche, it will appoint two ambassadors to deal with matter (ASV, SS 15, fol. 15v).

1440: 26 April
Jacopo Antonio Marcello and Andrea Donato embark with Sforza from Venice to go to Padua (Sanuto 1733, 1093–94).

1440: 3 June
Sforza crosses Mincio to follow up a naval victory of Stefano Contarini's, and will subsequently take Rivoltella, Lonato, Salò, and other places (Hazlitt 1915, 1:930).

1440: 14 June
Sforza defeats Piccinino between Orzinuovi and Soncino, and finally re-lieves Brescia after 3-yr siege; proceeds to Mantovano, and thence to Adda by end 1440 (Hazlitt 1915, 1:930–31).

1440: 21 July
Stefano Contarini, captain of Venetian fleet, takes key site on the shores of Garda (Sanuto 1733, 1100; Dolfin, *Cronaca,* fol. 387v [276v] gives 20 July), winning effective control of the lake by August (Hazlitt 1915, 1:930; Mallett & Hale 1984, 99; see also Franzoi 1982, 231, 233).

1440: 10 August
Senate elects Jacopo Antonio Marcello as "ambassador" to go to Ravenna to hold that city in obedience (ASV, SS 15, 35; Barbiani 1927, 36); Mar-cello was in Romagna as Venetian *provveditore* with Cardinal Ludovico Scarampo, assisting papal army (Spretus *De amplitudine,* fol. 35v; and ge-nealogists).

1440: 7 September
In response to repeated requests, the Senate tells the ambassador of René d'Anjou that Sforza would be free to contract with him once a peace was arranged. Sforza in fact only contracted by René in 1442 (Perret 1896, 166–67; below, at 25 March), although René had made overtures to him on 20 November 1439 and 14/15 April 1440 (Osio 1872, 3.1:190–92, 202–3).

1440: 13 September
Jacopo Antonio Marcello ordered to return to Venice immediately, on pain of 500 ducats, and then proceed within two days on his assigned embassy (ASV, SMI 60, fol. 251v).

1440: 24 October–1441: February
Senate actions taken regarding situation in Ravenna. Michele Attendolo has been instructed to release troops needed. Jacopo Antonio Marcello has written (on 23 October) saying that the city no longer wishes to remain under the rule of Ostasio da Polenta. If he is not already there, he should take the troops provided by Attendolo and go to Ravenna immediately. Giovanni Leone will serve as *podestà,* and Jacopo Antonio Marcello must see to the city's defense; and while there, "cum illis prudentibus et cautis modis qui vobis videbuntur," he should find out what is the temper of the city. And if it appears that Ostasio is noxious to the citizens, steps must be taken to preserve the city in Venice's allegiance in any case; but if they are content with him, Jacopo Antonio Marcello should do nothing (ASV, SS

15, fol. 48v; Barbiani 1927, 36–37). Marcello marches to Ravenna with 2,000 foot, instructed not to let the city fall, and Ostasio da Polenta flees to Venice (1441) while city declares itself for Venice (Barbiani 1927, 38 ff.; Hazlitt 1915, 1:939–40; Romanin 1853–61, 4:203–5). Marcello's role in Venice is described enthusiastically and perhaps with some exaggeration in the Ravennate Desiderius Spretus's *De amplitudine, vastatione et de instauratione urbis Ravennae,* dedicated to that nobleman (Texts III.10).

1440: 10 November
Jacopo Antonio Marcello, armed "ambassador" to Ravenna, reports that the city is in the greatest peril and requires assistance if it is not to fall to the enemy's hands; Senate orders troops to be sent as quickly as possible and so informs Marcello (ASV, SS 15, fol. 50v; printed in Pasolini 1881, 86, #15).

1440: 26 November
Gattamelata's forces are reorganized; the sick captain will be granted a pension of 1,000 ducats per year for life in recognition of his services (Eroli 1876, 147; Soranzo 1957, 111).

1440: 15 December
Jacopo Antonio Marcello, having long served as *provveditore* of Ravenna ("diu steterit in serviciis nostris"), wishes to return to Venice for his health ("pro recuperatione sue sospitatis, cum aer Ravene sit ei plurimum nocivus"); Vettor Dolfin is elected to replace him (ASV, SM 1, fol. 9v).

1440: 18 December
Sforza is honorably received in Venice, where he has come to participate in the Foscari-Contarini wedding (Toderini 1875, 117).

1441: 10–11 February
Celebration of Foscari-Contarini wedding, with the companies of Sforza, Gattamelata, and Taddeo d'Este competing in tournaments for rich prizes (Sanuto 1733, 1100; Eroli 1876, 144–45; Hazlitt 1915, 1:933–35). Sforza is permitted to use Gattamelata's house in San Polo while his own was being repaired (Norwich 1982, 321).

1441: 14 February
Michele Attendolo da Cotignola (uncle of Francesco Sforza) made Venetian captain general (Soranzo 1957, 112; also Mallett & Hale 1984, 40).

1441: 21 February
Venetian Senate accepts submission of citizens of Ravenna; Ostasio da Polenta, with wife and child (his last surviving heir), exiled to Candia, where both the latter die later the same year (Hazlitt 1915, 1:940).

1441: 6 July

Senate letter to Jacopo Antonio Marcello, "our citizen in Monselice," expressing confidence in his loyalty, instructs him to go with up to ten horses immediately to Vicenza, at the Senate's expense and only for a few days, to accompany Sforza and proceed as far as the Adige to assess situation (ASV, SS 15, fol. 87).

1441: 21–31 August

At his palace in Venice, Sforza discusses matters of state (Toderini 1875, 118).

1441: 14 September

Jacopo Antonio Marcello ("fu Francesco") is elected to the Senate for one year (ASV, SGV 4, fol. 116v).

1441: 24–28 October

Wedding of Francesco Sforza and Bianca Maria Visconti outside Cremona, granted (with Pontremoli) to Sforza in dowry; on 28 October, the new couple entered Cremona to take charge (Ady 1907, 23; Cognasso 1955, 6:345; Eroli 1876, 147; Peyronnet 1982, 15).

1441: 20 November

Sforza negotiates Treaty of Cavriana (Sforza's camp) between Venice and Milan, assigning Cremona and Pontremoli for himself (Bianca Maria Visconti's dowry); the Venetian-Milanese boundary is established at the Adda and Venetian rights to Ravenna are confirmed (Eroli 1876, 147; Hazlitt 1915, 1:937–38; Mallett & Hale 1984, 40; Toderini 1875, 119); Sforza is "l'arbitre de la politique italienne" (Peyronnet 1982, 15).

1442: 23 February

At his palace in Venice, Sforza discusses state business (Toderini 1875, 118).

1442: 25 March

Sforza contracts to assist René d'Anjou to hold Naples for mutually satisfactory territorial settlements, promising to arrive by mid-May (Perret 1896, 167; Rubieri 1879, 1:340). Lecoy 1875, 1:204–6, dates this agreement from November 1441, and places Sforza with René through the fall of Naples in June 1442. According to Sanuto, Sforza was held in the Marche fighting Niccolò Piccinino and never succeeded in getting to Naples (Sanuto 1733, 1104; see below, 2 June).

1442: 3 April

Jacopo Antonio Marcello elected captain of Padua; subsequently canceled (ASV, CLN 7, fol. 45).

1442: 10 April

The Senate votes to bestow a gift upon Bianca Maria Visconti, then in Venice with husband Francesco Sforza, with a value of 500 to 600 ducats (Toderini 1875, 119).

1442: 3–6 May

Sforza and his bride Bianca Maria Visconti are in Venice (Toderini 1875, 119), and lavishly entertained by Doge and Dogaressa (Dolfin, *Cronaca,* 390rv [278rv]; see also Sanuto 1733, 1104): "el conte Francisco capitanio zeneral de la signoria con madonna Biancha sua moier venne a Venetia per la vignuda de la qual li fo fatto tutto lhonor che far se pottè con grandissimi triomphi, et venne madonna Biancha con le barche da Padoa fina a Santa Croce et la la monto suxo el buccintoro con madonna la dogaressa con piu de 200 donne vestide de panno doro ede seda con assaissimi notabil zolye et fu acompagnata con grandissimo triumpho fina a caxa sua, et folli aparechiata per stantia la casa del mag.co Gattamellata a San Polo et desmonta la ditta madona Biancha zoso del buccintoro al tragetto de San Benedeto, el conte se alloza ala sua caxa ala volta de Canal Grande. El zorno sequente che fo adi 4, madonna la dogaressa con il triumpho de le donne da Venetia anda per la ditta madona Biancha per terra vene da San Polo fin a San Marcho, . . . et intrate ne la chiexia de San Marcho li fono monstrate le zoije che e una notabil cossa da veder. Dapossa fu menata in sala nova dove era aparechiato da far collation, e dapossa fu acompagnata a caxa soa da madonna la dogaressa e da tute le donne de Venetia honorevlemente . . . et a di 6 [??] messer lo doxe li dono unum zoiello de pretio de ducatorum 1000 doro e fono acompagnadi fina a Malamocho con grandissimo honor, et poi . . . li passo a Ravenna et ando in la Marcha, et questo perche el conte sentiva che Nic.o Picinin se facea grosso de zente a Bollogna." The gift to Bianca Maria had been authorized by the Senate (see 10 April, above), and the couple had been formally invited by the Signoria in the person of Orsato Giustiniani, captain of Verona, on 14 April (Toderini, as above).

1442: 17 May

Jacopo Antonio Marcello is elected ambassador to Francesco Sforza and accepts; Senate letter responds with displeasure to Sforza's news that Pope Eugene IV had reached an agreement with Niccolò Piccinino (he was made *gonfaloniere* of the church), and informs Sforza that Jacopo Antonio Marcello has been chosen to serve as the ambassador to him as he had requested, as a sign of the paternal love they bear him "ut toti mundo innotescat" (ASV, SS 15, fol. 121rv).

1442: 2 June
René d'Anjou loses Kingdom of Naples to Alfonso of Aragon (Sanuto 1733, 1104; Lecoy 1875, 1:204–6). René escapes via Genoese ship to Florence, arriving in that city on 19 July. There he protests before Pope Eugene IV his contract with Niccolò Piccinino, enemy both to Sforza and to Venice; with Piccinino at war in the Romagna, Sforza had been unable (and Marcello with him) to prevent the fall of Naples; as Sanuto writes: "Il qual Renato di lì poi si partì sopra una Galera di Genovesi, e giunse a Pisa, e poi a Firenze. E fu alla presenza di Papa Eugenio IV lamentandosi molto di lui, perchè avea fatto Niccolò Piccinino Gonfaloniere della Chiesa. E per questa cagione il Conte Francesco non avea potuto venire in Puglia a dargli soccorso contro il detto Re Alfonso, e che per questo gli era stata tolta la Puglia, e poi avea perduto Napoli."

1442: 4 August
Jacopo Antonio Marcello, who had been elected ambassador to Count Francesco Sforza months ago ("iam pluribus mensibus"), is now at Monselice; as it is no longer necessary that he go on that embassy, he may renounce it without penalty (ASV, SM 1, fol. 112; ST 1, fol. 73v).

1442: 20 September
Pope Eugene IV invests René with all the privileges of king of Naples (although Alfonso of Aragon holds the city in fact); within three weeks, René sets out from Florence to return to France (where he arrives by 23 October), intending to return and recover his realm (Sanuto 1733, 1105; Manetti 1986, 119; Rubieri 1879, 1:353).

1442: 30 November
Alliance of Filippo Maria Visconti, Pope Eugene IV (abandoning René d'Anjou), and Alfonso of Aragon against Florence and Venice (the latter employing Francesco Sforza); further agreement between Eugene and Alfonso on 14 June 1443, officially protested by René in July 1445 (Lecoy 1875, 1:266–68).

1443
Jacopo Antonio Marcello di Francesco and Francesco Marcello di Jacopo Antonio marry respectively Luca and Anna di Bartolomeo da Leone (Fam. I.A.25–26).

1443
Death of Niccolò III d'Este occasions a collection of funerary epitaphs, possibly the oldest Renaissance example of this phenomenon (Fabbri 1983, 232–33).

1443: 9 January
Death of Gattamelata, by whose request the command of his company passes to brother-in-law Gentile da Leonessa and son Giovanni Antonio; the Senate confirms the concession, 9 February. He is buried with honors in the Santo in Padua, with funeral orations delivered by Lauro Quirini and (12 days later) by Giovanni Pontano (Soranzo 1957, 113–14); subsequently he is commemorated by a magnificent tomb within that church (completed 1453), and the equestrian statue by Donatello in the piazza outside (1448–50) (Eroli 1876, 148–53, 170–83, 185–94; Soranzo 1957, 113).

1443: 22 June
Michele Attendolo da Cotignola (Sforza's cousin) is received honorably in Venice and receives the *bastone* of command (Dolfin, *Cronaca,* fol. 396rv [285rv]): "adi 22 zugno zonse el mag.co signor Michiel da Codignola nostro zeneral capitanio et fono mandadi molti zintilhomini incontra in fina a Oriago et acompagnollo infina a San Zorzi Mazor . . . messer lo doxe lo aspettava cum tutta la signoria cum paraschermi assaissimi faciando grandissima festa et honor, et fu acompagnado sina ala sua stantia aparechiada fina alavolta del Canal quella fo donata al conte Francesco. Et poi per la signoria li fu fatto de grandi doni de arzenti et de altre cosse et folli fatto le spexe a lui et ala compagnia. . . . Et da possa per messer lo doxe li fu dado al alatar de messer San Marcho il confallon et fatto nostro capit.o zeneral." Venice had recently forged a defensive league against Milan for 5 years with Florence, Genoa, and Bologna, and attempted to recruit Sforza (Hazlitt 1915, 1:942).

1444: 16 October
Death of Niccolò Piccinino (Dolfin, *Cronaca,* fol. 401 [290]). Piccinino's death is placed by Francesco Filelfo (Ben. 11) soon after the crossing of the Adda in October–November 1446.

1446: 7 May
Jacopo Antonio Marcello is the third candidate elected to replace Ludovico Foscarini who has long been ambassador to Bologna, and may therefore be present in Venice; but his name is canceled like those of the previous two (who instead were elected to the Council of Ten) and Barbone Morosini is elected (ASV ST 1, fol. 190v). See below at 13 May for Marcello's election to a different office six days later.

1446: 8 May
News reaches Venice that Visconti troops have overrun Cremonese, taking Soncino and Ponte dell'Oglio. Captain general Michele Attendolo is or-

dered to ready his army (which had been in retirement), and Ludovico Foscarini is sent as ambassador to Milan to protest to Filippo Maria Visconti his violation of the peace; Visconti replies that he intends to have the Cremonese (Dolfin, *Cronaca,* fol. 404rv [293rv]).

1446: 13 May
Jacopo Antonio Marcello is elected *provveditore* with the captain general in the army (ASV, SS 17, fol. 18v). At an unspecified date this year, thus after this election, Marcello, with title *provveditore* to the army, is elected to the Senate *zonta* of 40 (ASV, SGV 4, fol. 130), with no confirming record of service in that capacity.

1446: 11 August
Ducal commission to Jacopo Antonio Marcello to go "prestissime" and "quanto celerius possibile" to assist the captain of Cremona (a city technically under Sforza's authority), invaded by Visconti's army, and promise of arrival of additional Venetian forces (ASV, SS 17, fols. 48v–49); a Senate letter to the captain general Michele Attendolo on following 22 August advising strategy is also sent to Jacopo Antonio Marcello (ASV, SS 17, fol. 53).

1446: 23 August
Senate letters to Michele Attendolo and Jacopo Antonio Marcello applaud recent securing of Cremona, about which they have learned from latter's communication of 20 August (ASV, SS 17, fol. 53v).

1446: 9, 11, and 12 September
Senate letters to Michele Attendolo with copies to Jacopo Antonio Marcello urge prompt action, to include crossing of Po by a portion of his forces, and express sympathy for his chest wound. Jacopo Antonio Marcello will arrange for doctors and proper care. Responding on the last date directly to Jacopo Antonio Marcello's letters of 7 and 8 September, and commending his "prudentiam ac diligentiam," the Senate gives minute instructions about tactical measures for the defense of Cremona and the payment and disposition of troops. A further letter is drafted to Jacopo Antonio Marcello on that same date instructing him to reach terms with Ludovico Gonzaga and Taddeo d'Este regarding their service with Venice (ASV, SS 17, fols. 58–59v, 60v).

1446: 28 September
With Jacopo Antonio Marcello present as *provveditore* with the army, Venetian forces under Michele Attendolo win a decisive victory against the fortified position held by Visconti's army on the Po island of Mezzano, lying two miles from Casalmaggiore in the area of Cremona, defending Sforza's

interest in that city. A full description of the battle and its heroes is provided by Sanuto, culminating with the capture of the Po bridge, the routing of the enemy in their camp, their attempted escape, and the taking of horses, prisoners, and booty: 4,000 horses, with their equipment, plus women and weapons, "fino le sue femine e munizioni . . . ed è stato un bel fatto d'arme de' belli, che fosse già fatto molti anni in Italia" (Sanuto 1733, 1121–22). Marcello reported immediately to the Senate in two letters dated at hours 20 and 21 on the day of battle. In the first he characterized the achievement: "Questa e la piu glorioxa victoria, che mai havesse la S. V., alla gratia del qual me reccomando. . . . Allegressì la Signoria V. fino alle viscere." The second declares that all is over: "Ad gaudium significo alla S. V. la gloriosa victoria obtenuta. . . . Dat. a cavallo . . ." (Daverio 1804, 201–2). For the Casalmaggiore victory see also Dolfin, *Cronaca*, fols. 404v–405 [293v–294]; Guarino 1915–19, 3:488; da Soldo 1733, 836; Argegni 1936, 2:201; Cognasso 1955, 6:369; Mallett & Hale 1984, 40; Romanin 1853–61, 4:210–11; the date is variously given as 25 and 27 September.

1446: 30 September
Senate letters to Jacopo Antonio Marcello and Michele Attendolo (copy to Jacopo Antonio Marcello) congratulate both on victory near Cremona (on 28 September); they should warmly thank the leaders responsible: "cunctis illis magnificis capitaneis et strenuis conductoribus nostris." Jacopo Antonio Marcello should further urge Attendolo to diligently exert himself, and if possible to cross the Adda (ASV, SS 17, fol. 62v–63).

1446: 1 October
Jacopo Antonio Marcello is elected *savio di terraferma* for six months (and is replaced on the following 31 March); in fact, he is with the army nearly without interruption through the following year (ASV, ST 2, fol. 4v).

1446: 9 October
Michele Attendolo, captain general of Venetian army, is granted honorary membership in the Venetian nobility (ASV, SP 2, fol. 37; Sanuto 1733, 1123).

1446: 18, 21, and 26 October
Ceasefire agreements made by Jacopo Antonio Marcello, in the field at Caravaggio, with localities of Ghiaradadda (Predelli 1876–1914, 4:300 [xiii.301]; 5:6 [xiv.10]). The Venetian army had taken Soncino, Romanengo, Treviglio, and Caravaggio in the space of 21 days.

1446: 20 and 25 October
Senate letter to Jacopo Antonio Marcello *provveditore* and Venetian ambassadors Federico Contarini and Andrea Morosini with army, responding to

Jacopo Antonio Marcello's letters of 16 and 21 October, as to whether it prefers that the army cross the Adda or proceed to Crema and its site of winter retirement; do what is most feasible (ASV, SS 17, fol. 67v, 68v).

1446: 5 November
Senate letter to Jacopo Antonio Marcello urges him to persuade Attendolo to keep troops in action and cross the Adda, attempting variously to take Lodi, Crema, the Ghiaradadda; thereafter he should stay with army and see to its satisfactory provisioning (ASV, SS 17, fol. 73rv).

1446: 6–7 November
Jacopo Antonio Marcello is knighted on the banks of the Adda (along with captains Pietro Avogadro and Antonio di Martinengo) by Michele Attendolo da Cotignola, Venetian captain general, after army crosses the river to precincts of Milan (Anonimo Veronese 1915, 5; da Soldo 1938, 66–67 [1733, 836–38]; Dolfin, *Cronaca,* fol. 405v [294v]; Guarino 1915–19, 3:488; Sabellico 1718, 662; Sanuto 1733, 1123); the troops cry "E anderemo a Milano!" (da Soldo, loc. cit.) and Jacopo Antonio Marcello is called the "conqueror of the Visconti" (Meiss 1957, 10). Visconti's commander Niccolò Piccinino died soon after these events.

1446: 10 November
Nominal date of a forged Sforza document attesting to the *donatio inter vivos* by which Visconti granted Sforza the dukedom of Milan after the former's death (Cusin 1936, 62ff.).

1446: 12 November
The Senate responds to communication of 7 November reporting the recent victory (the conquest of Cassano on the far side of the Adda). Attendolo is to be congratulated for succesfully crossing the Adda: "de felici transitu Abdue, et de prosperis progressibus exercitus nostri." Furthermore, he will receive the *castello* of Castelfranco (near Treviso) in fief. All other captains and *condottieri* should be congratulated: "et laudent et commendent eos de strenuis eorum operationibus" (ASV, SS 17, fol. 75v, 76). The Venetian army wreaks havoc in the milanese: "E i nostri corsero su pel Milanese, mettendo tutto a saccomano, e prendendo prigioni" (Sanuto 1733, 1122).

1446: 14 and 17 November
Senate letters to ambassadors and Jacopo Antonio Marcello *provveditore* (in the earlier of these letters he is for the first time entitled "miles") urging all necessary action for maintenance and encouragement of army (ASV, SS 17, fols. 76rv, 78v–79).

1446: 18 November
Carlo Fortebraccio in military action (Sanuto 1733, 1123).

1446: 29 November
Senate letters to *provveditore* Jacopo Antonio Marcello regarding fortification and provisioning of army, responding to his letter of 23 November (ASV, SS 17, fols. 84–85).

1446: 10 and 20 December
Senate letters to *provveditore* Jacopo Antonio Marcello, responding to his of 3 and 4 December, commending all: "nam quanto magis solicite vigilatur ad oppressionem hostis et status sui, tanto magis consolamur." Administative details (ASV, SS 17, fols. 91rv, 96v).

1446: 11 December
Jacopo Antonio Marcello is elected captain of Verona (ASV, MC, Ursa, fol. 160 [166]); that title held concurrently with that of *provveditore* with the army through 1448 (Predelli 1876–1914, 9:300 [xiii, #301]; 10:6 [xiv, #10], 8 [#18], 19 [#35, 38], 27 [#75]; Cicogna 1841, 18).

1447: 12 January
Jacopo Antonio Marcello, *provveditore* with army, writes daily ("quotidie") that it is not possible for him to handle necessary accounting himself: "quod non est sibi possibile ullo modo attendere ad receptionem et dispensationem pecuniarum, et tenere computa et attendere ad alia negotia occurrentia pro officio suo." Nobleman Bernardo Contarini quondam Niccolò is elected to assist Marcello as "solutor exercitus" in managing both money and supplies with a monthly salary of 50 ducats, etc. (ASV, ST 2, fol. 16).

1447: 25 January
Senate instructions to *provveditore* Jacopo Antonio Marcello regarding adjustments to the contracts with *condottieri* Taddeo d'Este, Gentile da Leonessa, and Tiberto Brandolini (ASV, SS 17, fol. 101).

1447: 23 February
Jacopo Antonio Marcello has permission to return to Venice, and two ambassadors should be elected to go to join the army in his stead (ASV, SS 17, fol. 108v).

1447: 3, 10, and 13 March
Senate letters to Jacopo Antonio Marcello, *provveditore* with army, in response to several of his, regarding the fortification of Treviglio, Cassano, and other sites in the Ghiaradadda (ASV, SS 17, fols. 114rv, 116rv). On the latter date, Orsato Giustiniani is commissioned to join Marcello as *provveditore,* and jointly with him help restore harmony in the army and

urge the fortification of Treviglio, Cassano, and other Ghiaradadda locations (ASV, SS 17, fol. 117–18).

1447: 20 and 31 March
Senate letters to Orsato Giustiniani and Jacopo Antonio Marcello, *provveditori,* regarding the incursion of enemy troops near Cremona, and urging fortification of their position (ASV, SS 17, fols. 119, 123).

1447: 31 March
Jacopo Antonio Marcello, who had served as *provveditore* for a long time ("in quo exercitio etiam promptissimus sit se operari ad omnem beneplacitum nostrum"), may return to Venice for 15 days to attend to business: "necessitates sue, tam spectantes ad facultatem suam, quam ad propriam personam." He is replaced as *savio di terraferma* (ASV, ST 2, fol. 26).

1447: spring
Janus Pannonius comes to Guarino's school at Ferrara, and stays through the summer of 1454 (Thomson 1988, 8).

1447: 19 March
Francesco Sforza signs new accords with Filippo Maria Visconti (Peyronnet 1982, 15).

1447: April
Venice closes all approaches to Sforza, stops his pay, proclaims him rebel, and confiscates his Venetian palace (Sanuto 1733, 1124; Ady 1907, 72; Greppi 1913, 331; Hazlitt 1915, 1:943–44). Sforza had been won over to Visconti, now in league with Alfonso of Aragon and pope.

1447: 29 April
Jacopo Antonio Marcello is ready to return to field as *provveditore* with our captain general, but there is pending against him a law case: "quendam sentenciam, que ad factum suum plurimum importat, que duci debet ad consilium de XLta." An extension is arranged through 27 October (q.v.), at which time the matter is resolved (ASV, ST, 2, fol. 29v).

1447: 1 June
Responding to communications from *provveditore* Jacopo Antonio Marcello dated 27 and 28 May, the Senate urges more diligent action against Romanengo; administrative details (ASV, SS 17, fol. 142v).

1447: 11 June
Having advanced on Milan from early May (through Soncino, Casalmaggiore, Cassano, and Lambro), the Venetian army unfurls its banners before the gates of Milan, where it stays three days before retreating, having failed to corrupt the garrisons at the Porta Orientale (Cognasso 1955, 6:377).

1447: 28 June
Terms of *condotta* granted Carlo Fortebraccio da Montone, son of Braccio, with 600 horse and 100 foot, to enroll in Venetian service (Predelli 1876–1914, 5:7 [xiv.16]; see also Sanuto 1733, 1125; Argegni 1936, 1:404–5).

1447: 13 and 15 July
Senate letters to Niccolò da Canal, ambassador with army, and *provveditore* Jacopo Antonio Marcello, urging prompt action in view of Sforza's advance; and to Michele Attendolo, with copies to da Canal and Marcello (ASV, SS 17, fols. 148v–49).

1447: 4 August
Sforza surrenders Jesi, his last possession in the Marche, to the pope for 35,000 florins; he is now free to march to Lombardy to support the beleaguered Filippo Maria Visconti (Hazlitt 1915, 1:944; Ady 1907, 30)

1447: 9 August
Sforza sets out for Lombardy from the Marche, learning en route of Visconti's death on 13 August (Cognasso 1955, 6:405–7; Peyronnet 1982, 15).

1447: 13 August
Death of Filippo Maria Visconti, Duke of Milan; the Ambrosian Republic is declared on 15 August, the day of his burial. The Visconti palaces and possessions sacked, distributed or sold over the coming weeks and months, the Republic even permitting (in January 1449) the carting away of the stones of the castle. Perhaps it is through contacts in Milan that Marcello eventually extracts from the Visconti possessions a set of illuminated playing cards to send to Isabella, wife of René (Meiss 1957, 2–3). For the interlude of the Ambrosian Republic, which endures until Sforza's conquest in 1450, see esp. Cognasso 1955, 6:396–446; Martines 1979, 140–48; Robin 1991, chap. 3.

1447: 17 August
Wishing Milan to be under the domination of neither Sforza nor Aragon, Venice sends secretary Bertuccio Negri to arrange peace with Ambrosian Republic, declared supreme at Milan, Alessandria, Como, Novara; Lodi and Piacenza will declare for Venice (ASV, SS 17, fol. 156; Guarino 1915–19, 3:488; da Soldo 1733, 843; Sabellico 1718, 667; Hazlitt 1915, 1:949). On the same date, Jacopo Antonio Marcello takes possession of Lodi for Venice, committing Venice to certain concessions and agreements and securing military positions; these are confirmed 12 October 1447 (Predelli 1876–1914, 5:8–12 [xiv.18]).

1447: 23 August
Draft of Senate letter congratulating Jacopo Antonio Marcello, *provveditore,* from whom news had been received of the army's entry into Lodi; the Senate looks forward to hearing soon of the capture of Crema; Jacopo Piccinino should be supplied for that purpose. Whether Crema is taken or no, Attendolo should proceed to ravage the Cremonese, so that Sforza, now en route, cannot take refuge there. But take care that no injury is done to the Milanese. Marcello's letter of 19 August just received, describing negotiations he is having with Piacenza (ASV, SS 17, fol. 158v).

1447: August
Venice suspends peace negotiations with Milan; Dolfin suggests because it sees the opportunities for more conquests: "alhora li altri legati cognosciuta la cupidita venetiana appetir al dominio de tutta Lombardia per la occasion dela morte del duca disciolta tal praticha tornorano a caxa." Marcello secures lordship of Piacenza on same terms as with Lodi (Dolfin, *Cronaca,* fol. 408 [297]).

1447: 30 August
The Ambrosian Republic leagues with Francesco Sforza, who would serve them on same terms he had accepted from Filippo Maria Visconti, and keep no cities for himself but Brescia; alternatively, should he take Verona from Venice, he would return Brescia to the Milanese (Ady 1907, 40; Cognasso 1955, 6:407). Sforza moves immediately to block access to Piacenza of Venice's river fleet (Dolfin, *Cronaca,* fol. 408v [297v]).

1447: 2 and 4 September
Letters to Michele Attendolo and *provveditore* Jacopo Antonio Marcello commending preparations and cautioning against any agreement with the Ambrosian Republic (ASV, SS 17, fols. 163, 164v–65).

1447: 12 September
Ludovico Loredan is commissioned as *provveditore* with army as Jacopo Antonio Marcello's colleague and backup to Gerardo Dandolo, new Venetian *podestà* of Piacenza (ASV, SS 17, fol. 166v–67).

1447: 25 September
Senate letters to Ludovico Loredan and Jacopo Antonio Marcello, *provveditori* with army, responding to latter's communication of 20 September. Now that Attendolo is prepared for the attempt, do everything possible to take Crema. If Sforza takes Piacenza, we should proceed to cause damage in area around Pavia (ASV, SS 17, fol. 168rv; there are no further explicit references to Jacopo Antonio Marcello in SS 17, who leaves the field at about this time to attend to business in Venice: see Sabellico 1718, 668,

and below, 27 October 1447). On the same date, the Ambrosian Republic, negotiating for peace, declares itself unwilling to accede to Venetian demand for Crema and Cremona and their territories, as well as Lodi; instead they want Lodi and Ghiaradadda (Hazlitt 1915, 1:950).

1447: 16 October–16 November
Sforza besieges and bombards Piacenza, preventing its rescue by Venice's river *armata* (Dolfin, *Cronaca*, fol. 409 [298]); taken by storm, it is abandoned on 16 November to a devastating forty-day sack (Robin 1991, chap. 3; also Cognasso 1955, 6:411–13; Romanin 1853–61, 4:215–16). On which Pannonius (1784, 1:179): "Quicquid avarities, quicquid violentia, quicquid/ Foeda libido potest, cumulum tunc venit in unum."

1447: 27 October
So that Jacopo Antonio Marcello may return to the army in the position he previously held, the Council of Ten intervenes to absolve him ("pro removenda infamia") in the legal action postponed the previous 29 April; but the proposal made to the Senate does not pass (ASV, ST 2, fol. 47v).

1448: early months
In service of Ambrosian Republic, Sforza besieges Lodi (held by Venetians) and ravages Venetian conquests in Ghiaradadda; meanwhile Venetians continue to hold Caravaggio and menace Cremona, defended by Bianca Maria Visconti (Ady 1907, 43–45; Cognasso 1955, 6:418; Peyronnet 1982, 17–18).

1448: 20 June
Jacopo Antonio Marcello is captain of Verona, executing a judicial decision (Predelli 1876–1914, 5:13–14 [xiv.26]).

1448: 16–17 July
Sforza surrounds the Venetian fleet of 70 vessels at Casalmaggiore on the Po, unsupported by captain general Michele Attendolo; ships burned by Venetian commander Andrea Quirini to prevent their being seized by the enemy (Dolfin, *Cronaca*, fol. 410 [299]; Ady 1907, 45; Hazlitt 1915, 1:952).

1448: 23 July
Draft of letter to "Jacopo Antonio Marcello militi," captain of Verona, instructing him to proceed "omni cum celeritate possibile" to join the army as *provveditore;* the privileges and salary of his magistracy will be reserved for him "ac si essetis in Verona" (ASV, SS 18, fol. 24). But he is not present with the army at Caravaggio during the siege or battle (see below, 22 September).

1448: 29 July

Francesco Sforza besieges Caravaggio, last Venetian stronghold in Ghiara-dadda (Ady 1907, 45–46; Cognasso 1955, 6:419; Peyronnet 1982, 18).

1448: 10 August

Three additional *provveditori* to the army are elected: Federico Contarini, Gerardo Dandolo, and Ermolao Donato (ASV, SS 18, fol. 28); all will be in the field at the disastrous battle of Caravaggio (see below, 15 September).

1448: 11 August

Statutes published of the Chivalric Order of the Crescent (motto "Los en croissant") founded by René d'Anjou, centered on cathedral church of Angers, Saint Maurice, ancestral burial place of his line and monument to warrior-saint. One of the most important of the late-medieval chivalric orders (following those of the Burgundian Golden Fleece, the English Garter), it was dissolved soon after its author's death (Lecoy 1875, 1:258, 530ff.; Meiss 1957, 3, 6–7; René 1845–46, 1:51ff.; Ricaldone 1986; Vale 1981, 51–62).

1448: 15 September

Francesco Sforza routs Venetians under Attendolo (with Colleoni) at Caravaggio, gaining access to the whole of the Bresciano and Bergamasco: it was "une des victoires les plus éclatantes du XVème siècle" (Peyronnet 1982, 18). The *provveditori* Ermolao Donato and Gerardo Dandolo are captured defending the Venetian standards which will now be displayed in the cathedral of Sant'Ambrogio in Milan. As Sanuto reports their capture, "i quali provveditori da molti furono avvisati a dover fuggire e salvarsi, e risposero di voler più tosto morire attorno le Insegne pubbliche, che fuggendo salvarsi con vergogna." Dolfin describes Sforza's vengeance: "conte Francesco seguendo la victoria messe tutto el stado venetian in exterminio facendosse signor de tutte castelle." Attendolo will be dismissed, imprisoned, and deprived of his Castelfranco fief for dereliction of duty. (Ady 1907, 46; Cognasso 1955, 6:419–20; Mallett & Hale 1984, 41; Romanin 1853–61, 4:217; see also Portioli 1871; full descriptions of the battle in Dolfin, *Cronaca*, fol. 410v–11v [299v–300v]; Sanuto 1733, 1128–29)

1448: 22 September

To repair the damage done at Caravaggio, Ludovico Loredan and Pasquale Malipiero, both holding prestigious title of Procurator of St. Mark, are sent as *provveditori* in field; Jacopo Antonio Marcello, then captain of Verona, is ordered to ride to Brescia (now targeted by Sforza), of which he is made *provveditore*, to pick up 30,000 ducats to be used to ransom prisoners, collect refugees, regroup the army, and prevent Sforza's advance (Dolfin, *Cro-*

naca, fol. 412 [301]; Sanuto 1733, 1129–30; Simonetta 1932, 246; Hazlitt 1915, 1:952; Romanin 1853–61, 4:217, 218). Marcello did stop Sforza, according to Navagero, describing the aftermath of the battle of Caravaggio: "E il conte Francesco proseguendo la vittoria passò nel Bresciano, dove acquistò in pochi giorni tuto quel territorio, e Salò con tutta la Riviera, le Vallate, e Asola, Lonado, e quasi tutto il territoria Bergamasco, andò poi sotto la Città di Brescia, nella quale era Provveditore Ser Jacopo Antonio Marcello, e non la potendo espugnare, la mise in assedio" (Navagero 1733, 1112c).

1448: 25 September
Senate's letter to three *provveditori* Ludovico Loredan, Pasquale Malipiero, and Jacopo Antonio Marcello, urging the defense of the rivers Mincio and, even more important, the Adige, against the enemy (ASV, SS 18, fol. 41rv).

1448: September–October
Ermolao Donato's secretary, Clemente Tealdino, one of the Venetian captives at Caravaggio, was an old acquaintance of Sforza's secretary Angelo Simonetta, who had reappeared at Sforza's side. Brought before Sforza, Tealdino was sent by that captain back to Venice with the request that either Jacopo Antonio Marcello ("da esso Conte ben conosciuto," Sanuto remarks) or Pasquale Malipiero be sent to Sforza secretly to arrange peace: "Noverat eum jam antea Angelus Simonetta, occulteque ad Sforciam perduxit; ab eo ille ad Principem et Senatum est missus, ut Sforciae nominae ab eis peteret, si pax cordi esset, mitterent secreto ad se Jacopo Antonio Marcello, aut Paschalem Maripetrem" (Navagero 1718, 674). Since Marcello was abroad (as captain of Verona), Malipiero was sent to Fornaci, near Peschiera, where Simonetta came repeatedly to discuss terms with him (Dolfin, *Cronaca,* fol. 412rv [301rv]; Navagero 1718, 674; Sanuto 1733, 1130; also Toderini 1875, 120).

1448: 3 October
Senate letter to *provveditore* Jacopo Antonio Marcello, captain of Verona, instructing him to send a small force via Garda to secure route to Brescia, and secretly to go to that city himself to rally its leaders against an eventual attack by Sforza; arrangements for funds and reinforcements (ASV, SS 18, fol. 46v).

1448: 12 October
The Senate is pleased with *provveditore* Jacopo Antonio Marcello's prompt obedience to its commands regarding Brescia. Now he should renew agreements (see 1438, above) with the da Lodrone family securing access through their lands to that city, then proceed to Brescia to rally the citizens.

If he learns that Sforza will not attack Brescia, however, but aims to cross the Mincio, Marcello should return to Verona to see to its defense (ASV, SS 18, fol. 53).

1448: 18 October
Sforza and Venice reconciled in Treaty of Rivoltella, negotiated by Pasquale Malipiero for Venice, Angelo Simonetta for Sforza. Venice agrees to aid Sforza to gain lordship of Milan, and to pay him 13,000 ducats per month (with an advance of 40,000), providing that Crema and Ghiaradadda be ceded to them, in addition to lands granted by treaty of 1441. Thus the westward limit of Venice is established at the river Adda: a line from which Venice will not accept retreat throughout the ensuing conflicts nor in the negotiations towards the final peace at Lodi (see below, 1454, January–April). It was further agreed at Rivoltella, Dolfin adds, that Sforza would recover his palace on the Grand Canal, which had been bought by the doge Francesco Foscari: "Tertio che al conte sia restituido la sua caxa la in Venesia laqual altre volti essendo nostro capit.o a lui fu donada per la sig.ria laqual compro messer lo doxe Foscari." Alternate terms offered by Ambrosian Republic immediately afterwards rejected by Venice. (Predelli 1876–1914, 5:16–18 [xiv.32]; Dolfin, *Cronaca*, fols. 412v–413 [301v–302]; Sanuto 1733, 1130; Ady 1907, 47; Cognasso 1955, 6:423)

1448: 21 October
In response to recent occurrences, Jacopo Antonio Marcello should go with a small infantry force to Brescia immediately, rendezvousing there with captains and *condottieri* in Venetian service (ASV, SS 18, fol. 57v).

1448: 15 November
Senate letter to Jacopo Antonio Marcello responds to his of 10 and 12 November, praising his diligence in attending to matters at Brescia: "et prudentiam et solicitudinem vestram plurimum commendamus et laudamus." Now he should proceed at the head of those troops he raised to join Francesco Sforza, and remain with him as long as necessary acting according to the terms of the agreement recently made (of which a copy is enclosed), keeping the Senate informed: "et sitis gubernator gentium nostrarum . . . , que omnes gentes nostre ad vestram sint obedientiam, et cum eis stetis apud illustrem comitem suprascriptam, et prout requirret, vos exercere debeatis, quemadmodum disponunt capitula, concordii facti, quorum copiam pro clarior informatione vestra, vobis mittimus his inclusam, et de rerum successu, de tempore in tempus, nos debeatis vestris literis advisare" (ASV, SS 18, fol. 62; Simonetta 1932, 259–60).

1448: 2 December

On the advice of Jacopo Antonio Marcello, *provveditore,* the *condotta* of Giovanni Catalano is renewed (Predelli 1876–1914, 5.19 [xiv.35]).

1448: 7 December

In the presence of *provveditore* Jacopo Antonio Marcello, Francesco Sforza names his captains and *condottieri* to be included in the terms of the league with Venice (Predelli 1876–1914, 5.19–20 [xiv.38]).

1448: 19 December

Senate deliberation and letter to *provveditore* Jacopo Antonio Marcello informing him of Senate action in response to petition of the Marquis of Mantua, Ludovico Gonzaga (ASV, SS 18, fols. 66v–67).

1448–1449

Giannozzo Manetti is Florence's representative in Venice, urging Venice to support René d'Anjou in displacing Alfonso in Naples (Barbaro 1884, 47; Branca 1977a, 107n7; Cagni 1968). Manetti's letters and orations from Venice are preserved in BAV, cod. Pal. Lat. 931, among them the eloquent *Oratio ad venetos* (pub. Wittschier 1968, 162–75) urging a Venetian-Florentine league to snatch the initiative "ab Hispanis et Catalanis et Celtiberis nationibus" (ibid., 172).

1448–1450

Donatello's monument to Gattamelata is erected outside the Santo (the church of the patron San Antonio) in Padua. During the same period, Giovanni Mario Filelfo (son of Francesco) holds office of *juge du palais* at court of René d'Anjou in Marseilles, where he organizes the library of the Dominicans at Saint Maximin and teaches Greek to the king (Agostinelli & Benadduci 1899, 7–8; Bargement 2:106; Favre 1856, 44–50; Lecoy 1875, 2:180; Manetti 1986, 125–26).

1449: January

Sforza outside Milan, accompanied by Jacopo Antonio Marcello: "Francesco Sforza con le giente sta sul Milanexe; insieme con lui miser Iacomo Antonio Marcello, governatore de le giente, che li havea data Venetiani, per lo accordo fatto e lo acquisto de Milano" (Anonimo Veronese 1915, 10; date corrected from other evidence).

1449: 22 January and 7 February

Jacopo Antonio Marcello's *volgare* letters from the army camp at Landriano and Moirago to the doge reporting that he had spoken with Francesco Sforza (whom he accompanied as *provveditore*) about the boundary dispute between Soncino and Orzinuovi, and that Sforza had acted to settle it in accord with Venetian league (Predelli 1876–1914, 5:27–28 [xiv.75]).

1449: 13 February

Senate letter to *provveditore* Jacopo Antonio Marcello in response to his recent information that Savoy, on behalf of the Ambrosian Republic, was advancing against Francesco Sforza. Jacopo Antonio Marcello is strictly to follow the terms of the agreement made with Sforza, and if Sforza engages with Savoy, the Venetian troops should also be engaged (ASV, SS 18, fol. 75).

1449: February–March

Sforza takes Tortona, Novara, Alessandria, and Parma, with Jacopo Antonio Marcello at his side and instrumental in winning the victory: "Zonta la nova a Venexia tutti fono in gaudio, tanto piu, quanto che per opera de Iacomo Antonio Marcello proveditor successe la victoria, lo qual cum cavalli 2,000 era andato a suo favori cum doi proveditori, li ambassatori Alvuixe Loredan, et Pasqual Malipiero, et questi cum Alexandro Sforza fratello a tuor molti luogi di la da Po havia mandato, obtegnudo in gran parte li dicti luogi dela da Po, et ben firmati, fece adunar le gente venetiane, et cum le sue unite va al assedio de Millan. Da la parte de Novarra Sforza have novita da francesi 6000 contra di quali el Marcello mandato cum Bortolamio Coion a quella impresa, represse tutti quelli monimenti" (Dolfin, *Cronaca*, fol. 415 [304]; also Cappellari, *Campdoglio veneto*, 3:31; Sanuto 1733, 1131).

1449: 24 February

Letter of Francesco Sforza to René d'Anjou, responding to latter's diplomatic approach of late 1448 via his emissary Honorat de Berre seeking alliance with Venice and Sforza that would also assist him in the recapture of Naples (Paris, Bibl. Nat., ms. Ital. 1585, fols. 7, 61; partially pub. by Buser 1879, 365–66; discussion in Lecoy 1875, 1:272–73n4, and Perret 1896, 214–15). Sforza reports that he had nearly conquered Milanese, and approached Milan; allied with Venice and Florence, he could do nothing without their accord, but would plead René's cause with them: "So certo, ch'el concepto et contentamento della I. S. de Venetia et cosi della Ex. S. de Fiorenza seria ch'el Reame de Sicilia fosse in mano et governo della prefata M.ta, como quella laquale reputano sia amica benevola et affectionata ad esse S.ie et della natione italicha, et non in mano de Cathalani et Barbari" (Buser 1879, 365). He further assured the king of his loyalty: "intendo de seguire quella volunta et dispositione verso dessa Mta quale segui il mio genitore et che ho seguito anchori mi per lo passato verso della Mta et della soa casa" (ibid., 366). He suggested sending an ambassador to Florence, and recommended to the king Jacopo Antonio Marcello, with him in his camp near Milan: "Il est des plus affectionnés à Votre Majesté, et jouit d'un grand crédit dans tous les conseils de la république de Venise" (Perret 1896, 215n4). According to the epitaph for Jacopo Antonio Marcello in the church of San Cristoforo della Pace in Venice, he had held from René the "Praefectura Maritima" of Naples from this year (text at Fam. III.C.4).

1449: 3 April

Senate letter to Jacopo Antonio Marcello, *provveditore,* who had sent on to them communiqués from Venetian *condottiere* Bartolomeo Colleoni. Jacopo Antonio Marcello should attempt to persuade Sforza "illis modestis et pertinentibus verbis que vestre prudentie videbuntur" not to venture against Savoy, but rather attend to the conquest of the Ambrosian Republic, which in his absence has been able to rally and resupply. Moreover, action against Savoy is likely to provoke a French incursion (ASV, SS 18, fol. 80v).

1449: 5 April

Jacopo Antonio Marcello, *provveditore* of the army with Sforza, at his camp at the Villa di Zibido near Milan, executes the *condotta* of Matteo da Capua in service of Venice (Predelli 1876–1914, 5:28 [xiv.79]).

1449: 18 April

Senate letter to *provveditore* Jacopo Antonio Marcello, acquiescing to Sforza's proposal to send a messenger to Alfonso of Aragon (ASV, SS 18, fol. 81v).

1449: 7 May

Senate letter to *provveditore* Jacopo Antonio Marcello, saying that the rectors of Bergamo had forwarded to them his coded letter ("in zifra") of 29 April conveying his suspicions about Bartolomeo Colleoni. Jacopo Antonio Marcello should go to Sforza and persuade him to remove Colleoni from the Savoy enterprise and send him to Milan, replacing him with some of Sforza's own captains (ASV, SS 18, fol. 86v).

1449: 24 May

Jacopo Antonio Marcello has spent many months as *provveditore* to Francesco Sforza, serving without salary, and has asked repeatedly to return because of pressing business: "et multociens pro nonnullis privatis rebus suis permaxime sibi importantibus requisiverit licentiam repatriandi." It is proper that an election be held for a replacement, so that someone else can start learning to handle the job: "ut et alii discant promptius in agendis nostris se exercere." The new *provveditore* will receive 50 ducats per month; other provisions . . . Marcello himself is relected (ASV, ST 2, fol. 110v).

1449: 2 June
Senate letter: Jacopo Antonio Marcello has conveyed Sforza's question whether the Senate could send on his behalf 300 horse and 300 foot, with a bombard, across the Po; and if they cannot at this time spare the horse, to do what is possible. The Senate will send the infantry force and bombard requested (ASV, SS 18, fol. 90).

1449: 11 June
Senate letter to *provveditore* Jacopo Antonio Marcello describing a letter brought to them by secretary Febo Capella that had been intercepted by the Milanese, revealing discussions between Florence and Sforza; Sforza's secretary Angelo Simonetta now in Venice confirmed this information (ASV, SS 18, fols. 90v–91).

1449: 27 June
Senate letter to *provveditore* Jacopo Antonio Marcello, from whose letter, and from Sforza's to Angelo Simonetta which the latter showed to them, it understands the count's intention with regard to the letter intercepted by the Milanese (see above, 11 June). Sforza should not think that Venice is deserting him, since the Serenissima has always intended "honorem et exaltationem suam" (ASV, SS 18, fols. 91v–92).

1449: 5 July
Renewal of *condotta* of Carlo Fortebraccio, with monetary settlement of a matter involving Braccio the elder (Predelli 1876–1914, 5:36 [xiv, 94]).

1449: 18 July
Ludovico Foscarini sent by Venetian Senate to Genoa to gain support for alliance of Genoa and Ambrosian Republic against Alfonso of Aragon who, ten days earlier, had declared war on Venice (Zippel 1959).

1449: 26 August
René d'Anjou names Marcello and Sforza to be respectively the 17th and 18th knights of the Order of the Crescent (Meiss 1957, 3; Lecoy 1875, 1:533; Perret 1896, 215n2). René himself was the second member enrolled in 1449, and Giovanni Cossa the third in 1450; Sforza and Marcello had been enrolled before 1453; early chapter meetings were held on the eve of the Feast of Saint Maurice (22 September) in 1450, 1451, and 1452 (Vale 1990, 56, 59).

1449: 15 September
Senate letter to Jacopo Antonio Marcello, *provveditore,* and Pasquale Malipiero and Orsato Giustiniani, ambassadors to Francesco Sforza: We have learned about the league made between Sforza and Carlo Gonzaga, and about Sforza's conquest of Lodi and Crema, for which his diligence is to be commended. All three of you, or at least Jacopo Antonio Marcello, should tell Sforza that we have been informed of the arrangement with Gonzaga, and that Crema should now be immediately ceded to Venice; as for his other conquests, we congratulate him: "ex paterna affectione, et amore nostro erga eum, magnopere, et ex corde congratulemur" (ASV, SS 18, fol. 118rv).

1449: 24 September
Venice leagues with Ambrosian Republic against Florence; Venice would get Crema and the Ghiaradadda, preserving its frontier at the Adda; Milan would retain Lodi and Como. Sforza would hold Piacenza, Pavia, Parma, and Cremona if he vacated territory within three weeks, which he does not do (Dolfin, *Cronaca,* giving 23 September, fol. 416v [305v]; Cognasso 1955, 6:439; Perret 1896, 217).

1449: 25 September
Senate letter to Pasquale Malipiero and Orsato Giustiniani, ambassadors, instructing Malipiero with Jacopo Antonio Marcello to present themselves to Sforza saying that Venice is unwilling to prosecute war further, which now costs 110,000 ducats monthly, and has disrupted trade (Giustiniani is absent securing Crema): We have written Alfonso of Aragon asking for peace, and have arrived at terms; we assure Sforza personally of our constant afection for him, and require his prompt response. Jacopo Antonio Marcello should immediately remove our troops, securing the cooperation of Bartolomeo Colleoni, quickly across the Adda into territories held by us. Malipiero should remain with Sforza, and if his response is negative, should go to Crema, inform us, and await instructions. A secretary is further appointed to deliver detailed instructions to Jacopo Antonio Marcello about the disposition of the troops, and assuring him that Sforza is included in the peace terms reached with Milan (ASV, SS 18, fols. 120v–121).

1449: 30 September
Sforza, with Venetian troops, is standing before the gates of Milan and expects to gain entry when Bartolomeo Colleoni (presumably as instructed by Marcello and in his company; see items above and below) withdraws, compelling Sforza to abandon for the moment his Milanese ambitions

(Cognasso 1955, 6:439). In a few important verse lines, Janus Pannonius describes Marcello's position (1784, 1:197, lines 2627–31): "Sed quamvis ipsos concors tam cura ligasset, / . . . Cum tamen id tacito mandasset curia jussu, Sforciadae extemplo Marcellus castra reliquit, / Officia anteferens privato publica vinclo [Although a harmony of will bound those men together, . . . still, since the Senate had commanded it by secret instructions, Marcello immediately left Sforza's camp, putting public duty before the private claim of friendship]."

1449: 3 October
Senate letter to Pasquale Malipiero and Orsato Giustiniani, ambassadors, and Jacopo Antonio Marcello, *provveditore* with Sforza, responding to their letters of 29 and 30 September, and congratulating them for their efforts. They are to express Senate's pleasure to Sforza, assuring him that the peace was made with benevolent intentions for all involved and for all of Italy. He must now observe terms, withdraw his troops, and cease any interference with the Ambrosian Republic. By now Jacopo Antonio Marcello will have crossed the Adda as commanded, as is necessary for securing the peace; and if has not done so, he must do so immediately, retiring Venetian troops in the Bergamasco or Bresciano (ASV, SS 18, fol. 123v). Learning of Marcello's actions, in accord with Senate instructions, "Lo Sforza se ne mostrò compreso da alta meraviglia e da non minore rammarico; ma gli disse che facesse pure il proprio dovere, com'egli avrebbe fatto il proprio" (Rubieri 1879, 2:178; see also Cognasso 1955, 6:440).

1449: 8 October
Sforza (hoping to settle the war before being forced to accept a disadvantageous peace) still has not committed himself to the peace terms offered by Venice (Dolfin, *Cronaca,* fol. 416v [305v]; Peyronnet 1982, 19–20).

1449: 15 October
Senate instructions to the rectors of Padua to order Jacopo Antonio Marcello to return to Venice immediately so that he can report about conditions in Lombardy. Marcello, recently *provveditore* to Francesco Sforza, had gone without the Senate's knowledge to Monselice via Brescia as he returned from the front (ASV, ST 2, fol. 120v). (See below, 8 November, showing that Marcello was still in Monselice.)

1449: 19 October
Jacopo Antonio Marcello, entitled "miles," is elected to the Senate *zonta* of 40; subsequently canceled (ASV, SGV, Miste 4, fol. 125v).

1449: 8 November
Jacopo Antonio Marcello is in Monselice, and is thus unaware of his elec-

tion as *provveditore* of Crema, and does not respond; the term of response is accordingly extended (ASV, ST 2, fol. 123). He subsequently proceeds to Crema and serves in that capacity until at least April 1452.

1449: 24 December
Having recalled ambassadors to Sforza Pasquale Malipiero and Orsato Giustiniani on 1 December (Toderini 1875, 120), Venice reaffirms its alliance with the Ambrosian Republic and sends its troops to break through to Milan ahead of Sforza (Cognasso 1955, 6:441–42).

1449: 27 December
Sforza reattacks Milan, and lays siege. The Milanese government offers a reward of 10,000 ducats to anyone who kills or mortally wounds their besieger. Colleoni, leading Venetian troops, fails to break through and withdraws beyond the Adda. Jacopo Piccinino, leading Ambrosian troops, attempts to assist the city (Cognasso 1955, 6:446).

1449–c. 1475
Michele Orsini is prior of San Antonio Abate (da Vienna) in Venice (King 1986, 415).

1450: January
Sforza is besieging Milan: "Grande fu la constantia de Franc.o Sforza in continuar lassedio contra Millan, e dato chel aldiva venetiani, millanesi, Alfonso re unanimi vignir contra de lui alla guerra, tamen stette constante alassedio de Millan, vedendo quelli non haver victuaria da alcuno" (Dolfin, *Cronaca*, fol. 417 [306]).

1450: 21 January
Ducal commission to Jacopo Antonio Marcello, chosen *provveditore* of Crema. His duties as governor of the area are outlined, and he is assigned a salary of 100 ducats per month; other provisions concerning staff, personal guard, etc. (ASV, ST 2, fol. 127).

1450: 23 January
It was decided the previous day that Jacopo Antonio Marcello should depart on his mission as *provveditore* to Crema, and is required to be there soon. An extension through 8 February is granted (ASV, ST 2, fol. 128).

1450: 25–26 February
Angry victims of famine, the citizens of Milan riot (turning decisively from one to another faction of their leadership), cut the Venetian ambassador to pieces, and invite Sforza to lordship of Milan: "el populo de Millan a furor corseno al palazo, et taiorono a pezi, per lo mezo de uno citadin de Trivellis messer Lunardo Venier, legato nostro in caxa sua digando che per sua caxo

morivono da fame; et alle hore 22 se dette Millan a Franc.o Sforza, cridando viva viva el conte Francesco, el qual venuto in Millan a di 26 Febrar . . . fu da tutti aceptato per signor, ando acompagnato da Carlo Gonzaga, et Alexandro Sforza suo fratello, et andato alla piaza intro in Santo Ambruoxo et subito uscite lassando governatur in Millan messer Alex.o suo fratello in la qual cita avanti che intrasse capitulo cum millanesi" (Dolfin, *Cronaca,* fol. 417rv [306rv]). Sforza orders the family of Venier released (they had been seized by the citizens). He was hoping to restore relations with the Venetians, whom he knew had been negotiating for months in Ferrara (via Pasquale Malipiero) terms of alliance against him with Alfonso of Aragon (see below, 3 March); that league was concluded 2 July (Dolfin, *Cronaca,* fols. 417v–418 [306v–307]). On 26 February, at Sforza's insistence, he was acclaimed duke by the assembled *popolo* (Cusin 1936, 70), but withdrew to await the formal arrangement of terms. For these events, see also titles cited at 1450: 25–26 March.

1450: 3 March
Senate letter to Jacopo Antonio Marcello, *provveditore* in Crema, responding to his of 26 February reporting the visit to him of Pisanello, an emissary ("familiaris") of Francesco Sforza, "ac expositionem per eum vobis factam, sub literis credentialibus ipsius comitis": Send your emissary to Cicco [Simonetta], Sforza's chancellor, at Lodi; or if Cicco is not there, to the governor of that city, saying that you wish to respond to Pisanello's proposals, and have him or another of Sforza's emissaries sent to you for that purpose. Tell him that you have informed us of Pisanello's message concerning the count's excellent disposition toward our regime, and assure Sforza of our affectionate disposition towards him (ASV, SS 18, fol. 169).

1450: 4 March
Ducal letter to Jacopo Antonio Marcello, *provveditore* in Crema, informing him of very valuable privileges in effect, having been granted that city 20 September 1449 (Predelli 1876–1914, 5:45–46 [xiv, 126]).

1450: 13 March
Senate letter to Jacopo Antonio Marcello, *provveditore* in Crema, responding to his letters of 7, 8, and 9 March reporting the visit of Sforza's emissary Pisanello, and commending him for his prudence and diligence in executing its instructions. The Senate knows that he is reluctant to be involved, but prefers that these matters be handled by him rather than any other: "Est tamen verum quod comprehendimus vos satis timorose intrare materiam istam, que res preter mentem et intentionem nostram procedit; nam cum sitis nobilis civis noster, et de vobis omnimodem fidem et confi-

dentiam capiamus, sumus bene contenti, quod factum istud potius transeat per manus vestras, quam per aliud medium, quod nullatenus faceret pro nostro dominio." He is therefore that if Pisanello or any other representative has come to him from Sforza, or comes in the future, to discuss particulars, find out exactly what the count intends and inform the Senate as quickly as possible: "et de quanto habebitis, studiosus eritis, per velocissimum caballarium, nos subito, vestris literis, reddere certiores" (ASV, SS 18, fol. 171).

1450: 25–26 March
Sforza makes grand entry to Milan on prior day, and is formally invested as duke of Milan on the next, following preliminary oaths by representatives on 3 March, ratification by general assembly on 11 March. (For Sforza's conquest of Milan: Catalano 1956, 7:1–14; Catalano 1983, 29–44; Cognasso 1955, 6:446–48; A. Colombo 1905; Cusin 1936, 70; Peyronnet 1982, 20–21; Toderini 1875, 120.)

1450: 28 March
Senate letter to Jacopo Antonio Marcello, *provveditore* in Crema, responding to his letter of 22 March reporting the visit of Sforza's chancellor Renaldo Testa Grossa, praising his prudence and diligence; especially because the Senate prefers these arrangements to be made by Marcello rather than any other: "Et tuto ne piase, et dechiaremove che molto piu ne piaseria, e piu tosto volsamo, che per la vestra via, e mezo, cha per alguna altra, queste cosse se tratasseno." An enduring peace is vital, and Marcello is at liberty to discuss proposals of ten or fifteen years or whatever term can be arranged. The Senate is to be informed promptly of all further discussions: "et de quello seguira, velocissime ne darete per vestre letere" (ASV, SS 18, fol. 175). A second letter reports to Marcello peace proposals made by the Florentine ambassador Angelo de Acciaiuoli; therefore, Sforza should now send his ambassador directly to the Senate. But if Sforza prefers that the agreement be made only with Marcello ("si . . . disponeret hanc pacem tractari per manus vestras, et non per aliam viam"), Marcello should proceed to do so, and keep the Senate informed (ASV, SS 18, fol. 175v).

1450: 31 March
Senate letter to Jacopo Antonio Marcello, *provveditore* in Crema, responding to his of 28 March about discussions with Matteo de Pesaro, Sforza's emissary. The terms of peace discussed are satisfactory, and Marcello should proceed; as the Senate prefers the matter to be handled by him: "Et ex nunc acceptamus, et contentamur, quod per manus vestras, res procedat" (ASV, SS 18, fol. 176).

1450: 7 April

Senate letter to Jacopo Antonio Marcello, *provveditore* in Crema, responding to his of 31 March and 3 April reporting progress of his talks via intermediaries with Sforza: We continue to think that this matter is best handled by you: "Est nostre intentionis, et volumus, quod res ista transeat per manus vestras, quum certissimi sumus, cognita fide et prudentia vestra, factum istud longe melius et facilius, per vos, quam per aliud medium, ad volutum exitum posse conduci." Try to find out exactly what Sforza wants, and inform us immediately ("per velocissimum caballarium"). Do what you can to maintain good relations among all the parties: "pro conservatione amoris, et optime dispositionis utriusque partis, utque tolleretur omnis materia scandali, quod inter subditos oriri posset" (ASV, SS 18, fol. 177rv).

1450: 11 April

Senate letter to Jacopo Antonio Marcello, *provveditore* in Crema, on his continuing peace negotiations: We are content that the Florentines be informed (ASV, SS 18, fols. 177v–178).

1450: 14 April

Senate letter to Jacopo Antonio Marcello, *provveditore* in Crema, responding to his of 9 and 10 April regarding negotations with Matteo de Pesaro: We are pleased with the progress made. In terms of territories, we require Soncino, Romenengo, Mozanego, Pandino, Cosso, Antignamo, and Fontanelle, so that we have control of the road from Brescia to Crema; but if you cannot negotiate all of these, you may omit Pandino, Cosso, Antignano, and Fontanelle. From your letter of 11 April, we understand how difficult it is for you to arrange this peace, but we believe it is the best course, and insist that you continue to attend to this matter, and ask you to protest no further: "Comprehendimus ex literis vestris diei xi instantis quantum difficilem vos redditis, quod concordium istud transeat per manus vestras. . . . Nos autem dicimus, quod sicut per alias vobis scripsimus, est omnino mentis nostre, quod materia ista per vos praticetur. Sumus namque certissimi per medium vestrum, summa prudentia, et fide omnia debere procedere, et pro quanto in vobis erit non deficiet omnis bona conclusio, et optimus exitus illius pratice. Ideoque mandamus vobis, quod amplius verbum ullum nobis non faciatis, quod praticam istam trahamus de manibus vestris" (ASV, SS 18, fol. 179).

1450: 17 April

Senate letter to Jacopo Antonio Marcello, *provveditore* in Crema, responding to his of 14 April describing continued negotiations with Matteo de Pesaro, and praising his diligence. Under no circumstances is he to leave, but he must continue the negotiations, as previously instructed: "sed sicut nobis scribitis, et non dubitamus vos facturum attendatis ad bonam custodiam et conservationem ipsius terre prosequendo, et continuando praticam illam sicut sepenumero vobis diximus quia sic omnino est nostra intentio" (ASV, SS 18, fol. 180).

1450: 23 April
Senate letter to Jacopo Antonio Marcello, *provveditore* in Crema, responding to his of 19 and 20 April (ASV, SS 18, fol. 182) concerning continued peace negotiations with Matteo de Pesaro, and wishing more precise information of matters under discussion: We are pleased with the general terms, and that Florence is involved; and if you can't arrange the territorial disposition we prefer, do the best you can (ASV, SS 18, fol. 182).

1450: 3 May
Senate letter to Jacopo Antonio Marcello, *provveditore* in Crema, responding to his of 27 and 28 April describing continued negotiations, and commending Marcello for having done nothing against instructions, but having done everything in Venice's best interest: "pro meliorando facta nostra, et bene conducendo praticam istam." The terms in general are satisfactory; if necessary, Soncino, Romanengo, and Mozanego may be sacrificed; let each keep what he has, and in the name of the Holy Spirit, conclude the peace: "quod qui habet teneat, contenti sumus et volumus, ut in nomine spiritus sancti concludere debeatis." Further requirements regarding property owed to Jacopo Piccinino and family of Leonardo Venier (ASV, SS 18, fol. 183v).

1450: 10 May
Senate letter to Jacopo Antonio Marcello, *provveditore* in Crema, responding to his of the 6 and 7 May reporting ongoing peace negotiations. The Senate wishes to underscore its fair intentions and long history of cooperation with Sforza even beyond stated terms (ASV, SS 18, fol. 184).

1450: 27 May
Senate letter to Jacopo Antonio Marcello, *provveditore* in Crema, responding to his of 23 May reporting ongoing peace negotiations: [By your letter] we are fully informed. Urgently press conclusion of peace and inform us promptly (ASV, SS 18, fols. 188v–189).

1450: 2 July
Dolfin reports the conclusion of peace between Venice and Sforza (Dolfin, *Cronaca*, fol. 418 [307]).

1450: 8 July

Senate letter to Jacopo Antonio Marcello, *provveditore* in Crema, responding to his of 28 June reporting progress of negotiations; territorial settlements (ASV, SS 18, fols. 199v–200).

1450: 11 July

Pasquale Malipiero and Jacopo Antonio Marcello elected *provveditori* with the army, with a salary of 100 ducats per month; 500 ducats penalty for refusal. Marcello is written and informed of the terms of his election (ASV, SS 18, fol. 201).

1450: 25 July

Senate letter to Jacopo Antonio Marcello, *provveditore* in Crema, responding to his of 11, 15, 18, and 21 July reporting conversations with Simone da Spoleto, Sforza's chancellor, and subsequently with Andrea de Birago and Angelo Simonetta regarding the duke's desire for peace: Inform them, as we have often said before, that it is our intention to live at peace: "mens et dispositio nostra . . . optima est bene vicinandi, pacificeque vivendi." And so continue to negotiate . . . (ASV, SS 18, fols. 203v–204).

1450: 4 August

Senate letter to Jacopo Antonio Marcello, *provveditore* in Crema, responding to his of 29 July regarding ongoing negotiations: Marcello is to be commended, but Senate is increasingly impatient with Sforza's terms, and cannot consent to them. We must stand with our earlier position, that each should hold what he presently has, and if Sforza will agree, the peace can be concluded (ASV, SS 18, fol. 206rv).

1450: 17 August

Senate letter to Jacopo Antonio Marcello, *provveditore* in Crema, responding to his of 8 August, evading the request made by Angelo Simonetta, who wishes to come to Venice to negotiate a peace, for a safeconduct. We prefer that you conclude the peace there, if Sforza is truly intent on peace as he so often says: "si . . . habet eam sinceram, et bonam intentionem ad pacem, et ad bene vicinandum nobiscum, quam totiens dici fecit." Once peace is arranged, he may come here and we shall willingly receive him. This letter won 92 votes, and is followed by another version, granting the safe-conduct, and permitting Simonetta to come to Venice, but only if he is in agreement with the peace terms already discussed. The second version of the letter gained only 23 positive votes. No further communications to Marcello appear among the Senate documents regarding the negotiation of this peace (ASV, SS 19, fol. 1v); but see above, 2 July, for Dolfin's belief that a peace was settled in this period; and below, 20 August, for an alternative approach to Sforza's refractoriness!

1450: 20 August
The Council of Ten has been informed by Jacopo Antonio Marcello, *provveditore* in Crema, that a volunteer had come forward offering to kill Sforza: "quod Victor de Scoraderiis, squadrerius comitis Francisci, est contentus occidere comitem Franciscum, et, sicut omnes intelligere possunt, mors illius comitis est salus pax nostra et totius Italie, quocirca attendendum est huic tanto bono" (CXM 14, fol. 1, pub. Lamansky 1968, 1:161–62). Marcello should be instructed to negotiate with the helpful gentleman (the vote is 13/2/1); but there is no evidence known to me that the letter was sent or that Marcello ever proceeded in this matter.

1450: after 29 October
Pasquale Malipiero instrumental in arranging peace with Alfonso of Aragon (Navagero 1733, 1114); see also above, 25–26 February 1450, at end. For Venetian diplomacy from this point through the following June, see L. Rossi 1905

1450: 1 December
Senate letter to Jacopo Antonio Marcello, *provveditore* in Crema, Pasquale Malipiero, *provveditore*, and Vettore Cappello, captain of Brescia, who had been instructed directly by the Senate and by instructions carried by the secretary Febe Capella to meet and make arrangements for the security and the Ghiaradadda and Bergamasco, etc.: We wish to be advised immediately about actions taken ("ut . . . nos vestris literis per vellocem et celerem caballarium subito advisetis"), and thereafter in full written form by Febe Capella. Further, if you are in full agreement about actions to be taken for the utility of our regime, proceed with them immediately (ASV, SS 19, fol. 26).

1450: 18 December
Senate letter to Pasquale Malipiero, provveditore, following up matter of 1 December (q.v.): We have received your account of the discussions held by you three, and you may now proceed to round up those suspected (of rebellion?) and imprison them wherever convenient on our side of Verona. You should go with Jacopo Antonio Marcello who is well-acquainted with the area: "qui, ut noscis, etiam rerum et hominum Glareabdue bonam cognitionem habet." This letter followed by a draft of a letter to Malipiero, Marcello, and Cappello urging arrest of suspects and detailing fortifications of area to be undertaken (ASV, SS 19, fol. 29rv).

1450–1451

Lauro Quirini is *auditor veterum* in Venice (King 1986, 419); Ludovico Foscarini is *podestà* of Verona; there he has relations with Isotta Nogarola, Giorgio Bevilacqua, among others (Degli Agostini 1752–54, 1:57; King 1986, 375).

1451: February

Venice's command appointed by ballot among three leading *condottieri* Colleoni, Piccinino, and Leonessa; latter won; Colleoni deserts.

1451: 12 February

Senate letter to Jacopo Antonio Marcello, *provveditore* in Crema, responding to his letter of 8 February in which was enclosed a letter from Sforza presenting a claim against Venice (ASV, SS 19, fol. 40).

1451: 25 February

Senate letter to Jacopo Antonio Marcello, *provveditore* in Crema, responding to his letters of 20 February; instructions about fortifications, provisions for army (ASV, SS 19, fol. 45v).

1451: 24 March

Senate letter to Jacopo Antonio Marcello, *provveditore* in Crema, responding to his letter of 19 March, authorizing the hiring of a new *condottiere* and advising on judicial matters. At same time and place, Jacopo Antonio Marcello and Pasquale Malipiero jointly elected *provveditori* to the army, with salary of 60 ducats (an unsuccessful version had stipulated 100) per month; other provisions (ASV, SS 19, fol. 128v).

1451: 28 April

League between Venice, Naples, Savoy, and Montferrat; Florence draws close to Milan (they are allied by July) and presses for French alliance (Ady 1907, 67; A. Colombo 1894, 81; A. Colombo 1906).

1451: 30 July

Florence and Sforza ally against Venice (esp. Colombo 1906, for terms). Soon Venice readies for war, and by year's end, "fu decreto rompere guerra al duca Franc.o de Millan" (Dolfin, *Cronaca,* fol. 420v [309v]).

1451: 1 December

Jacopo Antonio Marcello, *provveditore* in Crema, is instructed to proceed in a judicial matter (ASV, CXM 14, fol. 89).

1452: 9 February

Jacopo Antonio Marcello, *provveditore* in Crema, is instructed on a routine matter (ASV, CXM 14, fol. 98).

1452: 21 February
King Charles VII of France pledges to support the league of Florence and Sforza through 24 June 1453 (A. Colombo 1894, 81–82; Ilardi 1982; Lecoy 1875, 1:271; L. Rossi 1906).

1452: 5 April (Venice)
Jacopo Antonio Marcello sends René d'Anjou the Greek text and Latin translation (by Lauro Quirini) of the *De sacerdotio Jesu Christi,* with his own dedicatory letter (see Texts I.2).

1452: 10 April
Jacopo Antonio Marcello is replaced as *provveditore* of Crema (ASV, ST 3, fol. 23).

1452: 24 April?
Valerio Marcello born (Fam. II.D; IV.21.b).

1452: 27 April
Jacopo Antonio Marcello and Pasquale Malipiero were elected *provveditori* with the army, but Malipiero is abroad on another mission; another is elected in his place and as Marcello's colleague (ASV, ST 3, fol. 25).

1452: 28 April
Senate letter to Jacopo Antonio Marcello, *provveditore,* who should have by now joined with captain general Gentile da Leonessa, enclosing a letter giving information about the situation at Casalmaggiore, which he should discuss with Leonessa and Jacopo Piccinino. He should try to arrange concord between those two captains, and Carlo Gonzaga as well (ASV, SS 19, fol. 136).

1452: 28 April (Padua)
Jacobus Lulmeus sends Giovanni Barozzi, Bishop of Bergamo, the *De sacerdotio Jesu Christi* with a copy of Jacopo Antonio Marcello's letter to René, the names having been changed (Mercati 1939, 1:73, 82).

1452 after 5 April but before end May
Jacopo Antonio Marcello sends René d'Anjou a second version of the translated *De sacerdotio Jesu Christi,* with explanatory letter. Mention is made of the sickness of Isabelle of Lorraine, who died the following February (Texts I.3).

1452: 16 May
In a bold and unexpected strike across the Adda—"la sorpresa"—Venice in league with Alfonso of Aragon opens war on Milan and her allies (Fossati 1934). Sforza alerted Ludovico Gonzaga two days later "che venetiani in

tucto et pubblicamente hanno rocta la guerra con nuy, . . . et in ogni loco
dove hanno possuto fare damno," having accomplished "questo loro novità
assay secretemente, donde dovevano trovare li nostri disproveduti" (Fossati
1934, 400; also Catalano 1956, 7:30). Florentine citizens are expelled from
Venetian territories (and from Neapolitan as of 11 June); Pope Nicholas V
presses vainly for peace. Dolfin describes the Venetian army of 12,000 horse
and 6,000 foot, under Gentile da Leonessa, in the field as of 7 May (but A.
Colombo 1894, 83, makes the Venetian force 16,000 horse and 6,000 foot
vs. Sforza's 18,000 and 3,000 respectively); with Leonessa are the captains
Jacopo Piccinino and Carlo Fortebraccio. In lieu of Jacopo Antonio Marcello who was *provveditore* in Crema, Andrea Dandolo was *provveditore in
campo* (but see above, 28 April, when Marcello is sent to join Leonessa, and
below at 19 May, where he is in the field). During the campaign season
that follows, Sforza once again ravages the Bresciano (Dolfin, *Cronaca,* fol.
420v–421 [309v–310]; see also for the assault on Brescia during the 1452–
53 period, Peyronel 1990). Meanwhile in Tuscany, Sforza's brother Alessandro leads Florentine forces (while awaiting the assistance of René d'Anjou)
against Aragonese forces under Federico da Montefeltro (A. Colombo
1894, 84).

1452: 19 May
Jacopo Antonio Marcello and Tommaso Duodo, *provveditori* with army,
from camp at Covo grant privileges to city of Antignate, near Cremona,
which had voluntarily submitted to Venice (Predelli 1876–1914, 5:79–80
[xiv, 259]).

1452: August?
Jacopo Antonio Marcello, on his return from Crema, sees son Valerio for
first time (Fam. II.D.3–4, IV.22–29).

1452: summer through November
Venetian army in field under Gentile da Leonessa and Carlo Fortebraccio
da Montone; little contact with Milanese (Hazlitt 1915, 1:957); in September, Florentines ask King Charles VII to send prince of blood to assist them
and Sforza, and that aid is promised for the spring of 1453 (Lecoy 1875,
1:271).

1452: 31 October
Francesco Sforza, furious at the Venetians, declares war in a long letter (Simonetta 1932, 362), and hurls a challenge at them: the "sfida," in the ar-
chaic form of a bloody glove transfixed on a lance (Catalano 1956, 7:34).
The Venetians respond in kind the same day, charging Sforza and his allies
with disturbing the peace of Italy, and pledging reprisals against them, par-

ticularly against "those" (Sforza) who had drained the wealth of Venice to win an heiress and build an empire: "et eos praesertim, qui pecunia ipsius nostri Senatus uxorem sibi et imperium comparaverunt" (Simonetta 1932, 363).

1452: 31 December
Jacopo Antonio Marcello is elected *consigliere* (ASV, SGV 4, fol. 105).

1453: 1 January
The city of Crema having been severely damaged by Venetian troops under Carlo Fortebraccio, Tiberto Brandolini, and Carlo Gonzaga, it is to be compensated (Predelli 1876–1914, 5:76–77 [xiv, 249]; see also Anonimo Veronese 1915, 38; Argegni 1936, 1:404–5).

1453: 26 January
King Charles VII of France agrees to send René d'Anjou to Italy. René promises to arrive by 15 June. Venice meanwhile tries to discourage France from participating in the anti-Venetian League. (A. Colombo 1894, 86; Ilardi 1959, 137–41; Lecoy 1875, 1:273–75). On 27 January, Filelfo writes to René, arranging for delivery of letter by means of Giovanni Cossa (Manetti 1986, 124).

1453: 28 February
Death of Queen Isabelle of Lorraine, wife of René d'Anjou. René adopts the emblem of a bow with broken string in expression of his mourning, with Italian device (*Arco per lentare, piaga non sana*), and buries his wife in half-constructed sepulchral monument in church of Saint Maurice (Lecoy 1875, 1:262–63, 2:182; Mercati 1939, 1:77n2; Manetti 1986, 127). Soon hereafter Marcello will write a consolatory letter to René (see Texts I.4).

1453: March–May
Jacopo Antonio Marcello prepares a manuscript with Greek text and translation of Chrysostom's first homily *De statuis* for René d'Anjou in consolation for the death of Queen Isabelle (see 28 February above), and composes dedicatory letter (see Texts I:5).

1453: 1 April
Gentile da Leonessa dies after being wounded the previous 18 March at the siege of Manerbio; Jacopo Piccinino will inherit Venetian command (Anonimo Veronese 1915, 47; da Soldo 1733, 878; Sanuto 1733, 1147; Simonetta 1732, 634; Mallett & Hale 1984, 42; see below, 13 April).

1453: 3 April
Jacopo Antonio Marcello and Pasquale Malipiero are elected *provveditori* (with salary of 80 ducats per month, and other provisions) to go to the

army in Brescia and take responsibility following the death of Gentile da Leonessa, "de quo tantum dolendum est" (ASV, SS 19, fol. 191).

1453: 10 April

Commission to Jacopo Antonio Marcello and Pasquale Malipiero, about to go to Brescia as *provveditori*, consisting of instructions about the disposition of various captains and *condottieri* (ASV, SS 19, fol. 192).

1453: 11 April

Birth of Francesco Filelfo's son Olimpio (Fam. II.D.1, IV.21.a). Filelfo also assigns Valerio Marcello's birth to 24 April of this year; but see above at 24 April 1452.

1453: 13 April

Letter to Jacopo Antonio Marcello and Pasquale Malipiero, *provveditori* in Brescia, instructing them to propose to Jacopo Piccinino his assumption of role of captain general, with pertinent terms. This done, they should proceed immediately to Brescia and see to disposition of remaining troops. Then they should approach Giovanni Antonio Gattamelata, son of the hero and Gentile's nephew, and ask him to take over his uncle's company (ASV, SS 19, fols. 192v–93; cf. Anonimo Veronese 1915, 47).

1453: 21 April

The Florentine ambassador Angelo Acciaiuoli returns from France, saying that René d'Anjou will soon be sent to assist with Lombard war at head of 2,400 horse, under terms specifying a Florentine monthly payment of 10,000 florins; the Dauphin (the future King Louis XI), invited by Genoese exiles, will also come to retake that city (Ilardi 1959, 138–40; Ilardi 1982, 422–23; Lecoy 1875, 1:274).

1453: April–August

Ludovico Foscarini, as *podestà* in Brescia (King 1986, 375), writes the new Venetian captain Jacopo Piccinino, naming the Venetians in the field with him as "colleagues in danger"—Jacopo Antonio Marcello, Pasquale Malipiero, and Girolamo Barbarigo (Foscarini, *Epistolae,* ##74 and 81, fols. 90v–97v; also 103–106). On 1 August, he writes the Patriarch Lorenzo Giustiniani, deploring the military situation and ravages of the mercenary soldiers (#87, fols. 113–114v; see Picotti 1909, 26–28, and rpt. 1955, 210–12; Degli Agostini 1752–54, 1:62–63). Foscarini's role at this juncture is discussed in Porcellio 1731.

1453: 4 May

René d'Anjou leaves Anjou, with Giovanni Cossa, Neapolitan exile and seneschal of Provence, to gather forces for Italian expedition (Meiss 1957, 4 and passim). Sanuto reports that René comes to Italy with 4,000 horse, joins Sforza, and declares war on Venice; at which time the Venetian *provveditori* Marcello and Pasquale Malipiero arrive in camp (Sanuto 1733, 1147).

1453: 29 May
Fall of Constantinople. The news electrifies Italy, and encourages Italian rulers to think of peace.

1453: 1 June
Jacopo Antonio Marcello sends René d'Anjou a manuscript containing the *Life* of St. Maurice, plus epigrams, illuminations, and prefatory letter. The letter to Giovanni Cossa provides the date and Marcello's location at that moment in its closing: "Valete feliciter, vestri memores Iacobi Antonii Marcelli ex felicissimis castris D. D. Venetiarum Post captum Quintianum et Pontemvicum. kal. junii. mcccliii." The manuscript book (later counted in the inventory of the possessions of the Order of the Crescent in Anjou) presumably reached René and Cossa, or perhaps Cossa alone, while they were in Provence preparing for Italian expedition (see Texts I.6).

1453: 2 June
Sforza writes René urging haste in departure for the expedition to Italy: "perche le cose sono tanto bene adaptate et disposte quanto podesseno essere, vegnerà etiandio a reportare gloria fama et laude immortale" (A. Colombo 1894, 86, 110–11, at 110).

1453: 15 June
Date agreed upon by French and Florentines for René d'Anjou's arrival in Italy; but he is still in Provence (A. Colombo 1894, 86; Lecoy 1875, 1:271).

1453: 16, 17, 18, 23 June
Senate letters to Jacopo Antonio Marcello and Pasquale Malipiero, *provveditori* with army, instructing them to provide relief to the citizens of Verona, who have been unexpectedly attacked, to fortify the area (ASV, SS 19, fols. 198v–199v; ST 3, fol. 68v).

1453: 29 June
René, still at Aix in Provence, makes his testament preparatory to departure; intends burial in same tomb in the church of St. Maurice where Isabelle of Lorraine was recently buried, and arranges for continued supervision of Order of the Crescent commended to the same saint (A. Colombo 1894, 86; Lecoy 1875, 1:276n1).

1453: July 4
René writes Sforza from Sisteron, explaining delays in crossing Alps to Italy (A. Colombo 1894, 111; Lecoy 1875, 1:276, 2:272–73).

1453: 2 and 28 July, 25 August
Senate letters to the *provveditori* with the army, unnamed, but including
Jacopo Antonio Marcello; administrative matters (ASV, SS 19, fols. 203,
206, 210).

1453: 1 (or 3) August
René and Cossa with troops reach Ventimiglia by sea (A. Colombo 1894,
87; Lecoy 1875, 1:277).

1453: 9 August
René writes Sforza from Pieve del Tecco, asking that the captains Bartolomeo Colleoni and Andrea Birago be sent to help him break through the
passes closed to him by Savoy; Sforza responds encouragingly on 22 August. René subsequently makes steady progress, entering Asti on 24 August
(A. Colombo 1894, 87–89, 117–18).

1453: 31 August
Venice declines offer of French Dauphin (the future King Louis XI) to assist
them against Sforza and against the interests of his own father and his uncle, René d'Anjou (A. Colombo 1894, 89–91; Lecoy 1875, 1:277).

1453: 18 (or 19) September
René (accompanied by Colleoni) is honorably received at Pavia by Bianca
Maria Visconti, and is celebrated by Catone Sacco's oration; on 26 September, he will proceed to Cremona and thence to join Sforza's forces preparing
attack on Brescia (A. Colombo 1894, 101–2, 362; Lecoy 1875, 1:279). On
7 October, he is in Cremona, and is urged by Colleoni to leave the next
day to join the army. When he does so in fact soon after, he is assigned the
fifth and last place in the lineup, after Sforza, Ludovico Gonzaga, Bartolomeo Colleoni, and Tiberto Brandolini (A. Colombo 1894, 366, 369; Rubieri 1879, 2:279).

1453: 19 September
Senate letter to *provveditori* in army, unnamed, but including Jacopo Antonio Marcello, responding to theirs of 15 and 16 September reporting the
refortification of Cassano by Bianca Maria Visconti: our troops should
cross the Adda and inflict damage (ASV, SS 19, fol. 212v).

1453: 28 September
Senate letter to *provveditori* in army, unnamed, but including Jacopo Antonio Marcello, responding to theirs of 25 September reporting various matters; need to occupy Ghiaradadda (ASV, SS 19, fol. 213).

1453: 3 October
The Senate responds to peace tentatives sent by Giovanni Cossa, in which

the French offered to negotiate a settlement between Venice and Milan, expressing astonishment at French advance and her own preference for peace; at same time, it urges ally Naples to attack the Florentines in Tuscany (ASV, SS 19, 215; Agostini 1930, 236–37; Lecoy 1875, 1:280; 2:274–75; Perret 1896, 261).

1453: 10 October
René d'Anjou and Giovanni Cossa, dispatching heralds in full chivalric pageantry to the Venetian *provveditori* Pasquale Malipiero and Jacopo Antonio Marcello, formally declare war on Venice, claiming the justice of their cause: "Juste ergo movemur ut arma in Italiam feramus"; Malipiero and Marcello answer on 12 October that they have not the competence to reply, and refer René's statement to the Senate (A. Colombo 1894, 370–71; Lecoy 1875, 1:279–80, 2:275–77). On the same day, Pope Nicholas V calls for a general peace congress among the Italian states; negotiations proceed languidly for months without issue (Ady 1907, 70; Antonini 1930, 233; A. Colombo 1894, 376).

1453: 12 October
Senate letter to *provveditori* in army, unnamed, but including Jacopo Antonio Marcello, encouraging them to supply provisions, see to progress of troops (ASV, SS 19, fol. 218).

1453: 14 October–27 November
Allied French and Milanese forces reoccupy (among other localities of the Ghiaradadda, Bresciano, and Bergamasco) Bassano, Pontevico (where Simonetta said French soldiers committed atrocities), Manerbio, Rovato, Soncino, Romanengo, Orzinuovi; Sforza retired for winter via Bergamo and Crema to the Milanese; René retired via Cremona to Piacenza, arriving 7 December 1453 (Catalano 1956, 7:52; A. Colombo 1894, 371–74; Lecoy 1875, 1:280–81; Rubieri 2:280–83). During the very same weeks, Ludovico Foscarini, *podestà* of Brescia, attempts with Senate approval to negotiate a secret settlement with Sforza (Antonini 1930, 240–42).

1453: 9 November
Decision taken to write to Jacopo Antonio Marcello, Pasquale Malipiero, and Girolamo Barbarigo, *provveditori* with army, informing them that funds are available to hire more troops, followed by text of letter (ASV, SS 19, fol. 220v–221).

1453: 14, 22 and 27 November
Senate letters to *provveditori* with the army, unnamed, but including Jacopo Antonio Marcello, urging firm stand, advising on disposition of troops (ASV, SS 19, fols. 222rv, 224rv).

1453: 22 November
Francesco Filelfo writes René, apologizing for not having visited the king at Orzinuovi although Filelfo was only 5 miles distant (Manetti 1986, 124). Filelfo had left Naples to join Sforza's camp at Orzinuovi when he learned that René had arrived in Italy to aid Sforza (as above; also Rosmini 1808, 2:88). On the same date, an unnamed Venetian patriot ("veneto") who had volunteered to kill Sforza was apprehended (Antonini 1930, 243).

1453: end November–December
The Augustinian canon Fra Simone da Camerino opens on Venice's behalf secret peace negotiations with Sforza in Milan (Antonini 1930, 252). For Fra Simone's continued activity, resulting in the century's most important peace treaty at Lodi, see Antonini 1930; Canetta 1885.

1453: 16 December
Jacopo Antonio Marcello and Pasquale Malipiero, *provveditori* with the army, want to return to Venice and report important developments; in any case, the troops are retiring to winter camps. One only will be permitted to return, the choice to be made "per texeram, vel per concordiam"; they draw lots, with the result that Malipiero returns, Marcello stays, and without salary (ASV, ST 3, fol. 91v).

1453: 31 December
Senate decision that Gerardo Dandolo should go as *provveditore,* and colleague of Jacopo Antonio Marcello and Girolamo Barbarigo, with captain general Jacopo Piccinino (ASV, SS 19, fol. 233v).

1454: 3 January
Deserted by Florentines and Milanese, who had begun peace negotiations with Venice, René d'Anjou leaves Piacenza for France (of his entourage, only Cossa wished to remain). From Alessandria on 8 January, he writes Sforza disingenuously promising the return of René's son Jean d'Anjou with reinforced troops in the spring. René arrived in Aix in Provence by 9 February. King Charles VII was furious at his desertion of the cause, but was eventually calmed by the eulogies of René's performance from Sforza and Florence (A. Colombo 1894, 378–81, 397–98; Lecoy 1875, 1:283–86, 2:278–79).

1454: 14 January
Fra Simone presents to the Senate proposals for peace conditions following discussions with Sforza (ASV, SS 20, fol. 3; Antonini 1930, 256–57 and 285–86, doc. #8). The Senate is adamant that Crema must be kept for Venice, while Sforza is intractable on the same point.

1454: 19 January

Senate letter instructing Jacopo Antonio Marcello, *provveditore,* and other *provveditori* with army, to look into the recruitment of additional infantry, since "potentia unius exercitus, consistat principaliter in armigeris et famulis armatis" (ASV, SS 20, fol. 5).

1454: 4 February

Fra Simone da Camerino comes to the Senate with new proposals, representing Sforza, who is eager for peace: "quum ut dicit nullum maius desiderium habet, quam redire ad pristinam affectionem et amorem cum nostro dominio, extendens se circa hoc multis verbis." But he continues to insist upon having Crema, saying it is in the middle of his lands, and our possession of it might give rise to future difficulties; in exchange for Crema, he would grant us all the remaining lands of the Bresciano and Bergamasco. Fra Simone should return to Sforza, affirming our desire to live in peace, and agreeing with all the peace terms except those concerning Crema, which we must have, as we have repeatedly said; and if he is really interested in peace, he shouldn't even ask: "salvo quam de Crema cum Cremensi, quam sicut moltotiens diximus respectu honoris nostri, et fidei date Cremensibus fidelissimis nostris, non intendimus sibi dare; nec profecto debet eam velle petere, disponente ipso realiter et bono animo venire ad pacem" (ASV, SS 20, fol. 7v; Antonini 1930, 286–87, doc. #9). Sanuto describes the peace process thus: "E questi (Fra Simone) più volte andò su e giù, e parlava al Duca, e poi quì a Ser Paolo Morosini, il quale le riferiva tuto in Collegio" (Sanuto 1733, 1152). Dolfin reports more amply, that after Orsato Giustiniani and Cristoforo Moro in Rome had failed to secure a peace after nine months of negotiation, "Tamen non se resto tentar la pace per altri mezi, et vie de amici. Tandem per lo mezo de ser Polo Morexini el Savio, fo de san Zilio, cum la interposition de frate Simonito da Camerino heremitano confessor del duca et m.a Biancha sua moier, prior alhora de san Christophilo de Muran alhora egregio predicator che in quella quadragesima havea predicato a Millan alla corte del signore, inspirato da dio se interpose per la fede et devotion haveva el duca in lui, et indusse quello per modo chi sono contenti che fra Simoneto se interponesse a pratichar la pace cum modi et condicion honeste. De che habuto colloquio cum messer Polo Morexini sopra questo, et proposto la cosa in Pregadi, fu a quello dato licentia se pratichasse, et andato et tornato piu volte da Venesia a Millano, non se confidando de alcuno, stetino per piu zorni suspesi venetiani che questa fusse praticha similata, et per questo la Sig.ria dato le prestanze messe sua gente in expedition cavalli et pedoni, et comenciono da questo, che feceno repatriar li proveditori che erano in campo messer Pasqual Malipiero proc.or et Jacomo Antonio Marcello, apresso el conte Jacomo Picinin nostro governator. Dapoi fu mandato novo proveditor ser Girardo Dandolo che fu de ser Iacomo solo appresso el ditto governator, et altri capitanii de nostre gente unde visto el duca de Millan farse per la Signoria si vallide provision, et za reusciva la provision facta de trovar del danaro. Provide el duca mandar fra Simon cum celerita a Venezia et dette a quello in scriptis, cum che capitali voleva far pace cul la Sig.ria. Et veduto et inteso per la Signoria, fu confirmato tal pace doverse far, et contento che fra Symon tornase a Millano, et poi tornasse, o mandasse, la conclusion ferma del duca" (Dolfin, *Cronaca,* fol. 437v [326v]). On the same day, a Senate letter to rectors of Verona and Jacopo Antonio Marcello, *provveditore,* authorizing their providing the Marquis of Mantua (Ludovico Gonzaga) with a safe-conduct (ASV, SS 20, fol. 7v).

1454: 6 February
Senate letter: Jacopo Antonio Marcello, our *provveditore* presently in Verona, who has been in our service for many months, may return and be replaced (ASV, ST 3, fol. 99v).

1454: 18 February
Senate letter: Jacopo Antonio Marcello has fulfilled his responsibilities and may return (ASV, ST 3, fol. 101v).

1454: 18 March
Senate responds to Fra Simone da Camerino's peace proposals affirmatively: he should proceed to secure the peace (ASV, SS 20, fol. 12v–13; Antonini 1930, 290, doc. #13; with Sforza's proposals in ASV, SS 20, fol. 14v and Antonini 289–90, doc. #12).

1454: 23 March
In a letter to Cosimo de' Medici, Sforza reports on Fra Simone's discussions with him, logjammed on the central issue of Crema—its position within Milan's orbit, Venice's nonnegotiable demand: "Ve scripseme alli di passati come fra Simonetta era qui el quale stava pur fermo sul facto de Crema et che non haveva altro de novo; et ala partita che fece de qui che sonno hoge nove dì, nuy le dicessemo: fra Simonetto, voy non venete may qui non ma a dire *lassa Crema, lassa Crema,* parendo a voy che quando fusse acconzo el facto de Crema fusse facto ogni cosa, Ma el non è cossi, perchè lasciamo andare che nuy dovessemo lassare Crema, che Importa tanto al Stato nostro come voy vedete per essere In mezo del Stato nostro . . . " (Canetta 1885, 550–51).

1454: 28 March

Paolo Barbo is assigned to go to execute the peace agreed upon by Fra Simone, as above (18 March); the Senate is sending him a copy of the memorials and a summary of the peace terms "manu dicti fratris Simonis." He should meet Fra Simone in Brescia, assuring him of the Senate's intentions to sign the peace, then proceed secretly (in the garb of a friar, as it happened) to Crema using Sforza's safe-conduct. There he should sign the peace with Sforza or his representatives, and return within 8 days. The text of the agreement follows (ASV, SS 20, fol. 14; see also Romanin 1853–61, 4:225n2). Dolfin describes these events of 20 March through 14 April: "Unde a di 20 zuoba 1454 venne a Venixia secreto uno compagno de fra Symone che alcun non sepe ne intese, et fatto a saper all Signoria mandono a san Christofalo de Muran suo secretario, al qual fu dato le lettere de fra Symone el qual scriveva esser partito da Millan, et era rimasto a Bressa cum uno trombetta del duca, et chiamato in quel di pregadi in el qual mi Zorzi Dolfin da san Cancian me atrovi come official ali .x. officii, et lette le lettere de fra Simonete per lequal se offeriva la pace alla Signoria cum la conclusion de quelli capituli, consentando la Signoria a quelli mandar se dovesse nostro sindico et commesso secretissimo, quanto piu presto se potesse acio chel diavolo non impariasse tanti beni. Etiam per raxon che questo rechiedeva el ditto duca de Millan, unde fu deliberato in quel Pregadi, chel colegio havisse liberta mandar uno gentilhomo incognito stravestido insieme cum Michiel di Grassi secretario, et per el collegio fu deputato a tal opera messer Polo Barbo cavallier, fu de la parte balotte 180 de non 0 non sincere 0, che in tanto numero mai fu veduto nel conseio tanta union. El qual messer Polo in quella notte parti de Venesia in habito de fratte minore, et rivo a Bressa a di 30 marzo, dove atrovo frate Simone, et subito premando al trombetta al signor duca facendoli a saper come lera zonto a Bressa, i sindici mandati per la signoria per concluder la pace. Azonto el trombetta a Cremona dal s.or duca dette ordene che ognuna vegnisse a Lodi come luogo piu proximo a li confini de Millan, acompagnato messer Polo Barbo cum frate Simone, et Michiel di Grassi cavalcorono a Crema, dove trovorono messer Andrea Dandolo za molti mexi governador per la signoria in ditta luogo, per esser amado da tutto el populo de quella citade. Dove inteseno la deliberation del luogo de Lodi deputato per el duca de Millan, et che li secretamente devosseno andar, et partino da Crema a di 5 de april a hore do de notte venere e arrivono a Lodi a hore 4 de notte, stetteno fin al sabbato matina secreti, che alcun non sepe. Venne adoncha el duca Franceso Sforza, messer Anzolo Simoneta, messer Andrea da Birano, messer Guarnier da Castigion al albergo dove era messer Polo Barbo et frate Simone dove fu abrazato messer Polo Barbo dal duca Francesco, et fatto grate reco-glienze, et non volse che de li se partisseno, et exposto la caxone per laqual erano venuti in ditto loco vennino sopra i capituli, et strenzandosse sule difficulta, li mando sotigliando, scrivando quale in ditto loco, sabbato, dominica et luni di fin hore 2 de notte, stando indifferentia sempre su con-dition de capituli, chel duca volea restringer a suo modo. Aliquali messer Polo Barbo non consentiva, et piu volte in discordo ordino fusse posta sella a cavalli, et voleva partir in quella hora perche messer Polo Barbo have co-mission de concluder pace solo cum 12 capituli, et lui voleva etc. Tandem mediante lo auxilio de Dio, el duca Francesco concluxe contento el sizillo et sottoscrisse, et iuro ferma vallida, et perpetua pace cum venetiani et suo adherenti e colligadi, cum queste succinte, et summarie condicion che lui dava et restituiva alla Signoria tuti li luoghi tolti del territorio bressano berga-masco et valle de san martin chel duca havea occupado, dando liberamente Crema cum tutto el cremasco a venetiani, benche quella fussa in ieradada, el resto de ieradada romagnisse al duca de Millan. Dapoi fu publicata dicta pace a di 14 april domenega de lolivo, cum solemne procession in Venexia et per tutto el dominio venetian, et cosi del duca de Millan cum gaudio et consolation de tutti i populi, et son de campane, el di cum la notte e fuogi per tutte le contrade. Laqual guerra duro anni cinque, fu dapoi per longo temporo ocio, et quiete in Italia, maxime in Lombardia chel stato venetiano stette quieto da movimento darme fino a la guerra del duca Hercules de Ferrara" (Dolfin, *Cronaca,* fol. 438rv [327rv]).

1454: 9 April
Peace terms between Venice and Milan settled at Lodi (in the house of Francesco Sforza) by Fra Simone da Camerino and Paolo Barbo, Venetian ambassador (Antonini 1930; Canetta 1885; Romanin 1853–61, 4:225; see also above at 18 March). Venice retained all *terraferma* conquests as well as the prized Crema and Ghiaradadda cities. Demobilization quickly ensued. (Mallett 1979, 149; 1984, 43)

1454: 17 May
Senate letter: Fra Simone da Camerino has petitioned us in writing, for the honor of God and celebration of the peace, to fund the restoration and completion of the church and monastery on San Cristoforo da Murano, and henceforth entitle that island San Cristoforo della Pace; he further asks for exemptions from all taxes and fees for the churches of Santa Maria de Monte Ortone in Padua and Santa Maria de Campo Santo in Citadella (near Padua), our subject city. His petition is granted, with an allowance of

100 ducats per month for a two-year term for the restoration of the buildings on San Cristoforo, as well as a perpetual donation of 30 ducats per year for its maintenance. The new name of San Cristoforo della Pace is approved, with preceding provisions, by a unanimous vote (ASV, ST 3, fol. 114; Cornelius 1749, 1: 277; the ducal letter of 21 May formally extending these benefits in Cornelius 1749, 1:276; see also Sanuto 1733, 1045; Antonini 1930, 278; Romanin 1853–61, 4:225n2). The church thereby completed once bore on its walls an inscription to Jacopo Antonio Marcello (buried in the same building), and an image of the joined arms of Francesco Sforza and the Venetian Republic (Fam. III.C.3–7).

1454: 30 September
Jacopo Antonio Marcello elected as member of the *zonta* of 40 to the Senate; subsequently canceled (ASV, SGV, Miste 4, fol. 140).

1454: October
Janus Pannonius leaves Guarino's school at Ferrara, after having composed in the master's honor a *Panegyricus* in May/June. He proceeds to study canon law at the university in Padua through 1458, when he returns to Hungary (Thomson 1988, 19).

1454–
Colleoni returns to Venetian army as commander general, receiving his *bastone* of command directly from the Venetian ambassador and humanist Paolo Barbo, a negotiator for the Peace of Lodi, who delivers an oration commemorating the occasion (King 1986, 330); Jacopo Piccinino deserts to Milan; Carlo Fortebraccio is an increasingly key figure in campaigns of 1470s, until his death in 1479 (Mallett & Hale 1984, 41ff., 46, 149, 194, and passim).

1455: 26 January–25 February
Alfonso of Aragon and Pope Nicholas V respectively sign accords (stemming from April 1454 Peace of Lodi) to an agreement creating the "Lega Italica" that would secure political equilibrium on the peninsula and 25 years of peace. Corollary to both settlements was the recognition of Sforza's otherwise precarious title to the Dukedom of Milan, bringing to culmination the career of the only Italian *condottiere* to win a kingdom and start a dynasty. In recognition of the peace, marriage alliances are agreed upon between Alfonso and Sforza (Cessi 1942–43; Cusin 1936; Ilardi 1959; Soranzo 1958).

1455 (Ferrara)
Guarino Veronese dedicates the first ten books of Strabo's *Geography* to Pope Nicholas V (Texts I:9).

1456

Porcellio Pandoni publishes his *Commentaria Comitis Jacobi Picinini*, dedicated to King Alfonso of Aragon and Sicily, on the 1452 war between Sforza and Venetians, from the latter's perspective (Pandoni 1731; see A. Zeno 1752–52, 1:18–19). Lorenzo Zane dedicates to Giorgio Bevilacqua the *De difficilimae doctrinae palma capescenda*, dated "idibus decembris, ex Garda" (published in Degli Agostini 1752–54, 1:198–204; *Iter* 1:14, gives date of 1446, unlikely because of author's extreme youth at that date; see King 1986, 446; ms. version in BMV, cod. Lat. XIV, 113 [4709], bears date of 1456 at fol. 84).

1456: 11 June

The nobleman Girolamo Donato is sent to Rimini as Venetian representative to the wedding of Carlo Fortebraccio, *condottiere* in Venetian service, and Margherita, daughter of Sigismondo Pandolfo Malatesta (ASV, ST 4, fol. 9; also Anonimo Veronese 1915, 101n4; Argegni 1936, 1:405).

1456: 14 June

Sforza is granted a palace (formerly Gattamelata's) near the church of San Polo, in Venice, which he will exchange in 1461 for a palace on the Grand Canal (Beltrami 1906; Greppi 1913, 336–51). Sforza in turn grants Cosimo de' Medici a house in Milan, which will house the Medici Bank until sold by Lorenzo de' Medici in 1484 (Ady 1907, 71–72).

1457: 12 January

Death of Jacopo Foscari in Candia, precipitating deposition of Doge Francesco Foscari.

1457: 1 March

Jacopo Antonio Marcello, in Monselice, prepares a manuscript containing map, translation of Ptolemy, and dedication for shipment to René d'Anjou (see Texts I.8).

1457: 30 October

Pasquale Malipiero, *procuratore* of San Marco and former Marcello colleague, is elected doge.

1457: 1 November

Death of Francesco Foscari, regnant doge during the whole course of the Lombard wars, as his epitaph reflects: "Maxima bella pro vestra salute et dignitate terra marique per annos plusquam triginta gessi, summaque felicitate confeci. Labantem suffulsi Italiae libertatem; turbatores quietis armis compescui; Brixiam, Bergomum, Ravennam, Cremam, imperio adjunxi vestro. Omnibus ornamentis patriam auxi. Pace vobis parta, Italia in tran-

quillum foedere redacta, post tot labores exhaustos, . . . ad aeternam re-
quiem commigravi" (Sanuto 1733, 1165).

1457–before 22 April 1463
Pietro Perleone teaches in the San Marco school in Venice until his death
(King 1986, 416).

1457: 17 September and 1 October
Money is provided for Carlo Fortebraccio, *condottiere* in Venetian service
(ASV, ST 4, fols. 51, 52v).

1458
Having received his degree in canon law at Padua, and before returning to
Hungary, Janus Pannonius writes an elegy to Andrea Mantegna who had
recently completed a portrait of the humanists Pannonius and Galeotto
Marzio (Fabbri 1983, 230n8; 232n15; Huszti 1933; Thomson 1988, 20).

1458: 11 May, 8 June
Jean d'Anjou, son of René, takes possession of Genoa (Ilardi 1959, 147);
René responds to Sforza's congratulations on his son, Jean d'Anjou's, re-
conquest of Genoa (Lecoy 1875, 2:283–84); in October 1458, Giovanni
Cossa and the bishop of Marseille will attempt to negotiate an alliance with
Florence, for France; in March and October, 1459, French envoys are sent
for same purpose to Venice (Ilardi 152; Perret 1889).

1458: 13 July (Ferrara)
Guarino Veronese completes his translation of Strabo and dedicates the
whole to Jacopo Antonio Marcello (Texts I.9–10).

1458: 27 September–1459: 22 August
Jacopo Antonio Marcello appears on the Council of Ten in Venice, at times
with title of *capo* (ASV, CXM 15, fols. 161, 164v, 167, 169, 169v, 170,
176, 177, 177v, 178v, 181, 182, 183, 185).

1458: September
Giovanni Antonio Campano completes his *De gestis et vita Braccii* (the life
of Braccio da Montone), dedicated to Carlo Fortebraccio (Valentini
1924, 165).

1459: 15 February
Money is provided for Carlo Fortebraccio, *condottiere* in Venetian service
(ASV, ST 4, fol. 98v).

1459: 14 March–4 May
Andrea Mantegna is working on an "operetta" for Jacopo Antonio Marcello
when his services are sought by Marquis Ludovico Gonzaga of Mantua.
(During this period he is also working for the Venetian Gregorio Correr,

Abbot of San Zeno, on that institution's famous polyptych.) On 14 March, Marcello requests Gonzaga's permission to have Mantegna work 8 to 10 days more on unnamed work. Gonzaga agrees in letters back to both Marcello and Mantegna in March. The work for Marcello (conceivably the Strabo manuscript described in Texts I.9–10, but identified by one expert as the *Saint Sebastian* in Vienna's Kunsthistorisches Museum: Tietze-Conrat 1955, 10, 185, 200, and plate 35) is mentioned again in Gonzaga's letter to Mantegna of 4 May 1459 (Meiss 1957, 44–46; also Fabbri 1983, 230n8, both citing Kristeller 1902, 496).

1459: 17 July

The Senate affirms that Sforza is to be granted the house in Venice previously granted to Gattamelata, near the church of San Polo (see 1456: 14 June); Sforza's secretary Antonio Guidoboni is here and has already taken the keys and title: "habuit claves tenutam et possessionem." A document of donation should be drawn up (ASV, SS 20, fol. 187). On the same day, *condottiere* Carlo Fortebraccio is reaccepted into Venetian service (ASV, ST 4, fol. 114).

1459: 13 September (Venice)

Jacopo Antonio Marcello dedicates and sends to René d'Anjou the translation of Strabo completed for him by Guarino Veronese (see Texts I:9–10).

1459: 4 October

Jean d'Anjou, who had already reacquired Genoa for France in 1458, leaves that city with Giovanni Cossa and large force to undertake long struggle for reconquest of Naples, abandoned (after a major defeat at Troia in August 1462) only in 1464. In his absence, Milan assists Genoese rebels, who isolate the French garrison which eventually falls in July 1461 (Ady 1907, 74–76; Lecoy 1875, 1:292ff.).

1459: 4 October–1460: 31 May

Jacopo Antonio Marcello appears as *consigliere* (ASV, CLN 9, 167v–190v, passim; CXM 16, fol. 1v; SM 6, fols. 143–170v, passim; ST 4, fols. 124v–142, passim).

1459: 6 November

Senate response to bishop of Marseilles, who came before the Senate representing René d'Anjou, justifying René's action against Venice in 1453: "multis verbis honestare et iustificare quesivit adventum suum in italiam contra nos, quando eramus in bello cum presenti duce Milani." Then he turned to the matter of the Kingdom of Sicily, which he insisted was rightfully René's: "legitime et pleno iure spectabat eidem Regi Renato." That king has now undertaken its reconquest, and wishes assistance. The Senate insists that it always supported René, and as for the hostilities of 1453, all is forgotten: "quum et si ob id tunc in magna admirationem inducti fuerimus, tamen iamdiu omnium earum rerum obliti sumus." As for the assistance that is asked, we affirm that we are bound in friendship with the royal house of France, and that there is nothing further to say: "nec videtur nobis opus esse in hac re aliud esse dicendum" (ASV, SS 20, fols. 195v–96).

1460

Giovanni Mario Filelfo is made first master of the Venetian school of rhetoric (with the patronage of Doge Pasquale Malipiero), arriving in January–February. During this year, Filelfo, George of Trebizond, and Pietro Perleone compete for an appointment as public historian (which is not in fact filled); see Gaeta 1980, 40–42; F. Gilbert 1971, 278ff.; Pertusi 1970b, 302ff.; also Zippel 1956, for an earlier such episode. Filelfo's *Invettiva contro Pietro Perleone e Giorgio Trapezunzio* expressed his resentment against the two competitors (Gabotto 1892, 252–55).

1460: Easter through August

Jacopo Antonio Marcello, Valerio, and the Anon. Tut. with *famiglia* vacation in Monselice (Anon. Tut. G, 244–45; text at chap. 1n95).

1460: 15 April (Padua)

Maffeo Vallaresso writes Jacopo Antonio Marcello to thank him for a favor (Texts III.12).

1460: 14 May, Milan

Francesco Filelfo writes to Jacopo Antonio Marcello (Texts III.4).

1460: 20 June

The Senate assures the ambassador of René d'Anjou of its good will, and wishes that the Duke of Milan also live peacefully with the French, and wishes this information to be passed to the Duke of Milan (ASV, SS 20, fol. 9rv).

1460 early July

Niccolò Sagundino experiences a calamitous shipwreck and the loss of his pregnant wife, three children, and his library; thereafter renounces the chancellorship of Crete for which he had been chosen, and resides in Venice except for intermittent official missions (King 1986, 428); he is consoled by Perleone's *Epistola ad Nicolaum Sagundinum* (Perleone 1740).

1460: 10 July

Senate actions taken on behalf of Niccolò Sagundino, their loyal secretary, beset by misfortunes: "Omnibus notum est horrendum et miserabile infortunium occursum infelici et calamitoso servitori nostro Nicolao Sagundino, qui in proprio conspectu amissa uxore gravido, duobus filiolis masculis, et una filia, cum tota eius facultate vix tandem evasit cum quinque filiabus pro maiori parte grandibus et viro maturis ac uno filio masculo." Both he and a surviving son are guaranteed employment and dowry subvention for the surviving daughters (ASV, ST 4, fol. 149). See also Mastrodimitris 1970, 245; Babinger 1961, 36, 44–45.

1460: 4 December

Death of Guarino Veronese at age 86.

1461: 1 January

Valerio Marcello dies (Fam. II.C, IV.21.d) and is buried in San Giorgio Maggiore (Fam. III.E, IV.33).

1461: January (Venice)

Niccolò Sagundino composes a consolatory letter for Jacopo Antonio Marcello (Texts II.C.1).

1461: 10 January

Francesco Sforza exchanges his palace in San Polo for an unfinished one at San Samuele on the Grand Canal, property of Marco Corner, father of Caterina Corner, queen of Cyprus (Gullino 1983). In 1460, a plan and description had been made by Marco Corner of this "caxa in Sancto Samael sopra el Canalle grande"; on the date given, Marco di Giorgio Corner sold it to Sforza (acting through his agent Antonio Guidobono) for 20,000 ducats (Beltrami 1906, 9–10, 22–26). Sforza subsequently had it continued to his own design and "al modo venetiano." Work was suspended when only one corner had been completed, but it is still called Ca' del Duca (Beltrami 1906; Greppi 1913, 336–51; Huse & Wolters 1990, 20–21; Lieberman 1982, note plate 57; see also photo of Ca' del Duca in chap. 6, above). It was confiscated by the Venetian government for nonpayment of debts, and was eventually sold on 21 March 1528 to Giovanni Ludovico Dolce (Beltrami 1906, 26–27; also Douglas Lewis in Lytle & Orgel 1981, 363–67).

1461: 8 March

Death of Francesco Filelfo's son Olimpio Gellio (Fam. II.C.2, IV.21.a).

1461: 1 April

Death of Taddea, daughter of Jacopo Antonio Marcello (Fam. IV.17–18).

1461: 7 April

Date of George of Trebizond's consolatory letter to Jacopo Antonio Marcello (Texts II.C.2).

1461: 27 June (Milan)

Francesco Filelfo writes to Jacopo Antonio Marcello promising to fulfill the latter's (unstated) request (Texts III.4).

1461: 17 July
René d'Anjou has led a war fleet to quell Genoese rebellion, assisting son Jean d'Anjou, engaged in Neapolitan struggle. On this date a decisive defeat (aided by the Milanese) leads to permanent loss of Genoa to French, and marks René's last personal appearance in a military endeavor and last attempt to gain Italian sovereignty (Ady 1907, 74; Lecoy 1875, 1:328–30). René's brother-in-law and supporter, King Charles VII, dies a few days later (22 July).

1461: 9 August (Verona)
Date of Isotta Nogarola's consolatory letter to Jacopo Antonio Marcello (Texts II.C.6)

1461: 1 September
Approximate date for the composition of Pietro Perleone's *Laudatio* for Jacopo Antonio Marcello. That author writes (G, 191; text at Fam. IV.18) that five months had passed since the death of Marcello's daughter Taddea, which occurred on 1 April of 1461 (Texts II.C.10). Previously, Perleone had written a brief consolatory letter for the same death of Valerio (Texts II.D.21).

1461: 8 September
Giovanni Mario Filelfo has left Venice and relocated in Bologna (Castellani 1896, 369; Favre 1856, 93–95).

1461: 25 December (Milan)
Date of Francesco Filelfo's consolatory work to Jacopo Antonio Marcello (Texts II.C.3). Previously Filelfo had composed a Latin elegy on the same theme in the name of Francesco Sforza (Texts II.D.17).

1461–1462
Ludovico Foscarini is *luogotenente* in Friuli (in Udine) and is involved in a literary circle including the bibliophile Guarnerio d'Artegna (Degli Agostini 1752–54, 1:73; King 1986, 7, 12, 376; Picotti 1909, 36).

1462?
Francesco Filelfo composes a Greek elegy on the death of Valerio Marcello, and it is translated independently by Ludovico Carbone and Leonardo Grifo (Texts II.C.4, 5; II.D.19). Possibly in the same year, in Ferrara, Carbone composes his *Carmen* consoling Jacopo Antonio Marcello on the death of Valerio (II.D.16).

1462: 24 March
Ludovico Foscarini promulgates new statutes for Friuli, approved now by Senate (ASV, ST 5, fol. 4).

1462: 1 April (Udine)

Ludovico Foscarini writes a consolatory letter to Niccolò Canal, describing Jesus Christ's sadness at death of Lazarus (*Epistolae*, #196 [fols.226v–27v]).

1462: May

Date of (original) composition of Michele Orsini's *Opinio* in response to Francesco Filelfo's consolation of Marcello (Texts II.C.13); but see below at 26 August.

1462: 5 May

Death of Pasquale Malipiero, whose epitaph read: "Paschalis Malipiero dux pacificus" (Sanuto 1733, 1168–69).

1462: 9 and 11 May

Jacopo Antonio Marcello participates in the third, fourth, and final "hands" of the election of Doge Cristoforo Moro (ASV, MC-Regina, fols. 39, 39v; Sanuto 1733, 1171).

1462: 19 May

Jacopo Antonio Marcello selected as one of the officials charged to collect money from the salt office and "cum pecuniis in manu" buy necessary equipment for the imminent holiday tournament (ASV, CX 16, fol. 62v).

1462: 19 May–3 July

Jacopo Antonio Marcello appears with the title of *consigliere* (ASV, CXM 16, fols. 62v, 63, 64v, 66; SM 7, fols. 66, 67, 68, 69); on 1 June he is elected to that position through 5 July (ASV, CLN 10, fol. 63v).

1462: 13 June

Pietro Perleone is seriously ill, and is allowed to interrupt his duties to go the baths (King 1986, 416). His death is placed between this date and 22 April 1463, and probably closer to the latter date: his tomb bore the date 1463 (Affò 1794, 2:202; ref. courtesy of Prof. G. N. Knauer).

1462: 16 July

The Senate makes provisions for the situation in Trieste: "in rebus Tergestinorum." The naval blockade should continue; all Venetian officials in the area are to be informed. The Triestines may send their ambassadors to the Senate if they come in the spirit of repentance for their rebelliousness (ASV, SS 20, fol. 98).

1462: 26 August (Venice)

Date of transmission to Jacopo Antonio Marcello of Orsini's *Opinio* (Texts II.C.13).

1462: 11 October

Senate resolution: Urgent that the castle of Castronovo, currently held by our ally the Count of Goricia, be kept in our hands, since it stands on the

route to Trieste and Justinopolis; the Count of Goricia should be so informed (ASV, SS 20, fol. 115v).

1462: 12 October
Jacopo Antonio Marcello, first appearing as *luogotenente* in Friuli, is allowed
funds for repairs of the official palace (ASV, ST 5, fol. 20).

1462: 26 October
Senate letter to Ludovico Foscarini "our citizen" in Friuli, responding to his
of 23 October, advising him, together with the *luogotenente* (Jacopo Antonio Marcello, at this time), to choose a representative to take over positions
described ("oppidus Suera" and nearby "loci predicti"); the report on
Castelnovo is satisfactory (ASV, SS 20, fols. 118v–19).

1462: 15 November
Francesco Filelfo sends to Ottaviano Ubaldini della Carda a manuscript
containing his prose and verse consolations to Marcello, with dedicatory
letter (Texts II.C.3).

1462: 16 December
Ludovico Foscarini has returned from mission to Friuli (where Jacopo Antonio Marcello is *luogotenente*) to learn of emperor's intentions regarding
Trieste; now he is to be empowered to negotiate with imperial representative to purchase Trieste for 10,000 ducats (ASV, CX 16, fol. 81, pub. Cesca
1883, 24–25).

1463: 22 April
Pietro Perleone is replaced as teacher at the San Marco school, indicating
that he had died by this date. He had been ill since at least 13 June 1462,
q.v.

1463: 9 May (Modena)
Giovanni Mario Filelfo writes Jacopo Antonio Marcello referring to his pre-
vious works directed to the nobleman: a *consolatio* and *satire* against
Galeotto Marzio da Narni (see Texts, II.D.18, III.5).

1463: 15 July (Venice)
Date of the consolatory letter to Jacopo Antonio Marcello by the Anonymous Venetian (Texts II.C.12).

1463: 4 July–11 November
Venetians first surround, then besiege Trieste (Cesca 1883). Raffaele Zovenzoni (who had been a student of Guarino's at Ferrara, 1450–54, and was
present in Venice during period 1455–61) is public *rector scholarum* in Capodistria 1461–66, and precisely at time of Trieste siege, had ties with Jacopo Antonio Marcello and Vitale Lando, Venetian *provveditori* (Tremoli,
145–46; Ziliotto 1950, 21ff., 47).

1463: 8, 20 August
Senate resolution: The Senate finds the peace terms offered by the Triestine ambassadors unsatisfactory; inform our captains that they are not to make any agreements with Trieste (ASV, SS 20, fol. 119; Cesca 1883, 11–12, 27–28, 33–34).

1463: August
Count Antonio da Marsciano is sent with 1500 cavalry and increasing numbers of infantry to assist at Trieste (Cesca 1883, 12; Mallett & Hale 1984, 47); a small naval force also participates. See also Sanuto 1733, 1178; Scussa 1863, 94–95.

1463: 26 and 30 August
Senate provisions for military action against Trieste; arrangement for siege cannon, war galleys, disposition of *condottiere* under command of Vitale Lando, "our *provveditore.*" The rectors of Vicenza shall be instructed to send Carlo Fortebraccio there immediately (ASV, SS 20, fols. 180v, 182rv).

1463: 24 September
Senate instructs Jacopo Antonio Marcello, *luogotenente* of Friuli: when communication is received, he is to proceed as quickly as possible, with up to twenty horse, to Trieste (under Austrian control) and press the siege as best he can until reinforced by Carlo Fortebraccio: "quod recepto presenti nostro mandato equum ascendere debeat, . . . eundo quam citissime ad impresiam Tergestinam, operando et accellerando eam quo magis poterit, quousque Comes Carolus de Fortebrachiis illuc attigerit" (ASV, ST 5, fol. 51). Marcello's role at the siege of Trieste is noted by Anonimo Veronese 1915, 341; Cappellari, *Campidoglio,* 3:31; Malipiero 1843–44, 208; Navagero 1718, 723; Cesca 1883, passim; Mallett 1973, 144n91. Giorgio Bevilacqua's laudatory letter of 15 December on this subject is of little concrete use (see below, and Texts III.2).

1463: 27 September
Letter to Jacopo Antonio Marcello, *luogotenente* in Friuli, referring to letter of 24 September instructing him to depart immediately to the siege of Trieste. He is urged to do everything in his power to reduce the city to obedience: "quod civitas illa pertinacissima omnibus viis et modis possibilibus ad nostram obedientiam veniat, ac bellicis inquietationibus fortiter viriliterque expugnetur." Should the Triestines wish to negotiate to peace, he is to proceed cautiously and discreetly. If he must make some concessions, he is authorized to do so: "hoc in arbitrio vestro, quippe qui prudentissimus sitis relinquimus, faciundarum illarum honestarum, convenientiumque promissionum, que prudentie vestre videbuntur." The Senate has faith in his

ability to bring this city back under Venetian control: "Ut civitas illa in ditionem nostri dominii deveniat, quemadmodum de solita prudentia experientiaque vestra confidimus" (ASV, SS 20, fol. 190).

1463: October–November?
Composition of Carlo Fortebraccio da Montone's consolation to Jacopo Antonio Marcello, presumed from their association at Trieste (Texts II.C.7).

1463: 1 October (Padua)
Date of the consolatory letter to Jacopo Antonio Marcello by the Anonymous Student (see Texts II.C.14).

1463: 3 October
Letter from the Council of Ten to Jacopo Antonio Marcello *luogotenente patrie contra Tergestem*, responding to his of 29 September, with instructions to proceed, commending his diligence and sagacity, etc. (ASV, CX 16, fol. 100v). On the same day, a Senate letter to Marcello and Vitale Lando, *provveditori* "contra Tergestem," responding to Marcello's of 29 and 30 September and 1 October, and applauding their diligence in executing instructions. In order to succeed, you must completely seal off the city: "At quum ad obtinendum locum predictum, neccessarium iudicamus, quod quanto magis possibile sit, stringatur ex omni parte per modum, quod nullus succursus in eum ingredi possit, commemorandum vobis duximus, quod utile et necessarium esse tenemus, quod ex parte superiori tendente versus Forijulium fieri deberet una bastita, ponenda sub tali custodia quod omnino sublatus esset additus omnibus ingredi volentibus inter Tergestum." Reinforcements are on their way, and we have made arrangements for adequate provisioning of your troops (ASV, SS 21, 191, pub. Cesca 1883, 37–38).

1463: 19 October
Treaty drafted in Rome, allying Venice, Burgundy, and the Pope against the Turks.

1463: 24 October
Vitale Lando, with the army at Trieste, is wounded, and is to be replaced by Francesco Capello, who will join "our *provveditore* there" Jacopo Antonio Marcello (ASV, ST 5, fol. 57).

1463: 1 November (Udine)
Date of the Anonymous Tutor's *Perleone Supplement* (see Texts II.C.11).

1463: 3 November (Udine)
Date of the letter by Giorgio Bevilacqua introductory to his *Excusatio* in cod. V (fol. 6; see Texts II.C.15). The letter reveals that Bevilacqua, Mar-

cello's aide, has written the *Excusatio* as though it was written by his employer.

1463: 13 November, "ex foelicibus castris adversus Tergiestam"
Date of Giorgio Bevilacqua's *Excusatio* (presumably written by Jacopo Antonio Marcello, then *provveditore* with the army outside Trieste) (V, fol. 173; Texts II.C.15).

1463: 17 November
Upon intervention of Pope Pius II (previously bishop of Trieste, 1447–50), Venice grants Trieste harsh peace terms (Cesca 1883, 18–20; Tremoli 1983, 150).

1463: 4 December
Vitale Lando, Jacopo Antonio Marcello's colleague at siege of Trieste, has returned to Venice and is serving as *savio di terra ferma* (ASV, SM 7, fol. 140).

1463: 15 December
Date of Giorgio Bevilacqua's laudatory Latin letter to Jacopo Antonio Marcello on his role at the siege of Trieste (Texts III.2). Death of Jacopo Antonio Marcello follows after this date, probably by 21 March 1464, but possibly as late as July 1465 (Fam. II.B).

1463: 17 December
Truce between Austria and Venice, negotiated by the pope (Mallett & Hale 1984, 47). Ludovico Foscarini, Niccolò da Canal, Marco Donato, and Paolo Morosini are dispatched respectively to Rome, France, Burgundy, and Bohemia/Poland for the necessary negotiations regarding an allied offense against the Turks (Malipiero 1843, 22; for Foscarini's role esp., Degli Agostini 1752–54, 1:83–84; 96–97).

1463
Birth of Valerio II Marcello (Fam. I.A.19). Also death in the Morea of *condottiere* Bertoldo d'Este, in Venetian service since at least 1448, when his father Taddeo died (see below, 1464: March).

1463–1464
Giovanni Mario Filelfo removes from Bologna to Modena in 1463, returning to Milan in 1464 (Benadduci 1894, xxvii n20; Favre 1856, 98–102).

1464: March
Body of Bertoldo d'Este, mortally wounded at battle of Corinth during Morea campaign of 1463, brought to Venice, to be celebrated in an elaborate funeral with an oration delivered by humanist Bernardo Bembo (BMV,

cod. Lat. XI, 139 [4432], fols. 1v–32, followed by a consolation to Bertoldo's widow Giacoma da Leonessa at fols. 32–40; additional manuscripts in Giannetto 1985, 418, #3; see also Sanuto 1733, 1179; Mallett & Hale 1984, 46). Poems for his death by Bishop Pietro Barozzi (Contarini 1757, 213–17). Sigismondo Malatesta is sent to replace him.

1464: 21 March
Niccolò Marcello is sent to Friuli with title of *luogotenente* (ASV, CLN 10, fol. 96).

1464: 22 March
Death of Niccolò Sagundino (King 1986, 428).

1464: 11 July
Death at Modone during the Morea campaign of Orsato Giustiniani, Venetian *provveditore* and naval captain, according to Malipiero, "homo illustre, de grandezza d'animo e de richezze" (Malipiero 1843, 22). His body was back to Venice on 30 August. The citizen physician and humanist Giovanni Caldiera delivered his funeral oration in SS. Giovanni e Paolo, and the body was buried in tomb erected for him ("un arca bellissima marmarea") in Sant'Andrea di Lido (della Certosa) in the chapel constructed by his nephew Marino Giustiniani (Sanuto 1733, 1179–80; also Cicogna 1824–53, 4:629, dating the oration 4 August; King 1986, 61, 345; Vianoli 1680–1684, 662).

1464: 3 November
Francesco Filelfo asks Giovanni Diedo by letter if Jacopo Antonio Marcello had returned to Venice (Monfasani 1976, 176n203; Fabbri 1983, 246).

1465: 31 July
Luca da Leone, widow of Jacopo Antonio Marcello, presents their son Pietro and grandson Girolamo for ascription to the Balla d'Oro (Fam. I.A.13, 17, 26).

1466: 8 March
Death of Francesco Sforza, after imparting to his heirs the advice never to abandon the Venetian alliance: "lasciò per testamento a' figliuoli, che se voleano mantenersi in istato, mai non si partissero dalla benivolenza e dall'amore della Signoria di Venezia" (Sanuto 1733, 1177). Sabellico rated him thus: "se alcuno di questi che sono stati ai tempi nostri, per grandezza di animo, per felicità di fortuna, osse per alcun modo da essere comparato a Cesare Dittatore, lo Sforza veramente, ovvero niun altro, per mio giudizio merita di essere comparato a un tanto uomo" (cited by Cusin 1936, 5n2, from *Le historie venete* [Venice 1554], 196). Bianca Maria Visconti died the following 23 October (Toderini 1875, 122).

1466–1467 (Padua)

Ludovico Foscarini's letter to Giorgio Bevilacqua commenting on dedication to him of Bevilacqua's commentary on Cicero (Foscarini, *Epistolae,* #276, fol. 321rv; see Picotti 1909, 43).

1467–1468

Giovanni Mario Filelfo is teaching in Verona (Avesani 1984, 75–76; Cipolla 1954, 221; Favre 1856, 104–7).

1469: 2 December

Francesco Marcello presents his son Bernardo (grandson of Jacopo Antonio) to the Avogaria di Comun (Fam. I.A.14).

1471: 14 July

Testament of René d'Anjou orders once again the fulfillment of the wishes of Louis II, Louis III, and Giovanna II regarding throne of Naples, "quando erit in manibus nostris vel heredis nostris" (Lecoy 1875, 1:382n3).

1471: 12 September

Inventory of the furnishings of the knights of the Order of the Crescent held in the church of Saint Maurice in Angers in the care of the canons; among those for whom the *carreaux* (ceremonial cushions) are held are (in third place) the duke of Milan and (in fourth) "Messire Jacobo Antonio Marcello de Venise" (René d'Anjou 1845–46, 1:77; also Vale 1981, 58n133).

1473: 3 December

Pietro di Jacopo Loredan presents Andrea Marcello, son of Francesco and grandson of Jacopo Antonio, to the Avogaria di Comun (Fam. I.A.14).

1473–1474

Niccolò Marcello (of Santa Marina) is doge of Venice (see Fam. I.B.1; III.A.1).

1474: 2 December

Lorenzo, son of Jacopo Antonio, is presented to the Avogaria di Comun by Girolamo and Bernardino Marcello, grandsons of Jacopo Antonio (Fam. I.A.15).

1475

Editio princeps of F. Filelfo's *Consolatio* to Jacopo Antonio Marcello (Texts II.C.3).

1476

Death of Giovanni Cossa, "qui était la plus précieuse conquête faite en Italie par le roi René"; count of Troia in Naples, named grand seneschal of Provence by René and grand seneschal of Sicily by Jean d'Anjou in August

1460 (Lecoy 1875, 1:502). His tomb executed in Italian and notably secular style (Robin 1986, 168–69).

1479: 17 June
Death of Carlo Fortebraccio, one of Jacopo Antonio Marcello's consolers. Fortebraccio's son Bernardo succeeds to his father's Venetian appointment, and dies in turn in 1515, at the battle of Agnadello (Mallett 1979, 153; 1984, 194; also Anonimo Veronese 1915, 348; Argegni 1936, 1:405).

1480: 10 July
Death of René d'Anjou; buried in church of Saint Maurice, 18 August (Lecoy 1875, 1:426–27).

1480: October
Inventory presented to the chapter of St. Maurice of the goods of deceased knights deposited with the treasurer of the Order of the Crescent includes "un petit livret écrit sur velin, couvert de satin bleu, qui étoit un poeme latin, a la louange dudit Ordre, composé par Jacobo Antonio Marcello" (René d'Anjou 1845–46, 1:78).

1483
Marino Sanuto describes Monselice and the great house that had belonged to Jacopo Antonio Marcello in his *Itinerario della terraferma* (see chap. 3nn4, 5).

1483–1488
Equestrian monument of Colleoni by Andrea Verrocchio, erected in the Campo SS. Giovanni e Paolo, Venice.

1484
Death at battle of Gallipoli of Jacopo di Cristoforo Marcello, often confused with Jacopo Antonio Marcello (Fam. I.B.3)

1490: 18 May
Testament of Serena di Jacopo Antonio Marcello, widow of Francesco di Ludovico Loredan, naming children (Fam. I.A.23).

1493: 30 November
On the occasion of the marriage of Bianca Maria Sforza to Emperor Maximilian, Leondardo da Vinci's plaster model for the equestrian monument to Francesco Sforza is displayed in front of the Castello in Milan (Clausse 1909, 389).

1494: 12 January
Testament of Taddea di Jacopo Antonio Marcello, naming siblings by mother Fiordelise and Luca da Leone (Fam. I.A.23).

1497

Death of Michele Orsini (King 1986, 415).

1502

Leonardo da Vinci's wax model of a planned statue of Francesco Sforza is destroyed by French invaders (Portigliotti 1935, 178).

1509: 11 August

Venetian *condottiere* Tuzio Costanzo visits Marcello palace at Sant'Angelo (Fam. III.A.6).

1520

Marco and Valerio Marcello, sons of Jacopo Antonio Marcello, declare to the X Savi alle Decime that Monselice is uninhabitable.

1522?

Death of Lorenzo Marcello and Bernardino, son and (perhaps) grandson of Jacopo Antonio (Fam. I.A.15, 20, 21).

1527

Death of Cristoforo Marcello (of San Tomà), archbishop of Corfu, during sack of Rome (Fam. I.B.4).

After 1528

Death of Marco Marcello, son of Jacopo Antonio (Fam. I.A.20).

1529

Death of Pietro Marcello, son of Jacopo Antonio (Fam. I.A.18).

1531

Death of Valerio II Marcello, son of Jacopo Antonio (Fam. I.A.19).

1541

Publication of the Latin *De sacerdotio Christi* (second version) commissioned by Jacopo Antonio Marcello, together with dedicatory letter to René d'Anjou (Texts I.3).

1555: 1 December

Date of epitaphs for Jacopo Antonio and Pietro Marcello at San Cristoforo della Pace near Murano (Fam. III.C.3–6).

1588

Marcella di Pietro Marcello bestows on her son Ludovico all the possessions (including books) of her "camera" at Monselice (Barbantini 1940, 18).

1605

Antonius Olgiatus, first Ambrosian librarian (Milan) inscribes Michele Orsini's autograph *Opinio* (= cod. M), fol. 1v.

1676

Abbot Theodore Damadenus (Amaden) presents his eulogistic history and genealogy of the Marcello family to the nobleman Federico di Andrea Marcello. For the further history of this work, Fam. I.B.6.

1740

In Monselice, the *chiesetta* of Santa Lucia (adjoining the castello) is declared finished and open to the public by Vettore Antonio Alvise Marcello.

1753

Apostolo Zeno reports having seen the codex of Marcello consolations in a palace still belonging to that family (Texts I.15).

1767

Jacopo Morelli sees the codex of Marcello consolations in a Venetian bookshop (Texts I.15).

1768: 7 September

The Senate suppresses the order of regular canons of San Salvatore, occupying the ancient church and monastery of San Antonio Abate (da Vienna) (Da Mosto 1937–40, 2:125).

1776: 18 March

The codex of Marcello consolations are sold to Dr. William Hunter (Texts I.15).

1805: 8 June

Napoleon orders the destruction of church and monastery and even the island of San Cristoforo della Pace, the site to be joined to the island of San Michele da Murano and converted to a public cemetery (Fam. III.C.8).

1807: 7 December

Napoleon decrees the destruction of the church and buildings of San Antonio Abate (da Vienna) for the purpose of constructing the Public Gardens (Fam. III.B.5). In the same year, the codex of Marcello consolations passes to the University of Glasgow, its present location (Texts I.16).

1810

Castello of Monselice passes out of Marcello family ownership.

1841

At a meeting of a learned society of archeologists in Angers, there is discussed the renovation of the tomb of René d'Anjou, so utterly mutilated during the Revolution that from its parts local laborers could redecorate their cottages: "réduit en débris informes et jeté pêle-mêle sous les portiques du temple, jusqu'au moment où d'ignorants ouvriers, autorisés à s'en emparer, en formèrent des consoles, des cheminées et des vases grossiers" (René d'Anjou 1845–46, 1:cliii).

1935
The Castello of Monselice, having passed to the ownership of Count Vittorio Cini, is restored.

1972
Vittorio Cini donates the Castello of Monselice to the Cini Fondazione created by him in memory of his son Giorgio.

Texts

ᘓ

I. WORKS BY JACOPO ANTONIO MARCELLO
OR COMPILED AT HIS DIRECTION

1. The following are the works composed at the direction of Jacopo Antonio Marcello, in chronological order. Meiss 1957, 32 and 89n7, refers also
to other manuscripts sent by Marcello to René d'Anjou, French claimant
of the Neapolitan throne, possibly with dedicatory letters: (1) a manuscript
of Pomponius Laelius, *De arte grammatica;* (2) a manuscript of Quintilian
based on that recovered by Poggio.

1452: 5 April (Venice)
2. *De sacerdotio Jesu Christi,* Greek text (from Pseudo-Suidas) and Latin
translation (by Lauro Quirini), with prefatory letter to René by Marcello.
Rome, cod. Corsin. 839 (43 D 8), fols. 78–80. See Mercati 1939, 1:70–85;
also Meiss 1957, 89n8; *Le roi René* 1986, 126. Text of Marcello's introductory letter in Mercati 1939, 1:81–82; also Manetti 1986, 131–32. The
month and day are given in the manuscript. The year was inferred (by Mercati) from the reference made by Marcello to a new duty about to be assumed. This could be the provveditorial mission in which Marcello appears
by 28 April 1452 (see Chron.). Some time before the preparation and transmission of the manuscript, Marcello had commissioned Quirini to prepare
the translation and had sent him the Greek text. Marcello could have been
in Venice briefly, as the manuscript indicates, early in April, in between his
missions to Crema and to Gentile da Leonessa (see Chron. 1452: 28 April).
Lauro Quirini left Venice permanently for Crete soon after his work on
this volume (King 1986, 419). An earlier version of Quirini's translation as
addressed to Pope Nicholas V was published by Mittarelli 1779, cols. 982–
85. For the dedication to Pope Nicholas, see Kristeller, introduction to
Branca 1977a, 29; also Segarizzi 1904, 15–16. The Paduan university student Jacopo Lulmeo sent to the bishop of Bergamo, Giovanni Barozzi, the
texts of Marcello's letter and Quirini's translation, but with all names
changed on 28 April [1452] (Mercati 1939, 1:73, 82).

1452: April–May

3.   *De sacerdotio Jesu Christi*, second version, Greek and Latin texts (translator unknown, but described as "vir sane doctus et mihi perfamiliaris"), with prefatory letter by Marcello to René. See Mercati 1939, 1:73–74, 77, and n2; *Le roi René* 1986, 127. Published 1541 [Basel? Robert Winter?] (not seen); for which Mercati 1:78, 80.

1453: after 28 February

4.   Consolatory letter to King René on death of Isabelle of Lorraine, presumed lost. See Lecoy 1875, 2:182; Mercati 1939, 1:77 and n2, 82, 84; also Manetti 1986, 132.

1453: March–May

5.   Greek text and translation of Chrysostom's first homily *De statuis (De tollerandis calamitatibus)* prepared in March by an anonymous translator ("homo doctus et mihi perfamiliaris") at Marcello's direction. BAV, cod. Vat. Lat. 5145; Padua, Museo Civico, cod. CM 525, pt. 5. See Manetti 1986, 127; *Iter* 1:21, 2:331; Mercati 1939, 1:22ff., 77n2, 82–83. Chrysostom's work (previously also translated in an unrelated version by Ambrogio Traversari) in Migne, PG 49:15–34. Marcello composes dedicatory letter to René possibly in May, for which see Meiss 1957, 32 and 89n8; Mercati 1939, 1:82–83, with text at 84–85; text also pub. Manetti 1986, 132–33. The manuscript never received the illuminated initials planned, and was probably never sent.

1453: 1 June

6.   Latin *Life* of Saint Maurice, with prefatory letter, illuminations, and other items. Paris, Bibliothèque de l'Arsenal, cod. 940. See Martin 1898, 229–52; Meiss 1957, 2–17, 79–80; Vale 1981, 53–54. Marcello's letter to Cossa (fols. 1–5) and verses to René (fols. 35–37v) separately published by Martin 1898, 258–64. The letter to Cossa closes (at fol. 5): "Valete feliciter, vestri memores Iacobi Antonii Marcelli ex felicissimis castris D. D. Venetiarum, post captum Quintianum et Pontemvicum. Kal. junii. MCCCCLIII." The manuscript reached Cossa, and was inventoried among the possessions of the Order of the Crescent in the keeping of the canons of St. Maurice in Angers: "un petit livret écrit sur velin, couvert de satin bleu, qui étoit un poeme latin, a la louange dudit Ordre, composé par Jacobo Antonio Marcello, vénisien nommé cy dessus entre les Chevaliers . . . a l'entrée duquel livre l'on voyoit une forte exelente enlumineure la représentation de la chapelle des Chevaliers du Croissant telle que nous la voyons encore, et autour les seances des Chevaliers en leurs hatiz" (René d'Anjou 1845–46, 1:78); and again in 1505 (Meiss 1957, 15). Maurice,

patron saint of the Order of the Crescent, was martyred under Emperor Maximian with his companions of the Theban Legion at Sion-en-Valais in Gaul (France) on September 22, the obligatory assembly day of the Order (O'Connell 1962, 207).

7. Illuminations of the assembly (facing fol. 1, where the letter to Cossa begins), St. Maurice (fol. 34v facing fol. 35, where the verse to René begins), the portrait with coded message (fol. 38v), the elephant riddle (fol. 39); also decorative initials (containing miniature inset portraits of Marcello) at fols. 1 and 35. For the cryptogram (fol. 38v), Martin 1898, 243ff. For the identity of the illuminator see in addition to Meiss (who is the principal proponent of a Mantegna attribution), also Alexander 1977, 53–60 (who follows Robertson, below); Covi 1958; Fabbri 1983, 229–30n8; Goffen 1989, 106 and 282ff.; Lightbown 1986, 494–95 (who disputes the Mantegna attributions); Mariani Canova 1969, 14–16 (whose attribution is to an "Anonymous Venetian"); Robertson 1968 (who proposes Giovanni Bellini), 17–21, 28, 50. The arguments of Joost-Gaugier 1979 (November) for the Strabo illuminations (see below, I.9) are also relevant here. Reviewing the arguments of her predecessors Giuseppe Fiocco and Lino Moretti, writing in the same journal in 1958 (who propose attributions to, respectively, Marco Zoppo and Leonardo Bellini), she disputes the authorship of Mantegna and others and claims the miniatures for Giovanni Bellini. Eisler accepts that attribution for the St. Maurice illuminations as well as the later Strabo ones (Eisler 1989, 535–36). (Thanks to Dr. Rona Goffen, Dr. Christiane L. Joost-Gaugier, Dr. Cynthia Pyle, and Dr. Joanna Woods-Marsden for assistance with this matter.)

1457: 1 March (Monselice)
8. Ptolemy, *Cosmographia* [*Geographia*], Latin translation by George of Trebizond, with a *mappamondo* obtained by Marcello from Onofrio di Palla Strozzi, and Marcello's dedicatory letter (of 1 March) to René d'Anjou. Paris, Bibliothèque Nationale, cod. Lat. 17542; illuminated. The whole was prepared by Marcello while resident at Monselice, prompted by René's agent Ludovico Martelli of Florence (not Marcello; an error in De Mérindol 1987, 185); see Lecoy 1875, 2:194, for the king's interest in geography. Marcello's letter (fol. 1rv) is separately published by Martin 1898, 264–66; announced as published but does not appear in Manetti 1986; see 127, 133. See also Diller & Kristeller 1971, 226; *Iter* 3:266b; Lecoy 1875, 2:181; Meiss 1957, 30–32 and 88nn3,4. The letter is dated "ex Monte silicae prima martii mcccclvii." The illuminated initial is perhaps by a Mantegna assistant (Meiss 1957, 91n7), but this claim is disputable by the same

arguments offered against the Mantegna attributions for the Maurice volume. *Pace* Meiss, Marcello did not at this or any other time hold the pode-
stariate of Padua. For Trebizond, who had sent his contribution to Marcello
with his own dedicatory letter, see Monfasani 1976, 175–76n201. See E.
Bevilacqua 1980, 359, for a 1436 *mappamondo* according to Ptolemy prepared by Andrea Bianco, a Venetian collaborator of the famed cartographer
Fra Mauro Lapi: a generation earlier, Bianco's is considered "precocious."
For Ptolemy and the *mappamondo* tradition in the Renaissance, see esp.
Edgerton 1987.

1459: 13 September (Padua)

9.　Strabo, *Geography*, translated by Guarino Veronese, with dedicatory letters of Guarino to Pope Nicholas V and Jacopo Antonio Marcello and of
Marcello to René d'Anjou. Guarino's original autograph (probably completed 13 July 1458) is in Oxford, the Bodleian Library, cod. Canon. Lat.
301 (Summ. Cat. 18882). The illuminated presentation copy (completed
13 September 1459) is in Albi, Bibliothèque Municipale, MS 77 (formerly
Bibliothèque Rochegude, MS 4). For other manuscript versions, see Diller
1975, 129. See in general Diller 1975, 126–29; Diller and Kristeller 1971,
225–26; Fabbri 1983, 229n8; Giorgi 1742, 286ff.; Meiss 1957, chap. 2
and 81; Sabbadini 1964, *Vita,* 164–65, and *Scuola,* 126–30; Sabbadini in
Guarino 1915–19, 3:483–87. Illuminations (on fols. 3v and 4 respectively
of the Albi manuscript) depict Marcello receiving the volume from Guarino and René receiving it from Marcello; for their authorship (probably
Giovanni Bellini), see the discussion pertaining to the Saint Maurice manuscript, I.7 above. The illuminated initials (two in Mariani Canova 1969,
figs. 6 and 7), very early exemplars of the style sometimes called "littera
mantiniana" which later became typical for Venetian Renaissance manuscripts, strongly resemble the later initials of the Glasgow manuscript (see
below, I.12–16).

10. The text of Guarino's letters to Nicholas V and to Marcello are in Guarino 1915–19, 2:627–29 and 629–34 respectively (see also Berchet 1893,
for text of Guarino's letter to Marcello). The text of Marcello's letter to
René in Sabbadini 1909, 13–15, reprinted in Manetti 1986, 133–35. The
dedicatory letters appear in several manuscript versions. Guarino Veronese
began the Strabo translation commissioned by Pope Nicholas V in 1453.
Hard at work on the project in the spring of 1454, when Pannonius referred
to it in his panegyric of the scholar (Thomson 1988, 8, lines 731–33), he
had not quite completed the tenth book when that pope died on 25 March
1455 (Guarino 1915–19, 2:629, 3:487; Diller 1975, 126; Diller & Kris-

teller 1971, 2:225–33; also Meiss 1957, 32 and 89n9; *Le roi René* 1986, 127). Jacopo Antonio Marcello took over patronage of the project, which Guarino completed and dedicated to Marcello on 13 July 1458 (Guarino 1915–19, 2:629–34 and 3:484; also Berchet 1893; Diller & Kristeller 1971, 225–26; Meiss 1957, 33 and 89n10). Marcello had the final manuscript transcribed and illuminated and dedicated to René d'Anjou on 13 September 1459 (Sabbadini 1909, esp. 13–15).

11. The contemporary biographer Vespasiano da Bisticci described the series of events (da Bisticci 1970, 1:588–89): "Pregato di poi da papa Nicola, ch'egli traducessi Istrabone De situ orbis, et perchè gli era diviso in tre parti, l'Asia, l'Africa et l'Europa, gli dava per la sua fatica d'ogni parte cinquecento fiorini. Tradussene due, inanziche il pontefice morissi, et ebbene ducati mille. Morto papa Nicola, tradusse la terza parte, et voleva mandarla a qualche uomo, che gli donassi premio della sua fatica, perchè avendo più figliuolil e non molte sustanze, bisognava che si valessi colla sua fatica. Cercato in Firenze di mandarlo a uno de' principali di quegli tempi, trovandolo non disposto a dargli nulla de la sua fatica, la mandò a uno gentile uomo viniciano, che ebbe grandissimo animo a sodisfallo della sua fatica. Avutolo il viniziano, gli fece uno proemio et mandollo al re Rinieri." Francesco Sforza was meanwhile supporting Gregorio Tifernate's attempt to complete (never realized) his own translation of Strabo, begun in Rome for the same Pope Nicholas V when Guarino's translation appeared to that pontiff to be too slow in production (Guarino 1915–19, 3:485–87; Mancini 1923, 79–80, 86–87; Torrioli 1927, 38). On 22 September 1456, the duke of Milan wrote Ludovico Gonzaga, Marquis of Mantua, to borrow a Greek manuscript for Tifernate's use, but it was unavailable—perhaps already in Guarino's hands. A rare incunabulum (H *15087) edited by Raffaele Zovenzoni and dedicated to Jacopo Zeno was published in Venice in 1472 by Vindelino de Spira, containing both Guarino's and Tifernate's translations (Berchet 1893, 13n1; Bertalot & Campana 1975, 318; Mancini 1923, 79–80; Sabbadini 1909, 11). Zovenzoni's prefatory letter ("In absolutionem Strabonis inchoati proemium alterum") tells the whole story.

1463: after 13 November (Udine)
12. *Consolations for Jacopo Antonio Marcello* to René d'Anjou. Glasgow University, Hunterian Museum Library, MS 201 (U.1.5) = G. See for the manuscript and the following notes: Ker 1983, esp. 8–9 and 15, #XVII; *Sotheby* 1972 (with thanks to Sandra Sider); Thorp 1987, esp. 169; and Young and Aitken 1908, 142–43 (#201); also *Iter*, 4:28; Fabbri 1983, 231; Babinger 1962. Special gratitude is owed to Timothy D. Hobbs, P. D. Es-

creet, and Nigel Thorp (respectively Keeper of Special Collections, former Keeper, and Assistant Keeper, Glasgow University Library) for their enthusiastic and unstinting assistance; and also to John Monfasani for his meticulous reading and good advice. For list of contents, see below, section II.C.

13. A handsome parchment codex (366 × 245 mm.), well preserved, of 213 folios paginated as 426, 40 lines per page, bearing the title *De obitu Valerii Marcelli Nicolae Secundini et aliorum.* Written in an elegant hand, similar to that of the Albi Strabo (above, I.9–10). Frontispiece, marred by damp, in brilliant color, with blue background and gilt embellishment. Marcello arms (gold wave on blue background) in bottom border, and in the side borders portrait vignettes (left) of a boy (Valerio?) listening to a man with lion (Saint Mark?) reading (right), executed in penwork on gold background (Thorp 1987, 169).

14. Thereafter, component works open with 15 initials in fine classical style: "Exquisitely painted epigraphic capitals are set against a variety of colored backgrounds, including violet, mauve, grey and black, but also blue, red and green in a less funereal register. They contain delicate studies of flowers, animals, butterflies, figures, jewels, and other objects" (Thorp 1987, 169). Thorp concludes, on the basis of their advanced Renaissance style, that these were supplied no earlier than the 1480s, probably by Marcello's heirs; but Mariani Canova (1969, 18) identifies the closely related initials of the Strabo manuscript of 1458–59 as early examples of the Venetian Renaissance "littera mantiniana." Initials appear at pp. 1, 26, 38, 127, 130 [2], 134, 141, 161, 163, 175, 179, 189, 241, 269. Spaces left blank at 249, 295, 309 (a whole page) for illuminated initials and openings, never supplied; thus titles and incipits are missing at these pages. Marginals supplied pp. 1–241, 269–85, 309–42. Dates are given for six works: Filelfo's *Consolatio,* Mascarello's first letter, the Anonymous Tutor's *Perleone Supplement,* the letters of the Anonymous Venetian and Anonymous Student, and Bevilacqua's *Excusatio* (pp. 126, 162, 248, 268, 308, and 426). Dates for other works (as indicated in II.C below) and the identity of the author of the *Excusatio* are known from other manuscripts or editions only. A typewritten note from the bookbinders D. Cockerell & Son, dated November 1967 and pasted to the inside rear cover (alongside scraps of the original binding), describes the condition of the original manuscript to that year, when the book was cleaned, resewn and rebound.

15. The manuscript was seen by Apostolo Zeno as late as 1753 in the library of the Marcello family palace (A. Zeno 1752–53, 1:297), and by Jacopo Morelli in 1767 in a Venetian bookshop (Morelli 1889, 170ff.). In

the first edition of Morelli's work (Bassano 1800; not seen by me but cited most recently by Fabbri 1983, 231n11), he notes other of the consolatory works for Marcello existing outside of this volume, including Carbone's elegy, Pannonius's verse, the Grifo translation of Filelfo's Greek elegy, and Tifernate's epigram (see below II.D). From Venice the manuscript passed to the collection of Caesar de Missy, a German scholar of the New Testament and classical languages who served in England as chaplain to King George III. Following de Missy's death, his library was purchased entire on 18 March 1776 by the Scots physician and bibliophile William Hunter, known by contemporaries as a collector of coins, medals, shells, minerals, and the like, as well as books, as the physician to Queen Charlotte, and as the author of the gynecological work *The Anatomy of the Human Gravid Uterus* (1774). The Marcello consolations were part of Lot #1662 in the sale catalogue of auctioneers Baker and Leigh held on 18 March of that year (according to Ker 1983, 15, #XVII) or Lot #1664 (according to the Sotheby Catalogue of Sales 1972, part 1, reel 6; Sotheby absorbed the Baker and Leigh records).

16. Hunter died in 1783, having bequeathed his library to his nephew, to pass subsequently to Glasgow University, as it did in 1807. The Hunter library is the core of the present-day Special Collections at Glasgow, which includes some 650 manuscripts and 1,000 incunabula and ranks as one of the major British collections. The Marcello consolations were first noted in library catalogues from the 1830s, and fully described (but corrected here) by the 1908 catalogue begun by Young and continued by Aitken, cited.

II. CONSOLATORY WORKS TO JACOPO ANTONIO MARCELLO FOR THE DEATH OF VALERIO

Section A lists manuscripts and editions containing consolatory works. Section B is an alphabetical index (by author) of the twenty-three works by nineteen authors comprising the corpus of consolatory works; following each title is a number referring to the order in which those works are presented in sections C and D. Section C describes more fully the works contained in the Glasgow manuscript (G), and section D those works in our corpus that are not in G.

A. Principal Manuscript and Printed Sources

B   Berlin, Deutsche Staatsbibliothek, Stiftung Preussische Kulturbesitz, cod. Lat. qu. 557, fols. 3–108v. Formerly Phillipps 1019. See *Iter* 3:490b.

BMV 3727   Cod. Lat. X, 107 (3727). Owned by Marino Sanuto; see *Iter* 2:231.

BMV 4392   Cod. Lat. XII, 144 (4392). Mbr. XV, coat of arms. See *Iter* 2:258–59.

BMV 4451   Cod. Lat. XII, 137 (4451), containing *Opera* of Ludovico Carbone. From collection of Jacopo Morelli. cart. XV. See *Iter* 2:258.

BMV 4502   Cod. Lat. XIV, 266 (4502). Misc. XV, partly in the hand of Marino Sanuto.

BMV 4683   Cod. Lat. XIV, 246 (4683). Misc. XVI. See *Iter* 2:249.

F   Ferrara, Biblioteca Comunale Ariostea, cod. II, 135, fols. 85–119. See *Iter* 1:57–58. Related to G (Monfasani 1984, 236), but an inferior miscellany, compiled later, possibly originating in the circle of Ferrarese humanists that included Carbone and Guarini.

G   Glasgow University, Hunterian Museum Library, MS 201 (U.1.5). See I.12–16 above and II.C below for description.

M   Milan, Biblioteca Ambrosiana, cod. H 122 inf., fols. 2–28. Autograph of Michele Orsini. *Iter* 1:325.

MU   Munich, cod. Lat. Mon. 362. Misc. 1467. Fols. 1–142 and 151 written by Hartmann Schedel. *Catalogus codicorum latinorum monacensis,* rev. ed., 1.1 (Munich: sumptibus Bibliothecae Regiae, 1892), 94–95.

V   Verona, Bibl. Civica, cod. 1472 (Biadego #224). G. Biadego, *Catalogo descrittivo dei manoscritti della Biblioteca Comunale di Verona* (Verona: Stabilimento tipografico G. Civelli, 1892), 147.

VatF   BAV, cod. Vat. Lat. 1790, fols. 3–154v (autograph), dated 17 kalends decembris (15 November) 1462. Later than G, a rededication of the *Consolatio* to Ottaviano Ubaldini della Carda. *Codices latini vaticani,* ed. Bartholomeus Nogara, 3 (Rome: Typis polyglottis vaticanis, 1912), 267; see Fabbri 1983, 237.

VatP   BAV, cod. Vat. Chis. J VII, 215. Misc. XV. *Iter* 2:484.

VatS   BAV, cod. Vat. Ottob. Lat. 1732, fols. 1–13. See *Iter* 2:432; Mastrodimitris 1970, 145.

Abel   Nogarola, Isotta. *Opera quae supersunt omnia.* Ed. Eugenius Abel. 2 vols.; Vienna-Budapest: apud Gerold et socios, 1886.

Ben.   Giovanni Benadduci. *A Jacopo Antonio Marcello patrizio veneto parte di orazione consolatoria ed elegia di Francesco Filelfo e lettera di Giovanni Mario Filelfo.* Nozze Marcello-Giustiniani (31 January 1891). Tolentino: Stabilimento tipografico Francesco Filelfo, 1894.

Mon.   John Monfasani, ed. *Collectanea Trapezuntiana: Texts, Documents, and Bibliographies of George of Trebizond.* Binghamton, N.Y.: Medieval and Renaissance Texts and Studies, 1984: 235–48.

B. Index of Works

Anonymous Student [= Anon. Stu.], consolatory letter (14)

Anonymous Tutor [= Anon. Tut.], conclusion to Perleone *Laudatio* [= *Perleone Supplement*] (11)

Anonymous Venetian [= Anon. Ven.], consolatory letter (12)

Bevilacqua, Giorgio, da Lazise, *Excusatio adversus consolatores in obitu Valerii filii* (15)

Carbone, Ludovico, *Carmen . . . in consolationem de obitu . . . filioli sui Valerii* (Latin elegy) (16)

Carbone, Ludovico, translation of Francesco Filelfo's Greek elegy (5)

Filelfo, Francesco, *De obitu Valerii filii consolatio* (3)

Filelfo, Francesco, *Ad Iacobum Antonium Marcellum equitem aureum nomine Francisci Sfortzie Mediolanensium ducis consolatio de obitu Valerii filii* (Latin elegy) (17)

Filelfo, Francesco, Greek elegy (4)

Filelfo, Giovanni Mario, *Consolatio marcellina* (18)

Fortebraccio, Carlo, da Montone, *De obitu Valerii filii consolatio* (7)

George of Trebizond, consolatory letter (2)

Grifo, Leonardo, translation of Francesco Filelfo's Greek elegy (19)

Guarini, Battista, consolatory letter (9)

Mascarello, Montorio, dedicatory letter, *Dialogus consolatorius,* and consolatory letter (8)

Nogarola, Isotta, *Ad Jacopum Antonium Marcellum eius dulcissimi filii . . . in obitu consolatoria* (6)

Orsini, Michele, *Francisci Philelphi opinio de summa venetorum origine . . . improbata* (13)

Pannonius, Janus, *Epitaphium Valerii Marcelli,* and other consolatory
works (20)

Perleone, Pietro, *Laudatio in Valerium eius filium eximium* (10)

Perleone, Pietro, consolatory letter (21)

Sagundino, Niccolò, *De obitu Valerii filii consolatio* (1)

Strozzi, Tito Vespasiano, consolation (22)

Tifernate, Gregorio, *Oratio . . . de obitu Valerii filii,* with epigram (23)

C. Works Appearing in G

1. (pages 1–25)
    Sagundino, Niccolò. *De obitu Valerii filii consolatio.* INC.: Nec inepti
    nec incivilis omnino animi puto. DATE: Venice, January 1461 ["Ex
    Veneciis die . . . Ian. Ianuarii MCCCCLXI"] (F, fol. 105v); 1461
    (Mastrodimitris 1970, 145). OTHER MANUSCRIPTS: F, fols. 92–
    105v; VatS, fols. 1–13. COMMENTS: The date given by F is also sup-
    ported by Sagundino's reference to his own shipwreck and tragic loss
    (of July 1460; see Chron.) as having occurred "not long before" (G,
    3). VatS is very close to G, and could be its source.

2. (pages 25–38)
    George of Trebizond. Consolatory letter. INC.: Sepenumero, Iacobe
    Antoni Marcelle, ab aliis. DATE: Venice, 7 April 1461 (Mon.)
    OTHER MANUSCRIPTS AND EDITIONS: Mon., 235–48; additional
    ms. versions there cited, including F, fols. 85–91v, which the editor
    considers to be the best witness after G, and closely related to it.

3. (pages 38–126)
    Filelfo, Francesco. *De obitu Valerii filii consolatio.* INC.: Cupienti
    mihi aliquid ad te scribere. DATE: [Milan] 25 December 1461 (G,
    126; VatF, fol. 158; Filelfo 1496, fol. 44v). OTHER MANUSCRIPTS
    AND EDITIONS: Many manuscript versions (for some of which con-
    sult *Iter,* indices), including VatF, an autograph later than the text in
    G, prefaced by a letter (dated Milan, 15 November 1462; INC.: Se-
    rius respondi ad tuam epistolam) rededicating the work to Ottaviano
    Ubaldini della Carda (for whom Fabbri 1983, 237n35). Also several
    printings in the fifteenth and sixteenth centuries, beginning with au-
    tonomous edition(s) of 1475 (Rome), H12960 and 1476 (Milan),
    H12961; the corrected text in Filelfo 1496 (H12925), fols. [29]–44v
    used here. Partially printed (passage at G, 109–19) in Ben. 1–15.
    See ibid., xxvi n12; Fabbri 1983, 233n21 and ff.; McClure 1991,
    104–6, 109–11.

4. (pages 127–29)
   Filelfo, Francesco. Greek elegy. DATE: [1462] OTHER MANU-
   SCRIPTS AND EDITIONS: Fabbri 1983, 243–45; also many ms. versions, including VatF, fols. 155–58; and other printed editions.
   Translated by Ludovico Carbone (see below) and Leonardo Grifo (see
   section D, below). See Fabbri 1983; D. Robin 1991, 223, *Psychagogia*
   3.3; D. Robin 1984, 198 and n73.

5. (pages 130–33)
   Carbone, Ludovico. Translation of F. Filelfo's Greek elegy, with introductory epigram (at 130). INC.: O decus eximium; Valerium
   puerum nimis, O Iacobe, videris. DATE: [1462]. OTHER MANU-
   SCRIPTS: BMV 4451, fols. 16–18v; BMV 4683, fols. 139–41; BAV,
   cod. Lat. 8914 (see *Iter* 2:346); BAV, cod. Ottob. Lat. 1153, fols.
   226–28v (see *Iter* 2:427); and others, sometimes with verse preface
   to Ludovico Casella; see Fabbri 1983, 233ff. COMMENTS: Written
   at request of Duke Borso d'Este of Ferrara (G, 130: "compulit id
   facerem divi clementia Borsi / qui te ob virtutem miro est complexus
   amore"; IN MARGIN: Borsius dux Mutine).

6. (pages 133–41)
   Nogarola, Isotta. *Ad Jacopum Antonium Marcellum eius dulcissimi filii
   . . . in obitu consolatoria.* INC.: Memini me apud Plutarchum legisse.
   DATE: Verona, 9 August 1461 (Abel, 2:178). OTHER MANU-
   SCRIPTS AND EDITIONS: Abel, 2:161–78, who uses F, fols. 115–19
   as sole text.

7. (pages 141–60)
   Fortebraccio, Carlo, da Montone. *De obitu Valerii filii consolatio.*
   INC.: Non nihil mi forte tibi admirationis allaturum supicor. DATE:
   [1463: October–November] (inferred from reference to Trieste siege;
   see Chron.).

8. (pages 161–79)
   Mascarello, Montorio. Three consolatory works: 161–62, letter
   (INC.: Cum te audierim atque conspexerim; DATE: Venice, 1 February [G, 162]); 162–74, *Dialogus consolatorius* (INC.: Audivi te Marcelle clarissime); 175–79, consolatory letter.

9. (pages 179–88)
   Guarini, Battista. Consolatory letter. INC.: Apud Euripidem trag-
   icum haud ignobilem. DATE: Ferrara [no year] (F, fol. 114v). OTHER
   MANUSCRIPTS AND EDITIONS: F, fols. 109v–114v; Rome, Bibl.

Naz. Centrale Vittorio Emanuele II, cod. Varia 10 (619), fol. 360
(barely legible, not seen; see *Iter,* 2:360).

10.   (pages 189–241)
       Perleone, Pietro. *Laudatio in Valerium eius filium eximium.* INC.:
       Saepe mecum ipse considerans; and p. 241, Solunt plerimque pict-
       ores et ii qui celant. DATE: [after 1 September 1461]; see below.
       OTHER MANUSCRIPTS: B. COMMENTS: Dated by the author's ref-
       erence to the death five months before of Marcello's daughter Taddea
       (on 1 April): G, 191 (text in Fam. IV.18). He may have continued
       working on the *Laudatio* until his final illness and death, which oc-
       curred after 13 June 1462 but before 22 April 1463 (see Chron.).
       The work is unfinished, ending abruptly at G, 241. That Perleone
       died before the work could be completed is learned from the opening
       of the *Perleone Supplement* by the Anonymous Tutor, who reports
       that Perleone "acerbis interceptus fatis opusculo suo non ut optabat
       extremam manum imposuit." The writer will assume the mission of
       the dead man (G, 241). See item 11, following. Manuscript B is
       closely related to G, and may be its source, perhaps the author's auto-
       graph. At B, fol. 108v in a hand other than the scribe's is found this
       comment: "Haec laudatio imperfecta est, morte enim preventus fra-
       ter, eam absolvere non valuit." The hand may be that of Perleone's
       brother Jacopo, as G. N. Knauer will suggest in his study of Pietro's
       translation of the pseudo-Plutarchan *Vita Homeris* (with thanks to
       Prof. Knauer for his personal communications and kind provision of
       his typescript). If so (and if it is not a comment about another
       "brother" or friar who was the scribe), the statement confirms that
       death prevented Perleone from completing the *Laudatio.*

11.   (pages 241–48)
       Anonymous Tutor [= Anon. Tut.]. *Perleone Supplement.* INC.: So-
       lunt plerimque pictores et ii qui celant. DATE: Udine, 1 November
       1463 (G, 248). COMMENTS: Written by Valerio's tutor, closely re-
       lated to Perleone (see above, item 10). The date could be that of tran-
       scription rather than of composition, which could have been under-
       taken at any point after Perleone's death.

12.   (pages 249–68)
       Anonymous Venetian [= Anon. Ven.]. Consolatory letter. INC.:
       none; initial page blank for illuminated initial, title, and opening.
       DATE: Venice, 15 July 1463 (G, 268). COMMENT: The author is
       unknown to us because of the page left blank (and in the absence

of another manuscript witness), but was presumably known to the compiler. He is a resident or native of Venice.

13. (pages 269–94)

Orsini, Michele. *Francisci Philelphi opinio de summa venetorum origine . . . improbata.* INC.: Facit optima conciliatrix amicitie virtus. DATE: Venice, San Antonio Vienensis, 26 August 1462, but actually composed in May 1462 (as the colophon of M, written by Orsini, "manu propria," indicates; fol. 28). OTHER MANUSCRIPTS: M. COMMENTS: M is closely related to G, and is probably, as the author's own manuscript, its source. Antonius Olgiatus, first Ambrosian librarian, inscribed the work in 1605 (fol. 1v).

14. (pages 295–308)

Anonymous Student [= Anon. Stu.]. Consolatory letter. INC.: none; initial page blank for illuminated initial, title, and opening. DATE: Padua, 1 October 1463 (G, 308). COMMENT: The author is unknown to us because of the page left blank (and in the absence of another manuscript witness), but was presumably known to the compiler. He is a student or professor at Padua.

15. (pages 309–426)

Bevilacqua, Giorgio, da Lazise. *Excusatio adversus consolatores in obitu Valerii filii.* INC.: Expectaveram, dive rex et princeps serenissime (V, 7); none in G, as opening page is left blank for illuminated initial, title, and opening. DATE: Siege of Trieste, 13 November 1463 (G, 426; V, 173), in name of Jacopo Antonio Marcello, to René d'Anjou. COLOPHON at G, 426 in gilt and color: Vale dive rex ex foelicibus castris adversus Tergestum {V, Tergiestam} idibus November MCCCCLXIII. OTHER MANUSCRIPTS: V, fols. 7–173, with letter of Udine, 3 November 1463 (not in G; V, fol. 6), fols. 4–6. COMMENT: V is probably the author's autograph and the source for G, which relates to it closely but freely modifies word order. In G, the appearance is given that Marcello is the author from the blank initial page and the claims of the text itself. Bevilacqua's identity as author is established from the letter uniquely appearing in V at fols. 4–6. Not only is the telltale letter omitted from G, but also a sensitive passage discussing suicide as a remedy for grief (V, fols. 162v–171v).

D. Consolatory Works Not Appearing in G

16. Carbone, Ludovico. *Carmen in decus et laudem magnifici et illustris viri equitisque splendidissimi Jacobi Antonii Marcelli patricii veneti et*

in consolationem de obitu dulcissimi filioli sui Valerii. INC.: Imperii quondam multas rerumque potitus. Verse preface, INC.: Ite mei versus Venetum properetis ad urbem. DATE: Ferrara [1462]. MANU-SCRIPTS: BMV 4451, fols. 16–30v; BMV 4683, fols. 126–38; Berlin, Deutsche Bibliothek, cod. Hamilton 492, fols. 60–70v (not seen; see *Iter* 3:366a). See also Fabbri 1983, 235n28. In some cases headed by four-line verse of Tito Vespasiano Strozzi. Written at the request of Borso d'Este (BMV 4683, fol. 126).

17.   Filelfo, Francesco. *Ad Iacobum Antonium Marcellum equitem aureum nomine Francisci Sfortzie Mediolanensium ducis consolatio de obitu Valerii filii* (Latin elegy). DATE: [1461, written before the *Consolatio* of 25 December of that year; to the contrary, Fabbri 1983, 238]. EDI-TION: Ben., 17–23, and manuscripts there cited; also Fabbri 1983, 233ff.

18.   Filelfo, Giovanni Mario. *Consolatio marcellina* (so named by the author in his *Letter:* Benadducci 1894, 26). Presumed lost; see Benadducci 1894, pp. xx–xxi, xxvii n18, 25–26. Possibly written before Filelfo left Venice in 1461; see Chron. 1461: 8 September. Probably in verse.

19.   Grifo, Leonardo. Translation of Francesco Filelfo's Greek elegy. DATE: [1462]. MANUSCRIPTS: BMV 4683, fols. 142–44. See Fabbri 1983, 233ff.

20.   Pannonius, Janus. *Epitaphium Valerii Marcelli,* in Pannonius 1784, 1:519 (epigram #137); Pannonius 1985, 148–49 (#163). Other works consoling Marcello are believed to be lost: see Birnbaum 1981, 89 and 94n39.

21.   Perleone, Pietro. Consolatory letter. DATE: before September 1461, as it predates *Laudatio* begun at that time. INC.: Etsi calamitas . . . MANUSCRIPTS: F, fols. 106–109; MU, fols. 94–100 (fol. 95 lacking); VatP, fols. 103–106v; BMV 4502, fols. 218–22; also Padua, Bibl. del Seminario, cod. 126, not seen (see *Iter,* 2:9). COMMENTS: The Vatican and Munich manuscripts are closely related. The latter was written by Hartmann Schedel in Nuremburg, 1467 (see fol. 100).

22.   Strozzi, Tito Vespasiano. Consolation, apparently lost. See Carbone, *Carmen,* BMV 4683, fol. 137v (text in chap. 2n155).

23.   Tifernate, Gregorio. *Oratio . . . de obitu Valerii filii.* DATE: [probably 1461]. MANUSCRIPTS: Vicenza, Biblioteca Comunale Bertoliana,

cod. 7.1.31 (formerly 6.7.31), fols. 126v–131 (with epigram to Valerio on 131rv), for which *Iter,* 2:302 and Mazzatinti 1891–, 2:73–74n472; also Trent, Biblioteca Capitolare, cod. s. n. (temp. #258), unnumbered fols., for which *Iter,* 2:189; not seen. The epigram appears in several other manuscripts, and in an edition of the works of Decimus Magnus Ausonius of 7 December 1472, Venice (catalogue numbers GW 3090; BMC 5:211; IGI 1:144, #1097).

III. OTHER WORKS WRITTEN TO OR ABOUT JACOPO ANTONIO MARCELLO

1. Bevilacqua, Giorgio, da Lazise. *De bello gallico,* to Marco Donato. Florence: Bibl. Laurentiana, cos. Ashb. 292; Verona, Biblioteca Capitolare, cod. CCLXXXVI; BAV, cod. Vat. Lat. 5264. See *Iter* 1:84; 2:294, 332, 579; Avesani 1984, 64n2; Abel 1:cix–cx, n33.

2. Bevilacqua, Giorgio, da Lazise. Laudatory Latin letter (dated Udine, 15 December 1463 at fol. 47v) to Jacopo Antonio Marcello on his heroic role at the siege of Trieste. Autograph ms. British Museum, cod. Harl. 2640, fols. 1–47v, with Italian letter (of transmittal, dated 20 December 1463) at fols. 48–51.

3. Carrara, Giovanni Michele Alberto. *De bello Jacobi Antonii Marcelli in Italia gesto.* In G. B. Contarini 1757, 309–28. See Fabbri 1983, 229–31 and n9; G. Giraldi 1955, 127–28; A. Zeno 1752–53, 2:27–31.

4. Filelfo, Francesco. *Letters* to Jacopo Antonio (Milan, 14 May 1460; Milan, 27 June 1461). Filelfo 1502, xvi: fols. 116, 116bis.

5. Filelfo, Giovanni Mario. *Letters* (Modena, 9 May 1463; Verona, 7 September [1464?]). Both in BAV, cod. Vat. Chis. J.VIII.241, respectively fols. 123v–24v, 124v–25v. For the former, see Benadduci 1894, xx–xxi, text published at 25–26. This letter mentions *Satire* composed against Galeotto Marzio da Narni in defense of the author's father Filelfo, dedicated to Marcello; location not known to me.

6. George of Trebizond. Commentary on Ptolemy, *Cosmography,* with dedicatory letter [1460–62]. Oxford, Bodleian Library, cod. Laud lat. 111, not seen. Text of letter in Monfasani 1984, 248–51; see Monfasani 1976, 175–76n201. See also above, I.8.

7. George of Trebizond. *Comparatio Platonis et Aristotelis,* to Jacopo Antonio Marcello. Text of letter in Monfasani 1984, 251. Berlin,

Staatsbibliothek, Stift. Preussische Kulturbesitz, cod. lat. qu. 541, not seen. See Monfasani 1976, 175–76 and n201; *Iter* 3:490b.

8. Pannonius, Janus. *Panegyricus, ad Iacobum Antonium Marcellum Venetum,* in Pannonius 1784, 1:59–210; the *Carmen de itineribus C. Antonii Marcelli Veneti* (Pannonius 1580, 643–54; not seen) is excerpted from the *Panegyricus* for Marcello. Also Epigrams ##36, 79, 159, 209, 339, and 340 in Pannonius 1784 at 1:473–74, 495, 519, 551, 611 (= ##74, 110, 177, 214, 317, and 318 in Pannonius 1985, at 104–5, 124–25, 156–57, 170–71, 220–21): of these, the first and fifth bear distinctive titles, respectively the *Comparatio Marcellorum, Veneti et Romani,* and the *De versibus Marcelli a se latine expressis.* An additional ten-line poem for Marcello (*De Marcelli tropheo*) is published in Abel 1880, 125. Also dedicated to Marcello is a *Panegyricus in Renatum,* written in celebration of René's 1453 campaign (published by Abel 1880, 131–44). The *Carmen pro pacanda Italia, ad Imperatorem Caesarem Fridericum III* (Pannonius 1784, 1:211–31) is dedicated to René, having been commissioned by Marcello.

9. Rondo, Pietro. Letter to Jacopo Antonio Marcello, 1 December 1439 (Brescia). BMV cod. Lat. XIV, 267 (4344), fol. 48v. The miscellaneous manuscript was written by Marino Sanuto, who chose carefully to preserve this unusual letter.

10. Spretus, Desiderius. *De amplitudine, devastatione et instauratione urbis Ravennae,* to Jacopo Antonio Marcello. BMV 3727, preferred to editions of 4 September 1489: Impressum Venetiis per Matheum Capcasam Parmensem; and 1793–1796: ed. Camillo Spreti. Spretus's account repeated verbatim by Girolamo Rossi (Hieronymus Rubeus 1589, 626–28).

11. Traversari, Ambrogio. Translation of Chrysostom, *De consolatione ad Stagirium,* to Jacopo Antonio Marcello. See Mercati 1939, 1:83.

12. Vallaresso, Maffeo. *Letter* to Jacopo Antonio Marcello (Padua, 15 April 1460). *Epistolae,* 427–28.

13. Zovenzoni, Raffaele. Verses, from the *Istrias.* Manuscripts in Milan, Biblioteca Trivulziana (cod. 776), the dedication copy to Johann Hinderbach (Santoro 1958, 307; *Iter* 1:363); and Venice, BMV 4392, dedicated first to the Emperor Frederick III, who refused it; then Pietro Loredan (Ziliotto 1950, 21ff., 47; Tremoli 1983, esp. 162).

IV. FORM OF CITATION OF TEXTS IN NOTES

For excerpts of texts in G, G is the text normally presented (with its particular orthography). In three cases (the editions of Abel, Ben., and Mon.), the readings of the modern edition has been preferred to G. Manuscripts or editions collated with G are identified by their abbreviations as given above, section II.B. In the case of alternate manuscript versions, the reading is eclectic. Variants are shown thus: {F tibi}; {VatS tacendum}. Full title, date, and other manuscripts or editions available for each work (as available) are given above, section II.C–D.

Notes

ӿ

PROLOGUE

1. Mead, "Theoretical Setting—1954," in Mead & Wolfenstein 1955, 3.

CHAPTER ONE

1. For Valerio's birth and death, Fam. II.C–D; for the family palace, Fam. III.A.5–7.

2. Anon. Tut. G, 247; text in n118 below.

3. Bevilacqua, G, 379 (V, fol. 99): "Atque reliquum vitae tempus miserum mihi perpetuo sit illatum, et quanto mors isti foelicitatem aeternam et beatitudinem attulerit paradisi, tanto me pernicie affecerit sempiterna, et dum vita superfuerit, languore {G ac} diuturniori putrescam."

4. Chron. 1462: 12 October – 1463: 15 December.

5. For the consolatory works, see Texts IIC.1–15; see Texts I.12–16 for the codex in which they appear. For other collections, see Fabbri 1983, 232–33 and nn17–20 and sources there cited; also Kristeller 1956, 419–20 and n27; McClure 1991, 133–41. Fabbri counts thirteen such collections, apart from that for Marcello. Earlier collections for the ruler of Ferrara Niccolò d'Este (who died in 1442) or the humanists Gianpietro (d'Avenza) da Lucca (dead in 1457) and Poggio Bracciolini (dead in 1459) consisted of a scattering of verse and miscellaneous documents. Later collections, boasting works in a variety of genres and languages (Italian, Latin, Greek) include those for the rulers Pope Pius II (dead in 1462) and Cosimo de' Medici (dead in 1464; for it A. M. Brown 1961; A. M. Brown 1979, 40–41, 269–70), and to Federigo Montefeltro of Urbino for his duchess, Battista Sforza (dead in 1472). The genre culminates in another century and nation in the outpouring of literary tributes to Henry, Prince of Wales, son of King James I of England, who died in 1612 (Strong 1986).

6. Fam. III.A.1–4, esp. A.2.

7. Chron. at 1449: 24 and 25 September, 8 November; 1450: 21 and 23 January, 3 March; and following references until 1452: 10 April.

8. Perleone, G, 217–18 (B, fols. 59v–60): "Ad hanc autem bonam corporis habitudinem atque vivacitatem in filiis procreandam multum conferre utriusque parentis continentiam et temperiem quandam valitudinis et medici et philosophi tradiderunt. Sed de continentia parentum Valerii hoc loco taceamus, quam semper moderatam constantemque fuisse constat. Temperamentum vero Marcelli quo tempore genuit Valerium, ut ex etate et vita, et valitudine, et colore, et habitu, et dignitate ac maiestate corporis coniecturis, argumentisque colligere possumus, illud certe fuit quod a phisicis medium iustum et equatum appellatur."

9. Bevilacqua, G, 335 (V, fol. 41v): "Sic ego demum crediderim, quod ubi mater ex me viro filium hunc concipiebat, non formam aut figuram humanam aliquam contemplaretur, e qua similitudinem duceret, sed in ipsius mente species pulchritudinis eximia quaedam et singularis insidebat."

10. Bevilacqua, G, 330 (V, fol. 34v): "Verum antea quam infantem natum esse mihi nunciatum esset, O quot, quanta, quam diversa somnia, cum in cubiculo cubans solus obdormirem, nasciturum mihi marem filium elegantissima forma et omni virtutum genere refertissimum praedixere!"

11. Perleone, G, 211 (B, fol. 46): "Itaque ut a tempore quo puer in lucem est editus capiamus initium. Militie parenti re bene ac feliciter gesta nuntius allatus est, natum esse Valerium; quod ut in maxima rerum gestarum gloria illi iucundum et letum fuisse non dubito, sic certe infanti felicissimum prestantissimarum rerum omen arbitramur."

12. Fam. II.D, IV.21.b.

13. F. Filelfo, G, 41 (ed. fol. [29v]); for text see Fam. IV.24.

14. F. Filelfo, G, 41 (ed. fol. [29v]): "Recte enim qui supra aetatis rationem plurimum esset valiturus et ingenio et probitate, Valerius nominatur." See also Orsini, G, 286 (M, fol. 19); Anon. Ven., G, 255.

15. Bevilacqua, G, 330–31 (V, fol. 35v): "Quo ubi applicui, adventui meo Valerius filius adhuc inter crepundia obvolutus mihi oblatus est, quem ubi inter ulnas ad osculum accipio, quem que ut fieri solet, ad novum adventum meum evagire putassem, video istum mihi arridentem, et quo ad ei potis est, risu gestientem. Hunc ego conspiciens primo sum admiratus, qui tum eum illum esse cernerem, quem mihi tociens nocturnae quietes ostenderant, quem tociens in somniis fueram amplexatus, de quo mihi sonnia tam mirabiliter enunciarant. Pueri membra contemplor: frontem, oculos, nasum, ora, et faciem totam fixus admirar {G admiror}."

16. George, G, 27 (Mon. #6); for text see Fam. IV.26. See also text for Sagundino, G, 5 (F, fol.94; VatS, fol.2v) at Fam. IV.25; F. Filelfo, G, 41–42 (ed. fol. [29v]) at Fam. IV.24; Fortebraccio, G, 144, at Fam. IV.27; Guarini, G, 180 (F, fol. 110) at Fam. IV.28; text for Perleone, G, 212 (B,

fols. 47v–48) at Fam. IV.29; Bevilacqua, G, 330–31 (V, fols. 34v, 35v), at Fam. IV.23.b.

17. Surely an allusion in these events to *Iliad* 6.466–81.

18. F. Filelfo, G, 42 (ed. fol. [29v]): "Nunquam molestum se praestabat, sed horis per intervallum quasi constitutis lac modice capiebat, quo et corpusculum scite in proceritatem alebatur, et quoniam nulla esset praeter debitam stomachi concoctionem ei superfluitas, erat cute pernitida ac tersa, nullisque neque digestionis sordibus, nec alia purgatione naturae aut nimius aut gravis."

19. Anon. Ven., G, 251: "Illustrarem puerum et tuo sanguine et tibi similem virtutis imagine natum." Anon. Stu., G, 298: "Quamobrem tantopere admirandum non est si aliquam etiam maximam animi cordisque tristiciam accepisti ex huius filii cui accerbissimo obitu quem sicut prae caeteris diligebas, ita et in omnibus tibi simillimum videbatur, ipsa natura formasse, et a multis vera Iacobi Antonii Marcelli nuncupabatur imago: sic enim oculos, sic ille manus sic ora ferebat." Fortebraccio, G, 144–45: "Illud quoque non pretermittendum arbitror quod a natura ipsa nec frustra constitutum est, aptissimam videlicet membrorum eius proportionem insignemque et corporis et stature, proceritatem facile, tue simillimam, quod si in quoquam laudi unquam fuit in Valerio tuo magnopere extollendum."

20. Bevilacqua, G, 331 (V, fol. 36v): "Crescebat hic infans in pueriles annos tam formosus tam honesta liberalique facie decorus, tam venusta pulcritudine spectabilis, ut quemvis in tam compositae formae admiracionem excitasset." Similar comments by Fortebraccio, G, 145; George, G, 29 (Mon. #12); Orsini, G, 286 (M, fol. 19); Perleone, G, 220, 221.

21. An extended discussion of beauty follows in Bevilacqua, G, 331–34 (V, fols. 36v–39). The passage on the beauty of Jesus Christ is an inserted passage (in the original hand) in V at fol. 39; G omits it.

22. The feature-by-feature survey in Bevilacqua, G, 334–35 (V, fols. 39v–41v).

23. The discussion of Valerio's development of speech here and below: Bevilacqua, G, 344–45 (V, fols. 53–54).

24. Bevilacqua, G, 345 (V, fol. 54): "Nam in eo fuit semper summa verborum comitas, et incorrupta quaedam sermonis integritas, vocis suavitas atque dulcedo."

25. Hercules is noted as an example of precocious youth by Bevilacqua, G, 330, 351 (V, fols. 34, 61v); George, G, 26 (Mon. #2); Perleone, G, 213, 214, 216 (B, fols. 49–59). Bevilacqua also notes, among others, Cicero (G, 324; V, fol. 26v), Theseus and Themistocles (G, 357; V, fol. 68). George further notes Alexander and Marcellus, son of Octavia (G, 26;

Mon. ##2, 3); for Marcellus as an ancestor of the Venetian Marcello family, see Fam. I.B.9. Perleone further notes Midas and Plato, Erichthonius, and Moses (G, 213–16; B, fols. 49–59).

26. Anon. Ven., G, 253: "Erat . . . corpus praeter aetatem valida membrorum magnitudine, robore, firmitate, agilitate, mirabili quadam disposicione contextum; fulgebat in senili puero matura, gravis et libera frons."

27. Anon. Ven., G, 257: "Hoc more Valerius . . . cunctis in rebus virtute excesserat annos."

28. Guarini, G, 182 (F, fol. 110v): "Verbis supra aetatem prudentiam redolentibus et voluptatem et admirationem sepenumero concitabat." Sagundino, G, 4 (F, fol. 93rv; VatS, fol. 2): "Ubi lusus et cursationes et studia, multo sensatiora quam ut annis puerilibus conveniret?"

29. Perleone, G, 233 (B, fol. 91v): "Quid de acumine ad excogitandum et industria ad efficiendum dicam? que non modo illi pro etate fuerunt, sed etiam haud scio an tanta in eo supra etatem tamque admiranda fuerint."

30. Bevilacqua, G, 351 (V, fol. 61v): "Afficiebar totus iocunditate . . . in filio eiusmodi aetatis plani contemplarer, ut quod alii vel inviti virtutibus obsequi solent, qui vix nisi parentum reverentia vel praeceptorum moetu illis dari se paciuntur, hic sine ullo duce rectam per se viam ad virtutes et inire et tenere potuerit."

31. Nogarola, G, 138 (Abel, 2:171): "Summa ratione, magnitudine animi, moderatione, prudentia, eloquentia supra aetatem praeditus, ut omnibus quibus cognitus erat tanquam novum quoddam inauditumque miraculum videretur." Also Perleone, G, 220 (B, fol. 64rv): "Quid dicemus de Valerio nostro . . . qui . . . preter eius etatis rationem, et ceterorum infantium consueteudinem atque naturam, imagine patris et constantissimi quidem ac optimi patris oblata usque adeo in illam oculos et mentem et animum intenderit. . . . Certe fateamur necesse est aut aliquid magnum et excellens in eo infante latuisse aut divinam potestatem aliquid plusquam humanum in illo expressisse, neque enim sine magno Dei numine maxima signa in rebus humanis suam naturam excedentibus proveniunt."

32. F. Filelfo, G, 42–43 (ed. fol. 30): "In dies augescebat in Valerio cum sensu corporis mentis intelligentia, quam innata quedam prudentia que perite senectutis est propria, miro quodam incremento comitabatur. . . . Erat enim insatiabili quadam aliquid semper discendi cupiditate, eoque mentis acie ferebatur, ut aliquid boni quottidie supra annos, supra naturam assequeretur."

33. Orsini, G, 286 (M, fol. 19): "Et enim virilis puer corporis firmitate animique fidentia nunquam ociosus, velut sese maturioribus annis toler-

ando labori ad veram laudem prepararet." Perleone, G, 234 (B, fol. 95rv): "Valerius puer in puerili corpore virilem animum, virile robur, virile consilium gerens, . . . supra etatem . . . posset ceteros omnes viribus consilio atque ratione incredibili cum gloria superare."

34. Perleone, G, 220–221 (B, fols. 65v–66v): "Fuit Valerius iam usque ab infantia preter forme venustatem, magnitudine corporis atque membrorum adeo preter ceteros id etatis eximia, ut omnes admirati iudicarent illum nisi longo interiecto tempore pedibus non ingressurum. Verum ipsius rei vim atque naturam infantis generositate vincente, domi ludentes pueros Valerius spectans usque adeo gestu ac nixu corporis ad illorum congressum incendebatur, ut ludi miro desiderio et amore liquescere. Interdum etiam et animo deficere videretur. Itaque nondum expleto anno ingens illa generosi animi natura prius tulit corpus in ludos. . . . Atque preter omnium opinionem puer ipse per se nullo adminiculo ingrediens in aula cum ceteris ea contentione nitebatur, ut vix a mane ad vesperam posset in sinum a nutrice revocari, et quod maius visum est cum incredibili omnium admiratione expeditius et rectius fari cepit, quamque tertium aut quartum annum nati ante fuissent. Iam inde a teneris annis ostendens non dediturum se otio atque desidie corrumpendum, sed quantum illi roboris fuisset a natura tributum, tantum illud firmius redditurum studio exercitationeque fuisse." See also Mascarello, G, 178: "Nam cum haberet membra pro illa etate ingentia et ob hec putaretur non posse illum pedum plantis insistere donec biennium complevisset, tantus erat in puero ardor spiritus ac magnitudo animi tanta ut cum reliquos pueros ambulare cerneret, ac loqui audiret, ambulare cepit et loqui, hoc aperte testatur habuisse Valerium inatam animi magnitudine ac spiritus ardorem ingentem."

35. Bevilacqua, G, 350 (V, fol. 60): "Praestabat praeterea morum composicione, comitate, humanitate, benignitate, mansuetudine, adeo ut mirabile dictu sit, quam non modo sibi aequales, sed etiam natu maiores ad se diligendum, ad se amandum pellicere studeret."

36. Fortebraccio, G, 144; for text see Fam. IV.12.

37. Anon. Tut., G, 243: "Erat (ut nosti), Iacobe Antoni, natus ille tuus inter caeteros in schola patricios, ut inter minora sydera sol aureus cuius crinis in lacteam fluens cervicem radiabat. Oculi graves et venusti, regium supercilium, gene labella purpurea, totum denique corpus illud eburneum Veneris Iovem aut Cupidinem efingebat. Tanta vero membris alacritas inerat, tantum robur, tanta velocitas, ut in palestris in cursu semper victor evaderet. Quid in litterarum gymnasio? Sudabat interdum adiscendi fervore, cum caeteros condiscipulos hyems exagitaret. Adsidebat una Laurentius maximus frater natu minor, quem modo blandiciis, minis aliquando,

nonnunquam et crustulis et muscaciis alliciebat ut disceret. . . . Quare tanta mox benivolentia puerorum mentes allexerat ut eum omnis veneraretur ut dominum, observaret ut patrem, coleret ut animam. Exoriebantur saepenumero lites inter eos de pilla, de carceribus, de meta. Statim hic veluti dictator eas dirrimebat."

38. Perleone, G, 221 (B, fol. 68): "Atque prima illa infantis educatione pretermissa, que . . . eiusmodi nutrici commissa que proba et sobria et patriis moribus instituta etatulam illam fovere et alere, et ad incrementum maximi viri effingere rite posset." See also Bevilacqua, G, 346 (V, fol. 55v): "Immo cum magni interesse scirem quoquisque infans {V lacte,} quam puro, quam sincero {G lacte} enutriatur; et a qua frugi muliere, quos audiat domi cottidie, quibus cum loquatur a puero, quemadmodum patres, pedagogi, matres etiam loquantur."

39. Perleone, G, 225 (B, fol. 75v): "His igitur disciplinis et artibus iam usque ab infantia Valerius est institutus, hec maxima et latissima benevivendi in eo fundamenta sunt iacta, his documentis ad virtutem puerilis animus est informatus, ut aut tacendo que ceteri loquerentur audiret, aut loquendo et pauca et vera proferret, maxima profecto et firmissima non pueritie modo, sed omnium etiam etatum ornamenta et magnarum virtutum argumenta." The argument continues through G, 226 (B, fol. 78).

40. Bevilacqua, G, 348 (V, fol. 57v): "Plurimum enim interesse putavi semper a quo puer in tenera aetate doceatur, cum quo etiam sit consuetudo familiaritasque vivendi. Quando quae teneris mentibus fuerint infusa, ita insidere, ita radices immitere solita sint, ut si ea delere, melioraque super inducere volveris, non magis id coneris quam scriptores, qui non tam errores suos emendare possunt, ut non priorum vestigia semper appareant. Adeo inhaerere solent, et propter aetatis moliciem profunde inustam indelibilia esse, quae his annis puerorum mentibus imprimuntur."

41. Perleone, G, 226 (B, fol. 78v): "Raro enim vel nunquam fere accidit ut pernitioso puer aut adolescens ingenio sponte ac diligenter bonarum artium studia complectatur, nisi forte coactus et cesus. . . ."

42. Perleone, G, 226 (B, fols. 77v–78): "Nam cum multa et varia sint instituta et artes quibus genus humanum excultum atque illustratum videamus, nihil tamen rerum omnium humanarum excepta virtute, vel utilitate commodius, vel dignitate prestantius, vel firmitudine diuturnius est, quam excellentissima litterarum studia, quorum ea precipua et maxima iudicanda sunt que in eloquentia sapientie iuncta versantur. Hec enim in dubiis rebus consilium, in secunda fortuna ornamentum, in adversa presidium, in utraque maximarum rerum usum atque cognitionem prebent. Hec excol-

unt animum, ingenium acuunt, mentem erigunt, ac bono viro iter ad honorem et gloriam maxima sapienti post virtutem premia sternunt, {B atque ita sternunt,} ut non modo in civilibus officiis integre casteque versetur, sed illo etiam tamquam per gradus quosdam extructos ascendat, ubi virtus ac vite integritas, et religio et vera sapientia queritur."

43.   Bevilacqua, G, 347 (V, fol. 56v): "Consideranti mihi tamen quantum ad laudem {G ad} percipiendam colendamque virtutem litteris, ad quarum studium se homines {G iuvenes} contulissent adiuvarentur, et nihil filio deesset {G deesse potest} quin virtutibus omnibus conspicuus et omni ex parte perfectus illustraretur, {G mihi} visum est exquisitos illi conducere praeceptores a quibus bonas artes ab incunabulis institutus reddi."

44.   Perleone, G, 228 (B, fols. 81v–82): "Atque facere non possum quin hoc loco quantum Iacobi Antonii Marcelli diligentiam atque prudentiam admiror, tantum eorum parentum negligentiam . . . despiciam, qui cum in agro colendo, insternendis equis, in edificiis extruendis, in gubernanda navi, ceteris humilioribus officiis, eos deligere et magna mercede conducere soleant, qui eius artis peritissimi habeantur. In hoc autem maximo erudiendorum filiorum munere, ita incautos et negligentes atque socordes esse cognoscamus, ut sine ullo delectu cuicunque indocto atque insulso puerorum ingenia tractanda et formanda committant."

45.   Perleone, G, 228 (B, fol. 82v): "nihil perniciosius ingeniis esse imperito doctore, qui falsam et perversam sibi scientie persuasionem arrogans, stulticiam suam {B suam stulticiam} non veram doctrinam perdoceat."

46.   Anon. Tut., G, 242: "Quippe qui sextum vix agens annum primis litterarum elementis mihi traditur imbuendis, nec a meo latere prius quam a vita discessit. Verum enimvero liceat hic mihi paulo repetere longius observantiam simul et illum incredibilem suae pietatis ardorem quo me puer amplexus extuabat, et adeo extuabat, ut hilaris ipse me tristem nunquam aut hilarem tristis aspexit."

47.   Sagundino, G, 5 (F, fol. 94; VatS, fol. 3): "qua reverentia et veneratione preceptorem prosequeretur . . . explicari vix posset."

48.   Anon. Tut., G, 242: "Atque tu natum desyderas, dulcem ego discipulum; tu complexus recordaris et oscula, ego suavitatem et observantiam. Te maxima rerum gestarum gloria vivens illustrasset, me vero sua dicendi copia cunctis saeculis immortalitate donasset. Uter igitur iure nunc accusandus est, si cruciatur, si squalore capillum et barbam obducat, et atrato palliolo tectus domi tabescat in tenebris."

49.   Guarini, G, 181 (F, fol. 110v): "Tamen cum ad litterarium ludum se conferebat, tanta in eo modestia vigebat ut nihil minus quam militiam

optare, nihil magis quam bonarum artium studia affectare videretur, in eo quippe aderant omnia que ad consummandum oratorem postulari consueverunt."

50.　Bevilacqua, G, 349 (V, fol. 59v): "Cupiditate igitur discendi ita flagrabat, ita studiis incumbebat, ita haec litterarum bonarum rudimenta percipiebat, ut nullum disciplinarum genus esset, quod non ille {G ille non} sibi cognitum esse cuperet."

51.　F. Filelfo, G, 43 (ed. fol. 30): "Erat enim insatiabili quadam aliquid semper discendi cupiditate."

52.　Anon. Ven., G, 255: "quod in illa aetate mirabile visum est, somnum laborem inediamque contemnens, latinis et grecis litteris capescendis enixe operam dabat."

53.　Bevilacqua, G, 350 (V, fol. 60): "Adeo nihil inutiliter perire sibi cupiebat, ut vel horas quae apud caeteros esse ociosae solitae sunt, non nisi negocio virtuoso distribueret."

54.　Orsini, G, 286 (M, fol. 19): "Et cum illum aliquando sudorem somnum inediam contempnentem increparet illustris pater diceretque, Valerii, quando quiesces? Morte vel nocte, pater, ad hoc unum data mox respondisse cognovi."

55.　Sagundino, G, 6 (F, fol. 94v; VatS, fol. 3): "Ego vero ut primum convaluero, admonitis tuis parebo, nec me tantopere amplius ludendi studio dedam."

56.　F. Filelfo, G, 43 (ed. fol. 30): "Cum enim a matre quandoque increparetur, ut est ingenium muliebre erga filios indulgentius, ne tantam operam litteris daret, fieri enim posse, ut nimia animi cura in adversam valitudinem incideret, vix tandem ab eiusmodi studio tantisper dum mater aderat, veluti avulsus, tamquam ob {ed. ab} intelligendi ratione ad actionem se convertebat."

57.　Bevilacqua, G, 349 (V, fol. 59): "Quando id scire non videmur, quod non memoriter scimus, aut non facile reminisci possimus. Nec ullum est excellens hominis donum cercius, quam memoria, quae cuncta tenacissime servat."

58.　Fortebraccio, G, 145: "Eminebat . . . in eo . . . singularis memoria, ut quicquid a te pro eius etate seu a preceptoribus esse oblatum, seu ab aliis acceptum aut visum, captu mentis id tenacissime conservaret."

59.　Anon. Ven., G, 255: "omnia percepta diligentissimus puer tanta memoriae tenacitate servabat ut et longa poemata recensere, et multa secundo aetatis anno vix levi cognitione libata, octavo veluti proximo visa per singula posset memorando referre." Orsini, G, 287 (M, fol. 20): "Erat illi memoria tenax ita ut multa incunabulis fere visa, octavo anno velut ante oculos posita recenseret."

60. Guarini, G, 181 (F, fol. 110v): "Vox iocunda et clara, oris suavitas, pronuntiationis venustas gravitati coniuncta, in utraque lingua tanquam ad id natus esset litterarum omnium facilis expressio."

61. Perleone G, 227–28 (B, fol. 81): "Cum autem non nunquam hec bona in preclaris etiam ingeniis sine perito doctore corrumpantur, optimus ac diligentissimus pater . . . virum utraque lingua doctissimum domi conduxit."

62. Anon. Ven., G, 255; see n52 above.

63. Orsini, G, 287 (M, fol. 20): "Latinis tamen et grecis litteris cappescendis tempus omne a patre vel preceptore dictum tanta cura servabat ut nullo momento a lectione cessaret."

64. Bevilacqua, G, 354 (V, fol. 65): "Rerum omnium curiosus erat; scire conabatur, quod ei aetas denegaverat."

65. Perleone, G, 232 (B, fol. 90rv): "Agitabatur enim spiritus ille generosus incredibili quadam cupiditate semper aliquid discendi, investigandi, perscrutandi, non solum que preclara et admiranda intueretur, sed que etiam minima et usu trito communia essent, rationem eorum, vel a parente, vel a maioribus natu diligenter exquirens. Namque naves sepe ac triremes et biremes aliasque diversas navigiorum speties conspicatus, ita studiose querebat et quibus illa vocabulis appellarentur et rudentum atque armamentorum omnium nomina, et que ministeria nautarum, et ars in navigando gubernandoque esset, ut sepenumero earum rerum peritissimis eius ingenium admirantibus ratio in respondendo non suppeteret."

66. Perleone, G, 232 (B, fols. 90v–91): "Quid canes venaticas, aut generosos equos aspitiens, quam curiositatem adhibeat {G adhibebat} ut signa perciperet que spem portenderent illorum virtutis et animi celeritatisque future? quantum denique cognoscendi studium erat, que illorum esset alendorum cura, qui ve domandi equitandi, atque moderandi modus et ratio, quibus ad bellum, ac ceteros usus essent idonei? Age vero cum hospites, et amicos paternos ex continente Venetias ad patrem venientem {B venientes} modeste ac verecunde accepisset. Data loquendi occasione incredibile dictu est qua diligentia ab illis quereret urbium magnitudinem, situs locorum, numerum civium, mores patrios, et quid queque regio egregium et preclarum ferret."

67. F. Filelfo, G, 44 (ed. fol. 30): "Frequentabant, ut quottidie solent, innumerabiles prope viri amplissimas edes tuas, alii tui salutandi, alii negotii sui causa {ed. gratia}, quibus ille si forte aberas, confestim fiebat obviam

alacer ac letus. Quidnam vellent, sciscitabatur acuratissime atque permodeste, seque omnia patri cum primum revertisset domum renunciaturum pollicebatur. Et ita cuiusque intellecta adventus causa, neminem dimmittebat quem sibi non antea reddidisset singulari affectum benivolentia, cum aliis opera, aliis verbo, voluntate et diligentia omnibus inserviturum se ostenderet. Quotiens domum redires, occurrebat ad ianuam, teque reverenter salutato, dextram blandius apprehensam osculabatur, et quam fortunate respublica, et quam belle ipse haberes querere nunquam omittens; eaque deinceps addebat, que te merito in stuporem adducerent. Erant enim omnia prudentis senis non pueri verba."

68. Orsini, G, 287 (M, fol. 20): "Nam cum apud illustrem patrem quosdam Senatores audivisset pretoris a se creati socordiam exprobrare, absentibus illis oportune dixit ineptas querelas eorum qui damnant opera sua, quoniam se non illa damnare merito dici possint." Also Anon. Ven., G, 255: "Ex innumeris illud dum (si recte animo servas) is domi apud te clarissimos senatores varia de re publice diserentes, uniusque pretoris a se creati socordiam exprobrantis intelligens, clam illis ad te conversus, Cur pater, inquit (da veniam quaeso), tantis rebus perfecistis ignavum? aut cur ille recipiendo magis quam vos indigna tribuendo peccavit?"; and Perleone G, 224 (B, fol. 74rv): "Cum multi gravissimi senatores domum salutatum {G Iacobum Antonium Marcellum} venissent . . . in sermonem tandem inciderunt, quales eos deceat esse viros qui rem publicam gererent, quos cum vario sermone descripsissent, unus ex his occasionem nactus eo gravius se ferre inquit, quod maximum nescio quis gereret magistratum, qui longe ab eo esset alienus viro, quem suis sententiis ostendissent, atque propterea minus dignum cui eiusmodi provintia committeretur. Iam domo profectis senatoribus, parenti Valerius admirari se inquit, cum minus ille tante rei esset idoneus, cur talem ei civitas dignitatem detulisset?"

69. Orsini, G, 287 (M, fol. 20rv): "Unicum ex innumeris sed a me perceptum inditium memorabo. . . . Nam . . . cum viris etiam studiosissimis abdita, diligentissime rogaret quid esset celum, quid sol et luna, quid sidera, et cuius opera vel imperio moverentur, doctis responsis . . . haud facile sedens non minus ingenio quam puerili corpore luctabatur."

70. Perleone, G, 231 (B, fol. 88v): "Ita enim commode atque decore vel oppidorum oppugnationes, vel montes navibus superatos, vel pugnas et victorias suo ordine gestas pronuntiabat, ut non narrare sed gerere, non audivisse sed presens omnibus illis rebus adfuisse videretur." The reference to "mountains overcome by ships" can be no other event than the hauling of a Venetian fleet over Alpine foothills to Lake Garda, a deed attributed to Marcello, and discussed at greater length in chapters 3 and 4.

71. Bevilacqua, G, 357 (V, fol. 69): "Instabat ille, quo pacto, quibus auctoribus, inter has aquas, inter lacunas civitas nostra fundamenta iecisset, declararem; quaque audacia tam amplissimarum domorum et regiarum basilicarum moles in tam limosis paludibus struere fabricareque suaserit; an imperium rei publicae nostrae eo ritu quo nunc gubernatur a principio coepisset, an {G atque} unquam mutacio aliqua hunc regendi modum intercoepisset."

72. Bevilacqua, G, 350 (V, fols. 60v–61): "Spectabat ille magna continue, et . . . totam mentem et oculos ad consequendam gloriam coniiciebat."

73. Bevilacqua, G, 353–54 (V, fol. 64v): "Hanc unam esse sibi suadebat quae brevitatem vitae posteritatis memoria consolaretur; quae efficeret ubi {G ut} absentes adessemus, et mortui viveremus. . . . Hanc solam esse virtutis quae in laboribus periculisque versatur mercedem."

74. Perleone, G, 236 (B, fol. 98rv): "Sed iam ad gloriam . . . transeamus, cuius ardore Valerius ita semper fuit incensus, ut si cetera quoque leviora fuissent, huius tamen studio satis apparebat illius virtutem eximiam preclaramque futuram, propterea quod nihil sit quod magis comprimat luxuriam, desidiam, avaritiam, superbiam, ceteras malas artes, pro iis vero suadeat continentiam, laborem, liberalitatem, equabilitatem et reliqua quibus corpus et animus recte instituitur ad bene vivendum, quam laudis glorieque cupiditas."

75. Perleone, G, 238 (B, fol. 103rv): "Dum absente patre magnis imbribus ac turbulenta tempestate domi, ut fit Valerius a Matheo aliisque natu maioribus optimis viris et amicis in triumphorum ludum esset invitatus, paruisse illum et animi et obsequendi causa. Ubi dum in iactu Pandulphinum perciperet placendi studio vincendi sibi facere potestatem ridentem puerum ad Matheumque conversum venuste commodeque Virgilianum illud pronunciasse: At puer Ascanius mediis in vallibus acri / Gaudet equo, iamque hos cursu, iam preterit illos, / spumantemque dari pecora inter inertia votis / optat aprum aut fulvom descendere monte leonem [*Aen.* 4.157–9]." The incident was "often" described to the narrator by the jurist Matteo Pandolfini, one of Marcello's familiars.

76. Perleone G, 239 (B, fol. 104): "Erat quidem pestilentie suspitio quo tempore Iacobus Antonius decemvir creatus [Marcello held this office from 27 September 1458 to 22 August 1459; see Chron.], fugiens hominum coetus atque congressus in edes templo divi Antonii contiguas, que longo urbis secessu ab omni frequentia hominum domorumque absunt, se recepit ob eam familiaritatem que sibi est cum Michaele Ursino templi antistite, viro quidem ut nobilitate generis claro doctrinaque prestanti, ita

et moribus et liberalitate et omnibus officiis in amicos excellentissimo. Ubi dum pro more in templum quotidie rei divine causa proficiscitur, Valerius lateri patris inherens, re divina peracta, suspitiens in ara maiore statuam super sepulchrum armatam porrecto digito, Heus, inquit, pater, qui vir ille est armatus dextera hastam et veneta signa tenens? Cui pater, hic est, inquit, fili, Victor ille Pisanus patricius noster armis et rerum gestarum gloria {G gloriam} inclytus, qui suis armis suaque virtute bello genuensi rem venetam restituit, hostesque obsidentes sua industria et ingenio mira obsidione pressit. Cui subdens puer, o fortunatum, inquit, virum; et quando illa se ostendet dies, qua bene de patria merenti aliquis michi decernatur honos?"

77.　Fam. III.B.2.

78.　Text in n76 above. See also Anon. Ven., G, 255–56: "Dum statua sublimi Victoris Pisani . . . spectata diu, tanti muneris merita rogitando maturae virtutis intelligens, ad caelum fronte simul et voce versa, O liceat inquit Deus omnia potens, hoc immortale decus aliquando mereri!"; and Orsini himself, G, 287 (M, fols. 19v–20): "Venetiis in ede sacra beati Antonii Vienensis . . . meae curae commissa, Victoris Pisani maritimi ducis invicti et genuensium clodiano bello vere victoris, marmoreum sedet monumentum statua pedestri, gladio cincta et loricata sublime, hanc (ut aliquando solebat) Valerius puer ad me divertens, aspiciendo, cum sepe rogaret cui mortalium hec immortalis memoria deberetur, acciperetque non esse vulgare munus, sed rarum virtutis premium, non nisi pro ingentibus meritis in re publicam concessum, errectis oculis in celum, O faciant superi concusso pectore dixit, ut raros possim inter adesse viros, et cum illi supra quam ferret etas luctatio concursus equi et arma placerent."

79.　Fam. III.B.3–4. For Pisani's role in the war, Lane 1973, 189–96.

80.　Chron. 1443: 9 January, and 1438–40, passim.

81.　Perleone, G, 239 (B, fols. 104v–105): "Eadem quoque Patavii dixisse ferunt, cum illi querenti pater respondisset, statuam illam equestrem esse quam senatus Catamelate [i.e., Gattamelata] honoris virtutisque causa decrevisset."

82.　Perleone, G, 233–34 (B, fols. 92v–95): "Erant in area Marcellorum non longe ab edibus Iacobi Antoni forte eiusdem etatis pueri tres, inter quos et Valerium rixa et iurgio orto, cum certatim obstrepentes inter se obloquerentur, Valerium circumveniunt, qui ubi se vi defendisset, irati pueri de proximo divi Angeli foro collecta equalium manu clamoreque sublato in Valerium hostili modo impetum faciunt, qui re nova perturbatus magis quam perteritus, raptis ex humo lapidibus non effusa fuga terga vertens, sed sensim recedens ad edes urgentibus ac instantibus illis, lapides alternis brachiis intentans metu iactus irruentes hos {B hostes} a se prohibuit. Ubi vero in marmoreas schalas se recepit, ibi quasi redintegrata pugna constiterunt, clamoreque magno et contumeliosis dictis se invicem lacessentibus Valerio, ut nunc ignavissima turba adversum unum congrederetur, illis ut in campum et liberam aciem descenderet fugax et iners qui timore in arcem confugisset, clamor simul et strepitus et Valerii vox in cubiculum ubi pater aliique multi consedebant perveniens excivit, omnes trepidos ad fenestras cum iam Mattheus Pandulphinus vir modestissimus ac iuris interpres, forte in cenaculo non longe a schalis deambulans eodem excitatus clamore foras raptim se proripiens, Valerium solum adversus multitudinem de infimo gradu propugnantem prospexit, atque ad se receptum proclamans in puerorum turbam statim ad parentem deduxit."

"A quo iussus rixe ac tumultus initium dicere, flens inquit in palestra pueros equales meos cum superassem pater, invidia simul atque ira perciti, contumeliosa et indigna quedam adversus me insolentissime iactantes insultantesque pene in oculos ipsos involarunt, uni vero ex his graviter oculum pugno cum percucissem, reliqui vociferante sotio ultionem parantes, eam ut vidisti adversus me unam turbam conciverunt. At quid tu inquit pater animadvertens illos te petentes non fugiebas domum? Quod mihi turpe inquit puer et te parente qui fugere nunquam didicisti, et genere nostro indignum esse arbitrabar. Audivi enim te sepe quosdam ignavos graviter obiurgantem predicantemque prestare pugnando honeste mori quam fugiendo turpiter vivere. Volui igitur pater et mores tuos imitari, et dicta tua servare."

"At quid, inquit pater, pugnabas telo adversus inermes? Non ut quemquam, inquit Valerium, ferirem, sed ut lapides intentando metu vulneris illos arcerem, quoad me in tutum recepissem. Tum surridens pater macte inquit virtute fili, via hec est qua itur ad celum, ubi pro mortalibus immortales facti eamque vera est vivamus vitam. Sed tu cave post hac quicquam tale committas. Est enim temerarii non prudentis sine ullo negotio, nulla proposita publica utilitate vel gloria manifestis se periculis obiicere. At pro libertate, pro patria, pro salute communi, pro fide, pro iusticia, pro religione fortiter constanterque pugnare atque mortem ipsam non modo non recusare, sed ultro etiam appetere, id certe fortissimi et excellentissimi viri atque civis officium {G est}." Anon. Ven. and Orsini also allude to this incident at G, 255 and 286 (M, fol. 19) respectively.

83. Text in n82 above.
84. Text in n82 above.
85. Perleone, G, 213 (B, fol. 49): "Generosus animus pulcherrimo

quasi quodam virtutis et glorie simulachro . . . detentus, et sui similitudinem tamquam in speculo cernens, et quasi Narcissus quidam sua illectus
forma nequiret a copiosissimo virtutis fronte revocari."

86.   Perleone, G, 220 (B, fol. 64rv): "Quid dicemus de Valerio nostro,
aut quid potius non dicemus, qui . . . preter eius etatis rationem, et ceterorum infantium consueteudinem atque naturam, imagine patris et constantissimi quidem ac optimi patris oblata usque adeo in illam oculos et
mentem et animum intenderit, atque tanta constantia in ea permanserit,
ut ceteris neglectis atque contemptis solum patrem omni tempore vellet,
requireret, expeteret?"

87.   Anon. Stu., G, 297: "Diligit autem pater filium sicut artifex opus
suum, quantoque nobilitate et excellentia natura ipsa praecellit artem,
tanto et intensior est amor patris in filium; eo magis quo principium paterne virtutis active et principaliter ad formationem prolis accedat, mater
vero non nisi passive concurrat."

88.   Anon. Ven., G, 254: "Quicquid ocii puero . . . vel a praeceptore
dabatur vel a te, cuius a vultu pendere latusque servare pro singulari solacio
atque iocunditate ducebat."

89.   Bevilacqua, G, 344 (V, fols. 52v–53): "Annis augebatur cum tanta
sui in me patrem amoris vehementia, ut nihil esset in infante admirabilius.
Nundum balbutire, nundum verba frangere poterat, quod is emori videbatur; nisi ubi me domi continebam, inter ulnas meas resideret. Atque quocumque alio in loco esset, is tanquam flagello caederetur, dolore afficieba-
tur, illacrimabat, neque aequo animo pati poterat, nisi ubi ab me tractari se
conspiciebat. Immo si quandoque fastidio istius {G istius fastidio} affectus
in terram eum {G e sinu} remiseram, inter crura, inter pedes meos al-
ludebat, donec illius pellectus illecebris rursus inter amplexus susceperam.
Si forte aliquando vel molestia, vel perturbacione commotus eram {G
fueram}, cuius gratia eum ab me repulissem quasi nil aliud {G alius}, quam
de me cogitaret; ex insidiis, ut sic dixerim, inspiciebat; a cura, ab angore
molirer, ut rediret ad me, quo solo videbatur olectari. Noctu vero in lecto
nunquam a me seiungere se voluit."

90.   F. Filelfo, G, 44 (ed. fol. 30): "Cumque eras domi . . . abste longius
nusquam aberat, aut sedenti astabat, aut in ambulantem subsequebatur.
Deinde quidquid aut ageres, aut diceres observabat. Tum ipsum vultum
atque omnem corporis tui gestum conspicabatur acutius, sibique imitan-
dum proponebat. Tantaque animi voluptate in te contemplando afficie-
batur, ut eum gestientem aspiceres, quod si fortassis interdum te cogitabun-
dum, ut usu venire solet, animadverteret, attentissime tuos omnis et
oculorum et corporis motus considerabat tacitus. Deinde tum ex matre

tum e servis querebat, acciditne patri novi quippiam? Quid ita cogitat secum?"

91. Bevilacqua, G, 354–55 (V, fols. 65v–66): "Praesertim {G quae} fuit illud enarrandum qua arte, quo ingenio triremes per colles {illos} abruptos collibus impositos, per angusta praecipicia et invia omnia fuissent in Benachi lacum advectae. Quod ubi opera mea facinus illud {V et} excogitatum et perfectum audivit, tunc id {V ab} me voluit enudatum aperte intelligere, quasi quod gloriosum pater sibi ac posteris confecisset, ab eo cuius virtutem honori sibi et suis ducebat, vita moribus quae {G moribusque} se degeneraturum turpe putaret." Similar material at idem, G, 357 (V, fol. 69); text above at n71.

92. Orsini, G, 287–88 (M, fol. 20v): "Hoc unum tamen dixisse velim, Valerium puerum et Iacobantonio praestantissimo patre et Marcella familia nobilissima dignum, . . . quin et maiori laude recentibus annis matura virtute, preclarum nomen, multis illustribus Marcellorum nominibus addidisse. Nam si Marcelle familie decus insuperabile curabis inspicere, intelliges eam preter Iacobantonium etiam tot clarissimos duces, vel mari vel terra tulisse quot vix alie multe (nec obscure) viros habuere, et nunc quoque numero senatorum Fabiis equando sic fulget, ut ad parem exercitum confitiendum et viris et viribus posse sufficere videatur." Anon. Ven., G, 261: "Cum video summum rerum dominum voluisse primarium puerum perpetua corporis et animi valitudine firmum in Marcella familia quondam et in urbe romana et in sua veneta consorte praeclara in qua genus velut immortale manet plurimosque per annos stat fortuna ducum et avi numerantur avorum."

93. Bevilacqua, G, 348 (V, fol. 58): "Gaudebam filium opera mea, diligentia, cura, in tantam virtutem evadere, ut eum fore praedivinarem, qui maiorum meorum virtutes in se suo solerti ingenio esset collecturus, quibus posteritatem omnem nostram gloria rerum bene gestarum commendacione locuplectaturus esset."

94. Anon. Ven., G, 256: "Ut erat illi benigna vox plena laeticiae, plena veri nil nisi rectum probabileque complectens, olim iocose mentem sciscitanti affirmans malle se patrem morte prevenire quam sequi, causam requirenti spe poscentis reddidit multo maiorem. Nulla iactura, nulla clades inquit puerili corpore sublato cuiquam evenire potest nisi patri, cuius lacrimae, cuiusve suspiria non tam fugienda mihi quam morti praeferenda censerem. At pio genitore (horret animus memorare) nobis acerba morte direpto, quod mihi reliquum vitae, quod solamen, quod perfugium superesset, nisi mori? Ut inter quae brachia vivens iocunde quievi, moriens quoque dum sinerent fata iacerem. Heu quantum patriae moerorem,

quantos luctus, amicis, propinquis, et nostrae familiae daret? ut haud ambigue vita malim quam tantis cladibus optimo parente vel brevi mora et invise lucis querulo spacio carere." Also reported by Filelfo, G, 45 (ed. fol. 30); Fortebraccio, G, 146; Mascarello, G, 175; Orsini, G, 287 (M, fol. 20v); Sagundino, G, 5 (F, fol. 94; VatS, fol. 3).

95.   The following events are narrated in full by Anon. Tut. at G, 244–48; the arrival at 244–45: "Exorasti vir optime, nam paucis admodum diebus elapsis [after Easter] animi laxandi gratia Veneciis soluimus et universa familia Montem Sylicem versus navigamus. . . . Portus oppiduli tandem intramus, ubi mox cives primarii nobis obviam fiunt, ut una matronae cum coronatis de more virginibus aderat, enim et Luca Leona coniux tua femina spectatissima, quae eadem in navi devecta erat. Hic omnes in Valerium oculos coniciunt, omnes salutant, omnes amplectuntur et stupent. . . . Portam intramus haud infrequentiore cum pompa quam ii qui cum Aesculapio Romam ingressi sunt. Occurunt in primis incedentibus nobis augustae Marcellorum aedes et horti pheaces quos amoenissimis spirantes odoribus inter pomorum ramos aves indigene pe cantu demulcent. Illo me primo Valerius agit inde domus aulas et penetralia cunctosque recessus ostendit, ubi meo puer gaudens gaudio triumphabat." For Monselice, Fam. III.D.

96.   Anon. Tut., G, 245: "Vellem hic Iacobantoni liceret orationis huius filum abscindere, ne post hortorum tuorum delicias in spinosissimos anfractus ambo pariter irruamus. At nos susceptum iter impellit et quasi lapis e funda redire nescimus? In mense quintili Valerius gravi maxillarum dolore corripitur et totus fervet. Accersitur ex suburbio medicus et Matthaeolus physicorum princeps e Patavio volat attonitus ambo de scapulis sanguinem exanclare contendunt ferrum ampulas ignem vociferantur." In the Quattrocento, a "physicus" like "Matthaeolus princeps physicorum" held pride of place within the conglomerate medical professions that included also practitioners with little or no formal training, including women and Jews: see Park 1985, esp. 58–76 and 121, Table 4-1 (showing that physicians were paid more than 50 percent more than "all doctors"). For the summoning (by the very wealthy) of multiple doctors to the same case, ibid., 113. For the career of a prominent Venetian physician of the sixteenth century (Niccolò Massa), which might yet provide some clues about expectations in the earlier era, see Palmer 1981.

97.   Anon. Tut., G, 245 (continuing passage in previous note): "Ad haec generosus et delicatus puer expalescit et vulnus uti insolens timet. Tunc pater impensius oras ut si te simul et se salvos velit fortiter medicos ictus excipiat, quibus ille verbis accensus eum secultro flammisque porrexit ut insecandas verices Marius aut in urendam dexteram Scaevola videretur.

At nihil invitis fas quemquam fidere divis evadit emorbo Valerius, et singulari cura fovetur. Inde post paulo Venecias amne secundo relabimur, ubi recepta iam valitudine puer ad scholam ventitabat et amissi temporis iacturari moleste ferens ardentius studebat id resarcire quod egrotans intermiserat."

98. The following at Anon. Tut., G, 245–46 (continuing passage in previous note): "Instante salucius nostrae natalicio instaurata vi febris invadit Valerium, qua cum multum diu quam reluctatus puer ut illam clam te patre victor extingueret, haud prius cesit quam illius ante signum Deum agnosceret, Hectorem illum Homericum imitatus qui non prius Achilli subcubuit quam Apollinem quo cum homine se contrapugnantem inspexit. Quod ubi rescisti pater a curris consternatus et fervens morbo corpusculum senciens, evestigio medicos accersi iubes. Inprimis adest presto Gyrardus nostri temporis Aesculapius. Arteriam consulit, hanc satis offendit, arridet tamen et pallidulos demore parentes solatur, inter salubres herbarum succos exprimit unguentia strygiles et omnia medicae artis arma expediuntur. Nec tanta paenis cura fuit in ligando Menelai vulnere, quanta Gyrardi quum sudantem et anellum indigna Valerii valetudo redebat. Conspicabatur eum puer electulo veluti qui bimus primos vidisset, augende tunc spei gratia, pater? Hic est, inquis, Gyrardus ille, fili, qui vel extinctos in lucem vocat. Agnosco pater, inquit, hominem quem nostris olim in praediis hospitem accepisti." Accounts of Gerardo's visits also by F. Filelfo, G, 48 (ed. fol. 31); Fortebraccio, G, 145–46; Mascarello, G, 177; Perleone, G, 229–30 (B, fols. 85–86); Sagundino, G, 6 (F, fol. 94v; VatS, fol. 3).

99. Perleone, G, 230 (B, fols. 85v–86v); see text in Fam. IV.13.

100. Perleone, G, 230 (B, fols. 86v–87): "Obstupuit Gerardus hec audiens, et ore compresso et contracta fronte tacitus diu secum rem omnem mente atque cogitatione repetens, versus ad circumstantes admirari se inquit tantam in puero eiusmodi egrotatione presso rei multis ante annis geste memoriam tamque accuratam et singularem in rebus explicandis diligentiam et ordinem esse. . . . quod pater tempora secum dinumerans subdidisset, Valerium nondum tertium explevisse annum, cum ad Monsilicem hec visa et audita et gesta sunt."

101. Perleone, G, 230 (B, fol. 87rv): "Quid illud quod medico de morbi vi et natura querenti, et quibus doloribus ac perpetuis ne an remittentibus, et qua corporis parte, ac una ne magis quam alia et quo tempore nocturno vel diurno, et pransus ne, an ieiunus magis vexaretur, adeo memoriter ad singula diligenterque respondit, ut Gerardus ipse rursus in admirationem adductus, iurando affirmaret Avicenam signa eius morbi in eum modum, quo Valerius expresisset descripsisse."

102. Anon. Tut., G, 246: "Gyrardus interea cum calcerando phisico, ad Valerium ingrediuntur. Arridet puer advenientibus, vel quod opem sibi ferre iam frustra conentur, vel quod humanius eius membra torquaerent; nec id iniuria, nam pridie illius dici tonsor quidam immanissimus eius venas interflobotomandum novacula tam crudeliter excaverat, ut aspiciencium oculos atra bilis obstringeret. Haerent propius medici, tractant arteriam, mussant, urinam speculantur. Aiunt deteriorem paululum. Inter illa Iudeus adducitur . . ., a quo puer adeo perterritus est, quare iudeus ut ne tangi quidem ab homine pateretur, ille scaphium poscit, labrum distorquet acrius inspicit toga fundo subducta, secretus nescio quid cum reliquis agitat, et simul te consolari conati discedunt." For the place in the profession and society of Jewish doctors, Park 1985, esp. 71–75; Siraisi 1990, esp. 18, 29–31, 35–36, 58–59, 190. For the prejudice against Jewish doctors (in the name of piety), ibid. 54 for the saint Francesca Bussi, and Gardenal 1983 for the Venetian humanist and patrician, Marcello's contemporary Ludovico Foscarini.

Also F. Filelfo, G, 48 (ed. fol. 31) for Gerardo's medical treatments: "Confestim accersitur Gerardus medicus veronensis vir sane et doctus et amicus. Nam alii nonnulli veneti medici antea puerum curandum acceperant, qui quoniam desperarant de salute, se inde subtraxerant. Gerardus igitur cum venisset, omnium primum urinam in vitrea mathula conspicatur, quam et rufam videt et turbidam, deinde manibus apprehensis arteriolisque vitalibus contrectatis, reperit earum motiunculas perdebilis, ac raras et per intercapedinem se moventis. Contrectat extremos digitos pedum, deinde genua, demum partem vicinam cordi. Sentit omnia mortis viribus intercepta."

103. Bevilacqua, G, 377 (V, fol. 96rv): "Quod ubi ego perspexi, haud animum adverti miser quod interiturus esset, quod me patrem puer deserturus foret, incauto mihi in mentem non venerat. Egrotacionis inicium tum ludum ludificabilem esse credidi, et iam bonam valitudinem praesto affore illi putavi. Verum ubi eum in graviorem morbum inclinari protinus ego perpendi, hei mihi, quanta diligentia illum curandum duxi? Quantum illius curationem medicis commendavi? Quam assidue illorum operam ego coegi? Quae non modo lacrimis, sed lacrimarum rivulis pro illius incolumitate vota dicavi? Cuncta subselia paradisi me ambisse crediderim ut sanctos omnes mihi fautores eblandirem. Opem mortalium immortaliumque {G immortalium mortaliumque} mihi vocavi; inaniter omnia tentavi. . . . Monasteria universa civitatis nostrae contrivi, et viros omnes cuiusque observantissimae religionis Deo deditissimos rogando fatigavi."

104. Anon. Tut., G, 246: "Tunc omnis spes vitae nobis de puero peni-

tus exolevit. At ille sororem quae se singulari cura vel ab ipsis incunabulis educaxerat, unice tibi commendat. Omnia recipis et in illum fixo vultu stupes ut saxeus." See also G, 247, for another passage where Marcello is said to be "like a stone" upon recognition of his son's condition; text at n118 below.

105.   Bevilacqua, G, 423 (V, fol. 158): "Ego miser doloribus multiplicibus confossus loqui non poteram, nec tam suavibus verbis respondere."

106.   F. Filelfo, G, 47 (ed. fol. 30v): "His auditis puer nobilissimus quamquam erat toto corpore prostratus atque semianimus, perinde tamen atque collectis in unum dispersis et profligatis viribus sublato ad celum intutu in hec verba suavissimum os aperuit. Deus omnipotens Christe Ihesu redemptor noster, te quam devotissime precor per sanctissimam passionem tuam, te inquam clementissime rex glorie quam humillime obsecro per impollute Marie virginis tue pientissimae matris merita, ut hanc a me domine, qua tam vehementer affligor, egrotationem si tibi placitum est amoveas {ed. esta moveas} meque iucundissimo patri huic meo matrique dilectissimae restituas. At ego tibi liberatori humani generis quid sim pro tanto benefitio relaturus? Nempe ad perpetuum devotionis venerationisque mee studium omnia vestimenta mea ac reliquum omnem corporis ornatum dono do pauperibus." This vow also reported by Sagundino, G, 5 (F, fol. 94rv; VatS, fol. 3): "Egrotatione veroque tandem nature concessit, cum graviuscule habere cepisset, cumque {FVatS eumque} tu idempridem {FVatS identidem} hortatus esses creatori omnium Deo optimo eiusque gloriosissime matri quo sospitatem reciperet notum {F votum} aliquod faceret; pollicererisque te quidquid ipse vovisset sedulo et accurate persoluturum, conversus ad te, Quid voveam inquit, mi pater, equidem nescio ceteram universam rem meam egenis et inopibus lego."

107.   F. Filelfo, G, 47 (ed. fol. 30v), continuing the passage in previous note: "Que locutus mirabili cum animi affectu quasi extremo labore fessus ac lassus obticuit. Hic tu pater aliquanto exhilaturus {ed. aliquando exilaratus} tempestive subdidisti: Meum autem votum, Valeri mi suavissime, illud est, ut ego una tecum si convalueris, utar fusca veste, verum tu serica et in annum, at ego lanea idque in omnem vitam. Addidisti enim serica veritus quoniam puer uti semper consuesset leto quodam amoenoque cultu corporis, ferret tristius fuscam vestem. Sed audi {ed. avidi} obsecro tu, ut ceteri tecum audiant, quid is responderit. Absit, inquit, absit mi pater. Imo ego induar veste et {ed. omits et} fusca et lanea, sic enim decet, tu vero eleganti ut semper, atque senatoria. Nam in te non familie, ac tuorum solum, sed reipublice decus representatur."

For this vow see also Sagundino, G, 5–6 (F, fol. 94v; VatS, fol. 3), con-

tinuing passage given in previous note: "Voveras {F Voveas} proinde tu si
convaluisset vestimentis cum fusci coloris ut assolet induiturum, et ne forte
puero res molesta videri posset, quippe qui veste delicata et splendida semper uti consuevisset, adiiciendum statim in eius gratiam duxeras, eiuscemodi vestimenta, et si pro voto paulo incommodiore colore non tamen
viliave {FVatS vilia laneave} sed sumptuosa sericeaque futura, praeclaro
puer ingenio et sapientiore quam ut ad id etatus conveniret, Minime inquit
mi pater sericea, neque enim hoc pacto rite votum videretur absolui. Ad
hec oblivisci ne possis, quod sui ingenii speciem dederat, pridie eius diei
qua vita discessit?"

Also Anon. Ven., G, 257: "Quid cum tu piissimus pater voveres illum
(vita manente) gemis et auro distincta lacerna et picta tunicha dimissa
(humilitatis indicio) non nisi palidas vestes annum esse laturum, ad-
deresque (ne delicatus puer molibus assuetus, rudia penitus horrendo iniquo animo ferret) eas et si depressi terreique coloris, tamen sericas et ornatas
fore, non ne pulcherrimo ore soluto, super humana sentencia, dixit placere
sibi humile votum superbia contemnens additum ornamentum . . . placere
non posse?"

108.   Sagundino, G, 6 (F, fol. 94v; VatS fol. 3), text in previous note.

109.   Anon. Tut., G, 246: "Et alcius educto suspirio natum in te con-
vertis, qui qum lacrymantem conspicaretur, et tu mi pater, inquit, hic
ploras? haud hoc virum decet."

110.   Anon. Ven., G, 258: "Cave censere diucius, optime pater, lacrimis posse mea fata mutare. Cessa ob meam salutem vano dolore tuam
in praecipicium dare. Desine te magna rerum gestarum gloria magnum,
nunc tibi dissimilem turpi et indecoro luctu spectandum, et hac una excep-
cione probandum ignavo et maledico vulgo praebere." See also Filelfo, G,
46–47 (ed. fol. 30v): "Que adventantis luctuosissima mortis signa cum tu
coram aspiceres, non potuisti ita tibi moderari, quo minus pro paterni
affectus imbecillitate et lacrymis et gemitu animi sollicitudinem ostenderes.
Quod ille ita ut erat vi morbi mollequam deiectus, tamquam e somno excitatus, ubi animadvertit, febribus estuans lassusque anhelitu, quid agis, inquit, pater mi dulcissime? quid gemis? quid ita lachrymaris {ed. illachri-
maris}? Ita consolaris Valerium tuum? Pone queso lachrymas mi pater, pone
omnem animi curam. Bene nobis sperandum est. Nos Deus non destituet.
Cui tamen quidquid placuerit, id tranquillo atque leto animo feramus
necesse est. Quod si bonam valitudinem recuperaro, nunquam patiar, ut
eam nimia laudendi {ed. ludendi} exercitatione amittam, idque tibi bona
fide polliceor." Also Guarini, G, 182 (F, fol. 111): "Ille ut pius filius dextra
quam deficiente spiritu vix attolere poterat oculos abstergens te exhortaba-

tur ne casum tuum quem dominus Deus dedisset iniquo animo ferres potiusque dum liceret ad oscula suavissimi filii te infugientem {F inclinares et
fugientem} animam prono ore colligeres, ac te ipsum in reliquorum filiorum aspectu consolareris."

111.   Anon. Tut., G, 246: "Hac tu voce commotus ut amens erumpis
e cubiculo, secretusque fortunae tuae vicem adversam conquestus, acciris a
filio, ut a quo supremos amplexus petas."

112.   Bevilacqua, G, 423 (V, fols. 157v–58): "Modo me obsculabatur,
modo colla structis {G strictis} ulnis circundabat, modo me patrio nomine
appellabat, et manibus suis lachrymas mihi tergebat ab oculis."

113.   Anon. Tut., G, 246: "Accuris ulceratus et iam semianimum ac
pene frigentem Valerii vultum obscularis, et fletum comprimis inter haec
cruciatibus amplius urentibus, eum puer clamorem eduxit, quo parietes ipsi
concuti viderentur. Hic tu fili inquis eruminosae me iste voces excruciant.
Quod ubi puer audivit, et atrocius torqueretur, praesis tamen dentibus eas
doloris faces perferebat, quibus omnis sane stoicus ab heresi sua caesisset.
Vespertino mox crepusculo lingua riget ebecior et arteriae pulsus iam nullus
auditur." Compare the far more peaceful scene described by Filelfo, G, 47–
48 (ed. fols. 30v–31): "Dum {ed. Cum} hec scite serioque loquitur, mors
paulatim irrepens precordia frigore obsidet. Horret iam puer, ac tremit.
Nam quo magis animi magnitudine vincere nitebatur fragilitatem afflicti
corporis, eo magis febris immanitas membra prosternebat, ita ut demum
diceret sublatis ad caelum oculis. Miser ego, quis me liberabit {ed. liberavit}
de corpore mortis huius? Quamdiu claudar hoc seculi carcere? Quod ipse
audiens cum transfixus doloris iaculo, coepisses durius flere. Tunc ille: Quid
est mi pater, ut tanto te dolore conficias? . . . Implevi cursum, qui mihi a
domino datus est. Non hic vivitur nostro arbitrio. Peregrinamur quamdiu
sumus in vita. Que tamen vita certe non est, sed simulacrum quoddam
pure innocenterque viventibus, vite illius beate et sempiterne. Itaque stu-
dendum est semper {ed. semper est} ut quam properantius licet, redeamus
ad communem bonorum omnium patrem, qui mitis est et misericors. Sic
enim frui licebit corona iusticie, sic saturari eternis gaudiis; suavis enim
est dominus."

114.   Anon. Tut., G, 246: "Ex templo sacerdos accersitus adest can-
didatus crucem de more portans in manibus. Nos omnes hic flexi supplici-
ter preces concipere, vota protinus augere, recordari quatridianum in sep-
ulchro Lazarum. Hic sacerdos ex animis pene labellis crucem admovens:
respice puer inquit in faciem Christi tui. Quam penitus ille deosculans
trementi dextra pectuschulum feriebat, et haud quicquam locutus eam vim
lacrymarum effudit, ut cum linterio crux tota madesceret." Compare F. Fi-

lelfo, G, 49 (ed. fol. 31): "Assedit moderatissimo puero sacerdos, que is deliquisset {ed. dereliquisset} in vita auditurus. Que sunt eius errata? Unum id sane et maximum: quod dum post animi circa litteras et facundiam morumque disciplinam exercitationes assiduas, nihil otii sibi indulgens, exercet etiam corpus ingenue, ea est vi morbi correptus, qua ex hoc terrestri carcere ante in celestem patriam revocatur, quam per etatem posset flagitii foeditatem cognoscere. Miratus igitur sacerdos singularem integerrimi pueri bonitatem, quippe quem nulli reatui videret obnoxium, sed simplicis cuiusdam potius atque absolute probitatis speculum, dum eum iubet bene sperare, dum religionis more imposita capiti manu, omni culpa libere absoluit." Also Fortebraccio, G, 146–47: "Tandem cum morti esset proximus, illumque ad se piissimus omnium creator Deus evocaret, accedens spiritalis medicus ad egrum non infirmum, leniter rogare cepit, an suorum erratorum penitentia duceretur. Respondens Valerius ut quibat, iam voce titubante, sed mente ac sensu valido, penitet me inquit peccasse, si qua in deum hominesque deliqui, quibus dictis leniter pectus oraque percutiens, sese divino crucis signaculo quam devote munivit."

115. Anon. Tut., G, 247: "Ille coniectis in caelum oculis paululum suspirii vix efflans genas et ora composuit, uti qui dulcem in somnum abiret. Aedes vero tanta statim odoris suavitate fragrarunt, ut effusas illic ambrosiae simul et unguentorum omnium pixides dicederes. Illico tanti clamores exciti, tanta Valerii nominis vociferatio, tanti genarum et pectorum plactus auditi ut universa Marcellorum vicinia longe lateque reboaret."

116. Bevilacqua, G, 423 (V, fol. 158v): "O quantum corda tum ulcerata mihi mansere! O quantum corpus tum sine spiritu mihi, sine aliquo sensuum fomento collapsit! O quantum me omnis et cognatorum et familiarium turba cum filio tum extinctum credidere. Exclamare libet, sint immanes quicunque velint, sint impii, sint crudeles, filiorum funera siccis oculis contemplentur!"

117. F. Filelfo, G, 49 (ed. fol. 31): "Sunt ista profecto eiusmodi, quae hominum animos non commovere non possint {ed. possunt}."

118. Anon. Tut., G, 247–48: "Tunc vero pater exanimum nati corpus aspitiens, heres in multam noctem ut lapis, et illud tandem sigillo crucis obsignans, solus in tenebras fugis, lugesque validissime. Domus interea nigris atratur stragulis, at caelum festivis ornatur auleis. Pullatum palliolum moerens induis pater, at filius candida toga vestitur, ad divi angeli funus efertur Valerii. Valerius ipse angelus caelos triumphans ingreditur, et nos adhuc in terris excruciamur—nos infelices, nos erumnosi, nos omni calamitate sepulti vitam inviti trahimus."

119. Fortebraccio, G, 154: "Nulla enim aut dici, aut excogitari

prestantior dignitas potest quam cum Christo esse, cum beatissimis spiriti-
bus (ut ait quidam sanctorum) glorie conditoris asistere, presentem Dei
vultum cernere, in circumscriptum lumen videre, nullo mortis metu affici,
incorruptionis perpetuo munere letari. Quare si ab acta totius moeroris ca-
ligine, rem fideliter constanterque voluerimus considerare, letandum nobis
potius de filii tui Valerii morte quam dolendum esset, cuius anima ex hoc
carnis ut ita dixerim ergasculo liberata, ad celestem patriam beatissima evo-
lavit, et de his mortalitatis angustiis ad immortalitatis lata palatia perpetuo
gravisura conscendit." Sagundino, G, 24 (F, fols. 104v–105; VatS, fol.
12rv): "Dubitare ergo qui potes . . . Valerium tuum non perdidisse lucem,
sed veriorem clarioremque assecutum esse ex humili et depresso loco, in
celum emicuisse. In civitatem demigrasse excelsam . . . sacrosanctam, im-
munem, illesam, tutam, inexpugabilem, concordia, pace, tranquillitate
omni vigentem. . . . Non ille deseruit te, non matrem carissimam, non sua-
vissimos fratres destituit, sed omnes vos felicissimus puer in honore et gloria
insolido gaudio et eterna leticia prestolaturus antecessit."

120. Filelfo G, 55 (ed. fol. 32): "Quare inter nos et filios quos amisimus [speaking of Filelfo and Marcello and their two sons] non admodum
longa futura sunt divortia, modo demus operam quod in nobis est, ut una
cum illis quos tanto desiderio ardemus esse possimus"; idem, G, 63 (ed.
fol. 33v): "Non enim mortuus est Valerius, sed vite transegit conditionem,
ut qui mortalis erat factus sit immortalis. Ille nunc simul cum angelis quorum simillimus creatus est et gratia et pulchritudine et splendore faciem
dei videt, vultu quare velato {ed. vultuque revelato} sempiternam domini
gloriam ineffabilemque beatitudinem letus contemplatur et gaudens."

121. Sagundino, G, 24 (F, fols. 104v–105; VatS, fol. 12rv): text
above, n119.

122. Anon. Tut., G, 248: "At hoc non credebat forte Valerius, nec
in tanta felicitate sua squalorem ullum domesticum aut intestinos luctus
expectabat. Unde fit ut audiam nunc eum de caelo clamantem: O pater,
hec me pietas? Hoc ego te capillo? Hac barba? Pannosum lacrimantemque
cerno. Cine meae felicitati, congratularis sic me gaudens, o pater. Atqui
maluissem fili mecum hic esses, me oblectares et meae senectutis bacillum
et heres postreme fores. At hoc impii patris officium est summam liberorum
beatitudinem sua quantulacumque voluptate picisci. Nec si hereditatem
querit quem Deus omnipotens adoptavit ingravescentem aetatem tuam reliqui fratres mei, nepotesque suis amplexibus excipient. Et si christianus, si
Dei cultor es non minore gaudio pater afficieris unum te caelo angelum
peperisse, quam istos quinque rei publice cives reliquisse primarios."

123. Bevilacqua, G, 423 (V, fol. 158): "Modo me consolari [i.e., Va-

lerio] nitebatur, ut omnes dolores ego reprimerem et mihi suaderem deinceps filium habere in paradiso, et gloriosiorem ordinem adeptum quam venetorum Senatus illi fuisset unquam collaturus."

124. Bevilacqua, G, 379–80 (V, fol. 99rv): "Hinc tu cerne, Rex illustrissime, hinc arbitrare. Tot summi oratores ad me super obitu filii scripsere, atque suis eloquentissimis non epistolis, non orationibus modo, sed libellis delere mihi lacrimas et consolari enixe me conati sunt, qui necdum me permovere atque incitare potuerunt ut aliqua ex parte me a floetu revocarent."

125. Bevilacqua, G, 426 (V, fol. 172v): "Hos igitur consolatorios libellos, sic enim eos nunc nomino, hoc volumine ordinatim ut scripti et ad me dati sunt coniunctos ad te mitto."

CHAPTER TWO

1. Texts II.C.1. For background to Marcello's role as patron, see esp. Lytle & Orgel, 1981, contributions by Werner Gundersheimer, Charles Hope, and Douglas Lewis.

2. Mastrodimitris 1970; also Babinger 1961, 9–52; King 1986, 427–29.

3. Sagundino, G, 2 (F, fol. 92v; VatS, fol. 1rv): "Hoc nomine nunc factum, hoc meum ipse tueri possum, si quidem moerenti tibi et suavissimi et dilectissimi filii desiderio laboranti, forti tamen excelsoque animo incommodum et casum ferenti, atque moderatius et equius indies laturo, consolationem afferre constitui, cui magis ob virtutem animi gratulandum meritissimo videatur, quam ad dolorem leniendum remedia ulla querenda. Non tamen ob idem {F,VatS id} equidem non facile institutum hoc meum defendere posse videor, qui non ea ratione suscepi laborem hunc, quasi tu iis que sum allaturus indigeas, sed ut que mea in te sit voluntas intelligi explorarique possit. Quod si paulo serius hanc mihi operam desumpsisse cuipiam forte videor, est mihi ratio qua cur id factum sit non egre probare possim, neque enim ulla negligentia commissum id volui, quo desertor muneris in te mei, vel potius non acer et strenuus offitii custos videri possem. At primo quidem cedendum aliquantum mihi, et ut tempus aliquid inter laberetur ex industria permittendum putavi. Dum si qui sunt alii, ad quos hoc negotium attinere posset, plerosque autem litteratos et doctos tui nominis amantes studiososque scio, partes suas susciperent tuerenturque, ne insolens facinus ipse viderer facere, qui locum hunc aliis cupide intercipere, ac mihi arrogare inepte videri possem." Elsewhere Sagundino emphasizes the offering of the consolation as a sign of friendship: "Hanc ego consolationem tibi elucubravi, Iacobe Antoni Magnifice, non tam tui

consolandi et confirmandi, quam mee in te fidei et observantie ostendende nomine. . . . Quamquam maxime cupere in te potius leta atque iucunda, quam in lugubri et tristi, animi in te mei argumentum et testimonium edendi mihi facultatem fuisse prestitam." G, 25 (F, fol. 105rv; VatS, fol. 12v).

4. Sagundino, G, 3 (F, fol. 93; VatS, fols. 1v–2): "Moerore crede mihi atque dolore pene incredibili me affectum sensi, simul atque de obitu filii tui accepi nuntium, nec potui miser gemitus et lacrimas continere, casu {G enim} ingenui pueri, forma, ingenio, indole, natalibus illustris et clari non commoveri non potui, recordatus presertim tot filiorum iacturam, quam ipse non multo ante quod nosci momento temporis feceram."

5. Sagundino, G, 7 (F, fol. 95; VatS, fols. 3v–4): "Iure itaque casum tuum egre tulisti. Haud immerito doluisti, non iniuria lacrimarum affatim profudisti. Recte nos quoque qui te amamus, colimus, veneramur, vicem indoluimus tuam."

6. Sagundino G, 25 (F, fol. 105v; VatS, fols. 12v–13): "Verum posteaquam invitis et dolentibus nobis sors inevitabilis ita tulit, peto abste, perque humanitatem {FVatS et sapientiam} oro tuam {G et sapientiam}, opusculum hoc utcunque elaboratum, et si tuis nobilissimis factis non admodum aptum, et si tua expectatione non omnibus ex partibus dignum, voluntate tamen et fide edentis metitus, humaniter atque benigne accipias. In eo enim conficiendo, nihil diligentie, cure, studii, fidei a me pretermissum affirmo."

7. Sagundino, G, 2 (F, fol. 92v; VatS, fol. 1v): "Dum si qui sunt alii . . . plerosque autem litteratos et doctos tui nominis amantes studiososque scio." Full text above at n3.

8. For Perleone, King 1986, 416–17, and sources there cited. Recent additions to Perleone's bio/bibliography will be forthcoming by G. N. Knauer, who has kindly supplied me with the typescript in draft of his article on the subject's translation of the pseudo-Plutarchan *Vita Homeri*. See also *Iter* 4:491, for Perleone's translation of Isocrates' *Ad Demonicum*, dedicated to Brancaleo Grillus; and 621a and 660a for respectively a poem by Perleone and a letter to him from Bartolomeo Facio.

9. See Chron.

10. For the Venetian schools, see overviews by Labalme 1969, chap. 5; Ross 1976; Pastore Stocchi 1980; and sources there cited.

11. Texts II.D.21.

12. Perleone, Epistola, VatP, fol. 103; F, fol. 106; MU, fol. 94: "Etsi calamitates nostrae nunquam tam sero ad nos perferuntur quin sint celerius nostra voluntate, casum tamen atque obitum filii tui iam inde ab initio rei perlatum ad me voluissem, propterea quod nullum esset a me genus offitii

et dolendo et consolando pretermissum quod ab amicis in simili fortuna debetur. Ita ut quantum moeroris {MU doloris} mihi attulisset casus acerbitas, tantum detraxisset {VatP,F tempestiva} muneris nostri {MU nostra} satisfactio. Verum quando res in hunc locum perducta est, malui sero quam nihil ad te scribere, praesertim cum serum officium accusari non debeat, quando ignoratione rerum non negligentia sit praetermissum."

13.   Perleone, VatP, fol. 103v; F, fol. 106; MU, fol. 94rv: "Neque enim arbitror te dolere quod filium amiseris, quum natus erat moriturus, et necessitati resistere a tua sapientia sit alienum, sed quod et immatura et violenta morte {VatP eum} amiseris. Quibus sublatis non video quicquam superesse cur doleas. Atque si illud est immaturum quod ante suum tempus sit excerptum, id vero maturum quid {F quod} suo tempore cadat. Non est profecto filius tuus qui suo tempore concidit immature nobis ereptus. Neque enim potuit suum tempus appellare quod erat in numero annorum constitutum, sed illud duntaxat quo fati {MU fac ti} necessitate ducebatur. Omne enim hoc vivendi spatium quo vivimus non est nostrum {MU nobis}, sed eius qui nobis possidendum dedit. Ille tantum noster est dies quo morimur, ad quem quocunque tempore quis pervenerit is suum diem obiisse dicitur. . . . Ita filius tuus qui octavo aetatis anno mortuus est, ultimo senio mortuus est, si quidem illud erat ipsi ultimum vivendi spatium praestitutum."

14.   Perleone, VatP, fol. 104; F, fols. 106v–107; MU, fol. 96rv: "Imo si {VatP,F is} es qui semper fuisti beneficiorum gratus et memor, debes gratias Deo qui cum multos {VatP,MU et} egregios tibi filios, pudicam uxorem, patriam excellentem, genus illustre, opes, honores, dignitates, gloriam dederit, caeteris rebus omnibus tibi relictis, unum dumtaxat post multos annos repetivit filium quem, et caetera quae possides bona, iure ipsi {VatP adds ea} qua {MU qui} dedisset hora repetere licuisset. Est {MU et} profecto iniustus debitor, qui neget {F negat} quod creditum sit, ingratus qui invitus reddat."

15.   Perleone, VatP, fols. 104v–105; F, fol. 107v; MU, fol. 97rv: "At dices, Valerius meus invitus est mortuus. Equidem arbitror tres esse causas, quibus mortem plerique gravius ferant: quod {VatP,MU se} putent {MU putant} commoda huius vitae relinquere; quod vereantur quem {F quae} sint mortui locum habituri; quod filios et caeteros quos caros habeant et iucundos vitae praesidio privatos deserant. Horum nihil in filio tuo fuisse certum est. Neque enim erat vitae dulcedine illectus, quam nondum gustarat {MU gustarent}, nec de futura vita dubius, de qua vel {F nil} propter aetatem {F nil} omnino sentiebat, vel a te patre, a magistro, a caeteris quos

habebat vitae praeceptores, saepe audivisset, bonis viris et eius aetatis pueris, bene ac pudice educatis locum esse in coelo constitutum."

16.   Perleone, VatP, fol. 106v; F, fol. 109; MU, fol. 100: "Illud te rogo memineris te esse Iacobum Antonium, quem nunquam rebus adversis fractum, nec inimicis, nec fortunae. . . . Da igitur hoc dignitati atque existimationi tuae. Da hoc Valerio, qui te lugere non vult. Da caeteris denique filiis et amicis tuis omnibus, quibus profecto te merente geminatur dolor, et qui {F quod} filium amiseris, et qui {F quod} te lugentem videant."

17.   Fam. I.A.22–27; IV.17, 18.

18.   Texts II.C.2. For George of Trebizond, esp. Monfasani 1976; Monfasani 1984.

19.   For Giovanni Mario Filelfo see Agostinelli & Benadduci 1899; Castellani 1896; Favre 1856. For the school of rhetoric, see sources cited above, n10.

20.   G. M. Filelfo 1892.

21.   Favre 1856, 92.

22.   Texts I.8.

23.   George of Trebizond, G, 38 (Mon. #40): "Hoc breviter pro tua singulari virtute, pro tua inaudita humanitate, pro tuis in me meritis meaque in te pietate sicut fidelis debitor conscripsi. Que rogo ita libenter accipias sicut ipse libenter offero."

24.   George, G, 26 (Mon. #1): "Sepenumero . . . venit in mentem quamobrem prestantissime indolis adolescentuli puerique spem incredibilem pre se ferentis, anteaquam adolescentie peragant etatem, vitam cum morte soleant commutare."

25.   For Marcus Claudius Marcellus and namesakes, see Fam. I.B.9.

26.   George, G, 29 (Mon. #10): "Omnia enim animalia que citius ad opus suum peragendum perveniunt brevioris esse vite, et . . . arborum quoque genera plantarumque conspicimus brevissimo tempore flores ac fructum illa producere que brevissime vivunt, que diturnioris sunt vite diutius permanere antea quam aliquid de se ipsis producant."

27.   George, G, 37 (Mon. #38): "Tota enim perfectio nostra est ut non aliunde neque extrinsecus pendeamus, sed solummodo a se ipsis omnes rationes bene vivendi suspensas habeamus."

28.   F. Filelfo 1502, fol. 116bis: "Marchesius Varesinus et mihi familiaris et nominis tui observantissimus, id a me petiit verbis tuis, quod tuli equidem, ut par fuit, egerrime. Quippe qui in re laeta maluissem quam in lugubri et permolesta meam erga te benivolentiam experireris . . . Ego propediem quod cupis effectum dabo."

29. Robin 1991, 47; Robin 1984, 176; also Clough 1976, 35.

30. For Filelfo, see Robin 1991; De' Rosmini 1808 is still a good narrative; Garin 1955, 6:547–608; 7:539–97 for Milanese culture in the Visconti and Sforza eras respectively, passim for Filelfo.

31. Chron., 1420: 23 July.

32. For which see Robin 1983, and sources there discussed.

33. For Filelfo as tutor to Ludovico, Clough 1976, 39.

34. Robin 1991, chap. 2, for Filelfo's portrayal of his prince in the *Sforziad.*

35. Chron., 1448–50.

36. F. Filelfo 1502, fol. 116: "Accepi ex multorum sermone me tibi esse carissimum, quodque honorifice de me loqueris, sentisque peramice."

37. F. Filelfo 1502, fol. 116: "Cum enim in omnium voce didicissem magnum te esse virum eundemque perhumanum, et illorum apprime studiosum qui bonis artibus dediti, immortalitatem maxime et ipsi sequerentur, et aliis pararent."

38. Texts II.C.3. For judgments on the work: De' Rosmini 1808, 2:123–24; McClure 1991, 109–11; a discussion of Filelfo's moral philosophy with respect to his later *De morali disciplina* in Robin 1991, chap. 5.

39. Robin 1991, 122; Robin 1984, 203 and n14; Benadduci 1898, xix–xx; De' Rosmini 1808, 2:127. For Jacopo Bellini's study, perhaps of this basin as commissioned by Marcello, see Eisler 1989, 89 and 198, plate 87.

40. For the death of Olimpio, Fam II.D.1; IV.21.a–b. See also McClure 1991, 105n68 for subsequent losses in 1470 and 1475–76 of his adult son Senofonte and two other youngsters; ibid., 112, and Robin 1991, 249, for his net loss variously of seventeen or twenty of twenty-four children.

41. Fam. IV.21.a–c.

42. F. Filelfo, G, 38–39 (ed. fol. [29]): "Cupienti mihi aliquid ad te scribere, Iacobe Antoni Marcelle, quo tuus acerbissimus meror ille quem ex inopinato et immaturo obitu Valerii dilectissimi filii animo conceperas, aut tolleretur omnino, aut magna ex parte levaretur, eo difficilius consolationis genus est oblatum, quod paris egritudinis sotius accedens non minus ipse consolandus videar, quam te consolaturus. Quod enim consilium cuiquam sit daturus, qui sibi vix possit? Qua spe alteri videatur {ed. medeas}, qui ipse in morbo sit? Sum equidem eodem quoque transfixus vulnere, quo te video laborare."

43. The thesis of McClure 1991, 104–6.

44. McClure 1991, 31, for another case where an author (Petrarch) writes a consolation on commission, a professional writing for a patron.

45. F. Filelfo, G, 61 (ed. fol. 33v): "Scio me eo tibi dolorem facere longiorem, quo in dicendo sum longior. Verum cum video in {ed. tui} te Valerii quem tanto desideras opere veluti sagittis assidue vulnerari, et eo quidem animi vulnere quod dolore te conficit, institui non antea finem dicendi facere, quam ita te tibi restituero, ut {ed. adds me} mihi in luctu meo restitutum sentio."

46. F. Filelfo, G, 122 (ed. fol. 44): "Quare si Franciscum Philelphum tuum qui et ipse in simili casu est et te plurimum diligit, audire sequique institueris, Iacobe Antoni Marcelle, non modo non lugebis obitum Valerii filii sed gaudebis potius."

47. F. Filelfo, G, 123 (ed. fol. 44): "Omnes enim quibus es carissimus, tua causa dolemus, at fuerit {ed. fuerint} vel humanitatis cuius mirifice ab omnibus laudaris, vel liberalitatis tue, qua ceteros homines antecellis. Liberare nos tandem omni doloris aculeo, quod una sane re feceris, si te viderimus finem imposuisse tante doloris acerbitati."

48. Texts II.C.4.

49. Texts I.2, 3, 5, 8–11.

50. Texts II.C.5. For Carbone, Paoletti 1976; also Bertoni 1921, 112ff.; Frati 1910; Garin 1967, 69–70nn1–2; Gundersheimer 1973, 165–66; Piromalli 1975, 93–95.

51. Texts II.D.19. For Grifo (Griphus, Griffus, Griffi), see Cosenza 1962–67, 2:1678c. He is known as the author of many humanist opuscula (*Iter*, ad indices), including a verse celebration of the Sforza victory at Aquila (1424) dedicated to Francesco Sforza and his brother Alessandro (Grifo 1733); for other opusculi, dedications, and notes, ibid., ad indices. For Grifo's relation to Filelfo, Favre 1856, 88.

52. Texts II.D.17.

53. The judgment of Pellegrin 1969, 60. For Sforza's literary and artistic patronage, ranked below that of his counterpart in Naples, Alfonso of Aragon, but still significant, see Catalano 1983, 182–84; Peyronnet 1958, 41–44; Peyronnet 1982, 24; Santoro 1968, 33–35 (for his relations with the Simonettas) and 91–94. For Sforza's management of his literary portrayal through the patronage of humanists, and especially historians, Ianziti 1988.

54. F. Filelfo, Latin "Elegy," Ben. 20: "Nam memini mecum quo tempore bella gerebas / Legatus sociis missus ab hadriacis. / Nulla tuum poterat formido tangere pectus, / Nulla sagiptarum, nulla pericula necis."

55. Texts II.D.23. For Tifernate, see esp. Mancini 1923; Torrioli 1927; also Cosenza 1962–67, 4:3412ff.; Favre 1856, 74. Alternatively: Gregorio da Città da Castello, Gregorius Publius Tiphernas, Tifernas.

56. Texts I.9–11

57. King 1986, 428.

58. Tifernate, *Oratio,* fol. 126v: "Cum ad me admodum sero esset allatum Valerium Marcellum filium tuum e vita eossisse, eoque ex re non mediocriter esse permotum, veritus sum ne aut tardus essem si ad te scriberem consolandum, aut ineptus si te monerem, quem ego semper maximi animi virum et in omni re prudentissimum cognovissem, ut potius existimandum sit dolorem abs te, quam te a dolore esse superatum. Verum quia nec in secundis rebus amicus amico deesse debet, nec in adversis putavi ad me maxime pertinere, qui saepe in hos casus incidissem et te semper dilexissem, quod ego sentirem ad te breviter scriberem."

59. Tifernate, *Oratio,* fols. 126v–127v; text at chap. 6n45.

60. Tifernate, *Oratio,* fols. 128v–129: "An ideo tibi gravis et acerbus hic casus videtur, quia tu iam tibi effinxeras et in animum tuum induxeras Valerium cum aetate provectus esset in virum clarissimum evasurum, ad paternum et avitum decus perventurum, Marcellorum familiam illustraturum, civem Rei Publicae utilissimum futurum. Dic quaeso quis tibi hanc opinionem persuasit? . . . Quis inquam tibi haec ita fore promisit? cum haec ipsa vita quam vivimus tam periculosa sit et fallax, tot et tantis laboribus plena, ut infinita potius mala sint extimescenda."

61. Tifernate, *Oratio,* fols. 130v–131: "Sed cum multa sint quae in consolationem colligi possent, haec tamen familiariter ad te breviterque volui perscribere, non quo putarem magnopere te angi ac vexari (novi enim modestiam tuam et animi robur teque ita semper vixisse, ut potius a te alii quam tu ab aliis bene vivendi rationem et exempla sumant) sed ut qui meus in te esset animus ostenderem, quem ego cum sciam multis ac magnis virtutibus praestantem, non possum non multum diligere et admirari."

62. Texts II.C.6. For Nogarola, see esp. Avesani 1984, 4.2:60–76; King 1978; King 1991.

63. Chron. 1439: 20 November.

64. See n67 below, and G, 135 (Abel, 2:163–64): "Verum haec a me tibi deditissima inornate enunciata forsan magis acerbissimum hunc dolorem tuum emollient, quia me verae filiae officio fungi tua considerabit excellentia, cum maluerim ab omnibus audax et impudens, quam a te benignissimo patre et ab his qui me tuam humanissimam filiam ab ineunte aetate mea, ut dixi, pro tua in me et in Nogarolam familiam singulari caritate et mea in te reverentia cognoverunt iudicari, cum omnium virtutum merita bonum humilitatis exsuperet." Note also G, 139 (Abel, 2:174): "Testis est Verona nostra [of Marcello's greatness], in qua tam multa memoratu digna gessisti, ut in maximo discrimine suo tempore illius infelicissi-

mae cladis te tamquam imperatorem inter tot strenuissimos duces eligerent, illustris simulque senatus Venetus confirmaret tibique summam totius belli committeret."

65. For Rizzoni, Avesani 1984, 4:3:51–59. For Guarino and his circle, see Bertoni 1921; De' Rosmini 1805–6; Garin 1967, chap. 3; Piromalli 1975, 2.3; Sabbadini 1964. For Carbone, above at n50; for Bevilacqua, Guarini, Strozzi, and Zovenzoni, below at nn109, 150, 155, 78; for Carrara and Pannonius, see below, chap. 3, nn30 and 24.

66. Nogarola, G, 135 (Abel, 2:163): "Vereor tamen, ne multis appaream temeraria, quae inter tot oratorum, tot philosophorum agmina, qui te suis elegantissimis scriptis ac gravissimis sententiis consolari conati sunt, procedere et in media acie versari audeam."

67. Nogarola, G, 134–35 (Abel, 2:162): "Ego vero, quae te ab ineunte aetate mea amavi ut patrem, colui ut dominum, et felicissimum semper optavi, cum ex multorum relatione tuisque piissimis scriptis intellexerim, te pro obitu dulcissimi filioli tui Valerii in dolore ac moerore longe magis ac par est versari, temptare decrevi, si qua ratione dolorem hunc tuum, quo non possum admodum non dolere, aliqua ex parte lenire possem teque ad rationem revocare, ne, cum homines sumus, more Gigantum cum diis bellum gerere videamur." See also text above at n66.

68. Nogarola, G, 135 (Abel, 2:164): "Sed quo modo te consolabor, cum ipsa eadem consolatione egeam?"

69. Texts II.C.10.

70. Perleone, G, 191 (B, fol. 5v): "Quid Thaddee filie tue carissime mortem nunc explicem, femine quidem pudicissime, ac genero primario nupte filiorumque sobole fecundissimae, que ni fallor nunc quinto mense acerba morte subrepta est?"

71. Chron., 1461: 1 April; George, G, 36 (Mon. #34), text in Fam. IV.17.

72. Chron., 1462: 13 June; 1463: 22 April.

73. Texts II.C.10.

74. In G, pp. 211–40; many passages given in chap. 1, above, passim.

75. Perleone, G, 192 (B, fols. 8–9v): "Et quamvis non me fugiat hoc dicendi genus te moerore potius quam solatio afficere posse, propterea quod oratio, laudes, ac virtutes eorum quos caros et iucundos amisimus diligenter explicans dolorem augeat, inibo tamen hanc quoque rationem quando priore nihil profecimus, multique doctissimi et clarissimi viri te consolando in hunc usque diem laborem frustra suscepisse videantur. Tentandum enim esse duxi an stomachus tuus iamdiu morbi difficultate cuncta fastidiens hoc novum ut ita dixerim cibi condimentum valeat degustare, ac

dolori tuo medicinam afferre. Namque remedia temere ac sine ratione ten-
tata egrotantibus sepenumero profuerunt, et quod ratio et concilium non
potest, casus et fortuna sepe facit. Utque amantis animus maximis erumnis
sepe delectatur et quasi nutritur, sic forte animus tuus eger hac nova acerbi-
tate delectatus, in predicatione laudum illius quem unice dilexisti con-
quiescet."

76. Anon. Tut. G, 241: "Solent plerumque pictores et ii qui caelant
egregie vultus in marmore vivos, aut in tabulis edere, cetera vero corporis
liniamenta vel rudia vel intacta relinquere. Non quod opus ad calcem
efingere nesciant, sed qui neminem ausurum existimant id explere quod
ipsi incoeperint. Id quod si Parleo [Perleone] quoque conatus esset hac in
lucubratione consolatoria quam tibi mancham nuper inscripsit, eques illustris, erubescerem plane divinis fuis inceptis inertes admovisse digitulos;
et illud orationis filum quod ommisset emoriens non magis consequi posse
sperarem quam vel Aragne Minervam vel Apollinem Marsia. Verum hoc
provocationis genus orator ille modestissimus in medium nunquam tullit,
sed acerbis interceptus fatis opusculo suo non ut optabat extremam manum
imposuit, et perorationis membrum in quo Valerii pietatem complecteba-
tur ommisit. Quod ego munus inde mortui licet arduum non recusavi suscipere."

77. As I myself have done: see King 1986, 416–17; King 1987, King
1988, passim. The *Supplement* is described at Texts II.C.11.

78. Ziliotto 1950, 47 suggests this possibility, which accords with
Tremoli 1983, 144–45, and Ziliotto, 19, who place Zovenzoni in Venice
at some point between 1455 and 1460. For later contacts of Zovenzoni
with Marcello, see Chron., 1463: 4 July–11 November. Knauer suggests
that the continuator was Perleone's brother Jacopo: see Texts II.C.10.

79. Anon. Tut. G, 242; texts in chap. 1 above, nn46, 48.

80. Anon. Tut. G, 243; text in chap. 1 above, n37.

81. Anon. Tut. G, 244–45; texts in chap. 1 above, n95.

82. Anon. Tut. G, 245–47; texts in chap. 1 above, nn102, 104, 109,
111, 113–15, and 118.

83. Anon. Tut. G, 245: "Vellem hic Iacobantoni liceret orationis huius
filum abscindere, ne post hortorum tuorum delicias in spinosissimos anfractus ambo pariter irruamus."

84. Texts II.C.13. F. Filelfo's narrative to which Orsini responds at G,
107–9 (ed. fols. 41–42). For Orsini, see King 1986, 415–16.

85. Orsini, G, 269 (M, fol. 2): "Legi libellum sensu non corpore magnum a te nuperrime transmissum ad illustrem militem Iacobum Antonium
Marcellum et romane venustatis et venete nobilitatis decus, et iam sepe

lectum tam optabile fuit, tamque iocundum, multa doctissime disceptata, si non ingenio at certe memorie mandare tacitus etiam sine volumine mecum aliquando relego, et philosophi acumen et theologi lumen et oratoris ellegantiam miror."

86.   Orsini, G, 282–83 (M, fol. 15v): "Sed ex plurimis quas extra rem nostram non censeo repetendas Marcellam tibi gratissimam memorabo, in qua Iacobantonius Marcellus tui amantissimus nec litteratorum achademiae minus quam patriae pater."

87.   See letters to Orsini from Francesco Filelfo in 1462–64: Filelfo 1502, fols. 127v, 130v, 137v, 140rv, 142v, 149, 155v.

88.   Filelfo first mentions the *Sforziad* to Orsini in a letter of 5 June 1463 (Filelfo 1502, fol. 130v); then, having sent it, recalls it on 20 August 1463 (137v): "Sphortiados libros ita cupio ad me redituros, ut nihil fiat alienum a voluntate splendidissime equitis aurati, Iacobi Antonii Marcelli, cum primum ergo, et Marcello meo, et tibi mos gestus fuerit, facito, illi ad nos continuo revolent."

89.   For San Antonio da Vienna, see Fam. III.B. For the Marcello family's regular visits, Orsini, G, 287 (M, fol. 19v); see text at chap. 1, n78.

90.   Orsini was "ex generosa et iam diu maximis honoribus et dignatibus illustrata Ursinorum familia natum"; cited from the *acta* of the university at Padua in King 1986, 415.

91.   King 1986, 415; Cicogna 1824–53, 1:361; for Marcello's career, Chron. passim, and below, chap. 4.

92.   King 1986, 415; also Cicogna 1824–53, 1:362.

93.   Discussions in Orsini, G, 269–83 (M, fols. 2–15v) and 288–94 (M, fols. 21–28).

94.   For which see P. F. Brown 1988, chaps. 1, 6; Carile 1970; Cochrane 1981, 60–86; Fasoli 1970; Gaeta 1980; Goy 1985, chap. 1; Labalme 1969, chap. 10; Muir 1981, 65–102, esp 65–74; Pertusi 1970b; Zippel 1956. The discussion would soon be taken up in the *Cronachetta* and *De origine* of Marino Sanuto and Bernardo Giustiniani's *History of the Origin of Venice:* see Sanuto 1880, 7, 13, 28; Sanuto 1980, 9; Giustiniani 1722, i.3–4. See the following note for the myth of Venice.

95.   For access to a now vast literature on the Venetian myth, see Grubb 1986; Muir 1981, part 1; Queller 1986, chap. 1.

96.   Carile 1970, 91.

97.   Orsini, G, 276 (M, fol. 9): "Sic iam Veneti pates inexpugnabili situ perpetuo nominis et generis honore servato, in terrestem Venetiam et antiquam patriam diuturnis calamitatibus oppressam redentus, equo iure captare sua non aliena vexare merito dici possunt."

98. Orsini, G, 279 (M, fols. 11v–12): "Quorum testimonio credo satis aperte mostrari venetos non a galis sed ab henetis Paphlagonia pulsis et a troianis Antenore duce in Italia nominis et gentis originem habuisse, et hanc venetam libertatem supra millesimum annum a condita urbe illeso adhuc et inviolato iure manentem firmissimas inde radices accepisse."

99. Orsini, *De antiqua venetorum origine,* for which see Cicogna 1824–53, 5:525; Fabbri 1983, 232; *Iter* 2:332. Cicogna reports that the work was printed by Toscanella from the surviving Vatican ms., but could not locate the work; nor have I. For Morosini, King 1986, 132–40, 412–15; for Giustiniani (text, B. Giustiniani 1722), see Gaeta 1980, 45–65; Labalme 1969, esp. chap. 10; Pertusi 1970b, 306–18.

100. Discussion in Orsini, G, 285–88 (M, fols. 15v–20v).

101. Orsini, G, 286 (M, fol. 18v): "Audivisti et dignis laudibus celebrasti Valerii Marcelli nomen. Ego et viventem {M iuventem} et pene nascentem vidi. Et cum apud illustrem patrem quotidie versarer, tamen illius animi corporisque vigorum non pullulantem modo, sed presentes oculos ferme crescendo falentem, nova semper oblata causa mirabar; nec plurima quidem (non visa) credere, nec (visa memorando), non flere fas est." Further descriptions of Valerio's childhood at G, 287–88 (M, fols. 19v–20v), given in texts above, chap. 1, nn59, 63, 68, 78.

102. Discussion in Orsini, G, 290–91 (M, fols. 23–24v), ending at G, 291 (M, fol. 24v): "Sicque Marcellos antiqua probitate sublimes et priscis auctoribus et nostris et domesticis et peregrinis constat in veneta regione vetusta singulari prestantia floruisse, quorum indelebile genus scindens se sanguine ab uno in veneta urbe nunc romanorum certissima sede virtute, auctoritate, gratia fulget, multosque per annos, multa virum volvens durando secula vincit."

103. Orsini, G, 287–88 (M, fol. 20v): "Nam si Marcelle familie decus insuperabile curabis inspicere, intelliges eam preter Iacobantonium etiam tot clarissimos duces, vel mari vel terra tulisse quot vix alie multe (nec obscure) viros habuere, et nunc quoque numero senatorum Fabiis equando sic fulget, ut ad parem exercitum confitiendum et viris et viribus posse sufficere videatur."

104. Orsini, M, fol. 28; absent in G, which closes at 294: "Haec ad te Venetiis mense Maio scripta, familiaribus curis varia loca petendo, quieta diu magis quam neglecta reliqua; nunc demum tarda nec ideo minus amica mitto. Si quo verbo vel sententia lederis, corrige et emenda dissolve, lacera deleve, nam etsi propositum (se per ingenium licet) discere multa cedendo non (ut video multos) omnia cum superis etiam disceptando nescire. Venetiis vii kalendis Septembris mcccclxii. Michael de Ursinis, iuris civilis doc-

tor, prior Monasterii Sancti Antonii Vienensis s[. . .] Venetiis Paduae Utini et cetera manu propria."

105. Chron. 1462: 5 May.

106. For Foscarini, see King 1986, 374–77; for his role in Udine, Chron. at 1461–62; 1462: 24 March, 26 October, and 16 December.

107. King 1986, 12, also 7; Liruti 1760, 1:345–54.

108. Anon. Stu. G, 296: "Quod cum ita sit, existimans quoque apud te esse viros et vetustissimarum rerum disciplina doctissimos, et facultatum omnium cognicione praestantes: Leonardum ante alio Thomatistarum principem, et Hieremiam physicum peritissimum, Guarneriumque Martheniensem Latini decus eloquii, quos haec Foriiulii patria felicissima genitos educavit, infimae parvitati meae conveniencius iudicavi vulgaria nostra dicendi instrumento deponere et huius mori genus officii alcioribus ingeniis derelinquere, quae omnia multo facilius paucis consequi possent, quam ego sudoribus maximis et angustiis ea summis dumtaxat labiis degustare. Accedebat insuper Georgii de Lazisio non minus veneranda presentia, qui quantum ingenii viribus dicendi copia atque artibus elloquentiae praestet. Hoc uno tantum possum verissimo testimonio comprobare, quod dum puerulus essem, memini Iohannem Petrum Lucensem praeceptorem meum tam graeci quam latini sermonis interpretem, haec saepius cum discipulis meis verba dixisses, paucos se vidisse vel meminem, qui tam optime romanae linguae raciones atque instituta teneret quam Georgius iste cuius nunc mentio nostris versatur in manibus."

109. For Bevilacqua, Abel in Nogarola 1886, 1:xviii–xi, cviii–cx, nn32, 33; Avesani 1984, 4:2:60–66, and sources there cited, esp. 64–65n2; Cosenza 1962–67, 1:610c–611a; Guarino 1915–19, 3:139–41, 216–17, 226; Maffei 1731–32, 2:98; Weiss 1969, 193–94. For the noble Bevilacqua da Lazise family (distinct from the Veronese Bevilacqua family), see Cartolari 1854, 1:23. Also Bevilaqua, Bivilaqua, da Lazisio.

110. For Bevilacqua's career, see Chron. at 1436: 31 January, 3 April; 1437: 22 June, July. For his relations with the Nogarola sisters, see also Guarino 1915–19, 3:139–41.

111. For which see Texts III.1.

112. For the work to Foscarini, see Chron. at 1466–67. The *Flores ex dictis Beati Hieronimi collecti,* arranged by topics, in Budapest, National Széchény Library, ms. Clmae 458, possibly the dedication manuscript; see *Iter* 4:296a. The dedication to Barbaro is actually by the author's son Girolamo, as the work was left unfinished at Giorgio's death. See also Maffei 1731–32, 2:98.

113. See Chron. at 1456.

114. *Iter* 4:645a: Toledo, Archivo y Biblioteca Capitolares, cod. 96, 28.

115. Texts III.2; Chron. at 15 December 1463.

116. Abel in Nogarola 1886, 1:cviii–cix, n32.

117. Chron., 1450–51.

118. Chron. at 1439: 20 November; 1448: 20 June, 23 July, 22 September, 3 October; 1454: 4 February (end), 6 February.

119. So he signs a letter to his superior at V, fol. 4.

120. See those listed under Texts I; discussion in chap. 4.

121. Chron. 1463: 24 September.

122. A case nearly parallel is the circulation among the Sforza secretarial staff of the documents upon which were erected an official historical portrait: see Ianziti 1988, esp. chap. 4.

123. Texts II.C.7.

124. References to Trieste siege at Fortebraccio, G, 141–42: "Non nihil mi forte tibi admirationis allaturum supicor, magnifice Iacobe Antoni, tam sero ob immaturam acerbissimamque Valerii filii tui carissimi mortem, hoc consolationis offitium suscepisse, eo magis quo mihi tecum iam diu domi militieque singularis quedam consuetudo fuerit summa cum observatione coniuncta"; and 159–60: "Quod autem nos in hac ut cumque est consolatoria contulimus, non tantum id ingenio seu doctrina freti ut in initio dictum est egimus, quam ut offitio functi, veteri amicitie nostre satisfacere aliqua ex parte videremur. Scis enim me ut primum in castra veneta perveni, semper ut precipuum parentem, coluisse te, atque observasse, tuamque gravissimam auctoritate summa fide ac constantia prosequutum, quod idem mihi, dum spiritus hos reget artus, faciundum decrevi."

125. Texts II.C.8, 9.

126. For these last three, respectively Texts II.C.12, 13, 14.

127. Texts II.C.15.

128. For these events, Chron. 1424: 5 June; for Braccio, see Mallett 1974, 68–75.

129. *Iter,* ad indices.

130. Fortebraccio, G, 143: "Memini enim ob magnificentissimi ac preclarissimi parentis meo obitum quosdam ecclesiastice discipline doctissimos viros gravissimas coram me sententias consolando protulisse."

131. Chron. 1479: 17 June.

132. Chron. 1440: January; subsequently 1446: 18 November; 1447: 28 June; 1449: 5 July; 1452: 16 May; 1452: summer through November; 1453: 1 January.

133. Chron. 1456: 11 June.

134. Fortebraccio, G, 141–42; 159–60; see texts above at note 124.

135. Chron. 1463, 26 and 30 August, 24 September.

136. Fortebraccio, G, 142–43: "Militari itaque et incondita potius quam urbana eloquentia instructus aggrediar, nostra quippe disciplina ut scis aciebus struendis, castris metandis, milites ad pugnam cohortandis, ceterisque militaribus offitiis accommodatior forte quam consolandis amicorum moeroribus existimaretur. Conabimur tamen pro ingenii viribus aliquid in medium afferre, quo et ego amici offitio functus videat, et tu de mea integrati animi industria aliquid saltem consolationis, post ceterorum luculentissima et copiosissima scripta consequare. Non litterarum doctrina fretus, non his humanitatis imbutus studiis venio. A primeva enim ferme etate, rei militari deditus vix potui prima litterarum rudimenta percipere. Verum tamen quicquid mihi, natura duce, experientia, usu, ratione denique ipsa dictante succurrerit eius te participem faciam."

137. For Sforza's literary agents, Ianziti 1981, 1987.

138. See below, chaps. 3 and 4; Texts I for Marcello's commissioned works. For René, Lecoy 1875, 2:175.

139. See *Iter* 2:50, 438.

140. Mallett 1976; for Marsciano's role in the Trieste siege, also Chron. 1463: August. For *condottiere* patronage, also Joost-Gaugier 1988; Mallett 1974, 221–24.

141. Campano 1731; Tateo 1977, 333.

142. Fortebraccio, G, 143: "Nulla tamen te capiat admiratio, si aliqua inter loquendum de scripturis sacris afferentur testimonia. Memini enim ob magnificentissimi ac preclarissimi parentis meo obitum quosdam ecclesiastice discipline doctissimos viros gravissimas coram me sententias consolando protulisse, alios quoque epistolis suis idem fuisse factitatos. Ea omnia ab illis copiosissime dicta atque descripta memorie mandavi, que nunc pro arbitrio disposita in medium afferentur." Campano's description of Braccio's death, and the family's mourning: Campano 1731, 620:c–622:d.

143. Fortebraccio, G, 142: "Multos preterea et ingenio et doctrina excellentes viros sentiebam hunc tibi infixum et pene radicatum dolorem ab animo extirpare conatos diligentissime, quibus hoc consolandi genere quicquid dici excogitarive possit consumptum arbitrabar."

144. Fortebraccio, G, 158–59: "Si tecum his verbis deus ac salvator noster Christus Iesus ageret, quid responderes? Cur Iacobe Antoni fles, cur lachrymis indulges abimis precordiis, cur tam gravia trahis suspiria, dispositionem meam cur cecis querellis insequeris? Mihi de te bene merito gratie non parve agende essent, et tu terga vertis." Full discussion of these Christian themes at G, 152–59.

145. Texts II.C.8. For Mascarello, an old biography in Di Santa Maria 1772–82, 2:lxxv–lxxix, esp. for discussion of the subject's funeral oration for the Venetian *condottiere* Gentile Leonessa (1453). Mascarello received his license and doctorate in civil law at Padua on respectively 2 April 1432 and 25 October 1433 (Zonta & Brotto 1970, 1:280, #878, and 309, #963). An oration by Mascarello is appended to the 1477 edition of Giacomo Alvarotti's *In libros feudorum* (GW 1589, IGI 414), and is repeated in later editions through 1587 (Belloni 1986, 213). Manuscript orations and letters appear in *Iter* 1:333; 2:250, 312, 566, addressed to or about Leonello d'Este, Jacopo Alvarotto, and Ettore Pasqualigo; in 3:47b, 61b, 648a, where the author appears as a correspondent of Ludovico Foscarini and author of an oration for Marco Longo; and in 4:126b, 293a, where he is author of two orations including that for Longo. See also McManamon 1989, 279, for an oration on the death of Gian Francesco Capodilista.

146. Mascarello, G, 163: "Hoc tibi medicamentum eficacissimum fore arbitror, eques insignis virque magnanime, si ante oculos tuos quasi cernendum triumphum tuum posuero, hoc est tuarum ingentium laudum commemorationem." Prior to this statement is the opening of the dialogue (ibid.). Montorio asks Marcello whether he should attempt consolation: "Audivi te Marcelle clarissime dolore tabescere ob mortem filioli, tibique gratam fuisse epistolam quam ad te consolandi gratia misi. Quid si nunc tibi hunc dolorem penitus de corde tuo abolevero remediis de mea physica accersitis?" Marcello responds that, while the letter the former had already sent had soothed his grief, yet he is still unconsoled and requires further treatment: "Nihil maius mihi afferre posses, Montori carissime, tua illa pauca verba epistole quam ad me misisti, mirum in modum cor meum lenire ceperunt. Sed dum subit animum Valerii mei effigies illa divina pulchritudo celestis indoles preclaraque me in spem magnam erexerat redit qui abiisse videbatur dolor proinde si quod valentius habes, adhibe dolori meo solamen."

147. Mascarello, G, 173 ("Sed ut triumpho nostro supremam imponam manum"), 167 ("Aliud triumphi specimen aggredior"), passim.

148. Guarini's letter is that prefatory to his translation of Strabo; see Texts I.9–10.

149. Mascarello, G, 163; see text above at n146.

150. For Battista Guarini the Elder, for whom there are no complete recent biographies known to me nor a full edition of the *opera,* see the recent specialized studies of Piacente 1974; Piacente 1982; Rhodes 1974 (and sources cited, n1); Römer 1987; also a useful sketch in Bertoni 1921, 185–88.

151. Eng. in Woodward 1963, 159–78; Latin with Ital. trans. in Garin 1958, 434–71. See also Grafton and Jardine 1986, 124; Avesani 4:3:68 for Battista Guarini's relation to Maffeo Gambara, son of Isotta's sister Ginevra Nogarola.

152. Guarini, G, 180 (F, fol. 110): "Nunc autem mihi probasse velim talis filioli iacturam aut oblivisci, aut cum recorderis non commoveri difficillimum esse. Quis enim est sic omnis humanitatis et paterne {F patriae} dilectionis expers ut a lacrymis temperet, cum tali puero se orbatum esse cognoscat in cuius vultu tantum gratiae, in sermone tanta iocunditas inerat, ut qui viderent et audirent non admirari et laudare non possent? qui tantos ingenii praeferebat igniculos, tantum alte mentis et quod in ea aetate incredibile videbatur, tantum prudentiae ostendebat, ut non modo parentem, sed alienum quemvis ad se diligendum allicere posset."

153. Carbone describes this scene in his *Carmen*, BMV 4451, fol. 30rv (BMV 4683, fols. 137v–38):

Et nunc Borsinus Carbo iam audace iuncta
Cuius ab ingenio est conversa elegia Philelphi;
Qui cum hoc Ferraria recitaretur in urbe poema
Ad fletum, ad lacrymas, quercus et saxa coegit;
Ipse dedit gemitus lacrymasque Casella ciebat
Interpres summus Borsi, inviolabile robur,
Quo vigilante quidem secura Ferraria dormit
Urbis praefectus Paulus Costabile numen
Flevit, defensor populi magnusque tribunus
Bissenos inter sidus spectabile patres,
Strozzigenumque decus Nicolaus et inclitus heros,
Priscianus custos nummi, quaestor {4683, questorque} severus:
Deflevere gravesque senes {4683, senesque graves} iuvenesque diserti,
Mortem alii incusent, vita mihi carior est mors.

154. Gundersheimer 1973, 165; also Piromalli 1975, 93–94. For the elegy, Texts II.D.16.

155. For Strozzi, see Della Guardia 1916; Piromalli 1975, 95; V. Rossi 1964, 225–26, 228, 234. For his own consolation, Texts II.D.22. His awareness of Marcello's plight is concretely evidenced by his verse preface to the Carbone's consolatory *Carmen*; see Texts II.D.16. The other consolers named at *Carmen*, BMV 4451, fol. 30 (BMV 4683, fol. 137v):

Te sermone gravi doctus Trapesuntius ornat;
Te consolatur dulcis Sagundinus, eodem

Fortune telo quo tu perculsus amaro;
Parleo subtilis, noster Baptista Guarinus,
Et muliebre decus Nogarola Isotta puella;
Omnia collegit sapiens pleno ore Philelphus
Carmine solatus graico, prosaque latina;
Titus amor Phoebi Strozzae gloria gentis
Titus apollineus divino cuius ab ore
Dulcior hybleo defluxit copia melle.

156. Texts II.D.20.

157. Texts II.C.10–14.

158. Texts II.D.18. For Filelfo's movements after his stay in Venice see Chron. at 1461: 8 September; 1463–64; 1467–68. Texts III.5 for letters to Marcello.

159. Texts II.C.12.

160. Anon. Ven. G, 250: "Hoc ad te visendum proposito veni, limini primo concussum animum ex vultu tacito quodam quasi sermone collegi, necdum paenitus indulgens moerori meo, potui validis adiumentis obstare tuo."

161. For the works of G. M. Filelfo, Strozzi, Pannonius, respectively Texts II.D.18, 22, 20.

162. For Chiericati, Foa 1980; Gualdo Rosa 1971, 1–13; Paschini 1935.

163. Published by Gualdo Rosa 1971, 14–37; see also Tournoy 1970, 210n4.

164. Anon. Stu. G, 295–96: "In maximo fuit positus dubitacionis agone, quidnam mihi satius esset prosequendum, an in hac tui tanti doloris magnitudine sublevanda tibi nostras licet incultas et rudes litteras dare, an magis hoc sacrum pietatis officium silentio praeterire. Mobilitatem nostri puerilis ingenii varie hinc undique raciones et argumenta concitabant, vigebat siquidem amor et summa in te ordinis nostri dilectio persuadebat, ut hanc licet viribus meis imparem, tuis tamen in nos bene meritis dignissimam mihimet usurparem consolandi provinciam. Hortabatur deinde ne tanti ponderis gravitatem assumerem, innumera scriptorum ac ut rectius dicam voluminum multitudo, quae ex omni Italia ab illustribus atque clarissimis viris fuerunt eloquentia sua tuae regiae atque magnificae excellentiae dedicata. Quid enim iunior in hac tui casus adversi pertractanda materia, cum antiquis et iam perfectis oratoribus contendere ausim. Nihil arbitror fuisse ab eis intactum, quod tibi in nimia accerbitatis tuae mitiganda tristicia vel humana vel divina racio concludere posset. . . . Hi omnes, Iacobe

Antoni vir clarissime, cum ampliora tibi consolacionis munera prestare po-
tuerint unius solum diei spacio, quam ego si vitae meae cursu longissima
superioris aetatis tempora praeterirem, statueram omnino pristinae volun-
tatis munere propositum et ad nostra methaphysicae studia me conferre, ut
possum recto tramite sublimes theologiae gradus ascendere."

165. For Diedo, King 1986, 361–62.

166. Anon. Stu. G, 300: "Has ego nuper raciones adducens clarissimo
viro Francisco Diedo circa obitum infelicem atque accerbissimam dormici-
onem patris sui Ludovici, qui optime nosti quantum in senatu vestro clarus
evaserat, doloris sui magnitudinem non mediocriter consolatus sum. Est
enim vir ipse magni ingenii atque prudentiae, omniaque summa tem-
perancia ac discrecione considerat illud praecetoris divini atque celestis
muneris amplitudinem saepius mente revolvens post casum genitoris re-
mansisse sibi Creusam, non tam familiae suae atque inclitae urbis vestrae
quam etiam tocius matronarum Italiae ornamentum et decus quae cum
antiquitatis nostrae mulieribus in omni excellenciae gloria ac dignitate merito posset comperari."

167. Anon. Stu., G, 303–4; text at Fam. IV.20.

168. Bevilacqua, G, 400 (V, fol. 127v): "Ex quibus omnibus dicere
nunc velim ab istis eloquentissimis viris fuisse actum commode minus et
efficaciter minus excogitatum, qui tot vigilias, tot labores, tot lucubraciones
consumpsere, ut consolandi mei gratia non epistolas modo, sed codices {G
condices} ipsi componerent."

169. Bevilacqua, G, 409 (V, fols. 139v–40): "Caeterum ea quae ab
istis eloquentissimis viris mei consolandi gracia disertissime composita {G
et} luculenter apprime, et sentenciarum et rationis {G orationis} copia enar-
rata sunt, non dubito ex amenissimo {G amoris} sinu {V et} indulgenitis-
simo {G que caritatis} {V amoris} fonte ab iis {G his} fuisse deprompta quos
admirabili sapientia praeditos esse certo scio." He continues to praise their
works: "Quae si multo admirabiliori hominum quoruncunque opinionem
excederent, horum nemo tam suavibus verbis, tam firmis, tam innodatis
argumentis me nititur demulcere, et a tam gravi erumna aleviare, quin si
eadam fortuna mutetur et in eorum aliquem aequa ratione impetum vert-
erit, ita ut huiusmodi clade fungatur eorum ad me tam audaciori fronte {G
per} scripta et precepta ab {G ab} se protinus excidere non ignorem."

170. Bevilacqua, G, 413 (V, fol. 145): "Possent isti consolatores mei
quos in me consolando tanta ornavit eloquentia, ut undique se in dicendo
illustres reddiderint, nec unquam a Cicerone in eo libro in quo se ipsum in
obitu filiae consolari voluit tot loca excogitata, tot argumenta inventa fuisse
crediderim, quot isti exarata luculenter exposuerint {G exposuerunt}, mihi

exprobrare quod in refellendis his quibus me arguere obstinato animo laborant."

171.   Bevilacqua, G, 425–26 (V, fol. 171v): "Tu dive Rex igitur rationes meas ipse discerne, quas hac epistola mea non ut tot elegantissimos libellos in obitu charissimi filii mei erunnarum mearum consolatorios {G consolatoris} ingratos mihi fuisse ostenderem describendas duxi. Sunt enim tanta orationis elegantia compositi, ornatu tam eloquentissimo culti, tum gravitate sentenciarum et exemplorum copia, tum verbis suo loco tanquam in emblemate vermiculato commode compositis {V positus}, ut inter res illustres a maioribus nostris et priscis oratoribus aeditas certe annumerari possent. Sed ut potius haud indecore me gerere si nondum lachrymarum mearum rivulus desicatus fuerit praemeferrem."

172.   Bevilacqua, G, 426 (V, fol. 172v): "Hos igitur consolatorios libellos, sic enim eos nunc nomino, hoc volumine ordinatim ut scripti et ad me dati sunt coniunctos ad te mitto, quos maiestatem tuam ut legas et perlegas obsecro." Continuing: "Et si quid in his cognoveris elegantiae quod fore plurimum existimo, pro cuiusque meritis digna laudatione cumulabis. Hac epistola qua iis {G his} respondisse volui, tibi hoc iudicium . . . decrevi."

173.   See Texts II.C.15.

174.   Bevilacqua, V, fol. 4bis r: " Aequo animo te pusilanimitatis crimine lacessi non patior."

175.   Bevilacqua, V, fol. 6: "Sic epistolam scripsi quam abs te lucubratam fuisse, et a te divo Renato regi destinandum suasi. . . . Eam igitur nunc ad te do."

CHAPTER THREE

1.   Fam. III.D for the following.

2.   Chron., 1405.

3.   For the Marcello arms, Spreti 1928–36, 4:351–52.

4.   Sanuto 1881, 16–17; also Sanuto 1847, 33; cited Gloria 1862–65, 3:141. Elsewhere, Sanuto listed Monselice as one of the principal holders of sacred relics; from the loggia at the Rialto, one can go there by *traghetto de viazzi* en route to Arquà and Este (Sanuto 1980, 196 and n1; 175).

5.   Sanuto 1881, 16, 17: "Moncelexe è uno castello, situado sopra una monte . . . visto sopra el monte la caxa nostra antica, *apud vel contra* quella di Jacomo Antonio Marzello equite, *olim, nunc* di fioli."

6.   Barbantini 1940, 18: "con la Rocha grande del Chastelo de Moncelese, tutti li suoi libri e spezialmente tutte le sue scritture d'ogni sorte e tutti li fornimenti et adornamenti del suo camarin de Moncelese."

7.   Quoted by Gloria 1862–65, 139: "quadrato, massiccio, bruno, incoronato di merli, ma guasto per mecchiezza, per abandono, per mutilazioni, giunte e mutamenti."

8.   Barbantini 1940, 49: "fisionomia primitiva e in ispecie il duro aspetto medievale."

9.   Kaeuper 1988, 211–225 for the phenomenon of private fortifications and its psychological meaning in the late Middle Ages, esp. at 214.

10.   Romano 1987, 120–22, for Venice's neighborhood structure; Martines 1979, 31–33, 35–37, for urban fortresses and neighborhood clusters in other cities.

11.   For the notion of "self-fashioning" as a characteristic activity of Renaissance individuals, see Greenblatt 1980. For the concept of a "heroic ideal" in the Renaissance, see Weise 1961. Burckhardt 1958, esp. part 2, "The Development of the Individual," is the classic statement of the notion of individualism as the hallmark of the age of the Renaissance.

12.   Guarino 1915–19, 2:629–34; Sabbadini's commentary, 3:487–88. On Guarino's translation of Strabo, see Texts I.9–10. For Guarino, De' Rosmini 1805–6; Grafton and Jardine 1986; Sabbadini 1964. For his work in Verona, Avesani 1984, 31–50. For his circle in Ferrara, see chap. 2n65, above.

13.   Sabbadini in Guarino 1915–19, 3:488. For the Roman Marcellus, see Fam. I.B.9.

14.   Guarino 1915–19, 2:631: "Tu igitur, Marcelle vir sapientissime, ad tanta pericula propulsanda et malorum remedia excogitanda missus per silvestria loca et rupes iniquissimas transvolans ex insperato urbem intrasti civesque ac milites adeo animasti, ut te duce obsessum per id tempus vehementer ab hoste Roatum castellum, civitatis vere clavem et Brixiae columen, ex hostium faucibus eripuerint."

15.   Guarino 1915–19, 2:631: "invictus, velut Hanibal alter per alpes cursitans."

16.   Guarino 1915–19, 2:632: "quoddam humanis viribus maius et vix posteritati credibile facinus invasisti."

17.   Guarino 1915–19, 2:632: "tu vero animi magnitudine, mentis acumine, ingenio perspicaci terrestre iter stravisti navibus et loca per asperrima montanosque tramites in Benacum, . . . non mediocrem sane classem . . . induxisti."

18.   Guarino 1915–19, 2:632: "tu veluti Veronae dictator, vi redactis in potestatem montibus ab hoste possessis per invia loca rupesque vastissimas comitem ipsum Franciscum et militum quadraginta milium multitudinem incolumem perduxisti tantumque Picenino terroris incussisti."

19.   Guarino 1915–19, 2:633: "Testis est etiam insula Padi tuo ductu et auspicio in ea fusum profligatumque exercitum fuisse."

20.   Guarino 1915–19, 2:633: "unde inclyta illa et semper imperiosa Mediolanum suis in portis Venetorum affigi vexilla spectaverit."

21.   Guarino 1915–19, 2:633: "quo praeclaro et memorando facinore tuo auratae militiae et equestris ordinis insignia, magnanimitatis et fortitudinis tuae monumentum, meruisti et approbante exercitu adeptus es."

22.   Guarino 1915–19, 2:633: "Dux igitur Philippus tanta rerum permutatione commotus . . . mentem dolore saucius ex aegritudine morbum contraxit et paucos intra dies mortem obiit."

23.   Guarino 1915–19, 2:633: "Illud tua de continentia integritate innocentia occurrit saeculis omnibus celebrandum, . . . quod in tanta opum auri et spoliorum facultate atque licentia cum tui locupletandi praestaretur occasio, nihilo divitior domum revertisti; quin pecuniae publicae parcus ac sobrius administrator maiorem in contemnenda quam in adipiscenda pecunia gloriam collocasti."

24.   For Pannonius, see esp. Birnbaum 1981; Birnbaum 1988; Thomson 1988, "Introduction." See also Chron. 1447: spring; 1454: October; 1458. The Latin appellation "Pannonius" claims the poet for Hungary, though he was possibly Croatian. Many thanks to my student Christina von Koehler for sharing with me her preliminary work "Janus Pannonius," typescript, 1991. I did not have access to Jozsef Huszti, *Janus Pannonius* (Pécs, Hengary: Janos Pannonius Társaság, 1931).

25.   Pannonius 1988 (to Guarino); for works to Marcello, see Texts II.D.20, III.8, and chap. 4, following n184. Pannonius's verse includes many dedications to his friends from Ferrara: Galeotto Marzio, Battista Guarini, Tito Vespasiano Strozzi, Ludovico Carbone (Pannonius 1784, 1985 passim; for relations with Guarini also Abel 1880, 146–50, 203–15); also works to the Venetian secretaries Marco Aurelio (Pannonius 1784, 2:70–74) and Giovanni Sagundino (then adolescent), son of Marcello's consoler Niccolò (epigrams exchanged pub. by Abel 1880, 99–103).

26.   Pannonius 1784, 1:61: "Nempe togatorum generosus stirpe Quiritum / Marcellus, Venetae firma columna rei."

27.   Pannonius pursues the narrative in brief through the events of 1453, to the eve of the eventual peace, and thus is far more comprehensive in his vision than other Marcello panegyrists. Birnbaum 1981, 87–88 finds references in the *Panegyric* to a scandal which keeps Marcello sidelined, and sees Pannonius as Marcello's apologist, justifying his behavior to Venice's doge Foscari. But that reading does not square with events; nor do I see it quite that way in the text. Pannonius does refer to a problem Marcello faced

sometime after Casalmaggiore (1:177–78): and indeed, the Council of Ten intervened in Venice to clear his name in the fall of 1447, an incident which Pannonius might have had in mind (see Chron. 1447: 27 October). Later, the poet writes for Marcello a soliloquy (1:187–94), with much lament about the indignity of being excluded from battle. This soliloquy, set in Verona, seems to be placed at the time of the battle of Caravaggio— when Marcello, in fact, remained in Verona a distant spectator and eventual rescuer of the Venetian forces (see Chron. 1448: 22, 25 September; September–October; 3, 12 October). Of the "clandestine activities" that may have landed Marcello in jail (Birnbaum 1981, 87) I find no evidence and have been unable to check that author's source (94n26). For possible misbehavior in Marcello's career, see also below, chap. 4, nn123, 145.

28. Pannonius 1784, 1:473: "Si Marcellorum componas facta duorum, / Romani Venetus, vincet avi acta nepos." My translation, but see also Barrett's in Pannonius 1985, 105.

29. Pannonius 1784, 1:474: "Nunquam illi visas, toties hic contudit Alpes, / Vecta illi caesis, nulla carina, jugis. / . . . . Ille Syracusas trinis vix cepit in annis, / Verona huic trinos ante recepta dies." Cf. Pannonius 1985, 105.

30. Texts III.3. For Carrara, see G. Giraldi 1955; A. Zeno 1752–53, 2:27–31; Giraldi's intro. to Carrara 1967 (iii–li) recapitulates his earlier works. Giraldi (1955, 127) judges the *De bello* a "cosa da poco, scritto in età giovanissima," but full of echoes of classical epic.

31. Carrara 1757, 316: "Marcellus nostro in Regno victricia dudum / Signa tulit, nunc impunis mea maenia vasta[t]; / Magnificatque suum Imperium, multosque trucidans / Mincia, in arma furens subiecit."

32. Carrara 1757, 319: "Hi sensere Tubas primi, quantosque rugitus / Edere bis centum metu stimulante Leones, / aut possent Tigres, armati et unguibus ursi."

33. Texts III.1. Note also Bevilacqua's 1463 work to Marcello glorifying the latter's role at the siege of Trieste: see Texts III.2, Chron. at 15 December 1463.

34. Chron. 1441: 20 November, 1442: 3–6 May, and passim for the four-year period.

35. Nogarola, G, 139 (Abel, 2:174–75): "Testis est Verona nostra, in qua tam multa memoratu digna gessisti, ut in maximo discrimine suo tempore illius infelicissimae cladis te tamquam imperatorem inter tot strenuissimos duces eligerent, illustris simulque senatus Venetus confirmaret tibique summam totius belli committeret. . . . Testis est Brixia . . . in qua non minus . . . virtus tua enituit, cuius ductu et auspiciis tot et tanta gesta sint,

ut te propugnatorem, defensorem, conservatorem omnes tamquam e caelo missum semper appellent. Testis est denique Italia tota, cuius imperium tua singulari virtute et magnanimitate, dignitatem maiestatemque servasti, cui pacem, quietem, dehinc decus, honorem, libertatem restituisti."

36.   Fortebraccio, G, 148: "Casale maius tua opera, tua industria fortiter ac prudenter fuisse munitum atque defensum."

37.   F. Filelfo, G, 111 (ed. fol. 42; Ben. 4): "Frustrari enim hostis cum sua se vidisset spe ob unius Jacobi Antonii Marcelli consilium atque diligentiam, coactus est denique inde abducere suas copias."

38.   The battle described by Mascarello, G, 166–67.

39.   F. Filelfo, G, 111 (ed. fol. 42; Ben. 5): "Tum ipse, ut es ingenio acerrimo et animo ad res magnas atque periculosas invictus, te ultro quasi alter Scipio ad id negotii atque discriminis iturum polliceris."

40.   Bevilacqua, G, 402 (V, fol. 130v): "In me nescio quo modo versus Senatus me quasi fatalem provisorem creat, iubet copias omnes {V nostras} sine rei publicae nostrae detrimento e Brisia in agrum veronensem educere curem. Quod ubi audivi, et me designatum intellexi, principio color mihi immutatus est, me totum moetus increpuit, et ab me tam pium officium laeta duris admixta in tanta ambiguitate osita prohibebant. {V Mecum} Cogitabam mihi Brixiam esse per confragosa loca adeundum, evadandos amnes latos et profundos, brisiensem populum consolandum et spe subsidii praesto affuturi demulcendum. Exercitum omnem per vallem solis per asperrimas rupes, per confragosas cautes in agrum veronensem industria potius quam aliqua vi educendum. Sed nunquam me magis animi magnitudo deseruit."

41.   Described by Mascarello at G, 168.

42.   Perleone, G, 198 (B, fol. 20): "una tantum rei perficiendo ratio ostendebatur, ut Paride Lodroni regulo cuius opes et auctoritas inter montanos maxima erat consiliato, per eius loca transitus ad Veronam urbem peteretur."

43.   Perleone, G, 199 (B, fol. 21): "In tanto igitur metu, in re tam dubia ac prope desperata itur ad te, quod vel virtute vel fama, vel gloria vel fortuna tua nihil appararet tam arduum, tamque difficile, quod abste perfici atque obtineri posse non crederent."

44.   Bevilacqua, G, 404 (V, fols. 132v–33): "Verum ego qui rem hanc necessariam pro copiarum salute animadvertebam, me agricolam simulatus cum quo vestem commutaveram, clam omnibus ad Paridem proficiscor cui tum me ita dissimulans inde non arte discessi quam industria mea isti suaserim, mediolanenses oratores pellendos, atque ius societatis sancitum et amicitiae ista foedera cum venetis nostris exegerim."

45. F. Filelfo, G, 113 (ed. fol. 42; Ben. 7): "Nam impius iste Mahometus . . . , eodem machinamenti genere traducta classe per continentem a Bosphoro Constantinopolitanum in portum, inespugnabili illa nobilissimaque urbe potitus est cum maxima christianorum omnium iactura."

46. George of Trebizond, G, 32 (Mon. #21): "Solus enim per montes altos rupesque precipites . . . non exercitum tantum, ut Hannibal per Alpes, sed classem . . . ab Athesi fluvio in lacum Benacum traduxisti."

47. Fortebraccio, G, 150: "ipsum rerum ordinem, ipsa denique natura iura, mutata conspeximus . . . cuius id ingenio? cuius consilio actum est? nempe tue Iacobe Antoni."

48. Mascarello, G, 169: "Hic Marcelli virtus, hic ingenii lumen emicuit. Ad rem inauditam, ad rem que impossibilis videbatur animum tetendisti."

49. Perleone, G, 200 (B, fol. 24): "Qua in re quid prius, aut quid potius admirer ingenium ne tuum in excogitando acre, an industriam in efficiendo singularem, an rei miraculum inspectando inauditum? Iam naves a radicibus montis per aclivia et ardua loca vix qua eniterentur capree in altissimos, et quasi celo equatos montes machinis et ferramentis, magno militum clamore atque ingenti labore trahebantur."

50. Bevilacqua, G, 405 (V, fol. 135): "Te Marcelle admirabatur, te obstupebat, quod huius rei conficiendae cerciorem Senatum reddidisses."

51. Bevilacqua, V, fol. 136v (not in G): "Tui enim solius . . . , quia praeter omnium ingenia, qui id impossibile proculdubio asserebant, excogitatum atque perfectum." The whole enterprise is described by Bevilacqua at G, 405–7 (V, fols. 134v–37).

52. F. Filelfo, G, 115 (ed. fol. 42v; Ben. 9): "Tua igitur non minus diligentia, quam tanti imperatoris adventu ac viribus, factum videmus, ut et Verona obsidione illa ducali atque imminenti captivitate liberaretur, et Vicentinus Veronensisque ager omnis recuperatus immortales ageret tibi gratias."

53. George of Trebizond, G, 33 (Mon. #23): "Non obliviscaris quanto consilio, velocitate, celsitudine animi, cum Nicolaus Picininus agro Veronensi vastato ingenti fossa transitum rancisci Sfortie, cuius militari scientia etas nostra cum antiquitate potest certare, interclusit, et status inclite reipublice Venete nutaret et omnis spes salutis in transitu Francisci Sfortie sita esset, exire Veronam, ubi obsidebaris, potuisti et per montes saltusque Veronensium, qui ab hostibus tenebantur, victor Sfortie te coniunxisti et Suapis fovea superata statum reipublice in pristinum statum reduxisti."

54. Respectively at Fortebraccio, G, 149 ("Tu vero ut leo magnanimus et obsessa urbe Verona exire"); and Mascarello, G, 170 ("[Marcellus] sen-

tiens adventasse ducem fortissimum Franciscum Sfortiam, ut leo vincla indignatus, existi Verona").

55.   George of Trebizond, G, 33 (Mon. #23); see text above at n53.

56.   George of Trebizond, G, 33 (Mon. #24): "Taceo bis te tum Muntie, tum in Mediolanensibus burgis vitam Francisco Sfortie ab insidiis Francisci et Iacobi Picininorum consiliis tuis servasse." Mascarello, G, 172: "Francisco Sfortie nunc Mediolani duci bis vitam servasti tuis sapientissimis conciliis, que aptius in tuo sunt pectore conservanda quam a me scribenda, sit igitur triumphi tui portio preclara dux inclitus per te a crudeli morte servatus." Also Bevilacqua, G, 407 (V, fol. 137rv): "Haec atque alia huiusmodi ab me pluribus in locis gesta, vel ad salutem usque Sforciae Mediolani principis, dum imperium mediolani expugnare contenderet, providentia mea conservatam isti eloquentissimi viri commemorant."

57.   These statements respectively by Fortebraccio, G, 150: "Tunc comitem Franciscum Sfortiam in tue virtutis testimonium dixisse memini, Marcelle, tua non minus opera, at Veronam hodie quam virtute nostra recepimus"; and Mascarello, G, 171: "clara voce tunc testatus est Franciscus Sfortia, non a se magis quam a Marcello receptam esse Veronam."

58.   F. Filelfo, G, 115 (ed. fol. 42v; Ben. 10): "Quin etiam imperator ipse Franciscus, saepenumero aliisque permultis audientibus, quoties de tuis laudibus loquitur, loquitur enim et frequenter et perlibenter."

59.   F. Filelfo, G, 115 (ed. fol. 42v; Ben. 10): "Aufugit igitur bellicosissimus ille invictusque Nicolaus nec eum puduit clara voce testari apud Philippum Mariam, se ab uno patricio veneto, Jacobo Antonio Marcello, urbe Verona extrusum esse."

60.   F. Filelfo, G, 111 (ed. fol. 42; Ben. 5): "Franciscus Foscarus princeps ille . . . qui mirificae tuae divinaeque virtutis gravissimus iudex ac censor, et probaret tuam profectionem et magnam ex ea utilitatem ac laudem ad rempublicam perventuram certe speraret."

61.   Mascarello, G, 171: "Secutus est dux Marcelli consilium, pugnatum est, secuta est illa preclara victoria ut fere omnis hostilis exercitus caperetur."

62.   George of Trebizond, G, 33 (Mon. #24): "Taceo te causam eius victorie fuisse quam apud Casale Maius adversus Philippum Mariam consecutus senatus est cum dux exercitus Michael crus fregisset atque ideo tota vis certandi ad te convertisset."

63.   F. Filelfo, G, 115 (ed. fol. 42v; Ben. 10): "Nemo in tanto exercitu est inventus, qui prior flumen pervadere auderet."

64.   F. Filelfo, G, 116 (ed. fol. 42v; Ben. 11): "Hic tu, caeteris transitum detrectantibus, animo illo tuo infracto planeque Marcellus, repente

flumen eques ingrederis, reliquosque ut te sequantur hortaris; nusquamque deflectens inter altissimos rapidissimosque vortices, ante in ripa Insubrium visus es, quam alius quisquam ex tanto et militum et ductorum numero equorum ungulas aqua tinxisset."

65. F. Filelfo, G, 116 (ed. fol. 43; Ben. 11–12): "Tu enim unus, Jacobe Antoni Marcelle, . . . praecipuus auctor extitisti extremae calamitatis illius clementissimi atque optimi principis, qui non contentus Adduam superasse et amoenissimas late villas vicosque bonis omnibus refertissimos diripiendos militibus obiectasse, . . . voluisti etiam, ut vexilla ipsa signaque Venetorum ex illa celebri sublimique arce sua dux philippus, quantum oculi paterentur, posset coram adspicere . . . ut inde vehementi aegrotatione contracta post paucos menses in maxima regni clade vitam ipsam amiserit."

66. Fortebraccio, G, 151: "ex tanta spoliorum copia argenti aurique magnitudine, . . . nihilo locupletior domum reversus es, maiorem gloriam sane in contemnenda quam adipiscenda pecunias [. . .] imitatus Catonem illum Maiorem." (Cf. n23, above.)

67. Perleone, G, 209 (B, fols. 40v–41): "Nam cum pecunie publice non mitterentur militibus in stipendum, tu privata fide tantum auri et argenti uno die ab amicis contraxisti, ut deductus ex hibernis militibus omnem exercitum in armis paratum paucis diebus habueris."

68. Orsini, G, 284 (M, fols. 16v–17): "Nec ambique Marcellus et Romane probitatis et nominis et gentis, vel domi vel foris, vel paci vel bello clarus, maiorum suorum facinora memoranda renovasse videtur; dicereque fas est quicquid fortune virtutis et probitatis in omnibus Marcellis olim apud Romanos emicuit {M enicuit} nunc apud Venetos in uno Iacobantonio {G Marcello] fulgere."

69. Texts III.10.

70. Spretus, *De amplitudine,* fols. 34v–41.

71. Spretus, fol. 36: "Cuius quidem virtute precipua ac summa integritate ita omnia et bello et pace sapientissime administrata sunt, ut omnium civium nostrorum studia in venetorum benivolentiam ac devotionem summopere accensa sint, nec preter ipsorum imperium ullud aliud exoptarent."

72. Spretus, fol. 1v: "quem alterum ista in re. pu. Scipionem, aut tui generis patricipem M. Marcellum audeo dicere, cuius ductu et auspitio (ut caetera tua longe preclariora facinora sileam) nostra haec civitas e crudelissimis tyrannorum faucibus ad augustum venetorum descivit imperium."

73. Spretus, fol. 37: "tunc cives universi qui in forum ad Marcellum veluti ducem suum pro tutela convenerant."

74. See Fam. III.C.3–6.

75. Fam. III.C.4 for text.

76. See n35, above.

77. Damadenus, *De origine,* fol. 303: "Leonem venetum, Patriae symbolum imitatus est Iacobus Antonius . . . Marcellus. Leonem inquam alatum, uno pede terram, altero mare caleantem, capite ac reliquo corpore inter utrumque constitutum. Leonem imitatus est fortitudine, alas velocitate et diligentia, . . . capite, politica civitatis negotia intra mare et continentem sita, administravit." The lion of San Marco, symbol of the state, bestriding both land and sea, was an image commonly depicted. That by Caravaggio (painted in 1516) now in the Museo del Palazzo Ducale is most famous, but especially interesting here is the one painted by Donato Venetus in 1459, during our Marcello's lifetime and paid for in part by Marcello funds (as the arms, one of a sequence, depicted at the bottom margin signify); see Wolters 1987, 226–27 and figs. 239–40. For the "myth of Venice," see chap. 2n95.

78. Chron. for all dates.

79. Fortebraccio, G, 149: "per asperrimos colles iugaque montium, in agrum veronensem perduxisti, et quod mirabile dictu est, hieme asperi, adeo ut non nulli militum, in Sarche fluvio transitu, gelu diriguerunt et mortui marmoree instar statue immobiles constiterint." Also George of Trebizond, G, 32 (Mon. #19): "Veniat tibi in mentem, nobilissima Italie urbe Verona a Nicolao Picinino duce hostium occupata, imo repente rapta, viro temporibus nostris astucia, velocitate, robore animi, ceterisque virtutibus militaribus facile omnium principe, quibus consiliis duci exercitus Veneti persuasisti ut ex plano Arcus, Sarcha fluvio traiecto, idque in hieme adeo intensis frigoribus aspera ut non nulli peditum gelu deriguerint et mortui quasi marmoree statue sterint, Veronam per montes asperos atque invios exercitum duceret et in hostem repente irrueret."

80. For Guarino, see Texts I.9–11 and below; for Filelfo, chap. 2, at n39.

81. Sabbadini in Guarino 1915–19, 3:487–88, juxtaposes Guarino's references with passages from Cristoforo da Soldo, chronicler of Brescia (da Soldo 1938; Sabbadini refers to da Soldo 1732, passages from 792–843). Fabbri 1983, 246–50, and Monfasani 1984, 236, point out the minimal role assigned to Marcello in such sources as da Soldo again, Sanuto 1733, and Romanin 1853–61. For known events, see Chron. for these years.

82. The latter claim is made by Ludovico Merchenti, addressing a verse panegyric to Contarini's son preserved in the ms. *Benacus;* see Zeno 1752–53, 1:128; Zorzanello 1981, 2:311–12.

83. For the role of the *provveditore,* see Mallett 1973, 135–44; Mallett

1974, 88–90; Mallett 1984, 167–89; also Grubb 1988, 8, 172, and Menniti Ippolito 1984, for the provveditorial role in the establishment of Venetian civil power in respectively the Veneto and Lombardy. For another example of a Venetian nobleman active, like Marcello, in military ventures, P. Giraldi 1977.

84.   P. Giraldi 1977, 105.

85.   Bevilacqua, G, 401 (V, fols. 128v–29): "Ita me tanquam omnis res publica venetorum certam spem victoriae in me ac virtute mea {G ut verbis suis utar} collocasset, {G et} propugnatorem electum industria mea, celeritate, consilio, manus hostiles expugnasse, fudisse, dissipasse. Victorem totiens tanta gloria parta domum remeasse, atque victorissimis gestis meis nomen meum percelebre ab amicis sociisque imperii venetorum fuisse redditum? Tantam scientiam rei militaris adeptum, inter probaciores viros annumeratum, semper invictum, victorem semper extitisse ac me fama rerum gestarum et claritate nominis mei toto orbi factum illustrem?"

86.   Valentini 1924, 174n1: "Mitto ad te parentem tuum; non liniamenta solum . . . , sed loquentem, pugnantem et tandem nunc excitatum ab inferis in hanc demum ad te lucem exeuntem." The biography (completed September 1458) is Campano 1731; for which Valentini 1924; Tateo 1977; also Cochrane 1981, 52–53.

87.   See Cochrane 1981, 123, 98 respectively.

88.   See Cochrane 1981, 106–7.

89.   Decembrio 1731; Simonetta 1932; see also Cochrane 1981, 108–18; Ianziti 1981; Ianziti 1988. Note also the verse description of the Battle of Aquila (2 June 1424) by Leonardo Grifo, dedicated to Sforza, as victor: Grifo 1733, for which Lee 1978, 65.

90.   Robin 1991, chap. 3, excerpt at appendix B.

91.   See Cochrane 1981, 144–51, for the historians of Alfonso's reign; also Porcellio De' Pandoni 1731, for which see also Lee 1978, 185–86, and A. Zeno 1752–53, 1:15–21.

92.   See Mallett 1974, 46–47, for Machiavelli's portrayal; Green 1986 for a reconstruction of this "classical historical tragedy in its natural setting" (5).

93.   For judgments of this portrayal, Mallett 1974, 47–48. For the *condottiere* portrait generally, Campbell 1990, 60; Sleptzoff 1978, chap. 1. For equestrian monuments, Panofsky 1964, 84–85.

94.   Mallett 1974, 55, 56; Sleptzoff 1978, 10–13. The fresco of Hawkwood was followed up by Andrea del Castagno's of Niccolò da Tolentino in 1456.

95.   For the oration, see Sabbadini 1964, *Scuola*, 70.

96. Decembrio 1731 for Piccinino's; Di Santa Maria 1772–82, 2:lxxvii–lxxviii, for Gentile's; Giraldi 1955 for Colleoni's.

97. For Venetian state ritual, Muir 1981, part 3; P. F. Brown 1988, 165ff.; Molmenti 1910–12, 2:544–51.

98. McAndrew 1980, 9. See Paoletti 1893–97, 1:75–78 and 2:passim for monuments to doges and heroes; also Eisler 1989, 252–53; Huse & Wolters 1990, 159–60.

99. See Fam. III.B.

100. Mallett 1974, 62, 94; Molmenti 1910–12, 2:549; Paoletti 1893–97, 1:75; Sleptzoff 1978, 13–14.

101. Paoletti 1893–97, 2:160 and frontispiece; 145 and fig. 13, 274.

102. For these monuments, Molmenti 1910–12, 2:544, 546; for Capello's, also Paoletti 1893–97, 2:144–45, table 50.

103. Zorzi 1972, 2:393–401, at 393; Paoletti 1893–97, 2:144.

104. For the orations, Eroli 1876, 149–52, and Soranzo 1957, 113–14; for the burial and the will, dictating funeral arrangements, Eroli 179–83, 342–47; tomb inscriptions in Salomonius 1701, 356–57 (##23, 24, 26); Savonarola 1902, 33.1–7.

105. Eroli 1876, 185–94; Sleptzoff 1978, 17–22.

106. See esp. Janson 1967.

107. Paoletti 1893–97, 2:263–66; Sleptzoff 1978, 22.

108. Joost-Gaugier 1988.

109. Mallett 1974, 93.

110. Chron. 1438: 1 October; 1439: 23 November; 1446: 9 October; 1438: 8 October.

111. For Sforza's palaces, see below, chap. 4 at n207.

112. In addition to the works named, see Medin 1904, 85ff., for poetry in the vernacular celebrating Venetian conquests.

113. L. Giustiniani 1941; J. Zeno 1940.

114. Bembo, *Oratio in funere Bertholdi Marchionis Estensis;* Caldiera, *Oratio in funere Orsati Justiniani.*

115. Barbo, *Oratio in traditione insignium;* Navagero 1559.

116. Manelmi 1728; for Manelmi's account, Gothein 1932, chap. 7; also Cochrane 1981, 70, 78; for his brother's activity, Mallett 1974, 126–27.

117. F. Contarini 1623.

118. See for this point King 1986, passim, on the humanist spokespersons for the patriciate. See also Grubb 1986, 49–60 for the myth of the "good republic," and, for the contrary argument, Queller 1986.

119. Texts I.9–11 for the Strabo; I.7 for the possible authorship of the illuminations in the Strabo and Saint Maurice codices.

120. Chron. 1459: 14 March – 4 May.

121. For the lost portrait of the two friends, Birnbaum 1981, 14; Pannonius's elegy for Mantegna in Pannonius 1784, 1:276–78; 1972, 250–53.

122. Goffen 1989, chap. 3, n13 and 290; 192–93 and 291.

123. Eisler 1989, esp. 46, 197, 535–36, and ad indicem.

124. My thanks to Dottore Girolamo Marcello for pointing out the incongruity of Marcello's garb in this representation.

125. Meiss 1957, 38. For the paintings, ibid., 34–39.

126. Texts I.6–7.

127. For guidelines for costume and assembly, as specified in the statutes, Lecoy 1875, 1:532; also Meiss 1957, 6–7. For these illuminations, see also below, chap. 4, following n178.

128. For which see studies of the development of Renaissance portraiture, esp. Campbell 1990 (at 81 for profile portrait); Hatfield 1965; Lavin 1970; Pope-Hennessy 1966; Sleptzoff 1978, esp. chap. 1; Warburg 1987; Woods-Marsden 1987; also Goffen 1989, passim.

129. Meiss 1957, 19; see also Sleptzoff 1978, 27–28.

130. Meiss 1957, 18.

131. The images in these coins and medals were much reproduced in the art of the Renaissance; for Venice, see Weiss 1963. For the medallic source of this kind of portrait, also Woods-Marsden 1987; Pope-Hennessy 1966.

132. For this reading of the Piero portraits, see Baldwin 1987. Sleptzoff 1978, 28–30 also compares the Marcello and Montefeltro images.

133. Baldwin 1987, 17.

134. Goffen 1989, 192–93.

135. Ibid.

136. See esp. Warburg 1987 for the role of the patron in shaping the way the portrait subject is depicted.

CHAPTER FOUR

1. For the myth of Venice, chap. 2n95.

2. Fam. I.A.1–8 for the following.

3. Damadenus, *De origine,* fol. 303: "cum bellica virtute excelleret, et non nisi bella spirantem filium procreaverit."

4. Bent and Hallmark 1985, 224.

5. Fam. I.A.9–10.

6. Barzizza 1723, 85–87: "Oratio ad Petrum Marcellum episcopum patavinum in morte Hieronymi Marcelli."

7. Chron. 1413: 16 October.

8. Fam. I.A.24.

9. Perleone, G, 190–91 (B, fols. 4–6); for text see Fam. IV.1.b.

10. See Cenci 1968; King 1986, 283–87; Ventura 1979, 180; for the literature reflecting the role of the Venetian patriciate in these ecclesiastical positions, also Logan 1978.

11. After Marcello, Pietro Donato (1428–47); Fantino Dandolo (1448–59); Pietro Barbo (1459–60); Jacopo Zeno (1460–81); Pietro Foscari (1481–85); and Pietro Barozzi (1487–1507). King 1986, 283–84 (table 5) and "Profiles" for these figures.

12. King 1986, 402, 320–22.

13. For Venetian *terraferma* expansion, see the accounts in such standard histories as Cappelletti 1850–55, vol. 6; Cessi 1944, chaps. 6–7; Chambers 1970, 54–72; Hazlitt 1915; Kretschmayer 1920, vol. 2; Musatti 1919; Norwich 1982, chaps. 21–23; Romanin 1853–61, vol. 4. For Venetian rule of *terraferma* lands, Cracco & Knapton 1984; Grubb 1986, 72–82; Grubb 1988; Law 1982; Menniti Ippolito 1984; Mor 1963; Ortalli 1988; Tagliaferri 1981; Ventura 1979; Woolf 1962. For the cultural dimensions of *terraferma* expansion, King 1986, 217–19 and passim; Medin 1904, 85ff.; also biographies of two early *terraferma* rectors who were at the same time promoters of humanist culture, Gothein 1932 and Troilo 1932.

14. King 1986, "Profiles" for these figures at 323–25, 374–77, 361–62, and 335–39 respectively, and works there cited; for Bembo, Giannetto 1985 is now authoritative.

15. See Chron. for all dates.

16. Hazlitt 1915, 1:914–15.

17. In B. Giustiniani 1492, sig. L4rv; also Barbaro 1741–43, 2:174–76.

18. Da Soldo 1732, 793: "in tre giorni tutto da circo a circo a Brescia a otto miglia non rimase pure un sol cane nelle terre."

19. Chron. at 1438: 4 April, 13 June, 2 August.

20. Chron. 1438: 11, 16, 20 September; 2 October.

21. Chron. 1438: 24–28/29 September, 1 and 8 October.

22. Chron. 1438: 19 December; 1439: 6 and 15 February for the following.

23. Da Soldo 1938, 30; 1732, 808.

24. Franzoi 1982, 233.

25. Chron. 1439: 26 April.
26. Chron. 1439: July, September, October, passim.
27. Chron. 1439: 9, 12, 19, 20, 22–24 November.
28. Texts III.9.
29. Chron. 1439: 29 November, 10 and 31 December; 1440: 9 January.
30. Chron. 1440: 11 February.
31. Chron. 1440: 4 and 19 March.
32. Chron. 1440: 26 April, 14 June, 10 August.
33. For whom Texts III.10.
34. Chron. 1440: 10 August, 13 September for the following.
35. Text at Chron. 1440: 24 October – 1441: February.
36. Chron. 1440: 13 September, 24 October – 1441: February.
37. Chron. 1441: 21 February.
38. Chron. 1441: 10–11 February; also 1440: 18 December.
39. Chron. 1441: 6 July.
40. Chron. 1441: 14 September.
41. Chron. 1442: 3 April.
42. Chron. 1442: 17 May.
43. Chron. 1440: 18 December; 1441: 10–11 February, 21–31 August; 1442: 23 February, 10 April, 3–6 May.
44. Chron. 1441: 20 November.
45. Chron. 1441: 24–28 October; 1442: 3–6 May.
46. Chron. 1440: 7 September; 1442: 25 March. For René, see René d'Anjou 1845–46, 1:iii–cxlii; Coulet, Planche & Robin 1982; De Mérindol 1987; Des Garets 1946; Lecoy 1875; Perret 1896, 162–69, 214–17, 256–63; *Le Roi René* 1986. For the struggle over the throne of Naples, esp. Faraglia 1907; Léonard 1954; Peyronnet 1969; Pontieri 1958; Sabatini 1975.
47. For this phase of Sforza's career see esp. Catalano 1983, 5–17; Pontieri 1958.
48. Quoted by Lecoy 1875, 1:173n1. See also Chron., 1438: April.
49. Chron. 1442: 25 March, 2 June, 20 September.
50. Sanuto 1733, 1104; text at Chron. 1442, 2 June.
51. See below for Marcello's subsequent relations separately with Sforza and René. For links between the latter two, note the poetic celebrations of Porcellio de' Pandoni and Giovanni Mario Filelfo, which link the two rulers: see Manetti 1986, 122 and 125–26.
52. Chron. 1442: 4 August.
53. Chron. 1446: 7 and 13 May.

54. Chron. 1443: 22 June.
55. Chron. 1440: 2 January, 26 November; 1443: 9 January.
56. Fam. I.A.25–26, I.C, da Leone genealogy.
57. For the intermarriage of Venetian and *terraferma* families, Grubb 1988, 166–67; for a later generation, Olivieri Secchi 1987–89, 9.
58. Mallett 1974, 209.
59. Chron. 1456: 11 June.
60. Chron. 1443: 9 January; 1447: 25 January; 1452: 28 April, 16 May, and summer through November; 1453: 1 April. See also Eroli 1876, 156–57.
61. Mallett 1976, 204.
62. Eroli 1876, 156–57. Giacoma da Leonessa was left a widow in 1463, and honored by a consolatory address by the Venetian patrician Bernardo Bembo; see Chron. 1464: March.
63. Chron. 1446: 8 and 13 May, 11 August; also 7 May.
64. Chron. 1446: 11, 23 August.
65. Chron. 1446: 9, 11 and 12 September.
66. Chron. 1446: 28 September.
67. Franzoi 1982, 232.
68. Chron. 1446: 28 September.
69. Chron. 1446: 30 September.
70. Chron. 1446: 1 October.
71. Chron. 1446: 18, 21, and 26 October; and all dates specified below.
72. Chron. 1446: 12 November.
73. Chron. 1446: 9 October.
74. Chron. 1446: 12 November.
75. According to the panygyrists; also Chron. 1446: 6–7 November. From 14 November 1446 Marcello bears the title "miles" in Senate documents, which is the only benefit reaped from knighthood in the republic of Venice.
76. Chron. 1446: 10, 11, and 20 December; 1447: 12 and 25 January; 3, 10, 13, 20, and 31 March. The captain was one of two governors normally appointed by Venice to govern a subject city, the *podestà* tending to civilian, the captain to military business. In wartime, the captain's tasks resembled those of a hired general.
77. Chron. 1447: 23 February, 31 March.
78. Chron. 1447: 29 April.
79. Chron. 1444: 16 October; 1446: 6–7 November.

80. Chron. 1447: 13 and 15 July; 4, 9, 13, 17, 23, and 30 August for the following.

81. Chron. 1447: 13 August.

82. Chron. 1446: 10 and 20 December.

83. Chron. 1447: August.

84. For these perceptions of Venice, see esp. Rubinstein 1973; also Ilardi 1959, 131–37; Margaroli 1990, 529–30. Machiavelli's *Prince* often notes the greed and ambition of the Venetians.

85. Chron. 1447: 25 September.

86. Chron. 1447: 16 October – 16 November. F. Filelfo's *Sforziad* centers on Sforza's role in this event; see Robin 1991, chap. 3.

87. Chron. 1448: early months.

88. Chron. 1448: 16–17 July; for the following, 23 July, 29 July, 15 September.

89. Chron. 1448: 10 August.

90. Chron. 1448: 15 September.

91. Sanuto 1733, 1128–29; text in Chron. 1448: 15 September.

92. Chron. 1448: 22 and 25 September, 3 and 12 October.

93. Chron. 1448: 22 September.

94. Chron. 1448: September–October; for Simonetta, also 1437: 10 November.

95. For the Simonetta clan, who came with Sforza to Lombardy from the Marche, Santoro 1968, 33–35. Giovanni's work is Simonetta 1932, for whom also Ianziti 1981.

96. Chron. 1448: September – October.

97. Chron. 1448: 15 November, 18 October.

98. Chron. 1448: 15 November.

99. Chron. December 1448 – December 1449 passim.

100. Chron. 1449: January.

101. Chron. 1449: February – March.

102. Chron. 1449: February – March; also 13 February, 3 April, 7 May.

103. Chron. 1448–1449.

104. Chron. 1449: 24 February.

105. Perret 1896, 215.

106. Meiss 1957, 2–3.

107. Chron. 1449: 26 August, and 1448: 11 August, for the founding and nature of the Crescent.

108. Chron. 1449: 26 August; 1471: 12 September.

109. The award of the *praefectura maritima* is recorded in Marcello's epitaph: Fam. III.C.4.

110. Chron. 1449: 15, 24, and 25 September, 3 October for the following.

111. Chron. 1449: 25, 30 September, 3, 8, 15 October for the following.

112. Chron. 1449: 30 September.

113. Chron. 1449: 3 October.

114. Sometime ally, sometime enemy Sforza appears to have been a favorite of some other members of the Venetian nobility. Da Mosto (1983, 177) observes that Pasquale Malipiero opposed Foscari and was friendly to Sforza; Law (1982, 398 and n4) finds evidence that Sforza had admirers in Venice among the nobility and, indeed, Foscari's circle; Mallett (1974, 218–19) comments that Marcello curiously escaped the suspicion directed towards other patrician supporters of Sforza.

115. Chron. 1466: 8 March.

116. Chron. 1450: January.

117. Chron. 1449: 8 November; 1450: 21, 23 January for the following.

118. For the following, Chron. 1450: 25–26 February; 3, 13, 25–26, 28, 31 March; 7, 11, 14, 17, 23 April; 3, 10, 27 May; 8, 25 July; 4, 17 August.

119. Chron. 1450: 13 March; similar statements also at 1450: 28 March, 31 March, 7 April, 14 April, 17 April.

120. Chron. 1450: 14 April.

121. Chron. 1432: 5 May; 1441: 20 November.

122. Chron. 1453: end November – December; 1454: 14 January, 4 February, 18, 23, 28 March, 9 April.

123. For the failure of negotiations, Chron. 1450: 4, 17 August; for Dolfin's contradictory assessment, 2 July; for the assassination plot, 20 August. Birnbaum 1981, 87 and 94n26, sees Marcello as entangled in this assassination attempt, and perhaps later disgraced because of it or other secret operations. The evidence known to me (including that provided by Lamansky 1968, 1:161–62, whom she cites) does not support such claims. Similarly, she and Lamansky (vol. 2, index) identify the figure dispatched to Zara on an official mission on 17 August 1473 as Jacopo Antonio (already dead by this date), when the document itself (Lamansky, 1:185–87) clearly gives the name Jacopo Marcello (i.e., Jacopo di Cristoforo, for whom Fam. I.B.2–3).

124. The turf issues in these 1450 negotiations endure through the

1454 settlement at Lodi (Chron., at 9 April); a central condition for the Venetians was the retention of Crema, the securing of which was one of Marcello's principal achievements in the late stages of the Lombard wars (see Chron. 1454: 4 February; 23 and 28 March; also 1448: 18 October and 1449: 15 and 24 September for earlier territorial settlements along the same line of the river Adda; for the territorial issue, also Antonini 1930; Catalano 1956, 7:59–64; Santoro 1968, 44).

125.   Chron. 1452: 16 May.

126.   Chron. 1451: 30 July; 1452: 21 February, 16 May.

127.   For the following, Chron. 1452: 9 February; 10, 27, 28 April; 19 May.

128.   Chron. 1452: 31 October.

129.   Chron. 1452: 31 October.

130.   Greppi 1913, 327–31; Lorenzetti 1926, 600; Norwich 1982, 323.

131.   Chron. 1452: May – December passim, 31 December.

132.   Chron. 1453: 1, 3, 10, and 13 April for the following.

133.   Chron. 1453: 26 January, 21 April.

134.   For the statutes of the Order, Lecoy 1875, 1:530–32; René 1845–46, 1:51ff.

135.   Catalano 1983, 90; Lecoy 1875, 1:285; Ilardi 1982, 423.

136.   Chron. 1453: 2 June.

137.   Chron. 1453: 26 January, 21 April, 2, 15, 29 June, 4 July, 1 (or 3) and 9 August. Francophile Florence probably sought to "hire" such a figure as René because of its military unpreparedness: Mallett 1979.

138.   Chron. 1453: 18 (or 19) September.

139.   Marcello and Malipiero had been in the field since April (Chron. 1453: 4 May; 1, 16, 17, 18, and 23 June; 2 and 28 July; 25 August; 19 and 28 September; 10 and 12 October), with no military activity apparent until late September.

140.   Chron. 1453: 10 October.

141.   Chron. 1453: 14 October – 27 November.

142.   Chron. 1454: 3 January.

143.   Chron. 1453: 9, 14, 22 and 27 November, 16, 31 December; 1454: 19 January, 4, 6 February.

144.   See for example the sample in King 1986, 280–81 (tables 3 and 4).

145.   Ruskin 1906, 1:87. Fabbri (1983, 249–50) poses the explanation of Marcello's opposition to Foscari. Birnbaum (1981, 87–88) writes that he was disgraced and jailed as a result of involvement with "plots of ques-

tionable moral character," and that he commissioned Pannonius's panegyric to restore his reputation. I do not find that the evidence there cited sustains that interpretation (see also above, n123); but see Chron. at 1447: 27 October, when Marcello was involved in some possibly very minor legal problem; and also above at n123.

146.   Da Mosto 1983, 177. Malipiero was associated with the peace, perhaps by his own wish; the inscription on his portrait on the wall of the Maggior Consiglio in the doge's palace read: "Me duce pax patriae data est et tempora fausta." Compare this association of Malipiero with peace and the monument to the peace of the island of San Cristoforo, discussed later in this chapter.

147.   Chron. 1457: 12 January, 30 October, 1 November.

148.   Fam. I.A.33.

149.   Chron. 1458: 27 September – 1459: 22 August. He was also elected to the Senate *zonta* (Chron. 1454: 30 September), a minor position; but his name was subsequently canceled, and his other activities (see above) preclude his ever having served. For the following offices, Chron. 1459: 4 October – 1460: 31 May; 1462: 9 and 11 May, 19 May, 19 May – 3 July.

150.   Chron. 1462: 16 July, 11, 26 October, 16 December.

151.   For this incident see esp. Cesca 1883.

152.   Chron. 1462: 12 October; also 26 October.

153.   For Lando, King 1986, 385–86.

154.   Chron. 1463: 24 September.

155.   Chron. 1463: 27 September.

156.   Chron. 1463: 4 July – 11 November, 3, 24 October, 13 November, for the following. Marcello's particular role as director of bombardment is reflected in Bevilacqua's words of 15 December 1463 that in quick order he had torn the walls to shreds: "ut paucorum dierum intervallo magnam mura partem straveris ruinis." British Museum, ms. Harl. 2640, fol. 11, from laudatory letter listed at Texts III.2.

157.   Texts III.13.

158.   For Venice as "gerontocracy," Finlay 1978.

159.   Fam. II.B.

160.   For friendship as an alternative to the strain of continued role-playing imposed on those who belong to solidary groups (such as the Venetian aristocracy), see Wolf 1966.

161.   For the following, Chron. 1382–; 1409: 16 January; 1410: 19 May; 1420–; 1435: 2 February.

162.   Lecoy 1875, 1:502. Chron. 1476.

163. Lavisse 1900–11, 4:311. For the following, Chron. 1438: April; 1442: 2 June; 30 November; 1449: 24 February.

164. Chron. 1453: 26 January; 21 April; 4 May, 15 June, 18 (or 19) September, 10 October; 1454: 3 January, for the following.

165. For the following, Chron. 1458: 11 May, 8 June; 1459: 4 October, 6 November; 1460: 20 June; 1461: 17 July.

166. Chron. 1471: 14 July; 1480: 10 July.

167. Manetti 1986, 123; Chron. 1448–1450.

168. Lecoy 1875, 2:chap. 5, and esp. 175.

169. These works in René 1845–46, vol. 2. See also Coulet, Planche & Robin 1982, parts 2 and 3, esp. 149–64 for the tournament treatise; Ricaldone 1986.

170. Lecoy 1875, 2:182–97.

171. Manetti 1986, 123–24.

172. For the royal tomb, see below, chapter 6, discussion following n122.

173. For Marcello's relations with René, esp. Lecoy 1875, 1:273, 279, 336–38, 533, 536; 2:180–97. For contemporary Italian fascination with chivalric culture, see Grendler 1988; for the late-medieval cult of chivalry outside of Italy, the classic Huizinga 1954, chaps. 4–7; also Barbero 1986; Keen 1976, 32–45; Vale 1981.

174. See esp. N. Z. Davis 1983, for sixteenth-century France.

175. Chron. 1452: 5 April, 28 April (Padua), and after 5 April but before end May.

176. Texts I.2–3 for the two versions of the translation. For Quirini, Branca 1977a, 1977b, and sources there cited; also King 1986, 419–21.

177. Chron. 1453: 28 February. For Marcello's responses, below, see Texts I.4–5.

178. Texts I.6–7; Chron. 1453: 1 June.

179. For the interpretation of emblem and cryptogram, see Meiss 1957, 9–15, and Martin 1898, 243ff. The description which follows from Meiss, 9.

180. A device favored in this period by many princes, including Sforza and René himself (Ilardi 1987; Portioli 1871), and commonly used by secretaries employed in delicate missions (Neff 1981, esp. 48–49; see also Alban & Allmand 1976). It is not surprising that Marcello, a traveler in those circles, also availed himself of it; indeed, he had done so before, sending the Senate a letter "in zifra" (Chron. 1449: 7 May). For the documentary function of painting in contemporary Venetian culture, P. F. Brown 1988,

chap. 5, esp. 79. More on the portrait of Marcello in chapter 3, above, discussion following n128.

181.   Meiss 1957, 13; the cipher is decoded by Martin 1898, 243 ff. Marcello's curious relations with René at this juncture are not untangled by a reading of the *Panegiricus in Renatum* composed, at Marcello's request, by the poet Janus Pannonius.

182.   Chron. 1452: 21 February; 1453: 26 January.

183.   Texts I.6.

184.   So acclaimed by the early humanist Antonio Loschi; Loschi 1858, 32: "Jacob, militiae decus et lux una Latinae, / Quo duce terribili superata Bononia bello est." A sketch of this *condottiere* in Mallett 1974, 52–53.

185.   See Texts III.8.

186.   Pannonius in Abel 1880, 131, ll.3–4.

187.   Texts I.8 (for Onofrio), III.12 (for Vallaresso). For Matteolo, see text at chap. 1n96.

188.   Texts II.D.20, for the surviving epitaph; other works are lost. See also Birnbaum 1981, 82–86, for Pannonius's relations with Marcello. Pannonius also had close relations during his Paduan years with another Venetian, the future secretary Marco Aurelio: see his dedications, of 1 December 1456 and 28 February 1457, to Aurelio of translations from Plutarch in Pannonius 1784, 2:70–74.

189.   Trans. of Barrett 1985, 125, of Barrett's epigram #110; also Pannonius 1784, 1:495 (#79). Pannonius names respectively patrons and writers of antiquity.

190.   Trans. of Barrett in Pannonius 1985, 171, from epigram #214; also Pannonius 1784, 1:551 (#209).

191.   Trans. of Barrett in Pannonius 1985, 221 (#317); cf. Pannonius 1784, 1:611 (#339).

192.   Trans. of Barrett in Pannonius 1985, 221 (#318); cf. Pannonius 1784, 1:611 (#340).

193.   Trans. of Barrett in Pannonius 1985, 157 (#177); cf. Pannonius 1784, 1:519 (#159). I believe the sense is better and more consistent with the relationship between the two men if the Latin "Hoc tu magnanimo nunc es, Marcelle, Renato" is rendered "just so great-souled now are you, Marcello for René." The poet appears to be praising Marcello's *aristeia*, exercised for the king's benefit, but not the king's.

194.   For the Mantegna portrait and relations with Marcello at this time, see above, chap. 3, following n129, and the literature cited in Texts I.7.

195. For the above reasoning, Tietze-Conrat 1955, 10, 185, 200, and plate 35.

196. For the identification of Marcello as Bellini's patron, Eisler 1989, 38, 46, 183, 197, 207, 208, 217, 393, 535–36.

197. Eisler 1989, 197–99, plates 84 and 86, and 207.

198. Eisler 1989, 393.

199. Eisler 1989, 47 and 62, fig. 47.

200. Eisler 1989, 235; 223–51 generally for Bellini's role as joust planner, and 212–63 generally for military themes in his art.

201. For Giovanni Bellini's possible role as Marcello's illuminator, see esp. Joost-Gaugier 1979 and Robertson 1968, and the fuller discussion by the authorities cited in Texts I.7.

202. Texts I.8 for the following.

203. Texts, I.9–11.

204. Texts, I.11.

205. Meiss 1957, 34.

206. For the letters, Texts III.12, 4 respectively; for the conversations, see above, chap. 1, at nn67–69, n78, and following n82.

207. For Sforza's abiding concern with a palace in Venice, see Beltrami 1906, Greppi 1913, 326–31, and the references to Chron. which follow.

208. Chron. 1439: 23 November.

209. Chron. 1447: April; 1448: 18 October.

210. Lorenzetti 1926, 600; Norwich 1982, 323.

211. Chron. 1455: 26 January – 25 February; 1456: 14 June.

212. Chron. 1461: 10 January.

213. Lieberman 1982, plate 57. For the admixture of mainland style and its subsequent influence on Venetian palace architecture, Huse & Wolters 1990, 20–21; McAndrew 1980, 12–14.

214. For the negotiations, Chron. 1454: 14 January, 4 February, 18 March, 28 March, 9 April; for concessions granted, 17 May.

215. Fam. III.C for San Cristoforo. For Fra Simone's congregation, Walsh 1977; Walsh 1989.

216. Sanuto 1733, 1045: "gran predicatore, e uomo di santa vita."

217. 25 November; see Fam. III.C.

218. For Simone (born 1396), who migrated to Padua by 1432, and was made prior of Monte Ortone in 1436, see esp. Antonini 1930; Greppi 1913. For his relation to Foscari, Walsh 1989, 91. Walsh 1989, 95–96, challenges Dolfin's claim (followed by Greppi and most others) of Simone's intimate relationship to Sforza, and shows that the former dealt with the latter through the agency of another Augustinian friar, Agostino Cazzuli;

for the latter Walsh 1979. Yet there is ample documentary evidence of Simone's relationship to Sforza, before and after Lodi. Dolfin's key testimony is in his *Cronaca,* 437v (326v), text at Chron. 1454: 4 February. If there were a prior relationship developed in the Marche, the situation would parallel that of the Simonetta clan, who followed their lord from that region to Lombardy and remained loyal for two generations; see above, n95. For Fra Simone's role, special thanks to Dr. Patricia Labalme for much assistance.

219.   For the following, Greppi 1913, 335–50, based on letters in the Sforza archives in the Archivio di Stato, Milan.

220.   Greppi 1913, 337 and doc. #2, 353 (letter from San Cristoforo della Pace, 18 June 1454, some months before the actual donation): "O que honore, o que fama, farà a la S.a Vostra questo dono, questo é segno de gran dilectione et amore."

221.   For estimations of Sforza along the lines sketched here, see esp. Ilardi 1982, 442–47; Peyronnet 1982; Santoro 1968. Catalano (1956, 14–17; 1983, 44–48) reviews the development of historical judgments of his achievement. For the creativity of Italian political thought immediately at the hinge years of the 1450s when Sforza was a key figure, see Margaroli 1990.

222.   This discussion of place and entombment relies on Romano 1987, 112–18.

223.   Fam. III.C.7.

CHAPTER FIVE

1.   Tifernate, *Oratio,* fol. 126v: "[you] quem ego semper maximi animi virum et in omni re prudentissimum cognovissem, ut potius existimandum sit dolorem abs te, quam te a dolore esse superatum."

2.   Sagundino, G, 7–8 (F, fol. 95v; VatS, fol. 4rv): "Dolendum est quidem, sed non effrene neque inmodice, non muliebri et molli sensu, non perenni diuturnove luctu, non semper eodem dolendi tenore. Quis enim non nisi iniuria stulteque possit {VatS posset} eternum et immortalem sustinere dolorem? de re presertim caduca temporaria, fragili et suape natura mortali? Quod si hec rationis et consilii plena precepta quemvis hominem servare et sequi decet, quanto tibi amplius convenit, fortissimo atque clarissimo viro, qui tue singularis et rare virtutis iam inde ab ineunte etate, rebus maximis fortissime gestis, certissimum argumentum et locupletissimum testimonium edidisti?"

3.   Sagundino, G,14 (F, fol. 99; VatS, fol. 7v): "Collige itaque tibi te,

exicca iam lacrimas, comprime gemitus, mitiga et leni dolorem, circunspecta undique te quis ipse sis, quantus, ubi sis, quid deceat te, quid dedeceat {F deceat} cogita, quid homines de te sentire, quid expectare debeant tecum reputa, qua sis etate animadverte. Noli usque adeo indulgere dolori et lacrimis, ut dum egritudini isti tue satisfacere vis, tibi tuisque expectationi de te omnium satisfacere nequeas. Memoria queso repete et animo subiice tuo, qua virtute, qua sapientia, quo robore infatigabili corporis, quibus periculis, qua industria, qua nominis et fame celebritate, consilio, armis, imperio, dubiis rebus, dificillimisque temporibus rempublicam gesseris, quam inde domi et foris opinionem quam gloriam consecutus sis. Non convenit certe te ipsum nunc unius puerili {F pueruli} iactura facta, dolore frangi atque moerore consterni, lacrimis et luctu tabescere, una alterave eiuscemodi offensiuncula animo demitti et deiici."

4. Sagundino, G, 14 (F, fol. 99rv; VatS, fol. 7): "Vide quo loco, quo ordine, qua auctoritate vir sis, qua patria illustris et nobilis civis, omnium {F,G scilicet} florentissima, ditissima, potentissima, amplitudine ditionis imperii terra marique propagatione, optimo rei publice genere, prestantia patrum, numero virtuteque civium, maxima et in orbe urbe pene singulari. Turpe igitur est inter patres primarios, non modo senatorem verum etiam senatorium virum, ita domestica afflictari solicitudine, ita privato incommodo angi, ut rem publicam alicubi negligere et post habere videri {G haberi} possit. Illius {F, VatS vero} non tibi venit in mentem, quid tibi incumbat oneris, quis tibi sit respectus habendus? Marcellorum inquam claram et perantiquam familiam, inde a superiore Marcellorum romano sanguine ut mihi persuadeo ductam {VatS est}, ex qua ne plus {F, VatS plus ne} ornamenti ad te defluxerit, an ad eam ex te refluxerit satis constituere nequeo. {VatS Sed} debet ne in aliquem huius familie hominem, non dicam mollitudinis ulla labenda, sed vel suspitio cadere imbecillitatis?"

5. Sagundino, G, 19 (F, fol. 102; VatS, fol. 10): "Non ab re apud Lycios lata commemoratur lex, licere virorum nemini luctum et comploratiodem suscipere, nisi deposita toga virili, desumpta muliebri veste, certeque complorandi lugendique negotium mulierculis non viris convenire videtur."

6. Sagundino, G, 24 (F, fol. 105; VatS, fol. 12v); see text at Fam. IV.6.

7. For the meaning and function of "honor" in this period esp. Bitton 1969; Fichtner 1967; Huizinga 1954, esp. chap. 4; Peristiany 1965; Vale 1981, esp. chap. 1; Barbero 1986 reviews some of the literature.

8. George, G, 30 (Mon. #15): "Nunc illud restat ut rogem obsecremque te sine dolore nimio tanti adolescentuli perpetuam habere memo-

riam, quod equidem magis facio ut scribentis amici officio fungar quam quod credam dolore te acerbo acriter vexari. Cognovi enim te semper ratione optime vixisse et abste multa bene vivendi exempla sumi posse."

9.   George, G, 31 (Mon. ##16–17): "Deinde is tu es ut a te ipso . . . tu solus dolore turbatus te ipsum ignorabis? Valerius, puer tuus, moriens te flentem, ne mortis quidem amaritudine terroreque omnium summo superatus, ad considerationem tui te revocabat? Turpeque censebat esse si a rebus gestis tuis et gravitate pristine vite degenerares? Et tu vir, imo iam senex atque canus, non repetes memoria quis fueris, quis sis, que quotque gesseris, et quanta laude atque gloria ille puer ultimum spiritum trahens magnum animum et Marcellorum familie dignum gessit? Et tu vir belli pacisque artibus clarus, mari et terra probatus, domi et foris magnus, et in senatu Veneto prudentia, eloquentia, gravitate precipuus, hac perturbatione animi victus iacebis? Non facies scio."

10.   George, G, 34 (Mon. #26): "Hanc ego gloriam dico tibi iam contigisse nisi tu velis eam repellere. Hanc in te florere video, florescetque in dies uno omnium ore nisi tui ipsius obliviscaris, nisi tu tibi desis. Deeris vero tibi si non qui fueris, qui sis, quid te deceat, quid tibi turbe sit mediteris, sed dolore victus, lacrimis consumeris."

11.   George, G, 37–38 (Mon. #39): "Quasobres, Iacobe Antoni Marcelle, . . . ut merito iam inter illustres viros enumereris, hec ultima, si quanto acerbiora sunt tanto maiore animo feres, et preteritam confirmabus gloriam et futuram perpetuam reddes, sicut econtra, si dolore victus iacebis . . . , nec futuram consequeris, et acquisitam iam, imo stabilitam gloriam funditus evertes. Multi enim (parce mihi aperte loquendi) casu potius quam ratione atque animi robore invicto magnas abste res gestas esse putabunt. Non ergo aliunde sed a te ipso, ut hactenus fecisti, pendeas. A te ipso exempla collige. Te ipsum imitere. Tecum loquere. Tecum certa. Te ipsum vince gloriosumque tibi esse non dubita si sicut etate maior, ita virtute illustrior in dies efficiaris."

12.   Nogarola, G, 135 (Abel, 2:164): "Sed quo modo te consolabor, cum ipsa eadem consolatione egeam et omnis philosophiae ac religionis oblita terga dare visa sim, meque dolor et moeror, quem ex morte sanctissimae ac dulcissimae matris meae cepi, captivam ducant, ex qua incredibilem ac graviorem quam unquam existimassem concepi dolorem?"

13.   Nogarola, G, 137 (Abel, 2:169–70): "Cum igitur in omnibus servandus sit modus, . . . habenas rationis revocemus nec dolorem nostrum longius vagari sinamus. Tuque inprimis, vir clarissime, cum magna laus sit et admirabilis tulisse casus sapienter adversos, non fractum esse fortuna, retinuisse in rebus asperis dignitatem."

14. Perleone, G, 189 (B, fol. 3): "Saepe mecum ipse considerans, Jacobe Antoni Marcelle, magnitudinem atque gravitatem animi tui, mirari soleo quid sit, cur in maxima utriusque fortune varietate quam fortiter semper moderateque tulisti, nunc Valerii filii tui mortem gravissime feras."

15. Perleone, *Epistola,* cod. VatP, fol. 106v (F, fol. 109; MU, fol. 100): "Illud te rogo memineris te esse Iacobum Antonium, quem nunquam rebus adversis fractum, nec inimicis, nec fortunae. . . . Da igitur hoc dignitati atque existimationi tuae. Da hoc Valerio, qui te lugere non vult. Da caeteris denique filiis et amicis tuis omnibus, quibus profecto te merente geminatur dolor, et qui {F quod} filium amiseris, et qui {F quod} te lugentem videant."

16. Filelfo, G, 87–88 (ed. fol. 38), and G, 123 (ed. fol. 45): "In te florentissimi Senatus et bonorum graviumque virorum omnium oculi diriguntur. Quare tibi cavendum est, ne quid commisisse existimeris, qua propter reprehendi iure queas. . . . Quid igitur doleamus in gaudiis et gloria filiorum? At indulgendum aliquid fuit nature desiderio, ne si effervescenti ad huc vulneri remedia fortiora essent adhibita, dolor magis atque magis exagitatus incrudesceret. Qui enim recenti vulneri curationes adhibet validiores, dolorem exasperat magis quam lenit. Sed ecce annus iam tibi preterit. Satis nature imbecillitati, satis opinioni, satis offitio trubutum est. Iam ratione uti nos decet. Privatus dolor cum amicorum dolore tibi est digerendus. Omnes enim quibus es carissimus, tua causa dolemus."

17. Filelfo, G, 120 (ed. fol. 43): "Simus ne ingenio muliebri inferiores? Quot enim legimus mulieres, que obitum filiorum in {ed. omits *in,* adds *et*} constanti et infracto animo tulerunt?"

18. Filelfo, G, 123 (ed. fol. 44); for text see Fam. IV.4.

19. At G, 285 (M, fol. 18v).

20. Guarini, G, 181–82 (F, fol. 110v–111): "Quam quidem spem cum invida mors eripuerit, non tibi tantum sed universae quoque venetorum rei publice hanc calamitatem deplorandam esse censeo. . . . Nolim tamen existimes amplissime vir ita me dolori tuo indulgere, ut molliter aliquid effeminateque faciendum esse concedam. Nihil enim minus magnanimo viro dignum puto, quam supra modum angi afflictarique, presertim cum intelligam vehementer doloris acerbitatem ob peccata solum a deo esse tributam."

21. Mascarello, G, 163: "Cum te audierim atque conspexerim dolore lugenti afflictum ac consternatum ob filii dormitionem, dolui equidem cum rei publica. Causa tum tua consueveram enim te conspicere et magna cum leticia admirari huius glorisosissime civitatis sydus ac iubar eximium, dolebam tantum reipublicae decus tantum splendorem doloris nebula ob-

volutum, dolebam virumque summa veneratione complecterer dolore affectum in maximo. Huic rei pro virili succurrendum existimari."

22. Fortebraccio, G, 159: "Amicos tuos hoc onere libera qui tuo dolentes moerore die noctuqe excogitant."

23. Fortebraccio, G, 151: "Verum hec tibi impresentiarum ad memoriam perstringendo putavi esse revocanda, quo amplitudini tue cerneres congruere, te tantis rebus gestis tui similem esse oportere, paremque in hoc filii tui Valerii acerbissimo luctu exhibere prudentiam. . . . Quid iuvat superatis hostibus tantam de industria, magnanimitate, consilio tuo, gloriam deportasse, si domi a moerore superaris?"

24. Anon. Ven., G, 249; for text see Fam. IV.9.

25. Anon. Stu., G, 304: "Tu igitur tot tantisque virtutum ornamentis factus illustris in hoc quoque filii tui obitus accerbissimi negocio, minime debes ipsius solitae fortitudinis atque constanciae tuae vires amittere. Sed eo amplius moderanda est haec tanti doloris tui quo ut dixi meliorem vitae partem sortitus est, et ad casus huiusmodi fortiter tollerandos. Nostra ac preclara maiorum exempla non mediocriter impellunt. Legimus namque gentilium quosdam, dum sibi nunciati essent obitus filiorum sine ullo moerore atque tristicia hoc solum nunciis dedisse responsum, nihil doloris atque admiracionis velle suscipere, cum hoc semper firma cognicione perceperint eos a se corruptibiles fuisse genitos atque mortales."

26. Anon. Stu., G, 306–7; further passages at Sagundino, G, 15–18 (F, fols. 99v–102; VatS, fols. 7v–10); Nogarola, G, 136–37 (Abel, 2:166–69); Guarini, G, 183 (F, fol. 111v); Mascarello, G, 163; Fortebraccio, G, 147–48, 154–55; Anon. Ven., G, 251, 253; Carbone, *Carmen,* BMV 4683, fols. 135v–37 (BMV 4451, fols. 29–30). Bevilacqua gives these and other examples at G, 313–20 (V, fols. 12–20v); 338 (V, fol. 45); 383 (V, fol. 104): 386 (V, fol. 108): 387–90 (V, fols. 109v–114), 423–25 (V, 158v–160v). The figures posed for imitation are stock exemplars of classical and Christian virtue, but these authors (particularly Bevilacqua) may have been familiar with Giannozzo Manetti's *Dialogus consolatorius* (Manetti 1983), which gives a full roster of grieving parents, passim, esp. books 3 and 6.

27. For the latter, Cicero, *Tusc. Disp,* 1.42.102.

28. Filelfo, G, 121–22 (ed. fol. 44); Sagundino, G, 16–17 (F, fols. 100–101; VatS, fols. 8–9v). For Foscari, see also below, n49.

29. Bevilacqua, G, 310 (V, fol. 7rv): "Verum me tantus moeror afflixit, in tanto floetus langore fui consternatus, ut id minime facere potuerim, et semper inter angustias et afflictaciones oppraessus, nunquam dolores, nunquam gemitus excutere phas fuerit. Nunquam te litteris meis ad me {V

te} consolandum provocare licuerit, ab quo vulnerum meorum subsana-
tionis remedia sperassem."

30.   Bevilacqua, G, 310–11 (V, fol. 8rv): "Ego vero demum ad te scribere destinavi, et doloris mei causas quibus sum afflictus ostendere.
Quotque eloquentissimi viri, qui me nulla et propinquorum et familiarium, et si id summe conati sint, consolacione leniri perspexere, suis non
modo epistolis, sed libellis singulari doctrina et mira orationis facultate
compositis me solari studuerunt, declarare. Immo eos omnis quo ad me
tempore ordinatim dati sunt, in hoc volumine quos ad te mitterem, tum
scribi curavi, ut his perlectis atque rationibus angorum et molestiarum
mearum cognitis, doloris originem, et ex quo fonte scaturierit, quave causa
nunquam lacrimarum exsiccandarum potestas extiterit, intelligas. Atque
hac epistola mea te inter me et eiusmodi repraehensores censorem arbi-
trumque constituam, qui cum princeps haud minus iusticia et aequitate
quam imperio dignitateque celebratissimus sis, quod doleam, quod me {V
continuis} singultibus afficiam, quod iacturam meam illacrimer, ab me
nequaquam fieri ab re ipse cognoscas."

31.   Bevilacqua, G, 312 (V, fol. 10rv): "Et si haec omnia me a scri-
bendo reprimere deberet, tamen doloris flamma qua uror {V urar} indies,
et consolaciones summo studio a tam eloquentissimis viris lucubratae, quae
quamvis omnes mentis erunnas in quocumque altero evellere potuissent,
ut quantum mihi parum in tanto ulcere {V vulnere} profuerint, ne dicam
{dixerim}, subsanarint, ostendam, ad hoc faciendum impellunt. O tempus
accerbum, et exitio simile! O tempestatem erunnosam, et miseriarum com-
potem! O miseros dies, atque funestos, in quos me addictum esse, vicem
meam miserear, oportet! Hem {V Heu}, ad hoc adductus sum, ut an interitus {G interius} filioli mei Valerii mihi dolendus sit, an illius qui memoriae
suae nedum {ni dum} meo in corde construxit, obitus illacrimandus, in
discrimen a tam sapientissimis viris, qui ornatissima oracionis suae facultate
me in hoc defensionis mee certamen provocant, venire compellar. Hem {V
Heu}, nobilissimus filius meus e patris sinu, e matris complexu ereptus, et
in mortis praecipicium illisus {G illius} fuerit, nec flendi, nec lugendi mihi
locus praestabitur."

32.   Bevilacqua, G, 312–13 (V, fol. 11rv): "O mors impura et immanis! exclamare libet. Quid tam effrenatam violentiam in exicium tam
dulcissimi filii vertere tibi venit in mentem? O mors furibunda et quacunque execratione digna! Qua face exagitata, qua percita rabie tantam indolem, quae tantum futurum virum praeseferebat, invadere tibi venit in
mentem? O morsi {G mors} vipereis nodis {G nobis} innexa, qua furoris

insania, quo pestifero veneno repleta in tam nobilissimum filium exarsisti? Quo pacto in perniciem tanti pueri te praecipitare, quasi palmam clarissimam ex eius interitu esses relatura, tibi venit in mentem? . . . Num tu mihi filium hunc meum servare, ut eius dies in aliquam aetatem maturiorem diuturniores differre potuisses?"

33.   Bevilacqua, G, 336 (V, fols. 42–43): "Quam rem isti eloquentissimi viri qui ad me in tam funesto, tam accerbo funere consolandum amici officio fungi statuerunt, si sanius iacturam meam animo voluere voluissent, et erunnarum mearum habere racionem, non tam in me graves non tam severi consolatores, et animi abiectioris accusatores extituissent, sed in tam accerbissimo casu et indulgentiores et leniores se praestitissent. . . . Haud tanti laboris causam mihi praebuissent, ut tam amplissimis ingeniis disertorum hominum responderem, quibus cum summa sit dicendi gravitas, sitque cum gravitate luculentus iunctus ornatus, et eloquens argumentorum similitudinum et exemplorum copia, ut obruar dicendo necesse sit, ne si me excusare conatus fuerim eos refellere videar, sicque mea orationis tenuitate contemnar, quasi dicendo implere facultas non fuerit, quod summe fuerim enixus, quod erit impudentia. Sin forte taciturnus fuero quod crediderim urbanum, infancissimus existimer, in quorum altero vel insolentiae vel ingratitudinis accuser, in altero negligentiae. Verum his multo maiora elegantioraque fuere quae si quos modo nominavi eloquentissimis viris nota fuissent, quod in tam perpetuum luctum, in tam longum langorem ac floetum diuturnum educar, {V et} quod oculi in continuis lacrimis inundent, non in tantam admiracionis partem isti venirent."

34.   Bevilacqua, G, 407 (V, fol. 137rv): "Haec atque alia huiusmodi ab me pluribus in locis gesta, vel ad salutem usque Sforciae Mediolani principis, dum imperium mediolani expugnare contenderet, providentia mea conservatam isti eloquentissimi viri commemorant, quae etsi gloriam meam et laudem illustrent tamen omnia intelligo exarata ut me mollius, languidius, humilius, animoque demissiore ferre dolorem hunc omnes acclamittent, et viro huiusmodi esse incongruens tanti hanc doloris accerbitatem existimare, et filii obitum pendere animumque fortunae submittere, ut me sinam a gravissimi magnanimique viri proposito depelli, quasi nihil accidere mali forti viro posse, nec misceri posse contraria."

35.   Bevilacqua, G, 405 (V, fol. 134v): "Caeterum alterum mihi facinus incredibile industria mea, quod non negarim, gestum recensent atque exprobrant, quo me qui ordine senatorio natus sim, virtutum experimentis omni nobilitate clariorem aiunt, ut cum animi magnitudine atque rerum {V re} gestarum gloria omnes, per quos imperii nostri hostes domiti sunt, si non vicerim, at saltem aequarim, non possunt {G possint] me non admi-

rari, qui tantulae rei in obitu unius filioli me {G mei} succubuisse cernant."

36. Bevilacqua, G, 331 (V, fol. 36): "Nunquam cogitassem, in me tam accerbe, tam immaniter incessura, ut obitus hic tam immaturus mihi {V tam} molestissime flendus esset."

37. Bevilacqua, G, 341 (V, fol. 49): "Quae si mihi arrisit aliquando, et me {G foelicissimum} fecerit {V foelicissimum}, prole decorum, gloria habundantissimum, tantam postea calamitatem immiscuerit, ut in solius huius carissimi filii obitu me ab his {V iis} omnibus destitutum hoc tempore in extremum vitae usque reddiderit."

38. Bevilacqua, G, 338 (V, fol. 45v): "Quo modo igitur non ingemiscere non possum? {G Quo modo non illacrimari?} Quo modo non dolere? {V Quo modo non illacrimari?}"

39. Bevilacqua, G, 400 (V, fol. 127v); see text in chap. 2, n168. See also G, 379–80 (V, fol. 99rv); see text in chap. 1, n124.

40. Bevilacqua, G, 382 (V, fol. 102v): "Sed noli tu, Serenissime Princeps, contemnere; noli me idcirco flocipendere quod nullum lacrimarum solacium, nullum hactenus doloris moerorisque lenimen in obitu Valerii dulcissimi filii mei recepisse asseverem; et magis Orpheus inferos mulcere lyra flectereque potuerit, . . . Caesaris propositum Ciceronis oracione in alteram instituti animi partem cogi potis fuerit, quam ego a luctu, quam a floetu praecipua quadam incredibili{V que} {G omnis} eloquentissimorum virorum dicendi facultate et copia revocari. Amaritudinem enim meam non diffitebor, miro orationes melle circumlinierunt."

41. Bevilacqua, G, 425–26 (V, fol. 171v); see text in chap. 2, n171.

42. Bevilacqua, G, 425 (V, fol. 160v): "Haec mihi pensitanti mirum nimis videtur, quod isto sapientissimi viri in quo recipere me aliquam commendationem natura iubet, dannare me audeant et officium quod in superstice filio peramando praestabam reprimere me debere dicant. Si caeteri patres filiorum vita functorum exequias sumptibus immodicis quandoque parentant, . . . quo modo lachrymas quas ad conservandam filii memoriam dolor et erunna ex oculis natura impellente praemunt, oculis exstilare prohibeor?"

43. Bevilacqua, G, 387 (V, fol. 109v): "Quanto si aeque filios ac se ipsos vehementer dilexissent, indiem {G invicem} usque vitae suae novissimum defunctorum illorum memoriam haud unquam mente delessent, sed eos lacrimis non conservare {V sibi} non potuissent."

44. Bevilacqua, G, 422 (V, fols. 156v–157): "Mihi videntur isti eloquentissimi exhortatores dicere: Tu Marcelle filius tuus iugulandus est, iugulum securi suppositum carnificis ictum expectat. Sis necis filii tui spectator, et illius quem magis quam animam tuam amabas, in tam atroci oren-

doque spectaculo constans. Hoccine est, esse patrem? Hoccine humanitatem servare? Hoccine pietatem colere? Quae cum sint in quocunque
homine commendanda {G commendata}, in parente ac genitore ita de-
beantur ut in filium aeque ac in semet illam praeseferre devinctus sit. Amat
quis se, amet et filium oportet. Dolet quis ex aliquo infortunio sibi con-
tingendi {G contingenti}, dolet {G doleat} et filio necesse sit."

45.   Bevilacqua, G, 315 (V, fol. 157rv): "Evellit quis partem anime
meae, et ego non doleam? Cor meum mors ex hanc labit {G exhanelabit},
quod una cum filio efferat interrimendum, et ego ita mentis inops, ita de-
perditae fuerim, ut lapis sim? Omni sensu corporis caream? Nullum sit inter me et {G ac} animal brutum discrimen? Cur Deum potius non accusant,
qui mihi cor saxeum {G in pectore} non affigitur?"

46.   Bevilacqua, G, 423 (V, fol. 158v): "Sint immanes quicunque velint, sint impii, sint crudeles, filiorum funera siccis oculis contemplentur!"

47.   Bevilacqua, G, 357 (V, fols. 68v–69): "Lacrimis urgeor et affligor
angustia ubi video tale me filio sempiterne cariturum, et mihi tanti pueri
indolem exprimendam [esse], in qua quanto magis elaboro, tanto nulla me
satietas lassare potest. Nec defatigari possum {G defagari valeo} tantam familiae meae spem mihi fuisse praereptam lamentari, qua se futurum virum
admirabilem, et maiorum suorum exempla vel aequaturum, qualiacunque
fuissent, vel superaturum praeseferebat. Studeo iugiter ab me molestias has
{G has molestias} espellere {cispellere}. Miri nimis est qui {G quod} quae
solent in aliis temporis diuturnitate comminui me continue concudant, et
doloris amaritudo continue semper afficiat; et eam pocius in tanta iactura
cumulari quam residere sententiam {G senciam}."

48.   Clustered in G, 313–19; in V, fols. 12–20. For the Marcellus forebears, Fam. I.B.9.

49.   For the Foscari drama, the contemporary Zorzi Dolfin, *Cronaca,*
fols. 441ff. (330ff.) and near-contemporary Egnazio 1554, fols. 206–208v
(who also presents the exempla of Doge Leonardo Loredan, the Procurators
Luca Zeno and Domenico Trevisan); modern accounts by Berlan 1852;
Trevor-Roper 1961; Zannoni 1942.

50.   F. Filelfo, G, 122 (ed. fol. 44): "Num dux Franciscus aut vultum
mutavit unquam, aut verbum fecit ullum in tanta et tam atroci clade filii";
the passage continues, "quam coram quodammodo intuebatur. {ed. adds
Satis enim intuebatur} cum et filii vociferationes eiulatusque e proximo cubiculo audiret, et quod sit organi supplicium non esset ignarus. Cumque
post illius immanitatem truculentiamque supplicii coram videret allatum,
nam quo is {ed. quovis} modo duci potuisset, cui nulla corporis pars con-
sisteret."

51.   Bevilacqua, G, 387–88 (V, fols. 109v–110v): "Nam principatum iniens trium filiorum prolem quos antea genuerat habuit specie decoram, ex quibus duos inter dignitatis suae principia pestifero morbo consumptos amisit, alium quem in grandiorem aetatem educarat, et tanquam unicum relictum inter delicias et iocunditatum suarum ornamenta nutrierat, adultum inter saevissima tormenta cruciari vidit, et inter crudelia supplicia illius corpus dillaniari, vocem illius ad langorem usque dediti inter carnificum lassitudinem obstrepentem audivit. . . . Tamen inter utranque sortis mutacionem robustus pater animum bene institutum neque foelici fortunae laxavit, neque adversae submisit, immo in utraque magnanimus et fortis in dura aeque ac bona et foelici perfectus apparere visus sit. Eum aegritudo illa nedum senatum ingredi, sed ne pro eius quidem officio ad tribunal accedere, ubi expetentibus aures solent accommodari unquam retardavit. Sentenciam etiam libere quacunque de re, quae pro rei publicae utilitate diserebatur, cum admiratione omnium constanti fronte, solidiori lingua, tenaci mente dixit in senatu. Verum ubi usu evenit, ut e principatus dignitate removeretur, quod propter ineptam huiusmodi officio senectam factum fuit, non potuit ad tam subitam calamitatem non excandescere, non potuit sortem suam non deplorare, non potuit sine animi sui accerbo cruciatu tantum miseriarum suarum fatum non excipere."

52.   These examples at Bevilacqua, G, 410 (V, fols. 140v–141v); further classical examples through G, 413 (V, fol. 145).

53.   Bevilacqua, G, 413–15, V, fols. 145v–148v for these and other scriptural examples; Mary at G, 415 (V, fol. 148rv): "Quis abnegare poterit scribente Luca in evangelio, virginem sanctissimam Chrysti nostri matrem amarissimas lacrimas per longum tempus effudisse?"

54.   Bevilacqua, G, 417–19; V, fols. 150–153. See *Confessions,* 9.8–13; also Beyenka 1952, 31–43, for Augustine's experience of death.

55.   Bevilacqua, G, 419 (V, fols. 152v–153): "In obitu igitur matris si Augustino . . . se a lacrimis continere facultas non extitit, si dolor atque molestia {G eum} in genitrice vita functa confecit, adeo ut vir sanctus se in angores et lacrimas effuderit, cur isti consolatores disertissime me quia lachrimarum exsuperat {G exuberat} inundantia, tanquam pusilanimem et ex abiectiore animo stratum digitis . . . demonstrantes impetunt?"

56.   Consideration of suicide is a regular accompaniment to profound grief: see Parkes 1972, 52. For suicide in the pre-modern period, see Schmitt 1976, who notes (p. 4) that the word itself was not known prior to 1734. Bevilacqua, G, 417 (V, fol. 150): "Sic ego deinceps sine Valerio filio {V meo} victurus inaniter, vitam mallem cum morte commutare, et

ad ea loca proficisci, quibus vel illum intueri phas esset, vel si aspectus huiusmodi abnegaretur occasio, eo loci non esse gauderem in quo tam truculenter saevitum im me fuisset."

58. Bevilacqua, V, fol. 162v (not in G): "Nec me hoc accerbiori crimine impetant facundissimi consolatores isti, quo dolores meos augeant molestiori tormento, quod sempiternos mihi luctus et perpetuas lachrymas praeoptore maluerim, quam mortem, qua omnes has erunnas et diuturniores miserias ab me potueram excidere. Cum si mihi mortem ipse consciverim, omnes aegritudinum crudelitates ab me propulerim."

59. Bevilacqua, V, fols. 163–171, not in G. Petrarch also used Cato as a model in discussing suicide as a possible remedy for depression; see McClure 1991, 64.

60. Bevilacqua, V, fol. 166rv: "Quibus facillime responderi potest, quoniam hos quamquam antiquitas fuerit admirata, in ipsis tamen animi magnitudinem potius quam sapientiam aliquam laudatam intelligo. Quanquam si rationem diligentius animadvertere voluerimus, ne id quidem quappiam animi magnitudine factum rectius dicere poterimus. Cum omnes, qui se ipsos interemerint, magis culpandi sint, quam alios tolerare, vel eorum aut aspera aut saevera imperia aequo animo pati non possunt."

61. Bevilacqua, V, fols. 169v–70: "Quemadmodum de me possum attestari, qui nunquam in tantam imprudentiam, seu dementiam appellarim, ego deveni ut redio vitae me ad mortem coegerim. Nam mortem contennere, et hanc vitam odisse, ritum belluarum semper existimavi. . . . Ego vero mortem laudavi nunquam, de vita nunquam sum questus, quasi satis vixerim, aut nunquam mihi ratio constiterit, cur omnino sim natus."

62. Bevilacqua, V, fol. 171: "Non itaque me accusent ulli, si superstes in hac vita esse cupiam, cum non solum divinae voluntati obtemperare proposuerim, quae iniussu domini ex hac vitae statione neququam nobis exeundum statuit, sed naturam hanc sequendam esse duxi, quae nos immanium ferarum exemplo quod nobis faciendum sit, edocit."

63. Bevilacqua, V, fols. 161v–171v, not in G; the text is spliced at G, 425.

64. See esp. Bowlby 1979, esp. 81–102, "Separation and Loss within the Family," with Colin M. Parkes; Jackson 1986; Parkes 1972; Pigman 1985, "Introduction"; Rosenblatt 1983; Rosenblatt et al., 1976. Fundamental to all discussions of mourning is Freud's *Mourning and Melancholia*, in Freud 1957, 14:243–58.

65. Bowlby 1979, 56.

66. Bowlby and Parkes in Bowlby 1979, 93.

67. For Sagundino's loss and the deaths of Guarino Veronese, Olimpio

Gellio and Braccio, Chron. 1460: early July; 1460: 4 December; 1461: 8 March; 1424: 5 June. Nogarola refers to her mother's recent death in her consolatory letter; see above. The death of the mother of Janus Pannonius on 10 December 1463 was movingly commemorated by her son in the elegy *De morte Barbarae matris* (Pannonius 1784, 1:288–96; Pannonius 1972, 334–42), but not until after the date of the Marcello consolations: see Thomson 1988, viii, 14.

68. Anon. Tut., G, 248; see text in chap. 1, n122, as the angel Valerio rebukes his father from heaven. At the same place, the Tutor also rebukes Marcello for his unkempt hair and mourning dress; see text in chap. 6, n13. Carbone similarly commands Marcello to remove his mourning garb and cut his beard (BMV 4451, fol. 30v; 4683, fol. 138): "Letandum ergo {4683 ego} mihi tibi non est iure dolendum {4683 causa dolendi}, / Si sapis o genitor, cunctum deterge dolorem, / Lugubres depone habitus ac tristia quaeque / Nec patere incanam me propter crescere barbam / Ne haec res sola tuos possit maculare triumphos." This section of the Tutor's *Supplement* and Carbone's elegy both date from at least 1462, perhaps 1463, one or two years after the death. Molmenti 1910–12: 2:534, remarks that in this period there "had not yet entirely ceased the ancient custom" of wearing the beard uncut for a "certain time"—three years in mourning a father, two for a mother, one for a brother. But he gives no term for mourning a son!

69. Petrarch 1911, 84–85, in a passage referring not to loss but attacks of mental torment (*accidia*).

70. For the contemporary world, Parkes 1972, 122–23; for seventeenth-century England, Fraser 1984, 72.

71. Molmenti 1910–12, 1:467.

72. Seneca, *De cons. ad Marciam* 7.3; trans. Seneca 1958, 23. Two of Seneca's three consolations were for mothers. Note also his picture of his own grieving mother in *Ad Helviam* 2–3, 15–20.

73. For the following discussion, esp. King 1991, chap. 1.

74. Barbaro 1916, 41 (19): "Mirificas fruges esse perspicimus, quas optimae segetes pariunt. . . . Quod et ipsis hominibus accidere consentaneum est, ut ex claris mulieribus longe illustriores natos expectent." Molmenti 1910–12, 2:519–21 for elaborate birth rituals among aristocracy, a social manifestation of concern with female role.

75. Barbaro 1978, 223. In spite of the admonitions of Barbaro and other experts, few Renaissance mothers of elite classes in fact breastfed their children.

76. Savonarola 1952; for his career, Pesenti Marangon 1976–77.

77. Alberti 1969, 49. For this argument, see also the later Memmo 1563.
78. Alberti 1969, 50.
79. For father-son relations in Renaissance Italy, see esp. Goldthwaite 1968; Herlihy 1985, chap. 5; Jones 1956; Kent 1977; Kuehn 1982; Lugli 1909; Molho 1978; Ross 1974, 209–16; Tamassia 1971, chap. 8. For fathers in the family generally, see the titles cited below, n83. For the persistence of patriarchy into the eighteenth century, see also, for colonial America, Greven 1970; for France, Traer 1980.
80. An elaboration of the latter theme in Marsilio Ficino's vernacular letter to his brothers of precisely this era (6 August 1455): Kristeller 1937, 2:109–28.
81. Alberti 1969, 38.
82. Klapisch-Zuber 1985, for evidence relative to Florence.
83. The thesis argued by Ariès 1962 and De Mause 1974, and to varying degrees supported by, among others, Boswell 1989; Flandrin 1979; Marcus 1978; Mitterauer and Sieder 1982; Stone 1977; for Italy, the thesis is borne out by Ross 1974 and Trexler 1973–74a, b. For the contrary argument see esp. Fraser 1984, 72–76; Gittings 1984, 58–59, 81–82; MacFarlane 1986; Ozment 1983, 1990; Pollock 1983, 97–172; Rosenblatt 1983; Shahar 1990; Stannard 1977, 44–71. Stone 1974 and Elton 1984 review the arguments on both sides of the controversy.
84. Carmichael 1986, 41–53, 90–92; Flandrin 1979, 53; Gittings 1984; Stannard 1977, 54–57; Stone 1977, 54–66; for local data from Florence and Milan, Herlihy & Klapisch-Zuber 1985, 270–79; Albini 1983.
85. McClure 1991, 34–36.
86. McClure 1991, 39–42.
87. Petrarch 1966, 276.
88. Trexler 1975; Trexler 1980, 172–85.
89. Mazzei 1880, 1:247: "ora è il terzo dì, c'ho veduti morire due miei figliuoli . . . nelle mie braccia, in poche ore. Dio sa quanta speranza m'era il primo, che già l'avea fatto a me come compagno e padre meco degli altri."
90. Barzizza 1723, 186–87: "et ego, quo maximorum laborum, ac vigiliarum mearum fructum expectabam, illuc provectum cum sapientia, tum honoribus videbam."
91. Perleone 1740, 48–49: "Quod si gravissimam carissimi quondam filii tui, et viri, et doctissimi quidem viri aetateque floreritis jacturam, qui decem tibi erat filiorum instar, in quo tuae senectutis spem omnem collocaras fortissime tulisti, nunc unius foeminae, et per sexum imbecillioris, et

per aetatem jam morti propinquae, ac puellae unius puerulorumque duorum morte afflictaris?"

92. Da Mosto 1983, 188–89; Papadopoli Aldobrandini 1893–1919, 2:10–11.

93. For Cellini, Symonds 1935, 3:371; for Modena, N. Z. Davis 1988, 109–10; De Maio 1987, 282.

94. In addition to titles already cited above, see also Trexler 1974, Trexler 1980, 368–87.

95. Ozment 1983, 167–72; Ozment 1989.

96. Fraser 1984, 74.

97. Jonson, *Epigrammes,* 45.

98. Wooden 1982 for the sixteenth, Marcus 1978 for the next.

99. Montaigne 1958, 279 (2.8).

100. See Kent 1977, 55–58 for these figures. For other examples of the genre of paternal literature, Brucker 1967; Cicchetti & Mordenti 1985; Jones 1956.

101. Kristeller 1937, 2:113: "pare che ami il figliuolo più che sua propria vita . . . l'amore del padre inverso del figliuolo è el maggior amore che si possa immaginare infra tucti e mortali."

102. Respectively Starn 1971, at 415; Hale 1961, 172–73.

103. Alberti 1960–73; Alberti 1969; see also Ponte 1971.

104. From the 1472 *Ehebüchlein* (Nuremberg: Anton Koberger; facsimile rpt. Wiebaden 1966), quoted by Ozment 1983, 132.

105. Vergerio 1917–18, 1963; Vegio 1933, 1936; Vegio 1958; Plutarch, esp. *De liberis educandis* (*Moralia* 1); Quintilian, *Inst. Orat.*

106. King 1986, esp. 25–31; for the absence of the *ricordanza* in Venice, see P. F. Brown 1988, 88–89.

107. Rose 1977, the letter to Giacomo Barozzi (1597) at 172–78.

108. Rose 1977, 172: "Fu grande certò il desiderio mio d'allevar un'proprio figliuolo carnale, il qual mi fusse riuscito tale, qual vien da savii descritto esser un'figliuol nobilmente nato, et da saggio, e diligente padre, et dotti precettori instituito, ammaestratato, et ridotto huomo perfetto virtuoso. Il qual mio ardentissimo desiderio havend'io con ogni mio spirito tentato d'adempire in duo mei figliuoli carnali. . . . Nondimeno per mia mala sorte, et per loro inclinatione celeste . . . mi sono riusciti, non solo al contrario del desiderio mio, ma ancho . . . capitalissimi nemici et crudelissimi insidiatori della vita di me misero et infelice loro padre. . . . Onde finalmente . . . havend'io fatto elettione della persona vostra . . . io ho riposto tute le mie speranze in voi figliuolo mio carissimo."

109. See McClure 1991, chap. 5; McClure 1986.
110. For this incident, see McClure 1991, 94–98; Seigel 1968, 71–73; Tenenti 1957, 37–40; Witt 1983, 355–67.
111. The work in Manetti 1983; for which see Banker 1976; De Petris 1977; De Petris 1979; Langdale 1976; Manetti 1983; McClure 1986; McClure 1991.
112. Banker 1976, 358.
113. Banker 1976, 359.
114. For the following, Arnold and Gemma 1983; Ariès 1985, 51, 247–48; Burns 1991; Campbell 1990, 195, 196, 214; Finucane 1981, 54; Jackson 1986, 317–20; Gittings 1984, esp. 58–59, 80–82; Pollock 1983, 97–172; Taylor 1983. For the increased tolerance for grief generally from the late sixteenth century, esp. Pigman 1985.
115. Ariès 1985, 247.
116. Herlihy 1985, 114.
117. See descriptions in chap. 1 at nn26–37 and passim.
118. Guarini, G, 181 (F, fol. 110): "Necque mirari enim desino quod in tam tenera etate paternam animi magnitudinem redolebat."
119. Perleone, G, 220 (B, fol. 64rv); see text in chap. 1, nn31, 86. Similar comments also made by Sagundino, G, 3–4 (F, fol. 93rv; VatS, fol. 2); Orsini, G, 286 (M, fol. 18v–19).
120. Anon. Ven. G, 258: "Hic est quem tibi filium deus pro singulari munere, et inter mortalium optabilia summo concessit." Also 261; for text see chap. 1, n92.
121. George of Trebizond, G, 26 (Mon. #2): "Nam siquis, ut de ceteris gentibus mentionem non faciam, Grecorum Romanorumque historiam diligenter evolvere velit, paucissimos inveniet qui, cum animo ingenti fuerint et mirabilia prebuerint signa future spei maximarum gerendarum rerum, vix virilem etatem tetigerunt." See also chap. 2, discussion following n23.
122. George of Trebizond, G, 27 (Mon. #4): "Nam . . . Valerius tuus, in quo virtutum omnium numerus sedem habiturus facile videbatur, antea quam nonum attigisset annum raptus a manibus tuis est, raptus a gremio carissime genitricis, raptus a conspectu omnium amicorum, doloremque omnibus intulit qui aut te colunt, ut debent. . . . Nam cum in pueris communiter future virtutis specimen perspicere soleamus, in ipso singularum virtutum certiora signa elucebant ingenii vel, ut expressius, mirabilis cuiusdam intelligentie."
123. Anon. Stu., G, 298; text in chap. 1, n19.
124. Fortebraccio, G, 144–45; text in chap. 1, n19.

125. Perleone, *Epistola,* VatP, fol. 103v (F, fol. 106; MU, fol. 94); text in chap. 2, n13. See also chap. 2, discussion following n12.

126. Perleone, *Epistola,* VatP, fol. 104v (F, fol.107v; MU, fol. 97): "At dices, Valerius meus invitus est mortuus."

127. Perleone, G, 190–91 (B, fol. 4–6); see text at Fam. IV.1.

128. For the following discussion, see Fam. I.

129. See Bevilacqua's narrative at G, 319–20 (V, fols. 20v–21); text at Fam. IV.2.

130. See above, chap. 4, discussion following n56.

131. Anon. Tut., G, 248; text in Fam. IV.11. The number five could include not only sons of Jacopo Antonio, but his grandsons who were also nephews of Valerio.

132. Perleone, *Epistola,* VatP, fol.104 (F, fols. 106v–107; MU, fol. 96rv); Guarini, G, 182; texts respectively in Fam. IV.7, 10.

133. Sagundino, G, 24–25 (F, fol. 105; VatS, fol. 12v); text in Fam. IV.6.

134. Anon. Ven., G, 249; text in Fam. IV.9.

135. Tifernate, *Oratio,* fols. 129v–130; text in Fam. IV.15.

136. Filelfo, G, 119 (ed. fol. 43v); text in Fam. IV.16.

137. Anon. Stu. G, 303–4; text in Fam. IV.20.

138. George of Trebizond, G, 31, 36 (Mon. ## 15, 34): texts in Fam. IV.17a, b.

139. Fifty-three at Valerio's birth, Marcello is old enough to be considered an aging father, although the phenomenon may not have been unusual in the Venetian aristocracy. According to C. Gilbert 1967, Marcello's contemporaries would have considered him old by all accounts.

140. For the kind of role-reversal described here, see also Trexler 1974; Trexler 1975; Trexler 1980, 172–85. The incidents from the life of Valerio alluded to below are fully described in chap. 1.

141. The scene is described in full in chap. 1, following n14, with list of texts in chap. 1, n16. From nineteen authors of works of consolation, to reach the number sixteen I have subtracted Giovanni Mario Filelfo and Tito Vespasiano Strozzi, whose works are lost, and Ludovico Grifo, who translated Filelfo's Greek elegy but wrote no consolatory work himself. Special gratitude is owed to Bridget Gellert Lyons for her recognition of the phenomenon considered critical here of the exclusion of the mother.

142. For Sagundino, Babinger 1962, 321; information about the last two is provided by Professor G. N. Knauer who has most generously allowed me to consult the draft of his article on "Homer" destined for the CTC.

143. Bevilacqua, G, 330 (V, fols. 34v–35): "Tunc magistratum gerebam cum uxor quam Venetiis reliqueram infantem fuit enixa. Verum antea quam infantem natum esse mihi nunciatum esset, O quot, quanta, quam diversa somnia, cum in cubiculo cubans solus obdormirem, nasciturum mihi marem filium elegantissima forma et omni virtutum genere refertissimum praedixere! O quot noctibus in somnis visum {G sum} elegans pueri unius specimen ulnis amplecti, ora nati opobalsamo redolentiora {G reddentiora} suaviare, et inter oscula maiorem in modum laetari!"

144. Bevilacqua, G, 322–31 (V, fols. 24v–35v) passim.

145. See Goodich 1973–74, 286–87; Shahar 1982–83, 299; Weinstein & Bell 1982, 18, 20. Ianziti 1988, 74, points out that Sforza's humanist staff claimed that their patron's great destiny was preliminarily revealed in portents, signs, and dreams. And in his life of Dante, Boccaccio (1974, 441, #16) claims that the poet's mother, when pregnant, "per sogno vide quale doveva essere il frutto del ventre suo."

146. Goodich 1973–74, 287.

147. Weinstein & Bell 1982, 23.

148. For these events, see chap. 1, discussion at nn65–71.

149. For this incident, chap. 1, discussion following n82.

150. For the humanistic curriculum of the day, and use of tutors in households, see Grendler 1989, part 2, "The Latin Curriculum"; Grafton & Jardine 1986; Robey 1980–81; Woodward 1963.

151. For Zovenzoni, see above, chap. 2, n78.

152. D'Aubigné 1969, 385.

153. Cardan 1930, 142.

154. Stone 1977, 194.

155. See Ross 1974, 213.

156. Witt 1983, 282, and 356–67.

157. Alberti 1969, 47.

158. For the *ars moriendi,* see below, chap. 6n82. For the various deathbed scenes, see above, chap. 1, narrative following n103.

159. But note how twentieth-century leukemic children do prepare for their own deaths (Bluebond-Langner 1977), outpacing their parents in directness and attuned to authority figures who have replaced their own blood relatives.

160. Rosenblatt 1983, 91–96, 158–59.

161. Filelfo, G, 123–24 (ed. fol. 44): "Id autem facillime assequaris, si iisdem remediis in tuo isto casu uti {ed. ut} aliquando institueris, quibus ipse in obitu Olympii mei sum usus. . . . Plurimum tibi proderit non ad leniendam egritudinem solum, sed etiam ad letioris vite suavitatem, si om-

nem Valerii filii infantiam, si indolem, si ingenium, si corporis formam, si morum probitatem ac decus, si doctrine et eloquentie studium, . . . repetere tecum animo perrexeris. Nec enim esse debes oblitus, cum tuo ex collo Valerius penderet, cum te oscularetur, cum hereret in brachiis, et {ed. quo} magis garrula lingua balbutiebat, eo fiebat ipsa verborum offensione iucundior auditu."

162.   The argument of McClure 1991, esp. chap. 5.

CHAPTER SIX

1.   Anon. Tut., G, 247–48; text in chap. 1, n118.

2.   Anon. Stu., G, 299: "Sunt enim velut angeli Dei et innocentiae suae gloria dignissima coronati thronum supernae maiestatis ascendunt, ubi et tanto divinitatis splendore saciati pro nobis a quibus geniti sunt et qui remansimus in hac misera lacrymarum vale continuo praeces effundunt; quo in statu minime dubitandum est collocatum fuisse iamdiu Valerii tui spiritum generosum, qui cum nundum decem annorum complexus esset aetatem." The passage is preceded by the assertion that the dead, and particularly the youthful dead, go to an afterlife (to the Elysian fields, according to the Gentiles; to paradise, according to the Christians): "Consolari itaque non parum debemus cum videmus natos ac parvulos nostros ante viciorum et scelerum blandimenta gustata ex hac vita migrare." See also F. Filelfo, G, 63 (ed. fol. 33v); text in chap. 1, n120. Also idem, G, 122–23 (ed. fol. 44), text below, n20. Note Paulinus 1975, 328 (#591), writing of a dead infant in the late fourth century: "It is certain that the kingdom of heaven belongs to children such as you were in age, purpose, and faith."

3.   Anon. Stu., G, 303: "Adverse tamen fortunae iacula, huius mundi rerum dolores acerbissimos, infinita denique malorum genera ac multas condicionis suae propriae clades evaserunt."

4.   Anon. Stu., G, 303–4: "Hic autem . . . [filius] non alicuius sceleris vicio, non inter gentes barbaras aut procellosos pellagi fluctus, sed in maximo virtutum ornamento inter domesticos lares, regnantibus veneti sceptris imperii, te benemeritis rei publicae vestrae magistratibus ornatissimo gestarumque rerum gloria praeclaro, et quod sanctissimum puto, innocencia cordis atque optima rerum morum disciplina ex huius saeculi tenebris migravit ad astra."

5.   Fortebraccio, G, 154; see text in chap. 1, n119.

6.   Nogarola, G, 138 (Abel, 2:172): "Sciebat enim se ad meliorem vitam profecturum, ubi mors ultra non erit nec luctus neque dolor, et cum in hac vita tanquam advena esset et peregrinus, de exilio ad patriam, de miseria ad gloriam, de mortalitate ad immortalitatem pergere."

7.   Sagundino, G, 24 (F, fols. 104v–105; VatS, fol. 12rv): text in chap. 1, n119.

8.   Sagundino, G, 24 (F, fols. 105; VatS fol. 12v); text at Chap. 1n119.

9.   Anon. Stu., G, 299: text at n2 above.

10.   Mascarello, G, 179: "Tibi vero genitori est causa letandi quod habeas apud summum regem qui te miro amore dilexit ac diliget, qui cum sit regi dilectus ac regni particeps pro caro genitore exorare non desinit ut tuum ex ipsius discessu dolorem vertat in gaudium, ut tibi in hac vita que recte desideras cuncta succedant."

11.   Bevilacqua, G, 423 (V, fol. 158): "Modo me consolari nitebatur, ut omnes dolores ego reprimerem et mihi suaderem deinceps filium habere in paradiso, et gloriosiorem ordinem adeptum quam venetorum Senatus illi fuisset unquam collaturus. . . . Pollicebatur se assidue pro salute mea, {V et} pro matre sibi carissima, pro gratissimis fratribus salvatorem rogaturum."

12.   Anon. Tut., G, 248; text in chap. 1, n122.

13.   Anon. Tut., G, 248: "Adquiesco plane meis iis nescio quo pacto verbis Jacobi Antoni doloremque meum nedum leniri verum et in summam converti laeticiam sentio. Volo iam Valerii nostri felicitate congratulari, volo illius bono gaudere perinde ac meo. Tu vero vir optime, quid huic angelo respondebis? Quid horum quae dixit ibis inficias? Audebis amplius eum de caeli deducere. Capillum adhuc istum sordidum sines et in lugubri pallio te diucius macerans hanc lucem efugere voles? Hanc pater iniuriam filio facies? Quo si minus forte moveris at immortalis te Dei decretum absterreat, cui non assentire reluctari dicitur a suo se caelo perfodere, quod amentes aut desperati solent. Quare vir sapientissime tuum istum moerorem cum vestibus exue, nec te divinae diutius voluntati rebellem ostendas."

14.   Fortebraccio, G, 158–59: "Si tecum his verbis deus ac salvator noster Christus Iesus ageret, quid responderes? Cur Iacobe Antoni fles, cur lachrymis indulges abimis precordiis, cur tam gravia trahis suspiria, dispositionem meam cur cecis querellis insequeris? Mihi de te bene merito gratie non parve agende essent, et tu terga vertis. Cave ne meorum benefitiorum ingratitudine arguaris. Ego te genere, nobilitate, honoribus, opibus, rerum gestarum gloria fovi, atque provexi. Ego te ex primoribus urbis vestre constitui, uxore, liberis, cognatis, affinibus, amicisque fortunatum feci, ut tibi ad humanam felicitatem desit nihil. Nuper ex liberis tuis unum mihi adoptandum delegi, et ex tua ipsius sperata amplitudine ac mortali gloria, ad certam immortalemque beatitudinem transtuli. Quique tui filius nuncu-

pabatur in terris, nunc tum celestis regni mei hereditate, meum et dici et esse verius filium volui. Tu vero tanta in te sequi merita non advertens mecum hoc nomine videris indignari, tu iuditiis meis, ante mundi constitutionem predestinatis, obviam ire, tuis rebellibus lachrymis conaris. An mihi rerum omnium conditori, parva hec censenda erit iniuria? . . . Tu vero filium tuum Valerium meum esse factum doles, qui res hominum, qui deum qui eternis rego imperiis."

15. F. Filelfo, G, 59 (ed. fol. 33): "Quo enim et quanta quottidie accidunt in vita tristia miserabilia erumnosaque sola morte effugiuntur? . . . Quanto igitur Valerius tuus celerius excessit e vivis, tanto eius mors desiderabilior est censenda quod mali nihil neque nosset neque perpetrasset."

16. F. Filelfo, G, 60–61 (ed. fol. 33): "Cum tuus igitur Valerius ita egerit annos suos ut nullam ne minimam quidem senserit corporis contagionem, sed totius {ed. potius} esset et puritatis et bonitatis exemplum, non tam tibi lugendum est quod tali careas filio, quam immortales agende gratias {ed. gratiae} Christo Ihesu, quod illius te patrem facere sit dignatus, quo etiam aliquando patrono uti apud se possis."

17. F. Filelfo, G, 63 (ed. fol. 33v); text in chap. 1, n120.

18. F. Filelfo, G, 61 (ed. fol. 33); see text above in n16.

19. F. Filelfo, G, 107 (ed. fol. 41): "Iam sane tu Valerii benefitio qui nuper solum eras Venetiarum, celestis patriae factus es civis, ubi ullus {ed. nullus} est linori {ed. livori} locus, nullus obtrectationi, nullus contentioni. Quidquid enim bonorum acquirunt liberi non minus bonis parentibus quam sibi acquirunt. Quare cum pulcherrima et dilectissima tui portio celesta {ed. caelesti} re publica est donatus, potes etiam iure tu cum voles, velle autem semper debes, iura tibi filii vendicare."

20. F. Filelfo, G, 122–23 (ed. fol. 44): "Quare . . . non modo non lugebis obitum Valerii filii sed gaudebis potius, quoniam cum illo actum est optime. Exultat ille nunc inter angelorum choros perturbatione curaque omni vacuus, divine substantie visione fruitur. Tibique patri indulgentissimo, quo dum erat in terris, nihil sibi neque carius habebat neque iucundius, in celo domicilium parat."

21. F. Filelfo, G, 61 (ed. fol. 33): "Quid enim tantum lachrymarum effundis? quid adeo gemis, quid diutius doles?"

22. F. Filelfo, G, 38 (ed. fol. [29]); text at Fam. IV.21a.

23. F. Filelfo, G, 55 (ed. fol. 32): "Verum ea nobis offertur consolatio, quod non multum abesse possit, ut quos tanto animi ardore desideramus, coram liceat intueri, et tibi Valerium tuum et mihi Olympum meum, equalibus nobis equalis illos. . . . Quare inter nos et filios quos amisimus

non admodum longa futura sunt divortia, modo demus operam quod in nobis est, ut una cum illis quos tanto desiderio ardemus esse possimus." Birth and death dates at Fam. IV.21.

24.   F. Filelfo, G, 126 (ed. fol. 44v): "Quod si factum abste {ed. ab te} fuerit, non poteris non miro perfundi gaudio, cum intellexeris et tibi et filio consultum esse quam optime: illi quidem, quod post innocenter et bene actam seculi vitam eternam adeptus beatitudinem iam sibi nihil {ed. nihil sibi} sentiat formidandum, tibi vero, quod certo sperare liceat {ed. licet} a Valerio tuo paratam in celo sedem, ubi tu non post diuturnum admodum tempus tranquillam atque iucundam vitam una {ed. unam} cum illo per sempiternam gloriam sis acturus."

25.   For the theme of immortality, see McClure 1991, 109–111, and sources there cited. For Filelfo as a moral philosopher, see also Kraye 1981; Robin 1991, chap. 5. A dozen years after writing the *Consolatio*, and engaged on his *De morali disciplina*, Filelfo is less interested in the concept of the individual immortal soul: Robin, 156. Filelfo's discussion of immortality, reviewed below, lies within the humanist, moral philosophical tradition. Contemporary philosophers also engaged in discussions of the principle from a different disciplinary vantagepoint; see Eckhard Kessler's "The Intellective Soul," 485–534 in Schmitt 1988.

26.   F. Filelfo, G, 80–88 (ed. fols. 36v–38) for the following.

27.   F. Filelfo, G, 80–81 (ed. fols. 36v–37): "At {ed. Ad} quod omnes gentes communiter sentiunt, id quadam naturae lege fieri videtur. Quem quidem populorum omnium de animorum immortalitate consensum, ii omnes qui habiti sunt animo altissimo acerrimoque ingenio maiorem in modum confirmarunt. . . . Num se precipitasset in eternam {ed. Aetnam} Empedocles sine spe magna immortalitatis? Si falsum esset Theombrotus putasset quod de animorum immortalitate apud Platonem legerat, nunquam se de muro precipitem dedisset quo illam assequeretur? Que tanta cupido glorie Curtium, que tanta patrie caritas in illum terre hiatum potuisset immergere, si totum se periturum morte credidisset? Idem de Codro rege, idem de Philenis, idem de tribus deinceps Deciis, idem est de aliis quam plurimis existimandum, qui prudentia et virtute plurimum claruerunt. Ex quibus rebus cognosci potest animum non modo non interire cum corpore, sed ab eius vinculis solutum longe esse meliore statu vite."

28.   At F. Filelfo, G, 81–83 (ed. fols. 37–38).

29.   F. Filelfo, G, 82 (ed. fol. 37): "Num hec finxisset unquam antiquissimus ille divinusque poeta, nisi firmissimis rationibus compertum habuisset animos hominum cum discessum fecisset a corpore, per sese consis-

tere, nullaque tangi mortis suspitione?" The reference is to the *Iliad* 23.69–92.

30. F. Filelfo, G, 84–86 (ed. fol. 37v) at G, 85: "At non ea profecto narrasset vir gravissimus, nisi vera esse certo didicisset. Verum audiamus presbiterum Hieronymum virum ut trium linguarum eruditissimum ita veritate et sanctimonia nemini imparem. Is enim in iis que ad Eustochium et ad reliquas virgines scribit de regula vivendi in monasterio." For Paulinus's relations with Augustine, Lienhard 1977, 24–51 passim.

31. For the following, F. Filelfo, G, 86–87 (ed. fols. 37v–38).

32. F. Filelfo, G, 87 (ed. fol. 38): "Vivit inquam Iacobe Antoni Marcelle Valerius filius ille tuus, et vivit is quidem eam vitam que mutabilitati nulli subiecta est, sed eadem semper atque perbeata."

33. For the following, F. Filelfo, G, 88–104 (ed. fol. 38–40v). To a certain extent, the scholastic philosophers are subsumed under Aristotelianism, as Filelfo knows it. Filelfo made a lifelong study of the ideas of Aristotle and Plato, which he amalgamated; see Robin 1991, chap. 5.

34. F. Filelfo, G, 104 (ed. fol. 40v): "Nihil . . . habet animus noster in se mixtum, nihil concretum, nihil corporeum, nihil externum, sed sua quadam natura constat suaque vi, qua sentit, qua sapit, qua vivit ac viget, qua totus est Dei simillimus; quo fit ut neque dissolvi queat, nec secerni nec deleri, sed immortalis sit, potius planeque sempiternus. Quid ergo dolemus, Iacobe Antoni Marcelle, nobis ereptos filios? quid tam diu collachrimamur? quid querimur?"

35. F. Filelfo, G, 104 (ed. fol. 40v): "Prestantissima quidem inter virtutes et eadem splendidissima optimaque virtus a viris sapientibus iusticia iudicatur, nam neque domus neque respublica nec ipsum hominum genus vacare iusticia ullo pacto queat." For the following, G, 104–6 (ed. fols. 40v–41).

36. F. Filelfo, G, 105 (ed. fol. 41): "Qui omni sunt servitute inferiores imperant viris bonis, atque dominantur; honorantur impii, contemnuntur pii; qui doctrina valent et gravitate, ridiculo sunt, assentatores indocti habentur in precio. . . . Affliguntur viri iusti ab impiis, et ad mortem usque per omnem vite cursum acerbissime cruciantur. Qui autem vim, qui iniuriam, qui contumeliam inferunt, non modo poenam subeunt nullam pro sceleris magnitudine, sed in delitiis potius et voluptate vivunt."

37. F. Filelfo, G, 104 (ed. fol. 40v): "An unus fortasse tu inter patritios venetos sis inventus, qui divine iusticie diffidere velle existimeris? Hec enim venetis nobis laus est peculiaris {ed. veluti peculiarius}, quod mortalium omnium primi iustitiam colitis atque veneramini. Num Veneti iusti sunt {ed. sint}, Deus vero iniustus?"

38.   F. Filelfo, G, 106 (ed. fol. 41): "Cum igitur iam satis ostensum sit nullam esse neque necessariam neque honestam causam tam diuturni et tam vehementis doloris tui."

39.   Sagundino, G, 23 (F, fol. 104; VatS, fols. 11v–12): "Abdita et recondita penitus eruere et investigare animum inquam et mentem, vim absolutam et simplicem, . . . omni labe et macula, omni corporis colluvione secretam et separatam. . . . Animus contra sive mens, simplex omnino et immortalis, proinde pereunte corpore morienteque, ipse vivit et evolat suamque sedem que in celis est motu proprio, cunctis sublatis obstaculis querit. Ibi videndo contemplandoque creatore et domino omnium . . . finem suum adeptus ultimum acquiescit et beatissimus fit."

40.   The discussion of the Anon. Stu. at G, 298–303.

41.   Anon. Stu., G, 299: "fidei nostrae auctoritas divina confirmatur, in gloria sempiterna ac paradisi regno triumphali, qui electis omnibus a constitucione mundi preparatus est."

42.   Fortebraccio, G, 152: "Cum ex te genitum filium primo vidisti, an num sciebas esse mortalem? . . . Circonspice universum terrarum orbem et omnia que celi ambitu continentur, terrasque, tractusque maris celumque profundum, num ne morti ac corruptioni sese deberi profitentur? Celum ipsum tam preclarum, tam nobile, tam exornatum aliquando dissolvetur, sol, luna, ceteraque astrorum genera nequaquam permanebunt, terrestria cuncta animalia aquatica, volatilia, creatura denique omnis cum ipsa terra paulo post minime erunt."

43.   Fortebraccio, G, 153: "Immatura ergo illi mors non fuit quam divini decreti immobilis sententia maturam effecerat."

44.   Fortebraccio, G, 155–56: "Si tibi egrotante filio tuo Valerio, medicorum eximius aliquis pollicitus esset illum nequaquam esse moriturus, credidisses? Profecto Christo autem dicenti, resurget filius tuus, an non credemus? Indignissimum sane est, medico plus fidei adhibere quam Christo. Non lugendus est igitur, quem Christus Deus ac dominus noster resurrecturum promisit."

45.   Tifernate, *Oratio*, fols. 126v–127v: "Ego Jacobe Antoni nequaquam perspectem et in vita exercitatum hominem iudico, qui ullam in rebus humanis spem aut stabilitatem ponat, et quae caduca se et momentanea quasi solida ac diuturna existimet. . . . Videmus non modo singulos homines, qui brevissimae vitae sunt, sed clarissimas quoque civitates maximasque nationes, quarum nomen aeternum sperabatur penitus interiisse, ac nullam de se prorsus memoriam reliquisse. Nam ut de Romanis taceam, notum est enim in quas calamitates devenerint, quamquam vel soli cum reliquo terrarum orbe conferri potuerunt. Quanta vero in graecis ruina

facta sit, nemo est qui non videat, ut mihi consideranti quasi somnus quidam et umbra haec vita videatur. Ubi sunt tot et tanta graecorum ingenia? Ubi tot insignes civitates? Nonne omnia pone deleta sunt et extincta? Ut si in maximis rebus fortuna tantum potest mirari magna desinamus, quid est igitur quod tantopere afflictemur? Quid tantum insano iuvat indulgere dolori? Quid est quod tantum moeroris et acerbitatis ex unius morte pueri capiamus? Quasi putemus aut non infinitis nos subiacere periculis, aut non esse mortales? Nimirum profecto sumus delicati, ac nimium nobis ipsi indulgemus."

46. Nogarola, G, 140 (Abel, 2:176): "Eia igitur, illustris vir, abiciamus opera tenebrarum et induamur arma lucis, cogitantes nos homines natos esse ea conditione, ut moriendum sit, et qui morti repugnare conatur, divinae voluntati nititur repugnare, cui refragari impossibile est nec velle debemus."

47. For the following, Sagundino, G, 7–13 (F, fols. 95–98v; VatS, fols. 3v–7).

48. Sagundino, G, 7 (F, fol. 95; VatS, fol. 4): "Sed inquiet aliquis, quid affectus et sensum quocunque ducat, quocunque trahat et rapiat, nos sequi oportet, et laxis habenis appetitui temere ex currenti in morem ferarum {F ferarum mortem} parere et obsequi? . . . Ratio enim superne propterea indita est, ut concilio {F, VatS consilio} sensum regat, ut affectibus nimis lascivientibus modum faciat, ut velut in puppi sedeas {F, VatS sedens} clavumque tenens, appetitum regat et moderetur, qui et si per se consilii rationesque {F, VatS rationisque} exors est, aliquatenus tamen horum particeps esse videtur, propterea que imperata suscipere. Quod rationis dicto audiens esse potest, sapienter prospicientis et salutariter admoneretis, ut neque veluti per malatiam {F, VatS malitiam} navis huius vite inerter et segniter aquis lentis et immobilibus hereat {VatS herat}, neque periculose provehatur influctus et mare undosum et turbidum {VatS turbidinum} ferociter petat, immo vero utrumque malum declinans, medium amplectatur cursum, quo rebus omnibus salvis nullius iactura facta, ad finem et portum expetitum recte tandem appelli possit. Hoc est munus homini proprium, hoc a belvis homo differt, hoc ipso {F ipse} divinitatis particeps quodammodo sit {F fit}."

49. Sagundino, G, 8 (F, fol. 96; VatS, fol. 4v): "Id quod . . . te . . . diligenter et industrie facere intelligimus, ut iam nihil sit opus alienis preceptis, nihil admonitis, nullis omnino exemplis, tu te tibi ipse movitor {F monitor} et preceptor sic esse potes, ut aliis in te intuentibus, autor iure et dux bene fortiterque vivendi satis abundeque esse possis."

50. Sagundino, G, 8 (F, fol. 95v; VatS, fol. 4): "Quis enim non nisi

iniuria stulteque possit {VatS posset} eternum et immortalem sustinere dolorem? de re presertim caduca temporaria, fragili et suape natura mortali?"

51.   Sagundino, G, 11 (F, fol. 97v; VatS, fol. 6): "Ita vite ipsius comitem nostre ab ipso ortu, ab ipsis exordiis et primis liniamentis implicitam atque aptam, ut dies noctesque tum domi tum foris nobiscum ubique sit, nobiscum versetur, neque enim de repente in ipsam nos aut in nos ipsa, tamquam adventicia et foris accedens incidit et incurrit. Sed semper nobiscum congreditur, minutatim semper longius serpens procedit, ut ad signum et metam perventum est, sese offert atque apparet, et eodem momento et puncto temporis, eque extinguitur et extinguit, ut non magis deserere ipsa nos quam a nobis deseri videatur."

52.   Sagundino, G, 9 (F, fol. 96v; VatS, fol. 5): "Nam si natus esses Athenis, vel Thebis, vel apud Lacedemonios, leges instituta iura profecto civitatis et populi ubi natus esses, haud gravate subire deberes. . . . In communi ac {VatS hic; F hac} rerum omnium civitate natus, et nature sanctissimis fontibus vita hausta, leges et iura eius recusare contendis, et conditiones quibus in hanc lucem proditus es conaris infringere?"

53.   Sagundino, G, 10–11 (F, fol. 97; VatS, fol. 5v): "His rationibus mortem plerique non modo non timendam, verum etiam contemnendam existimarunt, et merito quidem. Quod enim quominus eveniat nulla ratione, nullo concilio impedire possis, quod rerum natura ordine atque cursu necessario est venturum, quod ubi advenit nihil mali, nihil incommodi videatur afferre, id quare tantopere timeatur impendens? Equidem non satis intelligo, ne timor atque solicitudo eiusmodi atque cura, non ex re ipsa, sed opinione errore concepta quodam, animus incutitur hominum. Qui quidem error ratione atque consilio, recto et indepravato iuditio, sapienti et forti viro tollendus est, et procul elimnandus fugandusque {VatS fugiandusque} penitus."

54.   Sagundino, G, 11 (F, fol. 97v–98; VatS, fol. 6): "Quo fit ut ratione et consilio predito homini, neutrum convenire merito videatur, nam neque mortem expetere quispiam et sibi per nephas tedio vite consciscere debet, nec timore atque solicitudine mortis vitam contaminare, inquietamque et anxiam reddere, cum vite commodis ut mortalis modice frui, et mortem impavide ad legem naturae atque adeo ad maximi principis omnium rerumque creatoris Dei prescriptum expectare futuram."

55.   Sagundino, G, 13 (F, fol.98v; VatS, fol.7): "Nunc me ad te vertam, te alloquar, te coram rogabo, quippe qui facile iam intelligis quorsum tot de vita, de morte, de nature legeque {F, VatS lege deque} conditione humana verba. Quid dicis, Iacobe Antoni clarissime, quid animo versas, quid cogitatione complexeris?"

56.   Bevilacqua, G, 391–92 (V, fols. 115v–16v): "Quorum aliquid ex hominis corpore evellere, facilius est hominem interficere, quam quod se {G est} ipsius proprium mutare posse naturam. Quam rem non in hominibus modo sed {G et} in omnibus rebus quae generatae sunt contemplari licet. Nam ut quicquid de {G e} terra ortum est, ut suis stirpibus id omne nitatur et in suo genere perfectum sit, natura esse voluit. Arbores et vites et quae his humiliora sunt tollere se altius e terra ut iubet natura non possunt. Alia semper virent, alia hieme nudata, verno tempore tepefacta frondescunt. Neque est unum, quod non vigeat interiore quodam motu, et suis in quoque seminibus inclusis, aut flores aut fruges effundat aut baccas omniaque in omnibus, quantum in ipsis sit, nulla vi impediente perfecta sint. Facilius vero et {G etiam} in brutis, quae in his de quibus diximus sensus a natura datus est, ex quo vis ipsius naturae perspici potest. Nam quas bestias nantes effecit, aquarum incolas esse voluit; quas volucres esse destinavit, caelo frui libero. Serpentes quasdam esse gradientes et earum ipsarum partim solivagas, partim congregatas, immanis alias, quasdam autem cicures. Nonnullas abditas terraque textas, atque earum quaeque suum tenens munus, cum in disparis animantis vitam transire non possit, manet in sua lege naturae. Et ut denique omnibus in rebus alius {G aliud} alii praecipui a natura datum est, quod suum quodque munus retineat, nec discedere ab eo potest. Sic homini usu evenit, ut quae natura illi ingenita sunt {V seu mista; G eum ista} ita compellant ut quamvis id magno studio contra nitatur, ab eo quod a natura infixum est et {G etiam} insitum sit, prorsus ipse vincatur."

57.   Bevilacqua, G, 395 (V, fol. 120): "Quod nullus unquam homo qui secundum naturam sentiret et saperet affectionibus istius animi . . . ac vacare posset atque non eas {G ea} pati, vel non dolere." Similar arguments also at G, 408–9 (V, fols. 138–39v).

58.   Bevilacqua, G, 395 (V, fol. 121v): "Qui videri se tranquillos, intrepidos, et immobiles volunt, atque dum nihil cupiunt, nihil dolent, nihil irascuntur, nihil gaudent, omnibus vehementioris animi officiis amputatis, in corpore ignavae et enervatae vitae consenescunt."

59.   Bevilacqua, G, 396 (V, fol. 122rv): "Tristiciam praeterea quandam animi aegritudinem {V Tullius G Cicero} diffinit, quae tanquam bona sit animi habitudo virtuti adversatur. Tristicia igitur virtuti contrariatur, nec cum ea simul esse potest."

60.   Bevilacqua, G, 396–97 (V, fols. 122v–23): "Nam cum homo ex animo et corpore compositus sit, id quod a {G ad} hominis vitam conservandam confert aliquod hominis bonum est, non tamen maximum, quia eo male uti potis sit, unde et malum huic bono contrarium in sapientem

derivare et moderatam tristiciam inducere potest. Praetera et si virtuosus sine gravi peccato esse possit, nullus tamen invenitur qui absque levibus saltem peccatis vitam duxerit."

61.   Bevilacqua, G, 398 (V, fol. 124v): "Insurgit sequens haec dubitacio, utrum floetus seu lacrimae tristiciae seu doloris et mitigandi et leniendi remedium esse possit, quod nonnullis absurdum videri solet {G potest}, et praesertim his qui tanta eloquentia sua me consolari conati sunt, et floetum hunc meum in quem vis omnis naturae me compellit, quoniam nullus effectus suae causae minuendae causa ipsa esse potest." The contrary argument continues through G, 399 (V, fol. 126).

62.   Bevilacqua, G, 425 (V, fol. 160v); text in chap. 5, n42.

63.   Bevilacqua, G, 425 (V, fol. 161): "Ut quem tutati fuerimus, dilexerimus, foverimus, eum {G cum} perpetua memoria teneamus absentium illorum reminiscamur, et lachrymis quod est et misericordiae et humanitatis signum conservemus."

64.   An excellent summary of the philosophical schools as understood in the Renaissance by Kraye in Schmitt et al. 1988, 303–86. For Stoicism, also Zanta 1914.

65.   Valla 1979.

66.   Witt 1983, 358–67.

67.   For the history of consolation, see esp. Buresch 1886; Calzaferri 1938; De Petris 1977; De Petris 1979; De Petris, "Introduzione," in Manetti 1983, xxvi–lii; Diekstra 1968; Favez 1937; Kristeller 1956; McClure 1986; McClure 1991, "Introduction"; Pigman 1985, "Introduction"; Tenenti 1957; Von Moos 1971–72. For Augustine, esp. Beyenka 1952; for Boethius, Courcelle 1967; Patch 1935; for the Augustinian and Boethian traditions esp., Courcelle 1971. For the continuation of the tradition in English verse and prose, see in addition to Pigman 1985, Sacks 1985, and Stein 1986.

68.   For Vitturi, see King 1986, 11, 19, 52, 445–46, and Fam. I.A.31. Barzizza 1723 contains many letters to Vitturi, as well as the one discussed below (pp. 141–43) to Vitturi and Valerio Marcello jointly. For Barzizza's Paduan career, see esp. Mercer 1979.

69.   Barzizza 1723, 141–43.

70.   Barzizza 1723, 145.

71.   Barzizza 1723, 85–87: the "Oratio ad Petrum Marcellum patavinum in morte Hieronymi Marcelli." It can be placed in 1412 or 1413 because of its reference to the prior death, considered "recent," of Bishop Pietro's father Francesco, who died in 1411. It must have been written after Barzizza's encounter with Girolamo in February 1412.

72. Barzizza 1723, 85: "Etsi verendum sit, Pater reverendissime, ne parente viro clarissimo nuper orbatus, nunc ad subitum nuncium de obitu Hieronymi fratris amantissimi animo deficias; tamen, cum me ad incredibilem, ac prope divinam animi tui modestiam retuli, nullum arbitratus sum malum post tantum incumbere, quod non sapientia tua aut moderetur, aut prorsus vincatur."

73. Barzizza 1723, 86: "Ego vero non illud audeo petere, ut nihil doleas; illud audeo, ut modeste doleas; quorum alterum, ut a tua humanitate alienum est, ita alterum sapientiae tuae esse judico." Valerio's son Giovanni Paolo is referred to in a final letter of Barzizza's to the father discussing the death of his own children: ibid., 186–88 (see above, chap. 5, at n90).

74. Pietro Marcello 1915.

75. The letter in Barbaro 1741–43, 2:127–33; Eng. trans. in King and Rabil 1983, 106–11.

76. Barbaro, in King and Rabil, 107.

77. Perleone 1740.

78. Chron. 1460: early July, 10 July.

79. Perleone 1740, 98: "nec amicos patricios Venetos, orbis terrae principes ad rerum omnium praesidium reliquisses, optimam profecto et pretiosam haereditatem ac in primis a parentibus post virtutem liberis tradendam."

80. King 1986, 427–29.

81. Perleone 1740, 79.

82. Barozzi 1531. For the genre of *ars moriendi,* see esp. Beaty 1970; Chartier 1976; McClure 1991, 116–31; Rainer 1957; Tenenti 1957 (for Barozzi, 95–97); for the contribution of Barozzi's contemporary, Girolamo Savonarola, Donald Weinstein's essay in Goffen, Tetel & Witt 1989.

83. Barozzi 1531, fol. 135v: "Et, cum alii studiis operam daturi, Patavium, alii Bononiam, Perusium alii, quidam superant Alpes, nonnulli mare traiiciunt, multosque ibi annos cum ingenti sumptu, et magnis degunt incommodis, et ut iuris civilis, aut pontificii, vel philosophiae, aut certe theologiae aliquid discant, . . . et nos Victoris nostri causa lamentabimur, quem sine labore, sine sumptu, sine incommodo, ab exilio praesentis vitae, in patriam coelestem ascendisse, ac bene habere, et omnia iam, quae scire intellectus noster potest, suis ex causis didicisse cognoscimus?"

84. Barozzi 1531, fols. 170v–171v.

85. Barozzi 1531, fol. 169rv: "Quibus tu ut vivis parentibus, sic etiam mortuis, omnia es: tutor, curator, procurator, praeceptor, pater. Nihil eis, te vivo atque incolumi, potest deesse."

86. Barozzi 1531, 174v: "Tuque in primis, qui cum tuis virtutibus,

tum hominum consensu, magnam suscepisti, et cura ut qui te die noctuque circunstant, consolatores officiosissimi, oculosque in te unum intentos tenent, dicant scire te non minus adversam fortunam constanti animo ferre, quam secundam."

87.   McManamon 1989; also, for Venice, King 1986, 44, 170, 177n241.

88.   Giuliani 1741.

89.   L. Giustiniani 1941.

90.   For Orsini's response to Filelfo, see above, chap. 2, following n84. The main discussions of Venice in Orsini's and Bevilacqua's works respectively at G, 269–82, 288–94 (M, fols. 2–15v, 20v–28), and 357–77 (V, fols. 68v–96). For the Venetian myth see above, chap. 2, n95.

91.   J. Zeno 1940; B. Giustiniani 1751.

92.   For some of these, see above, chap. 3, discussion near nn86–92.

93.   For the early modern development of autobiography, see esp. N. Z. Davis 1988; Schrenck 1985; Zimmermann 1971.

94.   Goodich 1973–74, esp. 287–88; Shahar 1982–83; Weinstein & Bell 1982, 18, 27.

95.   Goodich 1973–74, 288.

96.   Weinstein & Bell 1982, 24.

97.   Crantor's work is known from later authors, including Cicero: *Tusc.* 1.48; Plutarch *Ad Apollonium* (possibly pseudonymous) 102, 104, 114; see also Beyenka 1952, 3–4; Kassel 1958, 35–36.

98.   See also the consolatory letter to Cicero on Tullia's death by Servius Sulpicius Rufus, *Ep. ad fam.* 4.5, with Cicero's response at 4.6, and Cicero's own consolation of Titus, 5.16.

99.   *Confessions* 9.6 for Adeodatus's death, 9.11–13 for his mother Monica's; also Beyenka 1952, 31–43, for Augustine's experience of death.

100.   Paulinus 1975, 309–39; Latin text in PL 61 (1861):676–90. Thanks to Dr. Elizabeth Hill for her guidance in exploring Paulinus's contribution.

101.   The following from Paulinus 1975, 321–22, 327–28 (##381, 407, 545, 591).

102.   Lienhard 1977, 27.

103.   Quoted by Peter Brown 1981, 27n14, from Paulinus, *Carmen* 31.109–10.

104.   For the following, see chap. 5, discussion beginning near n85.

105.   McClure 1991, chap. 5; McClure 1986.

106.   McClure 1991, 94–98; Seigel 1968, 71–73; Tenenti 1957, 37–40; Witt 1983, 355–67.

107. Salutati, *Epist.* 3:420, as trans. by McClure 1991, 96.

108. Manetti 1983 is the text of the *Dialogus consolatorius,* with De Petris's valuable introduction at vii–ci; also De Petris 1977; De Petris 1979.

109. Manetti 1983, 6 (1.1): "Cum ex recenti et acerbo quodam Antonini mei funere me in Vaccianum solitudinis gratia contulissem, ibique vario consolationis genere, quoad poteram, me ipsum consolarer."

110. Two other interlocutors play minor roles; see Manetti 1983, intro. of De Petris, xxii–xxiv.

111. Manetti 1983, 46 (3.2): "Angelus quippe noster Stoicorum sententiam probat. Ego aurum scripta denegarem, si non nullas barbaras et efferatas nationes inneam, et sequor et probo"; the Italian version (originating with Manetti himself) states the point more clearly (p.47): "[Angelo] appruova la sentenzia degli stoici e io seguito l'opinione de' peripatetici come più conveniente all'umana natura." The theme is also expressed *passim.*

112. Manetti 1983, 12 (1.9): "Quid enim parentibus suavius, quid carius, quid denique dulcius quam salubris educatorum liberorum vita esse valeat non sane intelligo, quorum amissio sine quadam animi molestia contingere non potest."

113. Manetti 1983, 12 (1.10): "Tu parentibus ex filiorum morte, ac si e silice nasceremur, nequaquam dolendum esse arbitraris; ego autem fieri non posse reor ut parentes ex carorum sibi liberorum amissione ab ipsis presertim erumnarum incunabulis non mediocriter moveantur."

114. Manetti 1983, 214 (6.9): "Postea vero quam, sapientissimi viri, consilio vestro freti, lacrimis paulisper indulsimus, reliquum est ut filii nostri desiderium equanimiter toleremus atque propterea inmortali Deo gratias agamus, quanquam liberorum amissio acrius quam ceterarum rerum iactura torquere soleat."

115. Burckhardt 1958, 1:143.

116. For attitudes towards death in the late Middle Ages and early modern period, see Ariès 1974; Ariès 1985; Boase 1972; P. Brown 1981; Chaunu 1976; Chiffoleau 1980; Finucane 1981; Gittings 1984; Huizinga 1954, chap. 11; Le Goff 1984; Lorcin 1981; McManners 1985, esp. chap. 3; Stone 1977, esp. 206–15; Vovelle & Vovelle 1970; Whaley 1981; in Italy particularly, Cohn 1988 (for Siena); Goffen, Tetel & Witt 1989 (for Florence); Tenenti 1957 (also France). For tombs, esp. Panofsky 1964; for dogal tombs and funeral rites, Muir 1981, part 3, esp. 276. See also titles for consolation literature given at n67 above.

117. René 1845–46, 4:1–61, for which see Ricaldone 1986; for the *ars moriendi,* see above, n82.

118. René 1845–46, 4:10: "Le diable . . . ton cas poursuivra . . . pour toy mener avecques les perdans / Au puit d'enfer, là ou il te fera / Sentir tourment horrible que n'aura / jamais fin."
119. Huizinga 1954, 141.
120. René 1845–46, 1:xcii.
121. Lecoy 1875, 1:417.
122. Lecoy 1875, 1:262, 2:20–25, 2:387ff.; René d'Anjou 1845–46, 1:clii–cliii; F. Robin 1986; also F. Robin 1985. I am grateful to Dr. Paul Rosenfeld for his assistance with this Angevin tomb.
123. Coulet, Planche & Robin 1982, figs. 22, 42.
124. René 1845–46, 1:clii–cliii. At cliii, 8-line Latin verse; ll. 3–4, 7–8: "Marcescunt flores, mundi laudes et honores, / Gloria, fama levis, pomparum fastus inanis. . . . Mors, dominis servos, et turpibus aequat honestos, / Unus erunt tumulus, rex, pastor, inersque peritus." The painting (clii): The composition "fut de se représenter d'une manière emblématique, sous la forme d'un squelette revêtu d'un long manteau, assis su un trône resplendissant d'or, foulant aux pieds des tiares, des diadêmes, des globes, des livres, et méprisant ainsi tous les attributs de la grandeur, qui éblouit le vulgaire, ou de ces sciences périssables par lesquelles l'homme croit s'acquérir un nom immortel. Il semblait aussi que le spectre royal, appuyant sa tête hideus sur ses mains décharnées, cherchait à retenir sa couronne chancelante."
125. René 1845–46, 1:cliii; see Chron. 1841.
126. See above, chap. 4, following n211.
127. For the following, Clausse 1909, 388–91.
128. Janson 1967, 83 and fig. 23.
129. For the following see Chron. 1493: 30 November; 1502.
130. Fam. III.A.5.

Bibliography

꙰

SOURCES

Alberti, Leon Battista. 1960–73. *De iciarchia.* In *Opere volgari,* 2:185–286. Ed. Cecil Grayson. Scrittori d'Italia, 218, 234, 254. Bari: Giuseppe Laterza & Figli.

———. 1969. *The Family in Renaissance Florence (I libri della famiglia).* Trans. Renée Neu Watkins. Columbia, S.C.: University of South Carolina Press.

Anonimo veronese. 1915. *Cronaca di anonimo veronese dal 1446 al 1488.* Ed. Giovanni Soranzo. Venezia: Deputazione veneta di storia patria, Monumenti, Serie III, Cronache e diarii, 4.

Anon. Stu. (the Anonymous Student). See Texts II.C.14.

Anon. Tut. (the Anonymous Tutor). See Texts II.C.11.

Anon. Ven. (the Anonymous Venetian). See Texts II.C.12.

Augustine, Saint. *The Confessions.* Trans. Rex Warner. New American Library (Mentor).

Barbaro, Ermolao Giovane. 1943. *In funere Nicolai Marcelli Venetiarum principis.* In *Epistolae, orationes et carmina,* ed. Vittore Branca, 2:99–103. Florence: Bibliopolis. Also 1559, in *Orationes clarorum hominum,* 100v–103. Venice: In Academiae Venetae.

Barbaro, Francesco. 1741–43. *Diatriba praeliminaris in duas partes divisa ad Francisci Barbari et aliorum ad ipsum epistolae ab anno Christo MCDXXV ad annum MCDLIII.* Ed. Angelo Maria Quirini. 2 vols. Brescia: Joannes Maria Rizzardi.

———. 1884. *Centotrenta lettere inedite di Francesco Barbaro precedute dall'ordinamento critico cronologico dell'intero suo epistolario.* Ed. Remigio Sabbadini. Salerno: Tipografia Nazionale.

———. 1916. *De re uxoria liber.* Ed. Attilio Gnesotto. In *Atti e memorie dells R. Accademia di SLA in Padova,* NS 32:6–15.

———. 1978. "On Wifely Duties." Trans. Benjamin G. Kohl. In Kohl and Ronald G. Witt, eds., *The Earthly Republic: Italian Humanists on*

Government and Society, 177–228. Philadelphia: University of Pennsylvania Press.

Barbaro, Marco. *Arbori di patrizi veneti.* ASV, Miscellanea codici, I: Storia Veneta, RR. 17–23.

Barbo, Paolo. *Oratio in traditione insignium . . . Bartholomeo de Colionibus.* Florence: Bibl. Laurenziana, cod. Ashburnham 109 (181*–112*), fols. 26–27.

Barozzi, Pietro. 1531. *De modo bene moriendi.* To Marco Barbo. With three consolations (two to Cardinal Giovanni Michiel, Bishop of Verona, at fols. 118–146 and 146v–162v, and one to Cardinal Pietro Foscari, dated Belluno, 13 August 1481, at fols. 163–175v) and *officia.* Venice: In aedibus Io. Antonii et Fratrum de Sabio. The consolatory to Foscari also in G. B. Contarini 1757, 1:198–210.

Barzizza, Gasparino. 1723. *Gasparinii Barzizzii Bergomatis et Guiniforti filii opera.* Ed. Joseph Alexander Furiettus. Rome: Apud Jo. Mariam Salvioni Typographum Vaticanum.

Bembo, Bernardo. *Oratio in funere Bertholdi Marchionis Estensis* (1464), and *Consolatio* to widow Jacoba. Venice, cod. Marc. lat. XI, 139 (4432), fols. 1v–32 and 32–40 resp. Also BAV, cod. Vat. lat. 13709, fols. 272–307v.

Benadduci, Giovanni. 1894. *A Jacopo Antonio Marcello patrizio veneto parte di orazione consolatoria ed elegia di Francesco Filelfo e lettera di Giovanni Mario Filelfo.* Nozze Marcello-Giustiniani (31 January 1891). Tolentino: Stabilimento Tipografico Francesco Filelfo. Cited as Ben.

Bevilacqua, Giorgio, da Lazise. See Texts II.C.15, III.1, 2.

Boccaccio, Giovanni. 1974. *Trattatello in laude di Dante.* In *Tutte le opere di Giovanni Boccaccio,* 3:425–538. 2d ed. 10 vols. Verona: Arnaldo Mondadori.

Brucker, Gene, ed. 1967. *Two Memoirs of Renaissance Florence, The Diaries of Buonaccorso Pitti and Gregorio Dati.* Trans. Julia Martines. New York: Harper & Row.

Cagni, Giuseppe M., ed. 1968. *Giannozzo Manetti ambasciatore a Venezia, 1448–1450: Documenti.* Rome: Edizioni di Storia e Letteratura.

Caldiera, Giovanni. *Oratio in funere Orsati Justiniani Sancti Marci Procuratoris ad senatum populumque [Veneciis] habita in eclesia sanctorum Zoanis ac Pauli.* London, British Museum, cod. Addison 15406, fols. 91–97v.

Campano, Giovanni Antonio. 1731. *Bracchii Perusini vita et gesta ab anno [1368] usque ad annum [1424].* RIS/1, 19.5:429–622.

Cappellari Vivaro, Girolamo Alessandro. *Il campidoglio veneto.* 4 vols. Venice, cod. Marc. ital. VII, 15–18 (8304–7).

Carbone, Ludovico. See Texts II.C.5; II.D.16.

Cardan, Jerome. 1930. *The Book of My Life.* Trans. Jean Stoner. New York: E. P. Dutton.

Carrara, Giovanni Michele Alberto. 1757. See Texts III.3.

———. 1967. *Opera poetica, philosophica, rhetorica, theologica.* Ed. Giovanni Battista Giraldi. Novara: Istituto Geografico de Agostiini.

Cellini, Benvenuto. 1985. *The Autobiography of Benvenuto Cellini.* Trans. John Addington Symonds. New York: Modern Library (Random House).

Cesmicki, Ivan. See Pannonius, Janus.

Consolations for Valerio Marcello. See Texts II.A.

Contarini, Francesco. 1623. *De rebus in Hetruria a Senensibus gestis cum aduersus Florentinos, tum aduersus Ildibrandinum Ursinum Petilianensem Comitem, libri tres,* to Bernardo Bembo (1457). Rpt. of Lyon, 1562 edition by Giovanni Michele Bruto. Venice: apud Antonium Pinellum.

Contarini, Giovanni Battista, ed. 1757. *Anecdota veneta nunc primum collecta et notis illustrata.* Venice: Typ. P. Valvasensis.

Crivelli, Leodrisio. 1731. *De vita rebusque gestis Sfortiae bellicosissimi ducis ac initiis filii ejus Francisci Sfortiae vicecomitis . . . commentarius ab anno c. [1369] usque ad [1424].* RIS/1, 19.6:623–732.

Da Bisticci, Vespasiano. 1970. *Le vite.* Ed. Aulo Greco. Florence: Istituto Nazionale di Studi sul Rinascimento.

Damadenus, Theodorus, abbot. *Mare-caelum romano-venetum sive Marcellorum a Romani[s] principibus ad Venetos proceres ab anno u. c. CCXLIX usque ad annum Christi MDCLXXVI per annos MMCXXVII de patre in filium deducta progenies studio et opera Theodori Damadeni, Nobilis Belgae, S. Marthae abbatis commendatarii, Venetiis, anno salutis MDCLXXVI.* Latin (seventeenth-century) and Italian (eighteenth-century, trans. Vettore Marcello) mss. in the collection of Dott. Girolamo Marcello, Venice. Also Paris, Bibliothèque de l'Arsenal, MS 1211, not seen. Cited as *De origine.*

Da Soldo, Cristoforo. 1732. *Annales Brixiani ab anno MCCCCXXXVII usque ad annum MCCCCLXVIII.* RIS/1, 21:785–914.

———. 1938. *La cronaca di Cristoforo da Soldo.* Ed. Giuseppe Brizzolara. RIS/2, 21.3.

D'Aubigné, (Théodore) Agrippa. 1969. *Sa vie a ses enfants.* In *Oeuvres,* 383–463. Paris: Gallimard.

Decembrio, Pier Candido. 1731. *Vita Philippi Mariae Vicecomitis Mediola-nensium ducis tertii; Vita Francisci Sfortiae quarti mediolanensium ducis . . . [1401–1462]; Oratio in funere Nicolai Picenini.* Ed. Ludovico Muratori. RIS/1, 20.9/11:981–1090.

Dolfin, Giorgio [Zorzi]. *Cronaca di Venezia dall'origine dalla citt al 1458 di Zorzi Dolfin, q. Francesco da S. Canciano.* Venice, cod. Marc. ital. VII, 794 (8503).

Egnazio, Giovanni Battista. 1554. *De exemplis illustrium virorum Venetae civitatis atque aliarum gentium.* Parisiis: In officina Audoeni Parvi, via Iacobaea, ad Floris Lilij insigne.

Filelfo, Francesco. 1496. *Orationes Philelphi cum aliis opusculis.* Impressum Venetiis per Philippum de Pinzis Mantuanum, Anno Domini MCCCCXCVI primo kal. Iunii. H12925 [ex. Columbia University].

———. 1502. *Epistolarum familiarum libri xxxii.* Venetiis: ex aedibus Ioannis et Gregorii de Gregoriis fratres [Octavo Kal. Octobres].

———. See also Texts II.C.3,4; II.D.17; III.4.

Filelfo, Giovanni Mario. 1892. *Invettiva contro Pietro Perleone e Giorgio Trapezunzio.* In Ferdinando Gabotto, "Un nuovo contributo alla storia dell'umanesimo ligure," *Atti della Società Ligura di Storia Patria* 24:5–323, at 252–55.

———. See also Texts II.D.18, III.5.

Fortebraccio, Carlo. See Texts II.C.7.

Foscarini, Ludovico. *Epistolae.* Vienna, Österreichische Nationalbibliothek, cod. lat. 441.

Freud, Sigmund. 1957. *The Standard Edition of the Complete Psychological Works of Sigmund Freud.* Ed. James Strachey et al. 24 vols. London: The Hogarth Press and the Institute of Psycho-Analysis.

Garin, Eugenio, trans. and ed. 1958. *Pensiero pedagogico dello Umanesimo.* Florence: Giuntine-Sansoni.

George of Trebizond. See Texts I.8, II.C.2, III.6, 7.

Giomo, G. *Indice per nome di donna dei matrimoni dei patrizi veneti.* ASV, Miscellanea codici. 2 vols.

Giuliani, Andrea. 1741. *Pro Manuele Chrysolora funebris oratio (1415).* Ed. Angelo Calogerà in *Raccolta d'opuscoli scientifici e filologici,* 25:323–38.

Giustiniani, Bernardo. 1492. *Orationes et epistolae.* Venice: per Bernardinum Benalium. HC 9638.

———. 1722. *De origine urbis Venetiarum rebusque gestis a Venetis.* Ed. Joannes Georgius Graevius in *Thesaurus antiquitatum et historiarum Italiae,* 5. Lyon: Petrus Vander.

————. 1751. *Vita beati Laurentii Justiniani venetiarum protopatriarchae.* In *Sancti Laurentii Iustiniani proto-patriarchae veneti opera omnia.* 2 vols. Venice. Rpt. 1982: Florence: Leo S. Olschki.

Giustiniani, Leonardo. 1941. *Funebris oratio pro Carolo Zeno (1418).* In RIS/2, 19.6.2:141–46.

Grifo, Leonardo. 1733. *Conflictus Aquilani quo Braccius perusinus profligatus est, ad Franciscum Sfortiam libellus (2 June 1424).* In RIS/1, 25:465–78.

————. See also Texts II.D.19.

Guarini, Battista. See Texts II.C.9.

Guarino Veronese. 1915–19. *Epistolario di Guarino Veronese.* Ed. Remigio Sabbadini. 3 vols. R. Deputazione Veneta di Storia Patria. Ser. III: Miscellanea di Storia Veneta. Vols. 8, 11, 114 (= A, B, C). Venice: la Società. Anastatic reproduction 1967, Turin: Bottega d'Erasmo.

————. See also Texts I.9–12.

King, Margaret L., and Albert Rabil, Jr., ed. and trans. 1983. *Her Immaculate Hand: Selected Works by and about the Women Humanists of Quattrocento Italy.* Medieval and Renaissance Texts and Studies, 20. Binghamton, New York.

Lanfranchi, Luigi, ed. 1968. *San Giorgio Maggiore.* Comitato per la pubblicazione delle fonti relative alla storia di Venezia. Fonti per la storia di Venezia, sez. II: Archivi ecclesiastici, Diocesi Castellana. Venice: Il Comitato editore.

Lazzaroni, Giovanni Mario, ed. 1740. *Miscellanea di varie operette.* 2 vols. Venice: appresso Lazzaroni.

Loschi [De Luschis], Antonio. 1858. *Carmina quae supersunt fere omnia.* Padua: Typis Seminarii.

Lulmeo, Jacopo. See Texts I.2.

Malipiero, Domenico. 1843–44. *Annali veneti dall'anno 1457 al 1500.* Ed. F. Longo and Agostino Sagredo. ASI, Ser. 1, 7, part I and part II:1–720.

Manelmi, Evangelista. 1728. *Commentariolum de quibusdam gestis in bello gallico . . . Francisci Barbari . . . seu de obsidione Brixiae anni [1438] . . .* Ed. Joannes-Andreas Astezatus. Brescia: Typis Joannis Mariae Ricciardi.

Manetti, Giannozzo. 1983. *Dialogus de Antonini, sui filii, morte consolatorius.* Ed. Arnaldo de Petris. Rome: Edizioni di storia e letteratura.

————. See also under Wittschier, Heinz Willi.

Marcello, Jacopo Antonio. See Texts I, and passim.

Marcello, Pietro, elder. 1915. *Epistola consolatoria to Fantino Dandolo (January 1405).* In Remigio Sabbadini, "Antonio da Romagno e Pietro Marcello," 236–37. NAV, NS, 30: Parte I, 207–46.

Mascarello, Montorio. See Texts II.C.8.

Mazzei, Lapo. 1880. *Lettere di un notaro a un mecenate del secolo XIV.* Ed. Cesare Guasti. 2 vols. Florence: Le Monnier.

Memmo, Giovanni Maria. 1563. *Dialogo nel quale . . . si forma un perfetto Prencipe e una perfetta Repubblica.* Venice: appresso Gabri et Giolito de' Ferrari.

Merchenti, Ludovicus. *Benacus.* BMV, cod. Marc. lat. XII, 160 (4651).

Montaigne, Michel de. 1958. *The Complete Essays of Montaigne.* Trans. Donald M. Frame. Stanford: Stanford University Press.

Morelli, Giovanni. 1956. *Ricordi.* Ed. Vittore Branca. Florence: F. Le Monnier.

Navagero, Andrea. 1559. *Oratio in funere Bartholomaei Liviani, Veneti exercitus imperatoris.* In *Orationes clarorum hominum,* fols. 160–67v. Venice: In Academiae Venetae.

———. 1733. *Historia veneta italico sermone scripta ab origine urbis usque ad annum 1498.* RIS/1, 23.10:919–1216.

Nogarola, Isotta. 1886. *Isotae Nogarolae opera quae supersunt omnia,* with works of Angela and Ginevra Nogarola. Ed. by Eugenius Abel. 2 vols. Vienna-Budapest: apud Gerold et socios. Cited as Abel.

———. See also Texts II.C.6.

Orationes. 1559. *Orationes clarorum hominum, vel honoris officiique causa ad principes vel in funere de virtutibus eorum habitae.* Venice: In Academiae Venetae.

Orsini, Michele. *De antiqua venetorum origine.* BAV, cod. Vat. lat. 5280.

———. See also Texts II.C.13.

Osio, Luigi, ed. 1864–72. *Documenti diplomatici tratti dagli archivi milanesi.* 3 vols. Milan: Tip. di Giuseppe Bernardoni di Giovanni.

Pannonius, Janus. 1580. *Hodoeporicorum sive itinerum totius fere orbis lib. VII.* Basel: apud Perneam Lecythum. Not seen.

———. 1784. *Poëmata* and *Opusculorum pars altera.* 2 vols. Ed. Sámuel Teleki. Utrecht: Barthol. Wild.

———. 1972. *Janus Pannonius Munkai latinul es magyarul.* Ed. V. Sandor Kovacs. Budapest: Tankönyvkiadó.

———. 1985. *Janus Pannonius: The Epigrams.* Ed. and trans. Anthony A. Barrett. Corvina Kiadó [Hungary].

———. 1988. *Panegyricus for Guarino Veronese.* In Ian Thomson, ed. and trans., *Humanist Pietas: The Panegyric of Ianus Pannonius on Guarinus Veronensis,* 66–257. Bloomington Indiana: Research Institute for Inner Asian Studies.

———. See also Texts II.D.20, III.8.

Paulinus of Nola, Saint. 1975. *The Poems of Saint Paulinus of Nola.* Trans. and ed. P. G. Walsh. Ancient Christian Writers: The Works of the Fathers in Translation, 40. New York–Paramus, N.J.: Newman Press. Also *Opera* in PL 61 (1861).

Perleone, Pietro. 1740. *Epistola consolatoria ad Nicolaum Sagundinum.* In Giovanni Maria Lazzaroni, ed., *Miscellanea di varie operette,* 2:43–98. Venice: appresso Lazzaroni.

———. See also Texts II.C.10, II.D.21.

Petrarch, Francis. 1911. *Petrarch's Secret.* Trans. William H. Draper. London: Chatto & Windus.

———. 1966. *Letters from Petrarch.* Trans. and ed. Morris Bishop. Bloomington: Indiana University Press.

Porcelli de' Pandoni, Giannantonio. 1731. *Commentarii comitis Jacobi Picinini [Scipionis Aemiliani], sive Diarium rerum ab ipso gestarum anno MCCCCLII fervente bello inter venetos, et Franciscum Sfortiam Mediolanensium ducem, to King Alfonso I d'Aragona.* Ed. Ludovico Muratori. RIS/1, 20.2:65–154.

Predelli, Riccardo, ed. 1876–1914. *I libri commemoriali della republica di Venezia: regesti.* 9 vols. R. Deputazione Veneta di Storia Patria, Monumenti Storici, 3, Ser. I: Documenti, Vols. 1, 3, 7, 8, 10, 11, 13, 17. Venice: La Società.

René d'Anjou. 1845–1846. *Oeuvres choisies du roi René.* Ed. M. le Comte de Quatrebarbes. 4 vols. in 2. Angers: Imprimerie de Cosnier et Lachèse.

Rondo, Pietro da. See Texts III.9.

Rubeus, Hieronymus (Girolamo Rossi). 1589. *Historiarum Ravennatum libri decem, hac altera editione libro undecimo aucti . . . ,* Venetiis: ex Typographia Guerraea.

Rucellai, Giovanni. 1960. *Giovanni Rucellai ed il suo Zibaldone, I: "Il Zibaldone Quaresimale."* Ed. A. Perosa. Studies of the Warburg Institute, 24:1. London: The Warburg Institute.

Sabellico, Marcantonio. 1718. *Historiae rerum venetiarum ab urbe condita libri xxxiii, to Doge Marco Barbarigo.* In Apostolo Zeno, ed., *Istorici delle cose veneziane,* I. 2. Venice.

Sagundino, Niccolo. See Texts II.C.1.

Salomonius, Jacobus. 1701. *Urbis patavinae inscriptiones sacrae et prophanae*

. . . *quibus accedunt vulgatae anno [1644] a Jacobo Philippo Tomasino* . . . *additis historicis annotationibus* . . . *[1696]*. Padua: sumptibus Jo. Baptistae Caesari Typogr. Pat.

Sansovino, Francesco. 1968. *Della Venetia citta nobilissima et singolare.* (Orig. 1581). Additions by Giustiniano Martinioni [orig. 1663]; index by Lino Moretti. 2 vols. Venice: Filippi (Tipolitografia Armena).

Sanuto, Marino. *Cronica sanuda.* Venice: BMV, cod. Marc. ital. VII, 125 (7460).

————. 1733. *Vitae ducum venetorum, italice scriptae ab origine urbis sive ab anno [421] usque ad annum [1493] (Vite dei dogi).* RIS/1, 22.

————. 1847. *Itinerario per la terraferma veneziana nell'anno 1483.* Ed. Rawdon Brown. Padua: Tipografia del Seminario.

————. 1879–1903. *I diarii di Marino Sanuto, 1496–1533.* 58 vols. in 59. Ed. Rinaldo Fulin et al. R. Deputazione Veneta di Storia Patria. Venice: Visentini.

————. 1880. *Cronachetta di Marino Sanuto.* Ed. Rinaldo Fulin. Venice: Visentini.

————. 1881. "Frammento inedito dell'*Itinerario in Terra Ferma* di Marino Sanuto." Ed. Rinaldo Fulin. AV 22:1–48.

————. 1980. *De origine, situ et magistratibus urbis Venetae, ovvero la città di Venezia (1493–1530).* Ed. Angela Caracciolo Aricò. Collana di testi inediti e rari. Milan: Cisalpino–La Goliardica.

Savonarola, Michele. 1902. *Libellus de magnificis ornamentis . . . civitatis Paduae.* Ed. Arnaldo Segarizzi. RIS/2, 24.15.

————. 1952. *Il trattato ginecologico-pediatrico in volgare: Ad mulieres ferrarienses de regimine pregnantium et noviter natorum usque ad septennium.* Ed. Luigi Belloni. Milan: Società italiana di medicina interna.

Scardeone, Bernardino. 1560. *De antiquitate urbis patavii et claris civibus patavinis, libri tres.* Basileae: apud Nicolaum Episcopum juniorem.

Scussa Triestino, Vincenzo. 1863. *Storia cronografica di Trieste dalla sua origine sino all'anno 1695.* Ed. F. Cameroni. Trieste: Stab. Tipogr.-Litogr. di C. Coen Editore.

Seneca, Lucius Annaeus. 1958. *Moral Essays.* Trans. John W. Basore. 3 vols. Cambridge, Mass.: Harvard University Press; London: William Heinemann.

Simonetta, Giovanni. 1932. *Rerum gestarum Francisci Sfortiae Mediolanensium Ducis Commentarii.* Ed. Giovanni Soranzo. RIS/2, 21.2, fasc. 1–8. Also 1732: RIS/1, 21.2:165–782.

Sotheby. 1972. *Sotheby, firm, auctioneers, London, Catalogue of Sales (absorbs predecessor Baker and Lee bookdealers),* microfilm publication by Xerox

Univ. Microfilms, Ann Arbor, Michigan, 1972; 3 parts in 374 reels; 16mm. pos. micro. P.I (1734–1850), 71 reels; P.II (1851–1900), 148 reels; P.3 (1901–45), 155 reels.

Spretus, Desiderius. See Texts III.10.

Strozzi, Tito Vespasiano. See Della Guardia, Anita.

Tifernate, Gregorio. See Texts II.D.23.

Traversari, Ambrogio. See Texts II.D.10.

Valla, Lorenzo. 1979. *On Pleasure: De voluptate.* Trans. A. Kent Hieatt and Maristella Lorch. Janus Series, I. New York: Abaris Books.

Vallaresso, Maffeo. *Epistolae.* Cod. Vat. Barb. lat. 1809.

———. See also Texts III.12.

Vegio, Maffeo. 1933, 1936. *De educatione liberorum et eorum claris moribus libri sex.* Books I–III, ed. Sister Maria Walburg Fanning. Books IV–VI, ed. Sister Anne Sanislaus Sullivan. Washington, D.C.: Catholic University of America.

———. 1958. *De educatione liberorum.* Excerpt with Ital. trans. in Eugenio Garin, trans. and ed., *Pensiero pedagogico dello Umanesimo,* 171–97. Florence: Giuntine-Sansoni.

Velluti, Donato. 1914. *La cronica domestica.* Ed. Isidoro del Lungo and Guglielmo Volpi. Florence: G. C. Sansoni.

Vergerio, Pier Paolo. 1917–18. *De ingenuis moribus et liberalibus studiis adulescentiae.* Ed. Attilio Gnesotto. *R. Accademia di SLA in Padova, Atti e Memorie.* NS 34:75–157.

———. 1963. *De ingenuis moribus.* In W. H. Woodward, ed. and trans., *Vittorino da Feltre and Other Humanist Educators,* 93–118. Intro by Eugene F. Rice, Jr. Classics in Education, 18. New York: Teachers College, Columbia University. Orig. 1897: Cambridge: Cambridge University Press.

Vespasiano da Bisticci. See Da Bisticci.

Zeno, Jacopo. *Consolatio pro obitu matris,* to his brother Marino (Padua, 1 August 1434). London: British Museum Libary, cod. Arundel 70, fols. 169–74.

———. 1940. *Vita Caroli Zeni (1458).* Ed. Gasparo Zonta. RIS/2, 19.6:1–2.

Zonta, Gaspare, and Giovanni Brotto. 1970. *Acta graduum academicorum gymnasii patavini ab anno MCCCCVI ad annum MCCCCL.* 2d ed. 3 vols. Fonti per la storia dell'Università di Padova, 4–6. Padua: Editrice Antenore. Orig. Padua: Typis Seminarii, 1922.

Zovenzoni, Raffaele. See Texts III.13.

STUDIES

Abel, Eugenius (Jenö Abel). 1880. *Analecta ad historiam renascentium in Hungaria litterarum spectantia.* Budapest-Leipzig: F. A. Brockhaus.

————. See also Nogarola.

Ady, Cecilia M. 1907. *A History of Milan under the Sforza.* Ed. E. Armstrong. London: Methuen.

Affò, Ireneo. 1794. *Notizie intorni lo vita e le opere di Basino Basini.* 2 vols. Rimini.

Agostinelli, Lavinio, and Giovanni Benadduci. 1899. *Biografia e bibiografia di Giovan Mario Filelfo.* Tolentino: Stabilimento Tipographico Francesco Filelfo.

Alban, J. R., and Christopher T. Allmand. 1976. "Spies and Spying in the Fourteenth Century." In C. T. Allmand, ed., *War, Literature and Politics in the Late Middle Ages,* 73–101. New York: Barnes & Noble.

Albini, Giuliana. 1983. "L'infanzia a Milano del Quattrocento: note sulle registrazioni delle nascite e sugli esposti all'Ospedale Maggiore." *Nuova rivista storica,* 67:144–59.

Alexander, J. J. G. 1977. *Italian Renaissance Illuminators.* New York.

Antonini, Federico. 1930. "La pace di Lodi e i secrti maneggi che la prepararano." ASL, Ser. 6, 57:233–96.

Argegni, Corrado. 1936. *Condottieri, capitani, tribuni.* S. 19, *Enciclopedia Biografica e Bibliografica Italiana.* 3 vols. Milan: Istituto editoriale italiano (Bernardo Carlo Tosi).

Ariès, Philippe. 1962. *Centuries of Childhood: A Social History of Family Life.* Trans. Robert Baldick. New York: Random House (Vintage). French orig. Paris, 1960: *L'Enfant et la vie familiale sous l'ancien régime.*

————. 1974. *Western Attitudes toward Death: From the Middle Ages to the Present,* Trans. Patricia M. Ranum. Baltimore: Johns Hopkins University Press, 1974. French orig. 1974.

————. 1985. *Images of Man and Death.* Trans. Janet Lloyd. Cambridge, Mass.: Harvard University Press, 1985. French orig. 1983.

Ariès, Philippe, and André Bejin. 1985. *Western Sexuality: Practice and Precept in Past and Present Times.* Trans. by Anthony Forster. Oxford–New York: Basil Blackwell. Orig. 1982: *Sexualité occidentales.* Paris: Editions du Seuil/Communications.

Arnold, Dennis. 1983. "Alessandro Marcello," "Benedetto Marcello." In *New Oxford Companion to Music,* 2:1127–28. Oxford–New York: Oxford University Press.

Arnold, Joan Hagan, and Penelope Buschman Gemma. 1983. *A Child Dies: A Portrait of Family Grief.* Rockville, Md.: AspenSystems Corp.

Avesani, Rino. 1984. *Verona e il suo territorio, 4: Verona nel Quattrocento, Part 2.* Verona: Istituto per gli Studi Storici Veronesi.

Babinger, Franz. 1961. *Johannes Darius (1414–1494), Sachwalter Venedigs im Morgenland, und sein griechischer Umkreis.* Bayerische Akademie der Wissenschaften, philosophisch-historische Klasse, Sitzungsberichte, 1961, Heft 5. Munich: Verlag der Bayerischen Akademie.

———. 1962. "Notes on Cyriac of Ancona and Some of His Friends." JWCI 25.2:321–23.

Baldwin, Robert. 1987. "Politics, Nature, and the Dignity of Man in Piero della Francesca's Portraits of Battista Sforza and Federico da Montefeltro." *Source* 6.3:14–19.

Banker, James R. 1976. "Mourning a Son: Childhood and Paternal Love in the Consolateria [sic] of Giannozzo Manetti." *History of Childhood Quarterly,* 2:351–62.

Barbantini, Nino. 1940. *Il castello di Monselice.* Venice: Officine Grafiche Carlo Ferrari.

Barbero, Alessandro. 1986. "Guerra, nobiltà, onore fra Tre e Quattrocento nella storiografia anglosassone." *Studi storici,* Ser. 1, 27 (1986): 173–201.

Barbiani, Wilma. 1927. *La dominazione veneta a Ravenna.* Ravenna: Arti Grafiche.

Bassi, Elena. 1936. *Giannantonio Selva, architetto veneziano.* Padua: CEDAM (Dott. A. Milano).

———. 1976 [1978]. *Palazzi di Venezia.* Venice: la Stamperia di Venezia.

Beaty, Nancy Lee. 1970. *The Craft of Dying: A Study in the Literary Tradition of the Ars Moriendi.* Yale Studies in English, 175. New Haven–London: Yale University Press.

Belloni, Annalisa. 1986. *Professori giuristi a Padova nel secolo XV: profili bio-bibliografici e cattedre.* Ius commune, Sonderhefte, 28. Frankfurt am Main: Vittorio Klostermann.

Beltrami, Luca. 1906. *La "Ca' del Duca" sul Canal Grande, ed altre reminiscenze sforzesche in Venezia.* Nozze Alberto Albertini-Paolo Giacosa. Milan: Tipografia Allegretti.

Bent, Margaret, and Anne Hallmark, eds. 1985. *The Works of Johannes Ciconia.* Latin texts ed. M. J. Connolly. Vol. 24 in *Polyphonic Music of the Fourteenth Century,* ed. Kurt von Fischer et al. Monaco: Editions de l'Oiseau-Lyre.

Bentley, Jerry F. 1987. *Politics and Culture in Renaissance Naples.* Princeton: Princeton University Press.

Berchet, Guglielmo. 1893 (26 July). *Dedica alla Geografia di Strabone a*

Iacopo Antonio Marcello. Nozze Marcello-del Mayno. Venezia: Stab. tip. Ferrari.

Berlan, Francesco. 1852. *I due Foscari, memorie storico-critiche*. Turin: Tipografia G. Favale.

Bertalot, Ludwig, and Augusto Campana. 1975. "Gli scritti di Iacopo Zeno e il suo elogio di Ciriaco d'Ancona." In *Studien zum italienischen und deutschen Humanismus*, ed. Paul Oskar Kristeller, 2:311–32. 2 vols. Rome: Edizioni di Storia e Letteratura.

Bertoni, Giulio. 1921. *Guarino Veronese fra letterati e cortigiani a Ferrara (1429–1460)*. Biblioteca dell'"Archivum Romanicum," Ser. I, 1. Geneva: Leo S. Olschki.

Bevilacqua, Eugenia. 1980. "Cartografia ed esplorazioni nel secolo XV," in SCV 3.2:355–74.

Beyenka, Mary Melchior, Sister. 1952. *Consolation in Saint Augustine*. The Catholic University of America, Patristic Studies, 83. Washington, D.C.: Catholic University of America Press.

Birnbaum, Marianna D. 1981. *Janus Pannonius: Poet and Poitician*. Opera academiarum scientiarum ed artium slavorum meridionalium. Zagreb: Jugoslavenska Akademija Znanosti i Umjetnosti.

———. 1988. "Humanism in Hungary." In Albert Rabil, ed., *Renaissance Humanism: Foundations, Forms, and Legacy*, 2:293–334. 3 vols. Philadelpha: University of Pennsylvania Press.

Bitton, Davis. 1969. *The French Nobility in Crisis, 1560–1640*. Stanford: Stanford University Press.

Bluebond-Langner, Myra. 1977. *The Private Worlds of Dying Children*. Princeton: Princeton University Press.

Boase, T. S. R. 1972. *Death in the Middle Ages: Mortality, Judgment and Remembrance*. London: Thames & Hudson; New York: McGraw-Hill.

Boswell, John E. 1989. *The Kindness of Strangers: The Abandonment of Children in Western Europe from Late Antiquity to the Renaissance*. New York: Pantheon.

Bowlby, John. 1979. *The Making and Breaking of Affectional Bonds*. London: Tavistock Publications.

Branca, Vittore, ed. 1977a. *Lauro Quirini umanista: studi e testi a cura di Konrad Krautter, P. O. Kristeller, Agostino Pertusi, Giorgio Ravegnani, Helmut Roob e Carlo Seno*. Fondazione Giorgio Cini, Civilta Veneziana, Saggi, 23. Florence: Leo S. Olschki.

———. 1977b. "Lauro Quirini e il commercio librario a Venezia e Firenze." In *Venezia centro di mediazione tra Oriente e Occidente, secoli XV–*

XVI: Aspetti e problemi, ed. H. G. Beck, M. Manoussacas, Agostino Pertusi, 1:369–77. 2 vols. Florence: Fondazione Giorgio Cini.

Brown, Alison M. 1961. "The Humanist Portrait of Cosimo de' Medici, Pater Patriae." JWCI 24:186–221.

————. 1979. *Bartolomeo Scala, 1430–1497, Chancellor of Florence: The Humanist as Bureaucrat.* Princeton: Princeton University Press.

Brown, Patricia Fortini. 1988. *Venetian Narrative Painting in the Age of Carpaccio.* New Haven–London: Yale University Press.

Brown, Peter. 1981. *The Cult of the Saints: Its Rise and Function in Latin Christianity.* Haskell Lectures on History of Religions, NS 2. Chicago: University of Chicago Press.

Burckhardt, Jacob. 1958. *The Civilization of the Renaissance in Italy.* Trans. S. G. C. Middlemore. New York: Harper & Row (Torchbook). Orig. 1929.

Buresch, C. 1886. *Consolationum a Graecis Romanisque scriptarum historia critica.* Leipziger Studien zur classischen philologie, 9, Heft I.

Burns, Stanley B. 1991. *Sleeping Beauty: Memorial Photography in America.* Altadena, Cal.: Twelvetrees Press.

Buser, B. 1879. *Die Beziehungen der Mediceer zu Frankreich während der Jahre 1434–1494.* Leipzig: Verlag von Duncker und Humbolt.

Calzaferri, Bartolomeo. 1938. "La tecnica adottata dagli umanisti bergamaschi Gasparino e Guinforte Barzizza negli scritti d'indole consolatoria." *Convivium,* 10:425–38.

Campbell, Lorne. 1990. *Renaissance Portraits: European Portrait-Painting in the Fourteenth, Fifteenth, and Sixteenth Centuries.* New Haven: Yale University Press.

Canetta, Carlo. 1885. "La pace di Lodi (9 aprile 1454)." *Rivista storica italiana* 2 (1885): 516–64.

Cappelletti, Giuseppe. 1850–55. *Storia della repubblica di Venezia dal suo principio sino al giorno d'oggi.* 13 vols. Venice: G. Antonelli.

Carile, Antonio. 1970. "Aspetti della cronachista veneziana nei secoli XIII e XIV." In *Storiografia veneziana,* ed. Pertusi, 75–126. Florence: Leo S. Olschki.

Carmichael, Ann G. 1986. *Plague and the Poor in Renaissance Florence.* Cambridge History of Medicine. Cambridge–New York: Cambridge University Press.

Cartolari, A. 1854. *Famigli già ascritte al nobile consiglio di Verona . . .* Verona: Vicentini e Franchini.

Castellani, Giorgio. 1896. "Documenti veneziani inediti relativi a Francesco a Mario Filelfo." ASI, Ser. 5, 17:364–70.

Catalano, Franco. 1956. "La nuova signoria: Francesco Sforza" and "Il ducato di Milano nell politica dell'equilibrio." In *Storia di Milano*, 7.1 (1–224) and 7.2 (225–414). 17 vols. Milan: Fondazione Treccani degli Alfieri.

———. 1983. *Francesco Sforza*. Milan: Dall'Oglio.

Cenci, Cesare. 1968. "Senato veneto: *'Probae'* ai benefici ecclesiastici," in C. Piana and Cenci, *Promozioni agli ordini sacri a Bologna e alle dignità ecclesiastiche nel veneto nei secoli XIV–XV,* 313–454. Spicilegium Bonaventurianum, 3. Quaracchi-Florence: Typographia Collegii S. Bonaventurae.

Cesca, Giovanni. 1883. *L'assedio di Trieste nel 1463.* Verona-Padua: Drucker & Tedeschi.

Cessi, Roberto. 1942–44. "La 'Lega italica' e la sua funzione storica nella seconda metà del sec. XV." *Atti del R. Istituto Veneto di SLA,* 102.2:99–176.

———. 1944. *Storia della Repubblica di Venezia.* 2 vols. Biblioteca Storica Principato, 23–24. Milan-Messina: Giuseppe Principato.

Chambers, David S. 1970. *The Imperial Age of Venice, 1380–1580.* History of European Civilization Library. London: Thames & Hudson; New York: Harcourt Brace Jovanovich.

Chartier, Roger. 1976. "Les Arts de mourir, 1450–1600." *Annales,* 31:51–75.

Chaunu, Pierre. 1976. "Mourir a Paris (XVIe–XVIIe–XVIIIe siecles)." *Annales,* 31:29–50.

Chiffoleau, Jacques. 1980. *La Comptabilité de l'au-delà: les hommes, la mort et la réligion dans la region d'Avignon à la fin du Moyen Age, vers 1320 – vers 1480.* Preface by Jacques Le Goff. Rome: Ecole française de Rome.

Chojnacki, Stanley. 1973. "In Search of the Venetian Patriciate: Families and Factions in the Fourteenth Century." In *Renaissance Venice,* ed. John R. Hale, 47–90. Totowa, N.J.: Rowman & Littlefield.

———. 1985. "Kinship Ties and Young Patricians in Fifteenth-Century Venice." RQ 38:240–70.

———. 1986. "Political Adulthood in Fifteenth-Century Venice." *American Historical Review,* 91:791–810.

Cicchetti, Angelo and Raul Mordenti. 1985. *I libri di famiglia in Italia.* Rome: Edizioni di storia e letteratura.

Cicogna, Emmanuele Antonio. 1824–53. *Delle iscrizioni veneziane.* 6 vols. Venice: G. Orlandelli.

———. 1841. *Della famiglia Marcello patrizia veneta: narrazione.* Per nozze degli Orefici-Marcello. Venice: dalla Tipografia di G. B. Merlo.

Cipolla, Carlo. 1954. *La storia politica di Verona.* Rev. ed., Ottavio Pellegrini. Verona: Valdonega.

Clausse, Gustage. 1909. *Les Sforza et les arts en Milanais, 1450–1530.* Paris: Ernest Leroux, Editeur.

Clough, Cecil C. 1976. "The Cult of Antiquity: Letters and Letter Collections." In Cecil C. Clough, ed., *Cultural Aspects of the Italian Renaissance,* 33–37. New York: Alfred F. Zambelli.

Cochrane, Eric. 1981. *Historians and Historiography in the Italian Renaissance.* Chicago-London: University of Chicago Press.

Cognasso, Francesco. 1955. "Il ducato visconteo da Gian Galeazzo a Filippo Maria"; "La repubblica di S. Ambrogio"; "Istituzioni comunale e signorili di Milano sotto i Viscontei." In *Storia di Milano,* 6.1 (1–383); 6.2 (385–448); 6.3 (449–544). 17 vols. Milan: Fondazione Treccani degli Alfieri.

Cohn, Samuel K., Jr. 1988. *Death and Property in Siena, 1205–1800: Strategies for the Afterlife.* The Johns Hopkins University Studies in Historical and Political Science, 106th Series, 2. Baltimore-London: Johns Hopkins University Press.

Colombo, Alessandro. 1894. "Re Renato alleato del Duca Francesco Sforza contro i veneziani." ASL, Ser. 3, vol. 1, anno 21:79–136, 361–98.

———. 1905. "L'ingresso di Francesco Sforza in Milano e l'inizio di un nuovo principato." ASL, Ser. 4, vol. 3, anno 32:297–344.

———. 1906. "A proposito delle relazioni tra Francesco I Sforza e Firenze (luglio 1451)." *Rendiconti della R. Accademia dei Lincei, Classe di scienze morali, storiche e filosofiche,* Ser. 5, 15:551–60.

Colombo, Cesare. 1969. "Gasparino Barzizza a Padova: nuovi ragguagli da lettere inedite." *Quaderni per la storia dell'Università di Padova,* 2:1–27.

Cornelius, Flaminius. 1749. *Ecclesiae venetae antiquis monumentis nunc etiam primum editis, illustratae ac in decades distributae.* 10 vols. Venice: Typis Jo: Baptistae Pasquali.

Cosenza, Mario Emilio. 1962–67. *Biographical and Bibliographical Dictionary of the Italian Humanists and of the World of Classical Scholarship in Italy, 1300–1800.* 2d ed. 6 vols. Boston: G. K. Hall.

Coulet, Noel, Alice Planche and Françoise Robin. 1982. *Le Roi René: le prince, le mécène, l'écrivain, le mythe.* Aix-en-Provence: Edisud.

Courcelle, Pierre Paul. 1967. *La Consolation de philosophie dans la tradition littéraire: antecedents et posterité de Boèce.* Paris: Etudes augustiniens.

———. 1971. "La survie comparée des 'Confessions' augustiniennes et de la 'Consolation' Boécienne." In R. R. Bolgar, ed., *Classical Influences* on *European Culture*, A.D. *500–1500*, 131–42. Cambridge: Cambridge University Press.

Covi, Dario A. 1958. Review of Millard Meiss, *Andrea Mantegua as Illuminator. Renaissance News* 11:124–29.

Cracco, Giorgio and Michael Knapton, eds. 1984. *Dentro lo 'Stado Italico': Venezia e la terraferma fra Quattro e Seicento.* Trent: Gruppo culturale Civis-Biblioteca Cappuncini.

Cusin, Fabio. 1936a. "L'impero e la successione degli Sforza ai Visconti." ASL, NS 1, vol. 1:3–116.

———. 1936b. "Le aspirazioni straniere sul Ducato di Milano e l'investitura imperiale (1450–1454)." ASL, NS 1, vol.1: 277–369.

Damerini, Gino. 1969. *L'isola e il cenobio di San Giorgio Maggiore.* Venice: Fondazione Giorgio Cini by Verona: Valdonega.

Da Mosto, Andrea. 1937–40. *L'Archivio di Stato di Venezia, indice generale, storico, descrittivo ed analitico.* 2 vols. Bibliothèque des "Annales Institutorum," 5. Rome: Biblioteca d'Arte Editrice.

———. 1983. *I dogi di Venezia.* Florence: Giunti, by Aldo Martello. Orig. 1939: Venice: F. Ongania.

Daverio, Michele. 1804. *Memorie sulla storia dell'ex-ducato di Milano.* Milano: Presso Andrea Mainardi nella Stamperia a S. Mattia alla Moneta.

Davis, James Cushman. 1962. *The Decline of the Venetian Nobility as a Ruling Class.* The Johns Hopkins University Studies in Historical and Political Science, Ser. 80, 2. Baltimore: Johns Hopkins University Press.

———. 1975. *A Venetian Family and Its Fortune, 1500–1900: The Donà and the Conservation of Their Wealth.* Philadelphia: University of Pennsylvania Press.

Davis, Natalie Zemon. 1983. "Beyond the Market: Books as Gifts in Sixteenth-Century France." *Transactions of the Royal Historical Society,* Ser. 5, 33:69–88.

———. 1988. "Fame and Secrecy: Leon Modena's *Life* as an Early Modern Autobiography." *History and Theory,* 27:103–18. Rpt. of introduction to *The Autobiography of a Seventeenth-Century Venetian Rabbi: Leon Modena's Life of Judah,* ed. and trans. Mark R. Cohen with Howard E. Adelman and Benjamin C. I. Ravid. Princeton: Princeton University Press, 1988.

Degli Agostini, Giovanni. 1752–54. *Notizie istorico-critiche intorno la vita e le opere degli scrittori viniziani.* 2 vols. Venice: S. Occhi.

Della Guardia, Anita, ed. 1916. *Tito Vespasiano Strozzi: poesie latine tratte dall'Aldina e confrontate coi codici.* Modena: Tipografia editrice moderna Blondi & Marmeggiani.

De Maio, Romeo. 1987. *Donna e Rinascimento*. Milan: Mondadori.

De Mause, Lloyd. 1974. "The Evolution of Childhood." In *The History of Childhood*, ed. De Mause, 1–73. New York: Psychohistory Press.

De Mérindol, Christian. 1987. *Le roi René et la seconde maison d'Anjou: emblematique art histoire*. Paris: Leopard d'Or.

De Petris, Arnaldo. 1977. "Il 'Dialogus consolatorius' di Giannozzo Manetti e le sue fonti." GSLI 154:76–106.

———. 1979. "Giannozzo Manetti and His Consolatoria." BHR 41: 493–526

De' Rosmini, Carlo. 1805–6. *Vita e disciplina di Guarino Veronese e de' suoi discepoli*. 3 vols. Brescia: Nicolò Bettoni tipografia dipartimentale.

———. 1808. *Vita di Francesco Filelfo da Tolentino*. 3 vols. Milan: Presso Luigi Mussi.

Des Garets, Marie-Louyse. 1946. *Un Artisan de la Renaissance française au XVe siècle: le roi René, 1409–1480*. Paris: Editions de la Table Ronde.

Diekstra, F. M. N. 1968. *A Dialogue between Reason and Adversity: A Late Middle English Version of Petrarch's* De remediis. Assen: Van Gorcum.

Diller, Aubrey. 1975. *The Textual Tradition of Strabo's Geography*. Amsterdam: A. M. Hakkert.

Diller, Aubrey, and P. O. Kristeller. 1971. "Strabo," CTC 2:225–33.

Di Santa Maria, Angiolgabriello. 1772–82. *Biblioteca, e storia di quei scrittori così della città come territorio di Vicenza che pervennero fin'ad ora a notizia*. 5 vols. Vicenza: per Gio. Battista Vendramini Mosca.

Edgerton, Samuel Y., Jr. 1987. "From Mental Matrix to *Mappamundi* to Christian Empire: The Heritage of Ptolemaic Cartography in the Renaissance." In David Woodward, ed., *Art and Cartography: Six Historical Essays*, 10–50. Chicago-London: University of Chicago Press.

Eisler, Colin T. 1989. *The Genius of Jacopo Bellini: The Complete Paintings and Drawings*. New York: Harry N. Abrams.

Elton, G. R. 1984. "Happy Families." *New York Review of Books* 31.10:39–41.

Eroli, Giovanni. 1876. *Erasmo Gattamelata da Narni, suoi monumenti e sua famiglia*. Rome: coi tipi del Salviucci.

Fabbri, Renata. 1983. "Le Consolationes de obitu Valerii Marcelli ed il Filelfo." 3.1:227–50 in *Miscellanea di studi in onore di Vittore Branca*. Biblioteca dell' "Archivum Romanicum," Ser. I, vols. 178–81. 4 vols. in 6; Florence.

Facciolati, Jacopo. 1757. *Fasti gymnasii patavini*. Padua: Typis Seminarii, apud Joannem Manfré.

Faraglia, N. F. 1907. *Storia della lotta tra Alfonso V d'Aragon e Renato d'Angio.* Lanciano.

Fasoli, Gina. 1970. "I fondamenti della storiografia veneziana." In *Storiografia veneziana,* ed. Pertusi, 11–14. Florence: Leo S. Olschki.

Favez, Charles. 1937. *La consolation latine chrétienne.* Paris.

Favre, Guillaume. 1856. *Vie de Jean-Marius Philelphe.* In *Mélanges d'histoire litteraire par Guillaume Favre* 1:2–221. Geneva: Imprimerie Ramboz et Schuchardt.

Fichtner, Paula Sutter. 1967. "The Politics of Honor: Renaissance Chivalry and Habsburg Dynasticism." BHR 29:567–80.

Finlay, Robert. 1978. "The Venetian Republic as a Gerontocracy: Age and Politics in the Renaissance." JMRS 8:157–78.

Finucane, R. C. 1981. "Sacred Corpse, Profane Carrion: Social Ideals and Death Rituals in the Later Middle Ages." In *Mirrors of Mortality,* ed. J. Whaley, 40–60. London: Europa.

Flandrin, Jean-Louis. 1979. *Families in Former Times: Kinship, Household and Sexuality in Early Modern France.* Trans. Richard Southern. Cambridge, etc.: Cambridge University Press. French orig., 1976: *Familles: parenté, maison, sexualité dans l'ancienne société.*

Foa, A. 1980. "Chiericati, Leonello." DBI 24:682–89.

Fontana, Gianjacopo. 1865. *Cento palazzi fra i piu celebri di Venezia sul Canalgrande e nelle vie interne dei sestieri.* Venice: Prem. Stabilimento Tip. di P. Naratovich; rpt. Venice, 1934.

———. 1870–71. *Storia populare di Venezia dalle origini sino ai tempi nostri.* 2 vols. Venice: Giovanni Cecchini Editore.

Fossati, Felice. 1934. "Francesco Sforza e la sorpressa del 16 maggio 1452." ASL, Ser. 7, vol. 61.3:330–401.

Franzoi, Umberto. 1982. *Storia e leggenda del Palazzo Ducale di Venezia.* Verona: Edizioni Storti.

Fraser, Antonio. 1984. *The Weaker Vessel.* New York: Alfred A. Knopf.

Frati, Lodovico. 1910. "Di Ludovico Carbone e delle sue opere." *Atti e Memorie della Deputazione Ferrarese di Storia Patria,* 20.1. Ferrara: Tip. Sociale Zuffi.

Gabotto, Ferdinando. 1892. "Un nuovo contributo alla storia dell'umanesimo ligure." *Atti della Società Ligura di Storia Patria,* 24:5–323.

Gaeta, Franco. 1980. "Storiografia, coscienza nazionale e politica culturale nella Venezia del Rinascimento." In SCV 3.1:1–91. Vicenza: Neri Pozza.

Gallo, Rodolfo. 1944. "Una famiglia patrizia: i Pisani ed i palazzi di San Stefano e di Strà." AV, Ser. 5, 34–35:65–228.

Gardenal, Gianna. 1983. "Lodovico Foscarini e la medicina." In *Miscellanea di studi in onore di Vittore Branca*, 3.1:251–63. Biblioteca dell'"Archivum Romanicum," Ser. 1, 178–81 (4 vols. in 6). Florence: Leo S. Olschki.

Garin, Eugenio. 1958. *Pensiero pedagogico dell'Umanesimo.* Florence: Giuntine-Sansoni.

————. 1967. *Ritratti di umanisti.* Florence: G. C. Sansoni.

Giannetto, Nella. 1985. *Bernardo Bembo, umanista e politico veneziano.* Florence: Leo S. Olschki.

Gilbert, Creighton. 1967. "When Did a Man in the Renaissance Grow Old?" *Studies in the Renaissance,* 14:7–32.

Gilbert, Felix. 1971. "Biondo, Sabellico and the Beginnings of Venetian Official Historiography." In J. G. Rowe and W. H. Stockdale, eds., *Florilegium Historiale: Essays Presented to Wallace K. Ferguson,* 275–93. Toronto: University of Toronto Press.

Giorgi, Domenico. 1742. *Vita Nicolai Quinti Pontificis Maximis.* Rome: ex Typographia Palearinorum.

Giraldi, Giovanni. 1955. "Bibliografia delle opere di Giovanni Michele Carrara." *Rinascimento,* 6.1:125–43.

Giraldi, Philip M. 1977. "Tomaso Zen: A Venetian Military and Naval Commander of the Late Quattrocento (1435–1504)." SV, NS 1:109–118.

Girgensohn, Dieter. 1989. "Il testamento di Pietro Miani ("Emilianus") vescovo di Vicenza (+1433)." AV, Ser. 5, 132:5–64.

Gittings, Clare. 1984. *Death, Burial and the Individual in Early Modern England.* London: Croom Helm.

Gloria, Andrea. 1862–65. *Il territorio padovano illustrato.* 3 vols. Padua: Stab. di P. Prosperini. Rpt. Bologna 1974.

Goffen, Rona. 1989. *Giovanni Bellini.* New Haven: Yale University Press.

Goffen, Rona, Marcel Tetel, and Ronald G. Witt. 1989. *Life and Death in Fifteenth-Century Florence.* Duke Monographs in Medieval and Renaissance Studies, 10. Durham-London: Duke University Press.

Goldthwaite, Richard A. 1968. *Private Wealth in Renaissance Florence: A Study of Four Families.* Princeton: Princeton University Press.

Goodich, Michael. 1973–74. "Childhood and Adolescence among the Thirteenth-Century Saints." *History of Childhood Quarterly,* 1:285–309.

Gothein, Percy. 1932. *Francesco Barbaro (1390–1454): Frühhumanismus und Staatskunst in Venedig.* Berlin: Verlag die Runde.

Goy, Richard J. 1985. *Chioggia and the Villages of the Venetian Lagoon: Studies in Urban History.* Cambridge: Cambridge University Press.

Grafton, Anthony and Lisa Jardine. 1986. *From Humanism to the Humanities: Education and the Liberal Arts in Fifteenth- and Sixteenth-Century Europe.* Cambridge, Mass.: Harvard University Press.

Green, Louis. 1986. *Castruccio Castracani: A Study on the Origins and Character of a Fourteenth-Century Italian Despotism.* Oxford: Clarendon Press.

Greenblatt, Stephen Jay. 1980. *Renaissance Self-Fashioning from More to Shakespeare.* Chicago-London: University of Chicago Press.

Grendler, Paul F. 1988. "Chivalric Romances in the Italian Renaissance." *Studies in Medieval and Renaissance History,* 10:59–102.

———. 1989. *Schooling in Renaissance Italy: Literacy and Learning, 1300–1600.* Baltimore-London: Johns Hopkins University Press.

Greppi, Crescentino. 1913. "Le case degli Sforza a Venezia e Fra Simeone da Camerino." NAV, NS, anno 13, t. 26.2:324–58.

Greven, Philip J. 1970. *Four Generations: Population, Land, and Family in Colonial Andover, Massachusetts.* Ithaca: Cornell University Press.

Grubb, James S. 1986. "When Myths Lose Power: Four Decades of Venetian Historiography." JMH 58:43–94.

———. 1988. *Firstborn of Venice: Vicenza in the Early Renaissance State.* Studies in Historical and Political Science. Baltimore: Johns Hopkins University Press.

Gualdo Rosa, Lucia. 1971. "Un documento inedito sull'ambiente culturale padovano nella seconda metà del secolo XV: il "Dialogus" di Leonello Chieregati." *Quaderni per la storia dell'università di Padova,* 4:1–37.

Gundersheimer, Werner. 1973. *Ferrara: The Style of a Renaissance Despotism.* Princeton, N.J.: Princeton University Press, 1973.

Hale, John R. 1961. *Machiavelli and Renaissance Italy.* London: The English University Presses.

Hatfield, Rab. 1965. "Five Early Renaissance Portraits." *Art Bulletin,* 47.3:315–34.

Hayward, John and Elisabetta Antoniazzi Rossi, eds. 1980. *L'armeria del Castello di Monselice.* Cataloghi di raccolte d'arte, NS 14. Vicenza: Neri Pozza (Fondazione Giorgio Cini).

Hazlitt, William C. 1915. *The Venetian Republic, Its Rise, Its Growth, and Its Fall, A.D. 409–1797.* 4th ed. 2 vols. London: Adam and Charles Black. Rpt. 1966: New York: AMS.

Herlihy, David. 1985. *Medieval Households.* Cambridge, Mass.: Harvard University Press.

Herlihy, David and Christiane Klapisch-Zuber. 1985. *Tuscans and Their Families: A Study of the Florentine Catasto of 1427.* New Haven: Yale University Press. Abr. trans. of French 1978 ed.

Howard, Deborah. 1975. *Jacopo Sansovino: Architecture and Patronage in Renaissance Venice.* New Haven: Yale University Press.

———. 1980. *Architectural History of Venice.* London: B. T. Batsford.

Huizinga, Johan. 1954. *The Waning of the Middle Ages.* Garden City, New York: Doubleday (Anchor).

Huse, Norbert, and Wolfgang Wolters. 1990. *The Art of Renaissance Venice: Architecture, Sculpture and Painting, 1460–1590.* Trans. Edmund Jophcott. Chicago-London: University of Chicago Press.

Huszti, G. 1933. "Giano Pannonio." *Enciclopedia italiana* 16:970. Milan: Treves-Treccani-Tumminelli.

Ianziti, Gary. 1981. "A Humanist Historian and His Documents: Giovanni Simonetta, Secretary to the Sforzas." RQ 34:491–517.

———. 1988. *Humanistic Historiography under the Sforzas: Politics and Propaganda in Fifteenth-Century Milan,* New York: Clarendon Press of Oxford University Press.

Ilardi, Vincent. 1959. "The Italian League, Francesco Sforza, and Charles VII (1454–1461)." *Studies in the Renaissance,* 6:129–66.

———. 1982. "France and Milan: The Uneasy Alliance, 1452–1466." In *Gli Sforza a Milano in Lombardia e i loro rapporti con gli stati italiani ed europei (1450–1530),* 415–47. Milan: Cisalpina Goliardica.

———. 1987. "Crosses and Carets: Renaissance Patronage and Coded Letters of Recommendation." *American Historical Review,* 92:1127–49.

Jackson, Stanley W. 1986. *Melancholia and Depression: From Hippocratic Times to Modern Times.* New Haven: Yale University Press.

Janson, H. W. 1967. "The Equestrian Monument from Cangrande della Scala to Peter the Great." In Archibald Lewis, ed., *Aspects of the Renaissance: A Symposium,* 73–85. Austin: University of Texas Press.

Jones, Philip J. 1956. "Florentine Families and Florentine Diaries in the Fourteenth Century." *Papers of the British School at Rome,* 24, NS 5, 11:183–205.

Joost-Gaugier, Christiane L. 1979 (November). "A Pair of Miniatures by a Panel Painter: The Earliest Works of Giovanni Bellini." *Paragone,* 30, #357:48–71.

———. 1988. "Bartolomeo Colleoni as a Patron of Art and Architecture: the Palazzo Colleoni in Brescia." *Arte lombarda,* 84/85:61–72.

Kaeuper, Richard W. 1988. *War, Justice, and Public Order: England and*

France in the Later Middle Ages. Oxford: Clarendon Press of Oxford University Press.

Kassel, Rudolf. 1958. *Untersuchungen zur griechischen und römischen Konsolationsliteratur.* Zetemata: Monographien zur klassische Altertumswissenschaft, Heft 18. Munich: Verlag C. H. Beck.

Keen, M. H. 1976. "Chivalry, Nobility and the Man-at-Arms." In C. T. Allmand, ed., *War, Literature and Politics in the Late Middle Ages,* 32–45. New York: Barnes & Noble.

———. 1984. *Chivalry.* New Haven–London: Yale University Press.

Kent, Francis William. 1977. *Household and Lineage in Renaissance Florence: The Family Life of the Capponi, Ginori, and Rucellai.* Princeton, N.J.: Princeton University Press.

Ker, N. R. 1983. *William Hunter as a Collector of Medieval Manuscripts.* Glasgow: Glasgow University Press.

King, Margaret L. 1976. "Caldiera and the Barbaros on Marriage and the Family: Humanist Reflections of Venetian Realities." JMRS 6:19–50.

———. 1978. "The Religious Retreat of Isotta Nogarola (1418–1466)." *Signs,* 3:807–22.

———. 1986. *Venetian Humanism in an Age of Patrician Dominance,* Princeton, N.J.: Princeton University Press.

———. 1987. "An Inconsolable Father and his Humanist Consolers: Jacobo Antonio Marcello, Venetian Nobleman, Patron, and Man of Letters," in *Iter Festivum, Festschrift for Paul Oskar Kristeller,* ed. by James Hankins, John Monfasani, Martin Pine, and Frederick Purnell, 221–46. Binghamton, Medieval and Renaissance Texts and Studies.

———. 1988. "The Death of the Child Valerio Marcello," in Maryanne C. Horowitz, Anne J. Cruz and Wendy A. Furman, eds., *Renaissance Studies: Intertext and Context,* 205–25. Urbana-Champaign: University of Illinois Press.

———. 1991. "Isotta Nogarola, umanista e devota," in *Rinascimento al femminile,* ed. Ottavia Niccoli, 3–33. Rome: Laterza.

Klapisch-Zuber, Christiane. 1985. "Blood Parents and Milk Parents: Wet Nursing in Florence, 1300–1530." In *Women, Family, and Ritual in Renaissance Italy,* 132–64. Trans. Lydia G. Cochrane. Chicago: University of Chicago Press.

Kohl, Benjamin G. 1983. "Conversino, Giovanni, da Ravenna." DBI 28:574–78.

Kraye, Jill. 1981. "Francesco Filelfo on Emotions, Virtues and Vices: A Reexamination of His Sources." BHR 43:129–40.

Kristeller, Paul. 1902. *Andrea Mantegna.* Berlin-Leipzig: Cosmos.

Kristeller, Paul Oskar. 1937. *Supplementum Ficinianum: Marsilii Ficini Florentini philosophi platonici opuscula inedita et dispersa.* 2 vols. Florence: Leo S. Olschki.

———. 1956. "Francesco Bandini and His Consolatory Dialogue upon the Death of Simone Gondi." In Kristeller, *Studies in Renaissance Thought and Letters,* 411–35. Rome: Edizioni di storia e letteratura.

———. 1963–1991. *Iter italicum: A Finding List of Uncatalogued or Incompletely Catalogued Humanistic Manuscripts of the Renaissance in Italian and Other Libraries. Accedunt alia itinera.* 6 vols. London: Warburg Institute; Leiden: E. J. Brill. Cited as *Iter.*

Kuehn, Thomas. 1982. *Emancipation in Late Medieval Florence.* New Brunswick, N.J.: Rutgers University Press.

Labalme, Patricia H. 1969. *Bernardo Giustiniani: A Venetian of the Quattrocento.* Uomini e Dottrine, 13. Rome: Edizioni di storia e letteratura.

Lamansky, Vladimir. 1968. *Sécrets d'état de Venise: documents, extraits, notices et etudes servant a éclaircir rapports de la seigneurie avec les grecs, les slaves et la porte ottomane à la fin du XVe at au XVIe siècle.* 2 vols. Saint-Petersburg: Imprimerie de l'Académie Impériale des Sciences, 1884. Rpt. New York: Burt Franklin.

Lane, Frederic C. 1973. *Venice: A Maritime Republic.* Baltimore: Johns Hopkins University Press.

Lanfranchi, Luigi, ed. 1968. *San Giorgio Maggiore.* Comitato per la pubblicazione delle fonti relative alla storia di Venezia. Fonti per la storia di Venezia, sez. II: Archivi ecclesiastici, Diocesi Castellana. Venice: Il Comitato.

Langdale, Maria. 1976. "A Bilingual Work of the Fifteenth Century: Giannozzo Manetti's *Dialogus Consolatorius.*" *Italian Studies,* 31:1–16.

Lavin, Irving. 1970. "On the Sources and Meaning of the Renaissance Portrait Bust." *Art Quarterly,* 33:207–26.

Lavisse, Ernest. 1900–1911. *Histoire de France depuis les origines jusqu'à la Révolution.* 9 vols. Paris: Hachette. Rpt. 1969: New York: AMS Press.

Law, John E. 1982. "Un confronto fra due stati 'rinascimentali': Venezia e il dominio sforzesco." In *Gli Sforza a Milano in Lombardia e i loro rapporti con gli stati italiani ed europei (1450–1530),* 397–413. Milan: Cisalpina Goliardica.

———. 1984. "Lo stato veneziano e le castellanie di Verona." In G. Cracco and M. Knapton, eds., *Dentro lo 'stado italico': Venezia e la terraferma fra quattro e seicento,* 277–98. (= *Civis: Studi e Testi* 8.24).

Lazzarini, Vittorio. 1896. "La morte, il monumento di Vettor Pisani." NAV 11.2:395–401.

Lecoy de la Marche, Albert. 1875. *Le roi René, sa vie, son administration, ses travaux artistiques et littéraires d'après les document inédits des archives de France et d'Italie.* 2 vols. Paris: Firmin-Didot frères. Rpt. 1969, Geneva: Slatkine.

Lee, Egmont. 1978. *Sixtus IV and Men of Letters.* Temi e testi, 26. Rome: Edizioni di storia e letteratura.

Le Goff, Jacques. 1984. *The Birth of Purgatory.* Trans. by Arthur Goldhammer. Chicago: University of Chicago Press.

Léonard, Emile. 1954. *Les Angevins de Naples.* Paris: Presses universitaires de France.

Lieberman, Ralph. 1982. *Renaissance Architecture in Venice, 1450–1540.* New York: Abbeville Press.

Lienhard, Joseph T. 1977. *Paulinus of Nola and Early Western Monasticism, with a Study of the Chronology of His Works and an Annotated Bibliography, 1879–1976.* Cologne: P. Hanstein.

Lightbown, Ronald. 1986. *Mantegna: With a Complete Catalogue of the Paintings, Drawings, and Prints.* London: Phaidon/Christie's; Berkeley and Los Angeles: University of California Press.

Liruti, Gian-Giuseppe. 1760. *Notizie delle vite ed opere scritte da' letterati del Friuli.* 2 vols. Venice: appresso Modeso Fenzo.

Logan, Oliver. 1978. "The Ideal of the Bishop and the Venetian Patriciate: c.1430 – c.1630." *Journal of Ecclesiastical History,* 29:415–50.

Lorcin, Marie-Thérèse. 1981. *Vivre et mourir en Lyonnais à la fin du moyen âge.* Lyon: Editions da CNRS.

Lorenzetti, Giulio. 1926. *Venezia e il suo estuario.* Venice-Milan-Florence: Casa Editrice d'Arte Bestetti & Tumminelli.

Lugli, Vittorio. 1909. *I trattatisti della famiglia nel Quattrocento.* Biblioteca Filologico e Letteraria, N.II. Bologna-Modena: A. F. Formiggini.

Lytle, Guy Fitch, and Stephen Orgel, eds. 1981. *Patronage in the Renaissance.* Princeton: Princeton University Press.

MacFarlane, Alan. 1986. *Marriage and Love in England: Modes of Reproduction, 1300–1840.* New York: Basil Blackwell.

Maffei, Scipione. 1731–32. *Verona illustrata.* 4 vols. Verona: per Jacopo Vallarsi and Pier Antonio Berno.

Maggiolo, Attilio. 1983. *I soci dell'Accademia patavina dalla sua fondazione (1599).* Padova: Accademia patavina di SLA già dei Ricovrati.

Mallett, Michael E. 1973. "Venice and Its Condottieri, 1404–54," 121–45 in J. R. Hale, ed., *Renaissance Venice.* Totowa, N.J.: Rowman and Littlefield; London: Faber & Faber.

————. 1974. *Mercenaries and Their Masters: Warfare in Renaissance Italy.* London; Totowa, N.J.: Rowman & Littlefield.

————. 1976. "Some Notes on a Fifteenth-Century Condottiere and His Library: Count Antonio da Marsciano." In Cecil H. Clough, ed., *Cultural Aspects of the Renaissance,* 202–15. New York: Alfred F. Zambelli.

————. 1979. "Preparations for War in Florence and Venice in the Second Half of the Fifteenth Century." In *Florence and Venice: Comparisons and Relations,* 1: *Quattrocento,* 149–64. Florence: Nuova Italia.

Mallett, Michael E., and J. R. Hale. 1984. *The Military Organization of a Renaissance State: Venice c. 1400–1617.* Cambridge Studies in Early Modern History. Cambridge and New York: Cambridge University Press.

Mancini, Girolamo. 1923. "Gregorio Tifernate." ASI 81:65–112.

Manetti, Aldo. 1986. "Rapporti di Renato d'Angiò con alcuni umanisti italiani." In *Le roi René: René, duc d'Anjou, de Bar et de Lorraine, roi de Sicile et de Jerusalem, roi d'Aragon, comte de Provence, 1409–80: Actes du colloque international, Avignon, 13–15 juin 1981,* 119–35. Avignon: Université d'Avignon et des pays de Vaucluse, Faculté de lettres.

Marcus, Leah S. 1978. *Childhood and Cultural Despair: A Theme and Variations in Seventeenth-Century Literature.* Pittsburgh: University of Pittsburgh Press.

Margaroli, Paolo. 1990. "L'Italia come percezione di uno spazio politico unitario negli anni Cinquanta del XV secolo." *Nuova rivista storica* 74.5/6:517–36.

Mariani Canova, Giordana. 1969. *La miniatura del Rinascimento, 1450–1500.* Venice: Alfieri.

Martin, Henri. 1898. "Sur un portrait de Jacques-Antoine Marcelle, sénateur vénitien (1453)." *Mémoires de la société nationale des antiquaires de France,* 59 [= Ser. 6, vol. 9]: 229–67.

Martines, Lauro. 1979. *Power and Imagination: City-States in Renaissance Italy.* New York: Alfred A. Knopf.

Mastrodimitris, Panagiotis D. 1970. *[Greek title: Nicola Secundino, bios kai ergon]. (Nicola Secundino [1402–64]. Vita e opere. Contributo allo studio dei dotti greci della diaspora).* Athens: Ethnikon kai Kapodistriakon Panepistemion Athenon, Philosophike Schole.

Mazzarolli, Annibale. 1940. *Monselice: notizie storiche.* Padua: Tip. del Messaggero di San Antonio.

Mazzatinti, Giuseppe, and continuators. 1891–1980. *Inventario dei mano-*

scritti delle biblioteche d'Italia. 104 vols. and continuing. Forlì: Luigi Bordandini (1891–1911); Florence: Leo S. Olschki (1912–).

Mazzei, Lapo (Ser). 1880. *Lettere di un notaro a un mercante del secolo XIV, con altre lettere e documenti.* Ed. Cesare Guasti. 2 vols. Florence: Successori le Monnier.

McAndrew, John. 1980. *Venetian Architecture of the Early Renaissance.* Cambridge, Mass.: MIT Press.

McClure, George W. 1986. "The Humanist Art of Mourning: Autobiographical Writings on the Loss of a Son in Italian Humanist Thought (1400–1461)." RQ 39:440–75.

———. 1991. *Sorrow and Consolation in Italian Humanism.* Princeton: Princeton University Press.

McManamon, John M. 1989. *Funeral Oratory and the Cultural Ideals of Italian Humanism.* Chapel Hill–London: University of North Carolina Press.

McManners, John. 1985. *Death and the Enlightenment: Changing Attitudes to Death among Christians and Unbelievers in Eighteenth-Century France.* New York: Oxford University Press.

Mead, Margaret, and Martha Wolfenstein, eds. 1955. *Childhood in Contemporary Cultures.* Chicago: University of Chicago Press.

Medin, Antonio. 1904. *Per la storia della Repubblica di Venezia nella poesia.* Milan: Ulrico Hoepli.

Meersseman, G. G. 1973. "Seneca maestro di spiritualità nei suoi opuscoli apocrifi dal XII al XV secolo." *Italia medioevale ed umanistica,* 16:43–133.

Meiss, Millard. 1957. *Andrea Mantegna as Illuminator: An Episode in Renaissance Art, Humanism and Diplomacy.* New York: Columbia University Press.

Menniti Ippolito, Antonio. 1984. "'Providebitur sicut melius videbitur': Milano e Venezia nel bresciano nel primo '400." SV, NS 8:37–76.

Mercati, Giovanni. 1939. *Ultimi contributi alla storia degli umanisti.* 2 vols. Studi e testi, 90–91. Città del Vaticano: Biblioteca Apostolica Vaticana.

Mercer, R. G. G. 1979. *The Teaching of Gasparino Barzizza with Special Reference to His Place in Paduan Humanism.* Modern Humanities Research Association, Texts and Dissertations, 10. London.

Meyer, Alfred G. 1889. *Das venezianische Grabdenkmal der Frührenaissance.* Extract of the *Königliche preussische Kunstsammlungen,* 1889. Pp. 1–47.

Mittarelli, Giovanni Benedetto. 1779. *Bibliotheca codicum manuscriptorum monasterii S. Michaelis Venetiarum prope Murianum.* Venice: ex Typographia Fentiana.

Mitterauer, Michael and Reinhard Sieder. 1982. *The European Family: Patriarchy to Partnership from the Middle Ages to the Present.* Trans. by Karla Oosterveen and Manfred Hörzinger. Chicago: University of Chicago Press. German orig. *Vom Patriarchat zur Partnerschaft.*

Molho, Anthony. 1978. "Visions of the Florentine Family in the Renaissance." JMH 50:304–11.

Molmenti, Pompeo G. 1910–1912. *La storia di Venezia nella vita privata dalle origini alla caduta della Repubblica.* 3 vols. 5th ed., rev. Bergamo: Istituto italiano d'arte grafiche.

———. 1919. "Il monumento di Vettor Pisani." *Il Marzocco.* 19 October.

Monfasani, John. 1976. *George of Trebizond: A Biography and a Study of His Rhetoric and Logic.* Columbia Studies in the Classical Tradition, 1. Leiden: E. J. Brill.

———. ed. 1984. *Collectanea Trapezuntiana: Texts, Documents, and Bibliographies of George of Trebizond.* Binghamton, N.Y.: Medieval and Renaissance Texts and Studies. Cited as Mon.

Monselice. 1956. *Monselice nel VII centenario del suo duomo.* Ed. by Azione cattolica italiana.

Mor, Carlo Guido. 1963. "Problemi organizzativi e politica veneziana nei riguardi dei nuovi acquisti di terraferma." In *Umanesimo europeo e Umanesimo veneziano,* 1–10. Florence: Sansoni.

Morelli, Jacopo, ed. 1889. *Notizie d'opere di disegno nella prima meta del secolo XVI esistenti in Padova, Cremona, Milano, Pavia, Bergamo, Crema e Venezia, scritta da un anonimo di quel tempo [Marcantonio Michiel],* 2d ed.; Bologna: N. Zanichelli. Orig. Bassano: 1800.

Muir, Edwin. 1981. *Civic Ritual in Renaissance Venice.* Princeton: Princeton University Press.

Musatti, Eugenio. 1919. *Storia di Venezia.* 2d ed. 2 vols. Milan: Fratelli Treves.

Neff, Mary. 1981. "A Citizen in the Service of the Patrician State: The Career of Zaccaria de' Freschi." SV, NS 5:33–62.

Norwich, John Julius. 1982. *A History of Venice.* New York: Alfred A. Knopf.

O'Connell, J. B., ed. 1962. *The Roman Martyrology.* London: Burns & Oates.

Olivieri Secchi, Sandra. 1987–89. "Laici ed ecclesistici fra sogno ed ragione in un' accademia padovana del '500 gli Animosi." AV, Ser. 5, 130:5–30.

Orologio, Marchese. 1805. *Serie cronologico-istorica dei canonici di Padova*. Padova: nella Stamperia del Seminario.

Ortalli, Gherardo, et al., eds. 1988. *Venezia e le istituzioni di terraferma*. Terra di San Marco, Quaderni di studi, fonti e bibliografia, 2. Bergamo: Assessorato alla Cultura.

Ozment, Steven. 1983. *When Fathers Ruled: Family Life in Reformation Europe*. Studies in Cultural History. Cambridge, Mass.–London: Harvard University Press.

———. 1989. *Magdalena and Balthasar: An Intimate Portrait of Life in Sixteenth-Century Europe Revealed in the Letters of a Nuremberg Husband and Wife*. New York: Simon and Schuster.

———. 1990. *Three Behaim Boys: Growing Up in Early Modern Germany. A Chronicle of Their Lives*. New Haven–London: Yale University Press.

Palmer, Richard. 1981. "Niccolò Massa, His Family and His Fortune." *Medical History,* 25 (1981): 385–410.

Panofsky, Erwin. 1964. *Tomb Sculpture: Its Changing Aspects from Ancient Egypt to Bernini*. Ed. H. W. Janson. New York: Harry N. Abrams. Orig. Cologne: Grabplastik, 1964.

Paoletti, L. 1976. "Carbone, Ludovico." DBI 19:699–703.

Paoletti, Pietro. 1893–97. *L'architettura e la scultura del Rinascimento in Venezia*. 2 vols. in 4. Venice: Ongania-Naya Editori.

Papadopoli Aldobrandini, Nicolò. 1893–1919. *Le monete di Venezia*. 3 vols. Venice: Tipografia Libreria Emiliana.

Park, Katharine. 1985. *Doctors and Medicine in Early Renaissance Florence*. Princeton: Princeton University Press.

Parkes, Colin Murray. 1972. *Bereavement: Studies of Grief in Adult Life*. London: Tavistock Publications; New York: International Universities Press.

Paschini, Pio. 1935. *Leonello Chieregato, nunzio d'Innocenzo VIII e di Alessandro VI: note biografiche e documenti*. Lateranum, NS, 1, 3. Rome.

Pasolini, Pietro Desiderio. 1881. *Documenti riguardanti antiche relazioni fra Venezia e Ravenna*. Imola: Tip. d'Ignazio Galeati e figlio.

Pastore Stocchi, Manlio. 1980. "Scuola e cultura umanistica fra due secoli." In SCV 3.1:93–121. Vicenza: Neri Pozza.

Patch, Howard R. 1935. *The Tradition of Boethius*. New York–Oxford: Oxford University Press.

Pavanello, Giuseppe. 1905. *Un maestro del Quattrocento (Giovanni Aurelio Augurello)*. Venice: Tipografia Emiliana.

Pellegrin, Elisabeth. 1955. *La Bibliothèque des Visconti et des Sforza, ducs de*

Milan au XVe siècle. Publications de l'Institut de Recherche et d'Histoire des Textes, 5. Paris.

Peristiany, J. G., ed. 1965. *Honour and Shame: The Values of Mediterranean Society.* London-Chicago: University of Chicago Press.

Perret, Paul Michel. 1889. "L'Ambassade de Jean de Chambes à Venise (1459) d'après des documents vénitiens." *Bibliothèque de l'Ecole des Chartes,* 50:561–66.

———. 1896. *Histoire des relations de la France avec Venise du XIII siècle à l'avènement de Charles VIII.* 2 vols. Paris: H. Welter.

Pertusi, Agostino. 1970a. *La storiografia veneziana fino al secolo XVI: Aspetti e problemi.* Fondazione Giorgio Cini, Civiltà veneziana, Saggi, 18. Florence: Leo S. Olschki.

———. 1970b. "Gli inizi della storiografia umanistica del Quattrocento." In *Storiografia veneziana,* ed. Pertusi, 269–332. Florence: Leo S. Olschki.

Pesenti Marangon, Tiziana. 1976–77. "Michele Savonarola e Padova: l'ambients, le opere, la cultura medica." *Quaderni per la storia dell'Università di Padova,* 9/10:45–102.

Peyronel, Gianfranco. 1990. "Un fronte di guerra nel Rinascimento: esercito sforzesco e communità bresciane nella campagna del 1452–1453." *Nuova rivista storica* 74.5/6:537–609.

Peyronnet, Georges. 1958. "Il ducato di Milano sotto Francesco Sforza (1450–1466): politica interna, vita economica e sociale." ASI 116:36–53.

———. 1969. "I Durazzo e Renato d'Angiò, 1281–1442." In *Storia di Napoli,* 3:335–435. Napoli: Società Editrice Storia di Napoli.

———. 1982. "François Sforza: de condottiere à Duc de Milan." In *Gli Sforza a Milano in Lombardia e i loro rapporti con gli stati italiani ed europei (1450–1530),* 7–25. Milan: Cisalpina Goliardica.

Piacente, L. 1974. "Sul testo dell'oratio 'de septem artibus liberalibus' di Battista Guarini." *Giornale italiano di filologia,* 26.3:295–301.

———. 1982. "Tirocinio ed attività esegetica dell'umanista Battista Guarino." *Giornale italiano di filologia,* NS, 13.34 (1982): 67–82.

Picotti, Giovanni Battista. 1909. "Le lettere di Lodovico Foscarini." *Ateneo Veneto,* 32:21–49. Rpt. in Picotti, *Ricerche umanistiche,* Studi e lettere, storia e filosofia, 24, pp. 205–26. Florence: La Nuova Italia.

Pigman, G. W., III. 1985. *Grief and Mourning in Elizabethan England.* Cambridge: Cambridge University Press.

Piromalli, Antonio. 1975. *La cultura a Ferrara al tempo di Ludovico Ariosto.* Rome: Bulzoni.

Pollock, Linda. 1983. *Forgotten Children*. Cambridge: Cambridge University Press.

Ponte, Giovanni. 1971. "Etica ed economia nel terzo libro 'Della famiglia' di Leon Battista Alberti." In Anthony Molho and John A. Tedeschi, eds., *Renaissance Studies in Honor of Hans Baron*, 283–309. Florence: G. C. Sansoni; De Kalb, Ill.: Northern Illinois University Press.

Pontieri, Ernesto. 1958. "Muzio Attendolo e Francesco Sforza nei conflitti dinastico-civili nel Regno di Napoli al tempo di Giovanna II d'Angiò-Durazzo." In *Studi storici in onore di Gioacchino Volpe*, 2:787–883. Biblioteca storica Sansoni, NS, 31–32. 2 vols. Florence: G. C. Sansoni.

Pope-Hennessy, John. 1966. *The Portrait in the Renaissance*. Bollingen Series 35.12. New York: Random House.

Portioli, Attilio. 1871. "La giornata di Caravaggio: ed i sigilli di Lodovico III Gonzaga." *Periodico di numismatica e sfragistica per la storia d'Italia* 3:125–36.

Queller, Donald E. 1986. *The Venetian Patriciate: Reality versus Myth*. Champaign-Urbana: University of Illinois.

Rabil, Albert, Jr., ed. 1988. *Renaissance Humanism: Foundations, Forms, and Legacy*. 3 vols. Philadelpha: University of Pennsylvania Press.

Rainer, Rudolf. 1957. *Ars moriendi: von der Kunst des heilsamen Lebens und Strebens*. Forschungen zur Volkskunde, 39. Cologne-Graz: Böhlau Verlag.

Rhodes, Dennis E. 1974. "Battista Guarini and a Book at Oxford." JWCI 37:349–53.

Ricaldone, Luisa. 1986. "L'Arte del ben combattere e l'arte del ben morire in René d'Anjou." In *Le roi René: René, duc d'Anjou, de Bar et de Lorraine, roi de Sicile et de Jerusalem, roi d'Aragon, comte de Provence, 1409–80: Actes du colloque international, Avignon, 13–15 juin 1981*, 155–59. Avignon: Université d'Avignon et des pays de Vaucluse, Faculté de lettres.

Robertson, Giles. 1968. *Giovanni Bellini*. Oxford: Clarendon Press.

Robey, David. 1980–81. "Humanism and Education in the Early Quattrocento: the *De ingenuis moribus* of Pier Paolo Vergerio the Elder." BHR 42:27–58; 43:129–40.

Robin, Diana. 1983. "A Reassessment of the Character of Francesco Filelfo (1398–1481)." RQ 36:202–24.

———. 1984. "Unknown Greek Poems of Francesco Filelfo." RQ 37:173–206.

———. 1991. *Filelfo in Milan*. Princeton: Princeton University Press.

Robin, Françoise. 1985. *La Cour d'Anjou-Provence: la vie artistique sous le règne de René.* Paris: Picard.

———. 1986. "Quelques remarques sur l'art funéraire à la cour du roi René: De l'enfeu au sarcophage à l'italienne." In *Le roi René: René, duc d'Anjou, de Bar et de Lorraine, roi de Sicile et de Jerusalem, roi d'Aragon, comte de Provence, 1409–80: Actes du colloque international, Avignon, 13–15 juin 1981,* 160–73. Avignon: Université d'Avignon et des pays de Vaucluse, Faculté de lettres.

Le roi René. 1986. *Le roi René: René, duc d'Anjou, de Bar et de Lorraine, roi de Sicile et de Jerusalem, roi d'Aragon, comte de Provence, 1409–80: Actes du colloque international, Avignon, 13–15 juin 1981.* Avignon: Université d'Avignon et des pays de Vaucluse, Faculté de lettres.

Romanelli, Giandomenico, and Susanna Biadene. 1982. *Venezia piante e vedute, catalogo del fondo cartografico e stampo.* Venice: Stamperia di Venezia Editrice.

Romanin, Samuele. 1853–61. *Storia documentata di Venezia.* 10 vols. Venice: Pietro Naratovich.

Romano, Dennis. 1987. *Patricians and Popolani: The Social Foundations of the Venetian Renaissance State.* Baltimore-London: Johns Hopkins University Press.

Römer, Franz. 1987. "Eine 'Freundschaftsbrief' des Battista Guarini an Albrecht von Bonstetten." *Humanistica lovanianensia,* 36:138–46.

Rose, Paul Lawrence. 1977. "A Venetian Patron and Mathematician of the Sixteenth Century: Francesco Barozzi (1537–1604)." SV, NS 1:119–78.

Rosenblatt, Paul C. 1983. *Bitter, Bitter Tears: Nineteenth-Century Diarists and Twentieth-Century Grief Theories.* Minneapolis: University of Minnesota Press.

Rosenblatt, Paul C., R. Patricia Walsh, and Douglas A. Jackson. 1976. *Grief and Mourning in Cross-Cultural Perspective.* New Haven, Conn.: HRAF Press.

Ross, J. B. 1974. "The Middle-Class Child in Urban Italy, Fourteenth to Early Sixteenth Century." In Lloyd de Mause, ed., *The History of Childhood,* 183–228. New York: Psychohistory Press.

———. 1976. "Venetian Schools and Teachers, Fourteenth to Early Sixteenth Century: A Survey and a Study of Giovanni Battista Egnazio." RQ 39:521–66.

Rossi, L. 1905. "Venezia e il re di Napoli, Firenze e Francesco Sforza dal novembre 1450 al giugno del 1451." NAV, NS, anno 5, tomo 10:5–46, 281–356.

————. 1906. "La lega tra il duca di Milano, i fiorentini e Carlo VII re di Francia (21 febbraio 1452)." ASL, Ser. 4, vol. 5, anno 33:246–98.

Rossi, Vittorio. 1964. *Il Quattrocento.* 7th ed., rev. by Aldo Vallone. *Storia della letteratura italiana,* 6. Milan: F. Villardi.

Rubieri, Ermolao. 1879. *Francesco I Sforza.* 2 vols. Florence: Successori le Monnier.

Rubinstein, Nicolai. 1973. "Italian Reactions to Terraferma Expansion in the Fifteenth Century." In John R. Hale, ed., *Renaissance Venice,* 197–217. London: Faber & Faber.

Ruskin, John. 1906. *The Stones of Venice.* "Travellers Edition" (abridged). Collection of British Authors, Tauchnitz Edition, 3840. 2 vols. Leipzig: Berhard Tauchnitz.

Sabatini, F. 1975. *Napoli angioine: cultura e società.* Naples: Edizioni scientifiche italiane.

Sabbadini, Remigio. 1899. "Raffaele Zovenzoni e la sua *Monodia Chrysolorae.*" Nozze Fiorio/Murani. Catania: coi tipi di C. Galàtola.

————. 1909. "La traduzione guariniana di Strabone." *Il libro e la stampa,* 3:5–16.

————. 1915–16. "Antonio da Romagno e Pietro Marcello"; "Ancora Pietro Marcello." NAV, NS, 30.1:207–46; NS, 31.2:260–62.

————. 1964. *Guariniana* [photostatic reproduction of Sabbadini's *Vita di Guarino Veronese* and *La scuola e gli studi di Guarino Guarini Veronese*], ed. Mario Sancipriano. Turin: Bottega d'Erasmo.

Sacks, Peter M. 1985. *The English Elegy: Studies in the Genre from Spenser to Yeats.* Baltimore-London: Johns Hopkins University Press.

Santoro, Caterina. 1958. *I codici miniati della Biblioteca Trivulziana.* Milan: la Biblioteca.

————. 1968. *Gli Sforza.* Milan: Dall'Oglio.

Schmitt, Charles B., Quentin Skinner, and Eckhard Kessler, eds., with Jill Kraye. 1988. *The Cambridge History of Renaissance Philosophy.* New York–Cambridge: Cambridge University Press.

Schmitt, J. C. 1976. "Le suicide au moyen âge." *Annales,* 31:3–29.

Schrenck, G. 1985. "Aspects de l'écriture autobiographique au XVIe siècle: Agrippa d'Aubigné et sa *Vie à ses enfants.*" *Nouvelle Revue du XVIe siècle,* 3:33–51.

Segarizzi, Arnaldo. 1904. *Memorie della Reale Accademia delle scienze di Torino,* Ser. 2, 54 (Scienze morali, storiche e filologiche): 1–28.

Seigel, Jerrold. 1968. *Rhetoric and Philosophy in Renaissance Humanism: The Union of Eloquence and Wisdom, Petrarch to Valla.* Princeton: Princeton University Press.

Shahar, Shulamith. 1982–83. "Infants, Infant Care, and Attitudes toward Infancy in the Medieval Lives of Saints." *Journal of Psychohistory,* 10:281–309.

———. 1990. *Childhood in the Middle Ages.* London: Routledge.

Siraisi, Nancy. 1990. *Medieval and Early Renaissance Medicine: An Introduction to Knowledge and Practice.* Chicago: University of Chicago Press.

Sleptzoff, L. M. 1978. *Men or Supermen? The Italian Portrait in the Fifteenth Century.* Jerusalem: Magnes Press, Hebrew University.

Soranzo, Giovanni. 1957. "L'ultima campagna del Gattamelata al servizio della repubblica veneta (luglio 1438–gennaio 1440)." AV, Ser. 5, 60/61:79–114.

———. 1958. "Studi e discussioni su 'La Lega italica' del 1454–1455." In *Studi storici in onore di Gioacchino Volpe,* 2:969–95. Biblioteca storica Sansoni, NS, 31–32. 2 vols. Florence: G. C. Sansoni.

Spreti, Vittorio. 1928–1936. *Enciclopedia storico-nobiliare italiana.* 9 vols. Bologna: Forni Editore.

Stannard, David E. 1977. *The Puritan Way of Death: A Study in Religion, Culture, and Social Change.* Oxford–New York: Oxford University Press.

Starn, Randolph. 1971. "Francesco Guicciardini and His Brothers." In Anthony Molho and John A. Tedeschi, eds., *Renaissance Studies in Honor of Hans Baron.* Florence: G. C. Sansoni; De Kalb, Ill.: Northern Illinois University Press.

Stein, Arnold. 1986. *The House of Death: Messages from the English Renaissance.* Baltimore-London: Johns Hopkins University Press.

Stone, Lawrence. 1974. "The Massacre of the Innocents." NYRB, 21 (11 November): 25–31.

———. 1977. *Family, Sex, and Marriage in England, 1500–1800.* London–New York: Weidenfeld & Nicolson. Abr. ed. 1979: New York, etc.: Harper & Row.

Storia della cultura veneta [SCV]. 1980. *III: Dal primo Quattrocento al Concilio di Trento.* 3 vols. Vicenza: Neri Pozza. Cited as SCV.

Strong, Roy. 1986. *Henry Prince of Wales, and England's Lost Renaissance.* London: Thames and Hudson.

Symonds, John Addington. 1935. *The Renaissance in Italy.* 7 vols. in 5. New York: Modern Library

Tagliaferri, Amelio, ed. 1981. *Atti del convegno Venezia e la terraferma attraverso le relazioni dei rettori, Trieste, 23–24 ottober 1980.* Milan: Dott. A. Giuffrè Editore.

Talbot, Michael. 1980. "Marcello Alessandro"; "Marcello, Benedetto." In

The New Grove Dictionary of Music and Musicians, 11:647–48, 648–50. Ed. Stanley Saidie. London: Macmillan.

Tamassia, Nino. 1971. *La famiglia italiana nei secoli decimoquinto e decimosesto.* Milan: Multigrafica Editrice. Orig. 1914.

Tarducci, Francesco. 1899. "L'alleanza Visconti-Gonzaga del 1438 contro la repubblica veneta." ASL, Ser. 3, vol. 11:265–329.

Tassini, G. 1879. *Alcuni palazzi ed antichi edifizi di Venezia storicamente illustrati.* Venezia: Tipografia M. Fontana.

———. 1885. *Edifici di Venezia distrutti o volti ad altro uso.* Venice: Reale Tip. C. Cecchini

———. 1933. *Curiosità veneziane.* 6th ed., ed. Elio Zorzi. Venice: Ed. Scarabellin.

Tateo, Francesco. 1977. "G. A. Campano e la sua biografia 'umanistica' di Braccio." In *L'Umanesimo umbro: Atti del IX convegno di studi umbri, Gubbio, 22–23 settembre 1974,* 331–50. Perugia: Centro di studi umbri.

Taylor, Lou. 1983. *Mourning Dress: A Costume and Social History.* London and Boston: G. Allen and Unwin.

Tenenti, Alberto. 1957. *Il senso della morte e l'amore della vita nel Rinascimento (Francia e Italia).* Studi e ricerche, 5. Turin: Giulio Einaudi. Rpt. 1977.

Thomson, Ian. 1988. *Humanist Pietas: The Panegyric of Ianus Pannonius on Guarinus Veronensis.* Bloomington, Ind.: Research Institute for Inner Asian Studies.

Thorp, Nigel. 1987. *The Glory of the Page: Medieval and Renaissance Illuminated Manuscripts from Glasgow University Library.* Glasgow: Glasgow University Library, by Harvey Miller.

Tietze-Conrat, E. 1955. *Mantegna.* London: Phaidon Publications.

Tiraboschi, Girolamo. 1833. *Storia della letteratura italiana.* (1772–) Rpt. 4 vols. Milan: Niccolo Bettoni.

Toderini, I. 1875. "Le prime condotte di Francesco Sforza per Venezia." AV 9:116–29.

Torrioli, Ascanio. 1927. *Publio Gregorio Tifernate.* Urbino: Tipografia Melchiorre Arduini.

Traer, James F. 1980. *Marriage and the Family in Eighteenth-Century France.* Ithaca-London: Cornell University Press.

Tremoli, Paolo. 1983. "Raffaele Zovenzoni: un umanista sulle due sponde dell'Adriatico." In Vittore Branca and Sante Graciotti, eds., *L'umanesimo in Istria,* 143–65. Florence: Leo S. Olschki.

Trevor-Roper, Hugh. 1961. "The Doge Francesco Foscari." In Trevor-

Roper, ed., *Renaissance Essays*, 1–12. Chicago: University of Chicago Press.

Trexler, Richard C. 1973–74a. "The Foundlings of Florence, 1395–1455." *History of Childhood Quarterly*, 1:259–84.

———. 1973–74b. "Infanticide in Florence: New Sources and First Results." *History of Childhood Quarterly*, 1:98–116.

———. 1974. "Ritual in Florence: Adolescence and Salvation in the Renaissance." In Charles Trinkaus & Heiko A. Oberman, eds., *The Pursuit of Holiness in Late Medieval and Renaissance Religion*, 200–264. Leiden: E. J. Brill.

———. 1975. "In Search of Father: The Experience of Abandonment in the Recollections of Giovanni di Pagolo Morelli." *History of Childhood Quarterly*, 3:225–52.

———. 1980. *Public Life in Renaissance Florence*. Studies in Social Discontinuity. New York: Academic Press.

Troilo, Sigfrido. 1932. *Andrea Giuliano politico e letterato veneziano del Quattrocento*. Bibliotheca dell'Archivum Romanicum, Ser. I, Storia letteraria-paleografia, 18. Geneva-Florence: Leo S. Olschki.

Vale, Malcolm. 1981. *War and Chivalry: Warfare and Aristocratic Culture in England, France, and Burgundy at the End of the Middle Ages*. London: Duckworth; Athens, Georgia: University of Georgia Press.

Valentini, Roberto. 1924. "De gestis et vita Braccii di G. A. Campano: a proposito di storia della storiografia." *Bollettino della R. Deputazione di storia patria per l'Umbria*, 27:153–96

Ventura, Angelo. 1979. "Il dominio di Venezia nel Quattrocento." In *Florence and Venice: Comparisons and Relations*, 1: *Quattrocento*, 167–90. Florence: Nuova Italia.

Von Moos, P. 1971–72. *Consolatio: Studien zur mittelalteinischen Trostliteratur über den Tod und zum Problem der christlichen Trauer*. 4 vols. Münstersche Mittelalter-Schriften, 3:1–4. Munich: W. Fink.

Vovelle, Gaby, and Michel Vovelle. 1970. *Vision de la mort et de l'au-delà en Provence d'après les autels des âmes du Purgatoire, XVe–XXe siècles*. Cahiers des Annales, 29. Paris: Armand Colin.

Walsh, Katherine. 1977. "The Observance: Sources for a History of the Observant Reform Movement in the Order of the Augustinian Friars in the Fourteenth to Fifteenth Centuries." RSCI 31:40–67.

———. 1979. "Cazzulli, Agostino." DBI 23:182–84.

———. 1989. "La congregazione riformata di Monte Ortone nel Veneto." RSCI 43:80–100.

Warburg, Aby. 1987. "Arte del ritratto e borghesia fiorentina." In Warburg,

La rinascita del paganesimo antico: contributi alla storia della cultura, 109–46. Ed. Gertrud Bing, trans. Emma Cantimori. Florence: La Nuova Italia.

Weinstein, Donald, and Rudolph M. Bell. 1982. *Saints and Society: The Two Worlds of Western Christendom, 1000–1700.* Chicago: University of Chicago Press.

Weise, Georg. 1961. *L'ideale eroico del Rinascimento e le sue premesse umanistiche.* Naples: Edizioni scientifiche italiane.

Weiss, Roberto. 1963. "La medaglia veneziana del Rinascimento e l'Umanesimo." In *Umanesimo europeo e Umanesimo veneziano,* 337–48. Florence: Sansoni.

———. 1969. "Umanisti benacensi del Quattrocento." In *Il lago di Garda: storia di una comunità lagunale,* 2:191–202. 2 vols. Atti del congresso internazionale promosso dall'Ateneo di Sal. Sal: Ateneo di Sal.

Whaley, Joachim, ed. 1981. *Mirrors of Mortality: Studies in the Social History of Death.* The Europa Social History of Human Experience. London: Europa.

Witt, Ronald G. 1983. *Hercules at the Crossroads: The Life, Works, and Thought of Coluccio Salutati.* Duke Monographs in Medieval and Renaissance Studies, 16. Durham, N.C.: Duke University Press.

Wittschier, Heinz Willi, ed. 1968. *Giannozzo Manetti: Das Corpus der Orationes.* Studi italiani, 10. Cologne-Graz: Böhlau Verlag.

Wolf, Eric R. 1966. "Kinship, Friendship and Patron-Client Relations in Complex Societies." In Michael Banton, ed., *The Social Anthropology of Complex Societies,* 1–22. New York–Washington: Frederick A. Praeger.

Wolters, Wolfgang. 1987. *Storia e politica nei dipinti di Palazzo Ducale: aspetti dell'auto-celebrazione della Repubblica di Venezia nel Cinquecento.* Trans. Benedetta Heinemann Campana. Venezia: Arsenale Editrice. Orig. 1983: *Der Bilderschmuck des Dogenpalastes.* Stuttgart: Franz Steiner Verlag.

Wooden, Warren W. 1982. "The Topos of Childhood in Marian England." JMRS 12:179–84.

Woods-Marsden, Joanna. 1987. "'Ritratto al Naturale': Questions of Realism and Idealism in Early Renaissance Portraits." *Art Journal,* 46:209–16.

Woodward, William H. 1963. *Vittorino da Feltre and Other Humanist Educators.* Intro by Eugene F. Rice, Jr. Classics in Education, 18. New York: Teachers College, Columbia University, 1963. Orig. 1897: Cambridge: Cambridge University Press.

Woolf, Stuart J. 1962. "Venice and the Terraferma: Problems of the Change from Commercial to Landed Activities." *Bollettino dell'Istituto Storico per la storia e cultura veneziana* (continued as SV) 4:415–41. Rpt. in Brian Pullan, ed., *Crisis and Change in the Venetian Economy in the Sixteenth and Seventeenth Centuries*, 175–203. London: Methuen.

Young, John, and P. Henderson Aitken, eds. 1908. *A Catalogue of the Manuscripts in the Library of the Hunterian Museum in the University of Glasgow*. Glasgow: James Maclehose.

Zangirolami, Cesare. 1962. *Storia delle chiese, dei monasteri, delle scuole di Venezia, rapinate e distrutte da Napoleone Bonaparte*. Venice: Arti Grafiche e Vianelli.

Zannoni, Maria. 1942. "Il dramma dei Foscari nella Cronica di Giorgio Dolfin." *Nuova rivista storica*, 26:201–15.

Zanta, Leontine. 1914. *La Renaissance du stoicisme au XVIe siècle*. Paris: H. Champion, 1914.

Zeno, Apostolo. 1752–53. *Dissertazioni vossiane*, 2 vols. Venice: Giambatista Albrizzi Q. Gir.

Ziliotto, Baccio. 1950. *Raffaele Zovenzoni: la vita, i carmi*. Comune di Trieste, Celebrazioni degli istriani illustri, 3. Trieste: "Smolars"

Zimmermann, T. C. Price. 1971. "Confession and Autobiography in the Early Renaissance." In Anthony Molho and John A. Tedeschi, eds., *Renaissance Studies in Honor of Hans Baron*, 119–40. Florence: G. C. Sansoni; De Kalb, Ill.: Northern Illinois University Press.

Zippel, Gianni. 1956. "Lorenzo Valla e le origini della storiografia umanistica a Venezia." *Rinascimento*, 7:93–133.

———. 1959. "Ludovico Foscarini ambasciatore a Genova, nella crisi dell'espansione veneziana sulla terraferma (1449–1450)." *Bullettino dell'Istituto Storico italiano per il medio evo e Archivo Muratoriano*, 71:181–255.

Zorzanello, Pietro. 1981. *Catalogo dei codici latini della biblioteca Nazionale Marciana di Venezia non compresi nel catalogo di G. Valentinelli*. 3 vols. Florence: Olschki.

Zorzi, Alvise. 1972. *Venezia scomparsa*. 2 vols. Venice: Banca Cattolica del Veneto.

Index

⁂

Page numbers referring to appendixes and notes are given in *italics*.